The Most Ancient
of Minorities

Tempio Israelitico, Florence, 1882. Courtesy Stanislao G. Pugliese.

The Most Ancient of Minorities

The Jews of Italy

Edited by
Stanislao G. Pugliese

Prepared under the auspices of Hofstra University
Contributions in Ethnic Studies, Number 36

GREENWOOD PRESS
Westport, Connecticut • London

Library of Congress Cataloging-in-Publication Data

The most ancient of minorities : the Jews of Italy / edited by
Stanislao G. Pugliese.
     p. cm.—(Contributions in ethnic studies, ISSN 0196–7088)
   Includes bibliographical references (p.).
   ISBN 0–313–31895–6 (alk. paper)
   1. Jews—Italy—History. 2. Jews—Italy—Intellectual life. 3. Holocaust, Jewish
(1939–1945)—Italy. 4. Holocaust survivors—Italy—Personal narratives. 5. Italy—Ethnic
relations. I. Pugliese, Stanislao G., 1965– II. Series.
DS135.I8.M67   2002
945′.004924—dc21   2001040593

British Library Cataloguing in Publication Data is available.

Library of Congress Catalog Card Number: 2001040593
ISBN: 0–313–31895–6
ISSN: 0196–7088

First published in 2002

Greenwood Press, 88 Post Road West, Westport, CT 06881
An imprint of Greenwood Publishing Group, Inc.
www.greenwood.com

Printed in the United States of America

The paper used in this book complies with the
Permanent Paper Standard issued by the National
Information Standards Organization (Z39.48–1984).

10 9 8 7 6 5 4 3 2 1

In memory of the men—Jew and Gentile alike—massacred
at the Fosse Ardeatine outside of Rome
24 March 1944

Contents

Acknowledgments xi

1. Israel in Italy: Wrestling with the Lord in the Land of Divine Dew 1
   Stanislao G. Pugliese

Part I. Historiography and the Law 11

2. Legal Discrimination against Italian Jews:
   From the Romans to the Unification of Italy 13
   Sandra Tozzini

3. Modern Historiography on the Early Imperial Mistreatment
   of Roman Jews 35
   Dixon Slingerland

4. Archival Sources for the History of the Jews in Italy 51
   Micaela Procaccia

Part II. Medieval and Renaissance Italy 57

5. Florence against the Jews or the Jews against Florence? 59
   Michele Luzzati

6. Between Tradition and Modernity: The Sephardim of Livorno 67
   Julia R. Lieberman

7. Jewish Dancing Masters and "Jewish Dance"
   in Renaissance Italy 77
   Barbara Sparti

8. The Expulsion from the Papal States (1569) in Light
   of Hebrew Sources   91
   Abraham David

9. The Case of Ferdinando Alvarez and His Wife,
   Leocadia of Rome (1637–1643)   101
   Nancy Goldsmith Leiphart

10. Giovanni Di Giovanni: Chronicler of the Jews of Sicily   105
    Salvatore G. Rotella

Part III. Literature, Art, and Identity   117

11. Judeo-Italian: Italian Dialect or Jewish Language?   119
    George Jochnowitz

12. The Culture of Italian Jews and Shakespeare's
    The Merchant of Venice   123
    H. Wendell Howard

13. Emancipation and Jewish Literature in the Italian Canon   131
    Roberto Maria Dainotto

14. Assimilation and Identity in an Italian-Jewish Novel   139
    Lynn M. Gunzberg

15. Racial Laws and Internment in Natalia Ginzburg's
    Lessico famigliare   147
    Claudia Nocentini

16. Clara Sereni and Contemporary Italian-Jewish Literature   157
    Elisabetta Properzi Nelsen

17. Italian Synagogue Architecture and Italian-Jewish Identity 169
    Samuel Gruber

18. Italian-Jewish Literature from World War II to the 1990s   177
    Raniero M. Speelman

19. Italian-Jewish Memoirs and the Discourse of Identity   191
    Fabio Girelli-Carasi

Part IV. World War II and the Holocaust   201

20. Haven or Hell?: Italy's Refuge for Jews, 1933–1945   203
    Maryann Calendrille

21. "Di razza ebraica": Fascist Name Legislation and
    the Designation of Jews in Trieste   217
    Maura E. Hametz

22. Pope Pius XI's Conflict with Fascist Italy's Anti-Semitism
    and Jewish Policies   231
    Frank J. Coppa

23. The First Anti-Semitic Campaign of the Fascist Regime   247
    Luc Nemeth

24. Why Was Italy So Impervious to Anti-Semitism (to 1938)?   259
    Frederick M. Schweitzer

25. Rescue or Annihilation: Italian Occupation Forces
    and the Jews in World War II   275
    Yitzchak Kerem

26. The Priebke Trial(s)   289
    David Travis

Part V. Primo Levi   301

27. Deporting Identity: The Testimonies of Primo Levi
    and Giuliana Tedeschi   303
    H. Marie Orton

28. Narrating Auschwitz: Linguistic Strategies in Primo Levi's
    Holocaust Memoirs   315
    Eva Gold

29. The Tower of Babel: Language and Power in Primo Levi's
    Survival in Auschwitz   331
    Anna Petrov Bumble

Part VI. "The Language of the Witness":
Holocaust Survivors Speak   343

30. Dante Almansi, President of the Union of Italian
    Jewish Communities   345
    Renato J. Almansi

31. Reflections on an Italian-Jewish Life   353
    Lucia Servadio Bedarida

Part VII. Epilogue

359

32. The Survival of "the Most Ancient of Minorities"
   Stephen Siporin

361

A Selected Bibliography, 1996–1999
   James Tasato Mellone

369

Index

381

About the Contributors

393

Acknowledgments

This volume collects papers that were presented at a three-day international conference at Hofstra University in April 1999. More than sixty scholars from the United States, Italy, Israel, France, the Netherlands, Greece, and Scotland contributed to the success of an ambitious endeavor. The papers selected here for publication cover over 2,000 years of Italian-Jewish history, from ancient Rome, to contemporary developments concerning assimilation, literature, and identity.

It was a professional and personal honor to organize and direct this conference, and it gives me great pleasure to make these fine essays available to a wide audience. A project of this scale could not have been successful without the professionalism and dedication of many people. I would especially like to acknowledge the work of Natalie Datlof and her staff at Hofstra University's Cultural Center; the support of Jack and Helen Cytryn; the fine editorial staff at Greenwood Press (James Sabin, Margaret Maybury, and Betty Pessagno), as well as Nancy Lucas and Judith Antonelli. Professor James Tusato Mellone compiled the extensive bibliography; I thank him in the name of all students and scholars of the subject. A special word of thanks goes to Dr. Lucia Servadio Bedarida and Dr. Renato J. Almansi for their personal reminiscences in the section entitled "The Language of the Witness: Holocaust Survivors Speak." Lucia Servadio Bedarida celebrated her 100th birthday on 17 July 2000. Dr. Almansi passed away in January 2000; those of us who met him at the conference mourn his passing.

Finally, my thanks go to all the scholars whose participation and commitment made the conference, and this volume, possible.

S.G.P.

1

Israel in Italy: Wrestling with the Lord in the Land of Divine Dew

Stanislao G. Pugliese

An imaginative and perhaps apocryphal etymology translates the word "Italy" into Hebrew as "I-tal-Jah" or "island of divine dew." Popular tradition has it that the earliest Jews to settle in Italy, searching for an answer to their good fortune in finding such a place to live, found it in the very name of the country. By some strange philological twist of fate—and recalling the paternal benediction that Isaac bestowed on Jacob—it is revealing that the Hebrew name for the country has such poetic and symbolic resonance, for the morning dew is lovely to behold and necessary for life yet quickly dissipates in the harsher light of midday. Similarly, the history of Italian Jews has oscillated for two millennia between "benevolence and betrayal,"[1] between paganism and Catholicism, between humanism and anti-Semitism. Before the advent of Christianity, Jews had settled on the Italian peninsula. Italian Jews thereby constitute the oldest living Jewish community in the West. In the words of the historian H. Stuart Hughes, they are "the most ancient of minorities."[2]

Recent scholarship has generated an abundance of literature on the history and culture of Italian Jews, with several fine works in English.[3] Study of the nature and vicissitudes of Jewish identity has naturally coincided with this literature. Self-reflexive writing, by definition, seeks to answer the question of identity. This volume, while comprising a wide variety of chapters, has a connecting thread: as a people whose entire history and cultural memory have been dependent on, and defined by, the Word, how did Italian Jews define themselves on the Italian peninsula, and what strategies did they develop in response to their historical situation?

The history of Italian Jews is unique in the history of Europe. A Jewish colony existed in Rome 200 years before the birth of Christ; the Eternal City therefore represents the oldest Jewish community in the Western world.[4] Successive waves of immigration created dozens of Jewish communities in Italy. Depending on the time and the place, Italian Jews could expect tolerance, discrimination, persecution, or outright violence. Still, they fared better than their brethren in other parts of Europe. The Papal States of the central peninsula represented perhaps the most paradoxical situation, alternating between periods of toleration, benign neglect, and strident anti-Semitism. In the theology of the Catholic Church, the Jews played an ambivalent, although critical, role in the drama of human salvation.[5] As the "killers of Christ," they were to be punished and continually reminded of the bitter irony that they embodied: waiting hopefully for the coming of the Messiah, they failed to recognize him once he appeared on earth. Yet their existence was necessary, for they served as a reminder to the faithful and would one day repent of their sin and accept Christ, thereby hastening the Second Coming.[6]

The first ghettos were established in the sixteenth century in Venice (by decree of the Council of Ten in 1516) and by the papal bull *Cum Nimis Absurdum* in 1555 in Rome. The formation of the ghettos signified something more than merely the segregation of the Jews from Gentile society; gaining greater control over the Jews was necessary since their conversion to the one true faith was no longer to be put off or patiently hoped for. Instead, the ghettoization of the Jews can be seen as an attempt to hasten their conversion to Christianity.[7] By the early sixteenth century, the Spanish Bourbons, following the earlier Iberian example, expelled all the Jews from southern Italy. At the end of the eighteenth century, Napoleon's troops, carrying the torch of the French Revolution, had broken down the walls of the ghettos and burned the gates of the ghettos in the public squares of Italy. With the defeat of Napoleon and the restoration of papal rule in 1814, the ghetto was reestablished in Rome. The Risorgimento (movement for national unification) found wide support among the Jews of Italy. Giuseppe Mazzini, the moral conscience of unification, had written to the House of Savoy that "the Jews of Italy have an Italian heart . . . and are integral members of the Italian nation."[8] With the unification of Italy in 1870 the legal walls of the ghetto were dismantled.[9] After an emancipation that they directly associated with the House of Savoy and the constitutional monarchy, Italian Jews actively participated in the political and cultural life of the fledgling nation. Rapid integration and assimilation followed, characterized by the high rate of intermarriage. Due to the very high rate of literacy, Italian Jews were active in the intellectual and cultural professions such as law, medicine, journalism, and the academy. Two Italian Jews (Sidney Sonnino and Luigi Luzzatti) became prime minister, and several rose to prominence in the military, including Emanuele Pugliese—the most highly decorated officer of World War I. It would be almost impossible to conceive of an analogous situation in Germany, France, or even England.[10] It should be noted, though, that this traditional reading of Italian history as devoid of anti-Semitism has recently been challenged by two scholars, Lynn Gunzberg and Michele Sarfatti.[11]

When Benito Mussolini became prime minister in October 1922, Italian Jews had no unified position on the fascist regime. With the major exception of Rome, Italian Jews had successfully entered the middle class; therefore, their perception of fascism was determined by their socioeconomic status, rather than their religion. This was only natural, for the early program of fascism contained no trace of anti-Semitism; indeed, there were Italian Jews among the *san sepolcristi* (first fascists) when Mussolini formed the nucleus of the new movement in Milan on 23 March 1919. Jews participated at the highest levels of the fascist regime, as evidenced by Aldo Finzi (undersecretary of the Interior) and Guido Jung (finance minister). Anti-Semites like Roberto Farinacci and Telesio Interlandi were kept on a short leash. Mussolini even encouraged the Zionist movement in Italy, not through any sincere desire to further the cause but because he saw Zionism as a possible counterweight to British influence in the Mediterranean. As late as September 1934, Mussolini offered his own criticism of Nazi anti-Semitism in a contemptuous speech when he declared: "Thirty centuries of history permit us to regard with supreme pity certain doctrines supported beyond the Alps by the descendants of a people who did not know how to write and could not hand down documents recording their own lives, at a time when Rome had Caesar, Virgil, and Augustus."[12] Mussolini had a history of contradictory poses regarding the Jews; while he could take the charming, sophisticated, and brilliant Margherita Sarfatti as a mistress, he could also ominously write (as early as 1920), "Let us hope the Jews will be smart enough not to incite anti-Semitism in the one country where it has never existed."[13]

Many Italian Jews—as members of the bourgeoisie, not as Jews—were favorably disposed toward the new regime. Like their fellow citizens, they, too, were susceptible to the rhetoric of the dangers of a communist revolution in Italy. When the anti-Semitic legislation was passed in 1938, approximately 10,000 Italian Jews in a population of circa 50,000 (or one in three adults) were formally members of the Fascist Party. Of course, not all of these members were ideological fascists; many had joined the PNF (Partito Nazionale Fascista) in order to keep their jobs. A common sly reference at the time was to the PNF as "Per Necessità Familiare" (for family necessity). In addition, Italian Jews sensed more hostility from the Vatican than Mussolini's early regime; consequently, they saw fascism's conflict with the Vatican in a favorable light. Alfredo Rocco, minister of justice and one of the theoreticians of the fascist state, pushed for legislation in 1930–1931 that gave a coherent national legal status to Jewish organizations and their members for the first time.[14] As late as 1933, the Italian-Jewish scholar Arnaldo Momigliano, in a review of Cecil Roth's *The Jews of Venice* and later echoed by Antonio Gramsci, could speak of the "parallel nationalization" in which "the history of the Jews in almost every Italian city is essentially the history of the formation of their Italian national consciousness, which took place at the same time as the general Italian national consciousness."[15] Yet one scholar has argued that as recently as the 1970s and 1980s, "the perceived ambiguous nature of Italian Jewish identity still created tension in the lives of Italian Jews."[16]

After the unification of the new nation and the emancipation of the Italian Jews, adherence to Jewish religious practices rapidly declined, especially the observance of *kashrut* (Jewish laws of ritual purity and dietary laws).[17] According to Cecil Roth, Italy could count 108 synagogues, which conducted services twice a day in 1830; a century later, that number had dropped to 38, and those held services only irregularly.[18] A demographic study in 1976 discovered that while there had been eighty-seven organized Jewish communities in 1840, that number had dropped to twenty-two by 1970.[19] Andrew Canepa has argued that Italy's well-known lack of anti-Semitism and willingness to accept Jews into mainstream society came at a price: Italian Jews were expected to renounce the most overt expressions of their Judaism and conform to the dominant social mores.[20] Ironically, by the time that the Racial Laws were promulgated in 1938, the rate of intermarriage with Gentiles was nearly 50%. These sociological and demographic statistics, along with the work of Canepa and Gunzberg, suggest that Italian-Jewish assimilation was far more complex than previously thought and that Italian Jews may have been affected by a subtle social dynamic that suggests at least the possibility of a latent anti-Semitism. Italian Jews, in a psychic effort to compensate for this perceived "difference," were often more patriotic, nationalistic, and fascistic than their Gentile neighbors. Hence, patriotism became a "secular religion."

The positions of the Vatican and the monarchy on the "Jewish question" in Italy require a separate study. Suffice it to say that the Vatican oscillated between outright hostility and vague support of the Jews. Italian Jews, for their part, loyally supported the monarchy. Ironically, the same Vittorio Emanuele III who officially visited the opening of the new synagogue in Rome in 1904 and proclaimed, "Italy is a country without racial discrimination" thirty-four years later signed the Racial Laws.[21]

Those Racial Laws came as a shock in 1938. Scholars still debate the origin and evolution of fascist anti-Semitism, with some claiming that the laws were a direct influence of Hitler's Nazi Germany, while others contend that Mussolini unleashed the anti-Semites on his own.[22] Yet the Racial Laws had been preceded by ominous signs.[23] In May 1936 Hitler visited Italy and was accorded full honors. In 1937 Paolo Orano's book *Gli ebrei in Italia* appeared, spelling out the "official" position against Zionist Jews and making the transition from anti-Zionism to anti-Semitism. In July 1938, the country was stunned by the publication of the grotesque "Manifesto of the Racial Scientists," a document clothed in the language of positivist science. Among other "facts," the manifesto concluded that "[t]he population of modern Italy is of Aryan origin and its civilization is Aryan," that "[t]here now exists an Italian race," and that "Jews do not belong to the Italian race."[24] During the same month of July, the Office of Demography was ominously changed to the Office of Demography and Race, and in August a census was taken of Jews in Italy. In addition, fascist newspapers such as Roberto Farinacci's *Il Regime fascista* and Telesio Interlandi's *Il Tevere* stepped up their anti-Semitic diatribes, a sure sign that Mussolini himself had given them the green light to proceed. Farinacci, later "Inspector-General for Race" in the Republic of Salò, also had the distinction of publishing the "Protocols of the Elders of Zion" in Italian. The Vatican, not to be outdone in the arena of anti-Semitism, kept pace with the Jesuit organ *La Civiltà Cattolica*.

Ironically, the Racial Laws were a catalyst; Italian Jews, many of whom were neither observant nor familiar with Judaism, turned to their religious and cultural legacy. The memoirs, diaries, and recollections are unanimous on this point; by passing the Racial Laws, the regime in effect pulled Italian Jews out of their assimilated ways and their support for fascism and triggered a return to a "cultural memory." They were now forced to confront the question: What exactly was a Jew? How was identity to be conceived, especially after Italian Jews had almost all abandoned Hebrew, Yiddish, and the synagogue?[25] The answers were often paradoxical, contradictory, and ironic. One scholar has written that "the Italian Jew . . . considered his own religious crisis as a personal phenomenon: too profound to be healed by a single reform of ritual . . . [he] has found it possible to distance himself from religious observance, but has been firm about leaving intact the faith from which he was departing."[26]

Italian Jews were therefore in an ambivalent position, as they had been for most of their history on the Italian peninsula. What was to be their relationship to the state and Italian society? Debates raged within the Jewish communities. The question was sometimes framed as a choice to be made between assimilation (a complete absorption into Italian society, which demanded an abandonment of traditional Jewish culture and, ultimately, conversion to Catholicism) or integration (which would allow the Jews to fully participate in Italian society while maintaining their distinct cultural identity). Translated into the lexicon familiar to American scholars of immigration, it was a question of the "melting pot" of assimilation or the "salad bowl" of integration. Others argued over the question of Zionism and what it meant for Italian Jews. At the fourth Zionist youth conference in Livorno, held on 2–4 November 1924, the two fundamental positions were spelled out by Nello Rosselli, an advocate of integration, and Enzo Sereni, a fervent Zionist. What Sereni and Rosselli agreed on was that Judaism could not be constrained in a narrow definition. It had what might be called a "polyphonic" character; a single reading or interpretation was contrary to its history and its character, or, as Sereni himself put it, "[E]very attempt of ours to define it fails."[27] Enzo's brother Emilio eventually abandoned Zionism in favor of communism, which seems to bear out the point that many Jews were attracted to socialism and communism as a secular religion promising terrestrial redemption. Enzo never wavered in his beliefs and insisted that the Jews carve out a new state; accordingly, in 1927 he left a secure bourgeois life in Rome and helped found the Givat Brenner Kibbutz near Rehovot. With the outbreak of World War II, Enzo Sereni enrolled in the British Intelligence Service and performed missions in Egypt and Iraq. In 1944 he persuaded his superior officers to allow him on a dangerous mission, parachuting behind German lines. Tragically, he was captured by the Nazis, was tortured for four days, and perished at Dachau.[28]

Nello Rosselli was the historian brother of the more famous antifascist leader Carlo.[29] The Rossellis were related to the most distinguished Jewish families in Italy, such as the Nathans (Ernesto Nathan was mayor of Rome at the turn of the century) and the Pincherle family (the writer Alberto Moravia was a first cousin). While Carlo had actively engaged in the antifascist struggle, escaped from the penal island of Lipari, and established a new movement in Paris, Nello remained behind to carry the antifascist struggle through his scholarly work as a historian.[30] At the Livorno conference, Nello delineated what Judaism meant for him personally and also what political, social, and civil consequences derived from his position.[31] Rising before the Zionist majority, Nello Rosselli gave a memorable speech remembered by all those present and even grudgingly admired by the Zionists themselves as the most succinct and eloquent challenge to their position:

I am a Jew who does not go to Temple on the Sabbath, who does not know Hebrew, who does not observe any rituals of the faith . . . and yet I hold fast to my Judaism. . . . I am not a Zionist. . . . For the Zionists there is only one problem. . . . For me all the problems of life present themselves . . . as an equal torment to that of the religious problem. . . . The Jewish problem is not, and I do not feel it to be, the only, fundamental problem of my life. . . . I call myself a Jew because the monotheistic conscience, which no other religion has expressed with such clarity, is indestructible in me, because I have a very live sense of my personal responsibility . . . because every form of idolatry repels me; because I consider with Jewish severity the task of our lives on this earth and with Jewish serenity the mystery of the afterlife; because I love all men as it was commanded in Israel. And therefore I have a social conception which descends from our best traditions; because I have that religious sense of the family that, for those who look from the outside, truly appears as the fundamental and bedrock principle of Jewish society. I can therefore call myself a Jew.[32]

For the majority of Italian Jews, the questions raised by Sereni and Rosselli in 1924 did not assail them until 1938, yet so many Italian Jews participated in the antifascist cause that the question has arisen: Was there a strain of "Jewish antifascism," or are we limited to saying that there were "only" Jewish antifascists? The foremost Italian historian on the subject, Renzo De Felice insisted that there was no "Jewish anti-fascism."[33] Yet if we look at the leadership of the antifascist opposition, we find Umberto Terracini and Emilio Sereni of the Italian Communist Party; Giuseppe Emanuele Modigliani and Claudio Treves of the Italian Socialist Party; Eugenio Chiesa of the Italian Republican Party. All recalled the formative influence of Judaism on their early lives.[34] Other well-known Jewish antifascists include Carlo Levi, Leone Ginzburg, Max Ascoli, Vittorio Foa, and, after the war, Primo Levi. Levi, in fact, when arrested in the countryside in November 1943, confessed to being a Jew rather than admit his role in the partisan resistance, thinking this would be the safer course. To what extent did their Jewish heritage contribute to their political stance? Most did not address the question directly, but all shared the common assumption that the moral life intersected with civic concerns. Carlo Rosselli went so far as to insist that the precedents for his heretical conception of a liberal socialism were Greek rationalism and the messianism of Israel. Liberalism was rooted in a Greek rationalism that contains "a love of liberty, a respect for autonomy, a harmonious and detached conception of life," while socialism was the heir of a Judaic tradition stressing a completely terrestrial justice, "the myth of equality, a spiritual torment that forbids any indulgence."[35]

Yet neither Carlo nor his brother Nello made many more specific remarks concerning his religion. Like many of their generation, they had substituted a secular, civic religion, and this, combined with vestiges from Judaism, propelled them into opposing fascism. In a revealing memoir, their mother, Amelia, a noted playwright in her time, confessed the extent of her family's assimilation: "We were Jews, but *first and foremost* Italians. That is why even I, born and raised in that profoundly Italian and liberal environment, saved only the pure essence of my religion within my heart. Religious elements that were solely of a *moral* character: and this was the only religious instruction I gave my children."[36] That religious instruction was reflected in both the historical works of Nello and the political activism of Carlo. Translated into secular terms, it generated autonomy of thought, a stress on free will and the refusal to accept any truth as absolute. The Italian Jew may have lost the desire to strictly follow rituals and customs but clearly maintained a strong desire for social justice in the tradition of the Hebrew prophets. This is borne out by the many memoirs that have been written since the end of World War II. They are almost unanimous: when the Racial Laws were promulgated in 1938, they generated a fierce sense of pride in being an Italian Jew. Those who had long ago abandoned the synagogue returned, and young students began to pore over the ancient books once again. What they found convinced many that they had an ethical imperative to resist and fight. Gianfranco Sarfatti was twenty-two years old in 1943 when he wrote to his parents seeking refuge in Switzerland why he had returned to Italy and joined the Resistance:

Reflect that while it seems that all the world is collapsing and that the ruins must surely cover everything, your children . . . are looking toward the future and toward recon-struction, devoting all their forces to it. You are suffering; but millions of parents have been and are still in anxiety; and this must no longer be. And as I have recognized your sorrow in the sorrow of all suffering mothers and fathers, you must recognize your children in all the children and in all the young people who have been born into this world.[37]

This universalism and humanism are evident in the memoir literature of Italian Jews under fascism and for their entire 2,000 years in Italy.

Perhaps it is misleading to speak of a single tradition of Italian Judaism. Different cities had different Jewish communities; even within a city, Jews were further divided according to social class, degree of religious observance, place of origin, and date of arrival.[38] Many Italian-Jewish writers rarely spoke of their Judaism; Italo Svevo and Alberto Moravia spring to mind. Carlo Levi seemed more touched by the pagan existence of the southern Italians during his period of confinement there in 1935–1936.[39] For Primo Levi, it was science rather than Judaism to which he turned for a defense against the bombast and rhetoric of fascism; science was "clear and distinct and . . . verifiable," hence an effective "antidote to Fascism."[40] Natalia Ginzburg, wife of the Russian-Italian intel-lectual Leone Ginzburg, did not address her Jewish heritage until late in her writing career. Her *Family Sayings* of 1963 was an intricate web of concealment and disclosure; like Carlo Levi, she, too, remained "haunted by the ancestral theme of exile."[41]

Other writers testify to this new consciousness of a lost tradition. Dan Vittorio Segre, cousin of Ettore Ovazza, in his aptly titled *Memoirs of a Fortunate Jew* and echoing Amelia Rosselli, recounts that his parents "grew up in a climate of obsolete Judaism and of vigorous Italian nationalism and, as a result, shared all the virtues and prejudices typical of a generation of Jewish bourgeois sure of themselves, affluent, and respected, and totally unconscious of the dangers that lay waiting for them in the future."[42] Segre recalls that his father strongly opposed the Zionist movement, which to his mind undermined the patriotism of Italian Jews. Although the memoir sometimes approaches a nostalgic lament for a lost tradition, Segre approvingly quotes the Napoleonic king of Naples Joachim Murat, who once said proudly, "I am my own ancestor."[43]

Of all the twentieth-century Italian-Jewish writers, Giorgio Bassani forged the strongest ties with Judaism. "Jews . . . in whatever part of the earth, under whatever sky History scattered them, are and always will be Jews."[44] It may not be too far-fetched to suggest that all of Bassani's writing revolved around the question that he so simply puts at the beginning of his most famous work, *The Garden of the Finzi-Contini*, "For what on earth did the word 'Jew' mean, basically?"[45] That probing question pierces the hermetically sealed garden of the Finzi-Contini when the Racial Laws of 1938 become a reality. But the narrator is stunned that the question has to be posed; he and his fellow Jews had become banal in their ordinariness.

In a small literary masterpiece, *The Tiber Afire*, Fabio Della Seta recalls how the Racial Laws spurred radical questions about Judaism. In the context of persecution it was perhaps necessary, according to the author, to recall "the original and proud meaning of the name Israel: he who wrestles with the Lord." Following Martin Buber, Della Seta reminds us that "before each person, whatever his means and situation, the opportunity opens to attempt the absurd enterprise. And it is not only a possibility, but a duty as well."[46] That "absurd enterprise," the perennial task of Jews in Italy and throughout the Diaspora, is the creation of a relationship with the deity and, subsequently, the forging of a sustaining identity in a modern world that seems intent on obliterating all traces of that ancestral consciousness.

NOTES

1. The phrase is from Alexander Stille's *Benevolence and Betrayal: Five Italian Jewish Families Under Fascism* (New York: Summit Books, 1991; reprinted Penguin Books, 1993).

2. H. Stuart Hughes, *Prisoners of Hope: The Silver Age of the Italian Jews, 1924–1974* (Cambridge, MA: Harvard University Press, 1983), p. 2.

3. Still valuable is the essay by the distinguished historian Arnaldo Momigliano "The Jews of Italy," in *The New York Review of Books*, 24 October 1985. Of the many works that have appeared, see especially Hughes, *Prisoners of Hope: The Silver Age of the Italian Jews, 1924–1975*; Meir Michaelis, *Mussolini and the Jews: German-Italian Relations and the Jewish Question in Italy, 1922–1945* (New York: Oxford University Press, 1978); Susan Zuccotti, *The Italians and the Holocaust: Persecution, Rescue, and Survival* (New York: Basic Books, 1987); Stille, *Benevolence and Betrayal*; Nicola Caracciolo, *Uncertain Refuge: Italy and the Jews during the Holocaust*, translated by Florette Rechnitz Koffler and Richard Koffler (Urbana and Chicago: University of Illinois Press, 1995).

4. In September 1962, while preparing the way for a new road from Rome to Ostia, authorities uncovered the remains of a Jewish temple. *New York Times*, 28 September 1962.

5. For an examination of the role of the Jews in Catholic theology in the wake of the Protestant Reformation, see Kenneth R. Stow, *Catholic Thought and Papal Jewry Policy, 1555–1593* (New York: Jewish Theological Seminary, 1977).

6. David I. Kertzer, *The Kidnapping of Edgardo Mortara* (New York: Knopf, 1997), p. xii.

7. Ibid., p. 19.

8. Maurizio Molina, *Ebrei in Italia: un problema d'identità (1870–1938)* (Florence: La Giuntina, 1991), p. 70.

9. For the "juridical condition" of the Jews in Italy over the last two centuries, see Guido Fubini, *La condizione giuridica dell'ebraismo italiano. Dal periodo napoleonico alla repubblica* (Florence: La Nuova Italia, 1974).

10. Although it is true that Leon Blum became the first Jewish prime minister in France, this was not until the 1930s and with large crowds chanting, "Better Hitler than Blum!" in the streets of Paris.

11. Lynn Gunzberg, *Strangers at Home: Jews in the Italian Literary Imagination* (Berkeley: University of California Press, 1992); Michele Sarfatti, *Gli ebrei nell'Italia fascista* (Turin: Einaudi, 2000).

12. Quoted in Renzo De Felice, *Storia degli ebrei italiani sotto il fascismo*, 4th ed. (Turin: Einaudi, 1988 , pp. 138–139); and Zuccotti, p. 30.

13. Benito Mussolini, *Il Popolo d'Italia*, 19 September 1920, quoted in Gunzberg, *Strangers at Home*, p. 219.

14. De Felice, *Storia*, p. 127.

15. Quoted in Molinari, *Ebrei in Italia*, pp. 25–26.

16. Steve Siporin, "From *Kashrut* to *Cucina Ebraica*: The Recasting of Italian Jewish Foodways," in *Journal of American Folklore* 107 (424): 268.

17. Ibid., p. 269.

18. Cecil Roth, *History of the Jews of Italy* (Philadelphia: Jewish Publications Society, 1946), p. 506.

19. Sergio Della Pergola, *Anatomia dell'ebraismo italiano: Caratteristiche demografiche, economiche, sociali, religiose di una minoranza* (Rome: Carucci, 1976), p. 59.

20. Andrew Canepa, "Emancipation and Jewish Response in Mid-Nineteenth-Century Italy," *European History Quarterly* 16 (1986): 403–439.

21. Molinari, *Ebrei in Italia*, p. 15.

22. The most exhaustive work on the subject—based on archives in Israel, Italy, Britain, and the United States—is the Michaelis book. Because of a lack of any documentary evidence, Michaelis concludes that the anti-Semitic laws were not a result of direct pressure from Hitler. See also Zuccotti, *The Italians and the Holocaust*; Michael A. Ledeen, "The Evolution of Fascist Anti-Semitism," *Jewish Social Studies* 37, no. 1 (January 1975); Gene Bernardini, "The Origins and Development of Racial Anti-Semitism in Fascist Italy," *Journal of Modern History* 49 (September 1977): 431–453.

23. See Joel Blatt, "The Battle of Turin, 1933–1936: Carlo Rosselli, Giustizia e Libertà, OVRA and the Origins of Mussolini's Anti-Semitic Campaign," *The Journal of Modern Italian Studies* 1, no. 1 (Fall 1995): 22–57.

24. These are points 4, 6, and 9 of the "Manifesto of Racial Scientists." For more on the manifesto, cf. Stille, *Benevolence and Betrayal*, p. 70; Zuccotti, *The Italians and the Holocaust*, p. 35; De Felice, *Storia*, pp. 541–542.

25. This is the question that H. Stuart Hughes perceptively raises in *Prisoners of Hope*, p. 2. (Years later, Hughes revealed that "I derived more pleasure from *Prisoners of Hope* than from any other of my books." "Doing Italian History: Pleasure and Politics,"

Journal of Modern Italian Studies 1, no. 1 [Fall 1995]: 100.)

26. Attilio Milano, *Storia degli ebrei in Italia* (Turin: Einaudi, 1992), p. 374.

27. Mario Toscano, "Fermenti culturali ed esperienze organizzative della gioventù ebraica italiana (1911–1925)" *Storia Contemporanea* (December 1982): 957.

28. Zuccotti, *The Italians and the Holocaust*, pp. 268–270.

29. On the charismatic Rosselli, see Stanislao G. Pugliese, *Carlo Rosselli: Socialist Heretic and Antifascist Exile* (Cambridge, MA: Harvard University Press, 1999).

30. Nello Rosselli's first work was *Mazzini e Bakunin: 12 anni di movimento operaio in Italia, 1860–1872* (Turin: Einaudi, 1927); this was followed by *Carlo Pisacane nel Risorgimento italiano* (Genoa: Orfini, 1936); his *Saggi sul Risorgimento e altri saggi* was published posthumously in Turin by Einaudi in 1946. See also Zeffiro Ciuffoletti, ed., *Nello Rosselli: un storico sotto il fascismo* (Florence: La Nuova Italia, 1979).

31. A valuable study is Bruno Di Porto, "Il problema ebraico in Nello Rosselli," in *Giustizia e Libertà nella lotta antifascista e nella storia d'Italia* (Florence: La Nuova Italia, 1979), pp. 491–499. See also Zeffiro Ciuffoletti, "Nello Rosselli: storico e politico" in the same volume, pp. 439–482.

32. The entire speech was reprinted in the Zionist newspaper *Israel*, 20 November 1924, and later in *Il Ponte* 8 (1957): 864–868. Now in Ciuffoletti, *Nello Rosselli: uno storico sotto il fascismo*, pp. 1–5. A partial English translation appears in Zuccotti, *The Italians and the Holocaust*, p. 246.

33. De Felice, *Storia*, p. 433.

34. Terracini speaks about his Judaism in an interview found in Gina Formiggini, *Stella d'Italia, Stella di Davide: Gli ebrei dal Risorgimento alla Resistenza* (Milan: Mursia, 1970), pp. 414; on Emilio Sereni, see Ruth Bondy, *The Emissary: A Life of Emilio Sereni*, translated by Shlomo Katz (Boston: Little, Brown, 1977); for Modigliani and Chiesa, see Guido Ludovico Luzzatto, "La participazione all'antifascismo in Italia e all'estero dal 1918 al 1938," in *Gli ebrei in Italia durante il fascismo: Quaderni del Centro di Documentazione Ebraica Contemporanea* 2 (March 1962): 32–44.

35. Carlo Rosselli, *Liberal Socialism*, edited by Nadia Urbinati and translated by William McCuaig (Princeton, NJ: Princeton University Press, 1994), p. 6.

36. Amelia Rosselli, *Memoriale*, unpublished manuscript in the Archivio Rosselli, deposited in the Istituto Storico della Resistenza in Toscana, Palazzo Medici, via Cavour, Florence, Italy. Partially quoted in Nicola Tranfaglia, *Carlo Rosselli: dall'interventismo alla Giustizia e Libertà* (Bari: Laterza, 1968), p. 13.

37. Zuccotti, *The Italians and the Holocaust*, p. 269.

38. The point is made by Hughes, *Prisoners of Hope*, in reference to the Jews of Rome, p. 36.

39. Out of that experience came one of the greatest books of twentieth-century Italian literature and a masterpiece of amateur anthropology, *Christ Stopped at Eboli*, translated by Frances Frenaye (New York: Farrar, Straus and Giroux, 1947).

40. Hughes, *Prisoners of Hope*, p. 74.

41. Ibid., p. 112.

42. Dan Vittorio Segre, *Memoirs of a Fortunate Jew* (Bethesda, MD: Adler & Adler, 1987), p. 23.

43. Ibid., p. 10.

44. Giorgio Bassani, *The Garden of the Finzi-Contini*, translated by William Weaver (San Diego: Harcourt Brace Jovanovich, 1987), p. 14.

45. Ibid., p. 22.

46. Fabio Della Seta, *The Tiber Afire*, translated by Frances Frenaye (Marlboro, VT: Marlboro Press, 1991), pp. 83–84.

Part I

HISTORIOGRAPHY AND THE LAW

2

Legal Discrimination against Italian Jews: From the Romans to the Unification of Italy

Sandra Tozzini

INTRODUCTION

With few exceptions, discrimination has been legally sanctioned against Jews in Italy since the time of the Roman Empire. The Edict of Caracalla, issued in 212 C.E., officially gave Jews the status of full citizenship in the Roman Empire, protecting them from the legal abuses that they had endured previously. The edict, however, represented a brief window in time. Within less than 200 years and with the rise of the Christian emperor Constantine the Great, those protections waned, and Jews lost their status as equal citizens with their fellow countrymen. Occasionally, Jews were given citizenship status in certain geographic areas (as in Florence in 1437 and in Rome in 1430), but these were merely token gestures and were generally extended to a chosen few from whom the governmental body needed assistance. Not until the unification of Italy in 1861 were full citizenship rights again granted to all Italian Jews throughout the entire country. Over 1,600 years had passed for Italian Jews to regain the same legal status that they once had in 212 under the Roman Empire.

Although discrimination has been the rule, rather than the exception, the history of legal discrimination is a chaotic history. From the time of the Jews' first settlement in Italy approximately 2,000 years ago until the unification of Italy in the late nineteenth century, Italy has undergone a series of political, economic, and social changes. Because of this, the legal history is confusing, particularly when viewed solely from a chronological perspective. Furthermore, a chronological perspective focuses on causational issues, that is, *why* the discriminatory laws were enacted. Although historical events are certainly of interest in understanding the background that prompted such laws, they can detract from the *impact* that these laws had on the interaction (or lack thereof) of Jews with their surrounding countrymen.

The following analysis focuses on the *effects* of these discriminatory laws, rather than on causation. That is, what impact did these various laws have on the relationship that Italy had with its Italian Jews?

Here, social scientists can help explain the extent of the impact of such discriminatory laws. Social scientists have provided multiple models for describing assimilation, which Metzer defines as a process in "which ethnicity is not a basis of social differentiation and plays no role in the distribution of wealth, power, and prestige."[1] One commonly accepted model of assimilation was propounded by Gordon in 1964.[2] Although the model has been subject to some criticism, it has withstood the test of time and is still cited as one of the major models of assimilation.

More importantly, Gordon's seven-step model works particularly well in characterizing the effect of the discriminatory laws enacted in Italy. Gordon's model is well suited to this study because the model is not time-dependent.[3] That is, Gordon's model does not require a chronological sequence of events. Instead, Gordon describes a series of seven steps in which a minority group passes in the process of assimilation. However, under the Gordon model, the different steps need not necessarily follow one another. Thus, the *sequence* of steps in the assimilation process is not the critical issue. Rather, the degree of assimilation is dependent on the number of steps that a minority group has achieved.

By placing the long chronicle of anti-Jewish laws enacted in Italy in the framework of Gordon's seven-step assimilation model, the full impact of these discriminatory laws becomes much clearer. At various times throughout the past 2,000 years, laws have been enacted that counter each step of the normal assimilation processes, maintaining Jews as a distinct minority within the Christian host society.

GORDON'S SEVEN-STEP ASSIMILATION MODEL

According to the Gordon model, there are seven steps (or phases) through which a minority group must pass in order to become fully assimilated in the host or dominant society. These steps are:

1. Cultural Assimilation: changes in cultural patterns and adoptions of the host group's values.
2. Structural Assimilation: acceptance into the host group's cliques, clubs, and institutions.
3. Marital Assimilation: intermarriage between the host group and the minority group.
4. Identificational Assimilation: development of a sense of "peoplehood."
5. Attitude-Receptional Assimilation: absence of prejudice.
6. Behavioral-Receptional Assimilation: absence of discrimination.
7. Civic Assimilation: absence of power differences.[4]

In the context of discriminatory laws, only the attitude-receptional category is inapplicable. Because laws regulate *conduct* as opposed to thoughts or feelings, the attitude-receptional category does not apply when characterizing the effects of discriminatory laws. With the exception of this step, the model works well to classify the effects of the discriminatory laws that have been recorded in the literature. In short, analysis of these laws demonstrates the systematic exclusion of Jews from the rest of Italian society.

APPLICATION OF THE LAWS TO GORDON'S MODEL

Cultural Assimilation

Discriminatory laws directed at Jewish culture had their origins during pagan Roman imperial times. Historically, the primary focus of discriminatory laws directed at Italian-Jewish culture has focused on religious practices. Official positions of lawmakers oscillated throughout history between paternalistic toleration of Jews as an inferior race and overt hostility toward Judaism, expressed anywhere from religious restrictions, to forced baptism.

For a very brief period in pre-Christian times, Jews were granted freedom of worship under Julius Caesar and given special exemption from military service because of their dietary laws and in deference to their refusal to bear arms as well as to march on the Sabbath.[5] The emperor Augustus, in an edict on Jewish rights issued in 1 B.C.E., allowed Jews not only to practice their religion but to punish those who stole Jewish religious items by forfeiting their property to the state.[6]

Such religious freedoms were not to last for long.[7] Around the year 100, the emperor Hadrian forbade circumcision and applied this prohibition to Jews as well as all other groups in the Roman Empire that practiced it.[8] Hadrian's successor, Antonius Pius, relaxed the ban on circumcision by allowing Jews to perform it on their own children. However, should circumcision be performed on any non-Jew, the penalty was castration.[9] By 135 Rome prohibited—on pain of death— circumcision, reading the Torah, and eating unleavened bread at Passover.[10]

Septimus Severus (193–235), although generally favorable to Jews and permitting them to hold public office, did forbid conversion to Judaism (as well as Christianity).[11]

With the rise of Christianity, Constantine the Great declared Christianity the state religion in 315.[12] Not only was Christianity now the state religion, but any Jew who demonstrated anger against a Christian (who was a convert from Judaism) did so under pain of death by burning.[13]

In 339 Constantius II went even further and criminalized conversion to Judaism.[14] He also punished circumcision of slaves by making the offending party responsible for the damage to the slave as well as paying with his life for the transgression.[15] Theodosius the Great (379–395) forbade the building of new synagogues and permitted destruction of existing synagogues if their destruction served some religious purpose.[16] His successor, Honorarius (395–423), reaffirmed that existing laws against Jews and heretics were to be strictly construed.[17]

Apostolic canons of the early church prohibited Christians from taking oil to synagogues for celebration of Jewish feasts.[18] Proscriptions against conversion to Judaism promulgated at the Council of Orleans (533–541) were mild compared with the edicts of Leo III, who, in 722, outlawed Judaism and permitted forced baptisms.[19]

After a long period of overt hostility toward Judaism, the church changed its official position toward the Jews. With the ascendancy of Pope Gregory the Great in the late sixth century, the church became more tolerant of Judaism. Pope Gregory the Great issued the bull *Sicut Judeis*, which promulgated a paternalistic view of the Jews as being under the protection of the papacy. However, the underlying rationale of the change in policy was promoted not by humanitarian objectives but by a goal of achieving conversion through tolerance.

Around the turn of the fourteenth century, Pope Boniface VIII granted inquisitors the authority to treat born Christians who converted to Judaism as heretics, as set forth in the papal decree *Contra Christianos*.[20]

Similarly, in 1344 papal legates were given authority to institute proceedings against any Sicilian Jewish converts who reverted to Judaism.[21] In further attempts to prevent "backsliders," Pope Eugenius IV required neophytes to sign written promises abandoning all Jewish practices in return for abolishing the restrictions that the church had imposed upon Jewish converts.[22]

From the time of Pope Gregory the Great until around the fifteenth or sixteenth century, the church treated the practice of Judaism with relative tolerance, but Jewish converts to Christianity who reverted to Judaism were treated more harshly. From 1119 until the 1500s Jews were officially guaranteed the right to practice Judaism, in theory if not necessarily in practice.[23] For example, Pope Urban II urged that Jews should be tolerated.[24] However, papal tolerance was narrowly fashioned. For example, at the Fourth Lateran Council in 1215, Jews were prohibited from wearing their best clothes on Sundays or walking in public on special Christian feast days.[25]

During the reign of Martin V, the official papal policy of tolerance toward Jews began to waver. On 31 January 1419 Pope Martin V expressed tolerance toward Jews, reiterating the principles set forth over 800 years earlier by Pope Gregory the Great in *Sicut Judeis*, issued in 598.[26] Martin V reaffirmed this position toward the Jews in 1422, but in 1423 he repealed his earlier stance under pressure from influential Catholic preachers. He changed his position yet again in 1429, when he once again gave credence to the policies articulated in *Sicut Judeis* for Italian Jews.[27]

Martin V's ever-changing position may not necessarily have been a reflection of his own personal opinion but an advent of future change. During the 1400s Pope Eugenius IV required that Jews be compelled to attend sermons, with the hope of conversion.[28] In 1443 Eugenius IV revoked outright Martin's reaffirmation of the doctrine of *Sicut Judeis* almost twenty years earlier.[29] Although Eugenius IV's position was not as favorable to Jewish religious freedoms, it was merely a portent of things to come, with the oppressive *Cum Nimis Absurdum*, issued a century later.

Immediately prior to the issuance of *Cum Nimis Absurdum* (the papal bull so devastating to the plight of Italian Jews), Pope Julius III strengthened the force of an inquisitorial decree issued a year earlier and ordered the Talmud burned.[30] With the proclamation of the papal bull *Cum Nimis Absurdum* in 1555, Jews were allowed no more than one synagogue per community. In addition, all their accounting books were to be henceforth recorded in Italian and no longer in Hebrew.[31]

Although examples of religious freedoms granted to Italian Jews do occur at various points in history throughout the Italian peninsula, generally these expansive religious freedoms are limited to certain individuals and not expanded to the Jewish community as a whole. Furthermore, even where religious freedoms had been granted, they were usually short-lived. For example, in 1437 the Florentine government, in its *condotta*, or banking contract, with Abraham Datill, gave him special privileges of celebrating the Sabbath and other holidays, but these religious freedoms were not necessarily expanded to other Florentine Jews.[32] However, even these small concessions were reversed when the Florentine government was prosecuted by Datill's successors for allegedly violating the banking contract with the city.[33]

During the 1400s and 1500s, the Duchy of Savoy was a relatively safe haven for Italian Jews by comparison. Under religious privileges granted by Pope Martin V in 1418, Jews in the Duchy could not be penalized for practicing their faith as long as they did so in keeping with papal orders. Furthermore, under the special privileges, no Jew was to be baptized before the age of twelve against the wishes of the parents.[34] Later, during the 1500s, Jews in the Duchy were allowed to print and circulate Jewish publications as long as they were not listed in the *Index Librorum Prohibitorum*, the list of books banned by the church.[35]

However, these extensions of broader religious freedoms were the exception rather than the rule in sixteenth-century Italy. Even later in history, Jewish religious freedom was curtailed throughout many parts of Italy. For example, in 1660 the Jews of Genoa were compelled to post crucifixes on their doors, in violation of their own religious beliefs.[36]

The mid-1700s saw a return to severe papal restrictions on the religious practices of Roman Jews. In 1753 and 1754 police searched Roman ghetto homes for forbidden books, books either containing psalms or books designed for liturgical use in the synagogue. In 1775 a papal edict prohibited all Hebrew books, with few exceptions. The edict *Editto Supra Gli Ebrei*, promulgated by Pope Pius VI, required that no one "possess, buy, translate, sell, copy or otherwise dispose of any codex or book on the Talmud or any volume containing statements against industries of the Christian faith."[37] In addition, the edict prohibited Christian silversmiths from making any amulets, charms, or seven-branched candelabra. Neither were Jews allowed public cortege for their funerals.[38]

Even during periods when Jews were technically allowed to have a synagogue in their community, failure to abide by the specific regulations that governed their operation could prove disastrous. For example, in 1715 in Alba in the province of Piedmont, the Jewish community was celebrating the festival of Purim in the synagogue without benefit of a papal license. Because the Jews had violated the law, authorities interrupted the services and seized the menorah.[39]

Structural Discrimination

Structural assimilation refers to a minority group's acceptance into clubs and other institutions of the host society. Structural assimilation between a minority group and the host society necessarily involves social interaction. Without social interaction, acceptance into the clubs and institutions of the host society becomes virtually impossible.

Because many traditional trades have required admittance to guilds, historically they serve as the functional equivalent of social clubs for their time. For that reason, employment and occupational discrimination are forms of structural discrimination.

Social Interaction

Laws prohibiting social interactions between Christians and Jews are long-standing. The emperor Honorarius (395–423) excluded Jews from military as well as court functions.[40]

Early apostolic canons prohibited either the feasting or fasting of Jews and Christians together.[41] Because church teachings held that Jews were not to be superior to Christians, Gregory I (590–604) prohibited Jews from keeping Christian slaves or having Christian employees.[42]

The papacy continued to play a seminal role in keeping Jews and Christians socially distant. In 1215 Pope Innocent III reiterated the doctrine of Christian superiority over the Jews.[43] Later in history, Popes Eugenius IV and Calixtus III forbade Christians from using the services of a Jewish physician.[44] (Paul IV once again reiterated this long-standing prohibition against treatment of Christian patients in his papal bull of 1555.) Eugenius IV, in addition to banning Christians from taking any medications from Jews or Saracens, prohibited Christians from eating, drinking, or bathing with them.[45]

The most extensive prohibitions regarding social interactions between Jews and Christians were contained in *Cum Nimis Absurdum*, the papal bull of Paul IV, promulgated in 1555. In this bull, Paul IV disallowed the keeping of either male or female Christian servants by Jews, barred association between Christians and Jews on familiar terms, and prohibited Jews from being addressed by any title of respect (such as *signor*).[46]

However, the papacy was not alone in enforcing social distances between Jews and Christians. During the sixteenth century, the Republic of Venice had its own form of social police, the Esecutori contro la Bestemmia, a subcommission of the Council of Ten that regulated all forms of evil living, including sexual relations between Jews and Christians. Although sexual relations were prohibited between Jews and Christians, they were not considered as serious a matter if there was no possibility of pending marriage or conversion.[47] Lower down the administrative scale were the *Ufficiali al Cattava*, a lower board of magistrates whose duty also operated along the lines of a social police force; it was their job to keep social distances between Jews and Christians.[48]

Late in the seventeenth century, Friuli banned the employment of Christian servants or journeymen by Jews. Shortly before Friuli enacted its restrictions, the *Editto Supra Gli Ebrei* declared that Jews could not invite Christians into their synagogues and that Christians could not be employed to light the Sabbath fires, nor were there to be any familiar relations between Christian and Jew,[49] thereby ending any other form of social exchange.

Even in the eighteenth century, new restrictions were promulgated in order to keep Jew and Christian apart. The new severity toward Jews that arose during the papacies of Benedict XIV and Clement XIII went so far as to bar Jews from having their linen washed by Christians unless the linens were transported by specially licensed porters with unassailable religious convictions.[50]

Some small measure of social acceptance was finally attained by Jews in the Grand Duchy of Tuscany in 1767, when Jews were allowed admission to the Accademia dei Faticanti, a poetic society.[51]

Employment

Employment laws have been very reflective of the role in society that Jews needed to play at a particular time. Generally, employment opportunities for Jews have been very restricted. As a general rule, Jews were often either prohibited from participating in a lucrative occupation or pressed into the service of a less desirable job. Like other restrictive measures imposed upon the Jews, these restrictions vacillated over time.

Prohibited occupations. The emperor Honorarius (395–423) barred Jews from governmental service or the army but allowed them the practice of law, medicine, or the decurionate. Valerian III (425–455) reiterated Honorarius' exclusion of Jews from government service.[52]

In tenth-century Venice, Venetian ships were prohibited from transporting either Jews or their goods,[53] nor could Jews belong to guilds. Venetian Jews were restricted to the practice of medicine (albeit with some restrictions) and to dealing in secondhand garments as well as practicing usury.[54]

Despite the severe occupational restrictions that Venice imposed on Jews, other Italian communities were more liberal in their treatment of Jews. Even though Jews had been denied access to participate in fairs in many other areas in Italy, in 1331 in Ferme (near Ancona), Jews were allowed to participate in local fairs (which were of major economic importance to local communities). Similarly, in Parma Jews were allowed to practice any liberal trade. However, the practice of the trade was dependent upon payment of an annual tax.[55]

Pope Eugenius IV, the early fifteenth-century pope who instituted many new restrictions against Jews, also limited the numbers of professions open to Jews, promulgating a definitive list containing permissible occupations for them.[56] In 1451 Nicholas V reaffirmed the old exclusions that barred Jews from society and all "honorable walks of life."[57]

Although Jews had been categorically barred from treating Christians, exemptions were frequently granted. Special dispensations from popes or secular governments created special exceptions for certain specifically named Jews to practice medicine on Christians. For example, a papal dispensation issued in 1474 gave the Priori of Assisi permission to have a Jewish physician treat Christian patients of the town.[58]

The papal bull of 1555, *Cum Nimis Absurdum*, excluded Jews from dealing in corn or any other necessities of life. They could deal only in old clothes and secondhand goods.[59]

Later prohibitions on employment expanded the exclusions that already were in place. In addition to restrictions regarding kinds of employment, later prohibitions specifically restricted the places where Jews could work. With the establishment of the ghetto in Rome in the 1550s and its concomitant restriction on practicing a trade outside the ghetto, Jews were further hampered in their ability to obtain employment.[60] The spatial restrictions on trade evidenced in Rome during the sixteenth century were renewed in the middle of the seventeenth century when, in 1659, Pope Alexander VIII prohibited Jews from having shops or warehouses outside the Roman ghetto.[61]

A century later, a more liberal Trieste did allow Jews to keep their shops open on Christian holidays, an unheard-of practice a few centuries earlier.[62] However, not all cities were as liberal. Even after Trieste allowed Jews to conduct business on Christian feast days, Venice promulgated more restrictive laws aimed at the Jews. The *ricondotta* of 1777 barred Jews in Venice as well as any of its territories from any kind of manufacturing, employment of Christians and dealing in grains or any other type of foodstuffs.[63]

Permissible occupations. Permissible occupations were so restrictive that Jews had few employment opportunities in Italian society. Partially as a result of these restrictions, Jews were forced into banking as one of the few areas left open to them. Furthermore, Jews were pressed into service as moneylenders to circumvent the Christian prohibition against usury. Although the definition of usury was often unclear in earlier times, generally, "usury" was defined as lending money for profit.[64]

The early banking arrangements devised by the Jews circumvented the notion of lending money for profit, as they operated more as pawn-broking establishments. Banks were strictly regulated. Examples of the regulations imposed on Jewish bankers are contained in the Florentine laws of the fifteenth century, by which Jews were allowed to lend money only "ad pignus" (against a tangible object), not "ad scriptus" (against a written note).[65] Even with the limitations already imposed on Jewish bankers, these banking establishments were subject to additional controls. For example, in Assisi the city fathers required that Jewish bankers periodically shake out the clothing that had been pawned.[66]

Failure to abide by these strict banking rules could prove disastrous to the Jew who transgressed them. For example, the highest fine ever paid in Florentine history up until the mid-fifteenth century was the fine of 20,000 florins paid by the Jewish banker Salamone di Buonaventura for allegedly violating Florentine usury laws.[67]

Although these banking arrangements provided some Jews with employment opportunities that were otherwise unavailable, they did nothing to foster any harmony between Jews and Christians. Usury was a despised profession; it was strictly prohibited according to earlier Christian teachings. Usury was so despised that in 1179 the Third Lateran Council declared that usurers would be denied the benefit of Christian burial.[68] Even Dante put the Paduan bankers into one of the rungs of hell in his *Divine Comedy*.[69]

In spite of the early official Christian prohibition against usury for Christians, Jewish moneylenders did exist, often with the express permission of the pope. For example, moneylenders from Rome during the twelfth century relocated to communities outside Rome, often with a papal license allowing them to operate (as long as they did not charge excessive rates of interest).[70] Jewish banking was highly regulated, however, with *condotta* (contracts) entered into between the governmental body and the Jewish bankers, with control over rates of interest a key clause (*capitolo*) in any contract.[71] There were, however, certain advantages that Jewish bankers gained by these *condotta*, many of them bequeathing greater personal protections to the bankers who performed these services.[72]

However, even when Jews were virtually forced into lending, Italian society wavered in its acceptance of Jews in banking. For example, in 1456 the General Counsel of Assisi decided to call one to two bankers to its town in order to set up a lending bank.[73] A *condotta* was later given to a Jew to set up lending institution in Assisi. After he left, and the city fathers once again needed a lending institution, they proposed readmitting him to the town.[74]

The rise of Jewish moneylenders provided a service to the community. Generally, the Jewish moneylenders serviced the poorer elements of the community, so that even though Jews had a new occupation, they did not usually become major economic players in a society.[75]

With the rise of the Monte di Pietà, a church-based bank, first founded in Perugia in 1462, attempts were made to cut back on Jewish moneylenders.[76] For example, in the mid-1500s, Pope Paul IV hampered the ability of Jewish bankers by cutting the rates of allowable interest that Jews were allowed to charge from 24% to 18%.[77] Even so, church authorization of Jewish moneylenders remained in effect. In 1584 Cardinal Vastavillani issues a *tolleranza* (tolerance) that created a ten-year charter allowing Jews in the Duchy of Savoy to lend money.[78]

Certainly, the role of the Jewish banker was a critical one. Although borrowed money was used to fund more important societal needs, the role of the Jewish banker often helped with minor emergencies. The City Council of Cherasco authorized the *sindaco* (mayor) to secure a loan from the Jewish bankers to pay schoolteachers as well as pay for the costs of hay needed to feed the horses of the soldiers stationed in town.[79]

With a change in church policy toward the lending of money for profit, Christians entered the world of banking. Even though Jewish bankers were once considered a necessity, once they were viewed as competition for Christian bankers, restrictions began to appear. In Modena in 1767, Jewish bankers were suppressed when the Monte di Pietà was established.[80]

Marital Discrimination

The literature does not contain many references to antimiscegenation laws. Whether this lack of reference is due to a lack of renewed legislation or simply a lack of discussion by chroniclers is unclear. However, what is clear is that the legal restrictions on intermarriage were early entrants in the laws of discrimination against Jews, much earlier than other discriminatory laws (such as the wearing of badges). For example, Constantius II forbade future marriages between Jewish men and Christian women of the imperial weaving factory. In addition, the imperial order dissolved any current marriages existing between them.[81]

Early church councils were quick to ban interfaith marriages. For example, the Council of Orleans in 533–541 forbade intermarriage between Christian and Jew.[82] These early entries into the development of the discriminatory laws undoubtedly had a great impact. The dearth of references later in history may well be due to the strong societal taboos (such as existed in the United States between whites and African Americans) and religious taboos on behalf of both Christians and Jews regarding interfaith marriages, which would have lessened the necessity for legal intervention.

Identificational Discrimination

Gordon's concept of identificational assimilation focuses on a sense of "peoplehood." From a legal perspective, identificational discrimination keeps the minority group separate and apart from the host group. From the Middle Ages until the eighteenth century, numerous laws had been promulgated to make Jews visibly identifiable, barring any development of a sense of peoplehood between Jews and other Italians.

The hostility toward Jews was not just religious. From the time of the Middle Ages onward, Jews were viewed as *racially* separate, not merely as members of a different religious faith.[83] However, unlike some minorities that exhibit clearly visible, immutable characteristics, Jews were physically indistinguishable from the Christian community, absent some identificational badge.

The wearing of distinctive badges served another important social function besides merely keeping the groups from identifying a sense of communal peoplehood. It also served to inhibit sexual interaction between the two groups by identifying the Jews.[84]

Initial efforts at identifying Jews as different from the host society were the results of early church councils. The Fourth Lateran Council of 1215 required Jews to wear a ring-shaped badge.[85] As early as 1222 Frederick II enforced the new legislation from the Fourth Lateran Council, ordering all Jews to wear a distinctive blue badge in the shape of a *tau*, the Greek letter T. Although not enforced, Frederick also ordered that Jews grow beards as another indication of identification.[86]

From its origin as a religious enactment, the requirement of wearing badges later evolved into civic law as well. Civic statutes in Rome in 1363 required Jews to wear a distinctive badge, only this time the badge was identified as a *tabarro rosso* (red cloak). Only physicians were excused from the wearing of the *tabarro rosso*. Later revisions of the civil code, in 1430, were confirmed by Martin V.[87]

However, Martin V vacillated in this treatment toward the Jews and the necessity of their making their identity known. Martin V dispensed with the necessity of Jews in the Duchy of Savoy wearing badges, at the request of the duke.[88]

However, not all communities were as broad-minded as the Duchy of Savoy. Florence in 1439 enacted new *capitoli*. According to the Florentine government, Jews were not covered by the *capitoli* and were required to wear distinctive dress in Florence.[89] Even though an exception for the wearing of identificational garb was made for the Jewish banker Abraham Datill (who was being wooed by the Florentine government to set up a bank), none of the rest of the Jewish community benefited from this exception, and they were still required to wear identificational clothing.[90] A few years later, in 1445, Eugenius IV in *Super Gregem Dominicum* repeated the former church rule and echoed the law laid down in Florence that Jews were required to wear distinctive dress. A year later, Venice required that Jews wear their badges.[91] Nor was the wearing of the badge a phenomenon of the larger urban areas. Even communities as small as Assisi required the Jews in their communities to wear the badges designating them as Jews. In 1456 the Assisi General Counsel decided to require the wearing of the badge for its Jewish community members.

In the following century the papacy continued its assault. Pope Paul IV required Jewish men to wear yellow hats and women to wear a yellow veil.[92] The papacy was not the only authority still promulgating regulations regarding badges. In 1693 the Jews of Friuli were required to wear the badge with the creation of the ghetto there.[93]

The eighteenth century added new impositions regarding the wearing of badges. Popes Benedict XIV (1724–1730) and Clement XIII (1730–1739) mandated new code restrictions on Jews, extending the times when the Jews had to wear their badges. Under the new promulgations, Jews were forced to wear their distinctive badges even while traveling. The later *Editto Supra Gli Ebrei* of 1775 required that the badge be worn by both men and women.[94]

Although the papacy still appeared bent on the use of identificational badges, civil authorities began to ignore the rules requiring identificational badges. For example, by 1778 in Trieste, the enforcement of the wearing of badges had started to be neglected.[95]

Behavioral-Receptional Discrimination

Gordon defines behavior-receptional assimilation as an absence of discrimination toward a minority group. Discrimination has been described as actions toward a minority that include "avoidance, denial, threat, or physical attack."[96] The laws enacted in Italy that mandated that Jews be physically segregated from the Christian majority constituted legal behavioral discrimination.

Precedent for this type of legal discrimination is so ancient in Italy that it predates the Christian era in Rome. Furthermore, behavior-receptional discrimination lasted well into the nineteenth century in Rome, where papal authority maintained the ghetto of the "Pope's Jews."

History demonstrates that throughout nearly 2,000 years, banishment and coerced confinement often existed side by side in Italy. However, banishment as a legal remedy to the "Jewish problem" appears more commonly employed during earlier periods, with the use of ghettos more commonly utilized during later periods in history.

Banishment got a very early foothold in Italy. In the year 19 C.E., during the reign of the emperor Tiberius, Jews (along with the Egyptians) were expelled from Rome. The unacceptable religious beliefs of both groups (although substantively unrelated) were the rationale for the expulsion. The Roman Senate banished both groups to Sardinia to help the government fight the Sardinian outlaws.[97]

Banishment, however, was not to be confined to pagan Roman emperors. On 1 October 855 the Christian king Louis II, king of Italy, expelled all the Jews from his kingdom.[98] Centuries later, banishment was still employed against unwelcome Jews. In 1279 the podestà of Perugia expelled all the Jews from his city.[99]

The Catholic Church responded to the dissemination of Christian heresies toward the end of the twelfth century by reasserting its power and punishing transgressors, including Jews.[100] In 1215 Pope Innocent III issued a number of anti-Jewish laws, including the requirement that Jews were to remain in their homes with their shutters drawn on Easter and other special Christian holidays.[101] Although this confinement was temporary, it foreshadowed the later papal proclamations that established ghettos in Rome and the Papal States.

The subsequent institution of the ghetto was previewed in Sicily in the fourteenth century. In 1311 Fra Matteo da Ponsecco, inquisitor for the Kingdom of Sicily, was instrumental in controlling the location where Jews lived. The friar convinced the king to require that newly converted Jews live dispersed throughout the community with Christians so as not to be lured back into Judaism. Approximately thirty years later, this policy was reversed, and the neophytes were forced to live together for purposes of surveillance.[102] Although these living arrangements were not, strictly speaking, the ghetto conditions as instituted by the papacy in the sixteenth century, they did set a historical precedent for controlling where Jews lived.

In 1434 at the Council of Basle, Pope Eugenius IV decreed that Jews live in separate quarters.[103] His papal bull of 1445, *Super Gregem Dominicum*, established strict regulations of conduct between Christians and Jews, including the exhortation that Jews and Christians live separately, with Jews living in distinctly segregated areas.[104]

However, not until 1516 was the first ghetto officially established in Venice.[105] (Venice, not content with the formation of the ghetto in 1516, partially expelled its Jewish population in 1527.)[106]

Confinement to ghettos was accompanied by night watchmen, who controlled the opening of the gates to the ghettos in the morning and their closing at night.

The Genoese experience of ghetto confinement (although established during the next century) was not atypical. In the Genoese ghetto, special night watchmen called *massari* blocked the gates of the ghetto from 1 A.M. until dawn. Watchmen prevented direct contact (either commercial or sexual) between the Jewish residents of the ghettos and Christians.[107]

In the year following the establishment of the first ghetto in Venice, the papal bull *Cum Nimis Absurdum* proclaimed that Jews should live in ghettos.[108] However, the Roman ghetto was not formed until many years later. Between the time of *Cum Nimis Absurdum* and the formal establishment of the ghetto in Rome, Jews were exiled from Naples (1540),[109] Genoa (1550), and Venice (1550).[110]

Within a short time after these various expulsions, the ghetto in Rome became a reality. Although previous popes had advocated segregation of Jews from Christians, not until 1555 was the ghetto in Rome formally established by Pope Paul IV.[111] A year later, in 1556, a ghetto was established in Bologna.

The movement to confine Jews in ghettos continued to gain momentum. Ghettos were established in Modena in 1638, in Reggio between the years 1669 and 1671, in Gorizia in 1648, in Trieste from 1693 to 1695, in Turin in 1679, in Vercelli in 1724, and in Finale in 1736.[112] However, the establishment of ghettos was anything but uniform throughout the country. At the time that some ghettos were established, others were abolished, indicative of the disparate treatment that Jews received across Italy. For example, in 1679, at the time that the ghetto was formally established in Turin, it was abolished in Genoa.[113] However, by the time that Genoa abolished its ghetto, not many Jews remained. During the 1670s the attitude of the Genoese government resulted in the exodus of large numbers of Jews to the nearby towns of Livorno, Monferato, and Casale.[114]

Although attitudes in other locales gradually improved, the position of the papacy toward the Roman Jews hardened with the passage of time. In 1659 Pope Alexander VIII mandated that Jews could not leave the ghetto at night under penalty of a fine of fifty *scudi* or a public flogging.[115] The Jews of the Roman ghetto experienced a brief respite from confinement when they were liberated by Napoléon. But with the downfall of Napoléon, the Jews were returned to the ghetto.[116] Even immediately prior to the unification of Italy, the papacy continued to impose discriminatory restrictions on the Jews within its control. Between 1846 and 1878, Pope Pius IX reestablished all former restrictions against Jews in the Vatican state.[117] Not until 1870 was the ghetto in Rome formally abolished. Even then, its abolition contravened the wishes of Pope Pius IX, who wished to retain the formal institution of the ghetto.[118]

Civic Discrimination

Gordon defines civic assimilation as the lack of conflict in political power between the minority and the host society.[119] The multitude of laws aimed directly at Jews assured that they were not political equals. There were few periods from pre-Christian times until the unification of Italy when Jews enjoyed the status of citizens. Even fewer were the times when Jews were able to enjoy the privileges of citizenship, even if they had officially been granted the status of citizens.

The freedoms typically associated with citizenship that would equalize political power—property ownership, freedom to travel, ability to hold public office, fair taxation, due process in the courts, access to education—were generally denied the Italian Jews. As a general rule, the civil rights afforded Jews by the earlier Roman emperors were discarded with the rise of Christian emperors in the fourth century. Although civic freedoms became much more common during the age of Enlightenment, they were by no means universally present throughout Italy. Whatever civic freedoms Jews had prior to the unification of Italy were very much dependent on locale.

Freedom of Travel

Restrictions on freedom of travel took various forms throughout history. In some instances, the restrictions were temporary and (although humiliating) were not unduly burdensome from the point of view of their duration. For example, Jews were confined to their homes on Easter under the proclamation of Innocent III in 1215. Under the specific provisions of the papal declaration, Jews were to remain in their homes with the shutters drawn on Easter.[120]

However, in other instances, the restraint on travel was much more severe. The restrictions imposed on Jews by the Republic of Venice were a prime example. During the 1200s Venetians restricted the ability of Jews to travel. Venice excluded Jews from traveling on its ships because it viewed Jews as rivals in the trade business and therefore inhibited their ability to move freely.[121]

Reminiscent of Venice's earlier ban on freedom to travel, Pope Martin V issued a papal bull in the late 1420s denying ship captains the ability to transport Jews to the Holy Land.[122]

Later in time, however, the restrictive bans were removed in some parts of the country. The Duchy of Savoy, often more humanitarian in its treatment of Jews, granted Jews the freedom to travel (as well as freedom to live where it was both personally convenient for the Jews and convenient for the Duchy.)[123]

As other parts of Italy were yielding and granting more civil rights to its Jewish inhabitants, the papacy remained entrenched in its anti-Jewish position. Under the 1775 edict of Pius VI, Jews were not free to travel in carriages either in Rome or in its environs.[124]

Education

Although the literature does not contain extensive references to restrictions on secular education, access to education has traditionally been viewed as a key factor in minorities' seeking to escape the cycle of poverty. For Jews, however, education may not have provided much escape, as both secular and church officials barred them from most occupations. Even so, official proclamations impacted Jews' ability to receive a university education.

As a general rule, Jews in Italy were excluded from universities, with the exception of Padua, in which the first Jew to receive a doctoral degree graduated in 1409.[125] Martin V, who still generally supported the tenets of *Sicut Judeis*, officially permitted Jews to attend universities.[126] A few years later, Martin's successor, Eugenius IV, revoked the privilege of Jews' attending universities.

Other northern Italian areas, however, continued to be more liberal in their approach to education for Jews. The Duchy of Savoy allowed Jewish university students to receive the same honors and titles as Christian students were entitled to receive.[127] Modena specifically added regulations in 1780 that allowed Jews to attend public schools to study medicine.[128]

Criminal and Civil Rights

Except for the brief period when Jews were at least nominally considered citizens during the Roman Empire, they were not generally afforded the same legal protections as the rest of society, with respect to either criminal prosecution or civil rights. The disabilities that Jews suffered with respect to these rights and protections often extended beyond mere sweeping generalizations to very specific rights.

For example, the emperor Justinian in 531 forbade either Jews or heretics from offering testimony against orthodox Christians. However, Jews were allowed to offer testimony on behalf of orthodox Christians against one who was not a member of orthodox Christianity.[129] Thus, the testimony of Jews was selectively utilized, dependent not so much on the character of the witness (i.e., whether or not the witness was reliable) as on the character of the *defendant*. Thus, the testimony of the Jews was allowed to benefit orthodox Christians against non-Christians.

Criminal prosecutions were sometimes specifically targeted at Jews, especially during times of plague and natural catastrophes, because Jews were assumed to be the underlying cause of the problem. For example, authorities arrested some Roman Jews and charged them with putting a nail through a Eucharistic host, causing the earthquake and hurricane that occurred on Good Friday in 1021. These Jews were tortured in order to obtain confessions and later burned at the stake.[130]

At times, however, Jews were given more procedural protections to protect them from indiscriminate criminal prosecution. The edict issued by Pope Boniface VIII was an example of this extension of some criminal procedural protections. The edict, issued in 1229, allowed Jews a degree of protection against prosecution. Under the edict, Jews were accorded the right to know the names of their accusers during the papal inquisitions of the later thirteenth century.[131]

The proclamation of Martin V during the fifteenth century was also an example of an attempt at protecting Jews. Martin V, at the request of the Duke of Savoy, issued a decree that no Jew would be brought before either the ecclesiastical courts or secular foreign courts if they had settled in the Duchy prior to the commencement of the lawsuit.[132] However, the proclamation was restricted to the Jews residing in the Duchy and not to the Italian-Jewish population as a whole.

The *condotta* of 1437 between Florence and Abraham Datill, the Jew with whom Florence sought to engage in banking, protected him from charges of homicide without the express permission of the Council of Eight, the legislative body for the republic. In addition, the *condotta* required that all Jews of Florence would be treated as citizens under both civil and criminal laws. However, that protection was a mixed blessing for Jews at that point in history as it removed them from all church protections that were present at that time.[133]

The sixteenth century saw a shift in attitude by papal rulers regarding legal jurisdiction of the Jews of Rome, particularly with respect to the courts in which Jews were to bring their civil disputes. The Jews of Rome were allowed to utilize their own arbiters. These arbiters had primary jurisdiction in disputes, and their decisions were, at least theoretically, binding. In truth, however, the real source of the Jewish arbiter's power was a papal vicar or papal official who had to approve the Jewish arbiter's jurisdiction. This system of utilizing Jewish arbiters to resolve disputes was unique to Rome, however, and not authorized outside Rome.[134] Although the decision to use Jewish arbiters may have been beneficial for Jews, it did impose yet another wedge between them and the rest of society.

Although selective criminal prosecution of Jews had been criticized in the past, it continued to occur. Following close on the heels of the edict of Pius VI in 1775, *Editto Supra Gli Ebrei*, Roman rabbis were selectively imprisoned for failing to find the whereabouts of a Jew who was wanted by the police.[135]

Property

Restrictions against Jews' ability to own property have included prohibitions against both personal and real property, as well as the ability of Jews to inherit. The focus on prohibition against personal property appears to have occurred earlier in time, whereas the focus on later discriminatory property laws appears to have concentrated on prohibitions of ownership of real property. Historically, the degree of restriction of property ownership is very much dependent upon the hostility of the host society toward Jews at any particular time.

In early times, Jews had the right to own property. In ancient Rome, Jews formed communities, recognized as *collegia*, entities with rights, including the right to inherit property. These rights, however, were abolished by the legislation of later Christian emperors during the late fourth century.[136]

Under the imperatives of Constantius II, Christian slaves were to be taken from Jews, denying Jews the same personal property rights as Christians.[137] Not only did the ban on slave ownership discriminate against Jews in their ability to have the same property rights as non-Jews, but it also handicapped them in their ability to compete in an agrarian economy, which was dependent on slave labor.

The emperor Valerian III (425–455) allowed converted children of Jews to inherit property from their parents.[138]

Even the restricted property rights of the later Roman emperors were mild compared to restrictions that were subsequently imposed first by canon law and then by secular governing bodies. Jewish property rights in real property were totally abrogated in 545 by a church council promulgation that confiscated Jewish property and forbade Christians from selling their property to Jews.[139] In Venice during the tenth century, Jews were denied the right of ownership of either real property or slaves, as both were seen to be contrary to church law.[140]

Occasionally, the ban on real property ownership was relaxed. In 1437, in a move designed to benefit one individual, Abraham Datill (the Jewish banker who was viewed as vital to the needs of the Florentine economy), the Council of Eight of Florence allowed him to buy property up to the value of 500 florins.[141] Although Datill was allowed to buy property, the government still limited his property rights by setting a monetary limit on the amount of land that he could own.

Greater real property restrictions, however, were on their way. The restrictive *Cum Nimis Absurdum*, issued by Pope Paul IV in 1555, not only forbade future real property ownership by Jews but forced them to sell their currently owned property.[142] As would be expected from such a decree, the forced sale of the property resulted in severe losses to the Jews, who realized only about 20% of the value of the property.[143]

While many of the cities in other parts of Italy were slowly granting greater civil rights to Jews during the following centuries, the papacy remained entrenched in an anti-Jewish position. In 1775 Pope Pius VI issued his *Editto Supra Gli Ebrei*, which once again proclaimed that Jews were unable to own property. The edict specifically prohibited Jews from owning either shops or houses outside the Roman ghetto.

Taxation

Generally, Jews were taxed more heavily than Christians because they were not considered citizens and therefore not officially part of the community. Consistent with their unequal treatment was the disproportionate share of the tax burden that they shouldered. The rationale for taxation was usually either that the Jewish community was being taxed in conjunction with a special event (e.g., taxing the Jews on a Christian holiday) or that the Jews were viewed as foreigners, and the tax was a "living tax" for the privilege of living within the community. Often, the taxes collected from the Jews were used to support the church.

Examples of unfair taxation of the Jews span several centuries. The earliest examples of taxation during the Common Era appear to originate from church proclamations, with secular governments imposing taxes at a later time. For example, an early church synod, the Synod of Gerona (517), required Jews to pay taxes to the church in order to support it.[144]

The City Council of Genoa imposed a tax on its Jewish and foreign communities on 7 January 1134, requiring them to pay a "living tax" for the privilege of living within Genoa. The "living tax" was used to pay for the oil used to light the lamps of the San Lorenzo cathedral.[145] In 1215, in one of the many decrees issued by Pope Innocent III, another special type of tax was imposed on the Jews. The pope declared that Jews were to pay a special tax on Easter.[146]

There were, of course, exceptions so that Jews were not required to pay such exorbitant taxes. The Florentine edict of 1437, for example, which benefited the Jewish banker Datill, specifically exempted him from paying taxes (with the exception of paying *gabelle*, or excise taxes).[147] However, the edict did nothing for the plight of the other members of the Jewish community.

In the mid-1550s, the residents of the ghetto of Florence were required to pay a tax of two *scudi*. The tax was imposed on every Jew aged fifteen or older.[148]

Later on, as the winds of change began to blow, the imposition of taxes became more uniform between Jew and Christian. For example, in the progressive Duchy of Savoy, the duke declared in 1572 that Jews were to be taxed the same as Christian inhabitants of the Duchy.[149] Other cities slowly followed suit. In 1783 Parma and Piacenza exempted them from the special taxes that had been imposed on the Jewish residents of the cities.[150]

Public Office

Perhaps no area demonstrates the power disparities between Jews and the host society as well as prohibitions to holding public office. Restrictions relating to Jews' holding public office originate in Roman times, with similar prohibitions being reenacted at various points in history. With the unification of Italy, however, the situation changed, and Jews immediately held positions of power in the Italian government.[151] The road leading to that point, however, was a rocky one.

Septimus Severus (193–211 C.E.), an emperor more favorable to Jews than many of his predecessors, allowed Jews to hold public office. A year later, the Edict of Caracalla gave Jews the status of citizens.

However, access by Jews to official positions of power was short-lived. During his reign as emperor, Theodosius the Great (379–395) expelled Jews from any official gate positions or place of honor.

Later, Christian popes renewed these restrictions on access to official positions. In 1078 Pope Gregory VIII proclaimed that Jews could not hold public office. In 1215 Pope Innocent III revitalized the earlier prohibitions against Jews' holding office.[152]

Secular governments later imposed similar restrictions. Venetian Jews were barred either from holding any governmental position or from acting as a broker or agent for the government in the *ricondotta* of 1777. (The *ricondotta* was a renewal of the contract previously imposing restrictions on Jews in Venice.)[153]

Shortly after these restrictive measures were revitalized in Venice and Rome, other parts of Italy were expanding Jews' civil rights. In 1778 a member of the Jewish community became a representative on the City Council of Livorno, allegedly the first time that a Jew had held any sort of governmental position since the fall of the Roman Empire.[154] Not until Italy was unified in 1861, however, did Jews enter public life in significant numbers.

CONCLUSION

For nearly 2,000 years, Italy had enacted a plethora of laws aimed specifically at discriminating against its Jewish population. Reviewing even a few of the numerous laws through the lens of Gordon's assimilation model demonstrates the systematic exclusion of Jews from the Italian host society in which they lived. This systematic exclusion began during Roman times and extended almost uninterrupted until the Jews regained citizenship status with unification of Italy during the latter half of the nineteenth century. However, as history has painfully documented, in spite of full citizenship status in the nineteenth century, the worst page in discrimination against Italian Jews was yet to be written.

NOTES

1. M. Marger, *Race and Ethnic Relations: American and Global Perspectives*, 4th ed. (Belmont, CA: Wadsworth, 1997), p. 111.

2. Ibid.; J. Gonzales, *Racial and Ethnic Groups in America* (Dubuque, IA: Kendall/Hunt, 1990), p. 67.

3. Gonzales, *Racial and Ethnic Groups*, p. 67.

4. Ibid., p. 67; Marger, *Race and Ethnic Relations*, p. 111.

5. H. Leon, *The Jews of Ancient Rome* (Philadelphia: Jewish Publication Society of America, 1960), pp. 15–16.

6. A. Rosselli, "Something about the History of the Israelite Genoese Community from the Age of Imperial Rome to the Twentieth Century," http://194.244.85.178/pietremare/-hebrew.htm, p. 1.

7. Leon, *The Jews*, p. 10.

8. Ibid., p. 37.

9. Ibid., p. 38.

10. "An Overview of 2000 Years of Jewish Persecution," http://www.-religioustolerance.org/jud_pers.htm, p. 1.

11. Leon, *The Jews*, p. 43.

12. "An Overview," p. 1; "A Calendar of Jewish Persecution," http://www.hearnow.-org/caljp.html, p. 1.

13. "Medieval Sourcebook: Legislation Affecting the Jews from 300 to 800 C.E.," http://www.fordham.edu/halsall/source/300-800-laws-jews.html, p. 1.

14. "A Brief History," p. 1.

15. "Medieval Sourcebook," p. 1; "Jewish History Sourcebook: Jews and the Later Roman Law 315–531 C.E.," http://www.fordham.edu/halsall/jewish/jewishbook.html.

16. "A Calendar of Jewish Persecution," p. 1.

17. "Medieval Sourcebook," p. 2.

18. Ibid., p. 5.

19. "An Overview," p. 2.

20. B. Pullan, *The Jews of Europe and the Inquisition of Venice 1550–1670* (Oxford: Basil Blackwell, 1983), p. 59.

21. C. Roth, *A History of the Jews in Italy* (Philadelphia: Jewish Publication Society of America, 1946), p. 220.

22. Ibid., p. 271.

23. K. Stow, *The Jews in Rome* (Leiden and New York: E.J. Brill, 1995–1997), p. xxi.

24. F. Voll, "A Short Review of a Troubled History," http://www.jcrelations.com/-res/incidents.htm, p. 6.

25. Ibid., pp. 6–7.

26. A. Gow and G. Griffiths, "Pope Eugenius IV and Money-Lending in Florence: The Case of Salamone di Buonaventura during the Chancellorship of Leonardo Bruni," *Renaissance Quarterly* 42 (Summer 1994): 8.

27. Ibid., pp. 8–9.

28. Voll, "A Short Review," p. 10.

29. Gow and Griffiths, "Pope Eugenius IV," pp. 9–10.

30. Stow, *The Jews*, p. lviii.

31. Roth, *History of the Jews*, pp. 295–296.

32. Gow and Griffiths, "Pope Eugenius IV," p. 6.

33. Ibid., p. 2.

34. R. Segre, ed., *The Jews in Piedmont*, vol. 1 (Jerusalem: Israel Academy of Sciences and Humanities, Tel Aviv University, 1986), pp. 19–20.

35. Ibid., p. 479.

36. Rosselli, "Something," p. 1.

37. Roth, *History of the Jews*, p. 414.

38. Ibid.

39. Segre, *The Jews*, p. 1345.

40. "Medieval Sourcebook," p. 3.

41. Ibid., p. 5.

42. "An Overview," p. 3.

43. A. Eban, *My People: The Story of the Jews* (New York: Random House, 1984), p. 173.

44. "An Overview," p. 7.

45. Gow and Griffiths, "Pope Eugenius IV," pp. 9–10.

46. Roth, *History of the Jews*, p. 295.

47. Pullan, *The Jews*, p. 79.

48. Ibid.

49. Roth, *History of the Jews*, p. 414.

50. Ibid., p. 411.

51. Ibid., p. 425.

52. "Medieval Sourcebook," p. 3.

53. J.N. da Pisa, *Banking and Finance among Jews in Renaissance Italy* (New York: Block, 1962), p. 7.

54. Ibid.

55. Roth, *History of the Jews*, p. 115.

56. Gow and Griffiths, "Pope Eugenius IV," pp. 8–9.

57. Voll, "A Short Review," p. 10.

58. A. Toaff, *The Jews in Medieval Assisi*, vol. 148 (Florence: Leo S. Olschki, 1979), p. 92.

59. Roth, *History of the Jews*, p. 296; Stow, *The Jews*, p. xxxiii.

60. Stow, *The Jews*, p. liv.

61. Roth, *History of the Jews*, p. 331.

62. Ibid., p. 424.

63. Ibid., p. 415.

64. R. Felton, "Anti-Semitism and the Church," http://haydid.org/anitsemr.htm, p. 1; Pullan, *The Jews*, p. 2.

65. Gow and Griffiths, "Pope Eugenius IV," p. 5.

66. Toaff, *The Jews*, p. 151.

67. Gow and Griffiths, "Pope Eugenius IV," p. 1.

68. da Pisa, *Banking and Finance*, p. 4; Roth, *History of the Jews*, p. 98.

69. Ibid., p. 11.

70. Stow, *The Jews*, p. xxv.

71. Roth, *History of the Jews*, pp. 107–109.

72. Ibid., pp. 109–111.

73. Toaff, *The Jews*, p. 155.

74. Ibid., pp. 150, 188.

75. Gow and Griffiths, "Pope Eugenius IV," p. 8; Roth, *History of the Jews*, p. 107.

76. Stow, *The Jews*, p. 30.

77. Ibid.

78. Segre, *The Jews*, p. 645.

79. Ibid., pp. 391, 645.

80. Roth, *History of the Jews*, p. 415.

81. "Medieval Sourcebook," p. 1; "Jewish History Sourcebook," p. 2.

82. G. Grobman, "Classical and Christian Anti-Semitism," http://www.remember.org/-history.root.classical.html, p. 5.

83. Eban, *My People*, p. 171.

84. Rosselli, "Something," p. 2.

85. "An Overview," p. 3.

86. Roth, *History of the Jews*, p. 98; Eban, *My People*, p. 180.

87. Stow, *The Jews*, p. xxviii.

88. Segre, *The Jews*, pp. 19–20.

89. Gow and Griffiths, "Pope Eugenius IV," p. 8.

90. Ibid., pp. 9–10.

91. Ibid., p. 10.

92. M. Margolis, *A History of the Jewish People* (Philadelphia: Jewish Publication Society of America, 1945), p. 507.

93. Roth, *History of the Jews*, p. 337.

94. Ibid., p. 411.

95. Ibid., p. 423.

96. Marger, *Race and Ethnic Relations*, p. 70.

97. Leon, *The Jews*, pp. 18–19.

98. Voll, "A Short Review," p. 4.

99. Roth, *History of the Jews*, p. 120.

100. Eban, *My People*, p. 171.

101. Ibid., p. 173.

102. Roth, *History of the Jews*, p. 270.

103. Voll, "A Short Review," p. 10.

104. Gow and Griffiths, "Pope Eugenius IV," p. 8.

105. "A Calendar of Jewish Persecution," p. 2.

106. Margolis, *A History*, p. 509.

107. Rosselli, "Something," p. 3.

108. "An Overview," p. 4.

109. Ibid.

110. Ibid., p. 5.

111. Pullan, *The Jews*, p. 23.

112. Roth, *History of the Jews*, p. 328.

113. Rosselli, "Something," pp. 1–2.

114. Ibid., p. 3.

115. Roth, *History of the Jews*, p. 331.

116. M. Dimont, *Jews, God and History* (New York: Simon and Schuster, 1962), pp. 303–304.

117. "A Calendar of Jewish Persecutions," p. 2.

118. Voll, "A Short Review," p. 13.

119. Gonzales, *Racial and Ethnic Groups*, p. 11; Marger, *Race and Ethnic Relations*, p. 70.

120. "A Calendar of Jewish Persecutions," p. 73.

121. Roth, *History of the Jews*, p. 120.
122. Voll, "A Short Review," p. 10.
123. Segre, *The Jews*, pp. 478–479.
124. Roth, *History of the Jews*, p. 414.
125. Eban, *My People*, p. 227.
126. Voll, "A Short Review," p. 10.
127. Segre, *The Jews*, pp. 478–479.
128. Roth, *History of the Jews*, p. 425.
129. "Jewish History Sourcebook," p. 3.
130. Voll, "A Short Review," p. 5.
131. Stow, *The Jews*, p. xxvi.
132. Segre, *The Jews*, p. 72.
133. Gow and Griffiths, "Pope Eugenius IV," p. 5.
134. Stow, *The Jews*, p. xxx.
135. Roth, *History of the Jews*, p. 20.
136. Stow, *The Jews*, p. 20.
137. "Jewish History Sourcebook," p. 2.
138. "Medieval Sourcebook," p. 3.
139. Grobman, "Classical and Christian Anti-Semitism," p. 4.
140. da Pisa, *Banking and Finance*, p. 7.
141. Gow and Griffiths, "Pope Eugenius IV," p. 5.
142. Roth, *History of the Jews*, p. 295.
143. Ibid., p. 298.
144. Grobman, "Classical and Christian Anti-Semitism," p. 5.
145. Rosselli, "Something," p. 1.
146. Eban, *My People*, p. 173.
147. Gow and Griffiths, "Pope Eugenius IV," p. 8.
148. Roth, *History of the Jews*, p. 343.
149. Segre, *The Jews*, pp. 478–479.
150. Roth, *History of the Jews*, p. 425.
151. *Antisemitism World Report* (London: Institution of Jewish Affairs, 1997), p. 2.
152. Eban, *My People*, p. 173.
153. Roth, *History of the Jews*, p. 415.
154. Ibid., p. 425.

3

Modern Historiography on the Early Imperial Mistreatment of Roman Jews

Dixon Slingerland

In the course of research for my recent book,[1] I found a pattern of tendentiousness among modern historiographers that has distorted our picture of the relationship between ancient Jews and the imperial authority governing their lives. By means of incidental references, the book does call attention to this tendentiousness and its implications for our understanding of Roman-Jewish life under the early empire. The present study deals with these matters in a more systematic fashion.

We must keep in mind that Jews are but one of two elements in this discussion; the other, imperial power, is often the real interest of modern writers. In addition, the sources of discussion are those places where ancient writers intimated that the emperors behaved in a hostile manner toward their Jewish subjects. In such circumstances, someone was to blame. Either the Roman authorities mistreated subjects, or these subjects committed crimes deserving punishment. In light of this hostility to Roman and other Jews, scholarship has tended to justify the emperors at the expense of Jews. Moreover, it has done so as part of larger agendas. One of these intends to show the decency of imperial rule; that it acted negatively toward Jews with justification. Another intends to demonstrate the positive relationship existing between these people and Rome: only when they misbehaved did the authorities act against them. For the most part, however, neither agenda finds support in the ancient texts.

The tendency is an old one. Who killed Jesus? In their attempt to exonerate Rome, the Gospels blame Jews for Jesus' death. In Luke 22 the Jewish leadership wanted Jesus dead, but in the next chapter the fair-minded Roman procurator, Pilate, wished to set him free. Again, in Matthew 27:24–25 Pilate "took water and washed his hands before the crowd, saying, 'I am innocent of this man's blood; see to it yourselves.' And all the [Jewish] people answered, 'His blood be on us and on our children.'" (Revised Standard Version)

This claim against Jews as Christ killers is well known; less familiar is the charge that they wanted to kill St. Paul also. Historically and whatever the details, there is little doubt that he was executed in Rome by the emperor Nero. In the Acts of the Apostles, however, the imperial authorities consistently defend Paul—just as Pilate had tried to defend Jesus—against jealous, lying, treacherous, clamorous, riotous, violent, and even murderous Jews. Once again, Roman authority is exonerated.[2]

The heart of the present study is this characterization of Jews as sources of disorder and troublemaking. Both of the earlier New Testament examples tell part of the story. In terms of their assertion that Jews killed Jesus, the gospel writers were ancient historiographers, but many modern writers have accepted that evidence and made the same claim their own. Likewise, in accepting the twin claims of Acts that the Roman authorities were positively inclined toward the Christian leader Paul and that it was really troublemaking Jews who caused him so much hardship, modernity has been equally credulous.

Hence, in support of his view that Jews were a "peuple séditieux" Jean Juster cites, among his other prejudicial witnesses, this material from Acts.[3] Likewise, in support of the view that Caligula treated Jews in a deservedly bad way, Baldson implicitly appeals several times to Acts.[4] Gaston May's use of this New Testament image of violence-prone Jews is quite explicit.[5] Again, according to W.H.C. Frend, the second half of Acts makes clear that "the Apostles would arrive at a town and go to the synagogue where they would enjoy a first, favourable hearing. Then trouble would start," for "the Jews saw in Paul a deadly enemy." Conversely, "there was no clash between the Church and the Roman Empire."[6] Also following Acts, E. Mary Smallwood writes that "the way in which both Felix and Festus treated St. Paul when he was under arrest shows the Roman government in a good light. They were firm and impartial, and they were anxious to save their prisoner from merciless treatment at the Jews' hands and at the same time to prevent rioting."[7] Once again, at the expense of Jews, imperial Rome is exonerated. As can be shown case by case, that is largely the story of modern historiography on the subject of ancient Jewry under Roman rule.

Following are some general examples. Having referred to Smallwood, we may note her comment "that most of our information about Rome's dealings with the Jews and Judaism comes from Jewish sources. . . . To Roman writers the Jews mattered, and therefore were mentioned, only when they gave serious trouble."[8] Interpreting the Roman sources as witness to the troublemaking propensities of Jews and taking that interpretation as fact, Smallwood affirms this negative aspect of the Jewish character. Anthony Barrett also refers to the "intractable" nature of "the problems presented by the Jewish people as a whole," how they caused "ill will" with neighbors especially on account of "the rigidity of the Jewish faith."[9] As Vincent Scramuzza put it in 1933, "For one reason or another, the Jewish population scattered throughout the empire gave much concern to every emperor in the first century of the Christian era."[10] Stereotypical, too, is the comment of Margaret H. Williams about "turbulence-prone Jews," one of several supposedly "troublesome groups" in the Rome of Tiberius.[11] We return to this statement later.

Similarly, reading the mind of the Jewish ruler Herod Agrippa, Gaston May refers to the "touchy and irritable temperament of his subjects. He had penetrated the secret of the Jewish soul of those times, always disquieted and troubled, rebellious against all assimilation." Without indicating whose mind he next reads, May then claims that the same was true of Diaspora Jews. He thinks of Alexandria. When the emperor Claudius referred to Jews there as a potential world plague,[12] he meant that sedition could be expected to arise out of the overly large Jewish population of the city: "One might wish to refer to the measure to which the popular politics of today have given the somewhat barbaric name of containment (*contingentement*)." Apparently a buzzword of the 1930s in France, it has to do with the creation of population quotas. He provides a modern parallel: "The interdiction of which it is a question here makes us think of the measure advocated at this moment in Palestine by Arabs and directed against the Zionist immigration into Judea." Also assuming the general threat of Roman Jews, May believes that "their greatest reproach was their scoffing and restless spirit as well as their tendency to join themselves to groups of agitators who, by manifestations of anarchy, contributed to making the last hours of the Republic a period of endless trouble."[13]

An interpretation of Cicero's Republican-period defense of Lucius Flaccus, this last statement generalizes about Roman Jews living under the later realities of Claudius. In May's view, partially focused on modern fascism, these realities were positive: "One has neglected, forgotten, or turned to ridicule his [Claudius'] propensity for matters of law and the acts which the law dictated to him. Nevertheless, more recently one has ceased to place upon the first Caesars and their governmental role a judgment dictated by the prejudices and the rancor of their contemporaries and also, it must be said, by the modern adversaries of absolute power."[14] Untroubled by absolutism and apparently no adversary of its modern (1938) manifestations either, May makes little sense of Jewish miseries under Claudius except as the result of the imperial desire for legal order and the Jewish penchant for its opposite.

If May thinks that Jews tended to join other agitators, Heikki Solin sees them in the opposite light, for he refers to "the exclusivity of the Jews, the insistence upon their fundamental difference from all others."[15] Even so, he shares May's opinion about their anarchic tendencies: "The Jews [of Rome] were always a source of disturbance [*ein Ferment der Unruhe*], and so situations commonly arose in which the Roman officials saw themselves forced to resort to measures of punishment." Elsewhere, too, Solin generalizes concerning this Jewish *Ferment der Unruhe*.[16] Again, during the late 1920s Harvard's Giorgio La Piana refers to the "*temperamento inflessibile del giudaismo*."[17] Its "objectionable" traditions he contrasts with Christianity, that "new instrument of world domination fit to supersede" ancient Rome. Furthermore, Roman Jews orientalized the city. "Racial mixture" watered down the "vitality of the Latin spirit" and brought with it the eastern disorder that resulted in the "catastrophic transformation of ancient civilization."[18] Jews, in other words, played a part in the fall of the Roman Empire. In an unfortunate nativist article of 1916 the influential American scholar Tenney Frank had already clarified how this happened and what it might mean for modern America.[19]

Finally, picking up on La Piana's expression "world domination" and recalling the contemporary "Protocols of the Elders of Zion," we must mention Thaddée Zielinkski's 1926 article on the subject of "The Emperor Claudius and the Idea of Jewish World Domination." For their own benefit Jews sought to control the world, and the messianic age would bring it about. They were imperialists. Throughout the Mediterranean they were ready to revolt; indeed, under Caligula and Claudius at Rome and Alexandria, they did so. In both places, however, Claudius foiled their plot to dominate the world.[20] When we recall, however, that Rome's emperors were the real imperialists, that they, in fact, dominated the world, and that nothing in the ancient sources supports such an incredible construction, Zielinski's theory appears preposterous.

These incidental, stereotypical, and unsupported comments of modern historiographers[21] characterize the Jewish population of the Roman Empire in a uniformly unsympathetic way. Hence, since conclusions cannot rise above presuppositions, deductions drawn from this characterization are faulty. To demonstrate this, we turn to several instances scattered throughout my book where the presuppositions of modern writers obscure actual relationships between Jews and their emperors.

The tendency to demonstrate the well-intended, philo-Judaic orientation of the emperors appears in the modern interpretation of Suetonius *Augustus* 93:

He [Augustus] treated with great respect such foreign rites as were ancient and well established, but held the rest in contempt. For example, having been initiated at Athens and afterwards sitting in judgment of a case at Rome involving the privileges of the priests of Attic Ceres, in which certain matters of secrecy were brought up, he dismissed his councillors . . . and he heard the disputants in private. But on the other hand he not only omitted to make a slight detour to visit Apis, when he was travelling through Egypt, but highly commended his grandson Gaius for not offering prayers at Jerusalem as he passed by Judaea.[22]

This text asserts that Augustus approved some foreign rites, here the Eleusinian mysteries, but despised others—for example, the cult of Apis in Egypt and the Jewish cult in Jerusalem. Indeed, he commended his grandson, Gaius, for avoiding the latter.

Arguing Augustus' "good will toward the Jews," however, Harry Leon minimizes this affront by claiming that the emperor merely "refrained from showing himself too friendly to the Jews."[23] Suetonius wrote, nevertheless, of Augustus' contempt. Likewise, referring to "the first emperor's sympathy for the Jews," Vincent Scramuzza insists, again contrary to its plain meaning, that *Augustus* 93 deals not with the Jewish cult but with its spread, that is, with proselytizing.[24] Similarly, asserting that "Augustus was remembered by the Jews as a great benefactor," Menahem Stern claims that *Augustus* 93 is "not to be interpreted as the expression of a specific anti-Jewish attitude on the part of Augustus."[25] How the emperor might have been more specific is unclear. Remarkably, Williams employs *Augustus* 93 in support of her statement that "it had been Augustus' policy to favour the Jews." Equally odd is the position of

Frend: "The terse epigrammatic comment by Suetonius reads, 'He treated with great respect such foreign rites as were ancient, and well established, but held the rest in contempt.' In this case, the foreign rites included Judaism which he treated with marked favour both in Rome and the East."[26] Except as bogus attempts to establish Rome's first emperor as a philo-Judaic paradigm for his successors, none of these interpretations of *Augustus* 93 make sense. Whatever the motive, we are better served by Stern's other conclusion drawn from the same text: Augustus "had little sympathy for the Jewish religion."[27]

The situation with regard to the next emperor is equally interesting. That Tiberius gave Jews and Judaism a difficult time, particularly in Rome, is certain. Thus, Tacitus *Annals* 2.85 and Suetonius *Tiberius* 36 make clear that in 19 C.E. Tiberius expelled the practitioners of Judaism from Rome.[28] Introducing his 1915 analysis of this event, Max Radin writes, "Under Tiberius we hear of a general expulsion of the Jews, as afterward under Claudius. 'Expulsion of Jews' is a term with which later European history has made us familiar." Conscious of the events of the Christian Middle Ages, taken in by Philo's apologetically positive statement about Tiberius' treatment of Jews, reading Tacitus and related texts directly against themselves, and piling up vague hypotheses about individual foreign proselytes and/or practitioners of fraud, Radin concludes that Tiberius removed only these latter from the city:

> To suppose that all the Jews were banished by Tiberius involves an assumption as to that emperor's methods wholly at variance with what we know of him. A very large number of Jewish residents in Rome were Roman citizens. . . . A wholesale expulsion of Roman citizens by either an administrative act or a senatusconsultum is unthinkable under Tiberius. Exile . . . was a well-known penalty for crime after due trial and conviction, which in every instance would have to be individual. . . . No senatusconsultum could have decreed a general banishment for all Jews, whether Roman citizens or not, without contravening the fundamental principles of the Roman law.[29]

Unthinkable or not, the plain sense of the ancient texts is that just such a major expulsion of Roman Jews, citizens and others, did occur. Wishing to affirm the rights of these citizens but forced to account for the unsupportive evidence of the sources, Radin seeks to preserve the goodness of Tiberius and the lawful place of Roman Jews. He does this by singling out individual Jews, especially proselytes, as the criminals rightfully expelled from the city. Thus, having rejected the same ploy in the apologetic of Josephus,[30] Radin nevertheless returns to it. Jews, proselytes at least were responsible for their own expulsion. Exonerated, however, are the good Jewish citizens and emperors.

Leon does the same thing. Admitting that "under Tiberius . . . the Jews fared less well," he still insists that this emperor "is now known to have been a high-minded and capable ruler."[31] Hence, Tiberius' hostility toward Roman Jews arose in part because of his evil prefect Sejanus.[32] We must ignore at this point, of course, that Tiberius himself gave Sejanus his position of influence.[33] Furthermore, Leon insists that "the practice of Judaism was no crime in Rome at that time nor, indeed, at any time under the pagan emperors; and Tiberius . . . was a strict observer of the Roman law." Why then did the emperor take action in 19 C.E.? It was probably because of the fraud described in the otherwise doubtful account of Josephus.[34] Following good Roman law, therefore, Tiberius removed non-citizen Roman Jews.[35] The result of this analysis is like that of Radin. Seeking to preserve the basic justice of the emperor as well as the legitimate place of Judaism in Rome, Leon turns to the apologetic account of Josephus to find four Jewish culprits responsible for the massive Tiberian measures against Roman Jews. In fact, 19 C.E. had nothing to do with Jewish culpability. The autocrat Tiberius had the power to act against foreign cults in Rome, and in that year he chose to do so.

Williams sees these events in a different light but with results similar to those of Radin and Leon. In her view, the entire Jewish population of Rome, including proselytes, was expelled.[36] For what reason? She, like Leon, presupposes that it had nothing to do with the repression of Judaism: "At no time, not even in the darkest days of the second century, did the Roman authorities ever dispute the right of Jews by birth to practice their ancestral religion."[37] Hence, her question:

Why should a princeps who in A.D. 19 was still making strict adherence to Augustan precedent the guiding principle of his administration apparently have reversed Augustan policy so totally in the matter of the Jews? For there is no doubt that it had been Augustus' policy to favour the Jews . . . and that the Jews in Rome were generally happy under his administration. The good-humoured tone of the many references to the Jews and their ways in the works of the main Augustan poets shows just how relaxed the general climate of opinion was about this ethnic minority. . . . Augustus' surviving words reveal a man who regarded Jewish ways as odd rather than obnoxious—suitable material for pleasantries and puns.[38]

In other words, Tiberius followed Augustus in his positive treatment of Jews, a treatment that Williams discovers, in part, by reversing the sense of *Augustus* 93, and that also was contradicted by the brutality of the Augustan poets, who, in her view, were only joking about Jewish donkey-worshipers, murderers, and cannibals.[39] In fact, Tiberius' measures represented a reflection rather than a reversal of Augustus' own antipathy toward this segment of the Roman population.

Williams asks, "Why?" Ignoring the hostility of Augustus and his friends as well as the sense of the relevant texts that those expelled were Jews unwilling to give up their religious rites, Williams seeks an explanation congruent with her positive estimation of imperial attitudes toward Jews. Thus, contradicting her own observation that "the Romans . . . did not like *externae religiones* very much" and rightly rejecting the apologetic account in Josephus, Williams moves on to what she calls, accurately, "a more oblique approach." Following Tacitus, she then points out that Tiberius acted intentionally against Roman Jews and that some of them were subjected to "a savage punishment." She also recognizes that this prohibited Jews from practicing their religion.

Disregarding the ramifications of that observation, however, she conjectures: "If we make the not unreasonable assumption that the penalties proposed by the Fathers were neither totally irrational nor willfully unjust, then we must conclude that, in Roman eyes at least, the Jews had committed offenses on a scale and of a gravity commensurate with the heavy sentences that were handed out. . . . What can those offenses have been when so many thousands were involved?"[40] Thus, assuming the rationality and justice of the imperial authorities (i.e., starting with a presupposition hardly obvious from the ancient references), she can account for the 19 C.E. measures only by imagining that some terrible Jewish offense compelled the reasonable and just Tiberius to take action.

Now, however, she must discover the crime that they committed. She begins, therefore, with the correct view that Jews constituted a significant portion of Rome's population. More questionable, however, is her next contention that they were an "easily identifiable element in the population of Rome," that there was an "easily recognizable Jewish element in the crowd," and that it "formed a distinct and clearly identifiable element in the crowd on the Palatine." The operative term is "crowd." Williams has in mind, like Gaston May, Cicero's tendentious courtroom image of Roman Jews as a *turba*, in Williams' translation, and, from the perspective of Cicero, rightly, as "an unruly bunch." She writes, "Images of crowding and turbulence are worth noting." This is "an unfavourable aspect" of Roman Jewish behavior.[41]

What this really constitutes is a stereotype of turbulence-prone Jews, troublemakers. Of that claim there is no hint in our ancient descriptions of the 19 C.E. events. Nevertheless, reaching back to the rhetoric of Cicero almost a century before, Williams uses that stereotype to decipher those events:

> Given this evidence for the distinctly high profile of the Jews of Rome and their well-attested propensity for unruly behaviour, a question naturally enough presents itself. Could circumstances have arisen in A.D. 19 which might have impelled the Jews to take to the streets in such numbers and in such a manner as to alarm the authorities and force them to adopt the repressive measures outlined above?[42]

Assuming this "well-attested propensity for unruly behaviour" and accepting that repression was the necessary imperial response—Tiberius preferred to be nice to Jews—Williams moves to an additional assumption concerning circumstances that might have produced a renewal of bad behavior.

The first of these circumstances is poverty; it "was as much a hallmark of the Roman Jew as was his propensity for unruliness." That is, "In Roman eyes, rightly or wrongly, the Jews were perceived as a poverty-stricken bunch." The second is the generalization that the early years of Tiberius constituted "a period of enormous hardship for the poor of Rome and, in consequence of this, a tense and turbulent time." She writes, "It would not have been lost upon the authorities that the worst riots tended to occur at the times when food ran short." What links Jews to the supposed unrest among the poor of Rome in this period? As Williams admits, nothing: "That the Jews took part in this unrest cannot, of course, be proved. But, surely, it is not unlikely." In other words, the turbulence-prone poor of Rome mysteriously limit themselves to turbulence-prone Jews, the involvement of whom is undemonstrated, and they alone are expelled. It is no wonder, then, that Williams imagines an additional circumstance: recent inundations of the Tiber may have flooded Jewish homes and synagogues and resulted in Jewish agitation.[43] Again, however, she offers no evidence. Maybe, therefore, Tiberius' political vulnerability in 19 C.E. caused him to strike out against the poor masses of Rome.[44] Maybe, but maybe not. There is no evidence, and, were there, it could not account for the present matter, Tiberius' expulsion in 19 C.E. not of the Roman masses but of Roman Jews. The sources make reference neither to Jewish turbulence nor to any of these other imagined circumstances.

That, however, is not the end of the story, for one other element in the argument of Williams makes clear her tendency to blame the Roman-Jewish victims of religious represssion for their own travails. Specifically, though a fragment of Dio certainly refers to the same repression, Williams takes it to apply to a contemporary, but different, measure of Tiberius against Roman Jews. Dio wrote, "As the Jews had flocked to Rome in great numbers and were converting many of the natives to their ways, he [Tiberius] banished most of them."[45] To imagine two major expulsions of Roman Jews in a three-year period, both clearly religion-driven, is difficult. For present purposes, however, that is not the point. Of interest instead is Williams' interpretation of Dio. He described "the immigration of a group of Jews who were causing a public nuisance by their aggressive proselytizing activities." Here the operative phrase is "public nuisance," concerning which Dio wrote not a word. That language recalls instead the stereotypical image used already to justify Tiberius. Shortly, therefore, she associates Roman Jews with other "obnoxious minority groups." That is, "Repeated attempts at frequent intervals to curb the activities of obnoxious minority groups are a fairly common feature of Roman history." Perhaps, but here Williams reads that image of Jews into Dio, for she cannot read it out of him. It was, she decides, "troublesome immigrants Jews"[46] who were at fault in the present case. Troublesome Roman Jews preceded or followed troublesome Jewish immigrants to Rome.

This brings us to the conclusion of Williams' study: "Tiberius' action was simply the conventional response of a beleaguered administration to a group which was deemed to be posing a threat to law and order."[47] As compared to troublemaking Jews, after all, Tiberius "was a stickler for law and order in any circumstances."[48] Hence, in a case where the texts suggest something quite sinister about imperial rule, Williams defends the absolute authority of Tiberius. Specifically, separating the event in Dio from the one described by Tacitus, Suetonius, and Josephus, she nevertheless resorts to the same troublemaking nature of Roman Jews, citizens and recent immigrants alike, to account for the just measures of the emperor.[49]

These portions of the scholarly debate about the 19 C.E. Tiberian actions against Roman Jews are revealing. They presuppose the propriety of such steps: Tiberius had nothing intrinsically against Roman Jews or their religion. On this assumption, blame necessarily falls on the recipients of those measures. The question then becomes, what did Roman Jews do to deserve such treatment? Beginning with conjecture, however, means that conjecture is the result. Perhaps, on the one hand, they were uniformly troublesome; on the other, maybe only individual Jews (proselytes, foreign Jews, Jewish criminals, flooded-out Jews, Jews belonging to one troublesome synagogue, poor Jews) deserve blame for the misery of their banished brothers and sisters. What the ancient sources really tell us, however, is that in 19 C.E., as part of his measures to drive the Jewish and Isiac cults from Rome, Tiberius ordered Roman Jews practicing their religious rites to leave the city. It is that simple. If, therefore, on account of devotion to their god, blame legitimately fell on Roman Jews, they do deserve the criticism of modern writers. If, however, the real problem was religious prejudice combined with absolute power, responsibility falls elsewhere.

Turning to the next emperor, Gaius, we find the situation of recent historiography a bit different. Few scholars are sympathetic to him. As a result, it has been unnecessary to account for the miseries that he inflicted upon several Jewish communities by claiming that a good, philo-Judaic ruler was forced to unpleasant measures by Jewish mischief. It is to some instructive exceptions, therefore, that I wish to point. Thus, Hugo Willrich affirms the basic sanity and quality of Caligula's rule.[50] Confronted by this emperor's widespread anti-Jewish measures, therefore, Willrich's 1903 study devotes considerable space to Gaian Jewish policy.[51] Following his imperial predecessors, Gaius began as a friend of Jews.[52] He also claimed divine status, but this was traditional. Though he thundered against Jews for refusing to worship him, he did not compel them to do so.[53]

Hence, although Gaius later used the same measure in Jerusalem and its environs, this emperor did not, contrary to the eyewitness testimony of Philo, instigate the placement of his image in the synagogues of Alexandria. Because they wanted their Jewish enemies to appear to oppose the imperial cult, the Alexandrians did this on their own. Moreover, the prefect of Egypt, needing local support and not wanting to hinder the spread of that cult, enabled the desecration of the Jewish houses of prayer. To this interpretation, however, Willrich adds a strange conclusion: "To what extent he [the prefect] was correct in doing this, to what extent the Jewish behavior justified his own behavior, that, unfortunately, we cannot say since Philo persistently acts as if the Jews were pure victims without any blame in the whole conflict."[54] This is odd, because, to defend the original philo-Judaism of Gaius, Willrich already blamed the Alexandrians and the emperor's own prefect for these Jewish miseries. Furthermore, he blames them again for the pogrom that soon overtook Alexandrian Jews.[55] Hence, the insinuation of Jewish responsibility for the desecration of their own houses of prayer is doubly questionable, first, because a defense of Gaius' original philo-Judaism does not need it and, second, because nothing in the ancient sources supports it.

Finally, Willrich claims that the imperial attempt to convert the Jerusalem cult center into a *Gaiustempel* was, in light of Jewish provocation at Jamnia, entirely in accord with good Greco-Roman principles.[56] Here, too, however, his conclusion is curious. Aware that Gaius' death precluded continued anti-Jewish actions in Judea, he writes, "From this danger the Jews have learned [*haben nicht gezogen*] no lesson. On the contrary, the apparent proof that Yahweh does not abandon [*verlasse*] his people strengthened their opposition against the

Roman authority until the time came when a Herodian could no longer help and even Yahweh did not help."[57] Present-tense verbs aside, this statement is problematic in at least two different respects. First, it assumes that all Jews ("the Jews") extrapolated from Gaius' death their god's perpetual protection; of such a general interpretation; however, it provides no evidence. Second, it fails to identify the lesson that "the Jews" failed to learn. What, after all, could they have discovered from Gaius' attempt against the temple in Jerusalem (or the synagogues in Alexandria, for that matter) except that, as objects of Roman rule, they and their religious devotion were vulnerable to the whims of imperial power? Subject peoples knew that already.

Another scholar of interest in this regard is J.P.V.D. Balsdon. Writing in 1934 as a fellow of Exeter College, Oxford, Balsdon acknowledges his debt to Willrich and then points out the nearly contemporary application of Roman imperial historiography. He refers, that is, to a negative 1894 German study of Gaius, the apparent goal of which was to attack Kaiser Wilhelm II. Later it was translated into English, he says, as part of the British anti-German propaganda of World War I.[58] We are forced to wonder, therefore, what modern implications Balsdon saw in his own rehabilitation of the same emperor. In any case, examining his chapter "Gaius and the Jews," we soon meet an unexplained comment about "Jewish prejudice." Then, in reference to the Diaspora, we encounter the stereotypical, unsupported, and highly anachronistic ideas of new Roman colonies containing "their *quota* of Jews" and older eastern cities to which Jews "were attracted by the prospects of money-making."[59]

Moreover, Jews "were stubborn, and when disputes arose, unyielding, and they had a strong weapon which they were prepared to use unscrupulously—the threat that, if they were not honoured, they would revolt." Balsdon characterizes all Jews under Roman rule as stubborn, unyielding, haughty, and unscrupulous. They were also "sagacious." That is, they recognized the services of Rome in protecting them from Greek enemies: "The like achievement of British rule in India in keeping the peace between Moslem and Hindu at once springs to mind."[60] The good Roman Empire was peacekeeper in the East between unruly Jews and Greeks; the good British Empire of 1934 was peacekeeper in Indian between unruly Muslims and Hindus.

Turning to the Alexandrian pogrom of 38 C.E., Balsdon continues with an a priori assessment of the situation: "In Egypt, Cyrene, and Cyprus the largest and most troublesome sections of the Jewish dispersion lived side by side with the most unruly riff-raff of the Greeks." These Greeks were somewhat justified in their agitation; Jews, however, were "self-satisfied," and "their influence in business was increasing" under Roman rule. Hence, "the young Alexandrians . . . now gave a specious demonstration of loyalty to the ruling house. They endeavored forcibly to set up statues of the Emperor [Gaius] in the Jewish synagogues." They then compelled the Roman prefect to support them in their next endeavor against the Jewish population of the city. Jews were murdered, houses were burned, and so forth.[61]

This is an interesting report. Having vilified Alexandrian Jews for their troublesomeness, greed, and self-satisfaction—closely paralleled by Carl

Kraeling's 1932 view of Jews in Syrian Antioch[62]—Balsdon provides evidence of two facts. The imperially appointed prefect of Egypt permitted Alexandrian Greeks, in honor of the imperial cult, to desecrate Jewish houses of prayer; he then participated in the pogrom that followed. Even so, later recognizing that Gaius "regarded the refusal of the Alexandrian Jews to honour his image as a piece of contumacious independence,"[63] Balsdon still ignores imperial involvement in the horrors of 38 C.E.

Similar participation he cannot deny when Gaius next decided to erect an image of himself in Jerusalem's temple precincts. As reasonable as Balsdon claims that he was, Gaius admitted his error and demanded only that Jews not oppose the erection of imperial images near Jerusalem. Here, however, Balsdon fails to appreciate that activities very much like this had just provoked the butchery of Alexandrian Jews. Hence, he is indignant that Philo warned of just such danger:[64] "This [erection of images] was eminently fair, and Philo's unreasonable criticism only indicates the impossibility of reconciling the eastern Jews to any sensible arrangement of give and take."[65] One Alexandrian Jew, supposedly unreasonable as compared to Gaius, now stereotypically represents the senselessness of "the eastern Jews." In sum, the emperor Gaius was not responsible for the sufferings of those Jews over whom he ruled. They themselves were. Granted, insofar as forcing the imperial cult on Jerusalem was concerned, he had probably not understood "the stubbornness of Jewish opposition." That, however, was perfectly reasonable, too. After all, "Jewish psychology was no less difficult for the Roman to understand than is Indian psychology for the Englishman."[66]

Finally, moving to the emperor Claudius, we may examine a single instance of the historiographic tendency to assume the blame of Jews for their own miseries under the early empire.[67] Earnest Cary's translation of Dio 60.6.6 reads, "As for the [Roman] Jews, who had again increased so greatly that by reason of their multitude it would have been hard without raising a tumult to bar them from the city, he [Claudius] did not drive them out, but ordered them, while continuing their traditional mode of life, not to hold meetings." More literally, the text translates as a classical *men-de* ("while-nevertheless") construction: "While he [Claudius] did not expel the again-having-become-excessive Jews (who as a result of the excess could hardly have been excluded from the city without a disturbance by their crowd), he did in fact order the practicing-the-traditional-life Jews not to gather."

Thus, Dio asserted the following: first, the Roman-Jewish population was again excessive by the time Claudius became emperor; second, it would have been hard for him to expel such a large group without disturbances; third, Claudius did not expel it; fourth, he did order those Jews practicing their religion not to gather. Hence, the text does not claim that there were Jewish disturbances. It does not claim that the new emperor intended to expel Roman Jews. On these matters it reflects only the much later cogitations of Dio that it was perhaps in order to avoid disturbances that Claudius had not chosen expulsion. Dio had in mind here his earlier account (57.18.5) of how Tiberius did expel Jews from the city. Cogitations aside, therefore, the factual claim of Dio was that, when he became emperor, Claudius prohibited gatherings of the pious and so acted against those who practiced Judaism. "The measure of Claudius . . . ," says Thoedor Mommsen, "was limited, in Dio's view, to the prohibition against carrying out their worship."[68] In 19 C.E. Tiberius had given the Roman practitioners of Judaism the option of desisting or leaving. In 41 C.E. Claudius renewed the order to desist; later, according to Suetonius *Claudius* 25.4, he followed it up with expulsion.

In light of these considerations, the conclusions of modern historiographers are curious.[69] Referring to "some public disorder or infraction of Roman regulations" behind Dio 60.6.6, Robert Jewett implicitly contradicts his source. Adding that "the specific cause for the disturbance in A.D. 41 is unknown,"[70] he would compel us to search for an unknown cause of an unknown disturbance. Arnaldo Momigliano is more complicated. With Jews "Claudius desired to remain on good terms." The emperor also "respects Jewish rights and is quick to safeguard them." This belonged to "his natural humanity in such matters." The problem is that in his Alexandrian letter of 41 C.E.,[71] Claudius "quite unexpectedly assumes a tone of the utmost violence toward the Jews, whom he accuses of 'fomenting a universal plague.' Historians have been bewildered," writes Momigliano, by the expected reversal in attitude.[72] He, however, is not. The explanation lies in the report of Dio. The 41 C.E. repression of Roman Judaism arose in response to proselytism: "There was, in short, a difference between general recognition of the Jewish faith—of the right, that is, to follow the Law of Moses—and the particular permission governing its exercise in a given city, and above all in Rome, when that exercise involved activities, like proselytism, that brought it within the ordinary jurisdiction of the magistrates charged with the protection of Roman religion."[73] In fact, the text of Dio does not refer to proselytism; it does, however, challenge Momigliano's claim that Roman Jews were free to practice their religious rites.

Having changed Claudius' prohibition of religious gatherings into a prohibition of Jewish proselytizing, Momigliano returns to his original intention of accounting for the bewildering hostility of Claudius' Alexandrian letter: "Nothing with which the letter deals . . . could justify Claudius in using such harsh language. The explanation may perhaps be that he was disgusted with the events in Rome which must recently have provoked or were about to provoke the measures recorded by Cassius Dio; or, perhaps better, that he resented being compelled to deal with the same nuisance of Jewish unrest in two different parts of the Empire."[74] Momigliano's goal is to justify the highly charged, anti-Jewish language of Claudius. Having denied the obvious sense of Dio 60.6.6 that Claudius intended to repress Roman Judaism, Momigliano now ignores his previous statement about proselytizing and turns instead to his own highly charged language. Claudius "may perhaps" have been "disgusted" with Roman Jewish provocations or with the "nuisance of Jewish unrest."

Which is it? Proselytizing or Jewish unrest? Dio mentioned neither. He wrote only that one of the emperor's first goals was to curtail the practice of Judaism in Rome. At about the same time Claudius referred to the Alexandrian Jewish community, already repressed by Gaius, as a potential plague and threatened further violence against it. Momigliano is correct, therefore, that the "harsh language" of the Alexandrian letter is justified by nothing within it. Thus, in spite of suppositions about the emperor's desire to remain on good terms with Jewish subjects, his respect for Jewish rights, and his "natural humanity," Momigliano's reworking of the ancient texts in that direction does not succeed. Claudius, in other words, may not be justified at the expense of his Roman or Alexandrian Jewish subjects.

E. Mary Smallwood's repristination of Momigliano does not change this. She, too, rationalizes the hostility of the emperor's letter by suggesting that it "may reflect his annoyance at having an outbreak of Jewish unrest on his hands in Rome before he had finished with that in Alexandria." She knows, however, that the text of Dio undermines this view: "Dio, by giving no indication of the Jews' offence, creates the impression that Claudius attacked them gratuitously. But such an action would be uncharacteristic of Claudius with his sense of justice and his concern for the underdogs of society. . . . Some unrecorded provocation must have occurred."[75] The key word here is "gratuitously": "Dio . . . creates the impression that Claudius attacked them gratuitously." This is not quite accurate, for the obvious sense of Dio 60.6.6 is that the new emperor wanted to cripple Jewish religious life in Rome. Hence, the real question becomes not what Roman Jews did wrong but what in the evidence supports Smallwood's claims of Claudian justice and concern for the underdog. In the present instance we find neither of these qualities. Both claims do make a kind of sense, however, as final examples of historiography's tendency to exonerate Rome's emperors at the expense of their Jewish subjects.

NOTES

1. H. Dixon Slingerland, *Claudian Policymaking and the Early Repression of Judaism at Rome*, South Florida Studies in the History of Judaism, vol. 160 (Atlanta: Scholars Press, 1997).

2. See my "'The Jews' in the Pauline Portion of Acts," *Journal of the American Academy of Religion* 54 (1986): 305–321.

3. Jean Juster, *Les Juifs dans l'Empire romain: leur condition juridique, économique et sociale*, vol. 2 (Paris: Librairie Paul Geuthner, 1914), pp. 182, 182 n. 2, 198, 199 n. 2.

4. J.P.V.D. Balsdon, *The Emperor Gaius (Caligula)* (Oxford: Clarendon Press, 1934), pp. 121, 124, 131.

5. Gaston May, "La politique religieuse de l'Empereur Claude," *Revue historique de droit français et étranger* 17 (1938): 39.

6. W.H.C. Frend, *Martyrdom and Persecution in the Early Church: A Study of Conflict from the Maccabees to Donatus* (1965; reprint Grand Rapids: Baker Book House, 1981), pp. 158–159.

7. E. Mary Smallwood, "Jews and Romans in the Early Empire," *History Today* 15 (1965): 315; cf. Slingerland, *Claudian Policymaking*, pp. 7–10.

8. Smallwood, "Jews and Romans," p. 233–234; cf. Slingerland, *Claudian Policymaking*, p. 10.

9. Anthony A. Barrett, *Caligula: The Corruption of Power* (1989; reprint New York: Simon and Schuster, 1991), pp. 183–184.

10. Vincent M. Scramuzza, "The Policy of the Early Roman Emperors towards Judaism," in *The Beginnings of Christianity*, edited by F.J. Foakes Jackson and Kirsopp

Lake, vol. 5 (London: Macmillan, 1920–1933), p. 287.

11. Margaret H. Williams, "The Expulsion of the Jews from Rome in A.D. 19," *Latomus* 48 (1989): 783.

12. Greek papyri in the British Museum known as the Papyri London 1912 [hereinafter P. Lond. 1912]; *Corpus Papyrorum Judaicarum*, edited by Victor A. Tcherikover, vol. 2 (Cambridge: Harvard University Press, 1957–1964), pp. 36-55.

13. Gaston May, "Politique religieuse," pp. 36–37, 34, 17 (my translations); cf. p. 23.

14. Gaston May, "L'activité juridique de l'Empereur Claude," *Revuew historique de droit français et étranger* 15 (1936): 66 (my translation).

15. Heikki Solin, "Juden und Syrer im westlichen Teil der römischen Welt. Eine ethnisch-demographische Studie mit besonderer Berücksichtigung der sprachlichen Zustände," in *ANRW* (*Aufstieg und Niedergang der römischen Welt*) 2.29^2:617 (my translation).

16. Ibid., pp. 686 (my translation), 690 n. 224.

17. Giorgio La Piana, "L'immigrazione a Roma nei primi secoli dell'impero," *Ricerche religiose* 4 (1928): 239.

18. Giorgio La Piana, "Foreign Groups in Rome during the First Centuries of the Empire," *Harvard Theological Review* 20 (1927): 329–395.

19. Tenney Frank, "Race Mixture in the Roman Empire," *American Journal of Historical Review* 21 (1916): 689–708.

20. Thaddée Zielinski, "L'empereur Claude et L'idée de la domination mondiale des Juifs," *Revue de l'Université de Bruxelles* 32 (1926–1927): 133–135, 137–138, 141–144.

21. Cf. J.N. Sevenster, *The Roots of Pagan Anti-Semitism in the Ancient World*, Supplements to Novum Testamentum, vol. 41 (Leiden: E.J. Brill, 1975), passim.

22. LCL translation by J.C. Rolfe; cf. Slingerland, *Claudian Policymaking*, pp. 47–49.

23. Harry J. Leon, *The Jews of Ancient Rome* (1960; reprint with new introduction by Carolyn A. Osiek, Peabody, MA: Hendrickson, 1995), p. 11.

24. Scramuzza, "Policy," p. 293.

25. Menahem Stern, *Greek and Latin Authors on Jews and Judaism*, vol. 2 (Jerusalem: Israel Academy of Sciences and Humanities, 1976–1984), p. 111.

26. Frend, *Martyrdom*, p. 89.

27. Menahem Stern, "The Jewish Diaspora," in *The Jewish People in the First Century: Historical Geography, Political History, Social, Cultural and Religious Life and Institutions*, edited by S. Safrai and M. Stern, Compendia Rerum Iudaicarum ad Novum Testamentum: Section One, vol. 1 (Philadelphia: Fortress Press, 1974–1987), p. 163; cf. Slingerland, *Claudian Policymaking*, p. 49.

28. Slingerland, *Claudian Policymaking*, pp. 21–23, 43–46, 50–62, 65–77, 86–87.

29. Max Radin, *The Jews among the Greeks and Romans* (Philadelphia: Jewish Publication Society of America, 1915), pp. 304, 308–309.

30. Ibid., p. 306. Williams, "Expulsion," pp. 775–778, also rejects Josephus here.

31. Leon, *Jews of Ancient Rome*, p. 16. His reference is to Frank Burr Marsh (*The Reign of Tiberius* [1931; reprint New York: Barnes and Noble, 1959]).

32. Leon, *Jews of Ancient Rome*, p. 16.

33. This was Philo's apologetic. Cf. Slingerland, *Claudian Policymaking*, pp. 71–72.

34. Josephus Flavius, *Antiquities* 18.65, pp. 81–84.

35. Leon, *Jews of Ancient Rome*, pp. 17–19.

36. Williams, "Expulsion," p. 773. In fact, as Slingerland, *Claudian Policymaking*, pp. 50–62, makes clear, it was the practitioners of Judaism who left.

37. Williams, "Expulsion," p. 770.

38. Ibid., pp. 773–774.

39. Relatedly, Anthony A. Barrett writes, "To the extent that there was anti-semitism among the Romans before Caligula, it generally took the form of fairly good-natured

mockery of what were considered their outlandish religious views. There is no evidence of serious anti-semitic outbursts under Augustus or Tiberius." Barrett, *Caligula*, p. 184. In fact, its helpless targets thought imperial mockery deadly. Cf. Slingerland, *Claudian Policymaking*, pp. 16–27.

40. Williams, "Expulsion," pp. 775, 778, 779.

41. Ibid., pp. 779, 780.

42. Ibid., p. 780.

43. Ibid., pp. 781–782. Simeon L. Guterman, *Religious Toleration and Persecution in Ancient Rome* (London: Aiglon Press, 1951), p. 149, conjectures that

it was probably because the synagogues had become *illicita* in the sense of disorderly that Tiberius and Claudius adopted restrictive measures against them. . . . Tiberius' act was, therefore, an administrative, repressive one; it did not touch on the legality or the illegality of the *collegia*. It was likely that Tiberius' efforts should also extend to putting down the Jewish synagogues which had also probably become centres of unrest.

The purpose of his study is to show that Judaism was a *religio licita* (legal religion). To account for events like those of 19 C.E., he exonerates both the emperor and the Jewish community by blaming individual Jews for disorder in the synagogues.

44. Williams, "Expulsion," p. 783.

45. Dio 57.18.5a (Loeb Classical Library translation by Earnest Cary).

46. Williams, "Expulsion," pp. 767–768.

47. Ibid., p. 784.

48. Ibid., p. 782.

49. Margaret H. Williams, *The Jews among the Greeks and Romans: A Diasporan Sourcebook* (Baltimore: Johns Hopkins University Press, 1998), pp. 98–99, takes the same position.

50. Hugo Willrich, "Caligula," *Klio* (1903): 459–467.

51. Ibid., pp. 397–419.

52. Ibid., p. 402.

53. Ibid., pp. 439–446.

54. Ibid., p. 403 (my translation).

55. Ibid., pp. 407–409. Later (p. 443), Willrich assumes that the punishment of Alexandrian Jews resulted appropriately from their rabble-rousing or treason (*maiestas*).

56. Ibid., p. 443.

57. Ibid., p. 419 (my translation).

58. Balsdon, *The Emperor Gaius*, pp. xv–xvi.

59. Ibid., pp. 114, 120–121. May, "Politique religieuse," p. 23, also presupposes that the spread of the Jewish Diaspora resulted largely from a hunger for wealth. Referring to the Assyrian conquest as a factor in the development of the Diaspora, he omits reference to the Babylonian, Persian, Greek, and Roman conquests of Israel. Though aware of it (p. 17), he fails to indicate that Jews typically left Judea for Rome as slaves in the service of some Gentile's quest for wealth. Barrett, *Caligula*, p. 184, too, supposes that "enormous commercial potential" brought Jews to Alexandria.

60. Balsdon, *The Emperor Gaius*, p. 124.

61. Ibid., pp. 125, 131–133.

62. Carl H. Kraeling, "The Jewish Community at Antioch," *Journal of Biblical Literature* 51 (1932): 131: "The foundation [of Antioch] afforded an opportunity for enterprise such as would unquestionably call Jews to the spot without delay." The reason for their decline was a "sense of their own self-importance" that may have brought about the Antiochian pogrom in the time of Gaius (p. 148).

63. Balsdon, *The Emperor Gaius*, p. 136.

64. Philo of Alexandria, *Legatio ad Gaium*, edited with an introduction by E. Mary Smallwood (Leiden: E.J. Brill, 1961), pp. 334–336.

65. Balsdon, *The Emperor Gaius*, p. 139.

66. Ibid., p. 143.

67. Cf. Slingerland, *Claudian Policymaking*, pp. 131–150.

68. Theodor Mommsen, "Der Religionsfrevel nach römischen Recht," in *Gesammelte Schriften*, vol. 3 (1905–1913; reprint Berlin: Weidmannsche Verlagsbuchhandlung, 1965), p. 411 n. 3.

69. I use here those scholars accurately separating the accounts in Dio and Suetonius.

70. Robert Jewett, *A Chronology of Paul's Life* (Philadelphia: Fortress Press, 1979), p. 37.

71. P. Lond. 1912.

72. Arnaldo Momigliano, *Claudius: The Emperor and His Achievement* (1943; new preface, 1961; reprint Westport, CT: Greenwood Press, 1981), pp. 30, 34, 37. Leon, too, in *Jews of Ancient Rome*, p. 23, notes the "unexpected severity" of Claudius' letter.

73. Momigliano, *Claudius*, pp. 32, 33.

74. Ibid., p. 34.

75. E. Mary Smallwood, *The Jews under Roman Rule from Pompey to Diocletian: A Study in Political Relations*, Studies in Judaism in Late Antiquity, 2d ed., vol. 20 (Leiden: E.J. Brill, 1981), pp. 214, 215.

4

Archival Sources for the History of the Jews in Italy

Micaela Procaccia

The long and uninterrupted stay of Jewish people in Italy, beginning during the last years of the ancient Roman Republic, has left a considerable mark on documentary collections in the peninsula. One may find historical documents concerning Jewish settlements since the fourteenth century (and even sometimes since the end of the thirteenth century). State archives keep these documents as well as the archives of the Catholic Church and the private archives belonging to noble Italian families.

For example, the first mention of a Jew living in a small town not far from Rome, Sermoneta, is in the register reporting the names of the citizens swearing an oath to the lord of the Annibaldi family, who ruled Sermoneta in the year 1294. You may read this record in the archive of the Caetani family, who succeeded them, as well as a particular *formula di giuramento* (form of oath) for Jewish witnesses in court. The same kind of form (with few changes) may be found at the end of many communal *Statuti* (charters, statutes) of small towns near Rome in the fourteenth and fifteenth centuries.[1]

From the beginnings of the fifteenth century, documentary sources about Jews In Italy become nuermous, and you can find them in almost every state archive. Italian provincial state archives in ever one of the ninety-four major cities and the forty local state archives in municipalities of particular historical importance hold documentation produced by the governing bodies of the country before and since Italy's unification. They also hold notarial archives older than 100 years and those of suppressed ecclesiastical bodies and religious corporations confiscated by the state. As a consequence it is possible to find specific documentation for the history of Jews in Italy in different forms.

The history of the Jews in Italy begins in Rome, but between the end of the thirteenth and the fourteenth centuries Jewish bankers coming from Rome migrated toward the communes, where their capital was more in demand and investment more rewarding. They pushed out into the surrounding territory, settling, often for the first time, in many cities of Lazio, Le Marche, Umbria, and

Tuscany. The communes entered into negotiations with those groups of Roman Jews and invited them to come and extend their operations (not only on a small scale) to the local financial markets. The records of the deliberations of the citizen's councils testify to the position of a Hebrew community in the town, as well as the so-called *condotte* (i.e., banking contracts, usually fifteenth and sixteenth centuries); special permission for travelers, moneylenders, physicians, and rabbis; or the *capitula* (containing the rules about the presence of Jews in a small or big town, also from the fourteenth century). From the arrival of the first moneylender, always followed by a doctor, a merchant, and so on, such documents reflect the attitude of the urban ruling classes toward the Jews.

Then, from the middle of the fifteenth century to the middle of the nineteenth, the chancelleries of various princes produced documents about the presence of Jews, sometimes a requested one, sometimes a rejected one. You can guess the different situation of Jews in every period and single city just by looking at the archival position of the single document. For example, in 1466 Borso d'Este gave permission to establish a synagogue in his capital, but, as he was troubled by ecclesiastical opposition, he gave orders to his *referendaria* (official) to be tactful; so he wrote a simple letter, not a decree. In 1556, Ercole II granted Salomone da Riva the privilege of opening a rabbinical academy in Ferrara with a formal decree, writing that he's doing such a thing "for the benefit of many Jewish and Christian students, foreign ones as well as our subjects." The two documents have the same effective value, but their different archival position is the result of a different political attitude.[2]

The chancellery of the Vatican state has peculiar characteristics so that the overlapping of diocesan structures with provincial ones results in diverse and complementary archives. A particular situation is that of documentary sources in Rome. As a result of the agreement made after the city was conquered by the new Italian kingdom's army in 1870, the documents produced by the church's state were divided in two groups: the documents of the Reverenda Camera Apostolica, the central church's state organism for the secular power of the pope, went to the state archive in Rome, while those documents regarded as concerning *spiritualia* (spiritual matters) were kept in the secret Vatican archive.

After the seventeenth century we find documents about ghettos and relationships between the ghetto inhabitants and the public authorities. From the middle of the nineteenth century we have records about the so-called age of emancipation and the active presence of Jews in the Risorgimento and in the Italian nation after unification. Trial documents are of particular interest; the tribunal's records reveal several Jews as defendants or as witnesses. In the archival series of the Tribunale criminale del Governatore (Criminal Court in Rome) in the state archive in Rome we may find also rare traces of the dialect of Roman Jews (recorded by notaries) as well as information about everyday life of Jewish people in the town.[3]

We find the same information in the notarial archives (from the fourteenth century): recording contracts, agreements (sale and purchase, marriage, apprenticeship, etc.) among Jews and among Jews and Christians, as well as testaments and inventories of properties of Jews. We may guess about relations between Jews and Christians in Italian cities, for instance, by the presence of a Jewish witness in a contract among Christians, or vice versa, and by existing business contracts among Jews and Christians. We may also catch echoes of the voices of Jewish people as found in some notarial documents testifying to the activities of a Jewish community.[4] The most famous Jewish notarial series are kept in the communal historical archive in Rome (not the state archive), the Archivio storico capitolino. These *protocolli* were written in Hebrew in the first years and then in Italian.

The use of Roman Jews to give depositions taken down by Jewish notaries— as Christians used to do—at least from the sixteenth century to 1640 provides us with various details about life inside the community. Those about women are of much interest, telling us about their high level of independence, even inside marriage, their relationship with men, and their engagement in culture and business. It may be of some interest to note that the Jewish notaries use a special form to justify broken engagements (not an uncommon event): the bride and the groom "neither love each other nor are fond of each other" (*non se amano né se vonno bene*).[5]

The historical archives of the Jewish communities in Italy keep records from the period of the ghettos to now. Documents about the ghetto are very interesting because one can see the Jewish point of view about the same topics in the state documents. We also have records of the religious *Confraternite* and of the *scholae* (synagogues), which were always quite divided by nationality (Spanish, French, Roman, Ashkenazi, etc.). We can see as well the building of a new Italian-Jewish way of life during the age of emancipation and the reactions to fascist policies.[6] I wish to mention only the archives of Jewish personalities kept in Jewish cultural institutes such as the Centro bibliografico of the Union of Jewish Communities in Rome and the Centro di documentazione ebraica contemporanea in Milan. I'll add just one more example of the importance of personal archives, not only for the history of the Jews in Italy but also for the history of Italy *tout-court*: the archives of Isacco Artom, Jewish secretary of Count Camillo Benso di Cavour and one of the most important Italian statesmen for foreign policy in the first years of the Italian kingdom, now in the Centro bibliografico in Rome.

As for the last period of the history of Jewish people in Italy, the Italian state archives hold several archival series that may be useful for historical researchers interested in the Nazi-fascist persecution of Jews in Italy. As is well known, the fascist racial laws of 1938 are considered the first step of the Shoah in Italy. According to Liliana Picciotto Fargion, thanks to these racial laws it was possible for the German army and SS, helped by the fascist Repubblica di Salò, to deport Italian Jews in the years between 1943 and 1945, without any preparatory measures.

The pursuance of the racial laws is very well testified to by the documents of the Ministero degli Interni, Direzione Generale Demografia e Razza (Ministry of the Interior, General Administration for Demography and Race) in the central state archives in Rome. This Direzione Generale was the central administrative body of the fascist state for racial policy. In the provincial state archives you may find similar series of local documents in the archives of *Prefetture* (local state organs). Documents concerning the actual deportation of Jews may be found in *Pubblica Sicurezza* (policy and public safety) in central state archives, as well as in *Questure* in the provincial state archives and in the records of the most important prisons (e.g., Regina Coeli in Rome and San Vittore in Milan).

The so-called Archival Law of 1963 lays down limits for consultation of documents kept in state archives; classified records relating to foreign and domestic policy may be consulted after fifty years from the date of the documents, and those concerning people's private affairs are available after seventy years. Documents kept in the personal files of the series mentioned earlier (especially those of *Prefetture* and Demografia e Razza) are considered among the latter group.

Authorization to consult these documents may be asked of the Ministry of the Interior, but, as a matter of fact, it has not been easy to get authorization in the last five or six years, and free consultation will be available only in the years between 2008 and 2015. In the last three years the General Archive Administration reached an agreement with the Union of Italian Jewish Communities about this problem. It is now beginning an experimental project that will make possible consultation of Demografia e Razza in the next two years, thanks to a database where researchers will find all the information kept in the documents except those identifying the single person concerned by the file (name, name of parents, etc.). We hope that this project will be the first step to a complete database concerning the pursuance of racial laws and the persecution of the Jews in Italy. During 1997 and 1998, a bitter quarrel took place between historians and the Ministry of the Interior on the subject as a consequence of the new Privacy Law, which restricted further access. As a result, new rules are to be prepared about historical research and privacy laws, and a new committee has been established of archivists, historians, and the Ministry of the Interior to solve the problems of denied access. As I have briefly noted, the Direzione Generale Demografia e Razza was an office within the Ministry of the Interior that was responsible, between 1938 and 1944, for the "design and implementation of administrative and legislative measures for the protection of the race."

The files currently kept in the Central State Archives (ACS) also include previously missing documents later found at Merano and, in 1993, returned to the ACS by the Union of Italian Jewish Communities. The documents actually held, however, do not amount to the entire archive of the Direzione Generale, which also had authority for population and citizenship matters. They are only a portion (approximately one-third) of the archive of its race division (Divisione razza).

Despite these considerable gaps, whose causes are only partly known, the archive is the only one on a national level for research on Jews' persecution in Italy. It consists of about 13,000 files on people who applied for exemptions from the anti-Jewish legislation, some to be declared "not belonging to the Jewish race," some to conserve their job, and others to be allowed to attend public schools and universities or to carry out trade activities. Finally, there are the non-Italian and stateless Jews who applied to stay in Italy beyond the period of time stipulated by the law. The documentation also include ex officio race verification, as well as authorizations for marrying foreign citizens. The latter does not concern Jews directly or exclusively.

As mentioned, the archive is not yet freely accessible. Therefore, the project aims at developing an inventory and identifying information in the documents useful for working out the original structure of the archive and for identifying the activities carried out by the office that created it.[7]

Not only did Italian Jews give us the only archaeological site outside the Middle East, synagogues, handicrafts, illuminated manuscripts, and a particular cultural heritage, but you may also find in Italy the most complete and various series of archival documents concerning Jewish settlements, testifying to this presence even where there are no more Jews, as in the hundreds of small settlements in central, northern, and southern Italy, where archives have kept for centuries the memory of the most numerous Italian-Jewish community of the Middle Ages, that of Sicily, whose story ended in 1492, when the decree of expulsion from the Spanish territories banished them (soon followed by Jews from the kingdom of Naples), but who continued in the *Scholae sicilianae* (Sicilian synagogues) in the other Jewish settlements in Italy, like that of Rome.[8]

NOTES

1. B. Migliau and M. Procaccia, *Lazio: itinerari ebraici* (Venice: Marsilio, 1997).

2. R. Segre, "La società ebraica nelle fonti archivistiche italiane," in *Italia Jucaica*, vol. 1 (Rome: Ministero per i beni culturali e ambientali, Ufficio centrale per i beni archivistici, 1983), pp. 239–250.

3. M. Procaccio, "Non dabara': gli ebrei di Roma nei primi cinquanta anni del Cinquecento attraverso le fonti giudiziarie," in *Italia Judaica*, vol. 6 (Rome: Ministero per i beni culturali e ambientali, Ufficio centrale per i beni archivistici, 1998), pp. 80–93.

4. A. Esposito, *Un'altra Roma; minoranze nazionali e comunità ebraiche tra Medioevo e Rinascimento* (Roma: Il Calamo, 1995).

5. K. Stow, *Jews in Rome* (Leiden and New York: E.J. Brill, 1995).

6. M. Procaccio, "I beni archivistici," in *La tutela dei beni culturali ebraici in Italia* (Bologna: I.B.C., 1997), pp. 32–33.

7. L. Garofalo and M. Procaccia, "The Project of the Italian State Archives concerning Documents Dealing with Persecution of Jews in Italy," in Jacques Fredj, ed., *Les archives de la Shoah* (Paris: Harmattan, 1998), pp. 623–627.

8. A. Esposito and M. Procaccio, "La schola siciliana de Urbe: la fine della storia?," in *Italia Judaica*, vol. 5 (Rome: Ministero per i beni culturali e ambientali, Ufficio centrale per i beni archivistici, 1995), pp. 412–423.

Part II

MEDIEVAL AND
RENAISSANCE ITALY

5

Florence against the Jews
or the Jews against Florence?

Michele Luzzati

It is certainly true, as the title of this conference suggests, that Italian Jewry is the oldest of the diasporic minorities. It must be remembered, however, that the distribution of the Jews in the Italian peninsula and in its two islands varied considerably over time. The only exception is Rome, where a Jewish presence continued uninterrupted from the second century B.C.E. until today. Limiting myself to the most noticeable phenomenon, I remind you that at the time of the Roman Empire and in the first ten centuries of the Middle Ages, that is, approximately until 1350, almost all Italian Jews lived in the southern part of the peninsula (Rome and southern Italy and Sicily).

But 200 years later, around 1550, Jewish settlements were all in central and northern Italy, beside Rome. Southern Italy and the two main islands, Sicily and Sardinia, had, in fact, followed the same path of the Iberian Peninsula; Jews living there had had to escape or to convert. There was, therefore, in the course of just two centuries, between the end of the Middle Ages and the beginning of the modern period, a complete geographical capsizing, which was decisive for (1) the survival of Italy's Jewish element, (2) the welcoming of Sephardic refugees (and, on a smaller scale, of Ashkenazi immigrants), (3) the Jewish mercantile activity between the Mediterranean and Europe's Atlantic coats, and mostly (4) the development of religious culture and European Jewish civilization. This alteration in the dislocation of the Jews, which led to a Jewish presence concentrated almost exclusively, as it is still today, in central and northern Italy, was fundamentally determined by the assertion and diffusion of the Jews' banking activity.

Starting from the thirteenth century, Jews coming from Rome and the south of Italy traveled up the peninsula and opened loan banks in hundreds of towns and semiurban centers. These Jews, who were present almost everywhere in small groups, went on to monopolize similar credit enterprises previously belonging to Christians, ensuring in this way the possibility to continue living on Italian soil, both for themselves and their descendants. The history of the assertion, between the 1300s and the 1500s, of these "bankers," who were often also scholars, doctors, and rabbis, constitutes one of the most controversial themes in the history of Italian Jewry.

One particular chapter of this history is confronted here, which serves to make it clear that the Jews were not "passive" subjects who were called to fill the "spaces" made by the withdrawal of Christians from lending at interest but "active" subjects who were able to negotiate their entry into the financial market of the cities and states of north and central Italy with tenacity and ability. The specific case looked at here is of great importance, because it deals with the arrival of Jewish bankers in the city of Florence, the most important Italian mercantile and financial center of the closing centuries of the Middle Ages, as well as the "capital" of the Renaissance.

As has been suggested, starting from the end of the 1200s, it was precisely thanks to the capillary diffusion of Jewish lending banks that an extraordinary increase in the number of Jewish settlements occurred in central and northern Italy. Of course, exceptions were not lacking, and among these was Florence, where Jewish moneylenders were allowed within the city walls only in 1437, a date quite late compared to the average of almost all the rest of central and northern Italy. Without investigating too much the reason for this prolonged absence of a Jewish settlement, the chronicles and the historiographic tradition have sustained that, for decades, Florence had put up a fierce resistance to the acceptance of Jewish moneylenders and, in fact, any Jews. The thesis of the hostility that the Florentine Republic had toward the entry of the Jews into Florence was happily sustained, moreover, on the basis of "ideological reasons" both by the Florentine-Italian and Catholic sides and by the Jewish side.

In the first case this thesis was welcomed, paradoxically, by two opposing positions. Indeed, it allowed the Florentine people's Catholic traditionalism to be exalted and to show how it was capable of preserving their city, for as long as possible, from the possible negative influences of Judaism. On the other side, the thesis of the Florentine government's hostility toward the Jews offered polemical arguments to anticlericals, who criticized the supposed excessive compliance of the Florentines toward particular religious orientations.

As far as the Jewish world is concerned, the supposed Florentine hostility has been regarded as plausible because, after all, it brought grist to the mill of the "lachrymose history of the Jewish people." Also with the presupposition of a Florentine "refusal" of a Jewish presence, the importance of the settlement of bankers and other Jews that took place in the city in the decades following 1437 has sometimes been too quickly underestimated.

In reality, the delay of the admission of Jewish moneylenders into Florence was not due to any hostility, either immediate or indirect, toward Jewish moneylenders or Jews in general. I show that the late establishment of a Jewish settlement in the city was not determined only by a possible hostility on the part of the Florentines, a hostility that was not really either greater than, or different from, that of the inhabitants of every other Italian center, who were always suspicious of all homogeneous groups of "strangers" and, more importantly, "strangers" who were actually non-Christians.

On the history of Florentine Jewry we have the work of Umberto Cassuto, *The Jews in Florence in the Age of the Renaissance*, still essential reading today even if published in the distant year 1918. Cassuto's research is limited, however, by the choice to consider only the "city" of Florence (i.e., defined by the perimeter of its walls) without extending the analysis to what happened in the whole of the lands that were also subject to Florence (i.e., the Florentine state in its entirety, which was completely subject to the government that ruled the capital city). If we take into consideration the whole Florentine state and not just the city, Jewish "bankers" were admitted here approximately a century before the year 1437, which marks the opening of Jewish banks in the city of Florence and the beginning of a Jewish Florentine settlement. In fact, since the middle of the fourteenth century the Florentine government had quite happily allowed the entry of Jewish moneylenders into the land under its dominion, for instance, San Gimignano, Cortona, and Montepulciano.

In the last two decades of the fourteenth century and the beginning of the fifteenth the number of centers in the Florentine state that were authorized—on the basis of specific conventions (*capitoli*) approved by the central government—to welcome Jewish bankers increased considerably; these centers included Volterra, San Miniato, Colle Val d'Elsa, Arezzo, Fucecchio, Pescia, Prato, and Pisa, as well as others. Also, we cannot exclude the possibility that before the end of the 1300s some Jewish moneylenders had exercised their activity in Florence.

In fact, with a *provvisione* (law) defined as *pro iudeis* (in favor of the Jews)—proposed by the Florentine government on 23 November 1396 and then approved by the Council (Consiglio) of the Captain and the Popolo (something similar to a parliament) on 28 November, with 155 votes out of 219 in favor—it was established that "from henceforth one cannot and must not, in any way, give to or concede to any Jews, a licence to lend at interest or usury in Florence" (de cetero aliqua licentia non possit nec debeat dari aut quoquo modo concedi alicui iudeo sive ebreo mutuandi et seu mutuari faciendi in civitate Florentie ad fenus vel usuram) if this did not come exclusively from the government (the Priori, the Gonfalonieri delle Società del Popolo, and the Dodici Boniviri).

This decision suggests that before the autumn of 1396 a few Jews had managed to obtain authorization from certain minor *Officia* (magistracies) to lend money in Florence, without intervention on the part of the government and Consiglio. By giving itself the direct power to allow the Jews their money-lending business in the city, the Florentine government also reserved the authority to fix, in the case of an agreement with the interested party, the rules that would have guaranteed the Jews' stay in the city.

These rules dealt with the "*habitatione, stantia et mora secura*" (the peaceful stay), the "*securitas*" (the safety), and the "*franchigia*" (the exemption from direct taxation) of the Jews and their property, the freedom to observe their feasts and ceremonies that were referred to in the Old Testament or that were celebrated and observed at the time of the Old Testament (que continentur in Veteri Testamento seu que tempore Veteris Testamenti celebrabantur et obser-vabantur), the possibility or not to buy property, and judicial and fiscal treatment (including the possibility of submitting the "bankers" to payment of a tax for the exercise of their profession). The government engaged itself to not oblige the Jews "ad portandum habitum singularem vel signum" (to wear a badge or a particular kind of dress). This *provvisione* shows that the Florentine government was clearly prepared to allow Jewish moneylenders to carry out their activity, even within the walls of Florence, and proves that at the end of the 1300s there was no intended ostracization of the Jews.

According to Umberto Cassuto, the decision of November 1396 was not effective simply due to the inability to prevent Christian moneylenders from continuing their business. But, in my opinion, Cassuto's claim that "the prohibition on the Christian's lending at interest" and "permission for the Jews" were strictly dependent on each other is too aprioristic. We see better further on how the nonarrival of the Jewish moneylenders in the city in the years after 1396 was probably not due to this reason suggested by Cassuto. Until January 1406 the relationship between the Florentine government and the Jewish money-lenders continued to run along the same lines as during the previous years; on one side, no Jewish bank had been opened in the capital, and, on the other, numerous authorized Jewish banks were operating in many subject centers.

In January 1406 there was a radical change, probably instigated by religious reasons; indeed, it was decided by the Consiglio to peremptorily prohibit, from 1 September of the same year, the Jews from lending at interest in any part of the state. If this prohibition had been enforced successfully, no Jewish settlement of any importance would have been able to survive, not only in Florence but also in any other area of the Florentine state. This new policy was, however, destined to be an immediate failure. The law of January was not abolished (and continued, in theory, to hang over the Jews of the Florentine republic as a sword of Damocles), but only a few months after its proclamation, Jews from various areas of the state obtained many exemptions from the law, and the result was the return to the previous situation.

To be allowed back to lend money in various localities, but not within the city walls, the Jews had to pay the sum of 2,000 florins, which proved very helpful to Florence, which was involved in the costly conquest of Pisa. In the first decades of the 1400s not only were there Jewish banks in many nearby towns—for example, Prato, which was only ten miles away—but also, as many documents show, Jews moved around freely in Florence itself, and in some cases they were perhaps authorized to reside in the city. The Jews were not, therefore, prohibited from entry to the city, so much so that it was in Florence that the representatives of Italian Jewry met in 1428. What was still not allowed within the walls of Florence, however, was the opening of lending banks, the only instrument that, at the period, could permit a durable settlement allowed to follow its religious practices and rules openly, freely, and collectively.

From research, we have no further information on the issue of the possible welcoming of Jewish moneylenders into Florence until 12 June 1430, when the Consiglio del Popolo gave authorization once more to the government to arrange, before 30 September of that year, for any Jewish banker who wished to do so to settle in the city. Once again there was no effective result. According to

Cassuto, "it is impossible to determine" why there was this renewed failure; he suggested the theory that it derived from "either the influence of Christian moneylenders" or "an innate adversity of the Jews" (although it is not clear why this should have existed inside and not outside the city walls). Also, Cassuto proposed again the idea of a rigid "correlation between the lack of Jews in Florence and the Florentine [Christian] citizens' continued money-lending activity." Once the deadline set for 30 September 1430 had passed, the proposal to call Jewish moneylenders to Florence was renewed on 14 November of the same year; this time the plan was to be carried out within six months.

Seeing that the initiative had not yet been realized, at the end of May 1431 it was proposed again, and this time a longer deadline was set; the commissioners charged with the negotiations were to have a year to carry them out successfully. On 22 November 1435 the summoning of the Jews was once more resolved favorably, giving another year (to the end of November 1436) to come to a solution. Misinterpreting the meaning of governmental decisions aimed at allowing real negotiations with the Jewish moneylenders, Cassuto maintained that the Florentines approved these deliberations to simply postpone "the introduction of the Jews" "till doomsday."

To explain why the decision to call the Jewish moneylenders ended finally on 17 October 1437, with the effect of letting them settle in the city for at least ten years, Cassuto hypothesized, on rather fragile foundations, that meanwhile the lending banks owned by Christians had, in fact, been revoked. Cassuto basically confirmed in this way the "theorem" that Jewish and Christian banks could not or should not "legally" coexist, and he suggested, perhaps in a philo-Florentine tone and despite the previously quoted hint of a possible "innate adversity of the Jews," that Florence's hostility was, more than anything else, due to the pressures of a "lobby" by the Christian moneylenders. In any case, then, even according to Cassuto's interpretation of the events, which was certainly not simplistic but careful and thoughtful, it was Florence that had acted versus the Jews.

In my opinion a different hypothesis must be adopted to explain the events that led to the introduction of Jewish moneylenders into Florence only in 1437. This hypothesis implies, in some way, a reversal in point of view; it involves asking ourselves not whether Florence wanted the Jews but whether the Jews wanted Florence or, at least, wanted to see under what conditions the Jews were prepared to open their banks in Florence. The problem then is found in the conditions of the agreements that the two parties were prepared to stipulate.

Even Cassuto highlighted that, in 1396, when the Florentines showed for the first time (as far as we know) that they were prepared to welcome Jewish moneylenders into the city, a maximum interest rate of 15% per year was demanded. The Jews operating in other centers within the Florentine state normally lent at 30% per year and, in particular cases, at a maximum of up to 40% and a minimum of 25%. Fifteen percent was therefore a rate that was absolutely unacceptable, and any agreement made between the Jews and the Florentine government on this basis was destined to fail. Clearly it was the Jews who in 1396 refused to enter Florence; indeed, they had not agreed to lend at a rate of 15%. Given that over the following years the deliberations of 23–28 November 1396 do not appear to have been canceled, we can presume that the obligation of having to lend at an interest rate that did not exceed 15% remained the obstacle to the Jewish bankers' accepting the Florentines' invitation to work in their city.

The main aim of the Florentines behind their negotiations with the Jews was certainly lowering the interest rate as much as possible for the benefit of the poor people; all the subsequent events of fifteenth-century Jewish moneylending in Florence show this. But if, in the way that Cassuto noted, rates of 30% and 40% were common in Florence, it was really unthinkable to force the Jews to lend at 15%. For this reason the "laws" passed from June 1430 to June 1435 offered the Jews the new opportunity to lend at a maximum interest rate of 20% instead of 15%. This may still have been a rate too risky for the Jewish operators. On 12 June 1420 the Consiglio of Florence had tried to enforce a limit of 25% on Christian moneylenders, but already in the spring of the following year it had been forced—with a *provvisione* unknown to Cassuto—to revoke this measure because all the city banks, except one, had closed their shutters.

Despite this, in 1437 the Jews ended up agreeing to a proposal to operate three different lending banks (which quickly became four) within the walls of Florence at the rate of 20%, which had been offered them since 1430. With this decision, after forty years of hesitating and negotiating, the Jewish money-lenders made their official entry into Florence, and from this date forth we can speak of, it not an official community, then at least a stable Jewish settlement in Florence.

In the absence of precise documentation on the discussions that took place during the years 1430–1436 between the Jews and the government, it is difficult to understand why, in 1437, when the Jews finally accepted the maximum rate of 20%, they were then prepared to come down five whole figures below the threshold that a few years previously their Christian colleagues had considered unsustainable.

Several possible explanations can be proposed, all made on the assumption that the interest rate, although certainly the most important point in any agreement between Jewish moneylenders and the cities or states that decided to summon them, was not the only element through which advantages or dis-advantages could be obtained for the Jewish side. In the case of the Florentine agreement, the first and foremost advantage obtained by the Jewish money-lenders in 1437 must be the concession of an absolute monopoly; other than the planned three or four Jewish banks, no other moneylender, either Jewish or Christian, would be allowed to operate within a four-mile radius of the city.

No other document supports the hypothesis that, prior to this, the Jews were guaranteed an absolute lack of competition in their lending on pledge in Florence. Second, although the three or four authorized banks belonged officially to four different groups of Jews, in actual fact the individual Jewish associations were linked to each other, thereby forming something like a syndicate, able to minimize the risks implied in the estimated minimum rate of 20%. Again, within only three years the Jewish moneylenders were expected to guarantee a capital of at least 40,000 florins, a huge sum considering that a wage earner's annual income was about 20 florins. Committed to living and working in Florence for at least ten years, the Jews could nonetheless be expelled prematurely following a sudden change in the political direction of the government, with great economic losses. Changes of this sort were usually caused by pressures exercised by certain religious groups that were opposed, on matters of principle, to any form of lending at interest, especially that carried out by Jews.

A sort of precautionary absolution from the pope could avoid this risk. We know from the preface of the aforementioned *provvisione* of 17 October 1437 that the Florentine government had recently asked for, and obtained, from Pope Eugene IV an explicit authorization to allow Jewish moneylenders in the city walls. It is not difficult to imagine that the concession of this papal authorization was one of the conditions requested also by the Jews. Finally, according to the terms of the 1437 *provvisione*, the Jews did not have to pay any tax in order to run lending banks in the city of Florence. This was an obvious advantage compared to what was common both for Christian moneylenders in Florence and for lending banks that Jews had opened in other places in the Florentine state and elsewhere.

As you will remember, in 1396 the Florentine government had kept for itself the prerogative to tax Jewish bankers who would agree to operate in Florence, and it is likely that during the course of the negotiations that took place between 1430 and 1436 the issue of the possibility of charging the Jewish "bankers" with a tax had been brought up. Outside ethical-religious considerations that could have pushed the government not to ask either Christian or Jewish lending banks for payment of taxes on an activity seen as immoral, it is obvious that there was a correlation between the maximum level of interest rates that the moneylenders had to respect and the possible taxing of their banks. The higher the maximum level of interest that could be asked (which in consequence meant an increase in earnings), the higher the tax that had to be handed over to the government, and vice versa. The Jews' acceptance of the minimum interest rate of 20% could, therefore, in 1437 be compensated for by the elimination of any fiscal imposition on their banks.

In certain aspects the title of this chapter is obviously paradoxical, because neither Florence nor the Jews were either unitary or univocal "entities." It is clear that in order to have a more reliable historical picture of the events that eventually led to the Jews' settling in the city on the Arno, we would have to analyze, on one hand, the various political, economic, and religious forces that circulated in Florentine life between the end of the 1300s and the beginning of the 1400s, and, on the other hand, the direction and prospects of the various Jewish groups nominated to become Florentines. In this sense, there was no "Florence versus the Jews" or "Jews versus Florence." What is important here is that it is not historically provable that Florence had a more rigorous anti-Jewish attitude than that of other cities, as the historical research had sustained until today, nor, as was provocatively suggested in the title of this chapter, that the Jews distrusted Florence. Like any other state or urban center in Italy, Florence imposed on the Jews its "own" set of conditions allowing them entrance, and, as in all other cases, the Jews considered and weighed at length the opportunity to comply with those conditions.

The only unusual fact is that the two "parties" confronted each other for so long and then reached an agreement in 1437 only after about forty years of negotiations. In the following years, decades, and centuries, many points of that agreement would be repeatedly questioned, but substantially it survived, showing a solidity that was perhaps due precisely to the length of time that it took to take form and to the patience and ability with which the Jews were able to carry out the negotiations.

In conclusion, it can be said that the convention of 1437 guaranteed in Florence an uninterrupted presence—which after 500 years is still alive today—of a group of individuals free to follow the Mosaic law. This age-old continuity gives a concrete sense to the presupposition, by which our conference was inspired, that Italian Jewry is the oldest of the diasporic minorities.

6

Between Tradition and Modernity: The Sephardim of Livorno

Julia R. Lieberman

After the expulsion from Spain in 1492 of Iberian merchant Jews and New Christians[1] and the forced conversions of Portugal in 1497, a number of European countries began to offer these exiles the opportunity to settle in their territories under favorable charters. Due to their expertise as merchants, Iberian Jews first settled in several Italian states, then in Holland, England, and southern France.

On the Italian peninsula in the sixteenth century, a number of states competed to attract Iberian New Christian merchants to their soils. The Medicean grand dukes of Tuscany, following previous examples in Venice and Ancona, created important major trade centers in Pisa and Livorno, with the intent of encouraging New Christians to live in these centers. In 1591 the Grand Duke Ferdinand issued the charter known as *La Livornina*, intended to increase population growth in Livorno but addressed primarily to Spanish and Portuguese New Christians. *La Livornina* granted Jews freedom of religion and worship, freedom of movement, administrative autonomy, protection from the Inquisition, and Tuscan citizenship. Under these favorable conditions, what started as a community of New Christians, with little knowledge of Judaism, quickly became a vibrant Sephardic community. Although the community never reached large numbers—about 2,500 people in 1700—Livorno became in the seventeenth century one of the most important centers of Jewish studies in Western Europe. Following the patterns of other Western Sephardic communities in the Diaspora, the Sephardim of Livorno founded an impressive number of institutions to take care of the community's various needs; in addition to the synagogue, the center of religious and social life, the community had a public school, the Talmud Torah, for boys up to fourteen years of age, which provided the finest Jewish education. There were also several *hebrot* (fraternities): the Hebra Ghemilut Hasadim, founded in 1642, which provided free medical care to the poor; the Hebra Ba'ale Teshuba, founded also about 1642, which was in charge of ritually preparing the dead for burial; the Hebra

Mohar ha-Betulot, or Hebra de Cazar Orfas e Donzelas, founded in 1644, which was a fraternity that provided dowries for both orphans and poor nonorphans, following the model of Venice; and the Hebra Malbish Arumim, founded in 1654, which was a fraternity that provided clothing and linen to poor students and teachers of the Talmud Torah school. For the study and commentary of the Torah, or Jewish law, there were several *yeshivot* or religious academies: Bet ha-midrash Valensin, Yeshivah Bet Ya'Aqob, and Yeshivah Reshit Hochma.[2] We know very little about secular cultural activities, but, at least on one occasion, a Spanish play was put on stage in honor of the Grand Duke Cosimo II and his wife, Vittoria della Rovere.[3]

In 1675 three young men and their mentor, Dr. Raphael Diaz, founded a literary academy entitled Los Sitibundos (The Thirsty Ones), a poetic name referring to its members' thirst for knowledge. Like many other Italian literary academies of the times, the Sitibundos chose an emblem, an open shell waiting for the morning dew, and a motto, "Ho, all who are thirsty, come for water" (Isaiah 55:1).[4] We do not know exactly how long this institution lasted, but at least on five occasions, discourses or sermons were delivered to a gathering of the academy and were later published in Amsterdam. This study deals with one of these sermons, delivered between 1675 and 1679.

The sermon is entitled Moral and Sacred Academic Discourse (Discurso Académico Moral y Sagrado), and its author is José Penso de la Vega, born in 1650, probably in Spain, who spent some time in Livorno, between 1675 and 1679, and died in Amsterdam in 1692.[5] Penso was a merchant and a prolific writer highly regarded by his Sephardic contemporaries. He wrote some works in Hebrew and Portuguese, translated several literary works by Emanuel Tessauro and other Italian contemporary authors from Italian to Spanish, and published extensively in Spanish. Penso's sermons delivered to the Sitibundos can give us an idea of the occasions when the members of the academy invited others to their gatherings: on Sinchat Torah or other festivals or on the death of a parent. The day when the sermon that I intend to study was delivered, the gathering of Los Sitibundos was composed of young men, or future fathers. The main goal of the sermon seems to have been to encourage these young men to play an active role in their children's education and to influence their wives to breast-feed their infants, instead of relying on tutors and sending them away to wet nurses. In addition, the sermon shows Penso's creative reading of biblical texts and familiarity with the Hebrew language, Talmudic texts, and secular Italian and Spanish literatures.

The discourse, as Penso calls this sermon, is based on the Torah lesson for the day when it was delivered, *parashah Hayey Sarah* (the life of Sarah) (Gen. 23:1–25:18). It follows the structure of the contemporary Sephardic sermon:[6] an introduction and the sermon proper, which is divided into six parts, three dedicated to men and to proving their obligation to teach their children and three to women and to proving their responsibility to wet-nurse them. In each of the six parts, the theme-verse, "and God had blessed Abraham in all things"[7] (Gen. 24:1), is contrasted with a *ma'amar*, another biblical verse or a rabbinic commentary, and with a diversity of other biblical passages in order to arrive at Penso's interpretation of the theme-verse: that God's most precious blessing to Abraham was making him the father of Isaac, and that fathers are obligated to teach their children and mothers to suckle their infants. It is important to notice that among the many biblical quotations that Penso uses to prove his points, there is also evidence that Penso interprets the role of parents, the relationship between husbands and wives, and, above all, the role of women both as mothers and as wives, in ways more in accord with contemporary courtly fashions than with traditional Jewish values.[8]

The sermon begins with an interpretation of the biblical quotation on Eve (pp. 7–14), "in pain you shall bear children" (Gen. 3:16). Penso focuses on the double meaning of the Hebrew biblical word *ezeb* (pain and wealth) and interprets it to mean that, although women give birth with intensive pain, their desire to give birth to a son overcomes their concern for the suffering and concludes that women who are barren and cannot give birth suffer much more intensely from the lack of children.

After the introduction, the sermon's purpose is stated, which is to prove the following six paradoxical statements:

1. A father who is not a teacher to his children is not really a father.
2. A mother who does not suckle her children is not really a mother.
3. A father who is also a teacher to his children is twice a father.
4. A mother who suckles her own children is twice a mother.
5. A teacher is a father, even if he has no children of his own.
6. A wet nurse who suckles children is a mother even if she has not given birth to children of her own.

For the sake of convenience and clarity, I will analyze first the three parts referring to men and then the three referring to women.

"A father who is not a teacher to his children is not really a father" (pp. 15–17). Penso begins illustrating what he considers good parenting with the metaphor of the musician tuning his string instrument; the string should not be so lax as to be dissonant nor so tight that it will snap.[9] Parental love should be a combination of affection and discipline, and the ideal father is, according to Penso, the one who knows how to discipline his children when necessary but who is not too strict with them. He selects three biblical fathers and compares their parenting style: Eli, who did not know how to discipline his children, Hofni and Pinhas; David, who was too strict with his son, Absalom; and Jacob, who was the ideal father in his love for Joseph. Of the three fathers, only Jacob was repaid by his son in old age, when he was fed by Joseph in Egypt.

The first father on whom Penso focuses is Eli, and there are two contradictory references to him: a rabbinic quotation that says that "anyone who thinks that Eli's sons committed a sin, is wrong" and a contradictory biblical one (1 Samuel 2:12), "Now Eli's sons were scoundrels; they paid no heed to the LORD" (p. 17). The explanation of this contradiction is, according to Penso, that although Hofni and Pinhas were Eli's children, he was not a real father to them because he did not know how to teach and discipline them. The proof, Penso says, is that when Eli was told all the terrible things that his children were doing, all he could say was: "Don't, my sons."[10]

In contrast to Eli and his inability to discipline his sons, Penso now focuses on Abraham and the biblical quotation that says about him: "Abraham was old, advanced in years" (Gen. 24:1). The Talmud, says Penso, interprets this repetitive description of the Patriarch to mean that he reached old age as a blessing from God, because he knew how to educate Isaac. Of Eli, it says: "Now Eli was very old" (1 Samuel 2:22), and the Talmud interprets that he became very old on account of the suffering inflicted on him by his sons, Hofni and Pinhas. As a final proof that only teaching makes a father a real one, Penso refers to Lot, when his daughters decided to commit incest with their father after saying that "our father is old" (Gen. 19:31). The daughters' decision to sleep with their father, Lot, was made, according to Penso, because he was old and drunk and therefore could not be a teacher to them any longer.[11]

The next part referring to fathers, "a father who teaches his children is twice a father" (p. 34), is proven on the basis of contrasting again the theme-verse and its repetitive reference to Abraham, old and advanced in years, with a new *ma'amar* and its repetitive way of saying that Isaac is the son of Abraham: "these are the generations of Isaac, son of Abraham, Abraham had Isaac" (Gen. 25:19). The Talmud interprets this repetition to mean that Abraham was able to beget Isaac in his old age because he was a prudent man and that, by begetting Isaac, he acquired two worlds: succession and eternity.[12] He was twice a father, once by begetting Isaac and again by teaching him.

Abraham is compared to King David (pp. 36–37) when he finds out that his son died and repeatedly exclaims, "O Absalom, my son, my son" (2 Samuel 18:33), as if to explain that he had tried to be both a father and a teacher to his son, but he failed because of Absalom's nature. When Abraham is ready to slay his son Isaac, the Lord repeatedly calls him, "Abraham, Abraham" (Gen. 22:19), as if to say: I want you twice a father, and if you pass this test, you will be a father and a teacher to your son Isaac.[13]

The last part referring to men, that teachers become fathers even if their students are not their own children (p. 39), focuses on three cases in the Bible in which the phrase "these are the generations" occurs. In each of these three cases, the biblical text promises to talk about a character but instead talks about another one. Numbers 3:1—"these are the generations of Aaron and Moses, . . . These are the names of Aaron's sons, Nadab, the first-born and Abiuh, Elazar and Itamar"[14]— it gives the names of Aaron's children, leaving out Moses, according to Penso, because it considers them as if they were Moses' children. Gen. 25—"these are the generations of Isaac, son of Abraham, Abraham begot Isaac"—also, instead of talking about the children of Isaac, as expected, says "Abraham begot Isaac," as if it considers them Abraham's own children.[15] Gen. 10:1—"These are the generations of Noah, Noah was a just man"[16]—instead of talking about Noah's generations, talks about his virtues because he can be a model and a teacher to his sons. According to Penso, then, the Bible follows this pattern in order to signal something great about Moses, Abraham, and Noah. The parts dedicated to fathers end with the two Talmudic laws that show the high respect accorded to teachers in the Jewish tradition: a son is required to stand when his father enters, but the rule is inverted if the son is a teacher, and a pupil is not allowed to call his teacher by his name (p. 41).

Although, in the sections addressed to men, one would expect to find the subjects that a father should or should not teach his sons, Penso instead gives a list of dos and don'ts referring to when to give or withhold affection, how strict fathers should be with their children, and how to be a model to them. In this sense, the sermon seems a bit removed in time from our sense of the meaning that we give today to teaching, but the dedication to their children expected of fathers, the role of affection in creating bonds in childhood that will make responsible adults, and the centrality of the family around the children all seem modern and contemporary as if the sermon were given in a Reform or Conservative synagogue in the United States today.

The three parts referring to women are, in my opinion, the most interesting ones of the sermon. First of all, it is important to notice that women clearly were not present while the sermon was delivered. Penso specifically says: if "they (*ellas*) could hear me today" (p. 25). Also, the sermon speaks more about Abraham, a male character, than about any other character, including Sarah (following the original biblical "life of Sarah"). But the essence of the sermon equally pays attention to men and women. Considering that women's voices are totally absent from seventeenth-century Spanish discourses, Penso's attention to women and their roles in bringing up children is very significant.[17]

The first part—"a mother who does not suckle her children, is not really a mother"—according to Penso, is easy to prove, as it has bad consequences when it is not done. His comments clearly reflect on the contemporary custom of sending newborns away, at times to faraway places, to be wet-nursed by paid women during the infant's first two years of life.[18] Penso focuses once more on the double meaning of the Hebrew biblical word *ezeb*, pain and wealth, in reference to Eve (Gen. 3:16), "In pain/wealth (*ezeb*) you shall bear children," and poses the rhetorical question (p. 25): If women try to bring wealth to their homes, how could they send away, to faraway places, their children, their most important wealth?

Then Penso selects cases of biblical women giving birth in difficult circumstances as proof of women's desires to become mothers (pp. 25–29): the Hebrew women in Egypt (Exodus 1:19), who would give birth without the help of midwives, for fear of the pharaoh's killing their babies; Hanna, Eli's daughter-in-law (1 Samuel 4:19), whom, the Bible says, prayed and prayed to the Lord for a male child; and Manoah's wife (Judges 13:2), who the Bible says, in a repetitive way, "was barren and had borne no children" but finally also gave birth to a son. In summary, Penso finds unexplainable the desire of women to be mothers and yet even more unexplainable that they do not try to suckle their children when, in his view, women become real mothers only if they suckle their babies.

Then Penso attempts to prove with three biblical examples—Eve, Michal, and Sarah—that women become real mothers only when they suckle their own babies (pp. 29–30). In the case of Eve, Penso says, one could argue that she had no choice but to nurse her children. The proof to the contrary is, however, in the names that she chose for them: Cain, meaning, "I have gained a male child with the help of the Lord," and Hebel, meaning nothing (Gen. 4:1). Penso's witty interpretation is that she gained nothing by giving birth because she needed to suckle her babies in order to gain sons. The next woman whom Penso selects is Michal (pp. 30–31), Saul's daughter, and there are two contradictory biblical verses: "So to her dying day Michal daughter of Saul had no children" (2 Samuel 6:23) and "Michal bore five children" (2 Samuel 21:8).[19] According to the Talmudic interpretation of this discrepancy cited by Penso, it means that Michal, on account of being a princess, did not suckle her own children and therefore never became a real mother. As proof that Sarah is the ideal mother, Penso points out that Abraham held a feast the day that Sarah weaned Isaac (Gen. 21:9), not when the child was born (pp. 33–34).

The second part referring to women—"women are twice mothers when they suckle their babies" (p. 37)—is proven with biblical references to Sarah and Hannah, using the plural when the singular would be expected:

1. Referring to Sarah, it says, "Sarah suckled children" (Gen. 21:7), meaning, according to Penso (p. 37), that Isaac became Sarah's son only when she nursed him.
2. Of Hanna, it says that she asked God for "seed of males" (a male child in the modern English version, 1 Samuel 1:11) because, as she intended to nurse him, she was asking for males: "wanted a son to nurse him, so that he would be twice a son" (p. 37). Again, Hanna also refers to her son Samuel as the child and not as her son (1 Samuel 1:22), because she knew that he would become her son only if she were to nurse him.
3. Of Sarah, the Bible says in a repetitive way that Abraham "cried and mourned" for her (Gen. 23:2) as if to affirm that she had been twice Isaac's mother, once by giving birth to him and the other by nursing him. Penso concludes that this is the meaning of "God blessed Abraham in all things."

The last part referring to women (p. 41)—"the wet nurse who suckles children is a mother"—is, according to Penso, clearly stated when the biblical text says that Sarah suckled children (Gen. 21:7) instead of saying Sarah suckled Isaac. The rabbis explain this to mean that Sarah suckled her neighbor's children. This is followed by a list of women who became substitute mothers to children to whom they had not given birth.

Eliezer, Abraham's servant, sends Rebecca away with her wet nurse as a substitute for her parents (Gen. 24:59). When Ruth gives birth to a son, her neighbors say "A son is born to Naomi" (Ruth 4:17), because Ruth's mother-in-law, Naomi, was its foster mother. Joseph dreamed that his father, as well as his mother and his brothers, would bow before him (Gen. 37:10). However, when the family gets reunited in Egypt, Rachel, his natural mother, was already dead. Instead, Bilhah, Jacob's wife, became a substitute for Rachel. Two women claimed before King Solomon that each was the mother of the same child (1 Kings 3:20). Penso interprets that the childless mother wanted to be a substitute mother by nursing the child.

In summary, nurturing babies, something that women do by choice, is higher than the natural ability to give birth. This high regard for women who nurse babies by choice is very different from the view expressed in other Spanish Renaissance discourses, where mothers are encouraged to nurse their own babies and to mistrust wet nurses. In Penso's view, suckling babies is so highly regarded that women, even childless ones, become mothers by the choice that they make to care for the helpless newborn.[20]

In conclusion, this sermon gives a picture of family life in the Sephardic community of Livorno in the seventeenth century. As with all sermons, the biblical models that it gives to parents can be understood only as ideals to emulate and not necessarily as representing what took place in real life. But the references to real life also seem to tell us much about what was happening to the Jewish family at the time. The purpose of the sermon was to advise parents to take care of their children's upbringing and education, instead of relying on others, tutors and wet nurses, to do their job. The concerns of the modern Jewish family in the twenty-first century—to find a balance between traditional Jewish values and the values necessary for success in the larger society—do not seem very different from the concerns expressed by Penso in his sermon, well over 300 years ago. It is considered common knowledge that modernity in Jewish life takes place in the Enlightenment, after the emancipation in the eighteenth century, but I believe that the question of modernity is worth pondering when referring to the Western Sephardim in the seventeenth century.

NOTES

1. Historians differentiate between Eastern Sephardim, those who left Spain in 1492 and settled in the Ottoman Empire, and Western Sephardim, those who either converted to Christianity and remained in Spain or went to Portugal and were forcibly converted in 1497, the Conversos or New Christians. During the sixteenth and seventeenth centuries, New Christians left the Iberian Peninsula and established communities in different parts of Europe. My study is concerned with the New Christians, or Western Sephardim. See Benjamin Ravid, "A Tale of Three Cities and Their Raison d'État: Ancona, Venice, Livorno," and "The Competition for Sixteenth Century Merchants in the Sixteenth Century"; Renata Segre, "Sephardic Settlements in Sixteenth-Century Italy: A Historical and Geographical Survey," in *Jews, Christians, and Muslims in the Mediterranean World After 1692*, edited by Alisa Meyuhas Ginio (London: Frank Cass, 1992). For an explanation of why Livorno prospered as a free port in the seventeenth century and then declined in the eighteenth century, when the nature of commerce changed and free ports were no longer needed, see David G. LoRomer, *Merchants and Reform in Livorno, 1814–1868* (Berkeley: University of California Press, 1987), pp. 19–22.

2. See Renzo Toaff, *La nazione ebrea a Livorno e a Pisa (1591–1700)* (Florence: L.S. Olschki, 1990). Little girls were included in the kindergarten program only in 1771 (see p. 340 n. 23).

3. See Julio-Félix Hernando Alvarez, "Teatro hispanojud'o en Toscana durante el siglo XVII," in *Los judaizantes en Europa y la literatura castellana del siglo de oro* (Madrid: Letrœmero, 1994), pp. 193–214.

4. For a study of the academy, see Cecil Roth, "Notes sur les marranes de Livourne," *Revue des Etudes Juives* (1931): 91, 1–27. I have studied very similar institutions in Amsterdam in *El teatro alegórico de Miguel (Daniel Leví) de Barrios* (Newark, DE: Juan

de la Cuesta-Hispanic Monographs, 1996), Chapter III: "Academias literarias y de estudios religiosos en Amsterdam en el siglo XVII." When Penso returned to Amsterdam, he was also very active in the literary academies there. The major source for the Sitibundos of Livorno is Miguel de Barrios' *Respuesta panegírica a la carta que escribió el muy ilustre R. Joseph Penso Vega, al muy sapiente doctor Ishac Orobio. Glossala Daniel Levi de Barrios, y presentala en la heroyca Academia de los Sitibundos* (Amsterdam: Yacob van Velsen, 5437 [1677]). Barrios' gloss indicates that the Sitibundos of Livorno was in existence since 1675. The last reference that we have of the Sitibundos is the sermon that Penso read when his mother died, in 1679.

5. The sermon has the following subtitle: *De Josseph Penso, hecho en la insigne academia de los Sitibundos, y dedicado al zelo y benevolencia del ilustrisimo señor Yshak Senior Texera, Residente y consejero de la reyna de Suecia en Hamburgo* (Amsterdam: Yahacob de Cordoba, 1683). I use a photocopy of the original from the Ets Haim Collection, now in Jerusalem, Israel. In addition to this one, Penso delivered the following sermons to the Sitibundos of Livorno: *La rosa* (Amsterdam: Yahacob de Cordoba, 1683), delivered on Simchat Torah, when Penso was Hatan Bereshit, or groom of Bereshit, and another member, Josseph Gonzales, was the Hatan Torah, or groom of the Torah; *Discurso académico*, dedicated to Gabriel Arias (Antwerp: n.p. 1683), when two other sermons were delivered; and the *Oración fúnebre*, delivered thirty days after the death of his mother, published in 1683 in Amsterdam by Yahacob de Cordoba. Except for the last one, which was delivered in the month of Av in 1679, the exact dates for the three other sermons cannot be determined. Because none of these works were published in Livorno, but rather in Amsterdam and Antwerp, and because there was another literary academy with the same name, Los Sitibundos, in Amsterdam, it is usually assumed that Penso delivered these sermons in Amsterdam. I am hoping to clarify this confusion with this study and another one to be published.

6. I would like to give thanks to Professor Rochelle Millen, from Columbus, Ohio, who, via e-mail, answered my questions on biblical quotations at the early stage of my reading of Penso's sermon. On the Sephardic sermon, see the two studies by Marc Saperstein, "The Sermon as Art Form: Structure in Morteira's Giv'at Sha'ul," *Prooftexts* 3 (1983): 243–261, and *Jewish Preaching, 1200–1800: An Anthology* (New Haven, CT: Yale University Press, 1982). Penso also uses the theme-verse and the *ma'amar*, but in Penso's writing also evident is the use of wit, or *conceptos*; therefore, as I show, the use of the *ma'amar* is far more elaborated than in the case of Morteira. Incidentally, Penso in his writings quotes Morteira very frequently. I have analyzed Penso's use of wit in "Estética conceptista y ética mercantilista de *Confusión de confusiones* (Amsterdam, 1688)" (in press).

7. For the biblical quotations in English, I use *The Tanak—The Holy Scriptures* (Philadelphia: Jewish Publication Society, 1988).

8. Although the most important source for Penso's sermon is Genesis, his interpretation that the end of marriage is to have children also derives from Tessauro's *Filosofia moral*, Book 14, Chapter 12, which deals with husband–wife relationships and where marriage is viewed in political terms as a small kingdom: man is king, and woman is queen. Tessauro's source is ultimately Aristotle's *Politics*. See for example, p. 12 of Penso's sermon: "son los hijos el principio de la felicidad de los casados, porque son el fin del amor los casamientos," and Tessauro's, *Filosofia moral*, pp. 325–326, "Los hijos son el principio de la felicidad de los casados: porque son el fin del amor conjugal." Penso elsewhere claims to have translated the *Moral Philosophy* by Tessauro. I have used a Spanish translation of Tessauro's work by Gomez de la Rocha y Figueroa (Lisboa: Antonio Craesbeeck de Mello, 1682).

9. "[E]s necesario no afloxar la cuerda, de modo que disuene; ni tirarla, de suerte que salte," p. 15. Penso played the harp and uses musical metaphors very often in his writings.

10. In the modern English biblical translation, Penso's "proof" is not as forceful as in the Spanish and Hebrew biblical quotations that he uses: "No mis hijos," without a pause, can be understood in more than one way; and in Hebrew also the negative particle *al* (aleph and lamed) is placed in front of "my sons," without a pause.

11. According to Eric Lawee, "The 'Ways of Midrash' in the Biblical Commentaries of Isaac Abarbanel," *Hebrew Union College Annual* (1996): 107–142, previous to the expulsion of 1492, biblical commentaries in Muslim Spain "treated Scripture as a text which at times reflected standard patterns of human discourse" (see p. 127), while under Christian Spain, the tendency was more toward finding mystical meanings in biblical discrepancies (see pp. 113–114). Penso's approach is closer to that of the Andalusian commentators.

12. See Midrash Rabbah, *Genesis II*, translated by H. Freedman (London: Soncino Press, 1961), p. 519. Penso's Talmudic quotation into Spanish differs slightly from the English translation.

13. "Dos vezes padre te quiero, dize Dios a Abraham, tan misterioso como benigno; para advertirte que lo que te pido de tu hijo, requiere gran constancia en él, para que se sugete a lo que te pido; muéstrate dos vezes padre, que enseñándolo como deves, saldrá gloriosa la Prueva, Inmortal la fama y Luzida la Educación: Abraham, Abraham" (p. 37).

14. The modern English version of the Hebrew Bible says: "This is the line . . ." But in Penso's quotation it says that "these are the generations." For a twentieth-century reading of these biblical formulas, see Robert Alter, "How Convention Helps Us Read: The Case of the Bible's Annunciation Type-Scene," *Prooftexts* 3 (1983): 115–130, which studies the formula from a literary point of view; and James L. Kugel's *In Potiphar's House* (San Francisco: HarperCollins, 1990), which traces the origins of the rabbis' attempt to explain the problematic use of the formula "these are the generations" in reference to Joseph (Gen. 37:2–3) and used later to explain other cases, when the same formula reappears in the Bible. These two studies have helped me understand the rabbinic background in Penso's Spanish writings, secular and religious. To begin with, Penso's literary sensitivity to reiteration of formulas is impressive, such as "these are the generations," which he renders beautifully into Spanish. I have also concluded that Penso's writings deserve our attention not only in reference to Penso's own writings but also because of what they tell us about Western Sephardim in general.

15. The modern English version says: "This is the story of Isaac."

16. The modern English version differs (Gen. 10:1): "These are the generations of Shem, Ham and Japhet, the sons of Noah." Penso's version says: "Estas son las Generaciones de Noah, Noah Varón Justo" (p. 40).

17. The absence of mothers in Spanish literature of the Golden Age is notorious. Ruth Anthony El Saffar in *Rapture Encaged: The Suppression of the Feminine in Western Culture* (London and New York: Routledge, 1994), pp. 66–68, explains the lack of women's voices in Spanish discourse, not only in fiction, as a result, among other things, of the repressive culture in imperial Spain. El Saffar's thesis is that the early beginning period, the sixteenth and seventeenth centuries, had detrimental consequences for women in general.

18. See the study by Valerie Fildes, *Wet Nursing: A History from Antiquity to the Present* (Oxford, U.K., and New York: Basil Blackwell, 1988), especially Chapters 5, 6. Fathers were the ones to make the arrangements with the wet nurses, and many babies were sent to the countryside; see Chapter 6. Penso clearly refers to the custom of paid women as wet nurses (p. 25): "si [las madres] procuran traer a casa la Riqueza, por que han de dar a criar los hijos fuera de casa, . . . y mandar muchas vezes [a los hijos] fuera de la tierra?" Since one of the meanings of *tierra* is country (according to Covarrubias), it seems to indicate that Penso is referring to the custom of sending babies outside Livorno. The reason that Penso gives for this custom is love for comfort on the part of women (p. 13): "[las mujeres]

desvelanse por ser madres, y dexan de ser madres, por no desvelarse? Por no tener una hora de inquietud, dexan de ser lo que anhelan de ser con mil horas de tormento?" The charter *La livornina* allowed the Sephardim of Livorno to have Christian wet nurses in their houses (see Ravid, "A Tale of Three Cities," p. 157). Penso, however, is clearly referring to the custom of sending infants away to wet nurses.

19. The modern English translation gives Merab, instead of Michal; however, it explains with a footnote, "Most mss. and the printed editions read 'Michal.'" Penso's accuracy in his biblical quotations is indeed impressive. I have yet to find an error in his quotations.

20. I am referring, for example, to the humanist Juan Luis Vives and his negative views on women, mothers, and wet nurses. See the study of Emilie L. Bergmann, "La exclusión de lo femenino en el discurso cultural del humanismo," in *Actas del X Congreso de la Asociación Internacional de Hispanistas* (Barcelona: PPU, 1989), pp. 365–372. Among the Sephardic Jews, midwives (*parteras*) and wet nurses (*amas*) are highly regarded because women fulfilling these jobs secretly allied themselves with one another and saved the lives of male Israelites (including Moses) in Exodus 1–2 (see Penso's sermon, p. 27).

7

Jewish Dancing Masters and "Jewish Dance" in Renaissance Italy

Barbara Sparti

Fifteenth-century Italy produced the earliest known treatises on the art of the dance.[1] Less known than their scientific, humanistic, literary, and artistic counterparts, the treatises provide choreographic descriptions and music of dances that were performed on public and private occasions. Moreover, they include the very first formulation of a postclassical theory of the dance,[2] with many of its basic principles still valid today. Nine of these treatises (plus assorted fragments) have survived, and others may yet come to light. Seven of them can be attributed (directly or indirectly) to Guglielmo Ebreo (William the Jew) of Pesaro, who, together with his Gentile teacher, Domenico of Piacenza, was the foremost choreographer, composer, theorist, *ballerino*, and dancing master of the fifteenth century.[3] His father, Moses of Sicily, was a dance teacher for the Malatesta family,[4] while his brother Giuseppe—together with a Christian—ran a music and dancing school in Florence. Guglielmo taught dancing, choreographed spectacles and organized festivities at courts such as that of the Aragons in Naples, Federico di Montefeltro in Urbino, and Francesco Sforza in Pavia and Milan. He danced with the six-year-old Isabella d'Este and corresponded with Lorenzo de' Medici. He was knighted by the Holy Roman Emperor Frederick III, and perhaps for this reason and because of pressure put on him by a zealous patron,[5] he converted to Christianity, taking the name Giovanni Ambrosio. He tried to persuade his brother to change his faith also, though without success.

Guglielmo's treatise *De pratica seu arte tripudii* (On the Practice or Art of Dancing) was written in 1463, shortly before his conversion. It begins with a theoretical defense of the dance, replete with classical, biblical, and humanistic references aimed at raising the status of dance and endowing it with the moral dignity required for it to rank among the pursuits of a prince. Written in Italian in the typical Renaissance format, it contains fundamental precepts, rules, and challenging exercises (*experimenti*) that give weight to Guglielmo's claim that dance was not only art but also science. The "Practice," or practical part of the treatise, consists of descriptions of thirty-one dances, composed by both Guglielmo and his master, Domenico, and the music for several of these.[6]

Dancing played a significant part in Renaissance society.[7] In the courts and republics, dancing was often a part of festivities for visiting dignitaries, for marriages, and for carnival. Balls offered an opportunity for the display of magnificent clothes and jewels (i.e., wealth and power), duly noted by diarists and ambassadors. Entertainments also featured *moresche*, mimed and danced interludes, and "ballets" performed during banquets and plays. Their allegorical, heroic-mythological, exotic, and pastoral themes, together with spectacular and expensive scenery and costumes, flattered and idealized the prince through symbolism and, in their ostentation, reinforced his image.[8] Not only the aristocracy engaged in dancing. The middle class attended schools where they learned a variety of dances, from the more traditional and "popular," to the "art" dances created by Domenico, Guglielmo, and others.[9] Besides teaching at schools, dancing masters, many of whom were Jews, gave burghers and gentlefolk private lessons in their homes.[10]

Despite all this dancing, the status of dance tended to be low.[11] References to dancing in court chronicles are sparse and brief, quite outweighed by the long, detailed descriptions of the courses of a banquet, the participants' dress, or the hall decorations. Many rich and important courts, ruled by powerful and magnificent princes, employed no permanent dancing master but simply borrowed one from a neighboring or friendly court when the need arose. While princes did dance at state weddings and at carnival celebrations, some even participating in *moresche*, both public dancing and private dancing seem to have been the prerogative of ladies and of young people. Moreover, dancing—like painting—was not one of the liberal arts, and the humanist curriculum, that "program for the ruling classes," ignored it and at times explicitly condemned it.[12]

As to the status of the dancing master himself, from the few records that have thus far come to light, the majority seem to have had an uncertain and ambiguous social position and been modestly, if not poorly, remunerated.[13] As for Guglielmo Ebreo, despite the high regard in which he was held by his patrons, despite the distance that he condescendingly and vehemently insisted on between himself and the "mechanicals" and "plebeians," despite the efforts that he took in distributing dedicatory copies of his treatise to various patrons and would-be benefactors, and despite his being made a knight of the prestigious Order of the Golden Spur, he nevertheless appears low on the list of retainers at the court of Urbino, was shipped off, much against his will, to serve the king of Naples for two years, and had his appeals for a position at the court of Milan twice turned down. Further evidence that dancing masters earned (at best) small reward comes from Siena, where dancing played a notable role in festivities in private palaces and in public squares as well as in plays and in schools. Tax reports of two dancing masters reveal that, in 1478, one had nothing taxable to declare, while the second, the son of Mariotto of Perugia (about whom we shall hear more), was, in his own words, poor, in 1509 "eking out a living" and "struggling to support" his family. Other documents—

contracts for setting up dancing and music schools and a petition put forward by a particular dance teacher—confirm that the dancing masters' livelihood, dependent as it was on the patronage of the local bourgeoisie, was often precarious.[14]

In this general scene of dancing in Renaissance Italy, what was the role of the Jews? That Jews danced is corroborated by three fifteenth-century miniatures from the Mantua-Ferrara area.[15] The earliest (1435) shows a wedding scene, the couple, in princely garb, being married by a rabbi and then dancing to the accompaniment of a typical fifteenth-century wind band. It is one of four miniatures in the *Arba'a Turim* (Four Orders), a legal work by Jacob ben Asher, written in beautiful italic-Hebrew script. It illuminates the third section, which deals with matrimonial laws.[16]

Another dance scene appears in the magnificent Rothschild Miscellany, now in the Israel Museum in Jerusalem.[17] It is an illustration for a *pizmon*, generally an auspicious blessing and in this case a nuptial hymn by Semeon bar Isaac.[18] The single lute player in the miniature indicates a small, private gathering. The composition of the image—three couples dancing neither side by side nor promenading one behind the other—is unusual and generates a feeling of movement. The position of the couples recalls Guglielmo's *ballo* "Colonnese." The relatively simple dress depicted here and throughout the Miscellany has been explained as a response to the Christian sumptuary laws intended to restrict the richness of Jewish dress and to the periodic exhortations of Jewish moralists and religious leaders to limit luxury and the splendor of weddings.[19] On the other hand, this relative plainness of dress could reflect the patron's own Ashkenazic background, undoubtedly more austere and less fashionable than the general taste of Renaissance Mantua. The most plausible explanation, however, is that since the artist (undoubtedly a Christian) had to provide over 300 illustrations, he probably chose an uncomplicated model that could be repeated throughout. A further point of interest is that this is the only codex that shows women in the white coif or veil (which covered hair and neck) characteristic of married Jewish women. The cone headdress, worn here by two of the dancers, was never adopted by Italian women and was used in Italy only by foreigners, thus further reflecting the Ashkenazic background of the manuscript's owner.[20]

Book III of a copy of the *Mishne Torah* (first written in the twelfth century by the Sephardic philosopher Maimonedes) is devoted to seasons and holidays. The illumination entitled "Zemanim" (Times) shows Sukkoth and Purim.[21] It is exquisitely fashioned and is the only known portrayal of a Purim festivity in the fifteenth century.[22] The provenance suggested by the Ashkenazic Hebrew script goes some way to explain the very northern-looking (even Germanic-looking) attire of the dancers: the men's outfits and the ladies' headgear. Both the instrument—the pipe and tabor—and its player, the Fool, were also common in Northern European life and iconography and almost unknown in Italy.

All three images, undoubtedly painted by Christians, show men and women dancing together and not in separate lines or circles as was Jewish custom (though not law) in the following century, especially among the Ashkenazi.[23] Indeed, there is nothing in the style or treatment to distinguish the miniatures from non-Hebrew depictions of dance of the same period.[24]

Further documentation of Jewish dancing comes from the description and illustrations of the 1475 wedding festivities of Costanzo Sforza, lord of Pesaro, to Camilla of Aragon, in which *l'università de li giudei* (Jewish community) took part.[25] A procession of youths carrying real date palms preceded the queen of Sheba, dressed in gold and enthroned upon a wonderfully constructed elephant ingeniously maneuvered by men hidden inside. Two other elephants carrying young women were followed by a throng of Jews of all ages, dressed *a la arabesca* in gold and silver or in long, many-colored garments. The queen of Sheba delivered an oration in Hebrew (which was translated into Italian) and presented a gift. Then came a *moresca* that featured a "Monte degli Ebrei," which produced twelve dancers miming the labors of the field. Emerging from the mountain, to which they then returned for each successive scene, the dancers hoed, planted, and reaped the crops with gilded implements, performing all the movements perfectly in time to the music. This favorite fifteenth-century theme, which would be taken up again in 1499 and 1501 at the Este court in Ferrara,[26] reflected the contemporary idealization of country life in poetry, music, and pastoral plays,[27] and symbolically represented the munificence of the prince. Indeed, the elderly Jew who called forth the dancers at the entrance of the mountain, recited:

"This generous lord whom you see [Costanzo]
Gave us this land to till well and gather its fruits."[28]

Cecil Roth and others after him have casually attributed the choreography for the Jewish community of Pesaro's *moresca* to Guglielmo Ebreo. However, nothing is known of Guglielmo's whereabouts in 1475, by which time, moreover, he had already converted to Christianity. The identity of the choreographer for the dancing and spectacles at Costanzo Sforza's wedding (and that of the Jewish community, if he were someone else) is still not known. However, recent archival research has produced the names and some information about other Renaissance Jewish dancing masters besides Guglielmo and his family. (Since much comes from court reports and notarial acts, we are often given seamy, if not criminal, details rather than the dance occasions and curricula that we might hope for.)

Mariotto of Perugia, whose son was referred to earlier as "eking" out a living by teaching in Siena, was well enough known to have a dance of his included in one of the versions of Guglielmo's treatise.[29] A Christian, he comes to our attention in a legal agreement drawn up against one Deodato Ebreo.[30] On 30 January 1471 Deodato promises not to give either public or private dancing lessons to men and women in Perugia for the entire time that Magister Mariotto is in town, unless he receives his permission to do so. On his part, Magister Mariotto promises to teach Deodato new dances on request. It is not at all clear how or why Mariotto won his suit. Was it simply because he was Christian, and Deodato was Jewish, or had Deodato been renting space at his school or been his assistant? What is significant is that both Christian and Jew shared the same dance repertoire and the same clientele—public and private, male and female.[31] In 1459 a dancing master in his late twenties, one Moise Ebreo, pretending to arrange certain *feste* (feasts) and *moresche* for the well-known Pecci family of Siena, used the occasion to steal and pawn forty ducats worth of clothing and silver cups to satisfy his gambling needs.[32] In contrast, the name of Leone Ebreo, a dancing master working in Perugia 100 years later, appears in a notary's report of 1574 as being owed, by the Christian Gaspare Belardini, the considerable sum of ninety-two gold scudi.[33] One can only speculate how Magister Leone was in a position of credit for such an amount.

Another, rather unexpected, informant on late Renaissance dance is the great Venetian scholar-rabbi Leone Modena. In his autobiography, *The Life of Judah*, Leone recounts that in 1580, at the age of nine, his studies in Ferrara included, besides Jewish law, some instruction in Latin, in playing an instrument, in singing, and in dancing.[34] In 1605 he lamented the death of his brother-in-law, who was (in this order) "upright and well liked by all, sociable, knew how to play songs, dance, and conduct business, and possessed wisdom and a knowledge of books."[35] In Leone's report of the marriage of his daughter to Jacob Halevi in 1613, he specifies that this favorite son-in-law was a dance (and music) teacher.[36] For Modena and his circle, at least, dancing was clearly not looked down upon.

With the Counter-Reformation and the Council of Trent, local decrees supporting the church's orders to limit intercourse between Jews and Christians became common.[37] Jewish dancing masters and dance schools with Jewish teachers were frequently targeted, thus furnishing us with another source of information (including names and places) and showing how prevalent an activity dancing was among the urban middle class. On 1 March 1576 an emissary of Pope Gregory XIII proclaimed that the Jews of Mantua were prohibited from singing, dancing, or acting in Christian houses or teaching any of these activities to Christians, without the explicit permission of the duke.[38] While Duke Guglielmo ordered that the regulations be adhered to, neither he nor his son Vincenzo kept all of the church's ordinances to the letter, so much so that in 1601 Pope Clement VIII complained that "Jews in Mantua rule many Christians."[39] In Milan in 1575 Cardinal Borromeo confirmed that Jews were not to teach singing or dancing to Christians and, moreover, that no Christian was to enter a synagogue or participate in any weddings or festivities of Jews or dance with them.[40]

That same year, Cremona witnessed apostolic visitors' reports based on "rumour and hearsay" and the interrogation of some fifteen people who "had been in the employ of Jews."[41] These state that Christian men continued to study dancing with a certain "Moise," even on Sundays during mass, and that this same "Moise," who had a school where he taught instrumental music and dancing, played for, and danced with, *donne cristiane* (Christian women) at carnival. At such festivities, Jews put on masks and danced and made music with Christians.[42] Furthermore, during Lent, which often coincided with Purim, Jews would sing, act, gamble, and dance, and many times Christians joined in the merrymaking.[43]

At the same time, regulations decided by the Jewish community show that here, too, there was a determination to limit contact between Jews and Gentiles who continued to dance in each other's houses. In 1580 the Jewish community in Padua decreed that no male or female Jew was to dance with any non-Jew ("on pain of a fine of two scudi for each transgression he or she commits"). Fathers were held responsible for sons and husbands for wives, and the rule applied no matter whether the dancing took place in Jewish or Christian homes.[44]

In spite of Counter-Reformation bans, one Jewish dance master had what appears to have been a most successful career. Isacchino Massarano was also a lutenist and a singer.[45] His name appears in the last two decades of the sixteenth century in connection with performances for the ducal courts and theaters in Mantua and Ferrara,[46] and there seems little doubt that there, at least, he was the leading choreographer of the time. He is best known for his *Gioco della Cieca*, the "Blindman's Buff ballet," mimed and danced and also sung by a chorus of four nymphs taunting a blindfolded Amaryllis in the third act of Battista Guarini's *Il Pastor Fido*. Work on this pastoral tragicomedy, "which took Baroque Europe by storm," was begun in 1591, and it was finally produced seven years later.[47] The dance scene was complex and made more so by the negative attitude of some of the dancers (of five listed—all men—one, at least, was Jewish) and the absences not only of dancers but of Isacchino himself.[48] Isacchino also collaborated with the well-known Jewish playwright and director, Leone de' Sommi, choreographing, for example, the dances for the *Favola boschereccia delle nozze di Semiramide con Mennone*, staged in 1591.[49] To date, little more is known about Isacchino's life, but certain facts (such as a payment made to him in 1599) suggest that he was, if not prosperous, certainly well established.[50] In January 1594, for example, disregarding prohibitions and severe penalties[51] for nonaristocratic Christians attending Jewish festivities, Duke Vincenzo Gonzaga, together with a large number of ladies and gentlemen, including his cousin Annibale, took part, all masked and costumed (undoubtedly for carnival), in a soirée at Isacchino's home.[52]

Before concluding, I would like to address the following questions. What *kinds* of dances did Jewish choreographers create? *Which* dances were taught by Jewish dancing masters? Finally, was there such a thing as "Jewish dance" in Renaissance Italy? Guglielmo invented "art" dances, which were intended for the nobility but were also taken up by the bourgeoisie. His *ballo* "Voltati in ça Rosina" was a "hit" for at least three decades, and one humanist compared its artistic worth to Jannequin's music, Leonardo's painting, and the poetry of Homer, Dante, and Petrarch.[53] While some of Guglielmo's dances are for four or more dancers, most are for a couple or a trio. Guglielmo also choreographed spectacles of mime and dance, similar to the one organized by the Jewish community of Pesaro that featured "rustics" performing the labors of the field, though none are described. Isacchino, too, was well known for the "ballets" that he composed for plays and the musical theater.

A contemporary of Isacchino's and a fellow Mantuan was the composer Salomone Rossi.[54] Included in his outstanding production of instrumental and vocal works is a considerable body of dance music, with a great number of *gagliarde* (galliards).[55] The *gagliarda* was the most popular dance of the sixteenth century, and it spread from Italy to the rest of Europe. It became ever more intricate and demanding, and contemporary treatises contain hundreds of variations, providing male dancers with an occasion to show their agility and prowess.[56] Rossi's *gagliarde*, which are musically complex, are, despite unusual and irregular phrasing, very danceable.[57]

Rossi's *gagliarde* do not differ, except in their musical sophistication, from contemporary Italian dance music; nor do Guglielmo's choreographies differ in style and content from those of Domenico. Isacchino's "ballets" were part of non-Jewish plays and musical productions. Moreover, the images of Jewish dance are in every way typical fifteenth-century miniatures in their depiction of festivities, dress, and behavior. Finally, as can be seen in the case of the Florentine school run by Guglielmo's brother Giuseppe and his Christian partner Francesco and in Mariotto of Perugia's rivalry with Deodato, the curriculum of dancing schools run by both Christians and Jews included the same dances. This, plus the popularity of Jewish dancing masters among Jews *and* Christians, leads us to the inevitable conclusion that, at least up to 1600, the dances in question (like other aspects of Italian-Jewish cultural life) were totally Italian and had nothing specifically "Jewish" about them.[58]

Many questions remain unanswered. Were the dancing schools run by Jewish dancing masters and attended by Christians also frequented by Jews? (This may well have been the case in the fifteenth and early sixteenth centuries.) Did, for example, Leone Modena's son-in-law teach Jews or Christians or both? Modena had learned dancing in pre-ghetto Ferrara as part of his Neoplatonic course of study and, by eulogizing his son-in-law, whose "profession was dancing," seems to suggest that the *kind* of dancing was similar.[59] Since the autobiography is set in a very Jewish context, it may well be that Jacob Halevi's dance students were primarily, or only, Jews. Would they have learned the contemporary Italian repertoire? Who would they have been in terms of age, sex, marital status, and economic and social background? It is hardly likely that after the Counter-Reformation many—if any—Jews danced at schools frequented by Christians, for we know from an order of the Mantua ghetto issued in 1610 that even Jewish men and women were no longer allowed to dance together except for one wedding dance.[60] A *pragmatica* of 1630 (from the same city) forbids dancing altogether, with the one exception, provided that permission was obtained from the minor council, of the *mitzwe-tanz*, customarily danced by Ashkenazi Jews, and then men and women danced with their own sex alone.[61] Does this mean that in the late sixteenth century, middle- and upper-class Jews were taught dancing exclusively in their homes? Is it possible that, starting in the early 1600s, as a result of the segregation imposed by both ecclesiastic and ghetto regulations, the dance repertoires of Italian Jews and Christians became distinct?[62]

Finally, why did so many Jews go into the dancing profession, a profession that seems to have been engaged in on the same basis by Christians and, moreover, one that brought Christians and Jews into close, if not intimate, contact?[63] A list of trades engaged in by the Jews of Mantua and presented in 1588 to the Inquisition includes *ballerini*,[64] though for many other towns there is no evidence regarding the existence of the profession. Is this in part due to historians' failing to see or note these presences, which, for Robert Bonfil, are "likely to multiply . . . [and] contrary to the persistent myth that all Jews . . . were money lenders or learned rabbis."[65]

The attention paid by current historiographers to the traffic in money "seems to have obscured, possibly involuntarily, the rich spectrum of trades followed by the Jews, thereby distorting their history in another way that it would be well to eliminate."[66] Traditionally, a "trade" was passed on from father to son, but when and why and where in Italy did the teaching of dance by Jews first begin?

NOTES

1. For a complete listing of the treatises, their present locations, a description of their contents, and biographies of their authors, see Barbara Sparti, *Guglielmo Ebreo of Pesaro: On the Practice or Art of Dancing* (Oxford: Clarendon Press, 1993; reprinted 1995), Chapter 1.

2. The ancient Greeks and Romans—for example, Plato, the rhetoricians Lucian (*On the Dance*), Libanius (*On the Dancers*), and Quintilian—discoursed on dance, seeing it, in part, as a representation of the movement of the heavenly bodies and, in part, as pantomime, gesture, and the expression of emotions.

3. For Guglielmo's life, see Sparti, *Guglielmo Ebreo*, Chapter 2.

4. To date, I have been unable to find out anything about Moses of Sicily.

5. Alessandro Sforza, lord of Pesaro. See Sparti, *Guglielmo*, p. 34.

6. Many aspects of Guglielmo's life and work were first discussed in 1987 in Pesaro, both in a conference dedicated to him and in the catalog of the accompanying exhibition. Maurizio Padovan, ed., *Guglielmo Ebreo da Pesaro e la danza nelle corti italiane del XV secolo*, Atti del Convegno (Pisa: Pacini, 1990); Patrizia Castelli, Maurizio Mingardi, and Maurizio Padovan, *Mesura et arte del danzare* (Pesaro: Gualtieri, 1987). The results of some further research were incorporated in my 1993 and 1995 editions of Guglielmo's treatise. Five of Guglielmo's dances were reconstructed by me and performed in a video as part of the exhibition *Gardens and Ghettos: the Art of Jewish Life in Italy*, organized by the Jewish Museum of New York in 1989–1990, curator Vivian Mann, in which a copy of Guglielmo's treatise was also on show. Despite all of this scholarship dedicated to Guglielmo, the most important books on the history of Italian Jewry written in the last two decades (by Ariel Toaff, Shlomo Simonsohn, Robert Bonfil, as well as Mark Cohen's edition of Leon Modena's *Autobiography*—see later) were unable to include any of the information, inasmuch as they had all been published a few years previously. The dance references given in these books are based on Cecil Roth's important, but frustratingly undocumented and often inexact, *The Jews in the Renaissance* (Philadelphia: Jewish Publication Society of America, 1959) and Otto Kinkeldey's seminal, but now obsolete, *A Jewish Dancing Master of the Renaissance: Guglielmo Ebreo* (New York: 1929; reprinted Brooklyn, NY: Dance Horizons, 1972).

7. See Sparti, *Guglielmo Ebreo*, Chapter 3.

8. For *moresche*, see B. Sparti, "Antiquity as Inspiration in the Renaissance of Dance: The Classical Connection and Fifteenth-Century Italian Dance," *Dance Chronicle*, 16, no. 3 (1993): 378–380, and her "The Moresca and Mattaccino in Italy—circa 1450–1630," in the proceedings of the conference *The Meeting of Cultures in Dance History*, edited by D. Tércio and Cruz Quebrada (Lisbon: Faculdade de Motricidade Humana, 1999), pp. 189–199.

9. See B. Sparti, "The Function and Status of Dance in the 15th-Century Italian Courts," *Dance Research* 14, no. 1 (1996): 52 n. 74.

10. Giuseppe Ebreo and his Christian partner, for example, stipulated that they could teach at their school or at their pupils' homes. Alessandra Veronese, "Una Societas ebraico-cristiana in docendi tripudiare sonare ac cantare nella Firenze del Quattrocento," in Padovan,

Guglielmo Ebreo, pp. 53, 55.

11. Sparti, "Function and Status," pp. 42–61.

12. For the program, see ibid., pp. 47–48. The quotation is from Lauro Martines' Chapter 11, "Humanism: A Program for the Ruling Classes," in his *Power and Imagination* (Baltimore: Johns Hopkins University Press, 1979/1988).

13. Sparti, "Function and Status," pp. 49–51. There were, however, some notable exceptions: Isacchino Massarano (see later in text) and the author of a well-known dance treatise, Cesare Negri, who worked in Milan at the end of the sixteenth century and owned a substantial home. See Katherine T. McGinnes, "At Home in the 'Casa del Trombone': A Social-Historical View of 16th-Century Milanese Dancing Masters," in the *Proceedings of the 20th Conference of the Society of Dance History Scholars* (Riverside: University of California, 1997), pp. 203–216.

14. Frank A. D'Accone, *The Civic Muse. Music and Musicians in Siena during the Middle Ages and the Renaissance* (Chicago: University of Chicago Press, 1997), pp. 649–51. D'Accone also gives examples of dancing masters who owned property, even while protesting poverty.

15. See B. Sparti, "Dancing Couples behind the Scenes: Recently Discovered Italian Illustrations, 1470–1550," *Imago Musicae* 13(1996): 22–33.

16. Ibid, p. 29 and Fig. 19. The work is in the Biblioteca Apostolica Vaticana, codice Rossiano 555, and the miniature is on fol. 220r.

17. MS 180/51, fol. 246v. For commentary and reproductions, see Sparti, "Dancing Couples," frontispiece and pp. 26–28.

18. There is no explicit reference to dancing in either the *pizmon* or marginalia. Dr. Seth Jerchower, research associate to the Special Collections Library of the Jewish Theological Seminary of America, who generously furnished me with information concerning the *pizmon* and was initially skeptical about the miniature's depicting dance, later agreed that this was probably a dance scene and an appropriate illustration for a wedding hymn.

19. First and foremost, see Thérèse Metzger and Mendel Metzger, *Jewish Life in the Middle Ages* (Seacaucus, NJ: Chartwell Books, 1982), pp. 132, 143, 147.

20. See Sparti, "Dancing Couples," pp. 29–32, for a discussion of the dress of the figures in this codex and for sources.

21. Ibid, pp. 22–26, Figs. 13 and 14.

22. Metzger and Metzger, *Jewish Life*, p. 256, state that compared to textual sources, "the evidence of the visual records is very poor indeed," and besides the miniature in question they mention only one other image (with men playing dice and drinking), now in the British Library.

23. Ibid., p. 132, claim, "Apart from married couples and close relations, rabbin forbade members of the opposite sex to dance with each other at balls." However, in Italy certain rabbis waived these "rules" at weddings and during Purim. See Zvi Friedhaber and Giora Manor, "The Jewish Dancing Master in the Renaissance in Italy, in the Jewish and Gentile Communities and at the Ducal Courts," in Padovan, *Guglielmo Ebreo*, pp. 16–17.

24. See Luisa Mortaro Ottolenghi, "Alcuni manoscritti ebraici miniati in Italia Settentrionale nel secolo XV," *Arte Lombarda* 60 (1981): 41; Cecil Roth, "The Decoration of the Hebrew Biblical Manuscripts," *Manoscritti Biblici ebraici decorati provenienti da biblioteche italiane* (Exhibition catalog), edited by A. Martelli and L. Mortaro Ottolenghi (Milan: ADEI-WIZO, 1966), p. 38.

25. An anonymous 1475 description of the entire wedding festivity, copied five years later by Lionardo da Colle and enriched with thirty-two miniatures, is located in the Biblioteca Apostolica Vaticana, codice urbinate 899, and edited by Tammaro De Marinis: *Le nozze di Costanzo Sforza e Camilla d'Aragona celebrate a Pesaro nel 1475* (Florence:

Vallecchi-Alinari, 1946). The description of the Jewish community's contribution appears on pp. 35–38. An English version of the events is given by A. William Smith, "Jewish Dancing in Wedding Pageantry at Pesaro, Italy in 1475," *Israel Dance* (*The Israel Dance Annual*) (1987/88). See also Friedhaber and Manor, "Jewish Dancing Master," pp. 18–19 Figs. 2–3; Castelli, Mingardi, and Padovan, *Mesura*, pp. 24–25, particularly Figs. 24–25.

26. The *moresche* were created for Carnival festivities and the wedding of Lucrezia Borgia and Alfonso d'Este. See Sparti, *Guglielmo Ebreo*, p. 55 n. 26.

27. William Prizer, in his "Games of Venus: Secular Vocal Music in the Late Quattrocento and Early Cinquecento," *The Journal of Musicology* 9 (1991): 18, points out that the "elite" interest in the popular text resulted in a "popularizing" or "conscious imitation of the popular manner."

28. De Marinis, *Le nozze*, p. 38. "Questo signor benigno che vedete [Costanzo]/ Questo campo ci ha dato colgier fructi/ A lavorallo bene."

29. Now in the New York Public Library's Dance Collection and known as the "Giorgio" codex.

30. In Ariel Toaff's *Gli Ebrei a Perugia* (Perugia: Fonti per la Storia dell'Umbria, 1975), pp. 89, 301–302.

31. In 1487 Deodato murdered the banker Angelo, son of Guglielmo, one of the wealthiest Jews of Perugia, in the local synagogue. Banned from the city after paying a sizable fine, he returned to Perugia two years later and, though pardoned by the victim's daughter, was prohibited from passing near or entering the city's synagogue. Ariel Toaff, *The Jews in Umbria*, vol. 3 (Leiden, New York and Köln: E.J. Brill, 1994), pp. 1026–1027.

32. Documents found and published by Timothy J. McGee, "Dancing Masters and the Medici Court in the 15th Century," *Studi Musicali* 17, no. 2 (1988): 215–216, 223–224. McGee points out (n. 30) that forty ducats "would have been enough to purchase a small house" and was slightly less than the "average yearly wage of a laborer at the time."

33. Ariel Toaff, *The Jews in Medieval Umbria*, vol. 3 (Florence: Olschki, 1979), p. 1370. In the sixteenth century, the scudo replaced the ducat and was worth about the same amount, D'Accone, *Civic Muse*, p. xxi.

34. See Mark R. Cohen's translation and edition, *The Autobiography of a Seventeenth-Century Venetian Rabbi* (Princeton, NJ: Princeton University Press, 1988), p. 86.

35. Ibid., p.103.

36. Ibid., p.108. I have been unable to discover where Jacob Halevi was living and practicing his profession.

37. Susan Parisi, in her "The Jewish Community and Carnival Entertainment at the Mantuan Court in the Early Baroque," *Music in Renaissance Cities and Courts: Studies in Honor of Lewis Lockwood*, edited by J.A. Owens and A.M. Cummings (Warren, MI: Harmonie Park Press, 1997), pp. 293–305, notes that in the late sixteenth century, the Jewish community in Mantua (the largest in Italy at this time) numbered a little over 2,300 inhabitants. Its ghetto was not established until 1612. Elsewhere, Jews had been expelled from Sicily (1492), from the kingdom of Naples (1541), from the Papal States—except for Rome and Ancona (1569)—and from the duchy of Milan (1597). "By the beginning of the 17th century Jewish populations were concentrated in the territories of Mantua, Venice, and to a lesser degree, in Tuscany and in Savoy. . . . Ghettos were established in Venice in 1516, Rome in 1555, Florence in 1571, Siena in 1571 . . . Verona in 1602, Padua in 1603 . . . Ferrara in 1624, Modena in 1638, Urbino, Pesaro, and Senigallia in 1634" (pp. 296–297). Parisi cites Robert Bonfil, *Jewish Life in Renaissance Italy* (Berkeley: University of California Press, 1994), pp. 63, 56–57, 71–72.

38. Shlomo Simonsohn, *History of the Jews in the Duchy of Mantua* (Jerusalem: Kiryath Sepher, 1977), pp. 114, 116.

39. Ibid., p. 116.

40. Shlomo Simonsohn, *The Jews in the Duchy of Milan*, vol. 3 (Jerusalem: Israel Academy of Sciences and Humanities, 1982), pp. 1597–1598.

41. Ibid., p. 1616.

42. Ibid., pp. 1613–1617.

43. Ibid. Christians taught music to Jews (e.g., the viola), going to Jewish homes and organizing concerts there. "These sins and offences detrimental to the Christian faith and the purity of soul and spirit of Christians are committed by Jews in Cremona. They are contrary to the injunctions contained in the Bull published by Pope Paul IV and the constitution of the regional synod" (p. 1617).

44. Quoted by Friedhaber and Manor, *Jewish Dancing Masters*, p. 17, where the source is given as Daniel Carpi, *Pinkas Va'ad Padua* (Jerusalem, 1974), p. 117.

45. Most information on Isacchino is based on Antonino Bertolotti, *Musici alla corte dei Gonzaga in Mantova* (Milan: Ricordi, 1890; reprinted Bologna: Forni, 1978), p. 63; Alessandro D'Ancona, *Origini del teatro italiano*, vol. 2 (Milan: Loescher, 1891; reprinted Rome: Bardi, 1971), p. 400. Susan Parisi in her 1989 dissertation "Ducal Patronage of Music in Mantua 1587–1627: An Archival Study" (Ann Arbor, MI: UMI, 1993), gives all the known references as well as a few other documentary citations, including a decree of 1610 (the last known reference to Isacchino) in which Duke Vincenzo grants him—on the basis of his fourteen years of service—the possibility of acquiring a butcher shop as a dowry for his daughter (p. 460). Isacchino, however, is here referred to as "della Profeta," and it is not at all clear if this is "our" Isacchino Massarano, who would presumably have been in Duke Vincenzo's service for more than twenty years. According to Parisi, in 1607 or earlier, Isaachino was given ducal dispensation regarding the yellow badge. In her "The Jewish Community," pp. 293–305, she reports: "By the early reign of Duke Vincenzo [1588], it was customary for Jewish citizens to host a production and reception for the duke and his court during the carnival season. A special tax was levied in the community itself to fund the event." Maurizio Padovan reprints letters and gives some of the archival references to Isacchino in his "Il Gioco della Cieca rappresentato alla Regina di Spagna nel Pastor fido," in *La Danza Italiana*, quaderno 1, 1998, esp. pp. 14–18.

46. For example, "Ingiusti Sdegni" (1583–1584) by Bernardino Pino da Cagli (cited in Padovan, "Gioco," pp. 14–15), staged and directed by Leone de' Sommi (see later in text).

47. Translated into many languages, a printed edition was in its 20th printing by 1602 (there would be a total of 110!). Ahuva Belkin, "Leone de Sommi's Pastoral Conception and the Design of the Shepherds' Costumes for the Mantuan Production of Guarini's Il Pastor Fido," in *Assaph*, Department of Theatre Arts, Tel Aviv University, 1986.

48. Judith Cohen, "Words to Dance and Music—Music to Dance and Words (The Case of the Gioco della cieca)," *Musikometrika* (1993): 5; Iain Fenlon, "Guarini, de' Sommi and the Pre-History of the Italian Danced Spectacle," *Leone de' Sommi and the Performing Arts*, edited by Ahuva Belkin (Tel Aviv: Asaph, 1997).

49. The pastoral ("Rural Tale of the Marriage of Semiramis and Mennon"), directed by de' Sommi, was by Mutio Manfredi (see Padovan, "Gioco," p. 14; n. 46 earlier).

50. For Bertolotti, *Musici alla corte dei Gonzaga*, "he was very rich" (based on one payment?), while D'Ancona, *Origini*, assumes that because the Duke attended a soirée at his home (see later in text), he was "uomo di ricco stato" (a man of high social status).

51. Twenty-five scudi, also for Jews attending Christian festivities.

52. They were certainly not disguised, as suggested by D'Ancona's interpretation of "incognito" (*Origini*, p. 400). The information is in a letter written by Alfonsino Gonzaga (AS [Archivo di State] Mn [Mantova] A.G., b. 2665, Alfonsino Gonzaga, 15 gen 1594). It is still not clear to which branch of the Gonzaga family (possibly Novellara) he and

Annibale belonged. I wish to thank Beth and Jonathan Glixon for their help in transcribing the letter:

The night of Friday the 13 there was a soirée at the home of Isachino who sings soprano and His Highness went and many other masqueraded gentlemen and ladies, and because of the narrowness of the room there was much pushing of one another, and even though His Highness was shoved he didn't say anything at all but Messer Anibal Gonzaga, who thought that that costumed reveler who was His Highness masqueraded whom he didn't recognize wanted to get in front of him, hit him in the chest, and His Highness returned the punch on his face, breaking his mask and butchering an eye, and for Messer Anibale's good fortune His Highness didn't grab the knife that was at his side as he wanted to as it [got stuck?] in his shirt, and so this case passed. Messer Anibale excused himself as best he could and left and the party continued. The next morning the Captain of Justice with all the police was at his house to accompany him to prison but they discovered that he had quite openly departed with all his family on his best horse.

53. Sparti, *Guglielmo Ebreo*, p. 43 n. 55.

54. See Don Harrán and Salamone Rossi, *Jewish Musicians in Late Renaissance Mantua* (Oxford: Oxford University Press, 1999).

55. See Don Harrán's critical edition of Rossi's *Complete Works*, 12 vols. (Neuhausen-Stuttgart: Hänssler-Verlag for the American Institute of Musicology, 1995). Vol. 13 is forthcoming (2002).

56. See B. Sparti's Introduction to the facsimile edition of Lutio Compasso's *Ballo della Gagliarda* (Freiburg: "fa-gisis" Musik-und Tanzedition, 1995), pp. 5–25.

57. The speaker demonstrated the basic *gagliarda* step and a few simple variations that she performed to one of Rossi's *gagliarde* called "Massara," which may well have been dedicated to Isacchino or his family.

58. Is it possible that there was a different sort of dance among the smaller, poorer Jewish communities? In David Reubeni's account of his travels in Italy in the early sixteenth century (David Reubeni, *Un ebreo d'Arabia in missione segreta nell'Europa del '500*, edited by Lea Sestieri [Genoa: Marietti, 1991]), there are accounts of Jewish women's playing harps and dancing to entertain him. In 1524, at the home of the doctor Moshe Abdurahim in Rome, the young daughter who read and recited the sacred Scriptures every day was on Saturday "full of happiness and danced with joy" (p. 112). In Pisa, David, the guest of R. Yehiel, was fasting. R. Yehiel's wife, mother, and grandmother and other girls danced for him to honor and gladden him and dispel sadness. He, however, refused their harp, flute, and dancing (p. 123). It is possible that these examples represent a different sort of dancing from that discussed in this chapter, that is, one that is truly Jewish and for women only. I wish to thank Michele Luzzati for this reference.

59. See nn. 34 and 36. Mark Cohen and Theodore Rabb, "The Significance of Leon Modena's Autobiography for Early Modern Jewish and General European History" (Cohen, *Autobiography*), p. 5, point out, "Despite the physical segregation of the Italian Jews in the seventeenth century, there persisted a rich cultural life that exhibited tastes and interests acquired during the Renaissance," using Modena's and Halevi's dancing as an example. They also point out (p. 6) that despite the physical barrier of the ghetto, "people moved in and out freely," which Modena "takes for granted. . . . Like so many other learned Italian Jews during and after the Renaissance, Modena had extensive relations with Christians as students, admirers, correspondents, and interlocutors."

60. Simonsohn, *History*, p. 373.

61. Ibid., pp. 535–536. The pragmatica was published five years later in 1635.

62. Other questions, such as the whereabouts of dancing schools where Jews taught, particularly in southern Italy, and hopefully more information about curriculum and students

await further research.

63. Cohen and Rabb, in their "The Significance of Leon Modena's Autobiography . . .," in Cohen, *Autobiography*, suggest that because of their "minority status" and exclusion from a variety of activities "such as most branches of general education," Jews had to "develop their own alternatives" (p. 13). Moreover, as I have pointed out, dance was considered by many a rather low and equivocal trade.

64. In Simonsohn, *Duchy of Mantua*, p. 272.

65. Roberto Bonfil, "Lo spazio culturale degli ebrei d'Italia fra Rinascimento ed Età barocca," in *Gli Ebrei in Italia*, edited by C. Vivanti, *Storia d'Italia Annali*, vol. 11 (Turin: Einaudi, 1996), p. 462. My translation.

66. R. Bonfil, *Jewish Life in Renaissance Italy*, p. 94.

8

The Expulsion from the Papal States (1569) in Light of Hebrew Sources

Abraham David

Unlike the anti-Jewish edicts of Pope Paul IV in 1555,[1] the expulsion of the Jews from the Papal States in 1569 left surprisingly little impact on contemporary Hebrew literature. Historians cannot say why so little material has survived. I intend first to briefly examine the historical background of this event and then to discuss the accounts found in the better-known printed works. Finally, I hope to show that there are untapped sources of information on this event and its aftermath.

BACKGROUND

Pius V was appointed pope in early 1566.[2] Shortly thereafter, in a special bull issued on 19 April 1566 (*Romanus Pontifex*),[3] he renewed the anti-Jewish edicts of Pope Paul IV. Thus, he canceled all the mitigating measures of his predecessor Pius IV (1559–1566). Regarding the edicts, Hebrew sources single out the "badge of shame" (the obligation to wear yellow hats), the forced ghettoization, and the great economic harm caused by the exclusion of Jews from banking, that is, from lending money at interest.[4]

Upon realizing that his measures were not effective because the Jewish population was scattered throughout the Papal States, Pius V took more drastic steps. On 26 February 1569 he issued the bull *Hebraeorum gens*,[5] which called for the expulsion of all Jews from the cities of the Papal States within three months. As a result of this edict, the ancient Jewish communities of central Italy located within the area of the Papal States disappeared almost entirely.[6] The exception was Urbino, an independent duchy within the region of the Papal States that refused to accept papal authority. Although the Jewish communities of Rome and Ancona were excluded from the decree, the Jews in those cities were forced to reside in ghettos.[7] Many of the expellees sought refuge in the duchy of Urbino and in Rome and Ancona. They also took refuge in cities in Italian principalities outside the

Papal States, including Ferarra, Mantua, Pesaro, and cities in the Lombardy, Emilia Romagna, and Tuscany regions. Others made their way to the east to the Balkans, Turkey, and the land of Israel.

THE EXPULSION IN HEBREW SOURCES

Although this event was a turning point in Italian-Jewish history in the second half of the sixteenth century, it seemingly left little impression on its contemporaries. Isaiah Sonne noted: "Whereas the decrees and persecutions by Paul IV left a strong echo in contemporary Hebrew literature, this literature passed over the expulsion decree of 1569 in silence. Not a single *qinah* (elegy) lamenting this expulsion is extant. It left no traces in Hebrew literature with the exception of the historical works *'Emeq ha-Bakha* and *Shalshelet ha-Kabbalah*."[8]

It is these accounts to which I now turn. Briefly, these contemporary reports devoted little space to the description of the expulsion and its results. I begin with Joseph Ha-Kohen:

5329. All the thoughts of Pius, may his evil name rot, were constantly how to do harm to the Jews. He expelled all the Jews in the Papal States in the month of May of that year, the third month [after the decree]. The heads of the [Jewish] communities fell at his feet to turn aside his evil plan, without any success. Like a deaf viper he refused to listen and they departed angrily. Only in the city of Rome and in Ancona did he leave them a small refuge, and there they reside to this day. The inhabitants of the rest of the cities settled wherever they could; each one going his own way.[9]

In his *Shalshelet ha-Kabbalah*, the well-known historian Gedaliah ibn Yahya gave a personal slant to his brief description of the events:

In [5]325 [should read 5326] an Alessandrian cardinal became pope; he was called Pius V. He commanded that the [Jewish] hat be yellow, the color of straw. He later ordered that all Jews leave his kingdom within a three-month period at the penalty of loss of life and property. And so it came to pass that not a Jew was left, except for a few who converted. Some one thousand households left, leaving most of their property behind because they could not take it with them. And the Jews became extremely impoverished, for their loans were left behind. I myself held promissory notes for more than ten thousand pieces of gold in Imola and Ravenna.[10]

From his concluding remarks it seems that Gedaliah ibn Yahya was forced to leave the towns of Imola and Ravenna in the Papal States and a substantial sum behind in the form of "promissory notes for more than ten thousand pieces of gold." Elsewhere, ibn Yahya writes that he was residing in Pesaro, in the duchy of Urbino, as early as 1567. It seems then that he was forced from his hometowns two years before the official expulsion, perhaps as a result of Pius V's renewal of Pope Paul IV's anti-Jewish measures.[11]

A later Hebrew source, dating from the early seventeenth century, also mentions the expulsion. This source, the anonymous corrector of Joseph Ha-

Kohen's *'Emeq ha-Bakha*,[12] raises two additional points not found in the earlier
accounts: (1) Before issuing the expulsion order, the pope consulted with his close
advisers, the cardinals. The cardinals, fearing the harmful effects of the expulsion,
advised against it. The pope, however, rejected their advice. (2) The pope accepted
the appeal of the rulers of Ancona to exclude this city from the expulsion decree
because of the central role that the Jews played in the economy of this port city.
The text follows:

> He held a council and suggested to the cardinals that all the Jews be expelled from the
> Romagna region. They advised him not to do so, saying it would bring harm to the kingdom.
> He replied: "I am the ruler and no one may oppose my power." Upon his orders it was
> announced in all the cities of his kingdom that in three months' time every Jew must leave
> all the cities of his kingdom, with the exception of Rome. Even Ancona was included in the
> decree. The people and nobles of Ancona went to him, declaring that it was to his advantage
> and profit to leave the Jews there because they controlled trade and he received a great deal
> of revenue from them due to their trade with other countries and with Turkey. Because of
> this trade the Jews had an excellent reputation, and he yielded to their request. Then all the
> Jews left Romagna and scattered over Ferrara, Mantua, Pesaro, and Urbino, and all the cities
> of Tuscany as well as in the region of Milan. They left their houses, and their fields and
> vineyards fell to strangers; they offered their residences as they were for less than half their
> worth. And the Jews were impoverished.[13]

Additional Hebrew sources, including documents preserved in several Jewish
communal archives, contemporary *responsa*, and more than two dozen letters,[14]
reflect the aftermath of the expulsion order. These documents describe the efforts
of the Jews from the Papal States to find refuge in other Italian cities. They also
shed light on the emergency fund-raising campaign to assist their resettlement
initiated by the leaders of the Jewish communities outside the Papal States.

I would like to discuss very briefly the nature of the evidence found in these
letters in particular. Most of them have been preserved in Hebrew *igronim*. *Igronim*
or *epistolaris* are compilations of exemplary letters chosen from various spheres
of Jewish life for use as correspondence textbooks. In the course of editing these
letters for educational purposes, the teaching of Hebrew language, and correct
literary style, most of the identifying details, like dates and names of people and
places, were omitted. Even in the absence of identifying details, however, these
correspondence textbooks, whose sixteenth-century representatives alone number
in the thousands, are of great historical value. They form an untapped treasure of
prime archival material that contributes greatly to our understanding of various
aspects of Jewish life in Italy.

The importance of these *igronim* was first recognized more than a century
ago.[15] Although certain studies of Jewish life in Renaissance Italy have made some
use of them, currently there is much greater interest in the discovery and
publication of these collections for the purposes of historical research.[16]

Most of the related Hebrew sources treat the adjustment of the expellees to their
new homes. The Jews of Rome, Ancona, Mantua, Ferrara, and Pesaro, for example,
made every effort to assist in the absorption of the refugees in Italy and/or to

provide financial aid to those who wished to leave Italy and settle in Ottoman lands. These efforts continued for several years after the expulsion.

Five undated documents, taken from three *igronim*, were published by David Kaufmann from his own collection, who mistakenly assigned them to the anti-Jewish decrees of Pope Paul IV in 1555. Careful examination of these documents indicates that they belong to the later episode of the expulsion of the Jews from the Papal States.[17] These five documents reflect the intensive efforts by the Jewish communities of Mantua and Pesaro, which were not under the control of the pope, to assist their fellow Jews by fund-raising efforts in other Italian-Jewish communities outside the Papal States. The purpose of the funds was to enable six hundred refugees from the Papal States presently in Mantua and an unspecified number of refugees in Pesaro to sail east to lands under Ottoman rule, including the land of Israel.[18]

In addition to this material, I have discovered and published more than a dozen letters from various manuscripts located in different collections.[19] These letters shed light on the condition of the Jews from the Papal States in the aftermath of the expulsion and on their resettlement in various locations in Italy and elsewhere. Most of the letters treat the monetary difficulties that prevented the provision of proper assistance to the refugees either to settle within Italy or to sail for points east. Almost twenty years ago I published three letters concerning the expulsion that I discovered in three different *igronim*.[20] The first letter[21] was sent by Jews from Rome to the rabbi or communal leader of an unidentified town in 1569, shortly before the expulsion. In this letter, the Jews from Rome described the fearful response to the expulsion decree: "Everyone speaks unceasingly of but one thing; that is, how, due to our many sins, the pope, may he be exalted, has agreed to expel all the Jews in his kingdom, both near and far, except for those now living here in Rome and in Ancona."[22] The letter continued: "For his eminence's scribe has already come to take a census of all the houses and their inhabitants, big and small, and the decree will be issued shortly." Therefore, the writers requested that the addressee immediately "send lobbyists here to Rome who have the power to stand in the king's court . . . but let this be as soon as possible."

In his account, the historian Joseph Ha-Kohen also mentions unsuccessful attempts to intercede with the pope: "The heads of the communities fell at his feet to turn aside his evil plan, without any success. Like a deaf viper he refused to listen and they departed angrily."[23]

As I noted earlier, only the Rome and Ancona Jewish communities were exempt from the expulsion decree. Evidently, many refugees arrived in these two cities, and the heads of the Rome and Ancona Jewish communities also undertook to raise funds to assist them.[24] We learn from a letter preserved in the archives of the Ancona Jewish community,[25] that the heads of the Mantua Jewish community donated "a sum of 100 gold *scudi*" to this cause in 1569. The writers also informed the addressees that they were collecting additional funds for the Rome community.

One letter was addressed to the *parnassim* and the heads of the holy congregation of Urbino by the communal leaders of Pesaro in 1571, about two years after the expulsion.[26] The correspondents asked for the cooperation of the leaders of the Urbino community in finding solutions for the safe resettlement of the refugees now living in Pesaro. The writers noted that they were unable to absorb them because of the policy of the Duke of Urbino, Guidobaldo della Revere II, who also ruled Pesaro. Although he had allowed the Jewish refugees to winter there, this was with the understanding that they would leave the duchy at winter's end. The writers wished to take an accurate census of the number of refugees in their city: "We chose to send this letter first to all the places where they dwell in order to determine the number of people who must depart." They also asked that the *parnassim* of Urbino cooperate in planning their journey to the east: "to have them leave with comfort, to find them rest, to provide sufficient boats." They also noted that it was necessary to give the travelers money and provisions for the journey, "even though our brethren in Ferrara have agreed to give each person leaving a sum of three gold *scudi*."[27]

A similar request was sent by the heads of the Pesaro Jewish community to the nearby communities of San Angelo, Fossombrone, and Senigallia.[28]

Other extant letters reflect the same difficult situation. An anonymous letter sent by the heads of a Jewish community in the Duchy of Urbino[29] indicates that public pressure, most probably from church officials in Urbino, induced the duke to change his mind and to order the expulsion of the Jewish refugees from the Papal States from his realm:

For after the exiles came under the wing of the government of our master the duke, may he be exalted, they said: "In his shade [they] shall be revived: They shall bring to life new grain. They shall blossom like the vine" [Hosea 14:8]. But the local public quarreled with them and wrote accusatory letters to his eminence the master, may he be exalted. And even though the leaders of our generation stood in the breach many times and succeeded in turning aside their destructive anger . . . [this time] his eminence our master acceded to them, for he was unable to withstand all those standing before him. He made a law, he issued a decree to hasten to expel the broken down ones in a certain month—indeed when he lets you go, he will drive you out of here [Exod. 11:1]—if they do not leave voluntarily.

Another two anonymous letters relate to the Duke of Urbino's expulsion order. In one instance,[30] the writers noted the arrrival of expellees from Urbino, originally refugees from the Papal States, in Ragusa (present-day Dubrovnik), an important port city on the Adriatic coast. On their outbound journey to the east in 1571 these refugees were taken captive at sea. The letter's writers noted that they sent two emissaries to effect the captives' release and that both the Venetian ruler, Alvise Mocenigo I, and the "ruler here," certainly the Duke of Urbino, "who sent them from his domain, for their residence in his kingdom is not worthy of the king's trouble," played an important role in their release. A brief description of this episode, with the addition of some details, is found in the works of Joseph Ha-Kohen: *Divrey ha-Yamim le-Malkhey Sarfat u-veyt Ottoman ha-Tugar* and *'Emeq ha-Bakha*:

And it came to pass in the month of March, which is the month of spring, that the Duke of Urbino expelled the Jews who had been expelled from the Papal States by the decree of the aggressor, the enemy Pius V. They went down to sea in ships bound for Turkey and when they were near Ragusa they were taken captive like a bereaved she-bear by the commander of the Venetian ships. He brought the old men, the women, and the children to land and set them free; at the same time, he transferred the young men to his sailing ships and worked them hard like slaves, and they had no savior on the day of God's wrath. The heads of the Jewish community sent messengers to the Venetian leaders regarding the unlawful violence done to them, and the old man answered them: "You have gone too far! After all, the elderly, the women, and the children were released and sent on their way, only the young men will serve us until the threat of war is removed. Then we will free them and send them to their homes."[31]

Reference is made to this episode in an arbitration document dating from 1572 that is presently housed in the archives of the Mantuan Jewish community,[32] and notes that some of the expellees who had been captured eventually made their way to Mantua. It cites "[t]he ever-increasing expenses because of the poor Jews expelled from Pesaro who boarded ship to go across the sea and due to our iniquities some were taken captive and several returned to this region. Some came here to Mantua on 2 September 1572."[33] The members of the Mantuan Jewish community debated the question of funding the support for these redeemed exiles.

Another letter[34] also deals with the fate of the redeemed exiles. This letter was sent via an emissary from the heads of an unknown Jewish community (probably in the duchy of Urbino, perhaps Pesaro) to another community. The emissary's task was to raise funds so that "those expelled by the pope" who had found refuge in their city could be sent to safety. The writers went on to describe the heartbreaking situation of these refugees in greater detail. Although they had already managed to send "almost four hundred people by way of ship to the Levant," others still remained in their city. The rulers of the city, most likely the Duke of Urbino or his representatives, were exerting pressure on them to send the refugees on their way as soon as possible: "His eminence our master has had a change of heart to plot against his servants, and he decreed that we must send away the broken down ones quickly, adding that if we did not send them away quickly he would send us out of his presence, that is, he will drive us away."[35]

In addition, we must note the resulting social tensions in the communities where the refugees found temporary or permanent refuge. The attitude of the local Jews to the refugees was ambivalent. In some places, the arrival and projected absorption of Jews expelled from the Papal States posed a threat to the social and economic standing of the local Jews. We know of requests by individuals and by communities to find alternative solutions for the expellees so that they would not become a burden on that community. Similar social tensions between exiles and local Jews existed in the period after the expulsion from Spain.[36]

The problems created by the arrival of exiles from the Papal States are reflected in a letter from an anonymous Jewish community to other communities in the Emilia Romagna region.[37] This letter expressed concern that unless they received substantial aid, the expellees would have to remain with them and would be unable to "to go east by sea," thereby endangering both the socioeconomic status of the local Jews and their own position as well. As they wrote: "Lest they do harm by coming to us and becoming a burden on us, for they may be ruined suddenly, heaven forbid, and inherit Gehinnom twice. They will be in dread of the fierce anger, heaven forbid."[38] Accordingly, the communal officials requested financial aid from the addressees to assist the refugees in proceeding to the east.

In another letter, which lacks any identifying details, the writers protest strongly the refusal of another community to allow the exiles to remain in their region even temporarily: "We were horrified to see that from among you arose individuals who stood at the right hand of the poor of our exiled brethren to denounce them. In order to prevent wayfarers from staying in their land they wrote evil writs and made iniquitous laws so that none of the exiles could come there, and those who came were liable to death."[39]

A different kind of social tension is reflected in two *halakic* decisions concerning the same case, a disagreement between the Jewish community of Ferrara and exiles from Bologna who had settled in this city. The question was whether the Ferrara Jewish community could force rich exiles from Bologna to contribute to the communal purse for the poor. The exiles argued that they had no obligation to participate in this philanthropic activity. Since the aid to the poor from Bologna was not arranged through the community, they did not feel obligated to assist the poor of Ferrara. One decision was issued by Abraham Menahem Porto Ha-Kohen, the rabbi of the community of Cremona.[40] Another, much more detailed one was written by Moses Provenzalo in Mantua in 1573.[41] On this case, writes Abraham Menahem Porto Ha-Kohen:

I see from the words of the query that from the time that the holy congregation of Bologna was exiled from its homes to find refuge in the holy congregation of Ferrara, from the first day on they [the poor among the exiles from Bologna] always cried out. They [the exiles from Bologna] are not obligated to contribute to the Ferrara charity fund unless arrangements are also made to assist the poor among the exiles . . . the Ferrara communal officials certainly cannot impose this on them.[42]

In conclusion, I would like to note that the expulsion from the Papal States also left its mark in the liturgical sphere. Three versions of a supplicatory prayer for the welfare of the expellees from the Papal States are found in a large collection of prayers for different occasions, both public and private, compiled by R. Abraham ben Daniel of Modena in the second half of the sixteenth century.[43] It reads: "May Your overwhelming mercy and grace be upon the members of your people who are leaving the rule of the pope, may he be exalted. He has exiled them from there."[44]

To sum up, despite the fact that much of the documentary material previously cited lacks identifying details, it can assist our understanding of the fate of the expellees from the Papal States, both during and after the expulsion. Some expellees found refuge with the assistance of Jews in other cities, including Rome, Ancona, Pesaro, Mantua, and Ferrara. In order to help the exiles continue their search for a safe refuge in Italy and abroad in the east, the Jewish communities in these cities were forced to appeal to other Jewish communities for financial assistance. Several sources indicate that the expellees who settled in Pesaro and were expelled from the Duchy of Urbino two years later fell captive to maritime pirates outside Italy and that their release was obtained with the cooperation of the Venetian powers.

I can only hope that future discoveries will shed more light on the Jewish reaction to the expulsion and its aftermath and on the fate of the Jews expelled from the Papal States.

NOTES

1. Paul IV ruled between 1555 and 1559. His attitude to Judaism and Jewish people has been extensively documented. See I. Sonne, *Mi-Paulo ha-Revii' ad Pius ha-Hamishi* (Jerusalem: Mosed Byalik, 1954), pp. 19–93, 139–164; A. Toaff, "Nuova luce sui Marrani di Ancona (1556)," *Studi Ebraismo Italiano* (Rome: Barulli, 1974), pp. 261–280; K. R. Stow, *Catholic Thought and Papal Jewry Policy 1555–1593* (New York: Jewish Theological Seminary, 1977).

2. Pius V ruled between 1566 and 1572. See *Lexikon für Theologie und Kirche*, vol. 8 (Freiburg: Heider, 1963), pp. 531–532.

3. This bull has been published in *Magnum Bullarium Romanum*, vol. 7 (Torino: n.p., 1862; reprinted Graz: Akademische Druck-u Verlangsanstadt, 1966), pp. 438–439.

4. On his edicts against the Jews, see Stow, *Catholic Thought*, index. On this point we can also learn from several Hebrew sources, such as Joseph Ha-Kohen, *Divrei ha-Yamim le-Malkhei Sarfat u-Malkhei Beit Ottoman ha-Tugar*, part 3 (two mss. located at the British Library in London), Or. 3656 pp. 175r-v, Or. 10387 (Gaster 1071) p. 459v. The same version exists also in his other historiographical work, *'Emeq ha-Bakha*, the edition of K. Almbladh (Uppsala: Uppsala University, 1981), p. 95; the anonymous corrector of this book mentions this event in the beginning of the seventeenth century (p. 99); Gedalyah Ibn Yahya, *Shalshelet ha-Kabbalah* (Venice: n.p., 1587), p. 117v. See also Sonne, *Mi-Paulo*, pp. 175–179; D. Carpi, "L'espulsione degli ebrei dallo Stato della Chiesa al tempo di Pio V e i processi contro gli ebrei di Bologna,' *Scritti in memoria di Enzo Sereni* (Jerusalem: Sally Mayer, 1970), pp. 145–165 (in Hebrew); Y. Boksenboim, ed., *Iggerot Melamdim* (Tel Aviv: University of Tel Aviv, 1985), pp. 272–279; and *Iggerot Yehudei Italia* (Jerusalem: Mekon Ben-Tsvevi, 1994), pp. 279–283; A. David, "Nuovi documenti sull'espulsione degli ebrei dallo Stato della Chiesa (1569)," *Italia* 10 (1993): 17–19 (in Hebrew).

5. This bull has been published in *Magnum Bullarium Romanum*, vol. 7 (Torino: n.p. 1862), pp. 740–742.

6. See Sonne, *Mi-Paulo*, pp. 204–214; Carpi, "L'espulsione"; A. David, "New Documents concerning the History of Italian Jewry under the Shadow of Sixteenth Century Catholic Reaction," *Tarbiz* 49 (1980): 376–383; David, "Nuovi documenti," pp. 17–36.

7. As Pius V states in his bull *Hebraeorum gens*: "Urbe Roma et Ancona dumtaxat exeptis, ubi eos solos hebraecos, qui nunc aes habitant, ad praedictam memoriam amplius excitandam prosequendasque cum orientalibus negotiationes mutuosque commeatus cum eisdem, permittimus tolerandos." Ibid., p. 741.

8. Sonne, *Mi-Paulo*, p. 204.

9. Ha-Kohen, *Divrei ha-Yamim*, Or. 3656 pp. 176v, Or. 10387 (Gaster 1071) p. 465v; *'Emeq ha-Bakha*, p. 95.

10. *Shalshelet ha-Kabbalah*, p. 117v.

11. See David, "Nuovi documenti," pp. 18–19.

12. *See* n. 4.

13. *'Emeq ha-Bakha,* p. 100.

14. *See* n. 17.

15. Among the scholars who used and published such sources was David Kaufmann, the head of the *Jewish* Theological Seminary in Budapest at the end of the nineteenth century, who published several letters in the 1980s. Some of them we discuss later.

16. I cannot proceed without mentioning the work of Yacov Boksenboim, who has published in Hebrew five volumes of letter collections over the past fifteen years: *Iggerot Beit Carmi* (*Letters* of Carmi family) [in Cremona 1570–1577] (Tel Aviv: University of Tel Aviv, 1983); *Iggerot Rabbi Yehudah Arie' mi-Modena* (Letters of Rabbi Leon Modena) (Tel Aviv: University of Tel Aviv, 1984); *Iggerot Melamdim* (Letters of Jewish Teachers) [in Renaissance Italy 1555–1591] (Tel Aviv: University of Tel Aviv, 1985); *Iggerot Beit Rieti* (Letters of Rieti family) [in Siena 1537–1564] (Tel Aviv: University of Tel Aviv, 1987); *Iggerot Yehudei Italia* (Letters of Jews in Italy) [selected letters from the sixteenth century] (Jerusalem: Mekhon Ben Tsvevi Italyah, 1994).

17. As Heinrich Graetz has shown, in *Geschichte der Juden* (Leipzig: n.p., 1891; Philadelphia: Jewish Publication Society, 1891), p. 372 n. 2.

18. *Kaufmann, REJ* 20, pp. 70–72.

19. *David*, "New Documents," pp. 376–383; David, "Nuovi documenti," pp. 22–36.

20. David, "New Documents," pp. 376–383.

21. Ibid., pp. 378–379.

22. Ibid., p. 379.

23. See n. 10.

24.   David, "New Documents," pp. 379–381; David, "Nuovi documenti," pp. 26–27.

25. *Cited* in Sonne, *Mi-Paulo*, pp. 210–211.

26. *Cited* in David, "New Documents," pp. 381–383.

27. *Ibid.*, p. 383.

28. *Ibid.*

29. *Cited* in David, "Nuovi documenti," pp. 28–30.

30. Ibid., pp. 30–31.

31. Ha-Kohen, *Divrey ha-Yamim*, Or. 3656 pp. 182v-183r, Or. 10387 (Gaster 1071) pp. 473r-v; *'Emeq ha-Bakha*, p. 96.

32. This document has been published by Sonne, *Mi-Paulo*, pp. 211–214.

33. *Ibid.*, p. 212.

34. Cited in David, "Nuovi documenti," pp. 32–33.

35. Ibid., p. 32.

36. See A. David, 'The Spanish Expulsion and the Portuguese Persecution through the Eyes of the *Historian* R. Gedalya Ibn Yahya," *Sefarad* 56 (1996): 52–54.

37. *Cited* in David, "New Documents," pp. 379–381.

38. *Ibid.*, p. 381.

39. Y. Boksenboim, *Iggerot Yehudei Italia*, p. 284.

40. The decision of this sage has been published by David, "Nuovi documenti,", pp. 27–28.

41. His *responsum* has not been published yet but is preserved in ms. Budapest, David Kaufmann *collection* A 582 (today this collection is in the possession of the Hungarian Academy of Sciences), no. 24.

42. *See* David, "Nuovi documenti," pp. 27–28.

43. Preserved in ms. London, Montefiore collection 251, pp. 366v, 368r, 369v.

44. *Ibid.*, p. 368r.

9

The Case of Ferdinando Alvarez and His Wife, Leocadia of Rome (1637–1643)

Nancy Goldsmith Leiphart

During the sixteenth through the eighteenth centuries, the fortunes of the Jewish population of Rome rose and fell with the occupant of the Chair of St. Peter. When times were bad, Jews were confined to certain cities and neighborhoods, forced to listen to sermons designed to convert them, made to pay tributes at the election of the pope, forced into footraces and other public humiliations, and at times expelled from their homes and communities. Their holy books were banned and burned, and most were restricted to a few precarious livelihoods that, although often essential to the local economy, might be lost overnight.

In the early seventeenth century the Roman Jews' numbers had swelled with the influx of the expulsion from the Iberian Peninsula and the Spanish possessions of southern Italy. Perceived threats from these crypto-Jews and *conversos*, to say nothing of Protestants, witches, and other heresies, necessitated stern measures by the Inquisition to ensure purity of the faith. Urban VIII, in whose reign this case takes place, was a great patron of the arts and letters and in some ways wished to emulate the great popes of the Renaissance, but he was not lenient with the Jewish people. Despite harsh measures and a zealous climate, relatively few Jews were actually put to death by the Holy Office. A case cited as one of the exceptions to this claim is that of Ferdinando Alvarez and his wife, Leocadia.

Their story is found in the Manuscript Collection of the Vatican Library, a brief, but highly dramatic, record of the couple's arrest, renunciation, sentence, flight, rearrest, and final judgment.[1] The document is known from several sources but has generated some confusion in names and dates.

The card catalog in the Vatican first leads one to Pastor's *History of the Popes*.[2] Pastor, in turn, refers to Antonino Bertolotti's *Martiri del libero pensiero e vittime della Santa Inquisizione nei secoli XVI, XVII, e XVIII* for an account of the crime and judgment by the Holy Office.[3] Abraham Berliner gives a short outline,[4] and Cecil Roth gives it a footnote in his *A History of the Marranos*, which relies on the particulars given by Bertolotti rather than on the Vatican manuscript.[5] The name Alvarez is, of course, a common one, and Ferdinando merits two separate entries in the *Encyclopedia Judaica.*[6]

The structure and details of this brief account give it the slightly literary flavor of a novella. The notary went to great lengths to show all the characters involved— Ferdinando and his wife and the inquisitors—in the most objective light.

I would like to thank Lila Yawn, the National Endowment for the Humanities, the Biblioteca Apostolica Vaticana, and the Centro Bibliografico dell'Unione delle Comunità Ebraiche Italiane in Rome for assistance with this chapter. Following is a transcription and translation of the notary's record:

An account of the Crime of Ferdinando Alvarez and of Leocadia his Wife, who abjured in Rome on 14 March 1643:

It came to the notice of the Tribunal of the Holy Office of Rome that Ferdinando Alvarez and Leocadia his wife, both Portuguese, had fallen into Hebraism; and therefore proceeding against them for this crime in the month of February of the year 1637, by order of the Holy Inquisition they were arrested [and brought] to the prison of the Holy Office; and having been examined about the circumstances of the case against them, their confession was soon exposed, and having undergone the punishment that they deserved, on the 19th day of March 1639 they abjured in the Church of St. Peter at 21 hours of Winter.

There was such a crowd of people who were present at this function that it was a strange and wondrous thing to see that at 19 hours not only was the church full but even its porticoes, and the way the stands were set up, one could believe that there might have been about 15 thousand persons there [at] the renunciation of both until a half hour of the night and they were condemned to Prison for five years with the reservation, however, from the abovementioned tribunal that [it] could diminish their sentence as in fact happened, as after serving two years they were reprieved and subsequently set free.

They left Rome immediately and went to Bordeaux in France where they remained for a period of two years and from there passed into Tuscany to Livorno, during which time Leocadia gave birth to a son, and there they lived happily. But the demon that had never left the possession of those unhappy souls, confirming in them their original conviction even though they had demonstrated repentance of their failings by their abjuration, caused Ferdinando to have his son circumcised;[7] this he followed with the intention to go to Venice and live more at ease amongst the Jews in that city.

However, having come to the attention of the Holy Inquisition of Pisa, which was quickly advised of what had happened, the most rigorous trial was held in which the recent circumcision having been verified, notice was given of this fact to the General Inquisition of Rome by whom the Guilty were brought to this city and the crime having been confirmed through the Accumulation of trials, they were turned over to the Governor with the protests of the lay-sister the Woman was forgiven by the Compassion of our Lord and returned to the Prison of the Holy Office, and Ferdinando her husband in that of Curte Savella[8] to then condemn him to death as he deserved. As the execution of the sentence approached the brothers of the Confraternity of Mercy went to the prison the night of the 13th March of the year 1643 to entreat him to die well.

When the guilty condemned man heard the grim news of his Death, he began to give to the Brothers signs of his damnation, twisting his shoulders and flying about as if possessed, not wanting to hear or to answer the good and loving persuasion of those Brothers; it was therefore considered wise to call in other clerics, even those of his own people, who labored with the greatest effort to bring him to repentance, but with no result at all; and to the latter he answered that he had no need of their words and said that if he had to die he wanted to die as a Jew and they should not try to persuade him to the contrary. Monsignor Giovanni Battista Spada[9] the Governor of Rome was immediately informed of the obstinate and perverse will of this man and so as the executor of the orders [he considered] whether it was more opportune to save that soul if it were possible or to punish him with the most rigorous penalty; then the Monsignor sent his delegate named Alessandro Argoli to confer with the delegate of the Holy Office to judge whether to burn him alive as unrepentant and promulgate his death; and gathering together by order of the Monsignor those counselors of the Holy Office who were in the palace with the above-mentioned Argoli, they decided that if he did not come to an open declaration to want to submit to the true faith they must dispense the most rigorous punishment as unrepentant, and [he] must be burned alive because he had publicly abjured his past error, and this sometimes sufficed for the guilty in similar cases to delay Death when they found themselves in such ordeals.

Accordingly the brothers of the Confraternity continued to assist him to prepare for death until he had reached the gallows; the Guilty man said in a loud voice these precise words: "I die and I will die willingly in the law of Moses." These words having been heard by the spectators, Argoli reluctantly gave the order for him to be burned alive but the unhappy and obstinate victim, when he grasped that sentence, wanted to anticipate the work of the executioner to hasten his Death, and having been placed upon a stool to tie him to a beam from which was attached the hood that he had around his neck, he gave a kick to the stool until he was miserably hung without the aid of the executioner, to the great terror of the bystanders by whom a fire was ignited around him.

The cadaver then was burned in the piazza of Campo di Fiore and the ashes thrown into the Tiber.

The End

NOTES

1. The manuscript is bound in the Sala Manoscritti, Urb. Lat. 1704 (x. xviii), 212 verso and recto. The volume contains a census and accounts of crimes and natural disasters in both print and manuscript. There is some confusion over the date. Ludwig Freihen von Pastor, *The History of the Popes*, vol. 19: *Gregory XV and Urban VIII*, translated by Dom Ernest Graf (London: Kegan Paul, 1938), p. 39, gives the date of the execution as 1640 and corrects an earlier source (Franz Heinrich Reusch, *Die Selbstbiographie des cardinals Bellarmin* [Bonn: P. Neusser, 1887]) in a footnote as having mistakenly given the date as 1643. Some of the numbering in the manuscript could be either. If the years of the case are added up, the execution may well have been in 1643, but this also depends on the reading of one or two instances of di/dui/tri (two/three). Cecil Roth, *A History of the Marranos* (Philadelphia: Jewish Publication Society of America, 1932), dates the case in 1640; Abraham Berliner, *Storia degli Ebrei di Roma: dall'antichità allo smantellamento del Ghetto* (Milano: Rusconi, 1992) (originally published in 1893 as *Geschichte der Juden in Rom von her altesten Zeit bis zur Gegenwart*), dates the case in 1643. One scholar may have been referring to the date of the abjuration, and the other to the date when the document was written.

2. Pastor, *History of the Popes*, p. 39. Pastor's footnote links the Vatican document to the judgment in Antonino Bertolotti, *Martiri del libero pensiero e vittime della Santa Inquisizione nei secoli XVI, XVII, e XVIII, Studi e ricerche negli archivi di Roma e di Mantova* (Rome: Tipografia della Martellate, 1891).

3. Bertolotti, *Martiri del libero pensiero*, pp. 123–126. The details in the judgment are quite different from those found in the Vatican document. For example, the condemned man is called Fernando; "Essendo tu Fernando figliolo di Giovanni Alvarez Porto, d'anni 80, stato indicato nel Sant'Offitio" (p. 123). The subject of Bertolotti's account had been tried before: "che alter volte fossi stato per il medesimo delitto di giudaismo processato nel Sant'Offitio di Coimbra e condennato fosti quivi carcerato" (p. 123). To further obscure the identification, the subject himself apparently attempted to deny his true identity: "e giuditialmente esaminato negasti il tuo nome proprio e dicesti esser veramente hebreo nato in Amsterdam e chiamarti Abram etc." (pp. 123–124).

4. Berliner, *Storia degli Ebrei*, p. 246. Berliner summarizes the case of "Abraham Del Porto, che . . . nella primavera del 1640 fu condannato al rogo in Roma." Immediately following (p. 247), he gives a fairly lengthy summary of the case of "i portoghesi Fernando Alvarez e la moglie Leocadia"; that is, he separates one case into two.

5. Roth, *A History of the Marranos*, p. 391 n. 6. Roth says, in part, "Thus in 1640 Fernando Alvarez, alias Abraham da Porto, was martyred at Rome." The name "Abraham da Porto" is never mentioned in the Vatican document. Roth, following Pastor, has conflated the two cases, cited one after another by Berliner, that of da Porto in Livorno and that of Alvarez in Rome, and made them the same person.

6. "Alvarez," in *Encyclopedia Judaica*, vol. 2 (Jerusalem: Macmillan, 1972), p. 796; "Inquisition, Papal States," ibid., vol. 8, p. 1400. The latter entry states that "in 1640, Ferdinando Alvarez alias Abraham da Porto, an old man of 76, was burned at the stake." Again, the document in the Vatican Library does not show him as an old man at the time of his death. That detail comes from the judgment cited in Bertolotti.

7. In Bertolotti's account of the judgment, *Martiri del libero pensiero*, Ferdinando ("Fernando") also has himself circumcised: "Che perseverando in questa perfidia andasti a Livorno, ove per mostrarti veramente hebreo ti eri fatto circoncidere in compagnia d'un tuo figliolo per passartene poi unitamente con la moglie e figli fra gli hebrei di Venetia" (p. 124).

8. I am grateful to Professor Michele Luzzati for this identification. The Corte Savella prison was closed later in the century by Pope Innocent X.

9. In his summary of the story, Berliner, *Storia*, p. 247, gives the name of the governor of Rome, which I transcribe as Spada, as "Spinola." Pastor, *History of the Popes*, vol. 29, p. 34 n. 6, gives the name of a Cardinal Spada as a member of the Holy Office under Urban VIII, from an *avviso* of 1624; and p. 38 n. 1 says, in part, "In 1640, Spada, the governor of Rome, came upon traces of a plot for poisoning Urban VIII."

10

Giovanni Di Giovanni: Chronicler of the Jews of Sicily

Salvatore G. Rotella

Persecution, then, gives rise to a peculiar technique of writing . . . in which the truth about all crucial things is presented exclusively between the lines. That literature is addressed, not to all readers, but to trustworthy and intelligent readers only. . . . It has all the advantages of public communication without having its greatest disadvantage—capital punishment for the author. . . . Therefore an author who wishes to address only thoughtful men has to write in such a way that only a very careful reader can detect the meaning of his book.

—Strauss, *Persecution and the Art of Writing*[1]

This chapter is based on a close analysis of Giovanni Di Giovanni's *L'Ebraismo della Sicilia*.[2] Its purpose is to present some of the highlights of the volume and to suggest a thesis that is just the opposite of the conclusion of previous readers who have dismissed Di Giovanni as a zealous, often wrong, priest carried away with his own biases.[3] On close reading one may argue that there may be more than one way to interpret the text, that under the clamor of the biases there is information that, given the time in which the text was written, could not be passed on in any other safe way.

L'Ebraismo della Sicilia was published 256 years after the expulsion of all the Jews from Sicily. This was the last formal step in making the island a homogenized Christian domain for the kings of Spain and for the many island Catholics who could not coexist with any other religion. The physical expulsion was followed by a process that aimed at eliminating any evidence of the presence of the Jews in Sicily, to the point that in Sicily, as in many parts of southern Italy, in the parlance of the common people "Christian" has come to signify human being. No victory could have been more complete symbolically, but, in fact, Sicily is hardly a paragon of Christian piety or of religious practice.

Di Giovanni's *L'Ebraismo* was the first and, to this day, perhaps the only extensive treatise devoted entirely to the story of the Sicilian Jews: how they came to the island, how they lived on it, and eventually, how they disappeared from it. The author tells the reader that he wants to base the truth of his work on incontrovertible facts and not on the hearsay and tales that abound about the subject matter. He also cites some of the documents that have come to constitute the Diplomatic Code of Sicily.

In the mid-1700s, the Inquisition was still present and active in Sicily. In the author's lifetime there had been auto-da-fés and burnings in Palermo. Di Giovanni, a prosecutor in the Inquisition, is, as his name denotes, of Jewish descent, hence, always suspect. As a trained priest and of some rank, he has had much opportunity to study the Jews and his own history. All vestiges of Judaism are fast disappearing from the island. It may not be too far-fetched to suggest that as a descendant from the Jews and as a practicing historian, he is caught between his ancestry and the reality within which he lives. The best service that he can render to his heritage is to keep alive the memory of the Jews so that their history is not hopelessly lost. A treatise on the Jews, however, would be suspect coming from someone so closely connected with the Inquisition. People feared the Inquisition. Why not, then, in the attempt to keep alive what is known about the Jews of Sicily, their faith, and their culture, cast his work in the most orthodox party line and provide posterity with a clear map of the truth to be found by the discerning reader and to be used at a more appropriate time? His fastidiousness to identify the many places where the Jews had lived stands out in contrast to the avowed goal of the Inquisition to cleanse Sicily of all traces of Judaism. In the same manner, his unasked-for justification for undertaking and publishing the work is a further attempt to protect himself from his superiors and his subordinates in the Inquisition.

There are two parts to Di Giovanni's volume. The first, comprising twenty-one chapters, is devoted to the story of the Jews of Sicily as one people. The second, comprising twenty-eight chapters, deals with each of fifty-seven communities of the island in which Jews were present. The dedication, a note to the reader, and the story of a fifty-eighth community discovered after the book had been given to the printer complete the volume. Part two, the story of the individual communities, is not examined in this chapter.

Di Giovanni, in the note to the reader, explains how he came to write the book. It is not the result of fancy. Its purpose is to complement the general histories of the Jews published by two other authors, both of them non-Sicilians, who either did not know about the Jews of Sicily or simply chose to ignore them.[4] As such, the first part of *L'Ebraismo* complements the universal history of the Jews. The author hopes that it may please and be of use to foreigners as well as Sicilians. The second part, instead, should be considered a "supplement to the history of Sicily"; as such, it should be "pleasing and of value to our compatriots more than to foreigners" (p. x).

Intellectually, Di Giovanni is aware that history in the eighteenth century is central to the concerns of society and that the future is dependent on the verifiable knowledge of the past. Much is lost because of time or the carelessness of human beings, but whatever record can be pieced together, Di Giovanni sustains, has intrinsic value: "An historian must save diligently those ancient records that he has managed to find and must not worry about the rest, those that, through none of his fault, have gotten lost." Even if incomplete, his history of the Jews of Sicily has value for those who "rightfully love antiquity." It brings forth a "collection of records before unknown" (p. xi).

He also makes an extraordinary effort to leave no doubt that he is in line with the popular beliefs that prevailed at his time among average Catholics about the Jews, the accursed nation, the perpetrators of all sorts of evil against other religions, and, above all, the seducers of Christians to convert them to their religion through the most awful ritual, circumcision. Party line and factual information can be kept separate by the attentive reader. One can also discern the transition from bias and fantasy, to facts, from invention, to history. The author can indulge in fantasy and bias and then, all at once, turn, as with the wave of the hand—or better, of the phrase—to verifiable truths. Speaking of the arrival of the Jews in Sicily, for instance, he recounts what can amount to a lot of hearsay but eventually moves on to the more factual: "Be that [the many stories that have been told about the first arrival of the Jews in Sicily] as one may want it, there is no doubt that the Jews have been in Sicily since the early centuries of our Religion" (p. 5).

The dedicatory statement of the book deserves careful attention. The fiscal inquisitor dedicates the work to Monsignor Bonanno, his superior, the bishop of the city of Patti, whose responsibility as Inquisitor General of the Holy Office, first deputy of the Kingdom of Sicily, and so on, is to keep the Catholic faith free of theological and practical error. Di Giovanni lists first five reasons that have *not* prompted him to dedicate his work to Bonanno. These five reasons, however, may be more important than the reason that he *is* dedicating the book to his bishop. Two are relevant to our discussion. The first one is "the illustrious clarity of blood which deriving from a high and limpid spring, even after many centuries, still flows in all its vigor in your veins." Di Giovanni, the descendant from the Jews of Sicily, addresses Bonanno, who does not have such a stain in his blood. The other is the goodness and prudence with which the monsignor has performed his duties; he has further ennobled the family from which he descends (once again the reference to family origin, pp. iii–vi).

L'Ebraismo, instead, is dedicated to Bonanno because its subject matter is the very essence of the monsignor's ministry. He must "maintain pure and free from any error . . . in this entire kingdom, the true cult of God's Church." To prove his adherence to the orthodoxy of common belief, Di Giovanni closes with the assertion that "Christianity has not had . . . a sect so contrary from which it must always guard itself as that of the blind, haughty and most obstinate nation of the Jews" (p. vii).

AN ANALYSIS OF *L'EBRAISMO*

For the purpose of analysis the twenty-eight chapters that make up Part One of *L'Ebraismo* can be divided up into seven sections: (1) when and how the Jews came to Sicily and their number on the island; (2) everyday life of the Jews of

Sicily; (3) the faith of the Jews of Sicily, their rights and privileges; (4) organization of the Jewish communities; (5) religious institutions of the communities; (6) conflicts between Jews and Christians; and (7) expulsion of the Jews from Sicily and aftermath.

From Common Belief to Historical Fact

There is a pattern in the structure and development of the work. Several chapters, almost as if to appease the Inquisition, open with a general categorical statement unrequired and unsupported by true historical analysis, the kind of statement that the Church has fed to the masses in its historical effort to "forcefully Christianize" the island.

Section one opens with the generalization that the Jews were so impious and behaved so badly that "they fell from the heart of God. The honorable title of God's chosen people was replaced by . . . [that of] the accursed nation" (p. 1). In section three, dealing with the question whether Jews could aspire to be judges, the assertion is made that "it is not right to give the dignity of such office to the Jews . . . as killers of God they have fallen in infamy." The Jew is taught to oppress the Christian; he learns from the Talmud that "if a Jew and a *goy* [Christian] appear in front of you in judgment if you can absolve and favor the Jew by following the Jewish law, absolve him, and tell the *goy*, that this is the way we judge. If you can absolve the Jew using the law of the *goyim* [of the Christian] absolve him and tell the *goy*, that this is ordered by your law. If you cannot absolve him using any of the two, resort to hairsplitting argumentations (*cavilli*)." The sixth section, in particular the discussion on usury, opens with the statement that the Jews believe that usury is "actually ordered by God" (p. 89). The final section, devoted to tensions between Jews and Christians and the expulsion, opens with the story of Torquemada, who breaks into the royal chambers in which representatives of the Jews were attempting to convince the king to revoke the edict of expulsion and shouts, "It was not enough that Christ was once bought by the Jews for thirty pieces of silver" (p. 195). There is also a statement in the same section that the people were so happy in Sicily after the Jews were gone that some started recounting the years, beginning with the year of the expulsion as "year one."

But then the author clearly sets aside the generalizations and passes on to recorded and verifiable facts. In Part One, he says that perhaps the notion of the Jews as the "fallen race" may belong more to a general history and that all he wants to accomplish in his work is to "let people know about the origin of the Jews in Sicily." The Jews could not be judges; however, they could practice medicine on Christians, in spite of the legal proscription. After a fantastic discourse as to whether death comes from the inside or the outside of the body and whether the physician, like the Angel of Death, causes the corruption of the body or the body becomes corrupt from inside out and whether after this corruption the soul departs from it, Di Giovanni concludes that the law against Jewish physicians' practicing on Christians was observed more in the breach; in fact, King Alfonso, who used the services of a Jewish physician, Bonavoglia da Messina, in 1450 regularized what was going on with an edict. Even the Dominican Fathers in 1489 received official dispensation to be treated by Jews.

Creating Doubt

Intentionally or not, there are segments of *L'Ebraismo* that, upon careful reading, could create doubt in the mind of the reader as to the true message of this text. Three examples should suffice to make the point. The first example may just be an oversight, but it is too obvious for the reader not to notice it. Early in *L'Ebraismo*, referring to the practice of the Sicilian Jews who called their synagogues *meschitas* (mosques), Di Giovanni states that this was something engineered on purpose by the Jews. During the time of the Saracens, the Jews, "clever and crafty," started referring to their place of worship as mosques instead of synagogues to escape attention and to place themselves at the same level as the rulers of the island. In the latter part of the book, in discussing the religious institutions of the Jews, Di Giovanni addresses frontally the reason that the Jews came to use the word *meschita*. This time there is no reference to "cleverness or craftiness of the Jews" but basically a very sound observation about the nature of the language spoken by the Sicilians. A reference is made first to the Saracen period, when there must have been quite an influx of Jews into the island, a time, also, when there was an expansion of Jews into smaller cities and the establishment of new communities, hence of new synagogues, "and they were referred to generally with the common name of *meschitas* (mosques)." In this the Sicilian Jews "were conforming to the manners of the Saracens, the rulers of Sicily," who referred to their places of worship as mosques. The Jews kept the name even after the expulsion of the Saracens from the island "in the same manner that the Christians in that same kingdom kept hundreds, if not thousands, of Saracen words. And here I must let the reader know that the Sicilian language is not a dialect by itself, but is a mix of Barbarian, Greek, Latin, Saracen, Norman, German, Provencal and Spanish words. Each nation that took turn in governing of the island left its own words" (p. 140).

Another doubt may be created in the mind of the reader by the second example, devoted to the discussion of almsgiving in the Jewish religion. Almsgiving is, in essence, a material manifestation of the virtue of charity, and charity supposedly is the Christian virtue par excellence. Here Di Giovanni shows open admiration for the Jews. "With the same sincerity that elsewhere we have discussed the evildoing of the Jews, we must admit that there was in them a love for each other. To live honestly, each individual had to make sure that he gave to others. Poor people and beggars were much more difficult to find among them than among us" (p. 133).

The third example has to do with the question of when the Jews came to Sicily. This seems to be quite important and intriguing for Di Giovanni. Why is it significant to know when they came? The offhand answer seems to be for the use of the Inquisition. We need to know, he maintains, because the longer they have been on the island, the longer has been the suffering of our "forefathers. . . . whose natural inclination was to detest the Jews."

Historically, the presence of the Jews in Sicily is attested by Philo, "credible writer," and by Josephus, "ocular witness." The fact that both of them were Jews is not mentioned by the author; they are historians. Pompey and Titus are mentioned next; both of them caused the dispersal of the Jews into the world. It is hard to prove for lack of "authentic writings" that the Jews came into Sicily because of the Diaspora. It is more likely that they came and kept on coming because Sicily is the largest island in the Mediterranean, and they simply chanced to land on it. "Be that as it may," Di Giovanni concludes that the Jews had been in Sicily for a long time. He even says that they were already there by early Christianity, as attested by the writings of Saint Gregory. Given the "natural disposition" of the forefathers, the issue of the presence of the Jews before the Diaspora is critical. With the birth of Christ, the Messiah, that orthodox Christianity turns the "chosen People" into the "accursed race." If the Jews were in Sicily before all this, as Di Giovanni seems to imply, they could be no problem for the "forefathers." They were just another one of the many different groups living on the island.

Usury and the Real Reason That the Jews Became Evil

In spite of all the other evil things that the Jews were accused of, usury, in a proper reading of *L'Ebraismo*, seems to be the core reason for their fall from grace and ultimate expulsion. A proper reading, however, seems to make the political rulers, the kings—and the Jews were historically the wards of the crown—the real culprits for turning the Jews into evil. Ultimately, in Di Giovanni's treatment of the Jews of Sicily, between usury and the expulsion there is a cause-and-effect relationship. Early Christianity forbade usury, the making of money on money. Since making money on money is also the essence of credit, a very valuable economic institution, the Jews were generally used as moneylenders. The Jews, "interpreting wrongly Divine Scripture, claim that usury is not only tolerated by, but actually ordered by God" (p. 158). How this is so Di Giovanni does not explain, but, with the usual turn of the phrase, he continues "Let's skip to an examination of what use the Jews of Sicily made of it [usury]. Mainly, because the *history* of *our* [emphasis added] ancient Jews may serve . . . as a clear disapproval of the error in which live the Jews of today who believe that usury is licit" (pp. 158–159). This is a very puzzling statement. First note that history disproves belief. On the surface it suggests also that it is not *our* Jews, but the Jews of today, who are not in Sicily and are not Sicilian, who are wrong.

But Di Giovanni wants us to examine the record, the history. Frederick II issued the first edict that permitted the Jews to engage in usury, but he imposed a limit of 10% interest. The Jews of Syracuse, however, on 9 May 1363 resolved, against the better judgment of the king, not to engage in usury. The Jews of Catania, on the other hand, paid no attention to the 10% limit and eventually incurred the wrath of the Crown, which decided to punish them severely, but in 1406 the Jews appealed to King Martin, feigned repentance for their sins, offered him a gift of money, and were forgiven.

Soon the practice of charging excessive interest became widespread to the point that in some places it reached 100%. If and when punished, the Jews would bribe the Crown and would continue in their evil way. It is no wonder, claims the author, that King Ferdinand made usury one of the reasons for the expulsion. Ferdinand is a different kind of king: "The greed and the dishonest behavior of the Jews had gotten so out of hand that all the wealth of the Christians would have been insufficient to satisfy the voracious avarice of that insatiable nation" (p. 162).

King Alfonso, Di Giovanni continues, did his best to cure the "diseased Judaism," not Judaism per se but the diseased part of it. On 20 December 1449 Messer Giacomo Sciarch was appointed by an apostolic edict to an office to control this evil practice of the Jews. King Alfonso confirmed the appointment with a royal edict on 11 February 1450. However, in less than one year, on 9 July 1450, the office was abolished. As usual, the Jews went to the Crown and with a gift of 10,000 florins bought the right to continue their evil practice unsupervised.

The Crown, then, is at the heart of the evil ways of the Jews. To get around the firm position of the church, the Crown, starting with Frederick II, used the Jews by giving them permission to lend money. Without control, greed sets in, and interest goes up to whatever level the borrower is willing or forced to pay. Apostolic power, Di Giovanni seems to suggest, understood well this process and appointed the Reverend Messer Giacomo Sciarch to keep the evil practice under control, but the greed of the kings undid it all. Only a king different from the others, Ferdinand, the avowed defender of the Catholic faith, can do the right thing. But the process of evil has reached the point of no return; he has no choice but to resort to the final solution, banishing all the Jews from his domain.

Expulsion as Inevitable: History, Facts, Fantasy

For Di Giovanni, the chronicle of the Jews of Sicily unfolds ultimately as a Greek tragedy. Certainly, that is the case with usury, but that story is told in historical terms, as evidenced by the precise account with dates and specificity as to how much it took each time to bribe the king. A similar dialectic of necessity and denouement seems to evolve also in other aspects of the story of the Jews of Sicily. The many popular stories involving the Jews develop according to a paradigm that goes from belief, to fantastic events, and ultimately to excess and from excess, to the "final solution." Excess justifies also the continuous vigilance over those who have "mended their ways" and changed, that is, converted. The "neophytes," as Di Giovanni called the converts, occupy a special place in the heart of our author.

The excess in practicing evil leads to the downfall of the Jews. Two stories are recounted to illustrate this point. They are stories that scare and, because they scare, can persuade the masses. These are not history; whatever incontrovertible facts exist in them are irrelevant to the thrust of the account. The first story, which dates but one year before the expulsion, may have actually happened, but the logic is faulty, and the motives attached to characters are, at best, fantastic. The second, which supposedly dates back to 1347, through the years has definitely taken on fantastic connotations; the factual record is a plaque that confirms the fantasy.

In 1491 in the city of Castiglione, the crucifix was being taken in procession through the streets of the town. As the procession passed the house of Bitone, a "high priest of the Jews," a stone thrown from one of the windows of the house hit the crucifix and broke the arm of the Christ. The irate Christians went into the house and pulled Bitone out, and two brothers, Andrea and Bartolomeo Crisi, killed him on the spot. Nowhere does Di Giovanni say unequivocally that Bitone had been seen throwing the stone. The two brothers eventually took themselves to see the king and were absolved of their act; in fact, they were praised for their summary justice. All they asked of the king was that he ban the Jews from Sicily. The year being 1491, one cannot help realize, if one believes in stories, the direct connection between the request of the brothers and the edict of 1492 (p. 175).

In the second story, a young boy in Messina every day on his way to the market had to pass by the ghetto. The boy was used to singing holy hymns, including the "Salve Regina," in honor of the Virgin. The Jews, annoyed by the songs of the *chechez* (the Jewish term for a Christian boy, which actually means animal or dirty thing), several times did their best to scare him. Unafraid because of his strong religious faith, the boy continued with his hymns. One night, however, on Good Friday, the Jews caught him and "tormented, flagellated, and crucified him," in the same manner as their ancestors had done to Jesus. To hide the body, the Jews threw it into a well but, by "divine intervention," the water of the well turned into blood and boiled over into the public square. The perpetrators were caught and executed; their heads were impaled on poles and left in the place of the crime. The horrible event was marked with an inscription on a marble plaque erected at the place of the murder that read: "Segnum Perfidorum Judeorum" (as a sign of the perfidy of the Jews). After the expulsion of the Jews, that marble plaque was placed on the facade of the Duomo. "We saw it (the marble) with our own eyes," concludes Di Giovanni, and he explains further that, according to a certain Placido Samperi, though the events had taken place long before, their memory remained so vivid that Ferdinand had them in his mind when he issued the edict of 1492. Di Giovanni wrote, "[F]or this then, and the other many evil deeds, were the Jews thrown out of this kingdom by Ferdinand King of Sicily called the Catholic" (pp. 176–178).

The temporal expulsion is but a prelude to the spiritual cleansing. Hence it is not the rejoicing over conversion but the concern with conversion that justifies the activity of the Inquisition for centuries. With historical perspective, Di Giovanni informs us that the fathers of the church maintained that true conversion must be voluntary and from within the individual, like a process of continuous purification, while forced conversion "deforms and stains" religion. The "neophites" are, on one hand, cause for rejoicing, as the number of Christians is increased; on the other hand, they are the cause of concern, as they may have not embraced the faith out of conviction but to hold on to their property and to remain on the island. Di Giovanni shows that there had always been in Sicily a kind and accepting attitude toward true converts. In fact, Saint Gregory had even seen the value of inducing conversion through temporal gain. He reduced the taxes for those Jews who worked the land of the Church, hoping to see them turn to Christianity, ordered that these converts be baptized during the Easter period, when the sacrament is not normally administered, and gave, free of charge, appropriate clothing for the baptism.

"We have other records from the years after, which clearly indicate that in Sicily there has always been respect for the Jews who have converted to our holy faith." Hence, after the edict of expulsion, the clergy of the island did their best to encourage conversions. Torquemada, in Spain, recommended that the Jews should not be encouraged to convert in order to avoid the edict; however, if there was evidence of a true desire to embrace Christianity, then every assistance should be made available to them. In the presence of true faith, there is no harm in reminding the Jews that they would be exempt from expulsion and could hold on to their property. Di Giovanni seems to suggest that even in this potentially happy situation, the good sense of the Church is countermanded by the temporal concerns of the Crown. The promise of the Church to the "neophites" of Sicily that they could stay on the island and hold on to property was countermanded by an order of the king. The converts could stay on the island, but as to property, they had to give 40% to the Crown and 5% to those deputies who oversaw the dispersion of all Jewish property.

CONCLUSION

What is the true purpose of Di Giovanni's L'Ebraismo? Is it, as some contend, the work of a prejudiced canon that can be easily dismissed? Our analysis raises some questions about such a simplistic conclusion. There is not enough evidence to conclude that it is the work of a crypto-Jew or that the key has been found to the way that the information was scrambled so that eventually one could read the book in a manner that would show unequivocally that the author is not prejudiced, if not outright anti-Semitic. Attentive reading, however, as attempted in this chapter, can create enough doubt and raise the possibility that in L'Ebraismo there is an inner voice that wants to suggest something that would be too dangerous to state openly and in a direct manner.

Further research is needed to find out if the book has an open structure and a hidden one that can change its tone. However, there is no doubt that several segments of the volume, especially the entire part on the governance of the Jewish communities in Sicily as well as the one on religious institutions, if lifted out of context, give a factual and informative account, free, or somewhat free, of the annoying repetition of the many tales that amount to no more than gratuitous bashing of the Jews, their religion, and their culture. Especially descriptive and quite informative is also the section describing Jewish holy days and rituals, including the observance of the Sabbath, Passover, Purim, the Feast of the Tabernacles, and the manner in which the occurrence of each holy day must be calculated; for instance, the Feast of Expiation "is to be celebrated on the tenth day of the seventh holy month, i.e. on the seventh day of the first month of the civil year." Like the description of the special garments that the Jews were expected to wear, from the most conservative ones prescribed by Mosaic law, to the Taled, to the Arbanqcanfot, in this section there is also a long description of the distinctive sign to be worn by the Jews imposed originally in 1366, the *Rotella rossa*.

There are too many inconsistencies in *L'Ebraismo* not to detect something of a pattern through which the author seems to *show* the reader what to take seriously and what to dismiss; or could it be that Di Giovanni, a prejudiced and good servant of the Inquisition, by truly attempting to be a historian, is caught between the fantasy of the common prejudices about the Jews and the incontrovertible facts that he has discovered in the course of his research and his thinking about the subject matter? Is he basically caught between the beliefs that the Church has used to Christianize Sicily and the rational approach that is implicit in being an historian?

Who does Di Giovanni prefer as a source and as a model in the treatment of the Jews? Unquestionably, it is Saint Gregory, the source that provided Di Giovanni with many incontrovertible facts about the Jews in the earlier history of Sicily. Di Giovanni gives a sober and balanced judgment about Saint Gregory's disposition toward the Jews: "As he [Gregory] did not want the Jews to be interfered with by the Christians; so he did not have patience with the Jews interfering with the Christians. In this the Great Doctor of the Church *is superior to the other saints*" [emphasis added]. Jews as well as Christians, he maintains, "venerate the saint because of his sweetness and clemency" (p. 16).

If fact is separated from common belief, and history from fantasy, the image that one ultimately gets of the Sicilian Jews from Di Giovanni's volume is of a group of inhabitants on the island who put up with much abuse, especially from the Christian religious fanatics who treated them as the "killers of their Christ." The Jews, when necessary, resorted to accommodation and compromise but never gave in when their religious principles and cultural values were attacked. Of the many groups that have inhabited the island, from the Barbarians, to the Greeks, the Latins, the Moors, the Normans, and the Sikelians themselves, none were able to withstand the impetus of the fierce process of homogenization undertaken by the Catholic Church. Only the Jews stood up to it and attempted to carve a niche in the society for themselves so that they could coexist but at the same time remain true to their own religion, until the kings of Spain and the Church joined in common cause and imposed the "final solution": expulsion or conversion.

NOTES

1. Leo Strauss, *Persecution and the Art of Writing* (Chicago: University of Chicago Press, 1988), p. 25.

2. Giovanni Di Giovanni, *L'Ebraismo della Sicilia, Ricercato ed Esposto dal Canonico Giovanni Di Giovanni, Inquisitore Fiscale della Suprema Inquisizione di Sicilia* (The Hebraism of Sicily, Researched and Exposed by the Canon Giovanni Di Giovanni, Fiscal Inquisitor of the Supreme Inquisition of Sicily), (Palermo: n.p. 1748).

3. Two interpretations along these lines are Isidoro La Lumia, *Storie Siciliane*, 4 vols. (Palermo: Edizioni della Regione Siciliana, 1969); B. Lagumina and G. Lagumina, eds., *Codice Diplomatico dei Giudei di Sicilia* (Palermo: Amenta, 1884). For La Lumia, the work, being by an Inquisitore Fiscale, cannot be trusted: "He is not a man of large and liberal views." Lagumina speaks of "some mistakes of Di Giovanni . . . and the lack of and limited use of documents" (p. vi). "Some documents are simply alluded to, or as is more generally

the case, were not understood, or understood poorly, or adulterated" (p. vii).

4. The authors referred to are Henry Basnage de Beauval, *Histoire des juifs, depuis Jesus Christ jusqu'a present* (Paris: Louis Roulland, 1710); Humphrey Prideaux, *Histoire des juifs et des peuples voisins* (Amsterdam: Henry de Sauzet, 1722).

Part III

LITERATURE, ART, AND IDENTITY

11

Judeo-Italian: Italian Dialect or Jewish Language?

George Jochnowitz

Judeo-Italian: Italian dialect or Jewish language? The answer is both, of course. Judeo-Italian is an Italian dialect or, rather, a group of Italian dialects, varying from one part of Italy to another but containing a number of words of Hebrew origin and a few lexical items from other sources. Most of the vocabulary is Italian; most of the grammatical rules may be found somewhere in the complex system of Italian dialects. Judeo-Italian is also a Jewish language, like Yiddish, Ladino, and Judeo-Persian. It was written in the Hebrew alphabet for most of its history. As in all Jewish languages, words for items connected in some way with religion come from Hebrew. According to the orthographic system used by Bene Kedem,[1] following Italian orthographic practices but with the addition of *ch* for the voiceless velar fricative and "for the velar nasal consonant, we find *sciabad* or *sciabadde* 'sabbath,' *chadan* 'groom,' *cala* 'bride,' *ta'anid* 'fast day,' all of which have analogs in Yiddish, using the standard YIVO transcription system: (*shabes, khosn, kale, tones*). The Judeo-Italian word for synagogue is *scola*, generally distinguished from *scuola* "school," just as Standard Yiddish distinguishes *shil*, "synagogue," from *shul*, "school." (Many, perhaps most, Yiddish dialects do not make this distinction.) In the United States, a new distinction has arisen in the English of East European Jews: *shul* and not *shil* is "synagogue," which is distinguished from school, simply the English word.

What is the difference between a language and a dialect? Max Weinreich is reported to have said that a language is a dialect with an army and a navy. If so, Judeo-Italian does not qualify. Neither do Yiddish and Ladino, for that matter. Perhaps Max Weinreich contradicted himself in his book *History of the Yiddish Language*. Writing of Judeo-Greek, which he preferred to call "Yavanic," he said that it was "a fusion language, the stock of which was mostly Greek, but in which the 'mistakes' vis-à-vis standard Greek are systematized, and it is therefore necessary to speak of a separate language of Jews, however similar to Greek."[2]

Ladino and Yiddish are considered languages rather than dialects because they have been separated, by and large, from Spanish and German and have evolved in separate directions. They were written in the Hebrew alphabet for most of their history, although Ladino has generally used the Latin alphabet since Mustafa Kemal Ataturk switched both Turkish and Ladino from the Arabic and Hebrew alphabets, respectively, to Latin script early in the twentieth century. Judeo-Italian shares with Yiddish and Ladino the fact that it was written in Hebrew characters until the twentieth century. It has produced a literature of its own.

Unlike Yiddish and Ladino, however, Judeo-Italian has never lost contact with the language that provided most of its vocabulary and most of its grammar. It is not simply a variant of Italian with a few borrowed words. It is a family of dialects, none of which quite coincide with the local dialects of Italian. In Roman dialect, for example, the masculine singular definite article is *er*. In Judeo-Roman, it is *o*, a form found in various parts of southern Italy but not itself Roman. It is often said that any local Judeo-Italian dialect corresponds to the Italian dialect of somewhere south of where it is spoken. The only problem is we can never locate the "somewhere." Different phonetic and grammatical features that are found together in the same Judeo-Italian dialect are not found together in other Italian dialects. Furthermore, there are sounds that are decidedly non-Italian: an initial velar nasal consonant, for example, in *ainare*, "to look at," and a voiceless velar fricative that can occur in consonant clusters, for example, *sciachtare*, "to slaughter according to Jewish ritual." The gap between Jewish and local dialects is most striking in Lombardy and Emilia-Romagna. Judeo-Mantuan and Judeo-Ferrarese have no front rounded vowels. In this respect, though certainly not in all respects, they are closer to central and southern Italian rather than to their northern neighbors. In Mantuan, as in many north Italian dialects, subject pronouns are reinforced; there is an unstressed form of the pronoun following the stressed form, for example, *mi a gh'eva, ti at gh'evi, lu al gheva*, "I was having, you were having, he was having," instead of the simple Judeo-Mantuan *mi gh'aveva, ti ghavevet, lu gh'ghaveva*.[3]

In Piedmont, on the other hand, front rounded vowels are heard in both Piedmontese and Judeo-Piedmontese pronunciation. Our written sources for Judeo-Italian fall into two categories: prayer books and translations of books of the Hebrew Bible, dating from the Middle Ages and Renaissance, written in Hebrew characters; and plays and poems of the twentieth century, spelled out in Latin characters following the spelling rules of Italian, with digraphs or diacritics used for sounds that do not occur in Italian. For example, Bene Kedem uses *ch* for the voiceless velar fricative and apostrophe (') for the velar nasal consonant, as already mentioned. Our twentieth-century works are self-conscious attempts to preserve dialects that are generally considered dead or dying. When Crescenzo Del Monte wrote in the 1920s, he was, among other things, trying to capture a language while it still could be done; when the theater group "Chaimme a sore 'o sediaro e 'a moje," an oddly titled organization whose name means 'Chaim, the sister, the chairmaker, and the wife,' writes and performs plays in Judeo-Roman today, it is doing the same thing Del Monte was doing seventy years ago. The contemporary works differ from the Renaissance texts in two significant ways: the alphabet and the absence of words of Hebrew origin in the old religious texts. The Renaissance books were translations from the Hebrew, and every word had to be translated. On the other hand, despite a gap of several centuries, all Judeo-Italian dialects lack a distinction between the masculine plural and feminine plural. Other grammatical and lexical similarities apparently survived for centuries. The word for "now" is *mo* not only in contemporary Judeo-Roman but in a prayer book published in Bologna in the sixteenth century. The third-person plural suffix *-eno* is another example of a grammatical feature relatively rare and localized in Italian but widespread in Judeo-Italian. In every Jewish language, words of Hebrew origin are sometimes combined with morphemes of other languages.

In Judeo-Roman, a male thief is *un ganavve*; a female thief is *una ganavessa*; the verb "to steal" is *ganavviare*, analogous to Yiddish *ganvenen*. Other times, morphemes of Hebrew origin are used as well, for example, Judeo-Roman *ganavimme* "thieves," Yiddish *ganovim*. In Yiddish, it is possible for a Hebrew suffix to be used with words that do not come from Hebrew; for example, the plural of *dokter*, "doctor," is *doktoyrim*. There was never a single name for the different varieties of Judeo-Italian. The Jews of Ferrara called their language *ghettaiolo*. I have never come across this name elsewhere. It is necessarily a word that postdates the establishment of the first ghetto, which happened in Venice in 1516. In Livorno the language was *bagito*, a word of unknown origin.

Judeo-Roman and Judeo-Piedmontese, which are quite different from each other, share a name: *Lashon Akodesh* in Piedmont, *Lescionacodesce* in Rome. This name, meaning "holy language" or "language of holiness," is traditionally used to refer to biblical Hebrew. The use of this term for a Jewish language reflects a somewhat startling semantic change. Although Jewish languages were used for prayer on occasion, the distinction between Hebrew and the local Jewish language was always one of great religious and cultural importance.

Although Yiddish and Ladino are almost certainly much younger languages than Judeo-Italian, Judeo-Italian has borrowed at least one word from each of them: *orsay*, "anniversary of a death," is from Yiddish *yortsayt*; *negro*, "wretched," is from Ladino. In Judeo-Italian, *negro* has nothing to do with people from Africa, nor does it mean "black," which is *nero*. In Ladino, similarly, *negro* means "wretched," not black, which is *prieto*, from Portuguese. The presence of a word meaning "wretched" brings us back to words meaning "thief" and "steal."

Judeo-Piedmontese *pegarie*, an offensive way of saying "to die, croak" is analogous to Yiddish *peygern*, with the same meaning and connotation.[4] The Hebrew component of the language is often used for things that one doesn't quite want to talk about. To get back to our question asked by the title, Judeo-Italian is a dialect or, rather, a group of dialects, of Italian. Most of its grammar, most of its phonology, and most of its vocabulary are Italian. Judeo-Italian is also a Jewish language. It resembles other Jewish languages in every detail, its use of the Hebrew alphabet for most of its history; its mixture of Hebrew and other (in this case, Italian) elements—often within the same word; the fact that its dialects have their own geographical patterns that do not agree with those of any other language; and its Hebrew component, including lexical items referring both to religious practice and to human foibles. There is no contradiction.

NOTES

1. Bene Kedem, "La Gnora Luna," *La Rassegna mensile di Israel* 6 (1932): 546–579.

2. Max Weinreich, *History of the Yiddish Language*, translated by Shlomo Noble (Chicago: University of Chicago Press, 1980), p. 62.

3. Giovanna Massariello Merzagora, *Giudeo-Italiano* (Pisa: Pacini, 1977), p. 28; see also Umberto Colorni, "La parlata degli ebrei mantovani," *La Rassegna mensile di Israel* 36 (1970): 70.

4. George Jochnowitz, "Religion and Taboo in Lason Akodesh (Judeo-Piedmontese)," *International Journal of the Sociology of Language* 30 (1981): 114.

12

The Culture of Italian Jews and Shakespeare's *The Merchant of Venice*

H. Wendell Howard

Commentaries on William Shakespeare's *The Merchant of Venice* abound, and almost all of them fall into one of two broad streams of critical approach. The first concerns itself with themes and allegory. The second emphasizes Shylock and the social issues of usury, legality, and ethics that he brings into focus. This latter thrust underlines the fact that even though the title suggests that the play's main character is Antonio, in truth Shylock is central to the drama. Because of this fact, "much legal effort has been spent in arguing the pros and cons of Shylock's case—most of it on the doubtful basis of modern English law."[1] Various other critics, still thinking largely in terms of England, argue that even though Shakespeare knew many details about Venice, in all probability he gathered them from hearsay over convivial cups.

Such speculation, surmise, and uncertainty stem from the fact that we know almost nothing about Shakespeare. He had no contemporary biographers; he left no personal account of his life. We have no Shakespeare letters, and we have no facts about what made him as careless of his fame as he appears to have been. Yet indefatigable scholarship concerning his time and his works has made him far less an enigma than he would otherwise have been. What is surprising in all this scholarship, particularly as it relates to *The Merchant of Venice*, is that it generally ignores the history and culture of the Jews in Italy, specifically in Venice.

Before we look at the ghetto in Venice to add to our understanding of Shakespeare's portrait of Shylock, we must first address the question of whether or not Shakespeare ever visited Italy. It is quite likely that Shakespeare was interested in making such a visit, for in his day Italy was the center of culture visited regularly by English men of science (Francis Bacon, for one), literature (Lyly, Munday, Nash, Greene, and Daniel, to name a few), and art (Inigo Jones, most notably). As for Venice specifically, as R. B. Parker notes in his edition of Jonson's *Volpone*, it was "the exemplar of wealth, sophistication, art, luxury, political cunning, and stringent government."[2] Furthermore, *Two Gentlemen of*

Verona, Romeo and Juliet, The Taming of the Shrew, Othello, and *The Tempest*, as well as *The Merchant of Venice*, attest to the great attraction that Italy had for Shakespeare as he created settings in Verona, Mantua, and Padua and drew characters from Milan and Naples.

Besides having the disposition to journey to Italy, he also had the opportunity. From the autumn of 1592 until the summer of 1593, all of the theaters of London were closed because of the plague that was raging in the capital. The Queen even ordered no plays for Christmas that season. Furthermore, the dramas of Italian scene that Shakespeare produced about 1596 have such definite local color and "such an abundance of details pointing to actual vision," as George Brandes says, "that it is hard to account for them otherwise than by assuming a visit on the poet's part to such cities as Verona, Venice, and Pisa."[3] For example, *The Merchant of Venice* is set in Belmont as well as Venice, and Portia's great house, Belmont, can easily be conceived of as one of the summer residences that the wealthy merchants maintained on the banks of the Brenta. Dolo, a town on the Brenta that had these residences, is twenty miles from Venice. Portia, speaking to Nerissa in the last line of act 3, scene 4, says that twenty miles is the distance that she must "measure" to reach the city. Then, when she sends a message to Padua by Balthasar, her servant, and instructs him to meet her at "the common ferry which trades to Venice" (act 3, scene 4), she is giving realistic, meaningful directions. In Shakespeare's time, there were no reliable guide books for travelers to use or for wishful travelers to read. In fact, as Michele Marrapodi observes, the vivid picture of Italy presented in the countless treatises, travel books, and travelers' reports in the English Renaissance "was often imaginary."[4] So the kinds of exact detail that we have just pointed out, as well as the scores of additional facts that other critics note, add weight to the probability that Shakespeare visited Italy. Karl Elze is one critic who argues vehemently and convincingly that Shakespeare visited Venice; thus, our examination of the ghetto of Venice to gain insight into Shakespeare's portrait of, and attitude toward, Shylock is not out of line.

Venice in the sixteenth century was a city of comparatively free and frequent intercourse between the Jews and the Christians, even though the two groups felt and demonstrated a deep hostility toward one another. The Christians had banned the Jews from "the arts and trades, from public office and military service, from the professions and from landowning."[5] They did, however, grant "charters"—the results of strained negotiations between the Jews and the Venetian municipal authorities—that gave the Jews a license to trade. Medieval Christian Europe, as the great rabbi and Talmudic commentator Rashi de Troyes makes clear, had prohibited general trade, so that trading in money became a matter of life and death. As early as the thirteenth century in Italy, money-lending at interest had become the strength and the power of the Jews, and by the time of the 1519 renewal of the Jewish charter in Venice, the Jews were as important as bankers, as Marin Sanudo says in his *Diarii*.[6]

We must observe here that, historically, Venetians distinguished three kinds of Jews: Levantine (eastern), Ponentine (western), and German. The Levantine Jews had lived and traded side by side with Venetians in the Venetian quarter of

Constantinople when Venice's power had been at its peak in Romania, that is, the domains of the Greek emperor that they thought of as the continuation of the Roman Empire. Some of the Levantine Jews had been given a kind of Venetian citizenship and were the ones who gave the name Giudecca to an island in Venice. These Jews ostensibly were limited by law to a year's residence in Venice, but in truth, great numbers of them settled, raised families, and engaged in trade there.[7] The Ponentine Jews, because the Venetian Board of Trade realized that their customs revenues would be greatly increased by the trade that the Jews would bring to the city, were given a contract that guaranteed their residence for ten years and their right to engage in international trade.[8]

The so-called German Jews, however—those who came to Venice primarily from other Italian cities—were a different story. They were the ones who were not entitled to participate in Venice's international trade and were the first Jews forced to act as pawnbrokers and lenders of money usuriously. These were the Jews who were as important as bankers in the fifteenth century because the Venetians, according to William Dean Howells, who cites Galliciolli's *Memorie Venete* as his source, enjoyed great wealth but engaged in profligate spending. Howells writes:

The ladies of that bright-colored, showy day bore fortunes on their delicate persons in the shape of costly vestments . . . covered with gems, glittering with silver buttons, and ringing with silver bells. The fine gentlemen of the period were not behind them in extravagance; and the priests were peculiarly luxurious in dress, wearing gay silken robes, with cowls of fur and girdles of gold and silver.[9]

The prodigality was so extensive that sumptuary laws were passed, but to no effect. Galliciolli says that huge fortunes were wasted and that wealthy families were reduced to begging. Thus, the Jews as moneylenders and pawnbrokers were absolutely essential to the Venetians, but, as one can readily imagine, they were even more detested because of the proud Venetians' dependence on them.

This economically prompted antipathy was wedded to an already existing religious hatred. First, the Venetians hated the Jews because that race, they argued, had crucified God himself. That hatred, in turn, was intensified by the Christians' view that lending money with interest was sinful. Pope Leo I in 443 condemned moneylending, and the Councils of Rheims in 1049, of Rome in 1059, and the Lateran Council in 1139 all added rulings to the *Corpus Juris Canonici* (Body of Canon Law) against the practice. The church's position on the Jews' lending money at interest was not so unequivocal, but perhaps the most frequently stated position was the practical one that said that since the Jews were considered lost souls because of their serious crimes of infidelity and perfidy, they might as well be moneylenders.

By the mid-fifteenth century, however, the Franciscan Friars Minor preached that anyone who practiced usury was an enemy of the people, and rulers or municipal authorities who allowed it deserved excommunication. Nonetheless, the social demands for moneylending were as strong as ever, so the Minorites developed the *monti di pietà*. At first the *monti* had the character of charitable institutions and were not in direct conflict with the Jewish moneylenders, but when the need to recoup part of their operating costs demanded that they charge interest, they took on more of the nature of a financial institution and thus became active competitors of the Jews.

To draw citizens away from the Jewish moneylenders, the Friars leveled false accusations against them, the most damaging of which were their several charges of ritual murder. Such false accusations had been made repeatedly in history, and the Minorites merely built on them. They said that the Jews killed little children, drank their blood, and then committed additional crimes against the Christians as epilogues to the murders. This slander had enormous power, and frequently during the unjust trials of the accused, their property was confiscated in anticipation of conviction. Many popes throughout the years issued bulls denouncing the accusations and even promising protection for the Jews. Nonetheless, the stories resurrected by the Franciscan Friars Minor hovered in the air and permeated the beliefs of the common people. Parenthetically, it is sad to note that, as recently as the 1950s, published accusations of the Jews' role in ritual murders were distributed in Venice with the church's imprimatur.[10]

The point of all this for our discussion is that the fear generated by the anti-Jewish campaign increased the number of *monti di pietà* and cut the Jews' moneylending activities, intensifying even further the Jewish–Christian hatred. Since the Jews paid extra taxes and were less troublesome politically than the Minorites, however, the authorities preferred them to the agitating friars and their *monti*. Thus, the Minorites' preaching and persecution never accomplished all that they intended, and in Venice proper "the pawnshops enjoyed a strong position because they afforded significant advantages to anyone needing a loan: the Jews asked no questions, they did not require official declarations of poverty, they appraised pledges generously, [and] they sometimes lent against written guarantee with no pledge."[11] The Minorites in the end found themselves only in the Venetian countryside.

Because the Minorites relentlessly proclaimed their views, they generated a discord that assured that the Jews could not be assimilated—if there was ever any thought that they might be. This anti-Semitism resulted in the Jews' residences being confined to an area that had been the location of a new foundry— "Ghetto Nuovo," *getto* literally meaning "to cast," or "a casting," and therefore "foundry." Mutinelli presents another derivation; he says that the term "ghetto" derives from the Hebrew word *nghedah*, a congregation. Whatever the source of the word, it designated the vilest and unhealthiest part of the city, which was walled in and whose gates were tended by Christians whose wages the Jews paid. At the curfew hour, the Jews, now without distinction as to place of origin, were locked in for the night—as they were on Christian holidays—purportedly to protect them from fanatics and to prevent scandal. Two barges with armed men watched the ghetto day and night, a bit more protection, one thinks, than mere scandal prevention required. The Jews were also obligated to wear "color" designations to make them immediately distinguishable from the Christians. Initially, the eastern Jews wore yellow Os and the western Jews wore red Os, both of which became colored hats when outer garments would hide the Os.

Some sources say that, eventually, the Jews all wore oilcloth hats as the required badge of discrimination.

The Jewish "side" of the ghetto is seldom mentioned, but there was one. While ghetto life may have been squalid and overpopulated—vast numbers of persons crammed into the limited acreage inside the walls—and even though the Jews "had no concept of liberty, equality, or the pursuit of happiness . . . they were [not] hopelessly downtrodden."[12] From the time when their forebears had been slaves in Egypt, the Jews had been "set upon, spat upon, mauled, and massacred,"[13] but the ghetto Jews were not slaves. The one freedom that they required for survival they had—the freedom to worship their God. Until the Messiah came, however, the "mission of the Jewish people was to work toward becoming 'a nation of priests and a holy people,' as the Haggadah admonished,"[14] and ghetto life provided an environment that was conducive to fulfilling such a mission. As Moshe Leshem says:

What held the Jews together was not simply the Law, custom, and fear. At bottom, what held them together was the conviction that theirs was the only true religion, that they alone among the nations had a covenant with God and a divinely inspired mission. In their eyes, the Jews were a very different and superior kind of people.[15]

We have already mentioned the Christians' belief that the Jews were perfidious infidels, and they hated to be constantly reminded that there was a "certain people," as Haman called the Jews in the Book of Esther (III, 8), who refused to accept Jesus as Messiah. So, to apply Disraeli's comments about the rich and the poor in Victorian England to the ghetto Jews and their Gentile contemporaries, they were two peoples "between whom there is no . . . sympathy; who are as ignorant of each other's habits, thoughts, and feelings as if they were dwellers in different zones or inhabitants of different planets."[16] Knowing these facts, we are not surprised then that the Jews in Venice in the fifteenth and sixteenth centuries—like the Jews almost everywhere else in Europe—did not think of the city and country in which they found themselves as their homeland. We have already noted that they had no permanent residence, that they were subject to all kinds of prohibitions, and that they were roundly hated. Moreover, their fatherland was the land of Israel, that place when they prayed "next year in Jerusalem" that was not a tangible but a spiritual nation. They were sojourners in the ghetto, and the only way out was into Christianity. Except for a relative few, this was not a way out, for to become a Christian meant to sever all ties to one's own people, nation, culture, and way of life.

In England from 1290 until the middle of the seventeenth century, the Jews were essentially excluded, although the research of Cecil Roth does indicate that in Shakespeare's time some Jews lived in England. They, however, were Jews who professed Christianity to circumvent the laws of exclusion[17] and who could not have provided a model for the character of Shylock. It may well be that the scholars—and there are several of them—who say that Shylock is largely Shakespeare's creation have in mind that England could not produce a prototype. The Venetian ghetto Jew could have, though, and that possibility, even when noted by scholars, has not been taken seriously. Leo Salingar, for example, says that "Shakespeare seems not to have heard about the ghetto."[18] His first argument is that, when Old Gobbo asks Launcelot, "Which is the way to Master Jew's?" (II.ii.31), he is assuming that Shylock lives in the midst of the Venetians. That conclusion a prior is not to go unchallenged, for the pawn-brokers and moneylenders had "shops," as Calimani has indicated, so Old Gobbo could be asking directions to any place where he might find Shylock, whom his son serves and for whom he has a present. The dictate that Jews wear special headgear to make them immediately distinguishable emphasizes the fact that they were routinely present among the Gentiles. Furthermore, Shylock makes clear that he is frequently in the Rialto, Venice's center of business, so Salingar's conclusion that Shakespeare knew nothing of the ghetto because of Old Gobbo's inquiry does not necessarily follow. Salingar also notes that Shylock's "Jewish gaberdine" that Antonio spits upon is not attire that his trusted English social historian, Thomas Coryat, mentions. Thus, he concludes, it is merely a theatrical costume that Shakespeare makes up. Contrary to that notion is the definition of gabardine presented in *The American Heritage Dictionary of the English Language*, which notes that a gabardine was a long garment of coarse fabric worn by Jews in the Middle Ages. It also points out that the term derives from one of several words that mean "pilgrim's frock" or "to roam." With a knowledge of the Venetian Jews having come from elsewhere, Shakespeare may well be using the term in a far more knowing and precise way than Salingar allows.

Further, when Shylock refers to himself repeatedly as a stranger, he may be encompassing an entire range of meaning, from being an outcast from Venetian society because he is not a Christian, to having come from someplace else geographically, to being a member of that spiritual nation Israel, all of which we have already discussed. Again, Shakespeare's use of the term "stranger," like his use of "gaberdine," hints at a precise knowledge that the ghetto in Venice could have provided.

Repeatedly, critics note that Shakespeare demonstrates a degree of sympathy for Shylock that cannot be found for Jews anywhere else in England in his day. John Russell Brown, for example, says that the "humanity" of Shylock can "command the whole sympathy of an audience,"[19] but he attributes that success solely to Shakespeare's imagination. No one, especially not I, minimizes Shake-speare's instinct of genius with which he seizes upon the "just representations of general nature," to use Dr. Johnson's words, but the explicit way that he reproduces racial characteristics in Shylock suggests a firsthand acquaintance with Jews.

Another scholar, George Brandes, calls attention to Shakespeare's emphasis on what is peculiarly Jewish in Shylock's culture. While Marlow, according to custom, made his Barabas revel in mythological similes, Shakespeare indicates that Shylock's culture is founded entirely upon the Patriarchs and the Prophets:

With what unction he speaks when he justifies himself by the example of Jacob! His own race is always "our sacred nation," and he feels that "the curse has never fallen upon it" until his daughter fled with his treasures. Jewish, too, is Shylock's respect for, and obstinate insistence on, . . . his statutory rights, which are, indeed, the only rights society allows him.[20]

His hatred is not ungoverned; he restrains it within its legal rights, like a tiger in its cage—or, as Brandes might have said, like a Jew in the ghetto. Shylock, to the inmost fiber of his being, is "a type of his race in its degradation."[21]

Finally, Shakespeare almost certainly did not share the belief that Shylock could be saved by compulsory conversion to Christianity, even though at the end of the trial that conversion is exacted. When Launcelot jestingly asserts that Jessica, as the Jewish Shylock's daughter, is damned, and when Jessica claims that she will be saved by her husband because he has made her a Christian, Launcelot then declares that making her a Christian in truth was not such a good thing because converting Jews to Christians raises the price of pork. Later, Jessica repeats Launcelot's observation to Lorenzo, enjoying the repetition of a joke. Had Shakespeare actually believed this English religious prejudice, he would not have jested about such a momentous event. Therefore, if our point is correct, why does Shakespeare have Shylock condemned into Christianity? It is possible that Shakespeare, as court dramatist to James I, could not present his true position undisguisedly because he would have been subject to censorship. Furthermore, a more open approval of Shylock would have alienated the British public. This is similar to the point that Draper makes about Shakespeare's use of the term "Duke" rather than "Doge" in the first act of *Othello*, set in Venice. Again, as a politically astute court dramatist, Shakespeare "preferred not to depict on the London stage a government in which the ruler had no power."[22]

Whatever readers, theatergoers, and scholars ultimately and individually conclude about Shylock, they have to agree that he is a most complex and dominating character. He is a man who suffers and triumphs and even at times speaks with great nobility. He resonates with life and convinces us with his humanness, albeit a villainous humanness. All of these characteristics have parallels in reality, and I suggest that Shakespeare may have been personally familiar with Venetian Jews who demonstrated them.

NOTES

1. John W. Draper, "Shakespeare and the Doge of Venice," *Modern Philology* 33 (1935): 78.

2. R. B. Parker, *Volpone*, edited by Ben Johnson (Manchester, England: Manchester University Press, 1983), p. 89.

3. George Brandes, *William Shakespeare: A Critical Study* (New York: Macmillan, 1909), p. 113.

4. Michele Marrapodi, "Introduction," *Shakespeare's Italy* (Manchester, England: Manchester University Press, 1993), p. 2.

5. Riccardo Calimani, *The Ghetto of Venice* (New York: Evans, 1987), p. 18.

6. Ibid.

7. Frederic C. Lane, *Venice: A Maritime Republic* (Baltimore: Johns Hopkins University Press, 1973), p. 300.

8. Ibid., p. 303.

9. William Dean Howells, *Venetian Life* (Boston: Houghton Mifflin, 1867), p. 191.

10. Calimani, *Ghetto*, p. 25.

11. Ibid., p. 27.

12. Moshe Leshem, *Balaam's Curse* (New York: Simon and Schuster, 1989), p. 17.

13. Ibid.

14. Ibid., p. 18.

15. Ibid.

16. Ibid.

17. Cecil Roth, *A History of the Jews in England* (Oxford: Clarendon Press, 1941), pp. 139–144.

18. Leo Salingar, "The Idea of Venice in Shakespeare and Ben Johnson," in Marrapodi, *Shakespeare's Italy*, p. 176.

19. John Russell Brown, "Introduction," *The Merchant of Venice: The Arden Edition of the Works of William Shakespeare* (Cambridge: Harvard University Press, 1959), p. xxxix.

20. Brandes, *William Shakespeare*, pp. 166–167.

21. Ibid.

22. Draper, "Shakespeare," p. 80.

13

Emancipation and Jewish Literature in the Italian Canon

Roberto Maria Dainotto

On 20 September 1870, the Italian artillery led by Captain Segre, a Jew, manages to breech, in defiance of papal authority, the now mythical opening of Porta Pia. Through it, the combat unit led by another Jew, Captain Mortara, enters and conquers Rome. The unification of Italy is finally accomplished, and the doors of the last Italian ghetto are sprung open. The event, not surprisingly, is saluted by Italian Jewry with little more than simple patriotism. "Temporal power is down!," writes the *Educatore israelitico*: "This is, no doubt, one of the greatest events of the century."[1] The victory against the pope meant for the Jews of Italy that the nation for which they had strenuously fought was constituting itself, de facto, as a secular state: citizenship was a civic right, independent of religious beliefs.

Only three years after the historical event, Tullo Massarani, among the first Jews to be elected senator of the newly unified nation, published his *Studi di letteratura e d'arte* (Studies on Literature and the Arts).[2] For the Italian senator, the publication was, of course, timely, as the new nation needed to create and establish its own legitimating literary canon of truly "Italian" writers. Moreover, for Massarani the question becomes one of creating, within such a canon, the very possibility for the emergence of a Jewish voice. Leopold Zunz's 1818 essay "On Rabbinical Literature"[3] had generated, all over Europe and even across the Atlantic, a true fervor. Attempting to propose a canon, not of "Hebrew" or "Yiddish," but rather of *Jewish* literature, the essay had driven scholars to find, within different national traditions, some specific contributions to the formation of a Jewish canon.

Stemming from the teaching of the old Hebrew texts, Jewish literature "attached itself," in Zunz's words, "to new, foreign elements" and to the very tongues of the different nations where the Jewish nation was scattered.[4] Jewish literature was a synthetic category, bearing witness to the very complexity of the Jewish Diaspora. Its history was a movement from Xemona's Middle Ages Arabic poetry, through the Spanish travel books of Benjamin de Tuleda, to Yiddish Poland, and to the

Latin prose of Spinoza.

Massarani was a representative of Piedmontese Jewry, a group that had pioneered emancipation and stressed, accordingly, the values of Italianness. For someone like him, what was lacking was the possibility, within these proposed canons of Jewish literature, to accommodate the singular experience of Italian Jewry. In fact, apart from a few, mostly unknown Renaissance Jews, a place for Italy had been far from secured in these canons. The way in which the whole question of "Jewish literature" had been posed was, for the Italian, fundamentally wrong. "Jewish Literature" seemed to mean, fundamentally, a sort of literature crystallized around the condition of the Diaspora. It was the literature of the wandering, homeless Jew, doomed to speak from a "foreign" land. The very secularization of such literature still tied to an original rabbinical tradition was the consequence of a Diaspora that had forced Judaism to be just a confession in a "foreign" state.

Italian Jewry hardly needed such a "Jewish literature." It could have its own Italian one. The secular condition of Judaism in Italy itself was not the consequence of the Diaspora but issued from the active participation of Italian Jews in the construction of a secular state that was perceived as all but "foreign." True, the Italian canon had not yet found any room to accommodate within itself the voice of the Jews. Yet, the situation, for Massarani, in an Italy that was giving unprecedented civil rights to its Jews, was destined to change. The sacrifice of the Jewish community for the unification of Italy, after all, had been rewarded by giving fair representation to it in the political body of the nation. Would not the body of literature, too, now start representing the Italian Jewish experience? The goal of Massarini's *Studi di letteratura e d'arte* becomes therefore twofold: to establish, first, a canonical body of Italian texts and, second, to prepare the growth of a new Italian literature representative of the Jewish experience.

What, precisely, could a *Jewish* experience in unified Italy mean? Arnaldo Momigliano, in a famous preface to Cecil Roth's *History of the Jews of Venice*, wrote that "The history of the Jews, in any Italian city, is, essentially, the history of the formation of their Italian national consciousness."[5] Antonio Gramsci had proposed, accordingly, the famous thesis of the *disebreizzazione*, a de-Jewishization, so to speak, of the Italian Jews.[6] Their opposition to the Catholic cosmopolitanism of the pope in the name of a secular state tolerant of all confessions had brought them, as a consequence, from the very subordination of their own Jewishness to a new civic and national identity. "Religion is no longer everything," maintained Flaminio Servi in his *Vessillo Israelitico*.[7] If the old Judaism of the ghetto had made religion, law, and social life coincide, the emancipated Jews of new Italy had to put their religious affiliation in the background and start developing a sense of national identity instead.[8] Jewish religion, David Levi maintained, had been replaced by a new "religion of Nation" in which "all faiths and beliefs unite, and fuse in one single faith, one single religion of the Country—of Italy."[9] In Eugenio Artom's words, "The history of the Risorgimento thus becomes the history of the Italian people . . . caught in the moment of the spiritual passage . . . from religious faith to the idea of the Nation."[10]

If the secularism of "Jewish literature" was then the secularism of the Diaspora, Italian secularism represented instead the possibility, before the messianic return to the Promised Land, of constructing a nation for the Jews to feel at home. Yet, one problem remained: Once the principle of a total and unconditional secularism of Italy had been proposed, defended, and finally affirmed, what could "being a Jew" mean? Could a Jew be defined as such, independently of all the beliefs and rituals that had constituted, so far, Jewish identity? Was not the claim of a separation between the sacred and the secular, in itself, a negation, as Alfonso Pacifici would have suggested, of a "Jewish singularity" that does not admit such distinctions?[11] If Christians should be Christians only in the church, and if Jews can be Jews only in the synagogue, and if both can be nothing but Italians in the civic space, what can an "Italian-Jewish" writer possibly be? How can the Jewish experience be brought within the secularized canon of Italian literature?

The theoretical problem facing Massarani is, no doubt, a rather complex one. The paradigm provided by the category of "Jewish literature," suggesting the possibility that sacred Hebrew literature can immediately or painlessly issue in a new, post-Hebrew, post-rabbinical, secular Jewish literature, is again of no help. For that matter, the very position of the Italian senator is problematic: the oath sworn in front of the Italian Senate prevents him from overtly taking the stance of partisan, Jewish-only interests and concerns. The year 1873, after all, is the very year of the Pasqualigo case—from the name of the liberal deputy who had accused Jewish delegates of having become a "*State within the State*," defending only their group's interests.[12] Massarani needs then to face what amounts to an impossible mission: the need to handle the most urgent problem facing postunification Italian Jewry without the support of any paradigm and by dissimulating it behind the compelling necessity of having to find models for the creation of an Italian canon.

Massarani's work then tries to single out "not so much exemplary, but rather . . . possible models for the youth of our country."[13] It wants to find deep motivations, rather than mere examples, for the fashioning of the entire Italian youth. Massarani, accordingly, begins by canonizing Dante, reviled until the previous century,[14] and now celebrated as the poet of the Italian nation. He also enlists, in his register of exemplary figures of national literature, other expected names such as Vico and Alfieri. However, Dante or the "ancient" Alfieri[15] might well function as canonical "examples" of nationalistic "expectations that may be used in subsequent situations,"[16] but such examples are hardly "possible" for the modern youth of 1873.

Massarani then tries to look elsewhere for more timely figures of exemplarity, yet where could Italy, which was oppressed by the foreign yoke until recently and whose arts decayed into coterie and vain artifice already in the sixteenth century, find anything more modern and valuable? The answer to this problem is in line with the status of literary studies at the time: in order to construct a modern national literature, Italy has to look at, and learn from, modern foreign nations. Already Mazzini had lamented that "Italy has long lost its old character. . . . It is necessary now that Italy reforms its Taste. . . . It is then inevitable that Italy studies foreign literatures, not in order to imitate one or the other, but to emulate them all . . . to learn from them."[17] The Italian canon cannot be the mere accounting of past exemplarities: it has to be a project for the future. It has, for this very reason, to start looking elsewhere for the "possibilities" that will be able to produce a new Italian literature and, within it, a new Jewish voice. The gaze should move, first of all, to the most modern and national literature of all—that of the German Romantics.

What Massarani sees in German Romanticism, however, might be quite different from what other Italian scholars of his generation had found in it. It was a commonplace of the times to single out in German Romanticism the very antithesis to French classicism. The Germans, with their accent on individuality, had contributed to reinforce a sense of specific national identity opposed to the abstract universalism of French thought.[18] Not altogether differently, Romanticism is for Massarani a "war" against "arrogant France" and its universalistic claims.[19] Unlike his contemporaries, however, Massarani seems to notice in French universalism a concept akin to that of a Christian ecumene: "different from it, German thought is instead comprehensive . . . synthetic: it can accommodate anybody, and all the infinite inclinations and attitudes of human nature. . . . It can welcome, as an organic part of the whole, all the most distant varieties of faiths and beliefs."[20] Romanticism is, in other words, a system of differences whereby different inclinations, different identities, and different religious beliefs can be accommodated. Against the univocal truth of French classicism, Romanticism provides a horizon within which "differences," such as the Jewish one, could well find their legitimate place.

Whereas Italian nationalists read—or misread—German Romanticism as the precursor of their own struggle, the Jewish Massarani misreads it as the palimpsest on which to graft the new Italian statutes of religious tolerance. To show how partial Massarani's view of German Romanticism was, it would be enough to mention here Novalis' rather intolerant libel "Christianity or Europe," or even the Romantic exaltations of the Christian Middle Ages and of Protestant gothic architecture. Massarani's was an instrumental use of Romanticism. The German model had to be the pure and perfect example from which a tolerant literature, accommodating all religious beliefs, could be initiated in Italy. Romanticism, moreover, was the very principle of secularism that had to stir a new crop of literary artifacts in the new Italy: "German Romanticism was the genius of tolerance, the principle that locked divine problems away in the sanctuary, and immersed, in the most complete way, humankind and reason into secular life."[21] With this secularization of the model, however, Massarani is back to the initial riddle: if religious identities have to be locked in the temple, what remains of the Jewish identity in the secular world? What is a Jewish writer *outside* the synagogue? At this point Massarani's argument cannot move further, if not by invoking a concrete example of a Jewish, but secular, even national, writer— Heinrich Heine.

This canonization of Heine in an Italian book of 1873 is not as obvious as it may now seem to us. First, Heine did not enjoy such canonical status even in his homeland.[22] France itself, which Heine had been desperately trying to please, was not sure at the time that the German Jew deserved to be considered as anything but a buffoon. In this context, Massarani's decision to devote no less than 135 of the 520 pages of his book to the "absolutely unique genius of Heine"[23] becomes even more relevant. Heine, whose unconditional love for Germany is continuously mentioned by Massarani, seems to provide the example of a complexly national and Jewish writer.

Massarani's first chapter on Heine begins with a peculiar announcement: "It is vulgar curiosity to look into domestic matters and nose into writers' lives. The biographer who starts losing time with biographical details—the more scandalous, the more appetizing—often loses appetite, at the end, for the artistic work itself. In order to avoid this risk, we will not imitate the biographer."[24] Such distrust for the relevance of any biographic detail in the evaluation of works of art is certain not to surprise the reader, accustomed to quite more radical announcements about the very "death of the author." What might still surprise you, however, is that the announcement is immediately contradicted by Massarani with the biographical notation that Heine is "escito . . . di famiglia ebraica" (born of a Jewish family).[25]

Rhetoric identifies this figure as *praeteritio*: one says something after pretending that one does not want to say it. The figure is said to be a particularly convincing one; what is eventually said possesses the character of indispensability—it could not be left unsaid, despite the speaker's most genuine intentions, and so, no matter how irrelevant biographical considerations might be for Massarani, this one is all too important to be omitted. Heine represents, indeed, the very "reconciliation"[26] of Jewishness and Germanness, of the poetics "of exile and sorrow" with the "brotherly genius" of the exuberant Germans.[27]

The passage could also be read, however, in a more literal, nonrhetorical way: because Massarani's account of Heine literally omits those biographical details "the more appetizing as they are more flavored with gossip and scandal." In fact, only through such omissions can Heine's youthful enthusiasm for nationalism be generalized, and his more mature aversion to German nationalism completely disregarded.[28] Most important, only through omissions can the "German poet who was born a Jew but who thought it necessary to pay the price of baptism for his entry into the wider cultural community"[29] of German nationalism be presented as a solution to a problem that he, instead, represents.

The same passage may lend itself to a third interpretive possibility. It is *exactly* because of his conversion to Christianity—a piece of biographical "gossip" that is certainly not unknown to Massarani's Jewish audience—that Heine becomes, if not an example, at least a possibility for the new Italian Jew to start thinking about the dilemma of his new identity, because, if Heine's example of conversion cannot—and should not—be followed, some sort of conversion of the "old" Jew into a new, Italian type remains, for Senator Massarani, an absolute necessity. If Judaism, in the secular Italy of 1873, remained only a confession, its fate would have been swallowed by the dominant faith of Italy. Judaism, in order to continue to exist, had to be more than a mere confession and reshape a novel identity for itself.

Only a few years earlier, in 1862, Giuseppe Revere, poet of the Jewish

Risorgimento and dear friend of Massarani, had already dramatized this same necessity of converting the old faith into something new:

Since I can read the divine code in its original language, I work hard to find in it whatever can make my faith stronger. However, what I am looking for is not exactly the faith of the ancients. On the contrary, I try to figure out and imagine the faith of our grandsons, who will undoubtedly find the utterances of the old wise men or teachers of Israel quite hard to swallow.[30]

The "ancient faith" that Revere tries to reaffirm is no longer, paradoxically, the faith of the ancients but that of future "grandsons." If Heine points out, for Revere, the necessity for such transformation to happen, lest the old faith become "hard" to understand and accept in the new world order of the nation-state, his example falls short of a valid solution, not only because Heine died, as Revere put it, under the weight of the cross that he had accepted with baptism[31] but because, in the unprecedented historical contingency of a nation-state—Italy—created and willed by the Jews, the very principle for transforming Jewishness has to be found within a national horizon.

Jewishness—the "similar origin" that Revere claims between himself and Heine—is subordinated to national identification that separates the German from the Italian more than the common origin would unite. Italy has created a new horizon for Judaism, which can scarcely ground its identity on preexisting origins, and has to invent new directions for the future. To rephrase this in Revere's culinary metaphor, it is not the *matzo* that unites but the Italian oil that separates from the German butter: "Furthermore, Heine loved lard and butter, and he wished his Germany could swim in all that grease. In this respect, I am the polar opposite of him: I am quite content to see my land frying in oil—domestic of course, and quite tasty."[32] What Jewish Italy needs is a new cookbook, a recipe whereby to concoct a new kind of identity. The example is set by Heine, but it is not a concrete model nor a possibility for an Italian diet.

Let me summarize the set of ambiguities that have cropped up so far in the attempt to construct a literary canon. They are symptomatic, I believe, of the Jewish condition in the age of the Risorgimento. Both Massarani and Revere represent an ambiguous oscillation between Judaism and nationalism, between secularism and tradition, and also between the commonplace of "the most ancient of minorities" and the desire for a future form of Judaism. Heine, the German nationalist who was also a Jew, or the Jew who also became a convert, is the symptomatic figure of this ambiguity; he represents, ambiguously, both the possibility and the danger of the secularization of Judaism. Even more ambiguously, he introduces the necessity to move away from previous examples and origins and start imagining a new form of Jewishness—ambiguously anchored to tradition and further from it—to fit the new Jewish condition in modern Italy. In sum, neither Massarani nor Revere provides us with a canon or even with a concrete recipe for a new Jewishness. The latter remains an ambiguously defined project for the future.

NOTES

1. Yoseph Colombo, "Il XX settembre 1870 nella stampa ebraica dell'epoca," in *1870. La breccia del ghetto. Evoluzione degli ebrei di Roma*, edited by Salvatore Foà (Rome: Barulli, 1971), p. 100.

2. Tullo Massarani, *Studi di letteratura e d'arte* (Florence: Le Monnier, 1873).

3. Leopold Zunz, "Die Judische Literatur," *Zur Geschichte und Literatur* (Berlin: Veit, 1845), pp. 1–37.

4. Gustav Karpeles, *Jewish Literature and Other Essays* (Philadelphia: Jewish Publication Society of America, 1895), p. 328.

5. Arnaldo Momigliano, "Preface," in Cecil Roth, *History of the Jews of Venice* (Philadelphia: Jewish Publication Society of America, 1930; reprinted New York: Schocken Books, 1975), p. ix.

6. Antonio Gramsci, "Ebraismo," in *Il Risorgimento* (Rome: Editori Riuniti, 1996), p. 209.

7. Flaminio Servi, "Giudaismo passato e presente," *Vessillo Israelitico* (1877): 48.

8. Maurizio Molinari, *Ebrei in Italia: un problema di identità (1870–1938)* (Florence: Giuntina, 1991), pp. 32–33.

9. David Levi, *Ausonia. Vita d'azione (dal 1848 al 1870)* (Rome: Loescher, 1882), p. 81.

10. Eugenio Artom, "Per una storia degli ebrei nel Risorgimento," *Rassegna storica Toscana* (January-June 1978): 138.

11. Molinari, *Ebrei in Italia*, p. 46.

12. Andre M. Canepa, "Il caso Pasqualigo," *Comunità* 174 (June 1975): 177.

13. Massarani, *Studi di letteratura e d'arte*, p. 520.

14. Carlo Dionisotti, "Varia fortuna di Dante," in *Geografia e storia della letteratura italiana* (Turin: Einaudi, 1967), pp. 255–303.

15. Massarani, *Studi di letteratura e d'arte*, p. 143.

16. Charles Altieri, *Canons and Consequences: Reflections on the Ethical Force of Imaginative Ideals* (Evanston, IL: Northwestern University Press, 1990), p. 101.

17. Giuseppe Mazzini, "D'una letteratura europea," in *D'una letteratura europea e altri saggi*, edited by Mario Sipala (Fasano: Schena Editore, 1991), pp. 70–71.

18. Federico Chabod, *L'idea di nazione*, 1979 ed. (Bari: Laterza, 1961), p. 18.

19. Massarani, *Studi di letteratura e d'arte*, pp. 208, 14.

20. Ibid., p. 201.

21. Ibid., p. 246.

22. Alfred Wener, "Introduction," in *The Sword and the Flame: Selections from Heinrich Heine's Prose* (New York: Thomas Yoseloff, 1960), p. 37.

23. Massarani, *Studi di letteratura e d'arte*, p. 208.

24. Ibid., p. 218.

25. Ibid.

26. Ibid., p. 295.

27. Ibid., pp. 296–97.

28. Werner, "Introduction," pp. 70–72.

29. S. S. Prawer, *Heine's Jewish Comedy: A Study of His Portraits of Jews and Judaism* (Oxford: Clarendon Press, 1983), p. 3.

30. Giuseppe Revere, "Persone ed Ombre," in *Opere complete di Giuseppe Revere*, edited by A. Rondani (Rome: Forzani e C. Tipografi del Senato, 1898), p. 179.

31. Ibid., p. 175.

32. Ibid., p. 177.

14

Assimilation and Identity in an Italian-Jewish Novel

Lynn M. Gunzberg

Seven years after the unification of Italy was complete, seven years after the final emancipation of the Jews of Rome on 13 October 1870, the journal *Il Vessillo Israelitico* (The Jewish Standard) of 1877 carried an editorial entitled "Giudaismo passato e presente" (Judaism Past and Present). Reflecting on the Jews' recently acquired equality with all other Italians, Flaminio Servi observed that "in light of the Emancipation, Judaism which once was primarily a religious phenomenon, had now to be redefined. Religion was no longer the be-all and end-all; rather, Jews should commit themselves to public life. The orthodoxy of the past was nothing more than an anomaly born of compulsory residence within the walls of the ghetto."[1] After centuries of confinement, Jews were free to react against the narrowness of their former lives and eagerly embraced Italian culture and internalized Italian history as their own. We have Gramsci's famous analysis of Italy's perceived "lack of anti-Semitism." The Risorgimento, he said, overcame traditional Jewish separatism, and Jews spontaneously sought to rid themselves of their off-putting Jewishness: "The formation of the Jewish national consciousness parallels the formation of Italian national sentiment among the Piedmontese or the Neapolitans or the Sicilians. It is merely one moment of the same process and could well symbolize it. Thus at the same time Jews residing in Italy became Italians."[2]

Indeed, just before the watershed year, from the pages of his newspaper *La Patria*, Salvatore Anau advised Jews that "every free Jew, assuming he sees the cross as a symbol of national liberty, should kneel before this sacred symbol until the whole country is saved."[3] Arnaldo Momigliano de-emphasized the role of religion in the Risorgimento by attributing this shift in mentality to a fundamental development in Italian culture, that is, the rise of the secular in direct opposition to Catholic cosmopolitanism. This fundamental development permitted the nationalization and "de-Jewing" of the Jews.[4]

Historians of this shift in identity describe the culture of the majority as an irresistible siren, the flame that beckons the moth and destroys it. Certainly, the result was the same. The old way of life was over, and, what is more, for all but the poorest its restrictions were no longer inevitable. Those who sought to hold the many Jewish communities of central and northern Italy together fought a losing battle; in the end, Italian culture was just much easier to digest. Ironically, perhaps, this was also the time of the construction of the monumental Italian synagogues of Rome and Florence. Nor did religious schools or Jewish charitable institutions suffer from this sea change in Italian-Jewish life. On the contrary, as Jews acquired the wealth to move out of Jewish quarters, Jewish institutions profited from their benefactors' newfound ability to support them with ever more substantial bequests. As Jews moved away from personal observance, they sought to strengthen these manifestations of their former lives that they might endure in their mission to educate and assist less fortunate Jews.

Into what kind of world did the Jews move? Were they welcomed into those parts of cities and towns (but primarily cities) that had been out-of-bounds for them just a short time before? Let us look briefly at Rome, the site of the final emancipation. Until the fall of the Papal States, Jews were still subject to attack. Indeed, their lives had changed little during the centuries of their segregation. They were limited to few professions beyond commerce. While their brethren in other, less restrictive parts of Italy enjoyed complete economic freedom after 1848, the Roman Jews were even more limited in their activities after Pius IX regained his throne in 1849, but in 1870 the age-old prohibition against noncommercial activities would pay off.

What was the condition of the Roman Jews at the time of their final emancipation? In 1861 almost half the population of the ghetto—that is, 2,200 people—were listed as indigent.[5] In 1868, a census was taken by the Jewish community in which the activities of all the Roman Jews were duly noted. The census counted approximately 5,000 Jews (the exact number is questionable). Of these, the census listed 2,010 (including children) as being without a trade. Only 56 were artisans, and, since Jews could not attend the university unless they ventured out of the Papal States, only 72 were involved in intellectual professions, with an additional 40 listed as students; 230 Jews performed manual labor, 125 were servants, and 11 processed and served food and wine. None were listed as agricultural workers, since Jews could not own land and were forced to live in the center of the city. Agriculture, so much a part of Italian life, was foreign to the Jews' urban existence. Overwhelmingly, however, commerce, primarily of fabric and used clothing mended by 991 seamstresses, provided 993 Jewish merchants with their livelihoods.[6] Even after 1870, the majority of Roman Jews persisted in their traditional professions, in part because few were wealthy enough to take immediate advantage of the newly available range of activities.[7]

When they left the ghetto, Jews occupied an anomalous, but potentially profitable, economic position with respect to the population at large. The commercial life of the city beyond the ghetto walls was, at best, poorly developed. A large percentage of the population was still involved in agriculture, and another was in the employ of the church. The nineteenth-century Roman poet Belli tells us that when they wanted to buy something, have their clothes mended, or buy other items at rock-bottom prices, Romans went to the ghetto. After 1870, when Rome became capital of Italy and its population underwent rapid growth, the bureaucrats and their families needed to buy clothes and other household furnishings. Undergoing little fundamental change, the Jews were able to fill a crucial niche by doing what they had always done. Those able to take advantage of this situation prospered. Let it be understood, however, that the majority of Roman Jews were poor, as illustrated by the following example: for Passover 1900, free *matzo* were distributed to 3,240 Jews, approximately half the population, who otherwise would have been unable to afford it.[8] Nonetheless, commerce marked the way to a better life for many Jews. A census from 1911 shows 56.6% of the Jewish population involved in commerce, as opposed to 11.6% of the total population.[9] Before 1870, a flourishing used-clothing market was set up weekly inside the ghetto in Piazza delle Scuole and Piazza Cenci. After 1870, the same weekly used-clothing market could be found on Wednesdays in Campo dei Fiori, where it was called the "mercato dei giudii" (Jews' market).[10] In addition to commerce as it was traditionally defined, establishing themselves as "Commissionari, Spedizionieri, Rappresentanti di case commerciali nazionali ed estere" (brokers, sales representatives, and shippers for national and international companies), Jews added a cosmopolitan dimension to commercial relations in Rome.[11] Thus, in Rome, even outside the ghetto, Jews were and remained indelibly identified with commerce.

So, the world into which the Jews ventured in 1870 and which they inhabited and tried to make their own was one in which, despite individual cases, as an identifiable group they continued to do things differently from their neighbors. These differences persisted well into the twentieth century. In 1911, 55% of the Italian population was still involved in agriculture, whereas only 8.1% of Jews were; 41% of Jews were in business as compared to 5.6% of non-Jews, and so on.[12]

These differences in approach to daily life permeated the consciousness and, therefore, the fiction and poetry of Italian-Jewish authors. The reader is continually struck by the power, almost a magnetic force, of what Natalia Ginzburg later called a "particularizing angle of vision"[13] to divide the world into a narrow space where Jews can feel entirely comfortable and a wider world where, though apparently assimilated, something whispers to them that they really don't belong.

Such was clearly the view of Enrico Castelnuovo in his 1908 novel *I Moncalvo*. Castelnuovo, who lived from 1839 to 1915, experienced the vicissitudes of the final emancipation and entry into Italian society. The Venetian writer grew up with little or no religious education and throughout his life declared himself a "lay positivist"[14] in favor of the liberal state under the stabilizing influence and traditional values of the historical Right. He viewed with alarm the growing power of a new aristocracy of bankers and speculators who were gradually overtaking the revered protagonists of the Risorgimento. A journalist, business professor, and spare-time writer of popular serial novels, Castelnuovo had frequent contact with those who were laying the groundwork for the so-called Third Italy, and he understood its attraction for Jews and others who had hitherto lived in poverty at the margins of society. The clash between Castelnuovo's own deeply held ideals and the irresistible pull of social climbing and careerism constitutes the plot of *I Moncalvo*, the story of an eponymous family of wealthy Jewish bankers led by Gabrio, their banker-patriarch, and their struggle to enter the aristocracy, despite its alliance with the church.

After emancipation, the Moncalvos leave their native Ferrara and move to Rome to be closer to the center of national power and, through conversion and subsequent marriage into a princely family, to launch their new life. Here in this burgeoning city the family is pulled into two hostile camps as if it were a microcosm of the society of the time: one branch, headed by Gabrio, made up of ambitious social climbers; the other represented by two family members, Gabrio's staunchly positivist scientist brother, Giacomo, and Giacomo's son Giorgio. Giacomo and Giorgio are nonobservant Jews who nonetheless are atavistically attached to the old religious values and untouched by the mania for the modern and the money that buys comforts, titles, and other social distinctions. In his role as spokesman for the author, Giacomo complains bitterly of his family's calculated conversations in an effort to wash away the "stain" of their Jewish identity. Their understanding clouded by their desire to enter into a world long forbidden to them, Jews like Gabrio believe it is just the mere fact of religious difference that keeps them from allying themselves with the likes of the Princes Oroboni, a family of equal wealth living just opposite them but seemingly light years away in terms of lineage, social standing, and access to power. Gabrio, the new kind of Jew, would probably not understand the full significance of the Princess Oroboni's shock at her dour and sickly son's desired alliance with the lively, outspoken, and Jewish Mariannina Moncalvo. Blind to certain obstacles and firm in his conviction that by simply playing by the rules (read: conversion) he could overcome aristocratic (read: Catholic) hostility to his family of Jewish upstarts, Gabrio confronts the Orobonis' poorly concealed disgust as a challenge. Gabrio's wife heads the list of converts, with Mariannina next.

With each Jew who renounces Judaism, Giacomo becomes increasingly embittered and detached from the family until one day he and his brother Gabrio decide to reveal their innermost thoughts on the subject and conclude that they have nothing more to say to each other. Gabrio the banker sets up a balance sheet of the pros and cons of his own conversion. One count in favor is the promise of papal benificence that will come his way the moment he sheds his Jewish identity. The reader is conditioned to recognize what Gabrio cannot see: that the arguments against conversion make far better sense. But the protagonist's vanity decides the outcome of his calculations, and he rationalizes his decision:

We are an anachronism . . . which doesn't mean we should simply disappear. On the contrary. We should take the healthy and vigorous fiber of our race and use it to revive the worn-out Western aristocracies, which, in the end, have more reason to live because they have deep roots in the land and in European history . . . whereas us, we are merely nomads.[15]

This "lowering of principles, this shipwreck of ideals . . . this mad race to seize ephemeral honors and riches" (p. 338), the author warns us, "bring only destruction and unhappiness to those who abandon the compass of their heritage and become fugitives from the ghettos that kept Jews from taking their rightful place at the helm of a golden world."[16] Castelnuovo's novel, then, is nothing less than "the bitter observation that the ideals which had always united Jews through centuries of hardship were fraying."[17]

Castelnuovo was not mistaken. In Italy at the turn of the century, the mechanism that promoted the greatest number of conversions was mixed marriage, which almost always resulted in renunciation of Judaism. The well-to-do were more likely to convert, and females were more likely to convert through marriage than males. The Ferrarese Moncalvo family is a good example; Gabrio's wife heads the list of converts to ease the way for her daughter, and Mariannina converts soon after. The behavior of the Roman Jews, however, was somewhat anomalous. More males than females converted, and conversions were common among the lower classes, perhaps because, being already marginalized, they were more culturally and, therefore, religiously vulnerable and anxious to seek a "way out" of their economic condition.[18] The well-to-do, like their counterparts elsewhere, being already in a position to seize professional opportunities open only to well-off non-Jews, were quick to shed their Jewishness. Maintaining tradition, then, fell largely to merchants and those allied with commerce, who by dint of their profession were economically independent. Sons of merchants were more likely to take over their fathers' businesses than the sons of fathers in other trades, thereby conserving more generally established traditions such as the paternal religion.[19]

Regardless of efforts on the part of certain classes of emancipated Jews, Jewish leaders feared that Judaism in Italy, which had never boasted large numbers of followers, might well be flickering out. In 1890 Samuel Margulies, the charismatic, Galician-born chief rabbi of Florence, set about to reverse the trend in his adopted city. He revived the nearly dormant rabbinical college—Margulies' non-Italian origin is itself an indication of the condition of Italian rabbinical studies—and promoted the creation of two journals, *Rivista israelitica* (Jewish Review) (1904–1915) and *Israel* (1916-1925).[20] Beginning in 1907 and inspired by Margulies, Jewish cultural societies, called Pro Cultura, were founded in several cities and towns, and in 1911 Florence hosted the first Jewish Youth Congress. That same year, Italian-Jewish communities were organized into a Consortium. The Consortium (also called Pro Cultura), youth groups, and journals all preached Jewish intellectual and cultural solidarity within the framework of rock-solid Italian allegiance.[21] The number of Jews influenced by Margulies and his followers was small, but this attempt at Jewish revival, combined with the position of prominent Jews in government, business, and the professions, disturbed wary nationalists.

The Jewish sentiment that most alarmed ardent nationalists, was, of course, Zionism. In *I Moncalvo* Zionism is represented by a certain Doctor Löwe, a German who tries to win Gabrio and his money over to the Zionist cause. Doctor Löwe

had seen with his own eyes how Jews were persecuted and was persuaded that anti-Semitism was deeply rooted in those countries, and that even if Jews were to acquire government favor and legal rights, nothing was likely to change much. . . . In those countries where Jews enjoyed civil rights and could aspire to be magistrates, ministers, and generals, Jews couldn't let their guard down, because, instead of weakening, from those countries where it is endemic anti-Semitism spreads to those that were once immune. . . . If it is not readily apparent, it is latent. It's noticeable even in Italy (pp. 63–64).

But Gabrio is not convinced, and neither were most Italian Jews. Despite the efforts of Margulies and others—establishing a Zionist Society as early as 1898, holding a Zionist Congress in 1901, discussing Zionism with the king in 1903, and in 1904 calling in Theodore Herzl to continue the conversation with the king—few Italian Zionists were moved to emigrate. Rather, they preferred to contribute philanthropically to further the creation of a Jewish homeland in Palestine and to benefit their Eastern European brethren scattered in the *shtetls* of Russia and Poland. For themselves, they had a homeland, one they called "noble" and "beautiful,"[22] in Jewish publications such as *L'Idea sionistica* (The Zionist Idea) and *Il Vessillo Israelitico*, and to which they owed their loyalty, their substance, their honor.

Those nationalists and others who weighed the Jews against the usual traditional values of morality and lineage and found them wanting encountered reassuring examples of Jewish moral insufficiency in *I Moncalvo*. One of these will stand for all: In their frenzy to buy into the good life, the new rich were altering the face of ancient Rome, destroying it by rebuilding it into their own shameless image. Castelnuovo relays a conversation between Gabrio and his real estate agent. Gabrio cannot conceive of investing in property only to let it drain his resources; instead, were he to buy a certain villa and the surrounding parcel of land, he would demolish the house and garden and build an apartment house. The agent is shocked: who would want to destroy one of the few green spots left in Rome? It would be a true shame, Gabrio agrees, but the urge to maximize profit cannot be denied; after all, Jews, he says, have business in their blood (p. 80).

Critics have speculated that *I Moncalvo* is an anti-Semitic novel and Castelnuovo, by extension, a Semitic anti-Semite. Given the tremendous challenges to Italian Judaism represented by massive assimilation following emancipation, should not Jewish writers create more positive images of Jews? What differentiates this work from the many examples of obviously anti-Semitic popular novels? The signature dichotomy between Christians and Jews with their myriad undesirable characteristics, found in such fiction, is well entrenched here, particularly as the Princes Oroboni contemplate admitting Mariannina Moncalvo to their family. What saves Castelnuovo's novel from reproducing all the characteristics of anti-Semitic fiction is the author's creation of some positive Jewish characters to balance Gabrio's shallow and rudderless family. The Christian characters are presented quite realistically without the trappings of impossible virtue familiar to readers of most fiction in which Jews and non-Jews confront one another. Indeed, the only completely positive Christian is a painter who looks about himself in disgust at the breakdown of civilization. Thoroughly unlikable Jews are, however, in the majority here, and the only Jew to emerge worthy of respect isn't even Italian, the German

Doctor Löwe.

Rather than anti-Semitic, this novel is just the opposite: deeply pessimistic about the effects of assimilation on the survival of Jewish culture and, given the ineluctability of the Jews' massive desire to partake of the opportunities offered by the dominant culture in Italy and elsewhere, about the basic survival of Judaism. Castelnuovo appears to weep for Jewish tradition in his depiction of the funeral of Gabrio's sister, Clara. The chanted prayers of ancient origin have comforted countless Jews the world over; now, however,

the prayers were chanted in an unknown language. These were the prayers that had resounded throughout Zion and along the rivers of Babylon, that had comforted the families of the Diaspora in their mournful exile. There was no corner of the world where their notes did not evoke the Holy Land. They brought peace to the Jewish dead from . . . Venice to Amsterdam, from London to New York, from Calcutta to Lisbon. Handed down from generation to generation . . . like precious essences they preserved the faith, hope, and dreams of a people, so that the further it fell the more determined it was to rise again. But these funeral chants [for Clara] gave rise neither to emotion nor affection; the guttural, sing-song notes rose and fell away like the jets of a fountain long-since abandoned by those wishing to slake their thirst (p. 248).

NOTES

1. *Il Vessillo Israelitico*, fascicle 1877, pp. 335–336; cit. Maurizio Molinari, *Ebrei in Italia: un problema di identità (1870–1938)* (Florence: Giuntina, 1991), p. 32.

2. Antonio Gramsci, "Ebraismo e antisemitismo," Notebooks 2 and 10, reprinted *Il Risorgimento* (Turin: Einaudi, 1966), pp. 166–169.

3. Salvatore Anau, *La Patria*, 9 September 1847, cit. Andrew M. Canepa, "L'atteggiamento degli ebrei italiani davanti alla loro seconda emancipazione: Premesse e analisi," *Rassegna mensile di Israel* 43, no. 9 (1977): 429.

4. Arnaldo Momigliano, *Pagine ebraiche* (Turin: Einaudi, 1987), p. 242, cit. Stefano Caviglia, *L'identità salvata: Gli ebrei di Roma tra fede e nazione (1870–1938)* (Rome: Laterza, 1996), p. 6.

5. Bruno di Porto, "Gli ebrei di Roma dai papi all'Italia," in *1870: La breccia del ghetto*, edited by Elio Toaff et al. (Rome: Barulli, 1971), p. 23, n. cit. Canepa, "L'atteggiamento," p. 420. For a more general depiction of ghetto conditions, see Rev. Dr. Philip, *The Ghetto in Rome, as It Was and as It Is* (Florence: Claudian Press, 1875), as well as Massimo d'Azeglio's classic and influential account of the Roman ghetto: *Dell'emancipazione civile degli Israeliti* (Florence: Le Monnier, 1848).

6. Caviglia, *L'identità salvata*, p. 9.

7. Roberto Bachi, "La demografia degli ebrei italiani negli ultimi cento anni," in *Atti del Congresso internazionale per gli studi sulle popolazioni* (Rome: Istituto poligrafico dello stato, 1931), p. 117, cit. Caviglia, *L'identità salvata*, p. 10.

8. Stefano Caviglia, "Vita economica e sociale degli ebrei romani dall'emancipazione (1870) agli inizi del XX secolo," *Rassegna mensile di Israel* 52, no. 1 (1986): 132, n. 32.

9. *Censimento Generale della Popolazione del Regno d'Italia al 10 giugno 1911* (Rome: 1915), cit. Caviglia, *L'identità salvata*, p. 10.

10. Samuel Schaerf, "Impressioni storiche sugli ebrei di Roma," in *Israel* (1928), cit. Caviglia, "Vita economica," p. 130.

11. Caviglia, "Vita economica," p. 131. For a fascinating sense of the scope of Jewish commercial activity, see, as Caviglia has done, the *Guida Monaci* for 1897 and subsequent years.

12. Livio Livi, *Ebrei alla luce della statistica: Evoluzione demografica, economica, sociale* (Florence: Libreria della Voce, 1920), p. 120.

13. Natalia Ginzburg, *Cinque romanzi brevi* (Turin: Einaudi, 1964), pp. 7–8.

14. *Dizionario biografico degli italiani*, vol. 21 (Rome: Treccani, 1978), p. 818.

15. Enrico Castelnuovo, *I Moncalvo* (Milan: Treves, 1908), p. 166.

16. Giuseppe Gallico, "*I Moncalvo* di Enrico Castelnuovo," *Rassegna mensile di Israel* 2d series 6 (1931): 206.

17. Ibid., p. 204.

18. Caviglia, "Vita economica," p. 126.

19. Ibid. See also Sergio della Pergola, *Anatomia dell'ebraismo italiano* (Rome: Carucci, 1976), Chapter 14: "La comunità ebraica," and his *La trasformazione demografica della diaspora ebraica* (Turin: Loescher, 1983); also E. Raseri, "La popolazione israelitica in Italia," *Atti della Società Romana di Antropologia* 10, no. 1 (1904): 1.

20. In 1925 *Israel* became *La rassegna mensile di Israel*, which is still published today. On the Jewish press, see Attilio Milano, "Un secolo di stampa periodica in Italia," *Scritti in memoria di Dante Lattes (Rassagena mensile di "Israel")* 12 (1938): 96–136.

21. See Attilio Milano, "Gli enti culturali ebraici in Italia nell'ultimo trentennio (1907–1937)," *Rassegna mensile di Israel* 12 (1938): 253–269.

22. *L'Idea sionistica* (Modena, 1901–1911) cit. Renzo De Felice, *Storia degli ebrei italiani sotto il fascismo* (Turin: Einaudi, 1961), p. 25.

15

Racial Laws and Internment in Natalia Ginzburg's *Lessico famigliare*

Claudia Nocentini

Lessico famigliare,[1] published in 1962, is probably the most famous of Ginzburg's books and needs very little introduction. It is openly auto-biographical, and the narrative is woven with linguistic idiosyncrasies, jokes, and memorable sayings peculiar to the family of the author, from her very earliest memories up to her second marriage.

Both in her foreword to the novel and in the preface of the following-year new edition of her works, Natalia Ginzburg stresses her feeling of creative freedom and openness in *Lessico famigliare*, a book that shaped itself effort-lessly out of memory: "*Lessico famigliare* is a book of pure, naked, uncovered and stated memory. I don't know if it is the best of my books: but it certainly is the only book I've ever written in a state of total freedom. Writing it was for me exactly the same as speaking."[2]

Although Ginzburg had written a total of six novels by the time she started *Lessico famigliare*, and most of them had strong autobiographical connotations, only in this novel does the focus shift from a more general, individual identity to a specific family identity, and the Jewish component of this identity has center stage for the first time. Yet, as both her parents were socialist and secular, the fact that her father's background was Jewish and her mother's Catholic seemed relevant, at first, only to the old paternal grandmother, whose initial and very short-lived fears about her daughter-in-law are part of the family oral collection of anecdotes. Since neither of the two religions is practiced, attention is focused on political involvement as the common ground between the parents. On the other hand, as the father figure is more prominent within the household, and one of his most conspicuous traits is his sense of stability and coherence, it is mostly his friends whose presence is felt within the novel; his colleagues and their families have a stronger and longer lasting appearance in the narrative, and many of their surnames imply that they are also of Jewish background. As the narrative progresses, and political belonging moves from a nostalgia of the years of early socialism to active antifascism, more specifically to the group of

Giustizia e Libertà, a crowd of friends from a younger generation begins to gravitate around the family, and again their background is mostly Jewish.[3]

The representation of the intimate comedy of family life is the main strength of the narrative. Paradoxically, the reader is drawn into its domestic atmosphere in the full knowledge that the subject matter comes from reality, yet, as the author suggests in the foreword, the reader is captivated by its novelistic dimension. This is in itself a great aesthetic achievement, as writing about real life, particularly about famous people in recent history, is a very difficult enterprise. The main artistic risk, it seems to me, is that once the filter of fiction is removed, great care needs to be taken to reassure the reader that the voyeuristic impulse, which lies perhaps at the bottom of much of our appreciation of literature, is kept well in check. Ginzburg does this admirably by starting her narrative with a barrage of parental prohibitions in nonstandard Italian, immediately creating a feeling of affectionate solidarity and of humorous surprise at the peculiarity of the language, which, although unfamiliar to the reader in its specificity, evokes similar experiences of odd usage due to generational (and often regional) distance. Once safety anchored on this basic common ground, the relationship between reader and narrator is one of trust; gossipy indiscretion and curiosity into the private life of famous people do not go as far as the phrasing with which they were taught table manners, while on a deeper level injunctions and prohibitions are the opening functions of the most ingrained of narrative forms: myths and fairy tales.

The representation of this slightly theatrical bourgeois interior is, on the whole, very realistic, with few concessions to the fantastic. The most notable one is the account of Filippo Turati's flight into exile, seen through the eyes of the writer as an eleven-year-old girl. The old socialist leader, whose legendary persona had already featured in the narrative, described as "big as a bear, with a great goatee beard,"[4] stays under a false name in the family apartment for a few days. The narrator realizes soon that whenever the doorbell rang, this strange guest hid away in his room: "He ran down the passage, trying to go on tiptoe, like a great shadow of a bear on the walls."[5]

Turati's flight in 1927 is the first direct graze with history, but its account is a memory of childhood consisting mainly of a bearlike figure and the laborious effort to match personal observation with an incompatible adult explanation. The departure itself, though, is a mixture of child and adult memory in the description of one of the helpers, Adriano Olivetti, whose hair was receding then but whose look of excitement is linked with later instances of danger.

He was starting to lose his hair and had an almost bald square head, surrounded by fair, curly locks. That evening his face and scanty hair looked wind-swept. His eyes seemed alarmed, but resolute and cheerful. Two or three times in my life I saw that look in his eyes. It was the look he had when he was helping someone to escape, when there was danger and someone to be taken to safety.[6]

Since the thread of the narrative lies in the memorability of the sayings but also the uniqueness of family events, fragmentation, repetition, and ellipsis play a very important part in this book, very often with a comic effect. In this case the detail of somebody's receding hair in a moment of pathos is humorous. There is only the mention of later danger, despite its wrapping of joyful admiration, to remind the reader of the gravity of this predicament, which in itself resulted in two arrests.

Comedy is the connective strength of the narrative. Even the undoubtedly higher moral standpoint of early antifascism is tempered by a strong dose of caricature, and the rightful disdain of the narrator's father appears a lot less self-righteous because of the passionate way that it enters the narrative.

My father always came home furious when he had encountered a procession of Blackshirts in the street, or when at the Faculty meetings he had discovered new Fascists among his acquaintances. "Clowns, impostors, buffoonery!" he would say as he sat down to dinner, and threw his napkin down, banged his glass down, and snorted with disgust. He would express his opinions out loud in the street to friends walking home with him and they would look round in terror. "Cowards! Negroes!" my father would roar when I got in and described their fear, and I think he enjoyed frightening them by talking aloud in the street; partly he enjoyed it, and partly he was unable to control his voice level, which was always very loud, even when he believed he was whispering.[7]

Comedy in this case protects the ego of the reader, whose political background is unlikely to be as sound as that of the writer, but it is probably to be seen as a reaction against the neorealist trend to depict antifascism in strong hagiographic terms.[8]

A representation of her experience of persecution during the fascist regime could be recognized in *Tutti i nostri ieri*, a novel published in 1952, but the autobiographical subject matter had been fictionalized in such a way as to portray the development of a political awareness within her own generation.[9] *Lessico famigliare* shows a similar narrative pattern in that it follows the steps of the narrator's family up to her departure from the family home (unlike a conventional *Entwicklungsroman*, though, what refers directly to the narrator is mentioned very laconically, and the final rite of passage is her second marriage), but the openness of the autobiography raises issues that the previous novel had dealt with less directly. In her earlier novel persecution on the grounds of race had been portrayed from the outside, while the environment of the main character had witnessed and suffered various degrees of political persecution. In *Lessico famigliare* these unavoidable questions are handled with admirable lightness of touch, and a lot of care is taken in presenting grievous events so as not to shock or hurt.

As long as the persecution is caused by political opinions, humor can intercede to rescue, if not the situation itself, at least its account: the middle-class concern of the narrator's mother, who fears people will think that she is related to a murderer when her taxi crashes in the vicinity of the prison;[10] the incongruous rhyming of events when, while two family members are under arrest for political reasons, a third is also arrested because he forgot to return to the barracks after a day's skiing with his girlfriend;[11] and finally, the confident antifascism with which both the mother and this very skier comment, on rhyming occasions, on how boring it all is when they have not even been arrested.[12]

Clearly, both political persecution and racial persecution are hateful, but whereas the former can be romanticized to a certain extent, the latter is too serious to be romanticized and engenders only pity and horror. In her foreword, Ginzburg admits that she has been selective: "There are also many happenings which I have remembered but passed over in writing this book. Among them is much which concerned myself directly . . . because memory is treacherous and books founded on reality are so often only faint reflections and sketches of all that we have seen and heard."[13]

Ellipsis is obvious with regard to the murder of her husband, when the account is as factual as possible, and feelings are neither analyzed nor mentioned. As the event is particularly painful and shocking, through a twice repeated use of prolepsis the narrator ensures that the reader is aware of his death before its main relation in the narrative. This strategic alteration of the story line through anticipation of later chronological material and a variation of narrative focus from the individual to the general are, together with the use of ellipsis, the narrative devices that Ginzburg employs to sew this patch of tragic events into a narrative of everyday normality.

Rognetta never had time to explain about Madagascar. I didn't see him again for many years, and I don't believe that Leone ever saw him again.[14]

The Publisher had a portrait of Leone on the wall in his room, with his head bent a little to one side, his spectacles half way down his nose, a thick mane of black hair, deep dimples in his cheeks, and his feminine hands. During the German occupation Leone had died in the German wing of the Regina Coeli prison in Rome, one icy February.[15]

The factual style in which Ginzburg eventually comes to relate the events leading to her husband's death is not unproblematic:

Leone was arrested in a secret printing-works. We had a flat near Piazza Bologna, and I was there alone with the children; I waited for him. The hours passed and when there was no sign of him gradually I realized that he must have been arrested. That day passed, the night, and the following morning. Adriano came and told me to leave at once since Leone had been arrested; the police might arrive at any moment. He helped me to pack and dress the children, and we hurried away to some friends who had agreed to take me in.[16]

Her exclusion of any mention of feelings from the text may appear almost manipulative to a contemporary reader in that it implies the transformation of unsaid into unsayable pain.[17] Clearly, pain may indeed be unsayable, particularly for an author who is most at ease with comedy, but it is also worth stressing that factual representation of tragic events was the norm in neorealist narrative writings. This reserve also reflected a more general attitude in Italian society at the time, as exemplified in the text by the description of Cesare Pavese and of the author's mother and their refusal to talk about the dead.[18]

References to racial laws[19] are extremely economical and are introduced through concern for the predicament of non-Italian Jews.

It did not look as if Fascism would end soon—or indeed ever. The Rosselli brothers had been killed at Bagnoles de l'Orne. For years now Turin had been full of German Jews, refugees from Germany. My father had some assistants in his laboratory. These people were stateless. We too might be stateless some day, compelled to wander from one country to another, from one police-station to another, without work or roots or family or home.[20]

With this brief and somber section Ginzburg announces the beginning of a general and personal tragedy. The narrative is divided not into numbered chapters but into forty-five sections marked only by an empty line. This is the twenty-ninth section, and despite the absence of dates, it refers to 1938 as it appears between the narrator's marriage and the anti-Jewish census (22 August 1938).[21] Memories of the war period are spread from section thirty-four to section forty-one. Over these twelve sections (29 to 41), racial laws are scarcely alluded to, and their consequences are hardly commented on, particularly when they affect the family:

Leone and I also sometimes talked of going to "Uncle Kahn in America." However they had taken away our passports. Leone had lost his Italian citizenship and was now stateless. . . . However at heart neither he nor I wished to leave Italy.[22]

My father now had lost his chair in the university. He was invited to work in an institute in Liège. He accepted and my mother accompanied him to Belgium.[23]

Any injustice directly hitting the writer is excised from the text. Yet it is also after her marriage that the characterization of the narrator becomes more focused, as the change of marital status is related to a distancing from her own family, and her own identity becomes more visible. Her shyness, her inability to ask her maid what to do, and her own female friends enter the narrative for the first time. While the allusions to racial laws become more insistent, they are paradoxically distanced from the narrator; it is her friends who are Jewish and ready to face an uncertain future, her father who has to leave for Belgium, her husband who is arrested any time the king sets foot in Turin. It appears as if the racial laws had affected everybody else but her, whose main problem is lack of domesticity.

As it was very tiring to have two small babies to look after, and Natalina was too distracted and excited to devote herself to them, my mother advised me to find a dry nurse. She herself wrote to some of the old nurses in Tuscany with whom she had kept in touch, and a nurse arrived just when the Germans had invaded Belgium. We were all very worried and not inclined to cater to a nurse, with her demands for embroidered aprons and wide skirts. Nevertheless although my mother was very anxious about my father, of whom we had no news, she managed to buy the aprons, and actually cheered up to see the big Tuscan nurse moving about the house in a wide rustling skirt. I felt very ill at ease, however and missed old Martina, who had returned to her village in Liguria because she could not get on with Natalina. I was ill at ease because I was permanently afraid of losing this nurse. I was afraid that she would consider us, with our simple ways, beneath her. In any case the big nurse with her embroidered aprons and puffed sleeves reminded me of the precariousness of my own position. I was poor and without my mother's assistance I could not afford a nurse, and I thought of myself as Nancy in *I Divoratori* [a novel by Annie Vivanti] when she watches her little daughter from the window being led along the road by their magnificent nurse, and knows that in fact all the family's money has been lost at the casino.[24]

In her dignified account it seems to me that the author is omitting a very direct reference to a particular racial law, whereby Jewish families could not employ "Aryan" servants, the same law that, as recorded in the police files,[25] did not allow her to keep a maid while interned in the Abruzzi. Her rendition of events could not be more evasive: "When my daughter Alessandra was born my mother stayed a long time with us. She didn't feel like going away again."[26]

By excluding from the text, if not suffering, at least these humiliating instances, Ginzburg manages to paint a picture of pity that implies, but does not express, blame. Perhaps the greatest omission of all is outrage at the intensifying anti-Semitism. Only one proleptic segment that interrupts the flow of the narrative at the time of Mussolini's declaration of war to reassure the reader about the return of her exiled brother in 1945 deals discreetly with this issue. In his peculiarly obsessive way, Mario is indignant and fascinated at the same time about an anecdote that predated the racial campaign and that concerned school anti-Semitism related by his mother.[27]

Mario liked this story enormously. He couldn't get over it, and he asked if it was really true. "I never heard such a thing," he said slapping his thigh, "never heard such a thing." My mother was pleased that he liked her story so much, but she became tired of hearing him repeat that teachers like that did not exist in France, and could not even be imagined. She was fed up with hearing him say, "We in France . . ." and hearing him attack the priests.[28]

Somehow, as this solitary evidence of indignation is linked to indirect, or at least less direct, experience of this odious phenomenon, the text conveys the impression that outrage is an inadequate reaction. But these are just projections, and I can't prove them any better.

Recollections of the time in internment in the Abruzzi are mostly limited to one section (thirty-seven) and appear, at least in part, as an affectionate memory, not unlike the many tales of migration from the cities that were a common feature of war experience in Italy. The additional gravity of her family's predicament as interned rather than evacuees, at least up to the German occupation, can be inferred only by comparison with the position of one of her brothers; Alberto, the former forgetful skier, who is also interned in the Abruzzi with his family, arranges to be moved to a northern village, and this is seen as an indication that he will be set free in the near future.[29] Of the many restrictions brought about by internment, Ginzburg mentions only one, again as referred mainly to others:

All day long "Spindleshanks" went up and down the street, walking along in a half-witted state and stopping to talk to people to whom she recounted her misfortunes, her gloved hands raised to the heavens. All the interned used to promenade up and down like this, taking the same walk a hundred times a day, because they were forbidden to go into the country.[30]

Of the many material hardships suffered by herself and her young family, nothing is said, partly perhaps because they belong to a time of general hardship, partly in order to keep a degree of proportion between the separate representation of her own experience and that of the rest of her original family, partly also because she had already written of this experience both in fictional and directly autobiographical style. Within these textual limitations, the representation of internment in the town of Pizzoli shows amicable relations with the villagers. It allows also for the brief but moving appearance of other interned foreign Jews and therefore for an indirect reminder of a rather underrepresented distress caused by the racial laws. While in her previous representation of restricted residence much attention was focused on the conditions of the south, the short treatment of this period in *Lessico famigliare* does not raise this issue again.

Perhaps Ginzburg's use of ellipsis was partly a self-protective measure, but clearly it succeeded also in allowing for a unique experience to be read with a degree of identification that would otherwise be very difficult to obtain. The influence of the Biblical precept "tell it to your children" is clearly traceable in contemporary narrative by Jewish authors and it is certainly beneficial in that it provides them with an immediate and tangible audience.[31] Publishing an account of an individual experience goes beyond the boundary of one's immediate family and helps to educate those who perhaps most need to be educated on such matters.

NOTES

1. Natalia Ginzburg, *Lessico famigliare* (Turin: Einaud, 1962). All quotations from Ginzburg are from *Opere, raccolte e ordinate dall'autore*, 2 vols. (Mondadori, Milan: 1986 and 1987). The translation into English is by D. M. Low: Natalia Ginzburg, *Family Sayings* (Manchester, England: Carcanet Press, 1984). I would like to thank Anna Laura Lepschy and Marie Orton for their helpful comments on my manuscript.

2. Ginzburg, *Opere*, vol. 1, p. 1133, my translation. Grignani confirms this statement on the evidence of the few alterations to the manuscript, now in the Fondo manoscritti di autori contemporanei dell'Università di Pavia. See Maria Antonietta Grignani, "Un concerto di voci," in *Natalia Ginzburg: La narratice e i suoi testi*, edited by Maria Antonietta Grignani (Rome: Nuova Italia Scientifica, 1986), p. 52.

3. "I am Jewish. It seems to me that anything that concerns the Jews concerns me personally. I'm only Jewish on my father's side, but I always thought that my Jewish half must be heavier and bulkier than the other." In "Gli Ebrei," Ginzburg, *Opere*, vol. 2, p. 643, my translation.

4. Ginzburg, *Opere*, vol. 1, p. 928; Ginzburg, *Family Sayings*, p. 30.

5. Ginzburg, *Opere*, vol. 1, p. 975; Ginzburg, *Family Sayings*, p. 68.

6. Ginzburg, *Opere*, vol. 1, p. 977; Ginzburg, *Family Sayings*, p. 70.

7. Ginzburg, *Opere*, vol. 1, p. 977; Ginzburg, *Family Sayings*, p. 72.

8. Clearly, it does not mean that the writer does not share her father's judgment. In a much later writing about Fellini's *Amarcord*, Ginzburg's views on inept antifascism are just as stern as her father's: "Another character in the film, the father, is inadequate and

cowardly when confronting the fascists. There are no real antifascists in this film. They are not there because this is a world which has not been reached by reason and thought" (*Opere*, vol. 2, p. 564, my translation). As to the reaction against a romanticized representation of antifascism, it might be useful to refer to Calvino's famous "Prefazione 1964" to Italo Calvino, *Il sentiero dei nidi di ragno, Romanzi e racconti*, vol. 1 (Milan: Mondadori, 1991), pp. 1192–1193. Both Natalia Ginzburg and Italo Calvino were editors for the publishing house Einaudi, and it seems reasonable to think that they shared similar views on the undesirability of positive heroes in literature. In *Lessico famigliare*, Ginzburg describes the early postwar literary atmosphere and alludes briefly and perhaps indirectly to this very issue: "the result was a confusion of language between poetry and politics which appeared mingled together" (*Opere*, vol. 1, p. 1065).

9. My analysis of this text and of a previous one, "Racial Law and Interment in Natalia Ginzburg's *La strada che va in città* and *Tutti i nostri ieri*," appears in *Forum Italicum* 21 (2001).

10. Ginzburg, *Opere*, vol. 1, p. 1000.

11. Ibid., p. 999.

12. Ibid., pp. 1000, 1016.

13. Ibid., p. 899.

14. Ginzburg, *Family Sayings*, p. 125.

15. Ibid., p. 132.

16. Ibid., p. 143.

17. Grignani points out the dramatic effect of Ginzburg's coordination in this passage: "La coordinazione con e, altra costante istituzionale della prosa piana e volutamente neutra della scrittrice, dal parlato sale a litania dolorosa di brevi enunciati in sequenza, tenuti insieme da una particella grammaticale che non vuole o non può spiegare il sentimento nascosto sotto l'orizzontalità sintattica" ("Un concerto di voci," p. 54).

18. Ginzburg, *Opere*, vol. 1, pp. 1054, 1061.

19. The wording "leggi razziali" (racial laws) is carefully avoided throughout and always substituted by mention of "campagna razziale" (racial campaign).

20. Ginzburg, *Opere*, vol. 1, p. 1029; Ginzburg, *Family Sayings*, p. 111.

21. "As for my friends' old father in the Via Governolo, at the beginning of the racial campaign he received a form in which he was told to state 'distinctions and special services.' He answered: 'In 1911 I was a member of the *Rari Nantes* club, and I dived into the Po in midwinter. Once when building operations were carried out in my house, the contractor Casella nominated me as foreman" (Ginzburg, *Opere*, vol. 1, p. 1036; Ginzburg, *Family Sayings*, p. 116). For more information about the census, see *L'ebreo in oggetto*, edited by Fabio Levi (Turin: Zamorani, 1991).

22. Ginzburg, *Opere*, vol. 1, p. 1038; Ginzburg, *Family Sayings*, p. 119.

23. Ginzburg, *Opere*, vol. 1, p. 1039; Ginzburg, *Family Sayings*, p. 120.

24. Ginzburg, *Opere*, vol. 1, p. 1043–1044; Ginzburg, *Family Sayings*, p. 124.

25. Alessandro Clementi, "I Ginzburg in Abruzzo," *Paragone* new series 17 (29 October 1991): 66–82.

26. Ginzburg, *Opere*, vol. 1, p. 1059; Ginzburg, *Family Sayings*, p. 137.

27. "My mother told him of something that had happened to a friend's little son, many years ago, before the war and before the racial campaign. This child was Jewish. His parents had sent him to a state school, but had requested the teacher to excuse him from religious instruction. One day this teacher was not in school and there was a substitute who had not been told. When the time for religious instruction came, she was astonished to see the little boy pick up his satchel and prepare to leave. 'Why are you going away?' she asked. 'I always go home when it is time for religious instruction.' 'And why?' he was asked. 'Because I do not love the Madonna.' 'You do not love the Madonna!' cried the mistress in horror, 'Do you hear, children? He does not love the Madonna!' All the

children joined in, 'You do not love the Madonna, you do not love the Madonna!' The parents were obliged to take away their son from the school" (Ginzburg, *Opere*, vol. 1, p. 1047; Ginzburg, *Family Sayings*, p. 126–127).

28. Ginzburg, *Opere*, vol. 1, p. 1047–1048.

29. Ibid., p. 1059.

30. Ibid., p. 1058.

31. From an interview with Marino Sinibaldi in 1990, it appears that this was not the author's intention when she wrote *Lessico famigliare*.

Ginzburg: "What surprised me the most about its success was that young people read it. I didn't expect this because I had not thought of young people at all. And yet they read it."
Sinibaldi: "Do you mean that you had thought of your contemporaries, people who could understand the background?
Ginzburg: "Yes, I thought of my contemporaries."

In Natalia Ginzburg, *É difficile parlare di sé: conversazione a più voci condotta da Marino Sinibaldi*, edited by Cesare Garboli and Lisa Ginzburg (Turin: Einaudi, 1999), p. 131, my translation.

16

Clara Sereni and Contemporary Italian-Jewish Literature

Elisabetta Properzi Nelsen

It is perhaps a little difficult to identify Clara Sereni's place within Italian-Jewish literature if we talk only about her early works. These range from novels such as *Sigma Epsilon* (1974) and *Casalinghitudine* (Housewifery) (1987), to the collection of short stories *Manicomio Primavera* (Insane Asylum Spring) (1989). Her place is easily grasped once we come to her novel *Il gioco dei regni* (The Game of Kingdoms) (1993).

This work employs autobiographical recollection as a way to capture the allure of a primal form of memory—an approach also used by other authors of contemporary Italian-Jewish literature such as Natalia Ginzburg and Giorgio Bassani. For them it was a means of conveying how it feels to belong to a family that is different from those that typify Italian society, but Clara Sereni uses it to retrace her family's past down to her parents' generation. In addition, she provides a sensitive historical background for the events that she writes about and carefully traces her family's own sense of Jewish identity.

The result is a tale of individual lives that together make up three generations in the writer's family. At the same time, these generations also witness many of the most salient historical events of this century: the revolutionary movements in Russia, World Wars I and II, Fascist prisons and Nazi concentration camps, Italian communism, and the Zionist dream. As it unfolds chronologically, the novel is constructed as a mosaic would be, so that each tile of a large picture also has an individual identity.

This chapter shows how Clara Sereni's novel is a representative type of Italian-Jewish literature. Indeed, it is representative because it strove at the end of the twentieth century to uncover moments in Jewish history that have too often been hidden from view or amalgamated into the background of Italy's cultural history.

The book opens with an introduction that is taken from oral Hassidic tradition. This recalls the Jewish leader Baal-Shem Toe, who sensed that misfortune was about to befall his people. To ward it off, he went into the woods, lit a fire, and recited a prayer. As a result his people were saved from harm. Years later, Rabbi Maghid of Mesritsh also went into the woods. He wanted to ask God to listen to his people, although he didn't know how to build a fire. No one had taught him, or perhaps he had forgotten. Still, he was able to recite the same prayer, and so the miracle of a people's deliverance was repeated. Later still, Rabbi Moshe Loeb of Sasow also asked God for help, but he could neither build a fire nor recall the prayer that he once knew. He did, however, remember the same place in the woods, and he hoped that memory of it would be enough to guarantee his people's salvation. Finally, another rabbi, Israel of Rizin, realized that he could not even find the same place in the woods any longer because he had never been told or had also forgotten. He therefore declared that the only thing that he knew how to do was to keep the memory of his people's history alive, though he wondered if that would be enough to ensure their deliverance.

The trepidation felt by these Jewish leaders is also what Clara Sereni feels; she is without precise information and has lost the religious beliefs that connect her to the ethnicity of her people. She does have some memories and the ability to bring others to light. It is this goal that she aims to achieve in *Il gioco dei regni*. Hence, the novel's function is to rekindle the memory of individual lives as well as the past of a whole people who have been struck by misfortune. In a parallel way, the novel also serves to celebrate the acts of courage undertaken by individual families and the community to which they belong. These are acts intended to ensure one's own safety and self-dignity. But the question that the author asks, as did Rabbi Israel of Rizin is, Will that be enough? Namely, will that be enough to keep the memory of this history alive when, as Sereni recognizes, we may no longer know how to pray or how to find a point of reference in relation to the Jewish identity of our past?

The novel is divided into six main chapters, which are, in turn, subdivided into various sections, each of which is associated with a different narrative technique or genre. Among these are narration in the first person, the historical narrative voice, epistolary prose, the diary form, and literary self-examination. In this way each character finds their own means of expression and communication, and the author is able to build a large structure without relying on a single narrative form.

At the same time, two family histories sometimes converge: one Italian and one Russian. Blending the two successfully, the sections alternate between families to show how parallel lives develop and unfold. For the most part, these lives are completely unknown to each other, although historical contingencies cause them to converge now and then.

The story of the upper-middle-class Sereni family is woven together with that of its Russian branch, the family of Xenia Shmulevics and her husband, Lev, both of whom are Russian revolutionaries. After Lev's death, Xenia is left with just her daughter Xeniuska, and so they leave for Paris and then Rome, where Xeniuska meets one of the Sereni sons. The novel's events involve numerous members of the Sereni family, but Emilio and Xeniuska are a couple shown in particularly high relief since they are the ones to whom the writer herself will eventually be born.

The distinctively Jewish quality of the family's past is relived by presenting the reader with the details of everyday life. These same details, however, are also those that are continually threatened and interrupted by the events of history and by their political and social consequences. A quality that is symptomatic of Sereni's writing, the details of everyday life are also at the heart of *Casalinghitudine*, even if that work is set during times of peace and democracy.

As nowhere else, the details of everyday life are typified by the scene that first introduces the reader to the Sereni family. That scene focuses on the Passover ritual that marks the religious identity of the family and its clan. Hence, the reader is presented with Alfonsa Sereni's father, Pellegrino, reading and singing, who bravely faces "the difficulties of Hebrew, overwhelming them with a sort of roughness and approximation, just like any other obstacle in his life" (p. 20).[1] In this way, we are presented from the very beginning with a characterization of the Jew as strong and ready to face any of life's misfortunes. In addition, the menu at the Serenis' Passover is significant in that it reinforces the traditions of dietary customs. It includes unleavened bread, bitter herbs, *stracciatella* with artichokes, and boiled meat with green sauce (even if Dalinda the cook mutters because their "ghetto" recipes aren't the same as the ones used by her mistress) (p. 20).

After this meal, which identifies the Serenis' ethnicity and religion, the author provides a chapter in which she explains the names of all the children born to Lello and Alfonsa Sereni over a seven-year period: Enrico, Velia, Lea, Enzo, and Emilio. The boys all have names that start with *E*, which stands for the initial letter of the word "Jew" in Italian (*ebreo*). Sereni adds that this fact also reflects a kind of dynastic perspective on the family. Lea has the only biblical name, and Velia's, which is Roman, represents the family's tie to a new national home as well as "another step into the Gentile world." This is explained further by Lello, according to whom Italy at the beginning of the twentieth century "seemed to welcome them with open arms" because it "was erasing the centuries-old discrimination against the Jews as something obsolete and therefore absurd" (p. 40). From Lello's point of view, this is the environment that will allow his descendants to live lives free from discrimination. Of course, he has no way of knowing that in years ahead, from 1938 to 1940, racist laws would be perpetrated by the Fascist government and that fear of persecution would again become synonymous with the mere fact of being Jewish.

Different from the dominant Christian mainstream, the theme of everyday Jewish life is also defined by the Sereni children's religious education, especially because they study Hebrew and the Torah and have their bar mitzvahs. At the same time, they are also characterized by lively intellectual development. Expressions such as "reading to the bursting point" and "greediness of books" are used to describe them, and their reading habits range eclectically from authors such as Benedetto Croce and Stendhal, to Hegel and Flaubert. Indeed, their knowledge of these authors not only indicates the depth of their intellectual pursuits but also places them among those in opposition to the dominant ideology of the day. Emilio (nicknamed "Mimmo" from early childhood) is especially precocious, and he is the one who becomes interested in Marxism at the age of eleven, accusing his brothers of being "stupid bourgeois followers of Hegel" (p. 123).

But *Il gioco dei regni* also emphasizes Jewish identity as a condition of difference or variation from the mean. This condition is experienced as opposition to a system of power that threatens it. Moreover, in this same context the metaphoric meaning of the novel's title is to be explored. Thus, the reader is led to ask: What is the game of kingdoms? Who plays it, and to what kingdoms does it refer? It is a complicated game that the Sereni children made up on the rainy days and winter afternoons during their childhood and adolescence. They conjured up imaginary kingdoms and countries of which they were the respective rulers and ministers. Each kingdom would produce its own newspapers and official state proceedings, as well as maps and guides of its cities. The fictitious countries even accounted for museums, postage stamps, and a mint to coin currency. Their newspapers were printed on a ditto machine, and political debates were timed according to an hourglass filled with blue sand, which allowed each participant an opportunity to talk. Adults participated, too, especially Aunt Ermelinda, who carefully observed her nephews, noting which among them would eventually become the Chosen One. The Sereni family's fondness for this game also shows that they realized the importance of never taking for granted what they had around them. In addition, by inventing it, they constructed a venue in which to train themselves intellectually while engaging in dialogue. A vigorously active process, this training was also supported by the strong ties linking all the family members together. Later, as the Sereni children grow up and differentiate themselves from their siblings, it becomes clear that the political and religious choices that they make as adults reflect the roles that they had played together in the game of kingdoms.

Mimmo Sereni is the one who will choose the most political path. In fact, his Marxist beliefs, which are expressed by his unconditional commitment to the Italian Communist Party, lead him to withdraw from the rest of his family and almost deny being Jewish. During World War II he takes refuge in the Holy Land, where he goes to start a new life, but his politics set him squarely against the creation of the new state of Israel. This is due to his belief in the preservation of a free Palestine. Mimmo is therefore an excellent example of the Italian Jew who believes more strongly in his political ideas as a catalyst for Italian social change than he does in the preservation of Jewry itself within Italian society. In the postwar years he then becomes one of the most respected members of the Italian Communist Party, which is partly in recognition of his tireless opposition to Fascism, his time spent in prison, and his forced periods of exile in Paris.

When much younger, he had once decided to change his name to "Uriel," referring to Ur, the city of Abraham. This was to signify his calling to go on a new biblical mission in search of the land of justice as Abraham had. Obsessed with orthodoxy, Mimmo thought of himself as a new Abraham. In this light, Jewish orthodoxy is a point of reference for him that he will later on exchange for communist orthodoxy. Still, the dilemma that Zionism and communism represent is not felt only by Mimmo. It colors every Sereni-family event, though he is the family member who metaphorically represents it more than any other. For him, the dichotomy that it sets in place is not just a matter of a political choice. It involves his personal search for identity and existential meaning. Consequently, it also involves his marriage to Xeniuska, or Loletta, which is the affectionate nickname that he gives her. Furthermore, his dilemma achieves poignancy because it shapes his emotions and defines his feelings of love. In this context, his love for Xeniuska implies that he teach her about philosophy and history in order to awaken her to his political cause: "Mimmo explained to Xeniuska about Russian populism and Zionism. He also explained Marx, Engels, Bakunin and the French Revolution. Using a light and affectionate tone typical of that used to tell fairy tales to children, he also told her about some Jewish wise men: Akiva, Meir, Hillel, Shamnai . . . and Elisha ben Avja. This man, who had read much and yet also had an impelling need for justice, finally acted without faith in God" (p. 204).

In the chapter after this quotation Sereni comes to her own conclusion about her father's controversial political opinions, but she leaves her reader with an unresolved issue. From a perspective at the end of the twentieth century, she reveals an almost postmodern view, since she finally embraces neither of the two political stances: "Zionism and Communism: these are words that have taken on different shades of meaning through the years. For those who are now twenty years old Zionism is identified with Israeli expansionism, and Communism with the flags that were hauled down from the Kremlin's golden domes" (p. 205).

In contrast to this view, when Mimmo and his brother Enzo were in their twenties at the beginning of the century, communism and Zionism had found a common denominator in the hope of creating a different world that would be both more just and more human. Sereni adds that each brother's political choices were based on personal feelings and inclinations, as well as on passions and fears, "unresolved psychological knots," and painful experiences endured. She also says that, ultimately, we can know very little about the brothers' intimate thoughts because they are men who chose to act. Consequently, they are men who used words to change the world around them, but not to talk about themselves. Sereni goes on to express other opinions about the past. She admits, for example, that those in her family made many mistakes, but she justifies their errors in light of the fact that the latter half of the twentieth century was "merciless" and that the enemy that they faced seemed undefeatable. In struggling with this enemy, injustice, some countered with balanced responses, and some made recourse to dogma. The latter is the case with Mimmo Sereni.

As a result, characters such as Enzo and Mimmo do not reflect a victimization of Jewish identity. Instead, theirs is an identity born from the strong sense of self that flourishes when nurtured by the members of a close-knit community. It springs from a profound sense of belonging both to one's family and to collective experiences, such as the political activism discussed earlier.

In treating the horrors of the Holocaust, Sereni also approaches from an oblique perspective, and she shows the reader, for example, how even apparently marginalized people become emblematic of such a persecution. One such character is Aunt Ermelinda, who struggles to maintain the routine of her existence even during times of extreme danger. Living in the midst of great confusion and moral disarray, she nonetheless discovers "a strong and solid law" inside her that enables her to hold on and survive. Another character like this is Giacomo Pontecorvo, Alfonsa Sereni's brother. Because his "accidental" death is both mysterious and ominous, it comes to embody the genocide perpetrated against the Jews.

However, Sereni does not focus on the Holocaust itself, and in this sense her novel is different from works by Natalia Ginzburg and Giorgio Bassani. Their novels recall those who did not survive it as well as those who did and who therefore have to remember as well as live with the burden of their memories. Sereni is surely familiar with Primo Levi's personal account in *Se questo è un uomo* (If This Is a Man), and she probably also recalls the tragic description of the trains loaded with Jews in Elsa Morante's *La Storia* (History), but instead of the scenes of destruction that these novels evoke, she has chosen to emphasize her characters' classical moral virtue and psychological fortitude. She recognizes that the horror of mass murder was organized to deliberately destroy the inner strength and self-dignity of human beings, but she chooses to denounce it indirectly. Her aim in this is to tell a tale of human strength rather than defeat.

This fact has to do with another aspect of *Il gioco dei regni*: the importance and function of its female protagonists. These are somewhat overshadowed by the Sereni brothers since they emerge to dominate major portions of the plot, but female characters, who are generally traced in lower profile, achieve more and more importance as the novel progresses. In this sense, Sereni has tried to retain elements from previous works, such as *Casalinghitudine*, that help to identify *Il gioco dei regni* as a form of the female novel or women's writing.

In fact, the female characters who fill in the Sereni family mosaic are the ones who support the whole family structure. Alfonsa is the matriarch and a kind of biblical mother who nourishes and preserves Jewish traditions. She is the center of the household and is like a vine that sends its roots deep into the domestic intimacy of her home. She guards her family's customs and serves as the repository of its value on a daily basis. She is also the mother who transmits the rules and prayers of her religion to her children, which is represented as a tree that is growing new branches. This metaphor is evoked during the same Passover meal described earlier. At one point, Pellegrino Pontecorvo looks at his pregnant daughter Alfonsa intently and realizes that she embodies the continuity of the family's roots: "He gazed on Alfonsa and on her prominent belly and breasts ready to nurse," and he realized that "the distance or the road between the old roots behind him and her new branches would continue to remain whole" (p. 21). Alfonsa retains her function as the trunk of the family tree throughout the novel, and she thus becomes the woman in whom her children recognize their own Jewish identity.

Later, she is left speechless and incapable of action after the death of her firstborn child, Enrico. Deprived of energy and the vitality necessary to face life anew, she starts to speak again and resume her habitual routine only because of her granddaughter Adale, to whom she sings a Jewish nursery rhyme. To relieve the pain of her son's death, she also goes through a brief period of alcoholism, but she discovers that she shares a kind of communion with her two daughters-in-law, Dvora and Xenia. They come to live with her after Enrico's death and Mimmo's arrest, and she enjoys a certain female complicity with them. Alfonsa is moved by their youth, vulnerability, and suffering, but at the same time she feels responsible for their welfare:

She feels like both laughing and crying, would like female complicity in sharing complaints and jokes, and craves to talk about her confused feelings. She also thinks that her duty is different from this and that she ought to be strong and persevering. . . . But she has also accustomed her family to this pattern, which they expect from her, so that her milk will flow like a river as long as they need it and for as long as their appetite requires its nourishment— just like Sarah's, the wife of hundred-year-old Abraham (pp. 271–272).

Parallel to Alfonsa's life is Xenia Pamphilova Silberberg's. She is Lev Silberberg's wife, the Russian revolutionary known as the "Ishtar terrorist." Xenia is also Xeniuska's mother. A widowed refugee first in France and then in Italy, she was raised in the Russian Christian Orthodox Church, though no longer a believer. Instead she is committed to the cause of the Russian Revolution, though her personality retains a strongly spiritual side. Communism becomes synonymous for her with solitude and sacrifice after her husband dies in prison, and she is forced to live in Russia. Consequently, she eventually comes to think that her previous terrorist activities only separated her from reality, which she finally comes to define as a daily routine linked to a warm existence of human affections. Moreover, Xenia is particularly defined by the special relationship that she has with her daughter Xeniusksa, named symptomatically after herself and whom she raises alone. These facts tend to emphasize her strong will and maternal attachment to Xeniuska, but Xenia is also very quiet and introverted. Sereni also proves that she has done her research on Xenia, who was her grandmother. She quotes from the book that Xenia wrote entitled *Mother and Daughter*, and she lingers on the controversial nature of their mother–daughter relationship, which is described most fully after Xeniuska's marriage to Mimmo.

At the novel's beginning Xenia's memories unfold without any order, and they appear as diary entries written in the first person. These function as flashbacks to her past. Later, when Xeniuska also becomes involved in Communist Party activities as a result of her marriage to Mimmo, it becomes apparent that she is repeating her own mother's experiences as a young bride. As a result, Xenia urges her to discontinue her party activities, but by doing so Xenia only manages to engender mistrust in her daughter. Although she will never convert to Judaism, Xenia feels that Israel fulfills all the expectations of a promised land, the land where her later years will be spent peacefully after a life full of sacrifices, inner torment, and reflection. Sereni intends to be very precise in pointing out that Xenia never became Jewish. In Na'an, inside the kibbutz, where she chooses to live , she writes her will and describes how she wants her funeral and burial. Sereni stresses the fact that Xenia "never forgot to not be Jewish" and that she longed to share the last part of her journey with her friends. "When the time came everything happened just like she had wished: music, flowers, special food, colorful clothes, the affectionate gravestone under the trees, a funeral without sadness just like the simple passing of a season" (p. 422).

In contrast to this, her daughter Xeniuska considers herself a communist first and a Jew second, just like her husband, Mimmo. In a sense, this perspective springs from her own experiences since her identity is constantly held up to that of her husband's, which fulfills a public political role. For this reason, her Jewish identity is camouflaged, in effect, by a political one. Called "Loletta" by her husband, Xeniuska dies of thyroid cancer in 1947. Clara Sereni is her youngest daughter.

As one can see in the lives of these women, Sereni has created what she has called an "uninterrupted female genealogy" that leads right down to herself. She also explains how she arrived at writing it. In the novel's last section, entitled "After the Story," Sereni tells how she met Giacometta Limentani, who is a writer, translator, and *mora* (teacher of Jewish wisdom). Limentani introduced Sereni to the midrash, the Hebrew exegesis of holy texts. "Drsh" is the root of this word, and it means "to interrogate" or "investigate." Hence, with this word in mind Sereni undertook writing "an intellectual game rich in surprises." This decision spurred her first trip to Israel, where she discovered her grandmother's writing in the form of diaries, notes for conferences, articles, essays, and letters. Feeling like a detective as she pored over these items, Sereni soon realized that her grandmother Xenia had had an intense relationship to writing, rather than a casual or occasional one. So in one sense her family biography really begins with her grandmother's activity as a writer—the same grandmother who became Jewish by choice.

This fact in particular leads Sereni to question her own identity, especially as it relates to her family's female genealogy. Therefore she asks herself: "Am I really Jewish if my mother and grandmother were not, at least from a legal point of view?" But this query is one that she answers by raising still other questions, which mostly concern her mother, whom Clara remembers only briefly during the last few months of her mother's life, when Clara was only two years old. Still, one of the things that she does recall is a sense of her parents' shared intimacy and her father's subsequent grief over his wife's death. This recollection leads Sereni back to herself. But she can now gaze back upon her former two-year-old self from a great distance, and from that vantage point she describes the meaning and feeling of being motherless. For her, without the love and sense of identity that a mother can provide, her mother's death also recalls the kind of loss associated with biblical orphans: those left proverbially alone and rootless. Therefore, it is obvious in this context how the mother–daughter relationship is important to women's writing and how giving birth and mothering are apt metaphors for the female writer's own book. Still, Sereni is not ultimately able to prove that her mother converted to Judaism before her parents were married, and so she concludes that she cannot claim to be totally Jewish. Nonetheless, she feels strongly attached to her family's heritage and to a sense of Jewish identity.

As the reader progresses through her novel, her reconstruction of women and children from the past is rendered in ever greater detail and nuance. Indeed, her family members seem to be the real people who they once were, not just literary re-creations. This is especially true of her ability to evoke the ephemeral, such as her grandmother's "beautiful voice, tenderly veined with a Russian accent"

(p. 446).

Sereni also asks her reader and herself to consider still other questions. Among these are (1) Am I a Jewish writer, or just another Italian contemporary author? (2) Do I belong to a specific Jewish literary tradition that is characterized by its own themes and style? and (3) Does Italy have its own Jewish literary tradition? The answers to these questions, from my point of view, bear repeating. In fact, many Italian writers from the early twentieth century and then later, during the postwar period, have been Jewish. Italo Svevo and Alberto Moravia were two of the first. Later, at midcentury, Natalia Ginzburg, Elsa Morante, and Giorgio Bassani, as well as Primo Levi and Carlo Levi, all published works of fiction, while Emilio Sereni became known as a poet. Several of them transcended Jewish themes in favor of existential or social issues. In addition, quite a few, like Mimmo Sereni, found personal and literary identity as intellectual militants in support of the Italian Communist Party.

Others writing about memory and recollection, such as Natalia Ginzburg and Giorgio Bassani, have addressed the issue of Jewish identity in lyrical and personal ways. On the one hand, Bassani's *The Garden of the Finzi-Contini* tells the story of a Jewish family swept away by the Holocaust. He framed this tale as a nostalgic recollection of love and youth that flowered amid an enchanted garden. It was the perfect and privileged refuge from threats from the outside world. On the other hand, Natalia Ginzburg's *Lessico famigliare* (Family Sayings) sought to recapture a lost Jewish culture by evoking it in the words, sayings, and "hieroglyphs" of her extended family's speech.

Elsa Morante, however, was one of the first writers to indict History itself and those who wield systems of power for their persecution of the weak and defenseless. These victims—including women, children, and Jews—share a common ground in that Morante sees them as a race of little creatures who are all in some way "different" from others. This same perspective—that of the persecuted—can describe Primo Levi's novel, too: *Se questo è un uomo* (If This Is a Man). Writing as one who witnessed the reality of genocide himself and survived confinement in a concentration camp, he retells his experiences there with realism and resignation.

But Sereni's work is different from all of these. Like Bassani and Ginzburg, she does give prominence of place to the function of memory, although this is really overshadowed by her factual and historical reconstruction of the past. Because of this, her writing can be associated with a new kind of historical novel that is principally written by female authors such as Rosetta Loy, Marina Jarre, and Marta Morazzoni.[2] Moreover, she occupies a prominent place in what I see as an existing Jewish literary tradition—a tradition that has been underestimated at times because it was mistaken for that of other genres such as the historical novel and the realist novel. Instead, this tradition is one with its own thematic and stylistic characteristics, such as a certain balance between humor and a concern for serious ethical issues—a balance that Sereni herself achieves in the creation of several characters in *Il gioco dei regni*. Other aspects of this novel can also be pointed to as part of a Jewish literary tradition: Sereni's lexical palette, for example, which makes regular reference to religious concepts and traditional customs. Indeed, mention of them is varied and recurrent enough that Sereni included a glossary to explain them at the novel's end. It covers terms such as *purim*, *shabbat*, *shema*, *teshuvah*, *kosher*, and *gheenna*. Yet the glossary is more than a curiosity since it may help to bring back to life a language that is still unknown to many Italian readers. Its existence is, in fact, a declaration that most of us still know very little about Jewish Italians and their traditions.[3]

On a more personal level, Sereni's novel also seems to represent the initiation of a learning process that the author had never explored before coming face-to-face with certain facts and emotions issuing from the discovery of her family history. The final result is an original and creative novel that is even provocative at times. In addition, it brings buried history to light that is unfamiliar to most readers—and this beyond its considerable value as biographical reconstruction. Moreover, Sereni's protagonists, both male and female, emerge in all their emotional complexity due to her ability to tell a story, without which her characters could never come to life—her manifest skill in rendering historical detail and factual accuracy notwithstanding.

Il gioco dei regni is an intriguing and unusual novel that looks at Jewish identity in the past from an honest historical perspective and does so while conveying a solid sense of reality. The protagonists are both winners and losers from time to time, but they are also voices and images that testify to the passage of time and its legacy: men who denied their own feelings in order to become role models and women who seemed resigned to their own subordination. These people, having led lives only apparently at the margins of history, are worth remembering.

NOTES

1. All the quotations are taken from *Il gioco dei regni* (Florence: Giunti, 1993). All translations are mine.

2. In 1997 Rosetta Loy published *La parola ebreo* (Turin: Einaudi, 1997); *First Words: A Childhood in Fascist Italy*, translated by Gregory Conti (New York: Metropolitan Books, 2000). This is one of her most recent works that can be considered a cross between the autobiographical novel and the historical essay. In it she recollects the years in which her own Catholic family and Italian bourgeoisie did not react against racist laws of the Fascist regime or develop any consciousness of the tragedy that was about to happen. Loy outlines the contours of what can be called a "gray zone" in which individual and collective memory are superimposed, and she thereby shows that the knots of a moral and historical dilemma are still very relevant.

3. In another short story, symptomatically entitled "Ebrei" (Jewish People), published two years after *Il gioco dei regni* (in 1995 in the collection *Eppure* [Yet] [Milan: Feltrinelli, 1995]), Clara Sereni again addresses the issue of historical ignorance of Italian-Jewish tradition. In this story, set initially during the period of Fascist racial laws from 1938 to 1939, a woman remembers her high school friendship with a girl who she eventually discovers is Jewish. While she is a teenager, this main female character does not understand why her friend, who is always called by her last name, Zarfati, does not keep her promise to invite her, the so-called *Gentile*, to her birthday party. Consequently, she feels betrayed in their mutual friendship, which is based on collaboration; they both study and amuse

themselves together. She feels that there is a difference between the two of them, even though this difference is never understood, not even when she is older and becomes a grandmother. In fact, later, sharing an afternoon with her granddaughter and one of her granddaughter's friends, she realizes that this little girl is Jewish because she cannot eat *prosciutto* (cured ham). As the little girl says, "We don't eat ham, we are Jewish" (p. 54), the grandmother is shattered and is hit by her own memories and by the cultural and racial differences that exist within her own society as something unknown, undecipherable, and frightening. She also tries to prevent her granddaughter from being disappointed in the future by her peers. She suggests to her granddaughter that it is better not to mix with people whom one doesn't know in order not to encounter strange customs of living. Hence, this female protagonist is used to present readers with the historical and social reality of a group that still exists in Italian society. Nonetheless, it is still received as strange, mysterious, unknown, dark, misunderstood, and therefore not to be trusted.

17

Italian Synagogue Architecture and Italian-Jewish Identity

Samuel Gruber

The Italian-Jewish community can boast, more than any other in the European Diaspora, of an unbroken chain of settlement and cultural cohesion dating back to ancient Rome. Since the third and fourth centuries C.E. at least, the art and architecture commissioned by Jews in Italy have reflected the tastes and talents of the surrounding majority culture. We can already see evidence of the amalgamation of the classical decorative language with Jewish meaning in the paintings of the Roman-Jewish catacombs, the mosaics of the synagogue of Bova Marina in Calabria, and the architecture of the synagogue in Ostia Antica. One net result of this ongoing process is that Jews in Italy became, at an early date, Italian Jews—influenced by, but distinct from, the Jewish cultures of *Sepharad* and *Ashkenaz*.[1]

Much of the cultural expression of Italian Jews is a product of this combination. Over the past four centuries there has been an especially rich architectural testimony to the fertile creative exchange between mainstream artistic language and adaptive Jewish use and meaning. More than in many other countries, Jews in Italy have been comfortable in their use of mainstream cultural expression, accepting it as their own. But in almost every period of Italian-Jewish history, the choices of Jewish patrons (and on occasion, artists) also convey something more: popular themes and styles are adapted to present new messages. Some of these were directed outward toward a non-Jewish audience. Others were more discreet and were intended to color Jewish sensibilities about cultural and political identity and allegiance.

One obvious case is the widespread use of pagan imagery in Jewish funerary contexts—dating from the Jewish catacombs in Rome to the Jewish Cemetery on the Lido of Venice—but the process of artistic appropriation can also be seen in architecture, where primarily design motifs, not illustrative or decorative imagery, are employed. As we will see, the popular adoption of Gian Lorenzo Bernini's spiral column motif from the Baldichin at new St. Peter's in Rome became one of the most popular design elements of synagogue arks during the

Baroque period. Other adaptations include the use of hidden light sources to illuminate the reader's table, as at the Scuola Canton Synagogue in Venice, a motif borrowed from Baroque altar and apse designs.

This process of stylistic appropriation and assimilation is in marked contrast to the Jewish artistic sensibility of the post–emancipation era, when Jews eagerly erected large, new synagogues in towns and cities of Risorgimento Italy. Here, deliberate attempts were made to compete in terms of siting and size with Christian churches and cathedrals, but attention was paid to incorporate stylistic innovations that made it clear to the viewer that these were not Christian foundations. Paradoxically, this overt expression through architecture of Jewish "otherness" occurred simultaneously with the greatest assimilation of Italian Jews ever. In the eighteenth century, when patrons preferred the popular styles of the day, they were still ghettoized.

While a large number of synagogues survive throughout the northern half of modern Italy, two geographically distinct areas—Piedmont and the Veneto—offer particularly rich collections of monuments, reflecting the long and relatively tolerant attitudes toward Jews in those regions. Jews were ghettoized but allowed to pursue a wide range of economic and cultural pursuits. Less restrictive than the ghettos of the Papal States, the Venetian and Piedmontese communities were forced to stay cohesively together but frequently interacted with their Christian neighbors. Because they are much less known, I focus on some of the Piedmontese synagogues. The prosperous Piedmontese community built numerous synagogues over a period of four centuries, many of which —such as those at Alessandria, Asti, Biella, Carmagnola, Casale Monferato, Cherasco, Cuneo, Ivrea, Mondovi, Saluzzo, and Vercelli—still survive.[2] Nothing is known of early synagogues in Piedmont, though there must certainly have been prayer rooms available to the Jewish communities that were formed or expanded in the fourteenth century following the expulsion of Jews from France. Synagogues were probably single rooms in the private houses of the wealthiest members of each community—the forerunners of the more elaborate ghetto synagogues from the period of the early eighteenth century, when ghettos were formally established in many towns. These ghettos were usually formed around a large, central courtyard from which most or all Jewish-occupied dwellings were entered, including the synagogue, as can still be seen at Chieri, Saluzzo, and elsewhere.

Known synagogues of Piedmont fall into two main groups. The first consists of smaller synagogues from before the emancipation of the Jews of the kingdom of Savoy in 1848. These are usually unmarked on the street and occupy residential-type buildings in the old ghettos. Sanctuaries were usually on upper floors, allowing greater security but also better lighting. Nondescript on the exterior, the sanctuaries are often ornately decorated within. Many are particularly noted for their richly carved Baroque and rococo arks and *tevahs*. These often incorporated twisted columns, a popular device from contemporary church architecture but adapted by synagogue designers to a new context. Bernini's columns are modeled after a much older set of twisted columns in the church that had previously marked the area reputedly over St. Peter's tomb. From at least the Middle Ages, these columns were believed to have come from Solomon's temple, and this, I believe, explains their popularity in synagogue design. Twisted columns are used in the Venice synagogues, too.[3]

Perhaps the most typical of the older synagogues is that of Cherasco,[4] because of its location, its approach, its articulation and decoration. It is one of a series of small upper-floor, square-plan sanctuaries with ornate, centrally placed *tevot* (reader's platforms). The Cherasco synagogue is on the third floor of a building entered through the ghetto courtyard of the small town. From a small stair landing one enters directly into the sanctuary, marked by a dedication plaque from Nathan and Abraham Benedetto. The inscription, dated 1797, reads, "I will wash my hands with purity, I will encircle your Altar, O Most High!" Below the inscription is a sink to allow the ritual purification before entering. On the wall to the right is the ark, with finely carved gilded doors, upon which are inscribed the Ten Commandments. The ark is impressive in its use of the twisted columns, which appear in three sizes: small colonettes flanking the ark doors; slightly larger columns supporting an inscribed entablature; and large columns that flank the cabinet proper and support an ornate Baroque, broken segmental pediment, in the center of which is set a small oval window, surmounted by a crown. The whole framing arrangement is similar to contemporary church altars.

The synagogue of Carmagnola[5] is entered from the street, and one immediately ascends a steep stair giving entry into a small vestibule that, in turn, leads directly into the prayer hall or, via another stair, to the women's gallery. The hall was a richly decorated, eighteenth-century space, similar to Christian confraternities but elegant, not overdone. The almost square room is open and airy. Benches line the walls except in front of the entrance door and the ark, which is set in the middle of the wall to the left of the entrance. The ark is relatively simple in design, a wooden cabinet with double doors flanked by twisted columns.

Each of the other walls has two vertical windows, closed by wooden shutters and surmounted by decorative stucco. On the walls between the windows are stucco cartouches with biblical verses in Hebrew. These would once have been richly gilded. The women's gallery is above the atrium and is separated from the main hall by a wooden balustrade. In the center of the space is an octagonal *tevah* with an elaborately carved, open canopy supported by eight twisted columns surmounted with Corinthian capitals, festoons, and garlands.

The most impressive of the early sanctuaries is the German-rite synagogue of Casale Monferrato,[6] built in 1595 in the center of the old ghetto but subsequently replanned and redecorated in the eighteenth century in a rich rococo style. The synagogue was completely restored in 1969 by the Soprintendenza ai Monumenti della Regione Piemonte, which declared it a national monument and opened it as a Jewish museum.

The synagogue was enlarged in 1662, and the configuration of the interior was substantially transformed in the eighteenth century. A massive pulpit, added in 1765, projects from the side wall on long, curved brackets above the heads of the worshipers—clearly an element inspired by contemporary church architecture. A new ark, installed in 1787, consists of three sections. Fluted Corinthian columns frame the central section, which protrudes, and they support elaborately carved frieze and cornice. The ark's side panels and attic section were added in 1866. Between 1853 and 1866 the building was further changed, in part reflecting new post–emancipation attitudes and desires. The *tevah*, ceiling, and seating arrangement were transformed, and a new entrance was made closer to the street beneath the women's gallery. The more traditional plan—squarer, with entry on the west—became longitudinal, much closer to the basilica arrangement favored after emancipation. The ark is set above three steps, and the *tevah* has been moved immediately in front, compressing both elements into a single focal point at the end of the long axis. The area in front of this new combined liturgical area resembles a church sanctuary, separated from the main prayer hall by ornate, wrought-iron grille and gates. Congregation leaders explained that since the site was oriented southwest, the new arrangement did not interfere with the traditional placement of the ark on the wall facing Jerusalem. They made no comment concerning the conflation of ark and *tevah*, an innovation that was becoming increasingly common in new synagogue architecture north of the Alps, but in Casale, the combination of elements appears to be more one of spatial practicality than of Reform tendencies.

The women's gallery had been expanded in 1720 and given delicate, gilded latticework screens, Hebrew inscriptions on the walls in rococo-style cartouches, and Hebrew letters in a painted sky on the elaborately decorated ceiling. All remind the visitor that this is a Jewish place of worship, worthy of an inscription based on Haggai 2:9, "the later splendor of this house shall be greater than the former."

Shortly thereafter, in 1832, a gift by Mordechai Segre enabled the rebuilding of the synagogue of Saluzzo,[7] located on the second floor of a house in the great court of the ghetto, a distinct section of the ghetto entered through a stone arch. A small entrance leads through a gilded wooden door into the sanctuary proper. The experience is extraordinary as one moves through the small opening into a surprisingly vast space, intended to hold up to 300 worshipers. This effect is accomplished by the height of the room, which is spanned by a flattened plaster vault. The entire space, lit by eight large windows, is open and unencumbered. At the entrance end of the hall four simple Tuscan columns support a women's balcony, separated from the main space by an elaborate grille-wall, which has a slightly semicircular projecting bay in its center (on line with the ark below). The top of the grille conforms to the contour of the vault, creating an unusual tension between this upper curve and the austere straightness of the supporting columns and their connecting entablature.

In many ways Saluzzo is a transitional stage between the small, square-plan, eighteenth-century synagogues and the large basilica-plan synagogue of the post–emancipation period. Here, for the first time in Piedmont, the benches are arranged in parallel rows facing the ark, as would become the norm in later synagogue design. Directly facing the entrance wall, again as in later synagogues, is the ark. While the location and exterior of the synagogue—on the top floor of a ghetto courtyard building—were traditional, the whole interior arrangement would have recalled to the congregants the disposition of a Christian church.

The second group of synagogues (referred to in Italy as temples) consists of a series of large, freestanding urban structures built after emancipation. These are public monuments, signaling a Jewish desire to be accepted within mainstream society and also expressing a Jewish belief in equality of religious status.

Nowhere was the new spirit of excessive celebration more clearly expressed than in Turin, where in 1859 the Jews of the city embarked on a massive building project that eventually threatened to bankrupt the community. The result, the towering structure now known as the Mole Antonelliana, after its engineer-architect Alessandro Antonelli, was sold by the community to the city in 1877 before its completion.[8] Today, the Mole is a symbol of Turin, much as the contemporary Eiffel Tower is of Paris, yet it also stands as the most visible Jewish monument in Italy. There is something of the Tower of Babel about it, signifying the ambition but futility of emancipation Jews, whose grasp was often greater than their reach.

The late nineteenth-century Piedmont synagogues are part of a Europe-wide movement. While they often emulate church buildings, almost all contain distinctive architectural or decorative details that clearly pronounce their Jewish identity.

Following the sale of the Mole Antonelliana, the Main Synagogue of Turin was begun in 1880 and inaugurated on 16 February 1884. The design competition of 1879 makes clear the ambitious needs of a post–emancipation Jewish community in a major city—it specified room for 1,000 men, with 700 seats, a women's gallery for 400, an organ, a choir area, a pulpit, a *tevah*, and an ark; in addition, offices and annexes were needed. The design of the multi-towered, Neo-Moorish style temple abandoned the Renaissance style of the Mole—and centuries of Italian tradition—instead using Islamic motifs, linking the building to many new synagogues of similar size being erected in countries north of the Alps. In Turin new elements, such as the Mameluke-inspired parapets and the four rectangular corner towers with bulbous domes, are in evidence. Architectural historian Carol Herselle Krinsky suggests that German and Austrian publications may have played a role in this, though the example of Florence, the largest new Italian synagogue, was also at hand.

For the first time it appears that Jewish patrons saw the classical Italian tradition as a foreign burden, an imposition rather than a natural inheritance. That the Islamic style should find favor in Italy—which as a nation still vividly recalled Saracen invasions of the Middle Ages and would soon embark on wars of conquest in North Africa—is truly remarkable.

Discussion leading to the erection of the great temple of Vercelli[9] began as early as 1864 in the paper *L'educatore israelita*, when members of the community broached the subject of building a synagogue better adapted to the growing community (then about 600) and for the prestige of the city. The architect, Marco Treves (1814–1898), was invited to study the project. He was a prestigious architect and a native of Vercelli, and had designed the classical-style synagogue in Pisa that opened in 1863. Treves' project was grandiose, but the community decided to spend even more than he projected. In size and cost it embodies all the communal aspirations of Turin, but in style it remains closer, in many elements, to Italian roots.

The synagogue is designed in the Moorish style and occupies the location of a previous sanctuary. Because of the size and cost of the project, work went slowly. Demolition of the earlier building and new construction did not begin until 1874, and the building was completed in 1878. To celebrate the occasion, the Jewish community struck a bronze commemorative medal in the tradition of Italy's Renaissance princes and popes.

The tripartite façade is influenced by synagogues erected in Central Europe in the mid-nineteenth century, such as the Templegasse Synagogue in Vienna (1853–1858)[10] and the Choral Temple in Bucharest (1864–1866),[11] which had a similar arrangement of a higher central bay and four small turrets. The Vercelli façade is only slightly less ornate than Vienna, employing a pattern of white and gray horizontal stripping. This recalls stripping on the Rumbach Street Synagogue in Budapest, designed by Otto Wagner, and many other synagogues[12] but also calls to mind many famous Italian cathedrals such as Orvieto and Siena, as well as scores of other churches built from the Middle Ages to modern times.

Inside, however, the style is more traditionally classical in the Italian manner, consisting of a long, central nave flanked by aisles separated by arcades carried on columns. These aisles, in turn, support galleries vaulted by three high barrel vaults set perpendicular to the main nave, recalling the immense arches of the Basilica of Maxentius in the Forum in Rome. The barrel vaults of the central bay help support and buttress a dome that rises on pendentives from the middle of the synagogue nave. The gallery walls are pierced with tall, round-headed windows in the end bays and by large, round windows in the central bay under the dome. The façade also has a large, round window prominently placed in its center. The nave terminates in a massive apse, open the full height of the building. Ark and *bimach* are combined within the apse and raised several steps above the floor level of the rest of the synagogue, reminiscent of the altar arrangement in Roman Catholic churches. Halfway along the nave a large wooden pulpit is wrapped around a supporting pier, similar to what is found in typical preaching churches throughout Italy. Only the decoration sets the building apart from contemporary Christian structures. True to the schizophrenic nature of Italian-Jewish identity in the nineteenth century, it is an odd mix of classical and Moorish elements and includes Hebrew inscriptions the length of the nave arcade.

As much as the Mole Antonelliana in Turin, the Vercelli synagogue speaks to the (perhaps overblown) aspirations of the emancipated Italian-Jewish community. The fact that the synagogue stands silent today, in desperate need of repair, is moving testimony to just how misguided those aspirations were. The Piedmontese Jewish communities had always been small, and with emancipation came migration and assimilation, reducing them even more. Even without the effect of the Holocaust, it is unlikely that a city like Vercelli, which had a Jewish population of only 275 in 1931, could have maintained a Jewish community large enough to need, and strong enough to support, a building of this size.

Today, the future of this building—like much of what is at the core of Italian-Jewish culture—remains uncertain.

NOTES

1. For a survey of Jewish art that amply illustrates the integration of Jewish and Italian themes and styles, including some of the sites mentioned here, see Vivian Mann, ed., *Gardens and Ghettos, The Art of Jewish Life in Italy* (Berkeley: University of California Press, 1989), passim.

2. The most complete description of the Jewish communities in Piedmont and their monuments is Anna Sacerdoti and Annamarcella Tedeschi Falco, eds., *Piemonte: Itinerari ebraici, i luoghi, la storia, l'arte*, illustrated with excellent color photographs by Giorgio Avigdor (Venice: Marsilio, 1994). This supersedes Anna Sacerdoti and Luca Fiorentino, eds., *Guida all'Italia Ebraica* (Genoa: Marietti, 1986). Some synagogues are discussed in J. Pinkerfeld, *The Synagogues of Italy* (in Hebrew) (Jerusalem: Mosad Byalik, 1954), and some arks are discussed in S. U. Nahon, *Ornamenti del Sefer Tora* (Jerusalem: Haderah, 1966).

3. On Bernini's Baldichin, see Irving Lavin, *Bernini and the Crossing of St. Peter's* (New York: New York University Press, 1968). On the history of the twisted columns, see R. Krautheimer, S. Corbett, and A. Frazer, *Corpus Basilicarum Christianarum Romae*, vol. 5 (Vatican City: Pontificia Istituto di Archeologia Cristiana, 1976).

4. See Sacerdoti and Tedeschi, *Piemonte*, pp. 74–79.

5. See D. Colombo and G. Tedesco, "Il Ghetto di Carmagnola," *Rassegna mensile di Israel* 27, no. 12 (1961): 536–549; Sacerdoti and Tedeschi Falco, *Piemonte*, pp. 53–59.

6. Much has been written on the synagogue of Casale. See G. Avigdor, "La sinagoga di Casale," *Studi Piemontesi* 1, no. 1 (1969): 94–96; D. Cassuto, "History of a Synagogue," in *Scritti in memoria di Umberto Nahon*, edited by R. Bonfil et al. (Jerusalem: Sally Mayer Foundation, 1978), pp. 176–195. *La sinagoga di Casale Monferrato: Cenni Storico—illustrativi* (Casale Monferrato: Edizione Comunità Israelitica, 1969) contains a reprint of Giuseppe Levi's *Le inscrizioni del sacro Tempio Israelitico di Casale Monferrato* (1914), which provides transcriptions of the Hebrew inscriptions with translation into Italian. A detailed discussion of the synagogue in English is found in Carol Herselle Krinsky, *Synagogues of Europe* (Cambridge, MA: MIT Press, 1985), pp. 345–348.

7. On Saluzzo, see Sacerdoti and Tedeschi Falco, *Piemonte*, pp. 125–131.

8. The history and architecture of the Mole Antonelliana are discussed in detail in Krinsky, *Synagogues*, pp. 374–377.

9. On Vercelli, see T. Sarasso, *Storia degli ebrei a Vercelli* (Vercelli: Comunità Israelitica, 1974); D. Colombo, "Alcuni appunti sul ghetto di Vercelli," *Rassegna mensile di Israel* 42, no. 7–8 (1976): 374–377; R. Bottini Treves, *Storia del ghetto di Vercelli* (Vercelli: Società Storica Vercellese, 1993); Sacerdoti and Tedeschi Falco, *Piemonte*, pp. 155–167. On the synagogue, see C. Caselli, "Il tempio israelitico di Vercelli dell Comm. G. Locarni," *L'ingegneria civile e le arti industriali* 14(1889): 8–15.

10. On Vienna's Tempelgasse synagogue, see Krinsky, *Synagogues*, pp. 191–194.

11. On the Choral Synagogue see ibid., pp. 153–154; Aristide Streja and Lucian Schwarz, *Synagogues of Romania* (Bucharest: Hasefer Publishing House, 1997), pp. 44–48.

12. On the Rumbach Street Synagogue, see Krinsky, *Synagogues*, pp. 159–162; Géza Komoróczy, ed., *Jewish Budapest: Monuments, Rites, History* (Budapest: Central European University Press, 1999), pp. 132–138.

18

Italian-Jewish Literature from World War II to the 1990s

Raniero M. Speelman

One of the most interesting features of modern Italian literature is the enormous contribution by authors of Jewish origin. In fact, as is more or less well known, many renowned poets and novelists, such as Italo Svevo, Umberto Saba, Giani Stuparich, Alberto Moravia, Elsa Morante, the numerous authors that bear the name Levi, and many others, are Jewish—even if not always according to halakic rules. Literary critics, though, are less scrupulous than rabbis and have never objected that Alberto Moravia's mother was a Gentile.[1] This Jewish presence is particularly strong among the authors from the Trieste region[2] (to the aforenamed, we could add Carlo Michelstaedter, Guido and Giorgio Voghera, Bruno Piazza, Bobi Bazlen, Ferruccio Fölkel, Susanna Tamaro, Paolo Maurensig). This can at least partly be explained by the history of the Hapsburg port on the Adriatic Sea and the close relationship with the assimilated "Mitteleuropean" Jewish culture of Vienna and Prague that the Triestines have always felt. Sociologically speaking, the Jewish middle class of Trieste, well acquainted as it was with the world of Freudian psychiatry and, at the same time, with "classical" Italian literature, played a major role as a vehicle of cultural exchange and cross-fertilization.

Other Jewish communities played no less an important role. Turin, for instance, cradle of antifascism and leftist thought, can boast an active and rather liberal *kehillah*, from which came Carlo Levi and Primo Levi, Natalia Levi-Ginzburg and her husband, Leone, Sion Segre Amar, the trade unionist Vittorio Foa, the scientist Tullio Regge, and many others.

We should note, however, that, before the Shoah references to Jewishness in literature are very scarce, even in the works of the Triestines, a situation not very dissimilar from that in Viennese culture (one could think of Schnitzler, Zweig, Kisch, and others), which is largely due to the high level of assimilation of the authors concerned.

In the first years after World War II this situation did not yet change. The general interest in written accounts of the horrors that the Jews had had to face was not very great. Though testimonies like Primo Levi's and Liana Millu's had been written, they were not considered worth publishing (the refusal to publish Primo Levi's *Se questo è un uomo* (If This Is a Man) in 1947 was a notorious mistake of Natalia Ginzburg).[3]

The only major author who in the 1950s had written about Jewishness, taking it as a chief theme of his works, is Giorgio Bassani, who is still considered one of the best-known and most important modern Italian authors.

All this changed in the next decenniums, first with the rediscovery of Primo Levi and the success of the second part of his autobiography, *La Tregua* (The Truce) (Turin: Einaudi, 1963), and afterward with the important novel *La Storia* (History) (Turin: Einaudi, 1974) by Elsa Morante, a novel that was at the center of the literary vanguard's discussion about the legitimacy of the modern novel as such but could likewise be regarded as an attempt to write a major novel about (nonreligious) Jews.[4] In an established, but less-known, author such as Alberto Vigevani, references to his Jewish identity are sometimes present, but as it were "in sordina," muted and more hinted at than proclaimed. This may be stated as well about the first works by Antonio Debenedetti.

Major literary activity began in the 1980s, a period of regained conscience for Jews worldwide and in Italy as well that goes on today. Certainly, the political situation of the state of Israel and its conflicts with the Arab countries and their terroristic activities partly account for the Italian Jews' choice not to hide themselves any longer in vague ideals of assimilation but to openly show their belonging to a greater community as well as to Italy. Italian Jews find themselves more exposed than before.

A survivor of the Shoah such as Primo Levi, having reached the age of retirement, returned to his wartime and Shoah experiences in books such as *Se non ora, quando?* (If Not Now, When?) (Turin: Einaudi, 1982) and *I sommersi e i salvati* (The Drowned and the Saved) (Turin: Einaudi, 1986), which have been read and appreciated in the whole world. At the same time, Italian literature was living a moment of great international recognition (sometimes called the "Eco effect" because of the success of Umberto Eco's *The Name of the Rose* [Milan: Bompiani, 1980; San Diego: Harcourt Brace Jovanovich, 1983]), which left space to young authors as well.

Let us now have a closer look at the last fifteen years' literary production and attempt to discover some developments and themes. At this point, a preliminary statement has to be made. There are, of course, no general overviews or databases of Italian-Jewish literature. Books and authors mostly have been found by systematically looking in specialized bookshops like Menorah in Rome, the best in the field, the museum bookshop in the Venetian ghetto, or L'altra in Perugia, which has a small Judaica section. Therefore, this contribution does not pretend in the least to be complete.

In recent years we have seen an extremely rich activity in all fields, from the narrative to (auto)biography, from philology to essays, and from poetry to divulgative works. We do not deal with the last two genres, although poet Emanuele Trevi and essayist and critic Elena Loewenthal have met with deserved recognition, and the older Franco Fortini, born Lattes, is a celebrity in both fields. Very interesting is the enormous material that has been published lately[5] about Jewish life and culture in Italy and abroad, ranging from history, to jokes and from interviews, to books about Jewish cooking. But it is with literary prose that we are here concerned.

A striking feature is certainly the impact of "immigrant" authors, such as Edith Bruck, Giorgio Pressburger and Nicola Pressburger, Elisa Springer, and Helena Janeczek, all of whom come from Central Europe, and who have become what the Italians call *casi letterari*, not least because of their excellent mastering of the Italian literary language. Of these, Edith Bruck has been active as an author from 1958, when her account of the Shoah, *Chi ti ama così* (Who Loves you So) (Venice: Marsilio, 1958) brought her some fame as an immigrant writer. The most frequent themes in her numerous subsequent works are those of the survivor of the Shoah in a world that still bears its ancient wounds and the relationship between the older and younger generations. Another recurrent theme is—not surprisingly for a Hungarian—Eastern Europe.

Helena Janeczek is an interesting case because she is a German Jewess of Polish origin and a daughter of survivors. In her (until this day) only book in Italian,[6] she lucidly describes her (and her mother's) intricate identity problem as a Polish Jew among German Jews, a Jew in Germany and a German in Italy. It is also a rare example of writing that is typical of "second-generation" survivors and that in Italy is much less frequent than, for example, in Dutch literature. It mainly deals with problems such as the communication between parents-survivors and (partly) victimized or spiritually maimed children.

The major writers among the immigrant ones are certainly the Pressburger brothers, of whom Nicola died in 1985, after having written two books with his twin brother. His presence can be felt, though, throughout Giorgio's fertile literary production—one need but recall the subject and title of *I due gemelli* (The Twins) (Milan: Rizzoli, 1996) and the manuscript of a short story accidentally discovered in a suitcase and published as the last of the novellas of *La neve e la colpa* (Snow and Guilt) (Turin: Einaudi, 1998).

Not only has Pressburger—I shall henceforward avoid the plural—never made a secret about being Jewish as well as Hungarian, but he has successfully exploited his somewhat exotic, albeit cosmopolitan, origin. If the point of departure of his works is the Eighth District of Budapest, the city's Jewish quarter, with its population of owners of small shops, merchants, and intellectuals, which forms the scenery of *Storie dell'ottavo distretto* (Stories from the Eight District) (Casale Monferrato: Marietti, 1986), the district with its haunts like the Café Emke returns as the background of many later tales, such as *La legge degli spazi bianchi* (The Law of the White between the Letters) (Casale Monferrato: Marietti, 1989), *Denti e spie* (Teeth and Spies) (Milan: Rizzoli, 1994), and the latest book, *La neve e la colpa*, creating thus a constant point of reference. Pressburger nearly always chooses Jewish heroes, such as Andreas, the protagonist of the certainly autobiographically inspired[7] bildungsroman *Il sussurro della Grande Voce* (The Whispering of the Great Voice) (Milan: Rizzoli, 1990), the girl Laura in the same novel, the physicians of *La legge degli spazi bianchi* who have to cope with curious neurological deseases, and the protagonist of *Denti e spie*, a Hungarian civil servant with somewhat suspect mansions and weak teeth who, wherever in the world he goes, always searches the telephone directories for Jewish dentists—of Hungarian descent, of course.

Pressburger's narrative is brilliant, often exuberant and passionate. Details are colorful and carefully selected, although the author never indulges in long descriptions. Unforgettable are the portrait of the shul in the Eighth District stories or the mountain walk of the four rabbi-physicians in the title story of *La neve e la colpa*. Humor is never far away; Pressburger prefers the humor of the understatement, particularly in *Denti e spie*, where he makes fun of the political culture of the then just "deceased" Warsaw Pact countries. The tale of teeth, by the way, is also very original from a narratological point of view; the stories are numbered according to the set of teeth and can be put in order according to various criteria: place in the mouth, chronology of extraction or caries, and so on, a concept possibily influenced by Italo Calvino.

Moni Ovadia was born in Plovdiv, Bulgaria. After a long career as an ethno-musician, he specialized in Jewish cultural theater shows. In 1996 he published the curious, very successful booklet *Perché no? L'ebreo corrosivo* (Why Not? The Corrosive Jew) (Milan: Bompiani, 1996), a kind of "transcription of a little show, a piece of oral writing destined for the stage." It is a composite of anecdotes, jokes, and reflection and must be considered a rare example—for Italy, that is—of typical popular Ashkenazic culture, the kind that one would expect to find in Yiddish.

From the Eastern Meditterranean,[8] though from families with ancient Italian roots, come Istanbul-born Marcello Lago, who has worked as a director of commercials, and Miro Silvera, who was born in Syria. In his first book, *L'ebreo narrante* (The Storytelling Jew), Silvera—like Saul Israel before him—clearly draws from the Arabic oral narrative tradition, whereas his second book, *Margini d'amore* (Margins of Love) (Milan: Frassinelli, 1994) is a quite normal book of short stories. Lago's novel, *A noi due* (Between the Two of Us) (Milan: Anabasi, 1993) is a most fascinating tale, which unfortunately never got the attention that it deserved, probably due to the publication by a small publisher.

The tale begins in an unexpected, nearly aggressive way as a settlement of accounts with "the Jew," the "nth attempt at the final solution of the Spectre of Auschwitz."[9] In much softer tones, though not without irony, is described the beginning of *Shabbat* in the Milanese appartment of the Levi-Vitale family, which "has never been persecuted" and comes from Istanbul. The mother's life in the old Ottoman capital is evoked in picturesque, nearly nostalgic terms: "with her straw hat and plissé skirt, she savours muffins and rose marmalade in the shadow of the Golden Horn, in the *meltemi* breeze." Why these memories from the shores of the Bosporus? "Are we noisome, by any chance? No. I want it only to be clear to you that not all Jews come from the East, even if in literature it looks like it."[10]

After this introductory and willfully deceptive chapter (we are still taken back to the world of war and Shoah, not to the shores of the Bosporus), the tale of Joshua Vitale, a professional musician traveling to Salzburg, is interwoven with the wartime past of his father, who has disappeared. The encounter with

Fries, a music-loving Austrian who once tried to save Vitale Sr., is the surprising central episode. Lago's debut, which joins autobiographic elements to fiction and humor to a sense of tragedy, contains the same intelligent mixture of literary writing and suspense that characterizes Paolo Maurensig's contemporary first novel. At the end of the book, Joshua rebels from his author in a Pirandellian manner and leaves the novel: "Now I hate what I've seen and cannot love who has shown it to me. For that reason, I go away. I leave your story forever."[11]

Maurensig is certainly another "case." The Gorizia-born author is a good example of what has been called a "frontier writer."[12] Until now, Maurensig has published four novels, the first of which, *La variante di Lüneburg* (The Lüneburg Variation) (Milan: Adelphi, 1993; translated by Jon Rothchild [New York: Farrar Straus and Giroux, 1997]), made his reputation. It is a weird novel that begins with a mysterious death in present-day Austria, the cause of which is told during travel by train from Munich to Vienna (by chance, the same way that Lago's hero travels to Salzburg). The story takes us back in time to the lanes of a Vienna that reminds us of Gustav Meyrink and other "mitteleuropean" writers. The book is fundamentally about chess and concentration camps, a strange combination at first sight, but the author uses the well-known idea that chess is a projection of life and as such may be involved in a struggle for life itself. The apotheosis is grand but grotesque, even if the literary use made of the Shoah will not delight everybody. In Maurensig's second novel, *Canone inverso* (Inverted Canon) (Milan: Mondadori, 1996), music is the theme, though not as a noble art but as a tyrannical discipline. The background is just as impressive as that of the first novel: a conservatory halfway between a prison and a monastery, a castle in the Austrian mountains, and, again, ancient Vienna. The suggestion of "Gothic" elements in both novels is very strong. Maurensig's third book, *L'ombra e la meridiana* (The Shadow and the Meridian) (Milan: Mondadori, 1998), is much shorter, more subtle, and vaguer. It's about a photographer who fixes in countless snapshots the last days of an old, dying man. Just as in his preceding novels, there is a link with the main character's past: the relationship between his mother and the now dying man. Thus, the book is a kind of *Auseinandersetzung*, a settlement of accounts. The latest novel, *Venere lesa* (Maimed Venus) (Milan: Mondadori, 1998), is a stylistically perfect tale of man–woman relationships between five characters, including the narrator. Music and chess recur as motifs, recalling the first books, but Jewishness is totally absent from the rather austere tale.

Jewish (identity) themes are important in many texts by Jewish authors,[13] and sometimes are dominant. Roberto Vigevani is certainly one of the most striking authors who have consequently treated this theme, sometimes in a really vehement manner. His most satirical novel, *Il principio della piramide* (The Pyramid Principle) (Milan: Adelphi, 1989) has been written under the pseudonym Ruve Masada.[14] Antonio Debenedetti has written in a much softer and intellectualist key, among other subjects, about the identity problem, which he surely feels as his own, having had a Catholic mother and a dominating father, the eminent critic Giacomo. The most autobiographical of his books, *Giacomino* (Milan: Rizzoli, 1994), gives an interesting, though somewhat chaotic account of his family life. Debenedetti's prior short novel, *La fine di un addio* (An End to a Farewell) (Rome: Editoriale Nuova, 1984) is an interesting, though not entirely successful, attempt to paint the artistic milieu of the 1930s, the epoch of progressive anti-Semitism culminating in the racial laws and, again, largely inspired by his own experience.[15] The journalist Fausto Coen wrote a beautiful novel about prewar life in an imaginary north Italian *kehillah*, *Quel che vide Màt Cùssi* (What Mad Cùssi Saw) (Genoa: Marietti, 1992). It is, in fact, a curious, rather "mitteleuropean" book that doesn't seem quite at home in Italian literature.

On the other hand, experiments in the manner of the "giovani scrittori" (young writers) can be seen in the fertile production of Alain Elkann, an author who in the last fifteen years has written at least a dozen books. The now very popular detective stories have an early representative in Paolo Levi, who is a slightly younger contemporary of Primo Levi and who wrote a long line of detective novels in the 1970s and 1980s before venturing upon a really Jewish novel like the family chronicle *Il filo della memoria* (The Thread of Memory) (Milan: Rizzoli, 1984). Even children's books have never been neglected by Jewish authors, from Elsa Morante's *Le bellissime avventure di Catarì dalla trecciolina* (The Most Wonderful Adventures of Catherine with the Little Braid) (Turin: Einaudi, 1942),[16] until the more recent works by Emanuele Luzzati, Susanna Tamaro, Isabella Lattes Coifmann, and Lia Levi. Midrashim and haggadah have been (re)written by Augusto Segre: *Abramo nostro padre* (Abraham Our Father) (Rome: Carrucci, 1982) and other collections,[17] and by Giacoma Limentani, the "grand old lady" of Italian-Jewish culture, who has written some fine novels as well.[18] Fantastic literature is represented by Fabio Carpi, who has written fairy tale-like works, by Arnoldo Foà and Lisa Morpurgo, and by Maurizio Cohen's debut, *La gabbia* (The Cage) (Venice: Marsilio, 1988), which is vaguely reminiscent of Franz Kafka. A talented work that maybe didn't get all the attention that it deserved, Cohen's novel is about two persons, the bureaucrat Manuel, who is annoyed by life and eagerly accepts to step out of it when he is injured in an accident, and Marçio, a savagelike individual who is somewhere between man and ape and lives in a zoo. Marçio gradually realizes that his past is a human one and takes the opportunity to escape, so as to discover his true identity—Manuel's. Cohen's discourse is essentially a moral one that touches upon questions such as the use of medical and scientific experiments and the sensibility of animals.

Another little-known, but very interesting, writer is Turin-born Massimo Ottolenghi, author of a novel and a collection of short stories, *La finestra di Kuhn* (The Window from Kuhn) (Cavellermaggiore: Gribaudo, 1994). Ottolenghi's pessimistic stories are extremely complicated, as they move to and fro between reality and imagination, present and past, memory and forgetfulness, interior and exterior experience. Jewishness is at the core of the metaphysical, Kafkaesque "Forse un processo" (Maybe a Trial), where the protagonist, who at the time of the Shoah has been an accomplice of evil, is confronted with the enduring character of evil. One could regard this tale as the key to the other stories, which all deal with "lost," tragic characters.

Traditionally, the historical novel has never been the literary genre to which Italian Jews have felt particularly attracted. Successful and attractive efforts to write novels dealing with the Jewish past, however, have not been lacking since the 1980s, when Guido Artom published the beautiful account of Astigian Jewry *I giorni del mondo* (The Days of the World) (Milan: Longanesi, 1981). After him, among others, Primo Levi and Sion Segre Amar explored the genre; in the last few years Sergio Astrologo with his masterly *Gli occhi colore del tempo* (Eyes of the Color of Time) (Genoa: Marietti, 1995), Sabino Acquaviva with *La ragazza del ghetto* (The Girl from the Ghetto) (Milan: Mondadori, 1996) and Lia Levi with *Tutti i giorni di tua vita* (All the Days of your Life) (Milan: Mondadori, 1997) have written very interesting works. We should distinguish between works that deal with Jewish history, such as Levi's *Se non ora, quando?*, and more "neutral" ones, such as Segre Amar's.

Sion Segre Amar's *Il frammento sepolto* (The Buried Fragment) (Milan: Garzanti, 1984) tells the life of a medieval monk and book illustrator. The story serves in the first place as a vehicle for learned excursions and quotes many texts, mostly taken from the anthology *Letteratura italiana delle origini* and other volumes of the Ricciardi text corpus as well as works by G. Scholem about Jewish thought. As a novel, it is less convincing, not only because it strongly betrays the influence of Umberto Eco's *Il nome della rosa*.[19] In spite of what the title suggests, Acquaviva's book is primarily about freethinking in sixteenth-century Venice, and the impossible love between the Catholic nobleman Alvise Cornaro and the fair Jewess Sara could have been more developed. As such, the book recalls Tomizza's documentary novel about the reformer Vergerio *Il male viene dal Nord* (Evil Comes from the North) (1984). Astrologo's novel is a vivid picture of prewar Turin but is a psychological, rather than a historical, novel, and the atmosphere is primarily intimate, even if the hero, "Monsù" Enrico Vitta, is an exuberant and expansive character.

Lia Levi's book is a voluminous one that describes the saga of a Jewish family in Rome from 1921 to 1946 and later. Although the subject matter is not new, the carefully reported rise to power of fascism and its subsequent relationship to Italian Jewry make it a fascinating novel. Levi does not introduce any innovations in the narrative field and writes (just as in her former works) in an easy, down-to-earth language. She manages to avoid noisomeness, thanks to a scrupulous construction of different characters, which, of course, represent various attitudes toward Jewishness, ranking from absolute assimilation, to a traditionalist outlook. Different as well is the fate of the main characters in the turbulent years of discrimination and Shoah: from emigration to the United States and exile in Switzerland to hiding in the country or fatalism. I think the chief quality of the novel is that of confronting the "normal" Italian public with the way that preceding generations treated their Israelite fellow Italians.

Maybe the most interesting phenomenon, however, is the hype of Jewish (auto)biographies that have appeared in the last fifteen years. Partly, these are works written earlier and published only now, but the fact they are being published means that a certain public interest for them must be there. This group of works consists of manuscripts left by members of the elder generation to their children—for example, the war memoirs of Marcella Levi-Bianchini (*E ora dove vado?* [And Where to Go Now] [Rome: Edizioni Associate, 1994]), Renzo Segre (*Venti mesi* [Twenty Months] [Palermo: Sellerio, 1995]) and Mario Tagliacozzo (*Metà della vita* [Half a Life] [Milan: Baldini & Castoldi, 1998])— or prepared for publication by serious philologists or researchers—for example, Aldo Zargani prepared the autobiographies of Davide Jona and Anna Foa, originally written in English, for publication;[20] Alberto Cavaglion edited the family history *Per via invisibile* (Invisibly) (Bologna: Il Mulino, 1998); *Una gioventù offesa. Ebrei genovesi ricordano* (A Wounded Youth. Genoese Jews Recall) (Florence: Giuntina, 1995) was edited by Chiara Bricarelli; the war diaries of Elena Morpurgo, Luisa Zaban, and Silvia Zaban, *Guerra, esilio, ebraicità: diari di donne nelle due guerre mondiali* (War, Exile, Jewishness: War Diaries of Women in Two World Wars) (Ancona: Il Lavoro, 1996), were edited by Paolo Magnarelli; and the anthology *Meditate che questo è stato* (Think About It That This Has Been) (Florence: Giuntina & *L'Unità*, 1996) was prepared by a team of eight people. Of course, most in this group are original memoirs, written by authors generally born between 1900 and 1930. The (sometimes) uneven artistic level does not compromise the documentary qualities of these works. We are informed about childhood and youth in prewar Italy, sometimes about ancestors and local *kehilloth*, about the implementation of the 1938 racial campaign and the difficulties that even "privileged" families had to cope with. In some cases, clairvoyant Jews emigrated to Palestine (as eloquently described by Max Varadi, Giorgio Voghera, Vittorio Segre, Bruno Di Cori, Aldo Zargani, and others), creating thus an Italian literature of *aliyah*, first of which is Ada Sereni's beautiful account *I clandestini del mare*.[21] A comprehensive study of Italian Jews in Erets Yisrael is Angelo Pezzana's *Quest'anno a Gerusalemme* (This Year in Jerusalem) (Milan: Corbaccio, 1997), which mostly consists of a long series of interviews but includes a historical essay by Vittorio Dan Segre, which is interesting for Jewish life in the home country as well.

Other works describe the adventurous lives of those who chose to flee before the Germans or the fears of those who hid themselves from them. Still other texts describe life in postwar Italy as members of a much diminished and still exposed group. The best account, albeit in the form of literary fiction, is Stefano Jesurum's *Raccontalo ai tuoi figli* (Tell It to Your Children) (Milan: Baldini & Castoldi, 1994). This tiny masterpiece touches upon all aspects of Jewish life in Italy: the rich history, the plague of fascism and Shoah, present-day life as a highly assimilated community but at the same time an isolated one, the special antiterrorist protection that it is forced to enjoy, the problem of education, and so on. We renounce all attempts at discussing individual works and name only these authors: Fulvio Anzelotti, Remo Bemporad, Angela Bianchini, Marcella Bianchini, Maria Casnedi, Antonio Debenedetti, Fabio Della Seta, Alain Elkann, Vittorio Foa, Guido Fubini, Eugenio Gentili Tedeschi, Donatella Levi, Franco Levi, Lia Levi, Rita Levi-Montalcini, Roberto Maestro, Arnaldo Momigliano, Elena Morpurgo, Virginia Nathan, Emanuele Pacifici, Cesare Rimini, Aldo Rosselli, Giancarlo Sacerdoti, Augusto Segre, Cesare Segre, Renzo Segre, and

(Dan) Vittorio Segre, Sion Segre Amar, Clara Sereni, Livio Isaak Sirovich, Susanna Tamaro, Liliana Treves Alcalay, Paolo Vita-Finzi, Luisa Zaban and Silvia Zaban, and Aldo Zargani.[22] Even the chief rabbi of Rome, Elio Toaff, wrote his own. *Perfidi giudei, fratelli maggiori* (Perfidious Jews, Elder Brothers) (Milan: Mondadori, 1987–1988) is a highly interesting book, full of adventure, and displays on more than one occasion a keen sense of humor as well. All these works continue an already established tradition that includes authors such as Primo Levi and Carlo Levi, Natalia Ginzburg, Ada Sereni, Guido Artom, and others but goes back to the end of the nineteenth century.

Jewish authors have written a bit more than goyish ones about family relationships, specifically, those between parents and children. From Elsa Morante (in all her novels), to Alain Elkann's and Lia Levi's constructed family dramas and from Giani Stuparich's touching novella *L'isola* (The Island), to Natalia Ginzburg's *Lessico familiare* (Family Sayings), Clara Sereni's *Il gioco dei regni* (The Game of Kingdoms), Sandra Reberschak's *Se anche tu non fossi* (Even If You Weren't), or Antonio Debenedetti's *Giacomino*, the essential relationship is that of the blood, seen from the point of view of different, often contrasting generations. In other words, having to cope with the precept from Torah to "tell it to your children"—which, significantly, is also the title of the already mentioned book by Stefano Jesurum—passing the blessings (and doom) of Jewishness to younger generations is a problem as well as a mitzvah. It is certainly one of the explanations of the Jewish preoccupation with auto/family biography and would merit detailed study.[23] This fact is enhanced by the relationships between two or more writing members of one family, as we shall see.

Susanna Tamaro is certainly one of the most successful contemporary writers, but she does not seem to give much attention to her Jewish heritage, except for some remarks in *Va dove ti porta il cuore* (Go Where Your Heart Tells You) (Milan: Baldini & Castoldi, 1994). In fact, her relationship to Christian culture is far more visible, thanks to her columns for the weekly review *Famiglia cristiana*. In her latest novel, *Anima Mundi* (The Soul of the World) (Milan: Baldini & Castoldi, 1997), Christian inspiration is made clear from the very beginning, a quotation from the Gospel of St. John. The book follows the schemes of a bildungsroman, with reminiscences of Andrea De Carlo's *Due di due* (for the two friends, Walter and Andrea, who are the main characters, and the death of the apparently stronger one), *Tecniche di seduzione* (Techniques for Seduction) (for the theme of the talented, but inexperienced, young writer who goes to Rome and is ensnared by the capital's cynical cultural scene), and *Uto* (for that of the angry young man who eventually becomes a sage). Whereas in De Carlo's works the city as such is contrasted to the country, Tamaro's novel is rather a "tale of two cities," Rome and Trieste. The austere city where the bora blows is not in the least a luring Siren, but it is genuine in its barrenness and hides undiscovered beauties in its Carso. By expressly referring to its "mitteleuropean" character, as well as to "mitteleuropean" literature—the first writer that Walter manages to name is Kafka—Tamaro recognizes her debt to Triestine and Austrian culture. The last part of the novel deals with Walter's enlightenment or conversion and is explicitly Christian in its mention of the parable of the lost son and that of the talents, as well as in its setting in a small mountain convent inhabited only by an ancient nun. The questions that the protagonist poses himself and her include the presence of evil and the use of intellectual gifts. Unhappily, the book, however moving it may be, seldom rises above the level of déjà vu. An interesting case of intertextuality should, however, be mentioned. Walter once finds a truck with lambs that are being brought to the slaughterhouse and exclaims in a moment of despair: "Do you understand? We are all on that truck, in that innocent pain! . . . It's waiting for us, with its motor switched on . . . it is always ready to leave, there's only one way, from the stable to the slaughterhouse."[24]

This passage clearly recalls the chapter "Il re dei giudei" (King of Jews) from Primo Levi's *I sommersi e i salvati* (The Drowned and the Saved), where the metaphor is that of the train waiting to bring the reader from the ghetto to the gas chamber. In Tamaro, the lamb can be read, of course, as reference to the Agnus Dei as well as Jonathan Demme's movie *The Silence of the Lambs*.

I think no book better expresses Tamaro's thought than *Non vedo l'ora che l'uomo cammini* (Dear Mathilde) (Cinisello Balsamo: Edizioni San Paolo, 1997), her collected columns for *Famiglia cristiana*. Tamaro's message is a simple and essential one. Modern life has sacrificed wisdom and love to materialistic ambitions and false ideas. People should concentrate upon spiritual growth and real values. All columns begin with a personal experience, which serves as a trampoline for reflection, and a conclusion. Thus, the "letters" written to a friend have the form of short sermons.

I suggest juxtaposing Tamaro's book with a stylistically quite different work, Clara Sereni's *Diario di un'ultimista* (Diary of an Ultimist) (Milan: Feltrinelli, 1998). At first sight, this book seems lacking in coherence or seems to be dealing, for the most part, with local or national politics. True as all this may be and difficult to read for outsiders, the whole book bears the mark of Clara Sereni's concern for the weaker groups in society, such as outcasts, disabled persons, and disoriented youth, a concern that may have its roots in her own experience as a "handicapped mother" (as she calls it) and in her family history and her belonging to a minority. This lends a unique warmth to the whole, which may excuse the seemingly chaotic structure. When Sereni advocates solutions, they are (just like Tamaro's) of a feasible, practical nature—just like the kitchen recipes of her curious booklet *Casalinghitudine* (Housewifery) (Turin: Einaudi, 1987).

An interesting feature of Italian-Jewish literary activity is the frequency of more writing members in a single family. We have writing brothers and sisters as well as parents and children (Italo Svevo and his brother, three generations of the Piazza family: Giulio, Bruno, Brunetto and Maria Luisa, Amelia, Carlo, and Nello as well as Aldo Rosselli, various members of the Sereni family, Elsa and Marcello Morante, Giorgio and Nicola Pressburger, Natalia, Leone, and Carlo Ginzburg, Giacomo and Antonio Debenedetti, the Bianchinis) or cousins (Giorgio Bassani and Gianfranco Rossi, Guido Artom, and Paolo Debenedetti), and so on. I'm sure this feature is not limited to Italian literature, but it is surprisingly strongly developed there.[25] If we were to look for an explanation, the accent that education among (Italian) Jews always placed on reading and written expression and the esteem in which literature is held may contribute to the answer.

The problem that remains is that of the Jewishness of the many works written by Jewish authors. It is not difficult to see that in many books of, let's say, Moravia or Elkann one cannot find the least trace of it.[26] It may lead us to conclude that all attempts to speak of Italian-Jewish literature are senseless or, at least, subjective (which for many critics has the same worth). One could respond, though, that nearly all abovementioned writers and most of all those who belong to the younger generations have touched upon Jewish themes or subjects in at least part of their literary production. To return to our examples, Moravia wrote *Il conformista* (The Conformist) (Milan: Bompiani, 1951) partly as a comment on the murder of Carlo and Nello Rosselli by the fascist secret police, the OVRA, and Elkann wrote two monumental works, *Piazza Carignano* (Milan, Mondadori 1985) about Jews and fascism and *I soldi devono restare in famiglia* (The Money Should Remain in the Family) (Milan: Bompiani, 1996), about cosmopolitan Jews between contemporary Turin, New York, and Israel, whereas in his intermediate novel *Rotocalco* (Milan: Bompiani, 1991) the search for Jewish identity is an important theme. Moreover, Elkann has published two interview-dialogues with Elio Toaff.

We have left aside in this swift overview many authors who do not belong to the situations (rather than groups) that we have just distinguished but have just written beautiful books, such as Sandra Reberschak and Rossana Ombres.

Even if Jewishness does not really play a role in a novel by a Jewish author, we may catch weak, but undisputable, signals as to his or her identity. This is, for instance, the case in Rossana Ombres' latest novel, *Baiadera* (Bayadere) (Milan: Mondadori, 1997). From the first page, a reference to "rabbines" provides us with a hint. Further on, a character named Montalcini leaves the country after having changed his name to Di Segni—both are, of course, typically Jewish names. We could point at quite a number of small facts. The novel is interesting from yet another point of view: the linguistic one. Just as Primo Levi in the introductory chapter "Argon" of his *Il sistema periodico* (The Periodic Table) (Turin: Einaudi, 1975; translated by Raymond Rosenthal [New York: Schocken Books, 1984]) focused on the Judeo-Piemontese dialect, so Ombres tries to capture as much of the hybrid language of her native Casale Monferrato as possible.

But there is more that characterizes Italian-Jewish literature. I believe that we can find in its pages a cosmopolitan spirit, curious of the world and humankind, centered upon people's intimate drama, as well as a profound reflection on life, people's dignity, and the many perils that threaten them. Many different voices meet in this continuing meditation, but they share an origin that may be half forgotten but is never despised.

Of course, this contribution is only a survey of some significant works. It is to be regretted that there have been few comprehensive studies on the field.[27] Even recent books such as *L'ebraismo nella letteratura italiana del Novecento*

(Jewishness in Twentieth-Century Italian Literature) (Palermo: Palumbo, 1995) and *Appartenenza e differenza* (Belonging and Difference) (Florence: Giuntina, 1998) mostly deal with deceased authors. In fact, most attention is still given to a very small group of celebrities: Svevo, Michelstaedter, Moravia, Morante, Carlo Levi, Primo Levi, Bassani, and Ginzburg. As far as known to me, few critical analyses have been dedicated to the work of, say, Giacoma Limentani, Lia Levi, or Alberto Lecco, each of whom has already published at least five books. At the same time, the theme of Jewishness and homosexuality remains yet to be studied: from modern classics such as Saba's *Ernesto* (Turin: Einaudi, 1975), Bassani's *Gli occhiali d'oro* (The Gold-Rimmed Glasses) (Turin: Einaudi, 1958),[28] or Morante's Davide Segre in *La Storia*, to the sad, but beautiful, books of Gianfranco Rossi, a writer still waiting for recognition,[29] Stefano Jesurum's subtle short novel about a brother and a sister *Soltanto per amore* (Only for Love's Sake) (Milan: Baldini & Castoldi, 1996), Debenedetti's *La fine di un addio*, or Lia Levi's *Quasi un'estate* (Nearly a Summer) (Rome: Edizioni e/o, 1995), the two subjects keep meeting. And not by chance: both are kinds of diversity, long subjected to persecution or discrimination and more or less taboo, that may assume the character of "metaphysical" suffering. For the time being, it seems primarily a task for us university teachers to guide our pupils toward these kinds of research.

NOTES

1. This might be partly due to the fact that (before the racial laws of 1938) often wealthy members of the Jewish bourgeoisie married a *shiksa*, but gave their children a fully Jewish education.

2. Cf., among others, G. Voghera, *Gli anni della psicanalisi* (Pordenone: Studio Tesi, 1980); F. Fölkel, "L'ebraicità triestina" in *L'ebraismo nella letteratura italiana del Novecento* (Palermo: Palumbo, 1995), pp. 27–32.

3. Bruno Piazza's account of Auschwitz, *Perché gli altri dimenticano* (Because the Others Forget), however, was published in 1956 by Feltrinelli, ten years after the author's death.

4. For Morante, Jewishness has a symbolic sense, more or less equivalent to being an underdog and a victim, rather than a cultural or religious one. This is illustrated by the character of Davide Segre, addict, homosexual, and, eventually, suicide.

5. The regional guides published by the Venetian publisher Marsilio deserve special mention.

6. Apart from her Italian autobiography, Helena Janeczek published poems in German.

7. One need but take into account Andreas' flight to Italy and his theatrical vocation.

8. To an older generation belongs Saul Israel (1897–1981), who immigrated to Italy from Selanik/Thessaloniki and wrote *Le leggenda del Re Horkham* (The Legend of King Horkham) (Milan: Adelphi, 1982), in the 1940s. The tale is largely inspired by Turkish popular culture (especially the so-called *eskiya roman*, or highwayman-novel). It deserves to be mentioned as a rare amalgamation of Islamic culture and Jewish skepsis; in fact, it introduces the philosophy of an imaginary sage called Bilmemne (equivalent to "I don't know") and offers a delightful defense of Doubt.

9. Marcello Lago, *A noi due* (Milan: Anabasi, 1993), p. 10. The translation of this and all other quotes and book titles is mine.

10. Ibid., pp. 20, 21.

11. Ibid., p. 155.

12. The Italian expression *di confine* indicates authors from frontier regions with a mixed culture who don't seem to belong to normal literary schools or movements. Most Triestine authors can be considered as such.

13. As well as by goyish writers, such as Rosetta Loy's interesting and extremely well timed *La parola ebreo* (Turin: Einaudi, 1997).

14. Cf. Elena Loewenthal, "La tentazione di esistere," in *Appartenenza e differenza* (Florence: Giuntina, 1998), pp.152–153.

15. Readers will meet, for instance, Bobi Bazlen and Umberto Saba, who often visited the Debenedetti's home.

16. Later published as *Le straordinarie avventure di Catarina* (Turin: Einaudi, 1959).

17. *I re di Israele* and *La scala di Giacobbe*, again published by Carucci in Rome.

18. Such as *Dentro la D* (Within the D) (Genova: Marietti, 1992).

19. For instance, in themes and motifs like the scriptorium, the burning of a witch, "illicit" intercourse, intertextuality.

20. Davide Jona and Anna Foa, *Noi due* (Bologna: Il Mulino, 1997).

21. Milan: Mursia 1973, reprinted a few years ago.

22. Some chose to do so in their new language, such as Davide Jona and Anna Foa, whose *Noi due* (Bologna: Il Mulino, 1997) was originally written in English.

23. For Elena Loewenthal, "La tentazione di esistere," in J. Hassine et al., eds., *Appartenenza e differenza* (Florence: Giuntina, 1998), pp. 147–159, Italian-Jewish literature "today is essentially, openly or between the lines, autobiographical" and is to be explained both by the wish to "hide oneself" and by the wish to state "I exist." For Alberto Cavaglion, in his introduction to the Italian edition of L. Valensi and N. Wachtel, *Memorie ebraiche* (Turin: Einaudi, 1996), "il libro della memoria," or *Yisker-biher*, belongs to an essential dimension of Jewishness but remains distinct from real autobiography.

24. Susanna Tamaro, *Anima Mundi* (Milan: Baldini & Castoldi, 1997), p. 174 (my translation).

25. One could recall the Herzbergs and Durlachers (both father–daughter) in Jewish Dutch and the Singer brothers in Yiddish literature.

26. A convincing analysis of Moravia's (partial) Jewishness is given by Micaela Procaccia, "L'ebreo Pincherle: Moravia tra indifferenza e rimozione," in J. Hassine et al., eds., *Appartenenza e differenza*.

27. Most valuable, among older studies, is Giorgio Romano, *Ebrei nella Letteratura* (Rome: Carucci, 1979), which contains a treasure of data concerning books that can hardly be found anymore. Famous is H. Stuart Hughes, *Prisoners of Hope* (Cambridge, MA: Harvard University Press, 1983), which primarily regards internationally affirmed authors, not forgetting, however, minor writers such as Augusto Segre or Davide Jona. Important as well is Lynn Gunzberg, *Strangers at Home* (Berkeley: Unversity of California Press, 1992), which mainly focuses on the image of Jews in Italian literature. Dr. Gunzberg wrote as well the section on literature of the prestigious Einaudi *Storia d'Italia. Annali 11. Gli ebrei in Italia*, edited by C. Vivanti (Turin: Einaudi, 1997), vol. 2, pp. 1577–1618, concentrating upon six novelists (E. Castelnuovo, I. Svevo, A. Loria, A. Vigevani, G. Bassani, P. Levi): "Alcuni romanzieri del Novecento." My own essay, "Dall'Argon al Carbonio: la letteratura italiana ebraica del dopoguerra," in *Gli spazi della diversità* (Rome: Bulzoni, 1995; Leuven: Leuven University Press, 1995), pp. 69–101, deals with the influence of Primo Levi and the Shoah, autobiography (e.g., Levi-Montalcini, Toaff), the birth of an Italian-Jewish novel (e.g., Artom, Debenedetti, Lecco) and some recent authors (e.g., Elkann and Clara Sereni).

28. Cf. Ada Neiger, "Modelli di difformità," in *L'ebraismo nella letteratura italiana*

del Novecento (Palermo: Palumbo, 1995), pp. 101–106.

29. Gianfranco Rossi unfortunately died on the same day as his cousin Giorgio Bassani, 13 April 2000. On his work, see R. Pazzi, "Ricordo di G. R.," and E. Testi, "G. R.: La scelta di essere se stessi," in *Quaderni della "Dante"* (Ferrara: Liberty House, 2000).

19

Italian-Jewish Memoirs and the Discourse of Identity

Fabio Girelli-Carasi

This chapter is part of a larger, ongoing research project that started, with a different perspective, several years ago. Because it is a work-in-progress, I present the blueprint for a comprehensive analysis, with hypotheses and several open questions and my initial attempts to formulate preliminary answers.

My research began when I first approached the world of the so-called Holocaust literature through the works of Primo Levi. Among the peripheral observations that I made in the course of my original study was the fact that Levi appeared to have received much higher recognition in the Anglo-Saxon world than in Italy, where, until a few years ago, he was still considered a *minore*, an author of lesser import, in the literary landscape. Besides the issue of the unquestionable value of Levi's work, I found it rather puzzling that Italians would *not* care to derive national pride from his success abroad. As we very well known, Italians are always seeking such recognition, as can be easily evinced, for instance, from the pride exuded by the media on the recent Hollywood triumph of Roberto Benigni.

An initial exploration of Italian literature, in particular, what is considered the standard canon, led me to the preliminary conclusion that Primo Levi was not assigned a preeminent position in the literary firmament because his work was outside the discourse of Italian literature. Its realm of belonging, I was convinced, was the Jewish discourse, a discourse of which Italian literature was completely ignorant. Lacking this context, Levi was reduced to an oddity, a strange and almost isolated phenomenon that escaped categorization and was therefore ex-centric, out of the mainstream, and to be handled as a separate entity.

The absence of a Jewish discourse in Italian literature does not mean that representation of Jews is totally absent from literary expression. As Lynn Gunzberg demonstrated in her seminal work *Strangers at Home: Jews in the Italian Literary Imagination*,[1] after the emancipation Jews have been depicted in literature, particularly in texts of "popular" literature, written mostly by non-Jewish authors, with results that can be easily imagined. Gunzberg's thesis is that these works reflect more closely a widespread anti-Jewish sentiment in the population, something that seems to contradict the presence at high levels of Italian society of preeminent Jewish personalities, politicians, military, and academics.

The "success" of the Jews probably originated the myth of Italians' being philo-Semitic, a gross generalization that borders on distortion and that has been enormously reinforced by a peculiar interpretation of the events in World War II. Just because "only" a third of Italian Jews were eliminated in the Lager or had to flee the country, and just because the genocidal fever did not reach the proportions that it did in Germany, France, and Central and Eastern Europe, the conclusion was that this was the result of a "benevolent" attitude. Just because "fewer" Jews were killed? I beg to differ and would like for a moment to subvert standard terminology to suggest that this operation amounts to a sort of homespun Italian "negationism," a comfortable position that denies the existence of anti-Semitism and that for the longest time in Italy took the connotation of default ideology.

To return to the main point, what I propose here complements Lynn Gunzberg's thesis and her conclusions. I submit that, although a "discourse about the Jews" may have been present, it was a discourse in which the Jews themselves were not allowed to participate, while a Jewish discourse proper has been absent from canonic literature and society.

"Discourse" is a comprehensive term that encompasses the production of meaning and the construction of significant texts, cultural, literary, and artistic, that, collectively, construct an ideology or an aesthetic. In literature, at least, it signifies a body of works that are interpreted, show marks of historical stratification, and reflect both a self-conscious and an unconscious vision of the world bundled within the definition of an identity. According to the standard tools of literary criticism that I chose to adopt, these works and the discourse that they would create are identifiable when they satisfy at least the basic test of "belonging," the cherished Italian *appartenenza*. The criterion of "belonging," thus, does not apply exclusively to topics, topoi, and themes but includes necessarily the notion of genre and, to use a softer term, even "tone."

As to the reasons that Italian literature doesn't contemplate a Jewish discourse, the standard hypothesis points to the historical circumstances, first of which is the extremely limited size of Italian Jewry through the centuries, a community that hardly ever exceeded 60,000 or 70,000 members. However, an intriguing opposite hypothesis could be offered based on the fact that, in rather stark contrast to the 70% or more illiteracy in the general population through the middle of the nineteenth century, practically all Italian Jews were able to read and write. The high literacy rate among Jews makes it not completely coincidental that, after the emancipation and in particular in the first half of the twentieth century, a significant portion of the publishing industry was controlled by Jewish owners, as was the case of Treves, La Nuova Italia, Lattes, Bemporad, and Mondadori.

Yet, even in these circumstances, we witness the failure of a Jewish discourse or even of Jewish themes to affirm themselves. Even Jewish authors or authors of Jewish descent were silent on Jewish themes and issues, with attitudes toward Judaism that ranged from the indifferent, to the dismissive, to the openly hostile, as were the cases, respectively, of Italo Svevo, Alberto Moravia, and Umberto Saba, to mention just some of the most representative voices. A particularly insightful analysis of this subject is contained in the volume *Appartenenza e differenza: Ebrei d'Italia e letteratura.*[2]

In the twentieth century, then, the historical absence of texts by Jews about Jewish themes arguably must be attributed to reasons other than the exclusion of Jews from the cultural and intellectual establishment. A possible explanation is that Italian Jews, historically, always wished "not to attract attention to themselves" as Jews, something that through the centuries they had learned was not in their best interest, for establishing a high profile would trigger unwelcome reactions against the whole community. Anyone reading the history of Italian Jews immediately realizes that the most salient events are, almost to the letter, the embodiment of the old proverb that the nail that sticks out is the one that gets hammered. I argue that this historically sedimented attitude most likely persisted even after the emancipation, resulting in a silence that pervades the literary world even today.

In support of this thesis, one could take into account the demographic stability of the Italian-Jewish communities to reach the conclusion that the so-called benign treatment of the Jews by Italians is more wishful thinking on the part of Italians than reality. This conclusion can be drawn from the observation that in the rest of Europe, Eastern as well as Western, Jewish communities flourished until they amounted to hundreds of thousands, if not millions, of individuals, while in Italy the number of Jews was always kept very small and in reality has declined progressively as a percentage of the total population. Genocide and large-scale pogroms were not necessary in Italy, one could suspect, because there was always some subtle kind of self-imposed population control mechanism at play. I don't believe necessarily in a vast anti-Jewish conspiracy to keep the number of Jews constantly low, but it is possible to envision a sort of "collective birth control" implemented by Jews who had realized that once the community went beyond a certain size, they would suffer repercussions. So, each community learned what its organic size was, above which it could not go. Jews learned to keep a low profile and to keep quiet.

As we move from the remote and quasi-remote past to more recent periods, the "hole" in the canon of Italian literature becomes harder to explain. I refer here to the absence of a discourse—historical, moral, metaphysical, and epistemological—emanating from the historically determinant experience of the racial laws of the Mussolini regime and the Italian-Jewish "contribution" to the death toll of the Shoah in Italian literature. To put it simply, Italian literature and, at large, Italian consciousness for the longest time did not have a place for a Jewish discourse, not even when a discourse emerged in the rest of Europe, in the United States, and in Israel, formulated in terms of what would be later labeled "Holocaust literature." There was very little place, in particular, for first-person accounts, for memoirs, for religious and philosophical meditations on the meaning of the Shoah, either in general or in reference to the Italian experience in particular. Obviously, among the Jews of Italy and in their publications these themes were widely debated and discussed. Oral history was preeminent, and a very firm form of consciousness existed. However, this hardly penetrated the discourse of society at large.

A confirmation of this situation is in Anna Bravo's essay "Gli scritti di memoria della deportazione dall'Italia (1944–1993). I significati e l'accoglienza." In a thoroughly researched paper, the author lists practically all of the publications on the theme of Jewish "deportation" and prefaces her findings with the observation that most of the works "could only count on small or very small publishing houses, too weak and too far from the cultural establishment to offer widespread distribution on the market and, consequently, obtain adequate recognition in the historical-literary environment."[3] Her thesis is that—significantly—historical research in Italy gave scant attention to the uniqueness of the Jewish predicament and that the ordeal of the Italian Shoah was subsumed under the "larger" rubric of the history of deportation to the German labor camps of Italian political prisoners, partisans, and draft evaders. In Italian historiography, Italian Jews are left with the role of extras in the representation of the drama of Italian suffering, as ratified by the new national ideology of the *Resistenza*. It is, in a way, the same sort of operation, a construction of text, performed by the Polish in Auschwitz, which was to be interpreted as a symbol of Polish suffering under the Nazis, with no reference to the Jews.

Or more dangerously, it mirrors the attempt by the Catholic Church and by the pope, John Paul II himself, to appropriate the Shoah for itself, using the argument that the Shoah was an offense against humanity, against "man," to use standard Catholic rhetoric. In that the Shoah was against "man," it follows that it was against Christ; therefore it was anti-Christian, and consequently it becomes part of the experience of Catholic suffering and martyrdom.[4]

The situation in Italy remained stable for some forty years, with a handful of titles published primarily, as we saw, by small, specialized houses. Of course, there was one major exception, and this exception was Primo Levi, Levi was the exception that confirmed the rule.

The landscape began to change significantly ten to fifteen years ago. The trickle of books became a steady stream, growing in size and relevance. In a crescendo that apparently is still to reach its peak, Italian publishers and readers "discovered" Judaism. Books on the Jews and Judaism started cropping up everywhere on the shelves of the poorly frequented Italian bookstores. It was a phenomenon that took everyone by surprise and that encompassed several genres of texts, from the journalistic, to the erudite historical essay, to the ongoing historiographical research, to the collection of personal stories. As Jews became a hot publishing item,[5] my task changed. It was no longer the attempt to explain why a Jewish discourse was absent in Italian literature but the effort of deciphering to what extent this production affected the direction of the Italian discourse on the Jews and if that amounted to the establishment of a Jewish discourse in the Italian consciousness.

The most tantalizing question was why the phenomenon is taking place at this particular juncture in Italian history. In a previous essay that I presented in October 1998 at a symposium at the State University of New York (SUNY) at Stony Brook, I formulated a tentative hypothesis that takes into consideration the major social changes that have taken place recently in Italy, the most relevant of which has been the arrival of immigrants. In this context, I contended, Italians began interrogating themselves about the myths and the truths of their proclaimed tolerance and antiracist nature in view of particularly hideous episodes of violence and a widespread attitude of intolerance. In order for this self-interrogation not to become self-referential and automatically autoexculpatory, Italians needed to turn to someone else for an answer from outside. The Jews could provide those answers, for, historically, the Jews of the Diaspora have always had the special and unwelcome task of functioning as the litmus test of the presence of racism in a society. My thesis was that Italy was witnessing the birth of the discourse of diversity and that within that discourse, for the first time, the Jewish discourse could be articulated and become part of the main discourse of Italian society about itself.

As clearly demonstrated in the volume *Ebrei in Italia: un problema di identità*[6] by Maurizio Molinari, there is no question that, starting at the very beginning of the nineteenth century, when the ideological construct of the Italian national identity was formulated, Italian Jews have felt fully and completely Italian, in terms of both their historical and existential consciousness. However, the Jews, in the consciousness of a Christian world, from the Middle Ages onward, have always represented the epitome of Otherness. Reflected in this historical Otherness, Italians are now trying to see, as in a mirror, the image of themselves. In the books written by Jews, Italians are looking for reassurance, hoping to hear, not surprisingly, good things about themselves.

It may not be completely coincidental that the shaping of a discourse of Otherness and diversity in Italy in 1994 found its first comprehensive treatment in the book *Gli altri*, whose author, Furio Colombo, a non-Jew, is nevertheless one of Italy's intellectuals closest to Jewish sensibilities.[7]

Another explanation as to the interest of Italians for everything Jewish has been offered in a conversation with Liliana Picciotto Fargion, arguably the foremost historian of the Shoah in Italy. According to her interpretation, Italians are reacting to a lack of a collective identity as a people and, in a time of confusion and uncertainty on what it means to be Italian, are looking at the Jews, fascinated by their certitude and the unwavering strength of their identity. One could thus conclude that in the books written by Jews on Jews, Italians are establishing the discourse of their identity. If this were the case, it would raise other, more complex questions, such as: Is the discourse of Italian identity at all compatible with the Jewish discourse? In other words, do the same books have the same meaning for non-Jewish Italians and for Italian Jews?

When I set out to read this new literary production, my goal was to apply a critical filter that would allow at least a preliminary categorization of the phenomenon. By now the landscape has become quite various. Some texts are historical and journalistic-type investigations, such as Alexander Stille's

Benevolence and Betrayal: Five Italian Jewish Families under Fascism.[8] Others are, improperly speaking, "guides to Judaism," as, for instance, *Essere ebrei in Italia*[9] by Stefano Jesurum, Elio Toaff's interview with Alain Elkann, *Essere ebreo*,[10] or Nedelia Tedeschi's *A domanda rispondo.*[11] A sizable portion of the texts that have been published are centered around the notion of identity, encompassing both the notion of Otherness and "diversity" and the consciousness of belonging. This is transparent even in the titles, which emphasize the complexity of the Italian-Jewish identity. A book of photographs is titled *La differenza invisibile.*[12] Others are the already mentioned *Ebrei in Italia: un problema di identità (1870–1838)* and the also mentioned *Appartenenza e differenza: ebrei d'Italia e letteratura.* The proceedings from "Il Nuovo Convegno" (1977) carry the revealing title *Identità.*[13]

A special place is occupied by the first-person accounts of the persecution and the Lager, the real "memoirs" of occasional writers whose only urge is to tell their story, to "bear witness," and to add another piece to the complex and never-finished mosaic of the Shoah documentation. My previous critical interest in Holocaust literature and a familiarity with the issues of autobiography led me to concentrate on those texts and to focus on the discourse of Judaism in terms of identity and its interplay with memory. In the development of this discourse in Italy, I believe that a crucial role, in textual terms, belongs to the work of Liliana Picciotto Fargion and her book, the monumentally researched *Il libro della memoria. Gli Ebrei deportati dall'Italia (1943–1945).*[14] This volume establishes without question the cognitive grid and the documentary scaffolding without which individual acts could again be relegated to the rank of "isolated" and unconnected voices. This is a crucial text in that it establishes as a subtext the notion of *participation* by the perpetrators in a vast machinery of extermination that was not only German or Nazi but also Fascist and therefore Italian.

In a parallel fashion, from a factual, nontextual perspective, the landmark historical event that imposed a Jewish discourse at the political and social level was the uprising of the Rome ghetto (a word I use with great affection), which followed the shameful and cowardly verdict in the Priebke case in 1996. This event was even more significant in terms of its meaning for Italian Jews than the murderous attack on the synagogue in Rome in 1982.

As I mentioned, the production has grown significantly over the last ten or fifteen years, with an acceleration in the last five or six. Among the texts that I analyzed, the most noteworthy are *Cara Sophie*[15] by Maria Sofia Casnedi and Fabio Della Seta; Elisa Springer's *Il silenzio dei vivi;*[16] Aldo Carpi's *Diario di Gusen;*[17] Lia Levi's *Una bambini e basta;*[18] Giuliana Tedeschi's *C'e un punto della terra . . .;*[19] Liana Millu's *Il fumo di Birkenau;*[20] Emanuele Pafici's *Non ti voltare;*[21] Liliana Treves Alcalay's *Con occhi di bambina;*[22] Ada Sereni's *I clandestini del mare,*[23] initially published in 1973 and reprinted in 1994. I could even include Angelo Pezzana's *Quest'anno a Gerusalemme,*[24] which contains interviews with Italian Jews emigrated to Israel, and the collection of personal stories in *Una gioventù offesa: Ebrei genovesi ricordano,* edited by Chiara Bricarelli.[25] Last week, the daughter of another author brought to my attention a text that I had seen listed in bibliographies but that I had not yet acquired: Carla Pekelis' *La mia versione dei fatti*, published in 1996.[26] My preliminary reading would place this text at the top of the list in terms of both historical and literary significance. I trust that in the future development of my work, I will devote much attention to this text, due to its relevance and intrinsic literary value.

The texts that I have mentioned represent a spectrum of experiences, sensibilities, and literary abilities that differ in scope, profundity, and urgency. My interest, however, was to see to what extent they contributed to the Jewish discourse and in what context. The first tentative conclusion is that these texts have the effect of "reconnecting" Italian Judaism with the experiences of the rest of Europe. This in itself could be the topic for a monster-size research project. As a general idea and, I hope, a useful provocation, I suggest that it is clear that very little is shared between Italian Judaism and the *shtetl* Judaism of Eastern Europe, which is the basis of American Judaism today, in terms of reciprocal knowledge. Time and again I heard anecdotes from American Jews who were stunned when they first found out about the existence of Italian Jews. One of my American friends, for instance, recalled being a child and telling fanciful and foolish stories, to which the family inevitably replied, "Oh yeah, and there are Jews in Italy," as a way to characterize something completely unreal. The distance and *rapprochement* between Italian Jews and other Jews is the subtext of identity, as appears, for instance, in Liana Millu's book, a text that is ambiguous at least, if not outright suspicious, in its reticence on Jewish themes. This reaches its peak in a series of episodes that clearly demonstrate the self-conscious decision on the part of the author to establish a distance between herself and the identification with the Jewish dimension. In describing an exchange among prisoners, she states: "I didn't understand German well to begin with, and she spoke it mixing it with that Yiddish dialect that to me sounded like the most horrible language on earth" (p. 47). On the occasion of Hanukkah, a clandestine celebration takes place, and Millu talks about the "perennial flame of *their* faith" (emphasis added).

At the individual level, the sense of identity receives quite a different treatment in Giuliana Tedeschi's work, in which the author describes the itiner- ary of its materialization. Talking about other inmates in the Lager, she describes a group of Jewish women from Salonika, in Greece. "'They are savages,' the French and Italians said with disdain. However, with their Mediter- ranean exuberance they were preferable to the Polish women, hostile and impenetrable" (p. 56). In a later episode the writer sees on the bed of a truck a bundle of overcoats with the Jewish star: "I saw these coats become alive, walk in the streets of the world: France, Belgium, Hungary. . . . And I felt on me the burden of the star that I had never worn" (p. 61). From this point the Jewish identity becomes total and paramount in her consciousness, as appears in several encounters with German guards and SS. Progressively, she is one of many "filthy Jews" (p. 86) to be gunned down, then the "filthy Jewish prisoner" (p. 101) at the presence of a purely Aryan SS. Her participation in the rituals of Rosh Hashanah is without reservations, and slowly we witness the recovering of a long-forgotten identity in the form of childhood memories, reminiscing about "ancient biblical traditions, with that element of a miracle that fascinated my childhood, but made me incredulous and doubtful during my youth years." The memory returns and so does identity: "'Bread and patience' says the proverb. And I accepted its wisdom" (p. 149).

Elisa Springer adds another piece to the mosaic, with a nonlinear narrative that intersperses flashbacks and foreshadowing and focuses the investigation of identity on the number tattooed on her arm. After the liberation, for years she had kept it hidden under a bandage. She tells the truth only when her sons asks about it, and from his reaction she derives the motivation to change her attitude, but at a great cost. "I wanted to hide the mark from other people's eyes, because I was wounded by their scorn and indifference. [My son] insisted: I should not feel any shame . . . I knew he was right but I could not find the strength to react and I was afraid I would be rejected by the others" (pp. 73–74).

Thus, the interplay of identity and memory slowly surfaces as the common denominator of these texts, a complex psychological dynamic portrayed with different attitudes, but all with the consciousness of performing the crucial task of the definition of the relationship between individual vicissitudes and the collective historical Jewish experience.

If identity is a crucial theme at the individual level, only when we read these texts in the context that they create, that is, within their particular discourse, do we begin to see the traces of the production of an original meaning that injects itself in the Italian discourse. This is the outline of a new interpretive and, arguably, hermeneutic paradigm, the very paradigm of what I called earlier the "revisionist" reading of Italian history. I use this term consciously and in a subversive way, but a way that I think is quite appropriate, in that this revisionism challenges the comfortable myths embedded in the negation of anti-Semitism in Italy, as explained by Anna Bravo when she claims that "the ideology of extraneousness of Italians in the persecution of Jews and in war crimes reaches its peak in the claim of innocence that goes hand-in-hand with the willingness to forget."

These texts put an end to the silence and the willingness to forget. The negationist attitude is challenged by these very documents, forcing the revision of the commonly assumed notion of a comfortable past. It is a challenge that only memory can bring, and in doing that, Italian memoirists perform the ultimate act of the most universal Jewish religious ritual, the most sacred, and the most uniquely Jewish after the Shoah: the act of remembrance.

The relevance of these texts goes beyond their documentary contribution. They fulfill the imperative that Liliana Picciotto Fargion defines in an essay contained in *Storia e memoria della deportazione*, when she reconstructs the origin of her book's title. *Libro della memoria* is the literal translation of the Hebrew "Sefer ha-zikaron," which indicated a type of book, written in the Middle Ages and after, that contained the names of people killed in the mas-sacres of the Crusades. By reconnecting to that tradition, "memory" ceases to mean individual and personal recollections. "Memory," even for Italian Jews, becomes the collective dimension of experiences and beliefs that have taken the connotations of a Jewish ideology and that often borders even traits of a Jewish secular theology. In this manner, Jewish identity is reconfirmed, without ever being questioned. Italian identity, too, is reconfirmed and remains unquestioned. The dialectic dimension of this encounter is played out in the memoirs, and the contribution of knowledge brought by the revision of history, rewritten by Italian Jews, forces a change in the Italian discourse. By virtue of this operation possible only to the possessors of a multilayered identity, an identity of belonging and Otherness, the discourse of Italian Jews has become part of and at the same time has changed forever the general discourse of what it means to be Italian.

NOTES

1. Lynn M. Gunzberg, *Strangers at Home: Jews in the Italian Literary Imagination* (Berkeley: University of California Press, 1992).

2. J. Hassine et al., eds., *Appartenenza e differenza: Ebrei d'Italia e letteratura* (Florence: La Giuntina, 1998).

3. In *Storia della memoria e della deportazione*, edited by Paolo Momigliano Levi (Florence: La Giuntina, 1996), p. 65.

4. This thesis reappeared in a piece signed by Luigi Giussani, head of the Catholic fundamentalist group Comunione e Liberazione, in the newspaper *La Repubblica* on 2 January 1999.

5. Personal communication with Liliana Picciotto Fargion, July 1999. In a recent conversation in Italy, she, in commenting on the phenomenon of so many publications about Jewish themes, jokingly mentioned an episode in which her daughter entered a bookstore in Milan and asked, with feigned exasperation, if they had *anything* other than books on Jews.

6. Maurizio Molinari, *Ebrei in Italia: un problema di identità (1870–1938)* (Florence: La Giuntina, 1991).

7. Furio Colombo, *Gli altri* (Rome: Nuova ERI, 1994; Milan: Rizzoli, 1994).

8. New York: Summit Books, 1991.

9. Milan: Longanesi, 1987.

10. Milan: Bompiani, 1994.

11. Florence: La Giuntina, 1996.

12. Alessandro Guetta and Ottavio Celestino (Florence: La Giuntina, 1988).

13. Florence: La Giuntina, 1997.

14. Milan: Mursia, 1991.

15. Udine: Paolo Gasparia Editore, 1996.

16. Bari: Marsilio, 1997.

17. Turin: Einaudi, 1993.

18. Rome: Edizioni e/o, 1994.

19. Florence: La Giuntina, 1988.

20. Florence: La Giuntina, 1986.

21. Florence: La Giuntina, 1993.

22. Florence: La Giuntina, 1994.

23. Milan: Mursia, 1973, 1994.

24. Milan: Corbaccio, 1997.

25. Florence: La Giuntina, 1995.

26. Palermo: Sellerio, 1996; *My Version of the Facts*, translated by Simona Pekelis McCray (Evanston, IL: Northwestern University Press, forthcoming).

Part IV

WORLD WAR II
AND THE HOLOCAUST

20

Haven or Hell?: Italy's Refuge for Jews, 1933–1945

Maryann Calendrille

The Hebrew word for Italy is said to describe a place that rests "in the dew of the gods," a paradise, a peninsula moistened with mercy. Yet is this idyllic image an accurate description of a country that lost 8,000 of its Jews during the dark years of Mussolini's fascism and war? At times, Italy did represent a haven for many Jews who found refuge there, if an uncertain one. But while many Jews were protected, others were turned away and suffered greatly under Mussolini's racial laws. For some, Italy was hell. During the German occupation (1943–1945) Jews were massacred or deported to their certain death. At other times, Italy must have been a frightening limbo; Jews interned at the Ferramonti concentration camp, for example, suffered malaria, malnutrition, and threats of deportation to the maw of Auschwitz, their precarious position left to the mercy of diplomatic leaders.[1] So what kind of refuge was it?

While we may be eager to agree that "it wasn't as bad as in Germany or Poland," to make a simple comparison would be troubling. Would we then be accepting the diabolical logic of Nazism as a benchmark? Would we be considering Auschwitz within the acceptable realm of the possible? While the Ferramonti camp, in southern Italy, was certainly not a killing center, it was a degrading, frightening, and threatening place and one that shouldn't have existed at all. Even if Italy's racial laws were only partially enforced, why were they enforced at all? How did they gain legitimacy?

The situation for Jews in Italy problematizes the definition of the Holocaust. The Italian signposts are often less obvious than the grotesque German crematoria, less blatant than the ubiquitous wearing of yellow stars. More subtle forms of anti-Semitism exist in Italy, however, as distinct markers along the continuum of historic and often brutal anti-Semitism. Every such marker within this continuum is significant to a more nuanced definition of the Holocaust.

We must begin our study, then, with the purity of a tabula rasa, for if we accept as evidence of the Holocaust only the black ash and oily smoke rising from the crematoria, we miss the more subtle and insidious steps that it took human beings to build and then use these repugnant contraptions against each other. What does it mean, then, that in 1940 innocent Italian citizens were brought in handcuffs to a remote and nearly deserted valley in Calabria to be interned at Ferramonti? What does it mean that a country without a strong history of anti-Semitism could have turned on its own citizens? What does it mean that Pope Pius XII made only the vaguest public objections while Roman Jews were deported to Auschwitz? With a more nuanced understanding of the subtleties of anti-Semitism and the Holocaust, we may realize that to wait to see the black smoke spewing into the sky above the killing centers is to have waited too long.

The picture of Italy is, therefore, a murky one; Italy did not share the same history of anti-Semitic hatred as Germany, yet Mussolini's race laws enacted in 1938 seemed to mimic those of Hitler. Official Italian policy after 1938 was clearly anti-Semitic; however, individual Italians often went to great lengths to protect both foreign and Italian Jews. While the Vatican might be accused of official inaction, many individual priests and bishops did protect Jews. As Mussolini tried to accommodate Hitler, Il Duce's military officers followed their own conscience in protecting Jews in Italian-occupied lands. The situation for Jews in Italy is complex and presents a paradox revealed by titles of various works covering this period: Joseph Rochlitz's film *The Righteous Enemy*, Nicola Caracciolo's *Uncertain Refuge*, Alexander Stille's *Benevolence and Betrayal,* and Lynn Gunzberg's *Strangers at Home*. While Italy can boast of its efforts to sabotage attempts to deport Jews to their certain death, Italy must also take responsibility for the loss of 8,000 of its citizens. While 42,000 of Italy's Jews did survive, 8,000 were murdered. There is no adequate rationalization for that.

The paradox of Italy continues today. More than fifty years after the war, monuments erected at historic sites commemorate lives lost under fascism. In the small southern village of Tarsia, three miles from the Ferramonti camp, a monument to victims installed in a tiny piazza reads: "To those of all faiths and religions who suffered." These conciliatory, yet vague, words seem to obfuscate Jewish identity once again. The complex and controversial trials of ex-Nazi Captain Erich Priebke (1996–1998) caused international uproar. The charges brought against him for his involvement in the Ardeatine Caves massacre in which 335 people were murdered, including seventy-eight Jews, in retaliation for a partisan attack on German SS in Rome in March 1944 sparked much debate. Today in Rome's Portico d'Ottavia, a bustling Kosher pizzeria serves midday meals to bearded men wearing long black coats and fedoras. In October 1943, during the German occupation, 1,259 Roman Jews were rounded up and held very near this spot before eventually being deported to Auschwitz. While contemporary Italians must wrestle with their individual consciences, we must question how a supposedly philo-semitic country could have allowed any part of the Holocaust to contaminate this place "in the dew of the gods."

Mussolini's brand of fascism certainly differed from Hiltler's anti-Jewish and anti-Christian assaults.[2] In the early years, Italian Jews were members of the Fascist

Party; Mussolini even condemned racism and anti-Semitism, but with Hitler's rise to power in 1933, a more lethal virus infected Mussolini's fascism. In the fall of 1936, he unleashed an anti-Semitic propaganda campaign, accusing Jews of spreading atrocious stories about the Third Reich, yet he still attempted to persuade Hitler to stop persecuting German Jewish subjects.[3]

Discriminatory legislation was delayed, however, while Mussolini prepared public opinion in Italy and tried to avoid conflicts with the Vatican. In a speech in Berlin on 28 September 1937, he claimed that Jewish opposition to the Ethiopian venture revealed the Jewish peril within Italy.[4] The next year Mussolini adopted racial laws to expel Jews from Italian public life. While the yellow Jewish star was not compulsory in Italy, and for a time Italian Jews were spared the ravages faced by Jews throughout Europe, a dangerous overture had been made: Mussolini broke with the West and committed Italy to the Rome-Berlin Axis. This would eventually prove fatal to thousands of Italy's Jews.

Italian historian Liliana Picciotto Fargion describes two distinct periods for Jews in Italy, marked first by the Italian alliance with the Germans during which the government's aim was to "discriminate, humiliate and persecute" Jews. The second phase under German occupation focused on separating and imprisoning Jews. In her view, rescuers were the exception to the rule: "Having honored those government officials who did not betray their own humanity . . . we must emphasize that no individual examples of generosity should or can detract from the monstrous state machinery that was placed at the service of injustice."[5] This machinery took the form, for example, of a special agency, Demografia e Razza, created in June 1938 to execute the anti-Jewish policy and to develop a special census to collect names, addresses and family group information.

This "monstrous state machinery" also took the form of Mussolini's version of race laws, which restricted Jews from attending or teaching at state-run schools, yet they were free to organize their own private community schools. Later, foreign Jews previously given Italian citizenship had it revoked. By 17 November 1938 other decrees were announced. Marriage between Jews and non-Jews was prohibited. Jews were forbidden to own or manage companies involved in military production or factories that employed over 100 people. Jews were forbidden to own land over a certain value; they could no longer serve in the armed forces or belong to the Fascist Party. Jews could no longer work in banks or insurance companies. Overall, Italian racial laws did cause severe economic hardship as well as moral deprivation for Jews in Italy.[6]

Great confusion ensued over definitions of who was a Jew, and with Italy's high rate of intermarriage and religious conversion, the situation was further complicated. Children of two Jewish parents could be considered Jewish regardless of whether the child had been baptized, which angered the Vatican. In cases of mixed marriages, the children were considered Jewish if they practiced Judaism but were not considered Jewish if they were baptized before 1 October 1938. Those children of mixed marriages born between 1 October 1938 and 1 October 1939 were given ten days to be baptized. Other exemptions included the immediate families of Jews killed, wounded, or decorated while fighting in Libya, World War

I, Ethiopia, and Spain. Those early members of the Fascist Party who joined between 1919 and 1922 were also eligible for exemptions.[7] Interpretation of these laws varied:

Local ordinances frequently denied licenses to small Jewish businesses, shops, restaurants, and cafes. A local decree in Rome revoked the licenses of rag pickers and second-hand clothes dealers. . . . The zeal with which these measures were executed varied from place to place, but the suffering was widespread and acute.[8]

Yet the very existence of these laws established a dangerous precedent.

Prewar conditions in Italy included food rationing and widespread civil unrest. Italian imports and consumption were greatly reduced, and in the winter of 1941 widespread hunger and demonstrations marked daily life. By March 1943 thousands of workers went on strike to demand higher wages, peace, and bread. This decline in living standards and general disenchantment with Mussolini's rule ultimately led to his overthrow in July 1943. Despite these conditions, immigrants continued to be drawn to the prospect of safe haven as conditions in other countries grew even worse.[9]

Jewish refugees found more lax visa policies and greater employment opportunities despite the fact that Italy was a fascist country.[10] A charitable organization was established in 1939 to aid Jewish refugees and provided food, clothing, medicine, and living allowances. The Delegation for Assistance to Jewish Emigrants (DELASEM) was directed by Lelio Vittorio Valobra, who suggested that the organization would actually help fascism by relocating thousands of Jews no longer able to work in Italy and by importing foreign currency to help support Jews. DELASEM was heavily funded by the Joint Distribution Committee of the United States and had the cooperation of the Italian government. The group aided rescue efforts that brought Jews from Italian-occupied territories into Italy.[11]

One of the organization's most noble actions was the successful rescue and protection of ninety-two Jewish children, refugees from Yugoslavia. The children were housed and cared for near Modena in an estate known as Villa Emma.[12] This effort took the cooperation of nearly all the residents of the small town, who, in fact, willingly gave of their time and services to feed, teach, and care for the children, incurring great risk to their own safety. As remarkable as this rescue story is, according to Susan Zuccotti,

[s]imilar events were occurring all over Italy. The ratio was the same everywhere: A handful of Fascist fanatics, like the one who led the Germans to Villa Emma and the others who arrested local priests and tried unsuccessfully to make them talk, were countered by hundreds who took in Jews, assisted them, or, at the very least, knew exactly where they were and kept quiet.[13]

Despite these early rescue activities, once Italy entered the war, many foreign Jews were arrested and interned in camps established to handle the growing numbers of immigrants. Threatened with expulsion or loss of citizenship, many Jews found themselves at the Ferramonti-Tarsia camp.

CAMPS IN ITALY

One of the largest of the fifteen internment camps in Italy was constructed in the malaria-infested Crati valley in the impoverished southern region of Calabria. The ninety-two-barrack camp known as Ferramonti-Tarsia was built expressly for the purpose of housing Jews, while all other places of internment utilized existing school buildings, ex-convents, or other public buildings. The barracks at Ferramonti were built, maintained, and supplied by the Eugenio Parrini firm, which had been engaged in a land reclamation project in the area. From 1,000 to 2,000 people were held there between 1940 and 1943.[14]

Conditions in the camp varied over the several years of its operation. The best that one could say is that prisoners were not forced into labor, though summers were brutally hot and winters cold and chronically damp. Indigent internees were given a government subsidy, yet another example of the bittersweet reprieve that Italy offered. At worst, prisoners suffered from disease (between 1940 and 1943, 820 cases of malaria were documented) and malnutrition.[15] On one tragic occasion, four internees were killed and many wounded when Allied planes bombed the camp on 27 August 1943, thinking it a military barracks.[16] While Ferramonti may have offered a reprieve to some, for others it was short-lived, and as the war dragged on, threats of deportations loomed.

The internees were subject to three roll calls daily, curfews, censorship of their correspondence, and restrictions on reading material and were prohibited from using cameras and radios. Despite these restrictions, the interned Jews organized their own kitchens, library, court, medical clinic, and synagogue. The neighboring peasants, at first fearful of the internees, due to their own isolation and "ancient sense of territoriality," gradually came to see the Jews as a "poor, unhappy, persecuted people"[17] probably not unlike themselves. Meanwhile, local fascists served as camp guards.

The camp director, Commissioner Paolo Salvatore, adopted a generally tolerant attitude toward his charges. According to one survivor, he was an "enlightened and kind person" who was later transferred (perhaps because he was too kind) and replaced by a more stringent fascist functionary. Boundaries between prisoners and guards seem to have blurred somewhat at Ferramonti. Commissioner Salvatore attended musical performances within the camp, inviting local dignitaries. Doctors among the interned sometimes also cared for sick villagers, and local peasants bartered with the interned, who, in some cases, had more resources than the peasants. The camp was eventually liberated by the British Eighth Army on 3 September 1943 and many internees later emigrated to the United States and to Palestine.[18]

Another, very different sort of camp represents a blacker notch along the continuum. Located in the northern city of Trieste, San Sabba, or La Risiera, as it was known, had been transformed from a rice-processing factory into a deadly prison camp when the Germans annexed the area. It claimed tens of thousands of prisoners, both Jews and non-Jews. A working gas chamber and crematorium consumed fifty to seventy corpses daily; death tolls ranged from 3,000 to 4,500. These were mostly partisans, however, as most Jews were gathered at La Risiera and deported to Auschwitz between October 1943 and November 1944. The exact number of deportees is not known.[19]

As the war dragged on, and increasing numbers of Italian troops were killed, resentment against Jews at home escalated. By August 1942 Mussolini ordered Jewish men to perform manual labor for practically no pay. Although this order was ignored in some localities, it was widely enforced in Rome. According to Alexander Stille, doctors, lawyers, and other professionals, perhaps showing Jewish spirit and dignity, actually took pride in this work and were not humiliated, as was intended.[20]

After Mussolini's fall from power on 25 July 1943, the situation for Jews in Italy grew ever more threatening. While the Allies controlled the south, headed by Marshal Pietro Badoglio, the north came under German control, headed by a reinstated Mussolini and the Repubblica Sociale Italiana government (RSI) at Salò. What ensued under occupation was a series of roundups, massacres, and, in some cases, deportations.[21]

Fargion divides events between 1943 and 1945 into three categories. First, between October and November 1943 the Germans, directed by SS Hauptsturmführer Theodor Dannecker (envoy of Adolf Eichmann), conducted autonomous lightning raids and rushed into the power vacuum. Second, from December 1943 till mid-February 1944 Italians managed the "Jewish question" through legislation and arrests. Finally, from mid-February 1944 to February 1945 the gravest violence erupted as a result of increased German imposition at Salò.[22]

The Germans' first targets were Roman Jews, who were attacked, according to Fargion, as a show of disdain toward the RSI, to defy the pope, weaken Mussolini's government, and thwart future negotiations.[23] The infamous 16 October 1943 roundup and arrest of Roman Jews had tragic results, yet Italian citizens and authorities attempted some resistance, hiding Jews and creating false ID papers. Testimony shows that taxi drivers literally forced Jews into their cabs as the arrests were happening and drove them to safety.[24] Herbert Kappler, head of Security Police Command, noted the resistance in his report to superiors. While higher levels of Italian authority seemed unaware of the actions, local citizens converged on the site where victims were held to offer aid and get news.[25]

By November 1943 Italy no longer merely applied German orders and the Nazis assumed direct authority. The manifesto of restored fascism declared all Jews foreigners and "belonging to enemy nationality." Italian fascists further distinguished between "citizen and subject." Once Jews were considered "subjects," further persecution ensued. Autonomous police orders under RSI sent Jews to internment camps, either local provisional ones or special ones created for this purpose, and seized Jewish property. Those with Aryan status due to mixed marriage were placed under special vigilance. After December 1943, Jews could no longer freely move about and were subject to arrest. On 5 and 6 December, Jews were arrested in Venice by Italian authorities, not the SS. The early morning raid included an attack on an old age home. A total of 150 men and women were arrested, separated, and taken to prison to await shipment to interment camps. Similar arrests by Italians took place in Ferrara, Florence, Siena, and Piedmont.[26]

During these arrests, some Italians did offer aid. Some police officials warned victims of imminent arrest; others helped hide Jews and confused files. "It is here, perhaps, better than anywhere else, that the dichotomy can be distinguished between organized powers and common people who could not understand how entire defenseless families could be dangerous enemies of the state," comments Fargion.[27] By the end of February 1944 the Fossoli prison, a principal internment camp near Modena, was run by Germans. This change in administration led to immediate deportations. The camp was closed in the summer of 1944 under threat of Allied advances and partisan attacks, and Jews were sent to Auschwitz, Buchenwald, Ravensbruch, or Bergen-Belson. Twenty convoys left with 5,734 people. In addition, 23 smaller convoys left from the Italian zone annexed to the Third Reich with 1,074 people. From the Italian island of Rhodes, another 1,805 were deported. The total number of deportees was 8,613, of whom 7,631 died; 291 Jews died in Italy, bringing the overall total to 7,922.[28]

THE ROLE OF THE POPE

Rome represented a safe haven to many Jews in hiding, but after the German occupation, the Vatican's Jews were ultimately abandoned. According to John F. Morley's account, Jewish lawyer Ugo Foa, president of the Jewish community in Rome, asked for the Vatican's help in protecting 150 non-Italian Jews. "The request was denied, and it was recommended that the 150 Jews flee from Rome in small groups led by an Italian-speaking Jew."[29] One month later, the SS demanded fifty kilos of gold in exchange for the safety of Roman Jews. While the Vatican is reported to have reassured the Jewish community that it would make up the difference of whatever amount the Jews could collect,[30] the pope's offer came in the form of a loan, not an outright contribution.[31]

The gold ransom episode created real terror for Roman Jews. The city, then under German occupation, suffered food shortages and lack of transportation, trapping Jews and non-Jews alike. German commander Major Kappler demanded the fifty kilos of gold, or he would take 200 hostages. Kappler told the president of the Jewish community, Ugo Foa, that Jews were enemies of Germany and would be treated as such.[32] Kappler was ordered by Himmler to liquidate the Jewish ghetto in Rome, but Kappler first began his own plan of extortion. He apparently felt that deportations were a waste of resources and feared that they would create resistance opportunities and disorder. It is still unclear whether he wanted to extort Jews for his own benefit or lull them into thinking that they could "buy off" the threat of deportation.[33] In any case, after much duress, slightly more than the requested amount of gold was finally presented to the Germans within the forty-four-hour period in which it was demanded,[34] but the terror did not end. Two weeks later, one of the most infamous events in the war against the Italian Jews took place.

The arrest of Jews in Rome marks a deep scar on the city, whose citizens thought themselves secure in the protection of the Vatican. In the early morning hours of 16 October, Italian-Jewish families awoke to the urgent ringing of doorbells and shouts: "'Jews! Run! Run! The Germans!'"[35] At first, people thought these armed Germans had come to order them to work assignments, and many men fled. It soon became clear, however, that their fate was more precarious. Women and children were ordered into the streets and quickly crammed onto trucks that transported them to an Italian military college at Via della Lungara, very near the Vatican. Some Jews managed to escape, but in all, 365 German soldiers and SS arrested 1,259 people, one-tenth of the city's Jews, in only nine hours. The captives were ultimately sent to their deaths at Auschwitz.[36]

To understand the actions of Pope Pius XII during the notorious events of the autumn of 1943, we might ask, What did the Pope know? When did he know it? Evidence suggests that Pope Pius XII could well have been aware of the 16 October roundup of Jews in Rome yet did nothing to warn them.[37] While train cars packed with 1,259 Jews sat at Rome's Tibertina station for forty-eight hours in full knowledge of the pope, he remained silent. More than a week after those train cars carried their victims to Auschwitz's crematorium the pope issued the following statement:

As is well-known, the August Pontiff, after having vainly tried to prevent the outbreak of the war . . . has not desisted for one moment from employing all the means in His power to alleviate the suffering which, whatever form it may take, is the consequence of this cruel conflagration. With the augmentation of so much evil, the universal and paternal charity of the Supreme Pontiff has become, it might be said, ever more active; it knows neither boundaries nor nationality, neither religion nor race.[38]

This, his only public comment regarding these events, seems little more than a carefully worded diplomatic palliative that ignores Italian citizens whose ashes were by then besmirching the sky. While it's been argued that the pope was perhaps fearful of a Nazi invasion of the Vatican and of ever more brutal retaliatory measures against both Jews and Catholics, the pope's silence at this most critical time clamors like a death knell for those driven from a country considered a safe haven. In Susan Zuccotti's words, it amounted to a "terrifying failure."[39]

RESISTANCE ACTIVITIES

The Jewish resistance movement in Italy was never a collective movement as in France and other countries. It was, rather, a movement of individuals. Early partisan efforts before 1938 were inspired by the writings of Neapolitan philosopher Benedetto Croce, who professed a "religion of liberty." In particular, Croce's article about Tullo Massarani,[40] a prominent nineteenth-century figure of liberal-democratic Judaism and already a model for radical and socialist Jews and non-Jews, served as a rallying cry for many.[41] Prominent Italian Jews Carlo and Nello Rosselli founded the movement known as Giustizia e Libertà in 1929, which served as a coordinating body for noncommunist opponents of fascism. It was a movement without a particular program, yet its members, highly educated, middle-class intellectuals, were democratic republicans committed to social justice, civil liberties, and international peace. Giustizia e Libertà suffered a terrible blow with the assassinations of Carlo and Nello Rosselli in France in 1937 but was reborn as the Partito d'Azione in 1943.[42]

Under German occupation, the Italian resistance movement took up arms, and partisans were often jailed, tortured, and killed. "The highest estimate of general Italian participants is 230,000, or .5 percent of a national population of 45,000,000. The lowest estimate of Jewish participation is 1,000 or about 2 percent of a total wartime population of 45,200."[43] Literary scholar, publisher, and supporter of Giustizia e Libertà, Leone Ginzburg was arrested on November 1943 and died in Regina Coeli prison. Rita Rosani, a twenty-four-year-old teacher in the Jewish school in Verona, was killed in September 1944 after Nazi troops surrounded and shot her. She was posthumously awarded a gold medal of honor by the postwar Italian government for her efforts as an "indomitable leader." The best of the academic community gathered in the Jewish schools, which "became little factories of anti-Fascism." Others awarded the gold medal of honor included Irma Bandiera, who was tortured and killed by Nazi troops; Lidia Bianchi, who refused a pardon and was killed; Irma Marchiani, who was captured and escaped, recaptured and killed. Vera Vassale escaped near capture by SS troops and fled with secret documents and continued to work behind enemy lines. Emanuele Artom, deeply influenced by Croce, was arrested on 25 March 1944 and died two weeks later of beatings in Nuove prison in Turin.

ACTIVITIES OF THE ITALIAN ARMY IN YUGOSLAVIA, GREECE, AND SOUTHERN FRANCE

The Italian military was instrumental in sabotaging Germany's plans for deportation and extermination of Jews in the occupied regions off the Italian peninsula. In early April 1941 Hitler quickly defeated the Yugoslav army in about two weeks. The area was divided into various regions: Germany controlled Serbia, Bulgaria took Macedonia, Hungary took Vojvodivia, and Italy controlled the Adriatic coast of Dalmatia. An independent state of Croatia was also established by the Italians and Germans as a Nazi puppet government. It was here that the terrorist bands of Ustasha originated.[44] Territorial friction ensued between Croatia and Italy.

Meanwhile, fierce Ustasha bands were massacring thousands of "foreign elements" in Croatia: first Serbians and then Croatian Jews. The Ustasha's vicious actions stunned Italian troops, who aided the Serbians and Jews. Two-thirds of 45,000 Croatian Jews were held in concentration camps in the summer and fall of 1941. Most were immediately killed by the Ustasha.[45]

Three thousand to 5,000 escapees fled to the Italian zone and were kept safe there. An Italian military inquiry had revealed gross atrocities: witnesses reported corpses of men, women and children hacked to bits strewn in huge piles. By

August 1942 a pact between the Ustasha and the Nazis meant the deportation of Croatian Jews, including those held in the Italian zone. By then, the Italians knew that deportation meant death, and Italian commander General Paride Negri refused to allow it: "'[D]eportation of Jews goes against the honor of the Italian Army,'" he said.[46] Italian officials wrote Mussolini regarding the horrible consequences of deportation. He replied that he had "'no objection" to their surrender.[47] The Italian Foreign Ministry then planned various delaying strategies.

A long and complex process of screening 3,000 refugees was begun to determine who could gain Italian citizenship. Under a broadened definition of citizenship, one became "Italian," for example, "by having performed advantageous actions for the Italian state."[48] When Hitler heard of this, in September 1942, he became furious. Italian officials met with Mussolini to request another denial of the deportation order based on establishing Italian autonomy from Germany. Mussolini agreed to postpone it. A second delay was initiated when the Italians decided to establish camps to contain the Jews in their territory. Unfortunately, this action was misunderstood by refugees, who, terror-stricken, committed suicide.

By early 1943 the Axis powers facing defeat increased attacks on Jews, thereby giving Italians more reason to protect them. The Italians also hoped to secure future negotiations with the Allies. Finally, Mussolini caved in to Hitler's pressure but simultaneously told the Italian Foreign Ministry to find a way to "pacify the Germans."[49] In other words, he allowed this office some autonomy in creating further delays to deportation, again demonstrating his duplicitous or oportunistic approach to the "Jewish problem." In May and June 1943, about 3,000 Jews were sent to the island of Rab in the northern Adriatic.

Defeat in North Africa signaled the Italian retreat from Yugoslavia, but attempts were made to continue to protect the Jews on Rab; however, shortly after the Italian armistice, the island was temporarily liberated by Tito's partisans, and most prisoners were evacuated to safe places. Many joined the resistance forces, but the island was quickly invaded by Germans, and whoever was left, roughly 204 old and sick, were deported.[50]

During the winter of 1942–1943 Jewish refugees living in the French Riviera had enjoyed the protection of the Italian army there, some since the fall of France in June 1940, but by spring 1942 the Vichy government began roundups for deportation to forced labor camps in the German-occupied zone. Italian consul-general Alberto Calisse contacted the Italian Foreign Ministry in Rome, which replied that it was not possible to permit the transfer of Jews. The Foreign Ministry sent a message to the Vichy government and occupied France, adamantly stating that only Italian officials could arrest or intern Jews. The Italians also refused to allow the letter J to be stamped on documents and refused to establish forced labor camps in its own zone. In fact, carabinieri were posted outside a synagogue to prevent arrests of Jews there. Both the Vichy government and the Nazis were outraged.[51]

German foreign minister von Ribbentrop met with Mussolini, who accused his generals of "sentimental humanitarianism" and said that he would send a special envoy to supervise the situation. The choice of this particular envoy is interesting; while the Germans were told that he was "'a most energetic man,'" they did not know that he was also a "stubborn humanitarian."[52] Inspector-general of Police Guido Lospinoso was sent to Nice to act as special commissioner for Jewish affairs with orders that the situation was to be rectified and that any military officers who protected Jews would be punished. Lospinoso's strategy, once he arrived in France, was to do nothing and avoid contact with the Nazis and Vichy officials. He was able to stall for five months.

Reports from a Gestapo chief in Paris noted that Lospinoso was working with Angelo Donati, a prominent Italian Jew living in France, to protect the 50,000 Jews in the Italian zone.[53] However, Lospinoso continued to stall and successfully held off the Germans by creating deceptions and exploiting jealousies among officers. After five months of delay, Lospinoso met with Nazi officials to say nothing more than that he was leaving for Rome to receive new instructions. Unfortunately, all Lospinoso's good work came to an end with the 8 September armistice. The Italians had planned an escape for the Jews, but the premature armistice announcement foiled the plan, and the Italians left the Cote d'Azur. Only a few hundred Jews escaped capture by the Nazis, who quickly rushed in.[54]

Once Greece was defeated in the spring of 1941, the country was divided into various zones of occupation: Bulgaria controlled Thrace and Germany had Crete, Macedonia, and a segment of Thrace and Salonika, where 53,000 Jews were trapped. Italy controlled the Ionic islands, part of the peninsula, and Athens, which had 13,000 Jews. Again, the Italian army refused to allow deportation of Jews from their zones and told the Germans to spare all Jews of Italian origin. Again a lengthy process of screening Jews for possible Italian citizenship began: any Jew married to a Greek in the Italian zone qualified for "naturalization," including the couple's "children," even those up to thirty years old. Those remotely connected to an Italian citizen or determined to have once done something "favorable" to the Italian nation or those with an Italian-sounding last name could qualify. This generous and imaginative awarding of citizenship, in fact, contrasted sharply with the situation on the peninsula, where the citizenship status of Italian Jews was being revoked.

The tactic worked for the duration of Italian occupation; however, once the Italian armistice was announced, and Germany occupied all of Greece, the Jews lost their protection. "Nearly half of the 3,500 Jews in Athens were deported in 1944; over 5,000 from the Greek mainland, and several thousand from other areas were also deported."[55]

Zuccotti speculates as to why the Italian army protected the Jews. These men witnessed daily the persecution and murder of the Jews, while Italians on the peninsula were mostly sheltered from such direct and brutal experience, so perhaps the military men were more motivated to act. Further, the Italian military desired the respect of the population under its occupation. Having been viewed as weak and defeated, the Italians sought honor, prestige, and independence from German authority. For whatever reasons that they acted, military officials did take numerous personal and professional risks and, according to Zuccotti, "restored a glimmer of honor to the shabby history of Fascist Italy. . . . They were brave, decent, and far too few."[56]

CONCLUSION

Postwar Italy remained plagued with many of the same problems of prewar Italy: food shortages, rampant inflation, depressed wages, and high unemployment. In addition, cities had been bombed and lives lost, and the specter of the Holocaust darkened the horizon. If we consider the German model of virulent Nazism on one end of the continuum, the Italian model seems like fascism of a "kinder, gentler" nation. But given that the Holocaust *did* happen in a country with little anti-Semitic history, in a nation with little interest in the extermination and total destruction of a people, we must ask what it means that it happened at all. The story of Italy during World War II should be heard as a warning that even the more "benign" countries harbor the evils of human self-destruction.

Recently, President Clinton advocated an expansion of Federal Hate Crimes law to include sexual orientation, gender, and disability, acknowledging that even here in the United States we are not safe from ancient hatreds. "Each of us," Clinton said, "wakes up every day with scales of light and darkness in our hearts. And it's up to each of us to keep these in proper balance." If the country that rests "in the dew of the gods" could lose 8,000 of its citizens, what does that portend for us?

NOTES

1. Carlo Spartaco Capogreco, "The Internment Camp of Ferramonti-Tarsia," in *The Italian Refuge*, edited by Ivo Herzer (Washington, DC: Catholic University of America Press, 1989), p. 172.

2. Meir Michaelis, *Mussolini and the Jews: German-Italian Relations and the Jewish Question in Italy, 1922–1945* (Oxford: Oxford University Press, 1978), p. 57.

3. Ibid., pp. 58–59.

4. Ibid., pp. 101–102.

5. Liliana Picciotto Fargion, "The Jews during the German Occupation and the Italian Social Republic," in Herzer, *The Italian Refuge*, pp. 109–138.

6. Susan Zuccotti, *The Italians and the Holocaust* (New York: Basic Books, 1987; reprinted Lincoln: University of Nebraska Press, 1999), pp. 36–39.

7. Ibid., p. 37.

8. Ibid., p. 40.

9. Roderick Phillips, *Society, State and Nation in Twentieth Century Europe* (Upper Saddle River, NJ: Prentice-Hall, 1996), pp. 315–316.

10. Klaus Voigt, "Refuge and Persecution in Italy, 1933–1945," *Simon Wiesenthal Center Annual, 1987*, pp. 14–15.

11. Alexander Stille, *Benevolence and Betrayal: Five Italian Jewish Families under Fascism* (New York: Summit Books, 1991), pp. 231–232.

12. Zuccotti, *The Italians and the Holocaust*, p. 65.

13. Ibid., p. 69.

14. Capogreco, "The Internment Camp," p. 161.

15. Ibid., p. 163.

16. Ibid., p. 173.

17. Ibid., p. 163.

18. Ibid., pp. 174–177.

19. Zuccotti, *The Italians and the Holocaust*, pp. 184–186.

20. Stille, *Benevolence*, p. 183.

21. Fargion, "The Jews during the German Occupation," p. 114.

22. Ibid., p. 116.

23. Ibid., p. 120.

24. Ibid., p. 122.

25. Ibid.

26. Ibid., p. 128.

27. Ibid., p. 131.

28. Ibid., p. 138.

29. John Morley, *Vatican Diplomacy and the Jews during the Holocaust, 1939–1943* (Philadelphia: New Ktav, 1980), p. 179.

30. Ibid.

31. Zuccotti, *The Italians and the Holocaust*, pp. 264–265.

32. Ibid., p. 109.

33. Stille, *Benevolence*, p. 193.

34. Zuccotti, *The Italians and the Holocaust*, pp. 110–111.

35. Stille, *Benevolence*, p. 202.

36. Ibid., p. 204.

37. Susan Zuccotti, "Pope Pius XII and the Holocaust: The Case in Italy," in Herzer, *The Italian Refuge*, p. 259.

38. Ibid., p. 255.

39. Ibid., p. 270.

40. Benedetto Croce, "Aggiunte alla letteratura della nuova Italia: Tullio Massarani," *La Critica* 36 (1938): 328–336; reprinted in Benedetto Croce, *Letteratura della nuova Italia* (Bari: Laterza, 1939), vol. 5, pp. 395–405.

41. Alberto Caviglion, "The Legacy of the Risorgimento: Jewish Participation in Anti-Fascism and the Resistance," in Herzer, *The Italian Refuge*, pp. 73–74.

42. On Carlo Rosselli, see Stanislao G. Pugliese, *Carlo Rosselli: Socialist Heretic and Antifascist Exile* (Cambridge, MA: Harvard University Press, 1999).

43. Zuccotti, *The Italians and the Holocaust*, p. 248.

44. Menachem Shelah, "The Italian Rescue of Yugoslav Jews, 1941–1943," in Herzer, *The Italian Refuge*, p. 206.

45. Ibid., p. 207.

46. Ibid., p. 209.

47. Ibid., p. 210.

48. Nicola Caracciolo, *Uncertain Refuge: Italy and the Jews During the Holocaust* (Urbana: University of Illinois Press, 1995), p. 62.

49. Shelah, "The Italian Rescue," p. 214.

50. Zuccotti, *The Italians and the Holocaust*, p. 79.

51. John Bierman, "How Italy Protected the Jews in the Occupied South of France, 1942–1943," in Herzer, *The Italian Refuge*, p. 220.

52. Ibid., p. 222.

53. Ibid., p. 223.

54. Zuccotti, *The Italians and the Holocaust*, pp. 88–89.

55. Ibid., p. 82.

56. Ibid., p. 100.

21

"Di razza ebraica": Fascist Name Legislation and the Designation of Jews in Trieste

Maura E. Hametz

"In light of the law of 13 July 1939 Italian citizens belonging to the Jewish race who are not exempted under the terms of RDL 17 November 1938 and who have changed their names to ones which do not reflect their Jewish origin must re-assume their original Jewish surnames," noted the prefect of Trieste shortly before the outbreak of World War II.[1] This statement reflected the struggle of officials in this northeastern border city to meet their administrative obligations in an environment of countervailing currents of nationalist assimilation encouraged by fascist policies of the 1920s and 1930s and racial discrimination contained in new provisions after 1938. Fascist legislation of the late 1920s had encouraged and even required the modification of names to suit nationalist purposes. Between 1927 and 1943 the names of an estimated 100,000 people, including many of the 5,000 or more Jews living in or near the city of Trieste, were "modified" under policies designed specifically to "Italianize" the multiethnic population of the former Hapsburg port.

Fascist decrees of January and May 1926 and April 1927 required those who "carried a surname originally Italian or Latin, but translated into other languages or deformed by foreign spelling or the addition of a foreign suffix," to restore the name to its original (Italian) form. Names of foreign origin could be Italianized on the request of the interested party.[2] Cases concerning the implementation of this legislation with regard to Jews can be found both among files of names "restored" to their Italian form by administrative fiat and among those "Italianized" on request. These name alteration documents show how and when the racial, anti-Semitic components of legislation were introduced on the local level, how officials responded to anti-Semitic measures, and how racial policies affected the daily lives of individuals.

In the 1930s, Arthur Ruppin, a sociologist of Jewish studies and lecturer at Hebrew University in Jerusalem, answered the question, Who should be called a

Jew? with an equivocal, It "depends on what is taken as criterion—religion, nationality, or race."[3] Unlike the oft-cited Nazi definition of Jewishness contained in the Reich Citizen's Law that relied on "blood" and heredity to establish affiliation, in Italy the Fascist Grand Council in October 1938 defined Jewishness based on a complicated mixture of religious, national, and biological factors.[4] Depending on their particular family histories and religious practices, those who were products of intermarriages might or might not be characterized as Jews.[5] Exemptions from prejudicial legislation were possible for those who had demonstrated loyalty to the nation. Members of the families of men who died, served as volunteers, or received the *croce al merito di guerra* (Cross of Merit in War) in the Libyan, world, Ethiopian, or Spanish wars; families of men killed, wounded, or disabled fighting in the fascist cause; families of those who had enrolled in the Fascist Party in 1919, 1920, 1921, or 1922 or during the second half of 1924; and families of members of D'Annunzio's Fiume Legions all merited special consideration.[6] After July 1939 Mussolini's agents could even Aryanize Jewish citizens "irrespective of services rendered to Italy or Fascism."[7]

Scholars generally agree that Italy's anti-Semitic legislation did not derive from direct German pressure but was linked to Italian foreign policy objectives with regard to greater Europe.[8] While closely related to Hitler's Nuremberg Laws in their form, the content of Italian policies reflected Mussolini's equivocal views on race. Inconsistencies in these provisions and the rather ambiguous stance of the Italian population in general toward racial anti-Semitism set the tenor for creative application of racial doctrines in the local context.

With regard to name change legislation specifically, Italian Fascist policy had little in common with Nazi policy. As early as 1932 Germans drafted laws prohibiting Jews from changing their names to conceal their religious identities.[9] At the same time in Italy in 1932 functionaries in Trieste acting on Fascist orders were zealously issuing name modification decrees erasing "foreign" identities, including those of the Jews. By August 1939 all German Jews were forced to add the names "Sara" or "Israel" to their given names to emphasize their racial background.[10] While in Italy the passage of racial laws in 1938 did spark anti-Semitic outbursts, including the demand on 1 June 1939 by the Bolognese fascist daily *Il Resto del Carlino* that Jews be compelled to relinquish such appellations such as Milano, Ravenna, and Viterbo, which were identical with Italian place-names, stringent measures to separate Jews or affirm their foreignness by name changes or modifications were never enacted on a broad scale.[11]

In Italy as a whole, while anti-Semitism was by no means absent, the general population's experience of the high degree of assimilation of Jews weighed against the racial prejudice inspired by ambiguous fascist pronouncements on the nature of *italianità* vague historical traditions of anti-Semitism and even eventual alliance with Nazi Germany. The passage of racial decrees caught the vast majority of Italians and especially Triestines by surprise.[12] The fact that Trieste's mayor was Jewish when the racial campaign began testifies to the fascist's lack of consistency and foresight with regard to the impact of impending discriminatory measures.[13]

Usually acknowledged as the third largest in fascist Italy, Trieste's Jewish population numbered somewhere between 4,500 and 7,700.[14] Disparities in researchers' estimates of the Jewish population in the city reflect the difficulties in identifying Jews, let alone studying their experiences. The population of the city comprised Jews of various ethnic and national origins, differing religious traditions (Sephardim and Ashkenazim, as well as those adhering to various levels of Jewish ritual practice), and varied ethnic backgrounds. It included children of mixed marriages, recent immigrants, and Jews of various social classes.

In his memoir of the fascist era, Dan Vittorio Segre emphasized the "social and ethnic mosaic of Jewish Trieste." He recounted a particularly poignant meeting between his uncle "baptized and a Fascist," "the epitome of economic success in authoritarian Italy," who came to Trieste from Piedmont after World War I, and Lionel Stock, a "confirmed Jew and Zionist," "the symbol of economic development in traditional Mittel Europa," a native of the region and the founder of a local distillery who had chosen not to flee with the Austrian collapse. In this encounter, Segre underlined the level of comfort, relative freedom, and degree of assimilation enjoyed by Triestine Jews of various political persuasions and cultural backgrounds.[15]

The diversity of the Jews in Trieste and the strong tradition of Jewish acculturation made it particularly difficult to define Jews in racial terms. The clash between biological conceptions and social constructions in the Italian understanding of racial identity was evident in the fact that the very meaning of the term "race" was ambiguous. Entries listed under *razza* in the *Dizionario Mussoliniano* reflected the variety of fascist usages of the word from 1919 to 1938.[16] Point Nine of the Manifesto of Race issued by Mussolini's government in July 1938 contended that "Jews do not belong to the Italian race and therefore cannot be assimilated," but this position was inconsistent with prior and subsequent statements.[17] Before the onset of the racial campaign, Mussolini employed the term to refer to the destiny or greatness of the Italian people in a manner consistent with the sense in which it had been used by such nationalists as Alfredo Rocco, who, in a speech delivered in Trieste in 1923, referred to population as the source of the nation's "greatest wealth" and "the greatest strength of all races." *Razza,* sometimes identified as *stirpe* (stock), implied the "body of the nation" defined in cultural, social, geographic, linguistic, or even spiritual or moral terms.[18] In an interview originally published in 1932, Mussolini denied the existence of any pure race. "Race is a sentiment, not a reality," Mussolini declared.[19] He naturally rejected the Nazis' "nordic racism" based on the pseudoscientific, biological doctrine professing the inherent superiority of Aryans over other groups, as German theorists saw Latins as a "mongrelized" race polluted by miscegenation traced back to the Roman Empire.[20] In fact, fascist policy discriminated against ethnic Germans in Italy. Name modification decrees originally targeted Germanic areas of the Trentino/Alto Adige, supporting the contention of many scholars that early fascist policy was more anti-German than anti-Jewish.[21]

With regard to anti-Semitism, "Jews," Mussolini said, "have acted well as citizens of Italy, and as soldiers have fought courageously. They occupy high posts in the universities, in the army, in banks."[22] While the fascist leader clearly distrusted financially motivated "world Jewry" and "resented manifestations of Jewish separatism in Zionism," before 1938 his policies were not necessarily anti-Semitic.[23] In a speech given in 1938 in Trieste, he distinguished between Italian Jews loyal to the state, whose contributions to Italy were "indisputable," and those who were "irreconcilable enemies of Fascism . . . committed to political separation."[24] Despite the fact that Trieste had been a seat of Zionist activity, publishing Zionist newspapers prior to the *redenzione* and afterward serving as the seat of the Italian Committee for Assistance to Jewish Emigrants, a tradition of irredentist activism on the part of several influential Jewish families and historical devotion to the Italian cause tempered anti-Jewish sentiment in the city. The Jewish question was only one aspect of the racial challenge, and the threat came only from those Jewish elements influenced by "foreign" affiliations or political ideologies.

Triestines were not strangers to biologically based theories of racial and demographic hierarchy. Historically, however, they were more prepared for these theories to take aim at Slavs. Corrado Gini's "cyclical theory of population" had defined the Slavic threat in biological as well as political terms. Differing reproductive capabilities explained how Italians as a "wealthier, more intelligent race with a glorious past should be unable to expand in the face of an intellectually and economically inferior one."[25] From this point of view, Jews native to Trieste shared the superior position occupied by their fellow Italians. Under fascism prior to 1938, Jews and non-Jews were brought together in the city not only by common economic interests promoted by the corporative state and support for the port but also by virulent political anti-Slavism encouraged as part of nationalist campaigns.[26] The depth of prejudice directed against Slavs was evident in fascist intellectuals' claims that name modifications in the northeastern borderland represented a "purification of the Balkan scourge which had polluted local populations." Slavic and pagan names had been adopted only in a blatant effort to cover the Italian heritage of the Upper Adriatic lands "civilized" by the Roman legions and the church, in particular, the see of Aquileia.[27]

Official name alterations initiated in the northeastern provinces in 1927 continued to be afforded to Jews wishing to "Italianize" their names as late as January 1938. An alteration was accorded to a trader born in Central Europe, a longtime resident of Trieste, who had requested a name modification for himself and his family in September 1937. The name change may have been an attempt on the part of the trader to mask his Jewish identity in an increasingly uncomfortable environment. There is no indication, however, that the granting of this modification caused any official concern. In 1941, two years after the 1939 decree ordering the annulment of modifications, the alteration was revoked.[28]

In fact, regardless of the year of issue of the name modifications, all revocations demanded by the 1939 statute seem to have been enacted in the autumn of 1941. A change granted to a trader's agent of Eastern European origin, whose wife was of a well-respected, ethnically Austrian Triestine family, was revoked in 1941, affecting his widow and children. The agent had received the name alteration decree in January 1928. A doctor who filed a name modification request through the Fascist Party in 1928 and was accorded the change in 1929 also lost the right to use the Italianized surname. The failure to crack down prior to 1941 was consistent with fascist inaction with regard to racial policy throughout Italian lands. Functionaries throughout Italy worked around and with racial policies according to the dictates of their consciences, personal preferences, or local practices rather than in a concerted national action. General humanitarian concerns and Italian suspicion of Germany were compounded in Trieste by traditional anti-German sentiments rooted in struggles of the nineteenth century against Hapsburg Pan-Germanism, particularly bitter local memories of World War I. The August 1940 "Report to the Duce on Demography and Race" from the Ministry of the Interior testified to the inconsistencies in the application of racial policies in Trieste. While in some sectors the laws had been carried out with vigilance, in others "the anti-semitic laws [had] not to this point been applied with severity . . . the Jews [had] been left in peace to their activities."[29]

Action on name modification petitions and revocations reflected local particularities. The administrative infrastructure set up to deal with Italianization was extensive. Under guidelines adopted in the late 1920s, functionaries required civil information including name, address, parents' names, place of birth, and occupation on name modification requests. Officials of the local Questura certified citizenship, residence, and civil status (single, married, widowed) and checked for criminal activity.[30] Although officials collected extensive information on individuals' socioeconomic situation and political leanings, religious or racial indication did not appear on forms filed for name alterations until after the passage of the racial laws in 1938, when records were centralized under the newly formed Direzione generale della demografia e della razza. Only in cases where proof of citizenship (hence, a copy of a birth certificate) had been required would it have been possible for the official actually acting on the petition to be able to ascertain the religious affiliation of persons affected by each decree issued prior to 1938.

After 1931, when the Comprehensive Laws on Jewish Communities centralized data collection, name changes that previously had been recorded in any number of centers maintaining birth or citizenship records were forwarded to central authorities of the local Jewish Commune. The fact that changes accorded to Jews became easier to trace did not seem to cause concern within the Triestine Jewish community. No evident racial discrimination emerged with regard to the granting of name modifications to Jews, nor did Jews seem to hesitate to call attention to their religious identity.

In fact, some used their Jewish heritage to evade compliance with official efforts to nationalize and Italianize the population. In 1932 a principal of one of the large insurance firms who desired to keep his family name in spite of its appearance on the list of names to be automatically returned to their Italian form used his Jewish identity to contest the modification decree. Providing officials with a "Hebrew" rather than "Hungarian" etymology for his surname, he convinced them that the name alteration decree issued by administrators to his family to "restore his name to the Latin root" had been drawn up in error. His name, Hebrew in origin, would not have been bastardized from an Italian form by any foreign official. The modification decree was annulled. With regard to this decision, the man's social position and influence likely worked in his favor. Jewish affiliation apparently carried no appreciable social stigma in Trieste in the early 1930s.

During World War II in Italian-occupied territories, including Greece and Tunisia, where Jews were influential in local economies, the Fascists hesitated to implement anti-Semitic policies for fear of provoking instability.[31] Similar concerns may have guided fascist actions in Trieste prior to German occupation of the city. Jews certainly did not escape discrimination in economic terms. Fascist measures restricting Jewish property ownership and participation in certain occupations, prohibiting Jews from positions in banks with national interest and in private insurance firms, and limiting industrial and commercial activities deeply affected Triestine Jews. Even *Il Piccolò*, the major daily in the city during the fascist period, noted the laws' negative impact.[32] By the time of the passage of the racial laws, private insurance companies in Trieste exercising a parastatal function under the corporative system had already begun revision and replacement of personnel. In September 1938 Edgardo Morpurgo gave up the presidency of Assicurazione Generali to Conte Volpi di Misurata. Arnoldo Frigessi, president of Riunione Adriatica di Securità (RAS), gave up management of the firm to Fulvio Suvich, a former fascist deputy and undersecretary of Foreign Affairs.[33] Social or economic privilege may have shielded influential Jewish families from the full effects of discriminatory measures, especially as regards such cultural or social manifestations of fascist policy as name modifications. For example, documents included in the folders of families bearing a Jewish surname of Germanic origin indicate that some had kinship ties to prominent families, Jewish and non-Jewish, in the region. None of the native Triestines who shared this distinctly Jewish surname prior to Italianization in the 1920s and 1930s had new Italianized names revoked in 1941. Curiously, in what appears an official omission of duty, the records concerning these individuals seem to have evaded scrutiny after 1938.

Some Jews did not shrink from official scrutiny even after the passage of the racial statutes. A Jewish sea captain proved bold enough to request a name modification in August 1941. The man's surname was not particularly ethnically Jewish, and his modification request, the simple addition of the letter *i* to the end of his name, seemed to reflect a desire for Italianization, not an attempt to conceal his lineage. Officials noted on his application that he was "of regular conduct (i.e., not a criminal), married with a Catholic wife and children, inscribed in the Fascist Party since 1933 and living in good economic conditions." "Once, an Israelite," he had obtained recognition as "not a member of the Jewish race." His petition for name modification was denied, but not on the basis of race. Officials claimed that the specific modification requested was inadmissible under the law (did not conform to specified norms for translation, modification of spelling, or transformation). As was standard practice in such cases, they did suggest a variety of other "legitimate" Italianized versions from which the petitioner could choose. The Jewish sea captain stood his ground, feeling that his position within the community was strong enough even in 1941 to debate with fascist officials and insist on the change that he wanted. Unable to reach an agreement with the man, officials filed the case away, and no change was accorded.

Foreign-born Jews without particular influence found themselves in a position more precarious than that of native Triestine or Italian Jews. As was consistent with Mussolini's suspicion of foreigners, fascist legislation discriminated specifically against Jews of foreign birth or those suspected of foreign ties. A fascist statute of September 1938 revoked the Italian citizenship of any Jews who took up residence in Italian lands after 1 January 1919 and required that these "foreigners" leave Italy within six months of the date of publication of the decree. Approximately 1,000 Jews in the local Triestine population were affected by this law.[34]

Prior to Trieste's annexation to Italy in 1919, the port had been under Austrian rule for more than five centuries. The names and even citizenships of those living in the city reflected the multiethnic composition of the Hapsburg state and the international flavor of the port. Those born in Trieste or other regions annexed after 1918 were considered native-born and had automatically gained Italian citizenship.[35] Ethnic Italians from parts of Istria and Dalmatia that were never part of the Italian state but were considered "unredeemed" territories were also eligible for citizenship in Italy,[36] yet many foreign-born residents of Trieste who had actually lived in the city for decades had been forced to file citizenship petitions after World War I. By the late 1930s, fascist officials waded through labyrinthine paperwork to ascertain individuals' status. The census of the Jewish population taken as required by the law of 22 August 1938 was supplemented in Trieste by a list identifying all Jews in the city whose names had been modified under nationalist legislation.[37] This list proved important for the execution of legislation regarding name modifications. In 1941 the case of a widow whose name had been changed in the late 1920s became a launching point for an official inquiry into the exact legal status of foreign-born Jews who had officially adopted Italian identities. The woman in question, along with many others in the Triestine population, had her Italian citizenship revoked on the basis of the September 1938 decree. The subsequent order of July 1939, which required that "Italian citizens of the Jewish race" reassume their original surnames, posed a conundrum for local officials.[38] By the time of the passage of the 1939 law, the woman's citizenship had already been revoked. "How should the matter be handled? Is the modification retroactive?" a local functionary queried the podestà. He took the same opportunity to ask for advice in cases where a person's surname had been changed, but in the interim the person had died. The podestà turned the case over to the local prefect.

The prefect's reply in late 1941 reflected the ambiguous and somewhat absurd realities of enforcement of the racial legislation on the local level. First, the prefect assured the local functionary that the statute applied only to those still alive; names of the dead were to remain untouched, but those of surviving family members should revert to their original form. Regarding the thorny question of citizenship, the prefect adopted a legalistic stance. Since the citizenship revocation preceded the decree requiring the repeal of name modifications, the official could not restore the original surnames of those who were no longer Italian citizens. The prefect's office was to be furnished a list of those who had been affected by the citizenship decree so that Jews who had been afforded name changes but had not been forced to relinquish citizenship could be differentiated from others. The irony of the situation was that foreign-born Jews whose names were "Italianized" kept the new versions but were no longer Italian citizens, while native-born Jews whose names had been modified lost their "Italianized" identities.

Not only were members of the Jewish community affected by the passage of racial legislation, but so, too, were those of mixed or uncertain origin and those married to Jews. For children of mixed marriages, nationalizing efforts often took precedence over racial concerns. The law permitted Italian citizens with Jewish fathers to substitute the Aryan (Italian) last name of their mothers provided they themselves did not profess to the Jewish faith. Non-Jewish Italians who bore traditionally Jewish last names but were not themselves Jewish were also permitted to alter their names.[39]

According to the Grand Council's resolutions of October 1939, paternity generally governed the race of the child. People born of Jewish fathers and foreign mothers were considered Jews.[40] In cases of mixed marriages, actual affiliation with Jewish practice and ritual figured into determinations of Jewishness. Those who professed to the Jewish religion were considered Jews, while those who professed to a religion other than Judaism prior to 1 October 1938 were not subject, by and large, to the discriminatory measures.[41]

The history of high rates of intermarriage muddied the "racial" waters in Trieste. The estimated rate of intermarriage for Jews in Trieste in 1927 was 56.1%, and intermarriage was especially prevalent among the "higher strata of society."[42] Prior to the racial campaign intermarriage had even been encouraged. An article attributed to Mussolini that appeared in *Il Popolo d'Italia* on 29 May 1932 urged that mixed marriages be "greeted with satisfaction by all who consider[ed] themselves good, sincere and loyal Italians." During the period in which nationalization efforts, including name modifications, were at their height in Trieste, the mixed marriage "constitute[d] proof of the perfect civic, political and above all 'moral' equality between all Italians, whatever their remote descent."[43] Although legislation of November 1938 prohibited marriage of "Aryan" Italian citizens to those of another race, the earlier standard for tolerance coupled with the high rate of intermarriage and the fact that early requests for name modification bore no sign of religious affiliation made officials' task to separate out those granted to Jews extremely difficult.

Fascist officials tended to be somewhat lenient with those born to parents of a mixed marriage. On 27 May 1942 a man in his early twenties, whose father had been granted a name change in 1927, asked that he be exempted from the revocation decree issued to his family. He pointed out to officials that his mother was a "Catholic Aryan" and offered proof that he was serving in the fascist army. His request for exception was not based in any of the criteria contained in the legislation. Yet on the day following his appeal, 28 May, the prefect conceded that the young man was "not a member of the Jewish race." In another case of mixed heritage, on a modification petition filed in 1939 the office of the Questura evaded the question of race altogether. When the request got to the mayor's office to be adjudicated, the official queried, "And the race?" "Born of a mixed marriage," was the vague response. Just over a year later, the name modification decree was issued.

In some cases where religious affiliation was unclear, yet it appeared that a petitioner might have been Jewish or at least of a Jewish background, local officials doctored records. Official respelling or correction of names written on petition forms was routine. In most cases it simply proved administratively expedient. To modify names automatically, officials were required to refer to a published list of names to be "restored" and to assign Italianized versions preapproved by a committee of local "experts."[44] The list of names could hardly be complete in the cosmopolitan city. Rather than referring any deviation in the original spelling of a surname to a special committee for consideration, officials altered the spelling of foreign names on original petitions so that they could process the petitions themselves. Sometimes these official respellings seem to have had a social or cultural purpose rather than an administrative basis. In one case in 1933 both the name and heritage of a banker's wife born in Austria were altered by the official. Not only was a modification in spelling made to her maiden name on the petition (a *j* was changed to an *i*), but her father's name, obviously Jewish in origin, was simply crossed out. On the eventual modification decree, her maiden name was neither the version that she wrote down nor the version to which the official changed it. It was modified from a third form, effectively masking a Jewish background.[45]

Non-Jewish women in mixed marriages posed a conundrum for fascist officials. Under Italian law a woman adopted her husband's surname on marriage. Name modification legislation allowed women to freely modify maiden names, which were often hyphenated to married names. In paternalistic fascist Italy, widows in particular had a right and a duty as part of their role as protectors of the family and home to carry on their married names in veneration of their late husbands. Wives and widows of Jewish men, it seems, bore no stigma even after the racial legislation came into effect. Like others, they rather routinely obtained modification of non-Italian maiden names and continued to bear their husbands' Jewish surnames. Their petitions to alter maiden names included indications of their husbands' religious background and usually bore the official report that "she is of the Aryan race" or "she is not of the Jewish race." Evidently, these women found it unnecessary to petition as non-Jews to have their Jewish married names modified.

In Trieste political sentiments were easily as important as religious affiliation, and in some cases political backgrounds seemed to have been of more concern to officials. In fact, information was provided by the Questura regarding the "moral" conduct of those seeking name modifications before any information on race was required. In routine cases before the passage of racial laws, a note from the Questura affirming that the petitioner was "of regular moral and political conduct" and describing the status of party membership accompanied name modification petitions forwarded to the local Prefecture. Even after 1938 officials may have remained more preoccupied with political than racial affiliations. A onetime official of the Russian imperial navy resident in Trieste applied in July 1939 for Italianization of his surname. A simple official note, "from the documents presented it is evident that [the subject] is not of the Jewish race," allowed the man to escape scrutiny under the racial laws. Emphasis in the file fell instead on the man's political affiliations. A short account of the man's life explained that he had fought against the Bolsheviks, arrived in Italy in 1922, joined the Fascist Party in 1926, and gained Italian citizenship in 1927. Clearly, in this case officials' fear of socialism and Bolshevism outweighed racial prejudice. The man who had arrived in Italy in 1922 was more suspect in 1940 due to the political color of his native country than he was due to possible ties to Judaism. He and his family were eventually granted the change that they had requested.

What conclusions can be drawn from the examination of legislation and official action in cases of name alterations in Trieste? It appears that the ambiguity of Mussolini's stance on race filtered down to result in inconsistencies in the treatment of individuals under racial policies. Mussolini's political differentiation between "loyal" Italian Jews and those who were affiliated with "world Jewry" reflected a general suspicion of enemies of the state. Some native Triestine Jews gained cultural sympathy from officials. Elevated political and economic status afforded some protection. Officials seemed to overlook records concerning the privileged and avoided subjecting them to inconveniences and the careful and thorough scrutiny to which the majority were subjected. The ambiguities evident in dealings with Jews were compounded in the assimilated community by the difficulties inherent in identifying Jews in the area that had been subject to fascist nationalization efforts since the mid-1920s. The fascist erasure of foreign influences had blurred clear lines of heritage and, in effect, had destroyed some evidence of Jewish affiliations or non-Italian origins in the interest of the creation of an Italian national community.

Fascist officials in Trieste, while compelled to make an effort to conform to national guidelines for treatment of Jews after 1938, did not zealously execute their duties. Especially in cultural and social realms in which national oversight might not be as thorough as in economic and political spheres, they acted on individual cases as ruled by the dictates of their conscience or perhaps their pocketbooks, creating a confused atmosphere of official intolerance and persecution alongside limited interference and even tolerance in private matters such as name changes.

This is not to suggest that the persecution of Jews in Trieste was limited overall. Gherardi Bon estimates that up to one-third of the younger Jewish population of Trieste fled after passage of the racial laws. Anti-Semitic violence in the city increased in the period from 1941 to 1943. Further, identification of both Slavs and Jews as antifascists promoted particular virulence of anti-Semitic campaigns based on nationalist zeal.[46] Fewer than half of the more than 5,000 Jews living in Trieste prior to the war remained in the city at the time of German takeover in 1943.[47] Yet, it seems that during the years prior to the Nazi occupation, discrimination did not engender aspects of social revolution as it did in Germany.

The experience of Jews in Trieste under the name change legislation seems to suggest that carrying out racial policies was not extremely high on local authorities' agenda. Certainly, after the passage of the racial laws in 1938 and with the increasingly close relationship to Germany, links existed between fascist anti-Semitism and Nazi extermination. Some local political and economic leaders adopted anti-Semitism only out of generic conformism; others used it in an attempt to be at the vanguard of the fascist regime or in an attempt to acquire personal advantage under the occupying Germans.[48] But these individuals' stances did not necessarily reflect the will or actions of the majority. Although Trieste was one of the first areas to turn to fascism in the early 1920s, racial laws and prescriptions lacked resonance for much of the population. Triestine officials did not lead the way in carrying out anti-Semitic policies. Latent anti-German sentiments may have been a factor, and the highly assimilated, cosmopolitan nature of those in the city may have also meant that popular anti-Semitism lacked particular bite. Finally, in Italian areas bordering the south Slav state, anti-Slav prejudice certainly competed with, if not outstripped, anti-Jewish sentiment. In the borderland, fascism perhaps found in the Slavs and even Germans more convenient targets for nationalist animosities and attacks.

The incongruities in fascist policy and practice were eliminated by September 1943, when Trieste fell under direct Nazi rule in the Adriatic coastland administered by the Gauleiter of Carinthia Friedrich Rainer. As such, the population was subject to the Nazi racial laws and policies formulated by the Citizenship and Race Section of the Reich Interior Ministry. On their arrival in the city in May 1945, the Allied Eighth Army discovered only 400 to 500 Jews remaining in Trieste.[49]

NOTES

1. Name modification decrees and revocations can be found in Archivio di Stato (Trieste)–Prefettura della Provincia di Trieste, Divisione I: Riduzione Cognomi Trieste, No. 11419 (1926–1943) (hereinafter AdS(TS)-PPT/DI-11419). Records dealing with name modifications are divided into two categories, alterations requested by petitioners and those carried out by administrative fiat.

2. For the texts of the 1938 and 1939 statutes, see Tito Staderini, *Legislazione per la difesa della razza* (Rome: Carlo Colombo, 1940), pp. 43–44, 136.

3. Aldo Pizzagalli, *Per l'italianità dei cognomi nella provincia di Trireste* (Trieste: Treves, Zanichelli, 1929), pp. 33–34.

4. Arthur Ruppin, *The Jews in the Modern World* (London: Macmillan, 1934; reprinted New York: Arno Press, 1973), p. 3.

5. See Staderini, *Legislazione*, p. 12.

6. Ibid., p. 25.

7. Ibid., p. 13.

8. Meir Michaelis, *Mussolini and the Jews: German-Italian Relations and the Jewish Question in Italy 1922–1945* (Oxford: Oxford University Press, 1978), pp. 254–255, describes the implications of Decree No. 1024.

9. Renzo De Felice, *Storia degli ebrei italiani sotto il fascismo* (Turin: Giulio Einaudi, 1993); Michaelis, *Mussolini and the Jews*.

10. Hans Josef Maria Globke, *In the Name of the Peoples, In the Name of the Victims* (Berlin: Press Centre Globke Trial, 1963), pp. 4, 9. By January 1938 such laws were actually adopted by the Nazis.

11. Ibid., pp. 9–12.

12. H. Stuart Hughes, *Prisoners of Hope: The Silver Age of the Italian Jews, 1924–1974* (Cambridge, MA: Harvard University Press, 1983), p. 5.

13. De Felice, *Storia degli ebrei*, p. 326; Enzo Collati, "Preface," in *La persecuzione antiebraica a Trieste (1938–1945)*, edited by Silva Gherardi Bon (Udine: Del Bianco, 1972), p. 9.

14. Silva Gherardi Bon, *La persecuzione antiebraica a Trieste (1938–1945)* (Udine: Del Bianco, 1972), p. 9.

15. Sergio Della Pergola, *Anatomia dell'ebraismo italiano: Caratteristiche demografiche, economiche, sociali, religiose e politiche di una minoranza* (Assisi: Beniamino Carucci, 1976), p. 60, Table 6. Della Pergola places Rome's Jewish population at 12,494, Milan's at 6,157, and Trieste's at 4,663. Sources used in Gerald Reitlinger, *The Final Solution: The Attempt to Exterminate the Jews of Europe 1939–1945* (Northvale, NJ: Jason Aronson, 1987), pp. 356–357, place the population at more than 5,000. De Felice, *Storia degli ebrei*, p. 10, counts more than 6,000. Carl Ipsen, *Dictating Demography: The Problem of Population in Fascist Italy* (Cambridge: Cambridge University Press, 1996), p. 191, places the Jewish population in Trieste second in Italy at 7,640.

16. Dan Vittorio Segre, *Memoirs of a Fortunate Jew: An Italian Story* (Northvale, NJ: Jason Aronson, 1995), p. 100.

17. Bruno Biancini, *Dizionario Mussoliniano: 1500 Affermazioni e definizioni del Duce su 1000 argomenti* (Milan: Ulrico Hoepli, 1940), pp. 175–176.

18. The "Manifesto of Race" appears in Michaelis, *Mussolini and the Jews*, p. 153.

19. Ipsen, *Dictating Demography*, pp. 53, 185.

20. Emil Ludwig, *Colloqui con Mussolini* (Verona: Arnoldo Mondadori, 1950), pp. 71–72.

21. Aaron Gillette, "La Difesa della Razza: Racial Theories in Fascist Italy" (unpublished manuscript, 1997), pp. 49–59.

22. Michaelis, *Mussolini and the Jews*, pp. 6–7, quotes, for example, Sir W. McClure on the attitudes of the Italians to Jews versus Germans. After 1938 the Germanic population of the Trentino/Alto Adige faced even harsher measures than those taken against minorities in Venezia Giulia; see Ipsen, *Dictating Demography*, pp. 138–139.

23. Ludwig, *Colloqui*, pp. 71–72.

24. Meir Michaelis, "Axis Policies towards the Jews in World War II," Fifteenth Annual Rabbi Louis Feinberg Memorial Lecture in Judaic Studies, Cincinnati, OH, 30 April 1992 (Cincinnati: Judaic Studies Program, 1992), p. 7.

25. Benito Mussolini, *Opera Omnia, Vol. 29: 1 ottobre 1937–10 giugno 1940*, edited by Edoardo Susmel and Duilio Susmel (Florence: La Fenice, 1959), p. 146.

26. Ipsen, *Dictating Demography*, p. 221.

27. Collati, "Preface," p. 9, discusses anti-Slavism in the city.

28. Angelo Scocchi, "I nomi pagani slavi e l'onomastica romana," *La Porta Orientale* (1932): 281.

29. Since records pertaining to the affairs of individuals remain protected by Italian privacy laws, no individuals can be named, nor can their identities be compromised. Unless otherwise indicated, documentation relating to all cases discussed later can be found in the records of petitions for name changes held in AdS(TS)-PPT/DI-11419.

30. De Felice, *Storia degli ebrei*, pp. 584–588.

31. Official "certifications" appear on all requests and officially issued decrees held in AdS(TS)-PPT/DI-11419.

32. Michaelis, "Axis Policies," p. 12.

33. Gherardi Bon, *La persecuzione antiebraica*, p. 73, n.

34. Ibid., p. 58.

35. Ibid., p. 115; Michaelis, *Mussolini and the Jews*, p. 171; Staderini, *Legislazione*, p. 16.

36. *Gazzetta Ufficiale del Regno d'Italia: Parte Prima Leggi e Decreti*, Anno 1921 (18 January): No. 14, Legge n. 1890. For clauses pertinent to the granting of Italian citizenship, see the text of the "Treaty of St. Germain, Part III: Political Clauses for Europe, Section VI: Clauses Relating to Nationality," Articles 70–78, in Carnegie Endowment for International Peace, *The Treaties of the Peace 1919–1923* (New York: Carnegie Endowment for International Peace, 1924), pp. 292–293.

37. Staderini, *Legislazione*, p. 30.

38. Gherardi Bon, *La persecuzione antiebraica*, pp. 89–91.

39. Staderini, *Legislazione*, p. 139.

40. Ibid., p. 140.

41. In direct contradiction to Jewish practice, where the mother's religion determines the child's, the father's Jewishness officially determined the race of the child in fascist Italy. Ibid., p. 12. This was further complicated by the fact that, according to some testimonies, false baptismal certificates were relatively easy to obtain. See Gherardi Bon, *La persecuzione antiebraica*, p. 110.

42. Ruppin, *The Jews*, pp. 320 (table), 323.

43. Quoted in Michaelis, *Mussolini and the Jews*, p. 34.

44. On actions of this committee, see Paolo Parovel, *L'identità cancellata* (Trieste: Eugenio Parovel, 1985), p. 25.

45. The underlying motivation here remains unclear.

46. Gherardi Bon, *La persecuzione antiebraica*, pp. 11–13, 114.

47. Reitlinger, *Final Solution*, pp. 356–357.

48. Gherardi Bon, *La persecuzione antiebraica*, p. 14.

49. Reitlinger, *Final Solution*, pp. 356–357.

22

Pope Pius XI's Conflict with Fascist Italy's Anti-Semitism and Jewish Policies

Frank J. Coppa

In the aftermath of the Holocaust the Vatican has been criticized for its policies toward the fascist dictatorships, including Mussolini's Italy.[1] It is recalled that Achille Ratti, while archbishop of Milan, had permitted the fascist banner to fly in the Duomo. Once pope, the collaboration was allegedly furthered by Pius XI's (1922–1939) failure to prevent the Catholic Popular Party from joining the Mussolini cabinet in 1922 and by providing the dictator with moral support during the Matteotti crisis of 1924–1925. He has also been castigated for concluding a concordat with the fascist state in 1929, thus legitimating the regime. During his tenure the achievements of fascism were often praised, and some suspected that the infallible pope concurred with the policies of the Duce, who claimed to always be right.[2] Critics also fault Pius for not condemning the invasion and conquest of Ethiopia.[3] Finally, the anti-Bolshevik crusade of fascism apparently found resonance in Rome, which embraced the regime as a natural ally against communism.[4] This allegedly resulted in an axis between pope and Duce.[5]

Generalizations concerning Catholic-fascist relations during the pontificate of Pius XI persist, influenced by political preoccupation and ideological considerations. Some maintain that Italian Catholics were temperamentally authoritarian, finding in fascism an approximation of their ideal society, dubbing Catholicism the fascist form of Christianity.[6] Since the concept of *Roma caput mundi* (Rome as leader of the world) was shared by pontiff and Duce alike, and both rested on the leadership principle, the church supposedly looked with favor upon the authority exercised by the Duce. Then, too, the supposedly similar mind-set of fascism and Catholicism on the position of women in society reinforced one another.[7]

Furthermore, some have assumed that the prevailing anti-Judaism in the pre–Vatican Council II church facilitated, if it did not provoke, the anti-Semitism of Nazi Germany and fascist Italy.[8] Jules Isaac, in his book *The Teaching of*

Contempt: Christian Roots of Anti-Semitism (1964), maintains that the church's doctrine of the contemptible character of the Jews paved the way for their persecution in the twentieth century.[9] Contemporaries such as Roberto Farinacci claimed that Mussolini's racist legislation was a logical culmination of the anti-Judaism of the church.[10] Writing in the columns of the fascist *Il Popolo d'Italia*, he insisted that Catholic practice provided the basis of fascist anti-semitism.[11] In the words of Gene Bernardini, anti-Semitism represented an undercurrent in Italian history flowing "from conservative sources within the Catholic church."[12] Confusion between anti-Judaism and anti-Semitism continues, with ultra-Orthodox Jews in Israel accusing secular Jews of being anti-semitic![13] If contemporary Jews can be branded anti-Semitic, one can understand how the charge might be launched against a church where anti-Judaism persisted. In fact, one scholar has written that Pius XI "offered few objections to the Italian racial laws,"[14] implying that he did not find fascist anti-Semitism reprehensible. She is supported by a number of Italian observers who claim that Pius XI "failed to assume a determined opposition against the racism of Fascist Italy."[15]

A less hostile evaluation notes that the concordat with fascist Italy was but one of the more than twenty concluded by Pius XI. It concludes that Catholics supported the regime when things went well but abandoned it when it challenged church practice by adopting a racist and anti-Semitic stance. At best, the relationship could be described as a "marriage of convenience" bound to end in divorce.[16] Others deny even this complicity, concurring with Giuseppe Dalla Torre on the incompatibility of fascism and Catholicism. They posit that a majority of Catholics, including those who collaborated with the regime, had serious reservations about its non-Christian methods, proto-pagan convictions, statolatry, and eventually its anti-Semitism, concurring with Monsignor Louis Picard that few practicing Catholics held positions of power in the party.[17] Furthermore, there is no evidence that Pius XI's Vatican ever objected to Mussolini's pro-Jewish policy during the first decade and a half of his regime. Finally, it is argued that the church began to disengage itself from fascism following the regime's adoption of racism.[18] The debate continues.

The charges that Pius XI was enamored of fascism and its policies, including anti-Semitism, have been resolutely challenged by those contemporaries who applauded this pope for speaking out against the fascists in the papal encyclical *Non abbiamo bisogno* (We Have No Need) of 1931 and his indictment of the Axis, which brought Nazi anti-Semitism to Catholic Italy. As the Roman sun burnished the Eternal City in late April 1938, the northern Italian Ratti worried less about the impending Roman summer than the prospect of a visit that had tormented him for months. Despite distinct papal disapproval, the Duce determined to welcome the Führer to Rome, converting the Axis from blustering rhetoric into dangerous reality. Early in May 1938, as Hitler commenced a visit to Rome, there was a decisive turn in fascist Italy's racial policy, much to the consternation of the pope, who immediately recognized that it violated Catholic universalism. Shortly thereafter, rumor spread that a Nazi commission ventured to Milan to assist the Italians in drafting their racist legislation, and the anti-Semitic Roberto Farinacci was appointed minister of state. In June 1938 the pope asked the American Jesuit John La Farge to draft an encyclical against racism.[19]

The eighty-one-year-old pope, exasperated that the racism and violation of human rights endemic to Nazi Germany were being transferred to Italy, which had remained largely free of this contagion, planned an encyclical condemning these moral evils.[20] Did the condemnations of racism and anti-Semitism in *Humani Generis Unitas*—the encyclical commissioned by the pope but never issued— reflect the thought of Pius XI? Finally published,[21] this document sheds light on the broader position and public posture of Pius XI on anti-Semitism in Mussolini's Italy, the focus of the present chapter. More broadly, it explores the relationship between Catholicism and fascism from 1922 to 1939.

Mussolini realized that during the initial period of his pontificate, which corresponded with the first year of fascism in power, Pope Pius XI had denounced racism as anti-Christian. In September the pope, a Hebrew scholar personally opposed to racist ideology, emphasized that "Christian charity extends to all men whatsoever without distinction of race."[22] At the end of the year, the Holy See pleaded on behalf of the persecuted Armenians.[23] Like Pius IX, whose name he assumed, Pius XI believed that "Jesus died for all nations without distinction, making all the beneficiaries of his suffering."[24] In 1923 he invoked prayers for those who had suffered during the war, regardless of nationality, class, or party.[25] In proclaiming the feast of Christ the King at the end of 1925, Pius XI specified that the spiritual realm of Christ included not only those within the church but all men.[26] Then in 1926, Pius XI condemned Charles Maurras' allegedly Catholic, but royalist, racist, and reactionary, Action Française, which was hardly distinguishable from fascism.[27] Two years later Pius XI denounced anti-Semitism when the Holy Office, with his approval, suppressed the Friends of Israel.[28] The suppression decree contains one of the most explicit rejections of anti-Semitism.[29] "The Holy See has always protected the Jews against unjust vexations," it read, and "particularly reproves hatred against a people once chosen by God, known as Anti-Semitism."[30] The pope virtually "put his money where his mouth was," entrusting the Italian Jew Bernardino Nogara with sole supervision over the Vatican treasury.[31]

It is true that during these years the pope negotiated with the fascists and in February 1929 concluded an agreement with Mussolini's Italy.[32] Likewise true, Pius was delighted that God had been restored to Italy, and Italy returned to God.[33] Some Italian Jews expressed concern once the concordat restored Catholicism as the religion of state, with one Jewish spokesman terming it "a moral pogrom."[34] However, their fears were allayed when this was followed by a comprehensive law which assured Jewish rights.[35]

Although fascist Italy remained a "model of tolerance" regarding the treatment of Jews, relations between Mussolini and the Vatican were often strained.[36] Early on, the Vatican contested the anti-Christian emphasis in fascist education.[37] To counter the bellicose fascist stance, the pope issued the encyclical *Divini Illius Magistri* (On the Christian Education of Youth) (December 1929).[38] Meanwhile, he cautioned the faithful to be leery of racism. "If there is in Christianity the idea of a mystery of blood," he observed in his Christmas message of 1930, "it is that not of a race opposed to other races, but of the unity of all men in the heritage of sin."[39] The papal encyclical *Non abbiamo bisogno* of June 1931 denounced fascist attempts to dominate all citizen organizations, youth groups, and private meetings, revealing that Pius would not abandon the younger generation to the regime.[40] While racism and anti-Semitism raged north of the Alps, the pope welcomed his old friend and collaborator De Fano, the chief rabbi of Milan, to the Vatican. The latter, aware of the pope's sentiments and actions, thanked Pius for his appeals against religious persecution. Pius did not hesitate to condemn those who fostered hatred and in 1932 called for planting "a hedge of protection around Israel."[41]

The pope was dismayed by Mussolini's increasing emphasis on totalitarianism and racism as he moved closer to Hitler's Germany.[42] During Pius' pontificate more than fifty protests were launched against the Nazi regime. Understandably, the Vatican deplored Mussolini's assertion that fascism and Nazism were parallel movements that shared a common weltanschauung. "Almost everywhere it is said that everything belongs to the State, that is the totalitarian State, as it is called; nothing without the State, everything for the State," the Pope complained. "There is an error here so evident, that it is astonishing that men, otherwise serious and talented, say it and teach it to the masses."[43] Pius XI's opposition to the doctrine of blood and race was reflected in the critical articles that appeared in *L'Osservatore Romano* and *La Civiltà Cattolica*. One of the articles in the Jesuit review claimed that the church had always opposed persecution.[44] In 1936 he dispatched Eugenio Pacelli (the future Pius XII) to the United States to silence the anti-Semitic radio priest Father Coughlin.[45] The elaboration of Nazi Germany's anti-Semitic policies led Pius XI to reconsider his attitude toward anschluss between Germany and Austria and strained papal relations with Mussolini's Italy. Throughout 1936–1937 Vatican Radio invoked prayers for the Jews persecuted by the Nazis. Thus, by the 1930s Pius XI had emerged as a powerful moral voice against fascism and Nazism.[46]

In June 1937 the pope placed Giulio Cogni's polemical book *Il razzismo*, which sought to popularize anti-Semitism in Italy, on the Index of Prohibited Books. At the same time, *La Civiltà Cattolica*, which occasionally issued anti-Jewish pronouncements, proclaimed that the church condemned all forms of anti-Semitism.[47] The Duce then shared the pope's position. "We are Catholics, proud of our faith and respectful of it," he confided to the Austrian chancellor Schuschnigg in 1937. "We do not accept the Nazi racial theories."[48] The following April the Sacred Congregation of Seminaries, of which Pius XI was prefect, condemned the pernicious racism championed by Nazi Germany and charged Catholic academic institutions to refute these erroneous theories.[49] The Catholic press deemed it an encyclical against racism![50] In July Pius XI stressed the absolute incompatibility between this nationalism and Catholicism, charging that the former opposed the spirit of the creed and violated the teachings of the faith.[51] Italian Jews told Neville Laski that the strong stance of the Vatican against racial heresy had worked to prevent the diffusion of racial ideology in Italy.[52] The pope had proven less successful in safeguarding Austria from this disease, deploring its extension there following the anschluss of 1938, which saddened him both as pontiff and as an Italian.

Early in May 1938, when Hitler visited Rome, the pope abandoned Rome for Castel Gandolfo, which was only seventeen miles away from the Vatican, but a world apart. The pontiff was scandalized by the prospect of the Führer's strutting in the Holy City. Indeed, the day that Hitler arrived, the Vatican journal *L'Osservatore Romano* ignored his presence, choosing to print instead the pope's April condemnation of racism.[53] Pius ordered the Vatican museum, which Hitler had hoped to visit, closed and forbade the more than 1,000 religious establishments in the Eternal City from displaying Nazi flags or symbols. The Romans followed the pope's example, showing themselves less than gracious to the Nazi visitors. "The Italians hardly hide their hostility to the Germans," wrote William L. Shire in his diary. "They watch them walk by and then spit contemptuously."[54] The Archbishop of Florence, Ellio della Costa, following the papal lead, closed the Duomo on the occasion of the joint Mussolini–Hitler visit to the city on the Arno and refused to decorate his residence for the occasion.

From Castel Gandolfo, the pope was distressed by the glorification of a "cross that was the enemy of Christianity."[55] Pius insisted that catholic meant universal and could be neither racial nor separatist.[56] Up to this point the Duce had shown restraint on the racial issue to avoid a clash with Pius XI, recognizing that racism violated the teachings of the church, which influenced Italians. However, Mussolini now determined to display his solidarity with Nazi Germany by adopting its racism, regardless of the consequences.[57] In mid-July 1938 the Fascist Manifesto on Race was issued, which included ten "scientific" propositions that were geared to prepare the way for fascist Italy's racial laws.[58] The anti-Semitic stance was a slap in the face of the church, which had acquiesced in the fascist seizure of power to prevent totalitarianism rather than promote it.[59] Convinced that the "devil Mussolini" sought to sabotage the concordat, the pope did not shy from a confrontation.[60]

Once anti-Semitism became an official doctrine of the fascist regime, an energetic response came from Pope Pius XI.[61] The old pope resolved to take additional steps to denounce fascist racist policies, making no secret of his compassion for the victims of persecution while condemning "hatred" of the people once chosen by God.[62] In June 1938 the pope talked with the American Jesuit John La Farge, the author of numerous books and articles on racism.[63] The pope had read and liked La Farge's *Interracial Justice*, published in 1937,[64] which denounced the notion of "pure race" as a myth that the church could not tolerate. Like Pius, La Farge insisted that the teachings of Christ proclaimed the moral unity of the human race, and his church offered all of humankind salvation. He warned that Christian social philosophy looked upon the deliberate fostering of racial prejudices as a sin. Consequently, it could not be ignored by the faith. La Farge posited that the universal church, which represented a living union of all humankind, had to combat racial prejudice, which destroyed the Creator's intended relationship of the individual to the rest of humanity.[65] Pius XI approved of La Farge's ideas, which reflected his own thought.[66]

To La Farge's surprise, Pius XI commissioned him to draft an encyclical to the universal church, demonstrating the incompatibility of Catholicism and racism. The pope, deeming the enterprise of the utmost importance, swore La Farge to secrecy.[67] Dismayed by the fascist attempts to ape Nazi anti-Semitism, Pius continued his condemnation of racism and those regimes that flaunted it. Like La Farge, the pope saw the need for a spiritual and moral treatment of the defense of human rights.[68] Pius XI knew what he wanted to say, outlining the topic and its method of treatment, while discussing its underlying principles with La Farge.[69] "Simply say what you would say to the entire world if you were Pope," Pius confided to La Farge.[70] On 3 July 1938 La Farge described his meeting of 22 June 1938 with Pius. He revealed that the pope had enjoined him to write the text of an encyclical condemning racism. Pius XI told La Farge that God had sent him, for he had been anxiously seeking someone to write on the topic. Responding to the pope's desire to have the encyclical quickly, Father Ledochowski, the Polish General of the Jesuits, suggested that La Farge collaborate with two other Jesuits: the Frenchman Gustave Desbuquois and the German Gustav Gundlach. The three prepared a draft in the summer of 1938 and in late September delivered the encyclical *On the Unity of the Human Race* to Ledochowski for transmission to the pope.[71]

This document, following Pius XI's suggestions and outline, condemned anti-Semitism as reprehensible and "did not permit the Catholic to remain silent in the presence of racism."[72] Before the onset of the horrors of the "Final Solution," the projected papal encyclical noted that the struggle for racial purity "ends by being uniquely the struggle against the Jews."[73] Fully aware that Pius XI deplored anti-Semitism in both Italy and Germany, the authors reported that such persecution had been censured by the Holy See in the past. "As a result of such a persecution, millions of persons are deprived of the most elementary rights and privileges of citizens in the very land of their birth, " the encyclical continued.[74] Indeed, the authors warned that anti-Semitism ultimately degenerated into a war against Christianity.[75] The encyclical focused on the evil of racism. "It is the task and duty of the Church, the dignity and responsibility of the Chief Shepherd and of his brother Shepherds whom the Holy Ghost has placed to rule the Church of God, that they should point out to mankind the true course to be followed, the eternal divine order in the changing circumstances of the times."[76] "The Redemption opened the doors of salvation to the entire human race," the encyclical continued, establishing a universal Kingdom without distinction between Jew and Gentile, Greek and barbarian.[77]

Pius XI continued to espouse the sentiments of the "encyclical" that he had authorized and inspired, upset by anti-Semitic policies that fascist Italy had adopted as it moved closer to Nazi Germany. The pope branded the fascist Aryan Manifesto of 14 July 1938 a "true form of apostasy," urging Catholic groups to combat it and initiating a chorus of opposition to the racism of the totalitarian regimes.[78] By this time many of the Catholic newspapers in Italy followed the lead of the pope and *L'Osservatore Romano* in denouncing racism, provoking fascist reprisals and confiscations.[79] During an audience with a group of nuns from Milan, Pius XI in the presence of his secretary of state Pacelli denounced this racism, referring to the encyclical that he was having prepared on this issue.[80] Pacelli did not care to, or dare to, ask the pope for an explanation. At the end of July, during an audience with the students of the Propaganda Fide, whose members hailed from thirty-seven nations, the pope praised their universal mission at a time when there was so much talk of racism and separatist nationalism. In the mind of Pius, the two were interrelated.[81] He insisted on the universality of the Catholic Church, repeating that humanity consisted of one family, the theme of his unreleased encyclical. He regretted that his *patria*, which had produced the first Jewish prime minister in Europe, had regressed by espousing Nazi racism, contrary to the beliefs and teachings of the church.[82] His antagonism had a substantial impact. Even Catholics who had hitherto tolerated fascism's Race Manifesto recanted once the pope proclaimed his opposition.[83]

Count Ciano, Mussolini's son-in-law and foreign minister, described the pope's speech as violently anti-racist.[84] From mid-July to mid-September 1938, an incensed Pius XI made four strong speeches against racism.[85] Throughout the year he decried fascism's anti-Semitism. Once again the papal intervention had an impact, constraining Mussolini to conclude that he could not forge an alliance with Germany "at the moment," for it would offend the religious sensibilities of Italians.[86] Unquestionably, the church's disapproval of Italian anti-Semitism continued "to haunt many Italians."[87] The German ambassador reported that the Italian rejection of Mussolini's racial legislation flowed from the fact that "it offended their Christian sense."[88] Small wonder that Italian Jews derived comfort from the pope's uncompromising stance against the "grave and gross error" of racism.[89] In Berlin, Hitler ranted against the anti-Axis machinations of the church of Pius XI.[90]

Although the Italian Foreign Office denied that its racism was imported from the Reich, the pope persisted in this belief.[91] Only at the end of his career did the Duce acknowledge that the pope had gauged the situation accurately.[92] Mussolini's adoption of Hitler's anti-Semitism stirred the aged pope to public wrath. He was outraged that the Italian press censured his attack on racism, while it included Nazi commentary. Pius XI had his nuncio to Italy, Monsignor Borgongini Duca, denounce Italy's racist legislation.[93] The pope preferred to speak of peoples rather than races. Human dignity, he repeated, rested in a unified humanity.[94] These papal positions guided the authors of the projected encyclical, and similar statements found their way into *Humani Generis Unitas*.[95] The Jesuit review *La Civiltà Cattolica* echoed the pope's sentiments, perceiving racism as fundamentally anti-Christian.[96] When Farinacci claimed that the Jesuits were allies against the Jews, the *La Civiltà Cattolica* rejected the contention, noting that its attitude toward the Jews had never been based on racist principles.[97] One journal described the pope's antiracist speech as initiating a *Kulturkampf* in reverse.[98] What is clear is that Pius' public stance was strikingly similar to the one enunciated in his pending encyclical.[99]

These talks and their publication in *L'Osservatore Romano*[100] provoked criticism in Italy and Germany, and in both the party press accused the pope of polemicizing and going beyond the realm of religion in discussing relations between the races, which they presented as a legal issue rather than a religious one. The pope responded in early September that he did not wish to provoke polemics but could not remain silent in the face of grave errors and the violation of human rights. Racism represented a religious and moral oppression as well as a civil one. His stance proved almost as intransigent as that of Pius IX, who had earlier warned that "no sort of conciliation is ever possible between Christ and Belial, between light and darkness, between truth and lies."[101]

Like the apostles, Pius XI insisted he had to bear witness to the truth.[102] Italy's racist legislation represented an attack on the church's teachings.[103] "No, it's not possible for we Christians to participate in anti-Semitism," the pope told a group of visiting Belgians on 6 September 1938. "Spiritually, we are Semites."[104] Meanwhile, Vatican Radio decried the unfortunate attempt to introduce racism into Italy as "a gross error," reminding the faithful that "the Jewish race served as a medium for the transmission of the Christian message to all nations."[105] In mid-September Roberto Farinacci denounced the pope's position on racism. "Religious questions may be the business of the Pope, but political ones are the exclusive province of the Duce," he wrote. He charged that the pope erred in condemning racism on religious grounds.[106] Farinacci's paper *Il Regime Fascista* continued to denounce the "Judeophile" policies of Pius XI, exposing him an ally of the Jews, communists, and Protestants.[107] The Duce himself warned the Vatican to cease its Judeophile campaign. "I do not underestimate his strength," the Duce thundered against the pope, "but he must not underestimate mine either."[108] The conflict escalated.

On 10 November 1938 Mussolini published a decree forbidding marriage between Italian Aryans with persons of "another race." This was followed by the Decree Law of 17 November 1938, "Measures for the Defense of the Italian Race," which, among other things restricted Jewish marriage, employment, and schooling.[109] Pius complained to both the king and Mussolini, writing that this represented a violation of the concordat of the Lateran Accords.[110] It was likewise deplored in the columns of *L'Osservatore Romano*.[111]

The fact that the pope relied on the concordat to press his case does not imply, as has been suggested, that he sought only to defend narrow ecclesiastical interests.[112] Rather, he felt that reference to the concordat provided the legal justification for protesting what the Duce considered "a purely political issue." He made public his displeasure in his Christmas allocution, once again attacking the measure as a violation of the concordat.[113] He did so despite the warnings of Count Ciano that the pope's denunciations of fascist racial policies made a clash between Mussolini's regime and the Vatican inevitable.[114] In fact, in the last months of the pontificate there was a marked deterioration in relations between the Vatican and the fascist regime.[115] Like La Farge, the Pope judged racism immoral and sinful.[116] At year's end the old and ailing pope again regretted that a cross other than the cross of Christ had been extolled in the Holy City.[117]

The New Year did not witness any improvement in relations between the Vatican and the fascist regimes, as an overworked and increasingly sick Pius prepared a message on church–state relations to be presented to the Italian bishops gathered in Rome for the tenth anniversary of the Lateran Pacts, 11 February 1939. In the interim the Vatican took steps to find positions for Jewish scholars and officials who had been dismissed, and in January 1939 at the pope's insistence, a similar request was transmitted to the cardinals of North America, accompanied by a personal letter on behalf of the persecuted by Pius XI.[118] Pius also spoke to the Diplomatic Corps accredited to the Holy See seeking visas for the victims of racial persecution under fascism and Nazism.[119] The British representative, who met with the pope at the end of the year, observed that following fascism's adoption of racism, which violated fundamental tenets of the church, he did not see "how the two systems can ever work in harmony together."[120]

In light of the Vatican's campaign against fascist racism and its efforts on behalf of the persecuted, one would have expected the appearance of La Farge's encyclical, which echoed the pope's sentiments, but no word arrived of its receipt by the pope or projected release.[121] It is believed that Pius XI received the document at the end of January 1939, but it is not certain if the pope read it before his death on 10 February.[122] Most likely he did not, even though the failing Pius XI was working on the draft of a speech to be presented to the bishops cataloging fascist abuses. He died on 10 February 1939, before he could deliver it.[123] The draft of this speech, later published by John XXIII, regretted developments in Italy while insisting on the unity of the human family.[124] The draft of the La Farge encyclical was likewise found on Pius XI's desk after his death, together with an attached note from Monsignor Domenico Tardini, indicating that Pius XI wanted the encyclical without delay![125] In light of Pius XI's condemnation of Italian anti-Semitism, it is not surprising that Mussolini was relieved by his death and supposedly blurted out, "Finally that obstinate old man is dead."[126] Some suspected that the Duce had hastened his demise.

While Pius XI was prepared to negotiate with the devil himself on behalf of the church, he did not shy from public denunciations while assuming the offensive on behalf of the church's creed and human rights. Indeed, his statement has often been taken out of context, for in 1929 he stated that he was prepared to negotiate with the devil when it came to saving souls.[127] His proclamation impressed Vladimir Jabotinsky, leader of the revisionist Zionist movement, who claimed that he was "ready to meet Satan if it will help the Jewish people."[128] Jews as well as Christians admired Pius XI. At his death, this pope was acclaimed as the champion of freedom against the totalitarian states.[129] "More than once did we have occasion to be deeply grateful for the attitude which he took up against the persecution of racial minorities and in particular for the deep concern which he expressed for the fate of the persecuted Jews of Central Europe," Bernard Joseph of the Jewish Agency wrote on 12 February 1939. "His noble efforts on their behalf will ensure for him for all time a warm place in the memories of Jewish people wherever they live."[130] Rolf Hochhuth, so critical of the "silence" of Pius XII, deemed it unfortunate that "on the very eve of the Second World War Pius XI, who was a very brave and resolute man, should have died."[131]

Pius XI did not hesitate to publicly condemn fascist anti-Semitism. During the course of the last two years of his pontificate, Pius XI had publicly characterized racism as scientifically unsound, a religious apostasy or heresy, and a totalitarian tendency in violation of natural law as well as the Christian creed.[132] This position was reflected in the encyclical that Pius XI commissioned. "The theory and practice of [racism] which makes a distinction between the higher and lower races, ignores the bond of unity," the 1938 document warned. Indeed, it added, "It is incredible that in view of these facts there are still people who maintain that the doctrine and practice of racism have nothing to do with Catholic teaching as to faith and morals and nothing to do with philosophy, but are a purely political affair."[133] In light of Pius XI's willingness to confront the totalitarian regimes on racism, one can assume that Pius XI would have issued the "encyclical," which reflected his stance on anti-Semitism, had he lived longer. In fact, a week before the pope's death, the Vatican newspaper published on its front page the antiracist speech of the American undersecretary of state.[134] Pius XI was not one to be intimidated by the Duce's warning that he would not tolerate any opposition to his racial policies.[135] Very likely his determined opposition to racism contributed to the subsequent systematic Italian resistance to Hitler's policy of genocide and the fact that more help was provided for the Jews in Catholic Italy than in any other country.[136]

NOTES

1. Gaetano Salvemini, exiled from Mussolini's Italy, from his chair at Harvard, fulminated against the philofascistic course pursued by the Vatican of Popes Pius XI and Pius XII.

2. Frank J. Coppa, "The Vatican and the Dictators between Diplomacy and Morality," in *Catholics, the State, and the European Radical Right, 1919–1945*, edited by Richard J. Wolff and Jorg K. Hoensch (New York: Columbia University Press, 1987), p. 199.

3. Paul I. Murphy with R. Rene Arlington, *La Popessa* (New York: Warner Communications, 1984), p. 139.

4. Anthony Rhodes, *The Vatican in the Age of Dictators, 1922–1945* (New York: Holt, Rhinehart, and Winston, 1973), p. 29; E.E.Y. Hales, *The Catholic Church in the Modern World* (Garden City, NY: Hanover House, 1958), p. 266; John P. McKnight, *The Papacy: A New Appraisal* (London: McGraw-Hill, 1953), p. 141.

5. John Hearley, *Pope or Mussolini* (New York: Macaulay, 1929), p. 44.

6. D. A. Binchy, *Church and State in Fascist Italy* (New York: Oxford University Press, 1941), pp. 85–86.

7. Lesley Caldwell, "Reproducers of the Nation: Women and the Family in Fascist Policy," in *Rethinking Italian Fascism: Capitalism, Popularism and Culture*, edited by David Forgacs (London: Lawrence and Wishart, 1986), p. 116; for a somewhat different interpretation, see Victoria de Grazia, *How Fascism Ruled Women, Italy, 1922–1945* (Berkeley: University of California Press, 1992), pp. 10–11; and Emiliana P. Noether , "Italian Women and Fascism: A Reevaluation," *Italian Quarterly* 23 (Fall 1982): 77.

8. For an examination of fascist anti-Semitism, see Renzo De Felice, *Storia degli ebrei sotto il fascismo* (Turin: Einaudi, 1961); Luigi Preti, *Impero fascista, africani ed ebrei* (Milan: Mursia, 1968).

9. Jacob Katz, *From Prejudice to Destruction, Anti-Semitism, 1700–1933* (Cambridge, MA: Harvard University Press, 1980), p. 321.

10. Meir Michaelis, *Mussolini and the Jews: German-Italian Relations and the Jewish*

Question in Italy, 1922–1945 (Oxford: Clarendon Press, 1978), p. 240.

11. *Il Popolo d'Italia*, 8 November 1938.

12. Gene Bernardini, "The Origins and Development of Racial Anti-Semitism in Fascist Italy," *Journal of Modern History* 49, no. 3 (1977): 431.

13. Deborah Sontag, "Plans for Rival Rallies on Religion Issue Stir Fears in Israel," *New York Times*, 12 February 1999, p.3.

14. Susan Zuccotti, *The Italians and the Holocaust: Persecution, Rescue and Survival* (New York: Basic Books, 1987; reprinted University of Nebraska Press, 1996), p. 51.

15. Antonio Pellicani, *Il Papa di tutti. La Chiesa Cattolica, il fascismo, e il razzismo, 1929–1945* (Milan: Sugar Editore, 1964), p. 103.

16. John F. Pollard, *The Vatican and Italian Fascism, 1929-1932: A Study in Conflict* (Cambridge: Cambridge University Press, 1985), p. 188.

17. Edward R. Tannenbaum, *The Fascist Experience: Italian Society and Culture, 1922–1945* (New York: Basic Books, 1972), p. 195 ; Giuseppe Dalla Torre, *Azione Cattolica e fascismo* (Rome: A.V.E. Stampa, 1945), p. 7; Maria Cristina Giuntella, "Circoli Cattolici e organizzazioni Giovanili fasciste in Umbria," in *Cattolici e Fascisti in Umbria (1922–1945)*, edited by Albertino Monticone (Bologna: Il Mulino, 1978), p. 31; J. Derek Holmes, *The Papacy in the Modern World, 1914–1978* (New York: Crossroad Publishers, 1981), p. 60; Binchey, *Church and State*, p. 164.

18. Michaelis, *Mussolini*, pp. 248–249.

19. La Farge had been sent by the editor of *America* to the International Eucharistic Congress at Budapest in April and on his way back stopped in Rome. John La Farge, *The Manner Is Ordinary* (New York: Harcourt, Brace, 1954), pp. 253–272.

20. The Jesuits who assumed the task were led by the American John La Farge, S.J., of *America*, who had written a series of articles and books denouncing racism and who was personally commissioned to write the encyclical. He was assisted by the German father Gustav Gundlach, S.J., who had written the 1930 article on anti-Semitism in the *Lexikon fur Theolgie und Kirche*, and the Frenchman Gustave Desbusquois, S.J., who served as the director of the *Action populaire*. Heinrich Bacht, S.J., translated the encyclical into Latin.

21. The reader will find the complete, abridged, French version of *Humanitas Generis Unitas* published for the first time in Georges Passelecq and Bernard Suchecky, *L'Encyclique cachée de Pie XI. Une occasion manquée de l'Eglise face à l'antisémitisme*, Preface, "Pie XI, les Juifs et l'antisemitisme," de Emile Poulat (Paris: Editions La Decouverte, 1995), pp. 219–310. It was translated from the original French by Steven Rendall and provided an Introduction by Garry Wills and published under the title *The Hidden Encyclical of Pius XI* (New York: Harcourt, Brace, 1997). My references are to the original French edition.

22. *Cum Tertio*, 17 September 1922, in Harry C. Koenig, ed., *Principles for Peace: Selections from Papal Documents from Leo XIII to Pius XII* (Washington, DC: National Catholic Welfare Conference, 1943) , p. 329.

23. Cardinal Gasparri to the Conference of Lausanne, 5 December 1922, ibid., p. 330.

24. Speech of Pius IX to a number of foreign women, in Pasquale de Franciscis, ed., *Discorsi del Sommo Pontefice Pio IX Pronunziati ai fedeli di Roma e dell'Orbe dal principio della sua prigionia fino al presente* (Rome: G. Aurelj, 1972), vol. 1, p. 65.

25. *Prope Adsunt*, 21 October 1923, ibid., p. 367.

26. Giacomo Martina, "L'Ecclesiologia prevalente nel Pontificato di Pio XI," in *Cattolici e Fascisti in Umbria (1922–1945)*, edited by Alberto Monticone (Bologna: Il Mulino, 1978), pp. 226–227.

27. Consistorial Allocution of 20 December 1926, *Discorsi di Pio XI* , edited by Domenico Bertetto (Turin: Societa Editrice Internazionale, 1959), vol. 1, p. 647.

28. Decretum De Conosciatione Vulgo, "Amici Israel" Abolenda, 25 March 1928, *Acta Apostolicae Sedis*, 20, pp. 103–104.

29. Passelecq and Suchecky, *L'Encyclique cachée*, p. 144.

30. *Acta Apostolicae Sedis*, 20, pp. 103–104.

31. Murphy, *La Popessa*, p. 76.

32. The Lateran Accords included three parts: a conciliation treaty, which terminated the Roman question and established Vatican City as an inviolable papal terrritory; a concordat, which regulated church–state relations in Italy; and a financial convention to provide compensation for papal territory annexed during unification. The texts can be found in Nino Trapodi, *I Patti lateranese e il fascismo* (Bologna: Cappelli, 1960), pp. 267–279. For an analysis of the documents, see Ernesto Rossi, *Il Manganello e l'aspersorio* (Florence: Parenti, 1958), pp. 227–236.

33. *L'Osservatore Romano*, 12 February 1929; *Il Monitore Ecclesiastico*, March 1929.

34. Murphy, *La Popessa*, p. 68.

35. Royal Decree number 1731, 30 October 1930, cited in Michaelis, *Mussolini*, p. 53.

36. Giuseppe Rossini, *Il Fascismo e la resistenza* (Rome: Cinque Lune, 1955), p. 48.

37. Ecco una, 14 May 1929, *Principles for Peace: Selections from Papal Documents from Leo XIII to Pius XII*, p. 388.

38. *Acta Apostolicae Sedis*, 21, pp. 730–753.

39. Pinchas Lapide, *Three Popes and the Jews* (New York: Hawthorn Books, 1967), p. 98.

40. Anne Fremantle, ed., *The Papal Encyclicals in their Historical Context* (New York: G. P. Putnam's Sons, 1956), p. 249.

41. Lapide, *Three Popes*, pp. 98, 100.

42. Bernardini, "The Origins," p. 434.

43. Address of 18 September 1938, *Principles for Peace: Selections from Papal Documents from Leo XIII to Pius XII* , p. 547.

44. "La questione giudaica," *La Civiltà Cattolica* 1936 (anno 87, vol. 4): 45.

45. Murphy, *La Popessa*, pp. 130–136.

46. Michael R. Marrus, "The Vatican on Racism and Antisemitism, 1938–39: A New Look at a Might-Have Been," *Holocaust and Genocide Studies* 11, no. 3 (Winter 1997): 379; Lapide, *Three Popes*, p. 96.

47. "La questione giudaica e l'apostolato cattolico," *La Civiltà Cattolica* (23 June 1937).

48. Michaelis, *Mussolini*, p. 35.

49. "Cronaca Contemporanea," *La Civiltà Cattolica* (9–22 June 1938); Patricia M. Keefe, "Popes Pius XI and Pius XII, the Catholic Church, and the Nazi Perseution of the Jews," *British Journal of Holocaust Education* 2, no. 1 (Summer 1993): 32.

50. Passelecq and Suchecky, *L'Encyclique cachée*, p. 157.

51. *Discorsi di Pio XI*, vol. 3, p. 770.

52. Michaelis, *Mussolini*, p. 243.

53. Lapide, *Three Popes*, p. 113.

54. William L. Shire, *Berlin Diary: The Journal of a Foreign Correspondent, 1934–1941* (New York: Knopf, 1941), p. 115.

55. Camille M. Cianfarra, *The War and the Vatican* (London: Oates and Washbourne, 1945), p. 122; Thomas E. Hachey, ed., *Anglo-Vatican Relations 1914–1939: Confidential Reports of the British Minister to the Holy See* (Boston: G.K. Hall, 1972), pp. 389–394.

56. Bernardini, "The Origins," p. 436.

57. Michaelis, *Mussolini*, pp. 146, 149, 173.

58. For the text of the manifesto, see Renzo De Felice, *Storia degli ebrei italiani sotto il fascismo* (Turin: Einandi, 1961), pp. 541–542.

59. Meir Michaelis, "Fascism, Totalitarianism and the Holocaust: Reflections on Current Interpretations of National Socialist Anti-Semitism," *European History* Quarterly 19, no. 1 (1989): 93.

60. Murphy, *La Popessa*, p. 103.

61. Marrus, "The Vatican," pp. 382–383.

62. Michaelis, *Mussolini*, p. 244.

63. See note 19.

64. Subsequently, La Farge published *The Race Question and the Negro: A Study of the Catholic Doctrine on Interracial Justice* (New York: Longmans, Green, 1943) and *The Catholic Viewpoint on Race Relations* (Garden City, NY: Hanover House, 1956), among other volumes, as well as a series of articles in *America* and *Interracial Review*.

65. John La Farge, *Interracial Justice: A Study of the Catholic Doctrine of Race Relations* (New York: America Press, 1937), pp. 12–15, 59–61, 75, 172–173.

66. La Farge, *The Manner Is Ordinary*, pp. 272–273.

67. Robert A. Hecht, *An Unordinary Man: A Life of Father John La Farge* (Lanham, MD.: Scarecrow Press, 1996), pp. 114–115.

68. La Farge, *The Manner Is Ordinary*, p. 273.

69. "Jesuit Says Pius XI Asked for Draft," *National Catholic Reporter*, 22 December 1972, p. 3.

70. Hecht, *Unordinary Man*, p. 115.

71. Ibid.; Passelecq and Suchecky, *L'Encyclique cachée*, p. 115.

72. Galleys of La Farge's copy of the encyclical *Humani Generis Unitas* were to be published in *Catholic Mind* of 1973 but never appeared. It was stored in the offices of *America* and uncovered by Professor Robert A. Hecht. In 1996 a copy of the hidden encyclical was published by Passelecq and Suchecky, *L'Encyclique cachée*. My reference is to the galleys of the encyclical for the *Catholic Mind*, p. 31, paragraph 123.

73. Galleys of La Farge's copy of *Humani Generis Unitas*, p. 33, paragraph 131; Passelecq and Suchecky, *L'Encyclique cachée*, pp. 283–284.

74. Galleys of La Farge's copy of *Humani Generis Unitas*, p. 33, paragraph 132; Passelecq and Suchecky, *L'Encyclique cachée*, p. 284.

75. Galleys of La Farge's copy of *Humani Generis Unitas*, p. 36b, paragraph 147; Passelecq and Suchecky, *L'Encyclique cachée*, pp. 292–293.

76. Galleys of La Farge's copy of *Humani Generis Unitas*, p. 38b, paragraph 154; Passelecq and Suchecky, *L'Encyclique cachée*, p. 296.

77. Galleys of La Farge's copy of *Humani Generis Unitas*, p. 34, paragraph 135; Passelecq and Suchecky, *L'Encyclique cachée*, p. 286.

78. *L'Osservatore Romano*, 17 July 1938, p. 1; Cianfarra, *War and Vatican*, p. 133–134.

79. Tannenbaum, *Fascist Experience*, p. 199.

80. "Alle Suore di Nostra Signora del Cenaccolo," *Discorsi di Pio XI*, vol. 3, pp. 766–772.

81. La Farge, *The Manner Is Ordinary*, p. 273.

82. Agli Alunni del Collegio di "Propaganda Fede," 28 July 1938, *Discorsi di Pio XI*, vol. 3, pp. 777–781.

83. *Il Regime Fascista*, August 27, 1938.

84. Poulat, in Passelecq and Suchecky, *L'Encyclique cachée*, p. 13.

85. 15 July, 28 July, 21 August, 6 September 1938, in *Discorsi di Pio XI*, vol. 3, pp. 766–772, 777–790, 793–798, 869–872.

86. Michaelis, *Mussolini*, p. 159.

87. Tannenbaum, *Fascist Experience*, p. 309.

88. Michaelis, *Mussolini*, p. 173.

89. Ibid., p. 243.

90. Meir Michaelis, "Fascism," p. 89.

91. De Felice, *Storia degli ebrei italiani sotto il fascismo*, saw a clear connection.

92. Michaelis, *Mussolini*, p. 155.

93. *New York Times*, 6 August 1938, 12 August 1938, 1 September 1938.

94. *Discorsi di Pio XI*, vol. 3, pp. 782–783.

95. In this regard, see sections 111 on race and racism, 112 on denial of human unity, and 116 on denial of true religious and moral values in the galleys of La Farge's copy of *Humani Generis Unitas* preserved in the offices of *America*, pp. 29b, 30, and in Passelecq and Suchecky, *L'Encyclique cachée*, pp. 274–276.

96. *La Civiltà Cattolica*, 10 August 1938.

97. *La Civiltà Cattolica*, 1 October 1938.

98. "Pio XI e un Appello," *L'Osservatore Romano*, 26 January 1961.

99. This is apparent from reading sections 106 to 110 in the galleys of La Farge's copy of *Humani Generis Unitas* preserved in the offices of *America*, pp. 28, 28b, 29, and in Passelecq and Suchecky, *L'Encyclique cachée*, pp. 272–274.

100. *L'Osservatore Romano*, 30 July 1938, p. 1; 22–23 August 1938, p. 1.

101. Maria Elisabeth De Franciscis, *Italy and the Vatican* (New York: Peter Lang, 1984), vol. 1, pp. 283–284.

102. *Ad Insegnanti di Azione Cattolica*, 6 September 1938, *Discorsi di Pio XI*, vol. 3, p. 796.

103. *New York Times*, 8 September 1938.

104. Passelecq and Suchecky, *L'Encyclique cachée*, p. 180.

105. Lapide, *Three Popes*, p. 96.

106. Michaelis, *Mussolini*, p. 240.

107. Ibid., p. 241.

108. Ibid., p. 181.

109. The text can be found in the *Raccolta ufficiale delle leggi e decreti del Regno d'Italia* (1938), vol. 4, 2946–2949.

110. " A proposito d'un decreto legge," *L'Osservatore Romano*, 14–15 November 1938.

111. Ibid.

112. Martina, "L'Ecclesiologia prevalente nel Pontificato di Pio XI," pp. 233–234.

113. Con grande, 24 December 1938, *Principles for Peace: Selections from Papal Documents from Leo XIII to Pius XII*, pp. 549–551; *Papal Pronouncements. A Guide: 1740– 1978*, vol. 2, p. 114; *New York Times*, 25 December 1938.

114. Galeazzo Giano, *Ciano's Hidden Diaries, 1937–1938* (New York: E. P. Dutton, 1953), pp. 140–141.

115. Michaelis, *Mussolini*, p. 251.

116. Hecht, *Unordinary Man*, pp. 103, 107.

117. *Discorsi di Pio XI*, vol. 3, p. 772.

118. "Pio XI e un Appello," *L'Osservatore Romano*, 26 January 1961.

119. Patricia M. Keefe, "Popes Pius XI and Pius XII, the Catholic Church and the Persecution of the Jews," *British Journal of Holocaust Education* 2, no. 1 (Summer 1993): 33.

120. Owen Chadwick, *Britain and the Vatican during the Second World War* (Cambridge: Cambridge University Press, 1988), p. 26.

121. Only after Pius XI's death was La Farge informed that the encyclical had been delivered to the pope and was among his papers. Ledochowski added that since the new pope had not yet had time to go over the "sundry papers left on his desk," it was "premature" to ask Pius XII what he planned to do with the draft. Castelli, *National Catholic*

Reporter, 15 December 1972, p. 8.

122. "Jesuit Says Pius XI Asked for Draft," *National Catholic Reporter*, 22 December 1972, p. 3.

123. *Acta Apostolicae Sedis* 51 (1959), pp. 129–135; *Papal Pronouncements. A Guide: 1740–1978*, vol. 2, p. 114.

124. "Il Testo Inedito dell' ultimo discorso di Pio XI presentato da Sua Santità Giovanni XXIII," *Discorsi di Pio XI*, vol. 3, pp. 891–896.

125. "Jesuit Says Pius XI Asked for Draft," p. 4.

126. Roger Aubert, *The Church in a Secularized Society* (New York: Paulist Press, 1978), p. 557.

127. Speech to the professors and students of the College of Mondragone, 14 May 1929, *Discorsi di Pio XI*, vol. 2, p. 79.

128. Deborah Sontag, "A Handshake Becomes More than a Symbol," *New York Times*, 10 February 1999.

129. Michaelis, *Mussolini*, p. 245.

130. Keefe, "Popes Pius XI and Pius XII," p. 33.

131. Patricia Marx Ellsberg, "An Interview with Rolf Hochhuth," in *The Papacy and Totalitarianism Between the Two World Wars*, edited by Charles Delzell (New York: J. Wiley, 1974), p. 115.

132. Passelecq and Suchecky, *L'Encyclique cachée*, p. 197.

133. Galleys of La Farge's copy of *Humani Generis Unitas*, p. 29b; Passelecq and Suchecky, *L'Encyclique cachée*, p. 275.

134. *L'Osservatore Romano*, 3 February 1939.

135. Michaelis, *Mussolini*, p. 198.

136. Michaelis, "Fascism," p. 317.

23

The First Anti-Semitic Campaign of the Fascist Regime

Luc Nemeth

The sight of a "Jewish" horse painted green in Roberto Benigni's film *Life Is Beautiful* is considered by spectators as normal—in the context of fascist Italy, of course—just as they consider "normal" what is shown in Vittorio De Sica's film *The Garden of the Finzi-Contini*. But often the same spectators, if you had met them before the show, would have told you: "No. There was no anti-Semitism in Italy before the Nazi presence." Both reactions are interesting; the first one proves to us that these spectators, when faced with the facts, recognize them, but their previous refusal to admit them attests to the existence of strong mental barriers. Even some scholars, though the main conclusions have been drawn by Meir Michaelis in the early 1960s,[1] will hardly admit that "until July 1943 the nature and extent of Fascist racial policy were determined by Mussolini"[2] and that Hitler thought it wiser not to interfere.

One barrier is the comparison with Nazi anti-Semitism; the fact that anti-Semitism, even if consistent with fascist ideology, is not a part of it; or the fact, recalled by George Mosse, that "Italian public opinion never accepted racist ideas."[3] At the beginning of the century, words like *cani* (dogs) might have been used by very ignorant people,[4] but they were a survival of a distant religious past—such words had been used to name all the unfaithful, Muslims as well as Jews[5]—and there was no physical violence. Nor had there been any anti-Semitism campaign such as the one that France had recently known with the Dreyfus case. This lack of a deeply rooted anti-Semitism was to be important, too, when the time came for deportations; Susan Zuccotti points out that while 6,800 Italian Jews were killed, 38,400 succeeded in surviving, a lower rate of victims than in most other European countries.[6]

Another barrier comes from the fact that anti-Semitism is usually seen as a passion, but in the case of Mussolini his only passion was himself. The thirst for power led him to say everything and its opposite on any subject. About the Jews, as about everything else, his attitude was "mostly opportunistic, influenced by circumstances."[7] In 1932, at a time when he wanted to pose as a protector of the

Jews, he declared: "Nothing will ever make me believe that biologically pure races can be shown to exist today."[8] Six years later, at the time of the promulgation of the racial laws, he said: "We must get into our minds that we are not Hamites, that we are not Semites, that we are not Mongols. And, then, if we are none of these races, we are evidently Aryans and we came from the Alps, from the North. Therefore we are Aryans of the Mediterranean type, pure."[9] An Italian who in 1937 had a talk with a British Jewish leader told him, "If philo-Semitism pays, he is philo-Semitic; if anti-Semitism pays, he is quite willing equally to be an anti-Semite."[10] Of course, to say everything and its opposite does not confer innocence: one anti-Semitic statement is enough to make a man an anti-Semite, but from a psychological perspective, one cannot consider Mussolini a pathological anti-Semite.[11]

Confusion comes from the word "anti-Semite" itself. If to be an anti-Semite means to act as such, the only thing that one can say is that "[f]ascism did not become officially anti-Semitic until Mussolini chose to make it so, with the racial laws in 1938."[12] But if to be an anti-Semite means to think as such, Mussolini obviously had prejudices that he sometimes expressed,[13] though some Jews, especially two women (Angelica Balabanoff and Margherita Sarfatti), were close to him, first when he was a socialist and then when he became a fascist. His links with Jewish bankers are not significant, from that point of view. His anti-Semitic statements from time to time, however, appear to be not so much an expression of a racial hatred—though he might have used the word *razza*—as connected with the stereotypical image of the Jews as bankers or of the Jews as masters of the world, either through capitalism or bolshevism. For instance, in 1919 he wrote, "In Russia 80 percent of the Soviets are Jewish; in Budapest, out of 22 commissioners of the people, 17 at least are Jewish. Would not Bolshevism, by chance, be the vengeance of Hebraism against Christianism? . . . World finance is in the hands of the Jews. . . . Race does not betray race."[14] The question is: Until what point did he believe what he had written? In October 1920 he dedicated an article to Zionism, concluding: "Let us hope that the Italian Jews will have the sense not to stir up anti-Semitism in the only country where it has never existed."[15] This tone is unpleasant, but he might have used the same one against other enemies or alleged enemies.

After the so-called march on Rome (October 1922), the priorities of Mussolini, now prime minister, were not exactly the same as previously, but the world, for him, was more than ever divided in two: people who were with him versus people who were against him. He thought it was better to have with him people whom he considered masters of the world—he firmly believed in the existence of an "international Jewry."[16] Then, as stated in Cecil Roth's *History of the Jews of Italy*, the attitude of the Jews to the fascist movement, at the start, had been indistinguishable from that of the general population: "If some of them, of some liberal political tendencies, abhorred it, others . . . were included among its earliest and more fervent supporters."[17] Such a situation is not surprising when one considers the social, economic, and cultural integration of this minority; a wide diversity of political opinions had to be expected, and neither religious nor "ethnic" factors seem to have determined the initial attitude. There were, though, potential points of conflict. One of them concerned Jewish moral values, which had not much in common with the fascist glorification of violence; the same can generally be said about newborn Zionism, which, far from being one more nationalism, as the fascists understood it, expressed ideals of human fraternity. A potential conflict came from the fact that the Jews were seen as a group by these fascists, who dreamed of being the only group controlling social life. But there was no anti-Semitic campaign during all of the 1920s, not even after the "full fascistization" of 1926. In 1928 Mussolini published an article that said," Now we ask the Italian Jews: are you a religion or a nation?"[18] but it was not followed by other articles. The temporary suppression of the weekly *Israel* in 1928 was the result of polemics concerning divorce. To sum up the first ten years of existence of the regime, one can say that in 1932 many people believed what the Duce declared to the journalist Emil Ludwig: "Anti-Semitism does not exist in Italy."[19] One might observe that when anti-Semitism does not exist, you do not have to say it does not exist! Or perhaps the real intent of this statement was: "I, Mussolini, do not need any anti-Semitism at the present time." He was then believed, and maybe he himself believed what he was saying. In 1932 he told Prince Starhemberg, the Austrian fascist leader: "I have no love for the Jews, but they have great influence everywhere. It is better to leave them alone. His anti-Semitism has already brought Hitler more enemies than is necessary."[20] According to Michaelis, Mussolini had decided "not to raise the Jewish issue, realizing as he did that anti-Semitism had no political value in Italy and that a clash with 'international Jewry' was most unlikely to benefit his regime."[21]

Hitler's rise to power was welcomed by the fascist press, both as the victory of a new fascist regime and as the emergence of a power that openly asked for a revision of the Versailles peace treaties. On the following day the newspaper *Il Tevere* wrote: "In the name of the new order that Europa claims, panting, we hail with sympathy the advent to power of Hitler, loyal friend of fascist Italy, admirer of Mussolini."[22] A point of disagreement between the two dictators was the anschluss (annexation of Austria), which Hitler had mentioned as his dream in the first lines of *Mein Kampf*,[23] but in 1933 Germany had not rearmed, and Italy was cooperating with the Western democracies. Concerning the German Jews, Mussolini disapproved the persecution of them, not for moral reasons but, as already said, because he considered it useless. On 30 March he cabled his ambassador in Berlin, Cerruti, about the Nazis: "The party's call for a fight against Hebraism, while it will not make Nazism stronger inside than it already is, will strengthen moral pressure and economic reprisals against world Jewry."[24] In the same cable he also gave Hitler advice to follow the example of fascist Italy, where there had not been any anti-Semitic campaign but where being a Jew was not an asset in getting an official position: "Every regime has not only the right but also the duty to eliminate from the command positions the elements not wholly trustable but to this scope it is not necessary—and it might even be harmful—to emphasize race."[25] The lack of anti-Semitic persecution in Italy also allowed him to boast about his own regime. Then, 1933 is not an ordinary time: it comes halfway between 1931 (after the bellicose anti-French speeches of 1930) and the Ethiopian War, a period in which the Duce tried (and largely succeeded) to appear as an element of peace in Europe.[26] Therefore, his hope in January 1933 was for a reconciliation between Hitler and the German Jews, of which he would have been the mediator—what a glory for this defender of the "Latin civilization"! Very soon he understood that such a project was unrealistic, considering the central position of the Jewish question for Hitler. Soon, too, he gave this new friend a symbolic satisfaction with anti-Semitic statements published in the newspaper *Il Popolo d'Italia*, which he controlled.[27] He also tried to court Western public opinion to appear as a protector of the German Jews. Five hundred refugees were accepted by Italy in 1933; this was not much compared with the 25,000 who were accepted by France, but in terms of comparison with Hitler and since "the evil-doing of one's neighbour often heightens, by contrast, one's own reputation for virtue" (as stated by Salvemini[28]), Mussolini benefited. Since he had no precise plans concerning his future relations with Germany, he needed, more than ever, to have a free hand as much as possible, which would have been impossible in a situation of an endless war between what he called "international Jewry" (including the Italian Jews) and Nazi Germany. The best solution for him would have been the voluntary departure of the nonfascist Jews for Palestine: no more Jews, no more "problem." This ambivalence explains why he was able to write, in the midst of the later anti-Semitic campaign, an article that was quite skeptical about Zionism but that ended with a revealing, "Anyway it is a solution."[29] He knew that the majority of the Italian Jews, who felt at home in their native country, had no desire to emigrate. It would be better to intimidate them for a long time.

As often happens in a vicious campaign, Mussolini did not use *Il Popolo d'Italia*. He used a paper that he had created in 1924, *Il Tevere*. According to an article published in the *Manchester Guardian* in 1927 dedicated to the major papers of the Italian press, *Il Tevere* "seems to be far nearer to the spirit of Mussolini, and far more accurate in its prophecies of his future conduct."[30] Alberto Moravia recalled that this paper was used for officious attacks against writers and intellectuals.[31] More recently, the historian Adrian Lyttelton remembered that this paper performed

a special function of some interest. It was inspired directly by Mussolini and it was encouraged to air themes and views (e.g. anti-Semitism) on which he did not wish to commit himself officially. He spoke with two voices, cautious, official, opportunistic in the *Popolo d'Italia* . . . : extremist, unrestrained and speculative in *Il Tevere*. He regarded *Il Tevere* as his own personal, unofficial organ, just as the *Popolo d'Italia* was his official one, and for this reason its opinions had always to be treated with respect by the others papers. . . . This type of informal control exercised through *Il Tevere* (and to a lesser degree some of the other extremist papers) was of a great importance in creating a climate of anxiety in which journalists wrote only what they knew to be safe.[32]

The anti-Semitic campaign of 1934 did not begin on racial grounds. A racial campaign would have been difficult in Italy; it might even have awakened old polemics against the *razza maledetta* (the damned race, i.e., the southern Italians), and this was not welcome for purposes of national unity. A campaign against the Jews as "masters of the world" was opposite the needs of Mussolini, who wanted to remain on good terms with what he called "international Jewry." Eventually, the campaign was based on the theme of impossible assimilation and of "dual loyalties." At the start it was allusive, consisting of ingenuous remarks usually published in a small spot on the first page, *Specola* (which means astronomic observatory); the periodicity of the attacks was irregular. What made these attacks very vicious was the method: the anonymous author quoted a Zionist paper with a short commentary and often published, some days after, an indignant Zionist protestation, presented as the best proof of "Zionist bad faith." This campaign began on 30 January by quoting a speech of a leader of a Zionist group of Rome, printed in the weekly *Israel*. The speaker, Augusto Levi, had said: "Anyone who believes to make himself useful to the country by fully assimilating, actually becomes an unproductive element; because in our soul lives our past, lives our story, live the ideals and the sacrifice of our ancestors, and these elements are those which are able to create spiritual values."[33] *Il Tevere*'s commentary was: "Here it would be the case to ask the orator for his I.D. card. If he is an Italian, as he is without any doubt, he is deeply wrong. In addition he is committing a bad action by inciting his coreligionists to not 'fully assimilate.'"[34] If ever an Italian Jew might have approved these lines, in the name of the assimilationist position, he should have paid more attention to the details. The first was the title of the article: "Ebrei" (Jews), not "Sionisti"; the second was the date of *Israel*'s incriminating issue, ironically reported as "2 Scevat 5694," which means 18 January in the religious calendar.

Eight days later, on 7 February, polemics with the Italian Zionist Federation concerned the same theme of assimilation, under the same title "Ebrei."[35] Until March the official target remained Zionism, but day after day this campaign became more and more anti-Semitic, not so much because of its content as because of its tone of intimidation and its attempt to make the Italian Jews appear "diverse." An example of this tone of intimidation is given by the article of 15 February; the title was "Sionismo e Patriottismo Ovvero: Carta Tanta (Zionism and Patriotism, or So much Paper). The article concluded: "These are the three observations here made to the Union of the so-called Italian, Israelitic Communities. But they are not the only ones. If the Union wants some others, we are in the position, with its own texts in hands, to confute her until the day of the creation of the kingdom of Israel."[36] On the next day, 16 February, the title was "Sionismo e Italianità Ovvero Della Perfetta Armonia" (Zionism and Italianity, or About Perfect Harmony).[37] On the first page was printed a facsimile of an article by the French anti-Semite Henry Coston, "A Bas le Pouvoir Occulte" (Down with the Occult Power).[38] One can here observe the perfect synchronism between this campaign and the one led at the same time by the anti-Semitic press in France from the start of the Stavisky affair. On 21 February, in a story titled, "Ancora Sionismo!" (Zionism Again!), the tone is a mixture of threat and ingenuity: "We want to know—and we repeat it for the thousandth time—how one can reconcile a Jewish nationalism with the Italian nationalism; how people can have two motherlands."[39] The next day, 22 February, the target was Albert Einstein; here also Zionism was supposed to be the enemy, according to the title—"Ciarle Sionistiche" (Zionist Boasts)—but the article mentions Einstein as "the inventor of relativity, who is not relativist at all when he deals with Judaism. . . . Not without some reason the German patriots had to make him pack his bags."[40] The next day, 23 February, the title is "Sionismo e Chiarezza" (Zionism and Clarity). The article welcomes the *Giornale d'Italia* for joining the anti-Semitic campaign.[41] On 24 February: "Ancora e Sempre Sionismo" (Zionism, Again and Ever).[42] Then, a pause of two weeks, but on 12 March the title was: "Alla Luce del Settemplice Candelabro" (Under the Light of the Seven-Branched Candlestick).[43] The alleged crime of a monthly, *Davar*,[44] was to have mentioned, as a tragic consequence of World War I, the fact that Jews of all countries had been led to kill each other. Commentary of *Il Tevere*: "Oh, poor Unknown Soldier, who believed in a heroic result of your sacrifice, the seven-branched candlestick was needed to enlighten your pitiful fate."[45] Between the middle and the end of March was a new pause because of the presence of the foreign press in Italy; an Italo-Austro-Hungarian conference had taken place on 14 March, and a plebiscite was organized on 25 March.

In the context of a plebiscite it would have been out of the question for the fascist press to mention that at the border of Ponte Tresa (Lugano) on 11 March, leaflets calling for a vote of "No" had been found aboard a car entering the country. The driver, Sion Segre, a member of Giustizia e Libertà in Turin, had been arrested; the passenger, Mario Levi, had dived into the river Tresa and succeeded in reaching Swiss territory. Some authors have speculated about a possible denunciation by an informer; Segre himself had doubts about a cousin of his, the famous spy Pitigrilli. Eventually, from the research that he did in the archives in Rome (Archivio Centrale dello Stato), the arrest of Segre appears to have been unplanned.[46] During the next two days the police arrested, in Turin, thirty-nine more people, including a good number of people named Levi (among them was Giuseppe Levi, a teacher of anatomy at the University of Turin, and the painter Carlo Levi, later the author of *Christ Stopped at Eboli*); there were also a pretty good number of people named Segre and some non-Jewish, too, like the antifascist writer Barbara Allason.[47] Jews were very active in Giustizia e Libertà in Turin. In the coat of Sion Segre the police had found a flyer of the Oneg Sciabbath (The Joy of Shabbath), a study group; Segre had not even thought of hiding it, because it had nothing to do with politics.[48] In a first step the police superintendent of Varese, who had strong anti-Semitic prejudices, might have sincerely thought that he was here faced with a "Jewish plot."[49] What is important is that the police soon realized that there was no such plot, and they even stopped questioning the arrested people about a link between religion and antifascism.[50] Segre himself has insisted that "the shadows of a supposed Jewish pattern of our conspirative activity, created by my ineptness as a conspirator who leaves for a mission and forgets to empty his pockets before leaving, and by the visceral anti-Semitic rage of the commissioner of Varese, faded very soon."[51] At the end of the month only sixteen people out of forty remained under arrest. On 30 March a communiqué of the official press agency Stefani informed the papers of the arrests of 11 March and gave the list of the sixteen names. The communiqué did not mention their religion—this was not usual in Italy—but the papers published it under titles like this one, in Turin's *La Stampa*: "Arresti di ebrei antifascisti (Arrest of Jewish antifascists): operanti di intesa con i furousciti (Who Acted in Accord with Political Exiles)."[52]

On the same day the Press Office of Mussolini, in its daily instructions, had ordered a communiqué to be published "about the arrest, because of an anti-Fascist plot, of 20 persons, most of them living in Turin, and out of which 18 are Jewish. One will give the communiqué some typographical importance."[53] What was new was the use of all the papers, not only *Il Tevere*. It was the first time that a public allusion was made to a supposed Jewish antifascism;[54] some personal attacks had already been made, usually against Carlo Rosselli (who in July 1933 had been mentioned as *ebreo* in *Il Popolo d'Italia*[55]), but there had never been generalizations, and this happened at the precise moment when most of those arrested had been freed and when it appeared that there were no serious charges against the others (except for Sion Segre because of the leaflets and Leone Ginzburg as the leader of the group). *Il Tevere* published this communiqué, too, but it also published a long article, whose title included a phonetic transcription of a Jewish prayer: "Lascianà abbà Biruscialaim ("L'anno prossimo a Gerusalemme") "Quest'anno al Tribunale Speciale" (Next Year in Jerusalem. This Year at the Special Tribunal). The article began as follows:

"Cowardly Italian dogs!," shouted Levi (Mario) when getting shelter in Swiss territory. He did not shout: "Cowardly fascist dogs!"; he specified "Italian," and, at such a moment, with the police running after him, for sure he did not select his words. The invective against the Italians was coming to him from the gut, from the "chosen" Jewish gut.[56]

The article ended with a reflection about this campaign:

What was the scope of the polemic that we have led in the last period, and which has been so lazily welcomed by the other organs of the public opinion? The scope was to establish, with Jewish documents in hand, that the Jew does not assimilate, because through assimilation he sees a diminution of his personality and a betrayal of his face. . . . Should we appear as ingenuous, we will remember that the best of past and present anti-Fascism are members of the Jewish race: from Treves to Modigliani, from Rosselli to Morgari, the organizers of the anti-Fascist subversion have been and are members of the "chosen people."[57]

Mario Levi had actually shouted "Viva la libertà,"[58] and nothing else. Anyone who could reason could see that this story of "Italian dogs" was fiction, not only because of the "dogs"—a word obviously chosen because of its ancestral connotation—but because of "Italians," as perfectly expressed by Aldo Garosci in his *Vita di Carlo Rosselli*: "As if in Italy it might have come to mind to a Jew to call his fellow citizens other than himself 'Italians.'"[59] Other people might have seen that the communiqué had been published on the first day of Passover, a date linked, in the anti-Semitic imagery, with the accusations of ritual murder but also a date that expressed the only visible difference between Jewish and non-Jewish Italians in Italy: the former celebrated Passover, and the latter, Easter. This article did not make Italy anti-Semitic, but the campaign had reached one of its goals: the Italian Jews were now anxious. Mario Levi's sister, better known as the writer Natalia Ginzburg, remembered how their mother repeated, "It is just like the Dreyfus case! It is just like the Dreyfus case!"[60] A later report of an informant of the OVRA (political police) indicates that

during the days of the arrests of last March, a true panic burst out. On a Friday evening, eve of the celebration, as the Jews feared there would be a demonstration in front of the synagogue or inside, there was a rumor that the police had been informed of it and had prevented it in time. The communiqué of the OVRA, published in all the papers with a title which underlined the word Jews, the very violent commentaries of *Il Tevere*, the polemics which followed, the fresh outburst of caricatures making fun of the Jews in the satirical papers, had created an atmosphere of "pogrom."[61]

(An interesting point in this report is that the communiqué is mentioned as having come from the OVRA; officially, from its signature, it came from the Stefani press agency.)

In April, as in May, other anti-Semitic articles were published, but none in June, because of the presence of foreign journalists in connection with the Hitler-Mussolini talks in Venice; one article on 13 July claimed the campaign was finished.[62] Then: nothing. This campaign had stopped, with the same suddenness with which it had begun. In August it seemed that Mussolini had found a new target—for a while, unfortunately—in Hitler, whom he described to Prince Starhemberg as "a horrible sexual degenerate, a dangerous fool."[63] In September he declared, "Thirty centuries of history allow us to look with some pity upon certain doctrines advocated beyond the Alps by the progeny of a people who did not know how to write and transmit the documents of its life at a time when Rome had Caesar, Virgil, Augustus."[64] The anti-Semitic campaign was almost forgotten when in November the trial for the arrests of March took place and ended with sentences that can be considered light, in the context of fascist Italy: three years of jail for Sion Segre Amar; four years of jail for Ginzburg.[65] What had happened?

Let us go back to the month of June. Mussolini, after he left Venice, thought that there would be no annexation of Austria (there might have been a misunderstanding since he pretended to understand German). But on 25 July the Austrian chancellor Dollfuss was assassinated upon Hitler's orders—a prelude to annexation—and Mussolini gathered four divisions at Brenner Pass; evidently it was enough, at least until 1938, but he did not trust his own army. He thought that he might need British and French help, which would not have been refused to him. An anti-Semitic campaign in Italy might jeopardize that help.

Once more, necessity had prevailed with the sudden end of this campaign. Mussolini's statement about "Hebraism against Christianism" already suggests the weight of opportunism. At that time (June 1919) he had just created, three months earlier, the *fasci di combattimento*; the interest of this old *mangiapreti* (priest-baiter), if he ever wanted his *fasci* to play a political role, was to support the church. In his 1920 attack against Zionism, the confusion between Jews and Zionists is obvious. In October 1920 Italian nationalism still hoped to get a small piece of the ruins of the Ottoman Empire,[66] and Mussolini agreed with Gabrielle D'Annunzio—through this condemnation of Zionism he wanted to appear as a defender of *italianità*. The 1934 campaign should not be seen as Mussolini's gift to Nazi Germany. An anti-Semitic campaign, besides the fact it had few consequences (considering the small number of Jews in Italy), was a gift that did not cost him much; it was also for the regime a way to please his own "extremists," unsatisfied because of compromises such as the alliance with the pope, the king, and so on, and unsatisfied, too, because at that time fascist Italy had no real enemy. Such a campaign was also a good way to intimidate the Jewish minority, not only as a potential factor of trouble in foreign politics but also as being quite a dynamic element among the antifascists.

Seen from abroad, this campaign remained quite overlooked.[67] A French official publication remarked that "for the first time, in Italy, an expression, through light, of anti-Semitism, will have been observed in the Fascist papers."[68] It could hardly have been presented as a "burning of the Reichstag": fascism had already had its burning of the Reichstag, against all opposition, with the Bologna assassination attempt on Mussolini of 30 October, 1926; it seems that here the goal was less repression than intimidation. Eventually this goal was not reached, and one can consider this campaign as quite counterproductive in the following ways:

- It made impossible, for a while, anything that might have looked like anti-Semitism.
- The Italian Jews, after the alert of March, saw a victory in the end of this campaign and in the "light" sentences of November. Facts proved that the Zionist militants had been right in courageously refusing to disband,[69] in spite of the strong pressure of the authorities.
- The fascist Jews just made themselves more ridiculous by creating, to "wash away the shame,"[70] a fascist Jewish weekly, *La nostra bandiera*; it lasted until the Racial Laws of 1938.
- The clandestine antifascist groups, especially Giustizia e Libertà, succeeded in attracting new militants among the Italian-Jewish community.[71]
- The antifascists in exile, who had campaigned for Carlo Levi and others, mentioned that he had been freed in their papers[72] and underlined the later end of the anti-Semitic campaign. Wisely, they did not make further use of it; to draw attention upon the Italian Jews more than necessary would not have helped them.
- Special mention has to be made of the Jewish antifascist militants (in exile or not). More than any others, they would have been ashamed to make political use of this campaign. For them, fascism had to be fought for what it was, as the negation of any freedom and not for the extra reason that it was able to be *also* anti-Semitic. They later became conscious of this aspect of fascism. One of the weak points of antifascism abroad was that it was often seen as an "Italian affair"; they helped to "universalize" the image of the fight[73] by recalling that fascism was a threat for all humankind.

One should also pay some attention to the publication in 1935 by the anarchist Camillo Berneri—one of the more famous later victims of the Stalinists in Barcelona—of a book titled, in French, *Le Juif antisémite* (The Anti-Semitic Jew),[74] an interesting book dedicated to the phenomenon of self-hatred, as observed in individuals like Weininger. Why did Berneri, who—as far as I knew—was not a Jew and who had so many other priorities, write such a book? For sure, it was also, for this militant, a way to tell the Jews that to deny their identity would be of no use. In other words, their place was among the anti-fascists.

In such conditions, can one blame the Italian Jews for having been blind? To those who know what followed, even some early statements of Mussolini sound strange (e.g., "Let us hope that the Italian Jews will have the sense not to stir up anti-Semitism in the only country where it has never existed"). It is an obvious fact that the Italian Jews were, from the start, in *liberté surveillée*, though a lot of them did not want to see it. To blame them excessively for this blindness would be to forget that, with such a regime, the entire population was in *liberté surveillée*. At any moment, in its opportunism, fascism might have allowed itself to act against any minority. Concerning the Jews, we even have a written admission of it. In his diary for the year 1937 (before the Racial Laws of 1938), Mussolini's son-in-law Galeazzo Ciano mentions a visit of the fanatical anti-Semite Preziosi in these terms: "December 29th—Conversation with Giovanni Preziosi. He wanted my support in organizing an anti-Semitic campaign, but I refused. I have no love for the Jews, but I see no case for action of this kind in Italy. At least not for the present."[75]

Far beyond fascist Italy, this opportunism also reminds us of an old reality. One does not need to be a fanatical anti-Semite to act against the Jews; there is also a "cold-blooded" anti-Semitism.

NOTES

1. Cf. Meir Michaelis, "The Attitude of the Fascist Regime to the Jews in Italy," *Yad Vashem Studies* 4 (1960): 7–41. The Italian version: "I rapporti italo-tedeschi e il problema degli ebrei in Italia," *Rivista di Studi Politici Internazionali*, no. 2 (April-June 1961): 238–282.

2. *Encyclopedia of the Holocaust*, edited by Israel Gutman, vol. 3 (New York: Macmillan, 1990), p. 1027.

3. Ibid., p. 1217, at "Racism."

4. Armando Borghi, *Mezzo secolo di anarchia* (Naples: Edizione Scientifiche Italiane, 1954), p. 336.

5. Salvatore Gattaglia, *Grande dizionario della lingua italiana*, vol. 2 (Torino: Unione Tipografico-Editrice Torinese, 1962), p. 627.

6. Susan Zuccotti, *The Italians and the Holocaust* (New York: Basic Books, 1987), p. xv.

7. *Encyclopedia of the Holocaust*, p. 1027.

8. Emil Ludwig, *Colloqui con Mussolini* (Milan: A. Mondadori, 1932), p. 73.

9. Benito Mussolini, *Opera omni*, edited by Edoardo and Duilio Susmel (Florence: La Fenice, 1959), vol. 29, p. 190.

10. Meir Michaelis, *Mussolini and the Jews* (Oxford: Oxford University Press, 1978), p. 408.

11. M. van Creveld, "Beyond the Finzi-Contini Garden," *Encounter*, no. 2 (February 1974): 47; Gene Bernardini, "The Origins and Development of Racial Anti-Semitism in Fascist Italy," *Journal of Modern History*, no. 3 (September 1977): 452.

12. Zuccotti, *The Italians and the Holocaust*, p. 25.

13. Leda Rafanelli, *Una donna e Mussolini* (Milan: Rizzoli, 1946), p. 49.

14. Mussolini, "I complici," *Il Popolo d'Italia*, 6 April 1919, p. 1.

15. Mussolini, *Opera omnia*, vol. 15, p. 271.

16. Jacob Dranger, *Nahoum Goldmann* (Paris: Editions Meteore, 1956), p. 226.

17. Cecil Roth, *The History of the Jews of Italy* (Philadelphia: Jewish Publication Society of America, 1946), p. 509.

18. "Religione o nazione?" *Il Popolo di Roma*, 29-30 November 1928, quoted in English in Michaelis, *Mussolini and the Jews*, p. 31.

19. Ludwig, *Colloqui con Mussolini*, p. 73.

20. Ernst Rüdiger Starhemberg, *Between Hitler and Mussolini* (London: Hodder and Stoughton, 1942), p. 93.

21. Michaelis, *Mussolini and the Jews*, p. 30.

22. "Hitler la nuova Germania e l'Europa," *Il Tevere*, 31 January 1933, p. 1.

23. Laura Fermi, *Mussolini* (Chicago and London: University of Chicago Press, 1961), p. 342.

24. Mussolini, *Opera omnia* (Rome: 1979), vol. 42, p. 36.

25. Ibid.

26. Gaetano Salvemini, *Mussolini diplomate* (Paris: B. Grasset, 1932), p. 329.

27. Renzo De Felice, *Storia degli ebrei italiani sotto il fascismo* (Turin: Einardi, 1961), p. 141. n. 1. A characteristic of this book is the length of its footnotes, but the note dedicated to this switch is astonishingly short: "Cf. 'Il popolo d'Italia, luglio agosto 1933" [*sic*]. Concerning its misleading statements about the campaign of 1934, see also Michaelis, *Mussolini and the Jews*, Appendix I, pp. 415–417.

28. Gaetano Salvemini, *Prelude to World War II* (London: V. Gollancz, 1953), p. 478.

29. Mussolini, *Opera omnia*, vol. 26, p. 172.

30. "Intellectuals of Fascism (I)," *Manchester Guardian*, 15 February 1927, p. 6.

31. Alberto Moravia, "Ricordi di censura," *La Rassegna d'Italia*, no. 12 (December 1946): 100.

32. Adrian Lyttelton, *The Seizure of Power* (London: Weidenfeld and Nicolson, 1973), p. 400. Besides *Il Tevere*, another paper, the *Giornale d'Italia*, was also sometimes used to intimidate the recalcitrant journalists. Giovanni Giglio, *The Triumph of Barabbas* (London: V. Gollancz, 1937), p. 288.

33. *Il Tevere*, 30 January 1934, p. 1.

34. Ibid.

35. *Il Tevere*, 7 February 1934, p. 1.

36. *Il Tevere*, 15 February 1934, p. 1.

37. *Il Tevere*, 16 February 1934, p. 1.

38. Ibid.

39. *Il Tevere*, 21 February 1934, p. 1.

40. *Il Tevere*, 22 February 1934, p. 1.

41. *Il Tevere*, 23 February 1934, p. 1.

42. *Il Tevere*, 24 February 1934, p. 1.

43. *Il Tevere*, 12 March 1934, p. 1.

44. Cf. Guido Valabrega, "Per la storia degli ebrei sotto il fascismo: prime notizie su 'Davar' (1934–1938)," *Il movimento di liberazione in Italia*, no. 107 (April-June 1972): 101–120.

45. Ibid.

46. Sion Segre Amar, *Lettera al duce. Dal carcer tetro alla mazzetta* (Florence: La Giuntina, 1994), p. 30, n. 1.

47. Babara Allason, *Memorie di un'antifascista* (Rome: Edizioni U, 1947), p. 160.

48. Alexander Stille, *Benevolence and Betrayal* (New York: Summit Books, 1991), p. 99.

49. Sion Segre Amar, "Sopra alcune inesattezze storiche intorno alle passate vicende degli Ebrei d'Italia," *La Rassegna mensile di Israel*, no. 5 (May 1961): 237.

50. Riccardo Levi, *Ricordi politici di un ingegnere* (Milan: Vangelista, 1981), p. 31.

51. Amar, *Lettera al duce*, pp. 45–46.

52. *La Stampa*, 31 March 1934, p. 1; or *Il Tevere*, 31 March 1934, p. 1 (under the title "Una retata di malfattori ebrei che svolgevano attività antifascista d'intesa coi furousciti di Parigi").

53. Michele Sarfatti, "Gli ebrei negli anni del fascismo," in *Storia d'Italia, Annali*, edited by Corrado Vivanti (Turin: Einaudi, 1997), vol. 11, p. 1659.

54. Luigi Salvatorelli e Giovanni Mira, *Storia del fascismo* (Rome: Edizioni novissima, 1952), p. 51.

55. Mussolini, *Opera omnia*, vol. 26, p. 32.

56. *Il Tevere*, 31 March 1934, p. 1.

57. Ibid.

58. Sion Segre Amar, "Sui 'fatti' di Torino del 1934 Sion Segre Amar ci ha scritto . . . ," in *Gli ebrei in Italia durante il fascismo*, edited by Guido Valabrega (Milan: Centro di Documentazione ebraica contemporanea, 1962), vol. 2, p. 132.

59. Aldo Garosci, *Vita di Carlo Rosselli* (Florence: Edizioni U, 1945), pp. 36–37.

60. Natalia Ginzburg, *Lessico famigliare* (Turin: Einaudi, 1963), p. 105.

61. Togo (pseudo. of René Odin), 10 November 1934, quoted in Amar, *Lettera al duce*, p. 89. The Jewish community in Turin was at that time about 4,000 members. Primo Levi, "Preface," *Ebrei a Torino* (Turin: 1984), p. 13.

62. "Quelli che stigmatizzano," *Il Tevere*, 13 July 1934, p. 1.

63. Starhemberg, *Between Hitler and Mussolini*, p. 170.

64. Mussolini, *Opera omnia*, vol. 26, p. 319.

65. Cf. for the text of the sentence "Tribunale Speciale per la Difesa dello Stato," *Decisioni emesse nel 1934* (Rome: Ministero della difesa, Stato maggiore dell'esercito, Ufficio Storico, 1989), p. 222–228.

66. Sergio I. Minerbi, *L'Italie et la Palestine 1914–1920* (Paris: Presses Universitaires de France, 1970), p. 29.

67. Garosci, *Vita di Carlo Rosselli*, p. 276.

68. *Bulletin périodique de la presse italienne*, no. 299 (10 April 1934): 20.

69. Michaelis, *Mussolini and the Jews*, p. 61.

70. Guido Valabrega, "Prime notizie su 'La nostra Bandiera' (1934–1938)," in *Gli ebrei in Italia durante il fascismo*, vol. 1 , p. 23.

71. Leo Levi, "Antifascismo e Sionismo: convergenze e contrasti (note e ricordi sui 'fermi' e suit fermenti torinesi del 1934)," in *Gli ebrei in Italia durante il fascismo*, vol. 1, p. 62.

72. "Une machination de l'Ovra qui s'effondre. Le peintre C. Levi relâché," *Giustizia e Libertà*, no. 1 (18 May 1934): 4.

73. Piero Treves, "Antifascisti ebrei od antifascismo ebraico?" *La rassegna mensile di Israel*, no. 1–6 (January-June 1981): 147.

74. Camillo Berneri, *Le Juif antisémite* (Paris: Editions "Vita," 1935). Italian edition, with a presentation by Alberto Cavaglion, *L'ebreo antisemita* (Rome: 1984).

75. Galeazzo Ciano, *Hidden Diary 1937–1938* (New York: Dutton, 1953), p. 52.

24

Why Was Italy So Impervious to Anti-Semitism (to 1938)?

Frederick M. Schweitzer

Part of the fascination about Italy and the Holocaust is the seeming paradox that Italy was the birthplace of fascism, the common denominator of which in its European manifestations was anti-Semitism, but that Mussolini's brand of fascism (down to 1938) was the exception to fascism's anti-Semitic rule. Despite Mussolini's embrace of Hitler and the Italian collapse and German occupation in 1943, 80% of Italian Jewry survived. Part of the story, also, is Italian sabotage of German genocidal aims and actions in the Italian-occupied areas of Europe (southeast France and in the Balkans) and North Africa. Only Denmark and, possibly, Bulgaria offer similar examples of resistance and survival. There is nothing comparable for Italy to the Nuremberg or Tokyo tribunals for war crimes and crimes against humanity. Part of the paradox is the continuing medieval posture of the popes down to the Second Vatican Council, notwithstanding Pius XI's 1938 cri de coeur that "spiritually we are all Semites"; therefore, Christians cannot be anti-Semites—it is "inadmissible."

Italy is probably the country most often invaded and fought over in world history. Jewish history in that crossroads peninsula spans over twenty centuries and six civilizations. Julius Caesar is reported to have said, "We are sorrowed to hear that decrees have been issued against our friends the Jews, which make it impossible for them to live according to their ancestral customs." Mussolini assured them at the time of the Concordat in 1929, "The Jews have been in Rome ever since the time of the Kings [presumably 2,500 years]. . . . They will stay here undisturbed."[1]

Italian Jewry is composed of several ethnic "layers." The oldest goes back to the second century B.C.E., Pompey's depredations in the next century, and Titus' captives and slaves from the suppression of the Jewish revolt a century later. In the Middle Ages merchant families went to Italy from far and wide on the Mediterranean shores. In the fourteenth century and after, Jews fled from Germany and southern France. Next came Spanish and Portuguese Jews, expelled, and then the Marranos, who fled after 1492. In the twentieth century came a stream of refugees from the Balkans, Nazi Germany, and North Africa. This has given rise to several varieties of Judaism, "Old Italian" or "Roman"; Ashkenazi or "German"; "Castilian"; "Catalan-Aragonese"; and "Levantine." Italian-Jewish communities, wrote Leone Modena in the seventeenth century, "are more different in their prayers than in anything else." In Cecil Roth's view, "Italian orthodoxy was at no time so rigid as it was north of the Alps."[2] For the most part, there was no conflict between the champions of the Jewish Enlightenment (Haskalah) and orthodoxy in the eighteenth century; in the nineteenth, since there was only slight development of the Reform movement, there was practically no conflict with Orthodox Judaism. In contrast to other Jewries in Europe, Italian Jews had participated in, and shared much of, the Italian secular culture (since the Renaissance). Thus since Italian culture was an integral part of their lives—a kind of common denominator—and because there were several gradations of religiosity that made them less uniform and standardized, Jewish communities had less to quarrel about and were more susceptible to pluralism. Therefore, in the period of emancipation, Italian Jews had less distance to cover on the road of acculturation and modernization.[3]

The modern story begins with the Italian Renaissance, when a lay, urban, and secular culture emerged, a trend that was confirmed by the experience of the Enlightenment and by the impact of the French Revolution and the Napoleonic conquest. In the interval between Renaissance and Enlightenment, the Counter-Reformation hit Italian Jewry severely. The ghetto regimen—with its gates and guards and curfews—came later than elsewhere to Italy and extended into the age of the democratic revolutions when Corregio was ghettoized in 1779, and it lingered on longer in Italy, in papal Rome to 1870. "Despite its many repressive measures [however], the Church in Italy never succeeded in implanting hatred of Jews amongst the Italian population."[4]

Poverty and degradation notwithstanding, education and culture flourished at a high level in the ghettos and were, or would become, a bridge to the world outside. It was, as Primo Levi said, that "special gift that history has linked to the Jews: literacy, culture, religious and lay, felt as a duty, a right, a necessity, and a joy of life."[5] Jews remained or became open to the culture outside the ghetto. The ghetto period actually brought some improvements in the fortunes of Italian Jewry; ghettoization was better than expulsions. Massacres and pogroms declined as did missionizing and forced baptisms, and accusations of ritual murder virtually ceased.[6]

Another bridge: Jews generally knew and spoke the same Italian as their neighbors, using the particular dialect of the province where they lived; among themselves they spoke neither Yiddish nor Ladino (which died out by the eighteenth century) but "Judaeo-Italian," which was mostly Italian but peppered with Hebrew words. A characteristic comment in explaining the absence of anti-Semitism has been that Italians, Jews and non-Jews, looked alike and had similar names—they also spoke alike, hence the frequent observation that Italian Jews were "more Italian than Jewish" or, as Weizmann remarked, that they were virtually "indistinguishable from their fellow citizens, except that they went to synagogue instead of to Mass."[7]

Almost from its start in 1789, the French Revolution spread spontaneously in Italy, well before it came on the shoulders of French troops. From the start, also, churchmen denounced the revolution as a Jewish plot against the church. The French revolutionists and Napoleonic conquests brought down the ghetto regime and wrought emancipation everywhere in Italy. Jews certainly joined enthusiastically with the French and with revolutionary crowds to end the old regime. "In no other country," writes Raphael Mahler, "did Jewish emancipation so *literally* mean destruction of the ghetto walls or arouse such spontaneous demonstrations of sympathy by Gentiles, as in Italy." For Jews, Napoleon's rule in Italy was, in a double sense, as historians have noted, a "false dawn."[8] Nevertheless, it was dawn.

Down to 1848, the Jewish condition in Italy was as bad as anywhere. In 1815 the old rulers, the old institutions, laws, prejudices, and discriminations returned. Jews committed themselves body and soul to the overthrow of the reactionary regimes, the expulsion of the Austrians, and the creation of a united Italy. They wrote, published, and distributed fiery patriotic literature and pamphlets, for they were a force in the printing business—one of the trades that they had pioneered in the Renaissance.[9] They subscribed their funds and joined revolutionary societies like the Carbonari and participated in a series of abortive risings in 1820, 1822, 1828, and so on. For this they were arrested, imprisoned, bankrupted, exiled, and killed, whether in battle or executed. Undaunted by repeated failures, in 1831 they took part in upheavals all over central and northern Italy. Although the revolutionary surge was initially successful in establishing liberal regimes that dismantled ghettos and extended civil equality to all non-Jews, Austrian armies quickly restored the status quo ante and summoned the hanging judges and the executioners. Many non-Jews entered the struggle of those years, the 1820s to the 1840s, with arguments for Jewish emancipation and scathing attacks on age-old degradation. Possibly the most eloquent and influential of them all was "On the Civil Emancipation of the Jews" (1847) by Massimo d'Azeglio. The debate, one-sidedly favoring emancipation, was perhaps best characterized by one of the contributors, G. B. Giorgini, when he inveighed against the subjection of the Jews as "a blot, a shame, an anachronism, in the constitution of a civilized people."[10]

In 1849 a Republic of Rome was proclaimed in which Mazzini was prominent. Several Jews were associated with him then and throughout his life. They served on the Republic's City Council, the National Assembly (one of whom, Giuseppe Revere, was the editor of Mazzini's paper *Italia del Popolo*), and the Defense Committee, and many were energetically active in the civic guard (a proposal to segregate them in separate companies having been turned aside). At Venice Daniele Manin, who was partly Jewish, proclaimed the Republic. Alas, French troops suppressed the Republic of Rome, and Austrian troops the Republic of Venice. A vindictive Pope Pius IX returned from exile and soon reverted to medieval and Counter-Reformation form by reinstituting a battery of familiar anti-Jewish laws. For some Jews these events meant, "Next year in Jerusalem but this year in jail!"

In the 1848–1849 revolutions, Jewish emancipation had been enacted almost everywhere in Italy; in the Counter-Revolution it was undone everywhere except in Piedmont-Sardinia. Even though that kingdom suffered a series of crushing defeats by the Austrian army, and the king had abdicated, the edict of emancipation stood, the Parliament declaring, "Religious differences do not affect the enjoyment of civil and political rights on the part of citizens who do not profess the Catholic faith, or their admission to civil and military office."[11] When Piedmont-Sardinia succeeded in uniting Italy 1858–1871, emancipation was extended to the entire peninsula, promulgated conquest by conquest as Sicily and Naples were followed by Venice and eventually Rome. All the leaders of the Risorgimento, apparently without exception, were well disposed toward the Jews, indeed philo-Semitic, which was certainly true of Mazzini, Garibaldi, and the mastermind of unification, Cavour, whose private secretary Isacco Artom was the first Jew to attain prominence in a public career and whose family was later ennobled.

In the period after 1850, full of vicissitudes, Jews were as active and committed as in the earlier years. They fought in every battle of the Risorgimento. They were engaged in underground activities, they marched with Garibaldi and the Thousand, Jewish volunteers from abroad like Charles Alexander Scott joined up, and the scroll of Jewish martyrs to the national cause grew longer until Rome fell in 1870. "The liberation of Italy and of Italian Jewry were completed by the same stroke."[12] In all of this, again in sharp contrast to Germany, Jewish contributions were duly noted and appreciated by the nation.

The Risorgimento was trenchantly liberal, secularist, and anticlerical. In Piedmont Cavour had ended the ecclesiastical privilege of benefit of clergy (whereby churchmen were not subject to the public law and courts), dissolved monasteries, and confiscated church lands. As Italy was united, these laws were extended to more and more of the country, provoking much uproar and many excommunications. Mazzini and Garibaldi were strenuous anticlericals, Garibaldi habitually referring to priests as "wolves." Pius IX's egregious *Syllabus of Errors* of 1864 propounded eighty theses or propositions that attacked nationalism, socialism, communism, and Freemasonry; denounced secular education, tolerance, and freedom of conscience; and condemned "progress, liberalism, and modern civilization." This provoked much indignation in the liberal ruling circles of the new Italy and underlay the law of 1866, by which almost all religious orders and congregations were dissolved, their property confiscated, and the monks pensioned off; cathedral chapters and bishops forfeited 90% of their capital property, and the priesthood became salaried officials of the state; seminaries were subject to state inspection and seminarians to military service. The state recognized only civil marriages, and in the public elementary schools it allowed religious instruction for the children only if parents asked for it. Clearly, to the makers of modern Italy the church was the enemy, especially once the Austrians were extruded (1866).

When the walls of papal Rome were breached on 20 September 1870 (thereafter celebrated as a national holiday) and the pope rendered himself "a prisoner in the Vatican," Pius IX refused to recognize the new state of united Italy, boycotted it as completely as possible, and forbade the faithful to vote in elections or participate in politics at all. The government's rejoinder was to abolish compulsory tithes and take over church charities, thus excluding the church from many of its traditional roles and functions. The Quirinal, the royal palace in Rome, lay under interdict. The only church that King Victor Emmanuel III built, it was said, was the new synagogue in Rome in 1904.

Unification having been attained under liberal auspices against the church, a cold war persisted between state and church for sixty years. Jews, however, were enthusiastic participants in the Risorgimento and strongly committed to the new Italy from the start. As one of them, Eugenio Artom, judged from the vantage point of the 1940s, Italy was unique among the European states in that it "effected its unification fighting against its own religion and . . . managed to achieve victory without any religious oppression."[13] If one were to sum up the Italian situation, it would be that Jews were closely associated with the cause of Italian liberation since the time of Napoleon and with that of national unification since Cavour. Anti-Semitism was associated with the enemy, with papal Rome, with persecutors and reactionary rulers everywhere who had opposed unification. The heroes of the Risorgimento and founders of modern Italy—again in sharp contrast with their counterparts in Germany—were liberal, secular, philo-Semitic. These are crucial considerations for the thesis of this chapter.

Not all was sweetness and light for the liberal, national, emancipatory cause, however. In the middle decades of the century Rome was regarded by the clerical Right as a Jewish conspiratorial center utilizing the unification movement as a front, employing Mazzini and his followers as puppets in the hands of "unknown superiors"; in Italy, as in France, there was full development of a Freemasonry that was rigorously devoted to republicanism and anticlericalism; its energetic part in the national movement of unification and campaign for the extinction of papal temporal power caused it to be attacked as Judaeo-Masonic conspiracy and devil worship. In fact, many Italian statesmen—Depretis, Crispi, and even kings—were Freemasons, and practically none were devout Catholics. Some Jews were prominent Masons. A famous one was Ernesto Nathan, a Freemason grand master and the mayor of Rome 1907–1913. To ultra-Catholics such developments were proof of the wide-ranging conspiracy.

In stark contrast to Austria, France, and Germany, there was no political anti-Semitism in Italy in the decades before 1914, since the clericals, under papal injunction, refrained from organizing themselves as a political party. Racism, such as that of Gobineau (who was not anti-Semitic), had to be imported. Some anti-Semitism spilled over into Italy from France in the 1880s and 1890s, for example, that of the Abbé E. A. Chabauty, which was the usual religious kind but did no more than reinforce the native Catholic variety; it had no influence on national politics. Pope Leo XIII (1878–1903) was not unsusceptible to anti-Semitism, as is suggested by his blessings upon Karl Lueger, the notorious anti-Semitic mayor of Vienna; the pope also supported the equally notorious Edouard Drumont and the anti-Dreyfusards in France, and he explained that the Jews were anarchists, Freemasons, and enemies of the Church. Leo fiercely attacked the conspiratorial

Masons but seems to have refrained from directly attacking the Jews, although he allowed other elements of the church to do so. The most extreme example was the Jesuits associated with *La Civiltà Cattolica*, especially R. Ballerini, S.J., and F. S. Rondina, S.J., in the 1880s and 1890s; they equated Freemasonry and Jews with all the calamities endured over 1,800 years, particularly the French Revolution and any and all contemporary wrongs and disturbances. Jewry, they said, was an "octopus" with its tentacles girdling the globe; they printed numerous ritual murder stories and scandalous accounts of corruption, violence, and chaos that blamed the conspiratorial Jews. All that is needed is translation into German for it to read like Hitler's vituperations or Julius Streicher's *Der Stürmer*. However, Italian Catholics were not much influenced by *La Civiltà Cattolica*'s anti-Semitic diatribes.[14]

In united Italy—unlike united Germany—there was no demand for Jews to abandon their identity and heritage in order to become fully accepted as Italian citizens. They could choose to assimilate to the point of disappearance or to preserve their Jewishness to the nth degree but enter social, political, and cultural life by either of these paths or some compromise route between them. Within the Jewish communities—variegated as they were—there were no linguistic or denominational barriers. Down to the period of World War I, as is often said, Jewish religious allegiance was declining. Yet most Italian Jews observed the great festivals and had their sons circumcised, bar mitzvahed, and so on; keeping kosher declined, but mixed marriages were few, and social life was confined to family and coreligionists. Jews experienced great social mobility, thanks to entry into the civil service, professoriate, and the professions—in this embourgeoisification they paralleled the ascent of much of the Gentile middle class. Jews moved to the large cities, and their birthrate declined. Inevitably, drawn into closer and more intimate contact with the host culture, they tended to weaken in attachment to their mores and traditions. Witness the erection at the turn of the century of those monumental "synagogue-cathedrals" in Turin, Florence, Milan, Rome, and Trieste. They epitomize a sense of Jewish belonging, of deep-rootedness, but also, because they were so little used—religious observance being more a matter for home—they testified more to the past than constituted a portal to the future.

As for anti-Semitism, there was none beyond the traditional medieval and Counter-Reformation kind of the church, which could and did target the Jew and Judaism as the emblems of modernity, liberalism, capitalism, socialism, and indeed, most of the things singled out in the *Syllabus of Errors*. But the first three of these elements were exactly what the Risorgimento represented, and anti-Semitism could hardly serve—so different from Germany—to mobilize the masses politically. Socialists did sometimes equate the Jews with Shylockian capitalism, just as some nationalists denied that Jews could be truly of Italian nationality, but in Italy's liberal environment and nonracist culture they were confined to the fringes. Only Zionism aroused criticism of a double loyalty, but very few Italian Jews were susceptible to Zionism's clarion call.

The great majority of Italian Jews rallied to the patriotic call of World War I. They felt that the war gave them the opportunity to express their gratitude to Italy and the monarchy for emancipation and equality. "Sacrifice in war became the ethical sanction of the national integration that had occurred, a sense of belonging now sealed with spilled blood."[15] Jews served quite out of proportion to their numbers and suffered high casualties; over 1,000 received medals for bravery. No less than Mussolini said in 1921, "I recognize that the sacrifice of Jewish blood during the War has been great, vast, and generous."[16] Many Jews saw it as the fourth war of Italian unification and independence. *Terre irredenta* (the unredeemed lands) of Trent, Trieste, and Fiume (acquired in the aftermath of D'Annunzio's fascist filibustering, it had to be renounced in 1946), where notable Jewish communities had long carried an Italian identity, were at long last redeemed, and the Risorgimento could be said to be complete.

Although it was among the victors of World War I, Italy emerged with a sense of grievance—symbolized by the abrupt departure of its foreign minister Orlando from the Paris peace conference—and suffered all the consequences of a war effort that it could not afford and the postwar chaos and dislocations. Frustration with the peace settlement, unemployment, inflation, and worker and peasant restiveness punctuated by radical socialist oratory took their toll. Such was the breeding ground of Mussolini's Fascist Party, founded in March 1919 and dedicated to everything for everybody: "We are reactionaries and revolutionaries, aristocrats and democrats, conservatives and democrats." In the 1919 election, Mussolini and his new party were routed, and the socialists came in as the largest single party in Parliament. The next two years—"the Red Biennium"—were turbulent: strikes, worker occupation of factories, peasant violence, and Mussolini's *squadristi* (blackshirt squads) implementing a reign of terror of murders, beatings, and torture. Mussolini had abandoned his erstwhile socialism and turned himself into the agent of the reactionaries, aristocrats, and conservatives and thus gained the support of the army, big business, landowners, and police. The comic opera sequel of "the march on Rome" brought Mussolini to the capital by train; there was no "seizure of power," for the king and prime minister ushered il Duce and the new praetorians to the seats of power in order to save the country from the Left that they feared so much. The dictatorship began to take shape in the next two years.[17]

In 1924 the Pro Cultura group founded in Florence in 1907 (one of several movements of Jewish religious and cultural revival) convened in Leghorn for its memorable fourth Youth Conference. The Matteotti murder intensified the crosscurrents blowing between the two poles of the group, Mussolini and Balfour. Matteotti was a moderate socialist deputy who gave a speech revealing the corruption and thuggery of fascist elections, whose murder (on Mussolini's orders, it eventually emerged) provoked an unexpectedly strong reaction in Italy; il Duce's response was to implement totalitarianism (of which he was the inventor) over the next year or two. No doubt with the news of Matteotti ringing in their ears, the group listened to Nello Roselli (who, with his brother Carlo, were to be "the most famous antifascist martyr[s]"[18]). He probably spoke for most Italian Jews, certainly the assimilated, educated, and well-to-do; for him Judaism was peripheral, he did not observe the Sabbath, he did not know Hebrew, and he was indifferent to tradition; his Jewishness inspired a vague responsibility for the Jewish community, and for him it was "precisely their Judaism that compelled Italian Jews to be more

Italian than the Italians themselves."[19] Rosselli was impelled to the path of antifascism by his Jewishness, inspired, he affirmed, by Judaism as the religion of freedom. Some exulted in the intensely nationalist fascist regime. Some, reacting to assimilation and denationalization, demanded a return to the traditional Judaism of Torah-true Jews and an end to "the degeneration of assimilation." Others, like Enzo Sereni, espoused Zionism and a national home.[20] Most Italian Jews seem to have felt themselves tugged in opposite directions, the weaker impulse toward Jewishness, the stronger toward *italianità* (Italianness), but the two essences could not be separated.

Jews reacted to Mussolini and fascism as did other Italians. Fascism was a Europe-wide phenomenon. It was, as G.D.H. Cole put it, "the ally of capitalism; but it was not the mere lackey of capitalist interests." It stemmed from the dislocations of World War I, the inflation, and the depression. Yet it was "not fundamentally an economic movement" but was characterized rather by superheated nationalism (*Nazionalfascismo*), militarism, and imperialism. It had its roots in the counterrevolution that went back to 1789, if not earlier. Renzo De Felice is correct in dubbing fascism "a preventive counter-revolution," a revolution from the Right directed against the so-called Bolshevik threat—actually it was directed as much against the liberal democrats and moderate socialists, who were themselves anticommunist. It drew on the middle, above all, on the lower middle, and eventually on the upper-middle classes. It enlisted wholesale war veterans and the young. Many fascists had been militant extremists, whether of Left or Right, in earlier incarnations. To Luigi Salvatorelli, as to John Weiss, it was never a "revolution" but simply a "revolt," a "counterrevolution."[21] A large proportion of Italian Jews, given that they were intensely patriotic and largely middle-class, was very susceptible to fascism's appeal. Like everyone else, Jews suffered the consequences of fascist totalitarianism, by which, as Mussolini said, the state is exalted as the absolute before which all else is relative.

As for Mussolini's attitude toward Jews, though in this he was from start to finish inconsistent and opportunist as in everything else, his words and deeds were, on the whole, reassuring and encouraging, especially in contrast to almost any leader whom one could care to name. An outer-directed man, he had no beliefs except power and would shift attitudes and stances as expediency dictated in Jewish questions as in all others. Mussolini was suspicious of "international Jewry," the bankers and the Bolsheviks, and also the Zionists. On the Russian Revolution he spoke with the accents of "The Protocols of the Learned Elders of Zion," asserting in 1919 that it was the work of "the Jewish bankers in London and New York [who are] bound by racial roots to the Jews in Moscow and Budapest."[22] In the same vein in 1937 he spoke of "the acid of Jewish corrosion" as the source of social decomposition in the United States and other countries, in contrast to the Italian, German, Russian, and Japanese peoples, who would, therefore, play decisive roles in the future.[23] Il Duce never ceased to be held in thrall by fears of the "Jewish international" and sought to make contact with "elders" and all-powerful "heads" of world Jewry. Probably the most accurate expression of his attitude was his remark, "I have no love for the Jews, but they have great influence everywhere. It is better to leave them alone."[24]

Zionism drew his ire because he perceived it as a British vehicle imperiling his Mediterranean ambitions and raising the bogey of the "dual loyalty" of Italian Jews. He supported the anti-British Revisionist Zionists of Jabotinsky, and he confided to the most famous Zionists of the day, Weizmann and Goldmann, "I am a Zionist."[25] All the while he delivered salvos calling Hitler "an imbecile, cad, and frightful babbler," and he attacked the racial ideology as a "delirium," since "[r]ace . . . is a feeling not a reality. . . . Nothing will ever make me believe that biologically pure races can be shown to exist today [1932]."[26] As though proof of his assertions, that same year he appointed Guido Jung as finance minister. To il Duce, the Führer's racism was "vulgar nonsense," and "Antisemitism is unworthy of a European nation . . . stupid and barbarous." Repeatedly, he proclaimed, "The Jewish problem does not exist in Italy."

Many German Jews (14,000 to 15,000) found welcome refuge in Italy. Toward Jews in the Italian colonies, Libya and Rhodes, policy was notably benevolent. When the Jews of Salonika came under Hellenizing pressure by the Greek government, Mussolini encouraged them to apply for Italian nationality. Jews from East-Central Europe were encouraged with grants-in-aid to study at Italian universities, and Mussolini endowed a professorship of Italian language and literature at the Hebrew University of Jerusalem. A striking instance of Mussolini's seeming goodwill was his self-designated role as mediator in 1934 between Hitler's government and the Jews of the Saarland, when its fifteen-year occupation ended, and the plebiscite restored it to Germany; the agreement permitted the Saarland Jews to exit with their possessions—"I shall compel Germany to allow the Jews of the Saar to depart with their money," il Duce assured Goldmann.[27] It would seem to have been richly deserved when he was selected a few months earlier by a group of editors of American Jewish magazines and newspapers as one of twelve Christians who are "the most outstanding in their opposition to anti-Semitism."[28]

There were bumps along the way, to be sure. In 1923 the Giovanni Gentile law made religious education in the public schools mandatory and thus exposed Jewish pupils to proselytizing. The atheist Duce lassoed church support by allowing crucifixes to adorn schoolrooms, appointing chaplains to party militias, abolishing Freemasonry, exempting clergy and seminarians from military service, increasing clerical salaries, and much else of the same tenor that reversed the state's anticlerical policies and practices since 1861. This trend climaxed in 1929, when the Concordat and Lateran Treaty were concluded with Pius XI, who called Mussolini "the man sent to us by Providence." The church finally recognized the existence of the Italian state and its acquisition of Rome and accepted the thirteen-acre Vatican in full sovereignty. In return, Catholicism was established as the state religion with government protection, church property was exempted from taxation, the Vatican invested heavily in Italian government bonds, mandatory religious education was extended to secondary education (and although non-Catholics could withdraw their children from the hour-a-day instruction, it was awkward and embarrassing to do so), Protestant evangelization was sharply reined in, and 11 February, commemorating the Concordat, replaced 20 September, when Rome had fallen in 1870, as a national holiday. Thereafter, Pius XI and *La Civiltà Cattolica* were polite and benevolent toward il Duce, and "no government in modern Italy had received so much ecclesiastical approbation."[29] These enactments were, however, "the only legal setback to Jewish parity in modern Italy" until 1938.[30]

The situation was rectified and Jewish suspicions mollified in 1930, when a law created for the first time a national organization, the Union of Italian-Jewish Communities, by which membership in the Jewish community was demanded of everyone of Jewish birth, local communities were required to join the Union and pay supporting contributions, the mode of election of the Union's leaders was spelled out, the role of the rabbis was defined, and the Union was declared to be under the "supervision" and the "protection" of the state. Thus, the grand rabbi of Rome became the grand rabbi of Italy.[31] Many of these provisions had been long sought by Jewish leaders, and the settlement was regarded as "a cordial and comprehensive resolution."[32] Nevertheless, the Jewish community, centralized as never before, fell more fully under the shadow of Mussolini's totalitarian control.

There had been five Jews among Mussolini's lieutenants in founding the Fascist Party in 1919; 230 (like the others, they all received certificates) joined him in the "march on Rome" in October 1922, and there were about 5,000 Jews in the party out of a population of about 45,000 in the country. They were disproportionately represented in the Fascist Party, as they were to be among the underground and Resistance in World War II. In 1930 Jews were very prominent as scholars, scientists and mathematicians, and professors—although about one-tenth of 1% of the population, they accounted for 8% of the university professors; they were also exceptionally prominent in politics and public life, most extraordinarily so in the last holy of holies to which Jews could be admitted, the army and navy officer corps. One of them was General Emanuele Pugliese, the most highly decorated officer of World War I, who commanded at Rome in 1922 and would have put down Mussolini's "march" had the king signed the order to do so. No Jews reached the highest positions of power in the government or the party, however, and none were admitted to the new Italian Academy; the 26 Jewish senators of 1923 had shrunk to 6 by 1938 (of about 350.)

From the start Mussolini and the fascist government persecuted national minorities, for the ideology proclaimed that there were to be no minorities, only Italians. These victims included the 200,000 Germans in Alta Adige/Südtirol, the half million Slavs in Venezia Giulia (Gorizia, Pola, Trieste, Fiume, Zara), and French speakers in the Val d'Aosta who were forcibly Italianized. Waldensians, Pentecostalists, the Salvation Army, and other groups were also subject to persecution.[33] To be sure, Italians, even the most brutal of them, could not have dreamed up Dachau, much less Auschwitz or Treblinka. Nevertheless, if there were no concentration camps, there were internment and detention camps; there were innumerable midnight knocks on the door by *squadristi*, beatings, tortures, and murders; there was a ubiquitous army of spies and informers.[34] So over the years there were plenty of signs, especially in 1936–1938, but Jews ignored them with the assurance that it could not happen there.

How to understand Mussolini's "Manifesto on Race" of July 1938 and all that followed from it?[35] While Mussolini's "kosher fascism" was an exception to the anti-Semitic rule, fascism "is normally and perhaps necessarily racist."[36] Mussolini often invoked the "Jewish international" and explained the decadence of the democracies—the "demoplutocracies"—as caused by the Jews. He had long flirted with the idea of the Aryan race and feared that "Levantine" qualities (a disposition for trade) came into Italy with the slaves brought by the Roman conquerors of Judaea. The Duce wanted a heroic, warlike national character and ruminated that it was essential to eradicate the nonheroic. In Ethiopia his racialist ideology and policies took form with the practice of apartheid and assertions of Aryan Italian superiority; that racialism propelled Mussolini's anti-Semitism. Still, as late as February 1938, he could say that there was no "specific Italian Jewish problem."[37] Apart from his moronic Aryan proclivities, his anti-Semitic offensive was a cynical tactic for cultivating his relationship with Germany and also with the Arabs. Hitler had cast his baleful shadow over Italy since 1933. With the wars in Ethiopia and Spain, a geopolitical shift occurred in the Mediterranean, and the African empire generated racist doctrines and stimulated Mussolini's latent desire to create the "new Italian"—this is the context in which the persecution of the Jews began in 1938 and opened the way to genocide at the hands of the Germans and some Italians (like Giovanni Preziosi) in 1943–1945.[38]

A question that arises is, Was the fascist dictatorship an aberration—what Salvatorelli called a "disease" and the "anti-Risorgimento" and what some designate the "parenthesis" thesis, that the fascist period was only a parenthesis in Italian history? Or was it the product of the Risorgimento, what is sometimes called the "revelation" theory, that everything in Italian history since Cavour led on to fascist totalitarianism?[39] Mussolini's anti-Jewish decrees were signed by an acquiescent king, approved unanimously by an acquiescent Chamber of Deputies, and accepted by the Vatican with the exception of the ban on intermarriage and without much resistance or reaction in the country at large.

In conclusion, I offer the following factors as explaining why there was no Holocaust in Italy. One set of explanations flows from the long-term weakness of anti-Semitism there. It is often said that the Jews of Italy were so few that they did not become a target. The fact of small numbers guarantees nothing, however, since anti-Semitism can flourish even when there are no Jews. The number of Jews went up in the decades before World War I, but their percentage of the population went down. More significantly, there was not much of a Jewish proletariat in Italy, for in contrast to Germany, Britain, the United States, and some other countries, in the late nineteenth and early twentieth centuries there was no large influx of Eastern European Jews, *Ostjuden*, many impoverished, many medieval in garb and appearance, and thus very noticeable to the host society as strangers and economic competitors. The argument that Italian Jews were so assimilated as to be disappearing is only partially valid, in the sense that Jews looked like, talked like, and behaved like Italians. But there is no necessary correlation between assimilation and tolerance; Germany affords a striking example of the opposite, the delusion that German Jews could be accepted as more German than the Germans themselves. Hitler himself pronounced that assimilated Jews are the "most dangerous," because they are disguised and concealed from view.

Nor is the argument convincing, famously advanced by Antonio Gramsci, of the "parallel nationalization" of the Italian Jews and Gentiles simultaneously during the Risorgimento, since the peasant masses and Catholic community were left out of that process, in fact, were not "nationalized" until the era of World War I, and thus the absence of mass/national anti-Semitic parties and movements cannot be explained by such categories.

The idea has also been advanced that Jews were not prominent in Italian economic life—so, in contrast to the German situation, anti-Semitism was denied an economic base. But, rather obviously, the economic profile of Italian Jewry was comparable to that of Germany; they were quite visible as bankers and entrepreneurs in railway building, rural electrification, development of waterways, textiles, building construction, insurance, and publishing, and a number of famous banks were Jewish-owned; in the professions also, as has been frequently remarked, as academics, civil servants, lawyers, and journalists and as newspaper owners, editors, and journalists, they were prominent indeed. While there were poor Jews, especially in Rome, the economic importance and prominence of Italian Jews cannot be doubted. Italian industrialization, coming only at the turn of the century, does constitute an economic factor in explaining Italy's anemic anti-Semitism; no howl of anguish went up from a lower middle class that was squeezed out and falling into the proletariat, in sharp contrast to the bawling *Mittelstand* (middle-class) in Austria and Germany. But such a lack of displacement should not be exaggerated, since there existed plenty of un- and underemployed teachers, lawyers, and doctors, but, unlike France or Germany, they did not turn into anti-Semitic agitators—agitators but not anti-Semitic. One should note, also, that imperialism—a potent source or reinforcement of racism—came late to Italy and was, moreover, when it came in the 1890s, a colossal failure—on the other hand, imperialism does stoke up racism and anti-Semitism, as illustrated by Mussolini's plunge into Ethiopia.

As a more fundamental point, the Italian ethnic stock was a homogeneous blend, since it had assimilated the last of its many invaders; cultural-ethnic minorities were few and minuscule, and there was no—or very little—paranoiac nationalism of the German *zerissenheit* (divisive) kind. Italians had no identity crisis; they swallowed the myth (one cannot help but smile) that they were a single ancient race whose genealogy went back to Romulus and Aeneas, that they were the direct descendants of the Romans of old, "the seed of Aeneas." There never was an Ostrogothic or Lombard myth comparable to that of the Franks in France or "our fathers the ancient Germans." "Modern Italy," wrote Leon Poliakov, "has not experienced anything like the Germanic blood cult or the imaginary racial conflicts which mark so profoundly the history of other western nations."[40] Thus, a decisive factor is that Italian nationalism had a cultural and historical basis and was quite devoid of racial foundations; it was a matter not of the Italian or Roman race but the idea of Rome, whether of the Caesars or of the popes. Perhaps that is why Italians, as is often remarked, are so genial and friendly. Italian nationalism may also have been softened by the heritage of classical humanism from the

Renaissance and the international outlook of the Catholic Church. Moreover, Jews were associated positively with the heroic age of unification and were the beneficiaries of its gift of emancipation; unlike Germany, where it dragged on for most of the century and the "love affair" was never requited, emancipation in Italy was debated publicly for a mere twenty or so years, and the gift was complete, for, once enacted, Jewish equality was never again questioned. It is true that there was an implicit obligation attached to emancipation, namely, assimilation and disappearance, but there was no attempt to collect on that promissory note, though indeed Italian Jews were flying down the primrose path of assimilation as fast as they could go. So while there were some anti-Semitic flutters from nationalists who suspected Jews of having a double loyalty and, among anarchists and socialists, it was largely the church that pumped the anti-Semitic bellows.

Religious/clerical anti-Semitism was without significant political influence, however, because churchmen desisted from organizing a political party to contend for power in the state, which they did not recognize; they were content, instead, to fall back upon journalistic means (like *La Civiltà Cattolica* and another forty or so newspapers and magazines) as their anti-Semitic vehicle. Only after 1904 (when the ban outlawing the Socialist Party ended, and a general strike induced the pope tacitly to withdraw the ban on political activity) was the Catholic *Popolari* Party organized by Luigi Sturzo, who was not an anti-Semitic firebrand. Thus, no party like the German Center or Austrian Christian Social Party emerged in Italy, where political anti-Semitism remained notably absent from the national scene.[41]

Thus, it may be said with Cecil Roth that down to 1848 "there was no European country . . . where the restrictions placed upon them were more galling and more humiliating. After 1870, there was no land in either hemisphere where conditions were or could be better. . . . Jews were accepted freely, naturally and spontaneously as members of the Italian people, on a perfect footing of equality with their neighbors. . . . There was thus no part of the world where religious freedom was more real, or religious prejudice so small."[42] Emancipation was enacted in law but, uniquely in Italy, prevailed in life as well—that is, until 1938.

NOTES

1. Sam Waagenaar, *The Pope's Jews* (London: Alcove Press, 1974), p. ix; Meir Michaelis, *Mussolini and the Jews: German-Italian Relations and the Jewish Question in Italy 1922–45* (Oxford: Clarendon, 1978), p. 53.

2. Leone Modena, quoted in Robert Bonfil, *Jewish Life in Renaissance Italy* (Berkeley: University of California Press, 1994), p. 217; Cecil Roth, *The History of the Jews of Italy* (Philadelphia: Jewish Publication Society, 1946), p. 492.

3. On this paragraph, see also H. Stuart Hughes, *Prisoners of Hope: The Silver Age of the Italian Jews 1924–1974* (Cambridge: Harvard University Press, 1983), pp. 10–11; Arnaldo Momigliano, *On Pagans, Jews, and Christians* (Middletown, CT: Wesleyan University Press, 1987), p. 238–240.

4. Raphael Mahler, *A History of Modern Jewry, 1780–1815* (New York: Schocken, 1971), p. 114.

5. Preface to Vivian B. Mann, ed., *Gardens and Ghettos: The Art of Jewish Life in Italy*

(Berkeley: University of California Press, 1989), p. xvi.

6. Bonfil, *Jewish Life*, pp. 71–73.

7. Michaelis, *Mussolini*, p. 3.

8. Mahler, *History*, p. 118.

9. Cecil Roth, *A History of the Jews of Venice* (New York: Schocken, 1930, 1975), Chapter 7. Jews had been jettisoned from Venice by 1700.

10. Roth, *Italy*, p. 464.

11. Ibid., p. 467.

12. Ibid., p. 473.

13. Andrew Canepa, "Christian-Jewish Relations in Italy from Unification to Fascism" in *The Italian Refuge: Rescue of Jews during the Holocaust*, edited by Ivo Herzer (Washington, DC: Catholic University of America Press, 1989), p. 30.

14. Norman Cohn, *Warrant for Genocide* (London: Eyre and Spottiswoode, 1967), pp. 33, 44, 47–48.

15. Mario Toscano, "The Jews in Italy from the Risorgimento to the Republic," in *Gardens and Ghettos: The Art of Jewish Life in Italy*, edited by Vivian B. Mann (Berkeley: University of California Press, 1989), p. 33.

16. Waagenaar, *The Pope's Jews*, p. 288.

17. John Weiss, *The Fascist Tradition: Radical Right-Wing Extremism in Modern Europe* (New York: Harper and Row, 1967), pp. xix–xxii, 36–45, 111–112.

18. Denis Mack Smith, *Italy: A Modern History* (Ann Arbor: University of Michigan Press, 1959, 1969), p. 429; they were murdered in 1937.

19. Ruth Bondy, *The Emissary: A Life of Enzo Sereni* (Boston: Little Brown, 1977), p. 53.

20. Renzo De Felice, *Storia degli ebrei italiani sotto il fascismo*, 3d ed., vol. 1 (Turin: Einaudi, 1961, 1972), pp. 105–111.

21. Renzo De Felice, *Interpretations of Fascism*, translated by Brenda H. Everett (Cambridge: Harvard University Press, 1977), pp. 37, 68, 123, 128–130, 183; John Weiss, ed., *Nazis and Fascists in Europe 1918–1945* (Chicago: Quadrangle, 1969), p. 21.

22. Waagenaar, *The Pope's Jews*, p. 288.

23. Ivone Kirkpatrick, *Mussolini* (London: Oldhams, 1964), p. 353.

24. Michaelis, *Mussolini*, p. 30.

25. Felice, *Storia*, vol. 1, p. 194, vol. 2, p. 618.

26. Emil Ludwig, quoted by Michaelis, *Mussolini*, pp. 28–29; cf. Leon Poliakov, *The Aryan Myth: A History of Racist and Nationalist Ideas in Europe*, translated by Edmund Howard (New York: Basic Books, 1971, 1974), p. 70.

27. Felice, *Storia*, vol. 1, pp. 169–170, vol. 2, pp. 614–615.

28. Michael Marrus and Robert Paxton, *Vichy France and the Jews* (New York: Basic Books, 1981), p. 316.

29. Smith, *Italy*, pp. 423, 440–441, 444.

30. Meir Michaelis, "Italy," in *The World Reacts to the Holocaust* (Baltimore and London: Johns Hopkins University Press, 1996), p. 518.

31. The law appears as document no. 2 in Felice, *Storia*, vol. 2, pp. 580–593.

32. Ibid., vol. 1, pp. 123–132.

33. Smith, *Italy*, pp. 430–431; Dennis Mack Smith, *Mussolini* (New York: Knopf, 1982), p. 163.

34. Weiss, *Fascist Tradition*, pp. 105–106.

35. The manifesto and other pertinent documents are reproduced in Felice, *Storia*, vol. 2, pp. 661–725.

36. Weiss, *Fascist Tradition*, p. 26.

37. Michaelis, *Mussolini*, p. 141.

38. Smith, *Mussolini*, pp. 220–222.

39. Luigi Salvatorelli, *The Risorgimento: Thought and Action*, translated by Mario Domandi (New York: Harper and Row, 1970), p. 183; Felice, *Interpretations*, pp. 25–26, 165–166.

40. Poliakov, *Aryan Myth*, pp. 55. The "Italian form of ancestor worship is Romanism [of the Caesars and the Popes]." Ibid., p. 59.

41. This summation owes much to Andrew Canepa, "Christian-Jewish Relations in Italy from Unification to Fascism," in *The Italian Refuge: Rescue of Jews during the Holocaust*, edited by Ivo Herzer (Washington, DC: Catholic University of America Press, 1989), pp. 13–33.

42. Roth, *Italy*, pp. 474–475.

25

Rescue or Annihilation: Italian Occupation Forces and the Jews in World War II

Yitzchak Kerem

Although in recent years, the Italian occupation in the Balkans in World War II has taken on more of an altruistic character through the uncovering of archival material, Italian military and governmental behavior during the Holocaust in North Africa was often brutal and genocidal. The purpose of this chapter is to analyze Italian behavior from recent research finds and to further expand upon the paradoxes in Italian behavior when juxtaposing rescue policy and actions versus involvement in mass killing and cooperation with Germany in instituting arrests and deportations, building labor and concentration camps, and furthering the death process of Jews.

Highlights of Italian behavior included refraining from handing Jews in Yugoslavia over to the Croatians for deportation; transferring Italian nationals or those Jews of Italian origin and Spanish subjects by military trains from Salonika in the dangerous German zone to the safe Italian zone in Greece in June–July 1943; and actively concerning themselves about the fate of the Jews in German zones and following their whereabouts. In the Balkans Italian diplomatic and military officials objected to the annihilation of the Jews, consciously opposed German and Ustasha plans to carry out the deportation and murder of the Jews of the region, and viewed their role as being obliged to protect the Jews. Official Italian policy for the Balkans was to oppose the persecution of the Jews.

In North Africa, in Tunisia, the Italian government sought to block French Vichy influence so that the latter would not carry out the Nazi death process against the Jews. However, in Libya the Italians set up labor camps for thousands of Jews where hundreds died from torture, terrible conditions, and hard labor. Whereas Italy sought to protect its nationals in Tunisia and Libya from forced labor and anti-Jewish measures, it permitted and executed great injustices against the other Jews. Did Italy have a different policy toward the Jews in North Africa? Was it an issue of race or skin color, a different attitude toward Africa, or a question of different personalities in authority? Were Italian scruples missing? Was Italy pressured by Germany, or were Italian officials and military personnel taking their jobs too seriously and not exhibiting prudence? Why did Italy not take positions and active roles in opposing deportations from Tunisia and Libya?

Both the historians Daniel Carpi and Meir Michaelis agree that the Italians saved Jews not for ideological or political reasons, but out of humanity.[1] Michaelis noted that while Jews were being rounded up and deported all over German-occupied Europe, those in Italian-occupied territories in Vichy France, Yugoslavia, and Greece found havens of refuge, until the Italian surrender to the Allied Powers.[2] Although Mussolini "broke" with his Jewish subjects in 1938 in order not to eliminate differences between the two Axis powers and created the image that he was willing to sacrifice the Jews for German friendship and partnership, he resented German intervention in Italian occupation zones. The Duce would not allow foreigners to discriminate between his subjects and would not "tolerate attempts on the part of France to use anti-semitism as a means of undermining Italy's position in Tunisia."[3] In August 1942, when Prince Otto von Bismarck, councilor of the German Embassy in Rome, requested that Rome take joint action with Germany against Croatian Jewry and send them to the East, Mussolini had no objection. General Mario Roatta, Italian military commander in Yugoslavia, and Luca Pietromarchi, the diplomat responsible for the occupied territories, did not agree and noted that the Jews were under their protection. They also thought that the Croats were behind the demands, not the Germans, and were ignorant at that point of the "Final Solution." Roatta argued that if the Jews were handed over to the Croats, there would be military and political repercussions, and Mussolini was convinced but needed to present the Germans with an excuse. In order to protect the Jews, Mussolini proposed to the Germans that the Italians would put the Jews in concentration camps and proposed that the Jews renounce their Croatian citizenship and property. After German foreign minister Ribbentrop tried to convince the Duce that drastic measures should be employed against the Jews under Italian occupation, Mussolini's subordinates convinced him to distance himself from Hitler's policy of genocide.[4]

During the unsystematic murder of Serbs and Jews by the Croat fascists from April 1941 to June 1942, Italian soldiers and officers acted spontaneously to resist the killings. From June to November 1942, the Italians failed to detect the beginning of the Final Solution. Italian diplomats did not understand at the time the meaning of what the Germans meant by the "resettlement" of the Jews and their "labor service."

Whereas the Italians usually were sympathetic to the Jewish refugees and assisted them, there was one Italian anti-Semitic incident in Split which is noteworthy:

On 12 June 1942 an ink bottle was thrown by an unknown person on the marble monument that was placed commemorating the entrance of the Italian army to Split. In reaction to this, a fascist group from the "Toscana" Battalion, accompanied by officers from the same unit, left at 6:30 P.M. the same day for the synagogue and totally destroyed it. They took the furniture outside and burned it, and pillaged many valuable items. The Jews present at the synagogue at the time were beaten. The Jewish merchant Ferdinand Fintzi was hit in the head by a butt of a rifle and was taken to the hospital for medical care. Likewise, many Jewish apartments were pillaged and many possessions were thrown into the street and tossed into the camp fire, which burned at the National Square. . . . Intervention by the Carabinieri prevented further plunder. However, store windows were broken and robbed. . . . At the place there were seen some firemen and secret police, and also the Italian Army soldiers who were there at the location, who joined in on these acts.[5]

The violence lasted until evening, and the damage included sixty apartments, the Jewish community's offices, documentation, and valuable religious ornaments. This atrocious attack was carried out by a unit of the fascist Italian militia, but it was condemned by the Italian army, which prosecuted Italian soldiers who participated and issued orders to prevent similar future activity. This was a fluke incident, one of a kind, that did not repeat itself.

In early November 1942, when Carabinieri General Giuseppe Pieche finally learned that the Croatian Jews from the German occupation were killed by toxic gas, he advocated to Rome that the Jews not be turned over to the Croatians since it meant death. When the Holocaust spread to Greece and France from November 1942 to June 1943, Italy tried to obstruct the process leading to the death of Jews in those countries. When Mussolini was overthrown, and Badoglio surrendered to the Allies, nothing more could be done for the Jews by the Italians.[6]

Whereas Pieche initially was willing to turn over the Jews to the Croatians since he thought that they spied for London, when he learned of the killings, he changed his position. In a similar fashion, the Italian governor of Dalmatia, Giuseppe Bastianini, in May 1942 ordered the army to expel Jewish refugees from that region. A year later, when Mussolini promised German ambassador Mackensen in Rome that he would order that Italy put an end to their policy of halting obstruction (on behalf of the Jews), the same Bastianini, as undersecretary of foreign affairs, urged Mussolini to reconsider since the Jews, without distinction, would be gassed. He stated, "Our people will never permit such atrocities to take place with their connivance."[7] Mussolini was so taken when Bastianini noted that the sole responsibility would fall on Mussolini entirely that Mussolini changed his decision. Bastianini informed Mackensen that he changed his position since the French police were "in cahoots" with the Jews.[8]

Jews who succeeded in escaping to the Italian areas of control fared better than in other parts of the former Yugoslav kingdom. Regarding the fate of the Jews in these Italian-controlled areas, Harriet Pass Freidenreich wrote:

While most of these Jews, whether natives or recent refugees, were eventually interned in Italian camps, they appear to have received better treatment. The Italian authorities saved them from deportation to the Reich as long as they were in command. After the capitulation of Italy, those Jews who fell into German hands were deported to death camps. Others, however, succeeded in reaching southern Italy, where they were able to remain alive in such camps as Ferramonte, which the Jewish Brigade later helped to liberate. A considerable number of Jews from the Italian zone, especially those who had been interned on the island of Rab, joined Tito's partisan forces.[9]

Regarding Italian policy toward the Jews in Greece, Michaelis summed up the rationale for Italy's resistance to the policy of genocide as follows:

In Greece, which the Germans had recognized as part of the Italian sphere of influence, it was necessary to safeguard "the complex of (Italy's) economic and political interests," largely represented by Italian Jews who had not only "attained prominent positions in the economic and financial field" but also "given constant proof of their *italianità*. Almost everything we have in the region is in the hands of the Jews and their removal would mean the irremediable loss of positions representing considerable Italian interests that we intend to preserve and defend."[10]

In Salonika two Italian consuls played valuable roles in rescuing Jews; the first was Guelfo Zamboni (11 April 1942 to 18 June 1943), and the second was Giuseppe Castruccio, who functioned as consul from 18 June 1943 until the consulate was closed by the Germans at the beginning of September 1943. Also valuable and instrumental in helping to rescue Italian and other Jews were Vice Consul, Captain Riccardo Rosenberg of the Italian Military Intelligence Service; Captain Lucillo Merci, the translator and liaison officer with the German authorities;[11] and the consulate staff members Stavile, Emilio Neri (who was the son-in-law of the previous consul Pietro Nobili Vitelleschi, who was removed in the second half of February 1942 since he was an antifascist), and Neri's secretary, Mrs. Gionio. Other members of "Rosenberg's Rescue Brigade" were the local Jews Mark Mosseri and Valeri Torres.[12] After the deportations to Auschwitz had begun in Salonika starting on 15 March 1943, the German officials notified the Italian consulate on 3 April 1943, that they had received stringent orders from Berlin to deport all the Jews who were Greek citizens even if they also were born as Italian citizens. The Germans would exempt from deportation only those who could prove without a doubt that they were Italian citizens. There were only 281 officially recognized Italian-Jewish citizens when the Nazis began the ghettoization process in February 1943.[13] The strategy of the Italian consulate was to give the Jews a document stating that their right to Italian citizenship was under investigation as a way of rescuing those who were of Italian background but formally lacked citizenship or any other Jews who were interested in acquiring Italian citizenship in order to save themselves from deportation to Poland. Zamboni appointed three teams to issue these documents very liberally. On 2 April 1943, without waiting for instructions from Rome, Zamboni instructed his Salonikan consular staff to act according to those liberal criteria. In Neri's car, Jews from Saloniki were smuggled to Platona, the beginning of the Italian zone some seventy kilometers southward, and from there they reached Athens by Italian military train. Merci acted as an armed guard for those fleeing, and he was ready to use his weapon if the need arose.

Zamboni had previously requested from the "Commanding Officer Salonika-Agean," Generalleutnant Kurt von Krenzki, to exempt from the 11 July 1942 registration for forced labor at Plateia Eleftherias (Freedom Square) a number of Greek Jews employed by two large Italian insurance companies whose work was considered essential.[14] On 5 January 1943 he reported to Athens and Rome that the Salonikan German consul had begun to amass information on the number of Jews with Italian and Spanish citizenship and their action and expressed the fear that new measures against Salonikan Jewry were being planned.[15] Already in June 1942 Zamboni was active in trying to protect the assets of the Italian Jews and prevent them from falling into Greek or German hands, detailed the assets of the thirty-five wealthiest Italian Jews in Salonika, and proposed the establishment of an official Italian governmental company that would control the property of the Italian Jews in order to protect it.[16]

Castruccio, who replaced Zamboni as consul, was also very liberal in issuing Italian citizenship to Jews. Italian papers were supplied to Jewish women who married Jewish men who were Greek citizens and to "minors" whose age was twenty to thirty. Any blood relation to an Italian citizen enabled one to receive an Italian identity card, and any Italian-sounding name also qualified. Daily the Italians sent the Germans a list of twenty names to release from the Baron Hirsch transit camp, where Salonikan Jews waited for the deportation trains to Auschwitz. In addition to Merci, two other Italian officers came to the camp and released Jewish women as if they were their wives. Neri and the Righteous Gentile, the attorney Dimitri Spiliakos, hid Jews in their homes and helped those Jews flee southward via Italian diplomatic and military channels. Also, the Italian-Jewish subject Shlomo Uziel was free to move about in Salonika and to Athens and helped the Italians greatly in their efforts to rescue Jews. The last group that the Italians could save consisted of 350 people, and they reached Athens on 19 July 1943 via an Italian military train.[17] The Italian diplomatic corps tried to save the 367 Spanish nationals remaining in Salonika, who lacked local professional diplomatic representation, but at the last moment the Germans arrested them on 29 July 1943 and prepared them for deportation to Bergen-Belsen on 2 August 1943. On 25 July, in Athens, Spanish ambassador don Sebastian Romero Radigales commented that the German authorities assured him that no action would be taken regarding the Salonikan Spanish Jewish nationals until an agreement was reached between the Spanish and German governments but that they also would not be transferred to Athens. In the end, the Germans deceived the Spanish, and the Italians had no possibility of helping these people.[18]

In July 1942 Zamboni noted that almost all of the wealthy Jews of Salonika had fled to the Italian zone by means of forged documents and other devices. In total, he estimated that 1,200 people had escaped southward to the Italian zone.[19] However, even the Italian diplomats had limitations when they had the best of intentions. The lawyer Saul M. Moisis, a Salonikan Jew and Greek citizen who had provided legal services for the Salonikan Italian Consulate for years, wanted to avoid deportation. Zamboni requested from the German authorities that Moisis, his wife, and daughter be exempted from being moved to the ghetto and from deportation. At first approval was received, but later the Germans announced to Moisis that his exemption was canceled. Moisis and his family tried to escape from

Salonika, were caught, and were condemned to death. At the last moment, the intervention of the Italian Consulate succeeded in annulling the death sentence. The Germans promised to release them from prison if the Moisis family was given an entry visa to Italy. Here is the end to the sad story:

The process of obtaining a visa was not simple since it was clear to all that Moisis and the members of his family were Greek citizens, and for the purpose of their transfer to Italy an Italian passport from the Foreign Ministry and an entry visa from the Ministry of the Interior would have to be obtained for them. Nevertheless, everything was obtained within a short time and in the middle of May Consul Zamboni   reported this to the German authorities and asked for the family's release to allow them to leave for Italy as agreed. According to Merten, Wisliceny then hastily and personally ordered them to be put on a deportation train. Merten himself informed Consul Zamboni of this some time after the deportation had been carried out.[20]

On 12 May 1943 Zamboni, attached to the Athenian Italian Diplomatic Mission, reported that Vital Hasson, the head of the Salonikan Jewish police and collaborator, was coming to Athens with several others on the initiative of the German authorities in order to trace Salonikan Jews who had fled to the Italian zone illegally, and then the German security services would demand their extradition. On 17 May Zamboni sent a telegram to Athens stating that Shlomo Uziel was due to visit the Athenian Italian Diplomatic Mission. It appears that Uziel was sent to Athens on an Italian military plane at the initiative of the Salonikan Italian Consulate to collect details on the Hasson scheme in order to sabotage the plan. On 27 May 1943 Deputy Foreign Minister Bastianini instructed Plenipotentiary Ghigi to notify the German authorities in Greece that the Italian government did not want the intervention of the German police and succeeded in foiling the German scheme.[21]

Castruccio notified the Italian authorities that the Jewish Nazi collaborator Vital Hasson, who viciously and actively had raped, killed, stolen from, and extorted numerous Salonikan Jews, was planning on escaping to Albania. In an act that was not so ethical but saved lives, Castruccio paid Hasson money to allow several Jews to escape from the Barion Hirsh camp and hence avoid deportation. Hasson knew that he had to switch sides in order to save himself and close ones, so he cooperated with the Italian consul. Based on the 1946 trial proceedings against Hasson in Athens, where he subsequently was executed, Carpi noted that "it may be learned that he requested and apparently obtained the Consulate's assistance in order to escape to Albania (a country which at the time was under Italian rule) and in return for this he helped in the escape of a few of the Jews mentioned above. (Referring to his wife, mistress, infant daughter, and a few members of his clique—Y. K.)"[22]

The Italian occupation in mainly the southern part of Greece and centered in Athens was very fair and humane to the Jews. Some Jewish student underground members were arrested in Athens for anti-Italian graffiti or sabotage but only briefly detained. The Italian governor Carlo Geloso promised that "as long as he is in power the Jews have nothing to fear." According to Bowman, he enacted no anti-Jewish measures, because he received no official Italian orders to do so and this made it possible "for larger numbers of Jews to participate in the Resistance in that area."[23] The "free" Italian zone was a place of refugee for thousands of fleeing Salonikan and other Jews of northern Greece. When Italian rule fell in September 1943, Jews in the Athens area were forced to go into hiding, and many looked for ways to escape Greece by boat or joining the Resistance. The Italian Jews who were arrested with Athenian Jews who reported to the synagogue on 24 March 1944 were sent to Auschwitz-Birkenau, and most did not return. Between 1941 and 1943 some 3,000-5,000 Salonikan Jews escaped to Athens in the Italian zone. In 1943–1944, there may have been as many as 7,000–8,000 Jews hiding in the Athens area. All this was initially possible because of the lenient Italian occupation until autumn 1943 and the base for resistance to the German "Final Solution" that the Italians had set up in Greece until the Germans fully dominated Greece.[24]

In the 1938 Italian racial anti-Semitic laws, Jews of foreign citizenship were forced to leave Italy and its protectorates. Some 2,000 Jews were stripped of their Italian citizenship since they had arrived in Rhodes after the 1923 Lausanne agreement and were forced to leave the island by January 1939. A delegation of Jerusalem Sephardic leaders arrived in Rhodes and succeeded in getting them only a month's extension. They went to the International Zone in Tangier and the Belgian Congo. They survived, unlike the 1,800 Rhodian Jews deported from Rhodes in late July 1944, who were mostly annihilated in Auschwitz-Birkenau. Most of the large concentration of about 1,500 former Corfiote Greek Jews and their descendants in Trieste, who had migrated since the large-scale 1891 blood libel in Corfu and retained their Greek citizenship, were allowed to stay in Trieste, and most of them died in the death camps. An estimated twenty to thirty families left Trieste after the 1938 proclamation "Manifesto della razza," stipulating that those who had arrived after 1919 would have to leave within several months. Some 1,300 to 1,400 Corfiote Jews remained in Trieste and as residents of the old ghetto area. In 1938–1939 there were several anti-Semitic events worthy of mention.

Signs were posted in bars and coffeehouses against admitting "those who take handouts, merchants, monkey grinders, gypsies, dogs, and Jews." Once Avraham Saloniccio and his wife were attacked on a Sunday promenade at the Aqueduct by a group of fascist university students, who painted the faces of the Jewish couple with black paint. Such gangs searched for Jews to taunt. Bank accounts of Jews were closed and seized by the authorities. Also telephones were cut, but not very many Jews had phones then. Also, the radio was shut down. Furthermore, gentile maids left their Jewish employers.[25]

In the case of Libya, there was no immediate order to expel the 1,600 Jews of French, Tunisian, and Moroccan citizenship and the 870 British subjects. Due to a lack of transportation, equipment, and internment camp space, the Italians arrested and imprisoned only some of these foreign nationals in September 1940 in the camps that they established in Tajura (by Tripoli), Buayrat al-Hasun (by Cyrenica) and Hun (150 kilometers south of Cirt). The foreign nationals were imprisoned until 1941.[26] In reality, only a few hundred British Jewish and Gentile citizens were imprisoned. As early as January 1939, the Italian Foreign Ministry suspended the issue of expelling English Jews since they did not want to darken relations with Britain. Once Italy declared war on Britain and France on 10 June 1940, keeping British Jews on Italian soil no longer remained a consideration. The Italian governor of Libya, Italo Balbo, was hesitant in 1939 to carry out fascist racial laws in Libya since he feared that it would create a great blemish on Italy's domestic and foreign prestige. Mussolini responded in writing to Balbo's protests that he (Balbo) could keep Jewish Libyans employed in hospitals, in tobacco industries, and as government clerks but that the "[n]on-indigenous Jews, that is those with metropolitan citizenship, should be given the treatment they receive in Italy under the recent laws."[27] More startling was Mussolini's next line, "I therefore authorize you to apply the racial laws as above, remembering that though the Jews may seem to be dead, they never really are."

On 7 February 1942 Mussolini personally ordered the "clearing out" of the Jewish population of Libya.[28] Aside from British subjects, the Jews of Cyrenica and Tripolitania were to be distanced from the battle regions and put in concentration camps in the Tripolitania Range. First, beginning in May 1942, the small communities were cleared out, and Benghazi was the last community depleted. In practical terms, by late July 1942, 591 Jews had been "cleared out" of Benghazi, Cyrenica, and sent to the Giado internment camp that had been set up for Libyan and Italian Jews. The remaining 33 Jews were waiting to leave. At the end of June, the Jewish population transfer was halted since Giado lacked adequate facilities. Some Jews were sent to another camp established for foreigners at Gharian. There were transportation problems, and Jews had resisted. However, by the end of June 1942 a total of more than 2,500 Jews had been evacuated from Cyrenica and interned in Giado.

On 28 June 1942 the Italian governor of Libya, Rodolfo Graziani, published an order that went into effect as of 11 July 1942 and equated the legal situation in Libya to that of Italy regarding the obligation of Jewish men of draftable age to report for civil service. Registration for men between ages eighteen and forty-five began, and 4,000–5,000 Jewish men from Tripoli were to be drafted, but only 3,000 were recruited from the Tripoli area and were sent to the Sidi Azaz camp ten kilometers from Homs. Due to a lack of infrastructure for this quantity of men, most were released, and only some 1,000, mostly professional laborers, remained. Some 350 of the latter were eventually sent to the Bukbuk Camp by the Egyptian border near Cyrenica. Those sent to this camp in Tobruk, where they were abandoned at the time of the Axis withdrawal and had to march back to Tripoli through the desert. Most of the Jewish prisoners in Sidi Azaz were from Tripoli, but there were also several dozen men from Homs. Other Jews had been released for medical reasons, as incompatible, or if they were employed by Italian contractors working for the state. Some of the Jewish forced laborers were transferred before the British conquest to an Italian military camp in the suburbs of Tripoli for hard labor and were forced to unload truckloads of weapons and transfer them to warehouses.[29] In Sidi Azaz relations between the Jewish Libyan prisoners and the Italian soldiers were good, for the most part. The Italian guards often exempted the Jews from work on the Sabbath, and they often ate together. Once, a Jewish Libyan prisoner got into a violent argument with an Italian soldier, and the latter shot the Jew, Camus Zango, to death. The soldier was not punished but removed to another camp. After this incident, the Jews refrained from arguing with the Italian soldiers.[30]

In spring 1942 the Italians built in Yefren, as in the neighboring Gharian, a small prison camp for the Jews of Cyrenica that had been exiled to the Tripolitanian Range at the command of Mussolini. The prisoners at Yefren, as in Gharian, were moved to houses on the side of the mountains and guarded by Italian soldiers. These Cyrenican Jewish prisoners suffered greatly from primitive conditions. The biggest camp set up during the expulsion of Cyrenican Jewry was Giado. There some 2,600 Cyrenican Jews were imprisoned, and some 562 died from starvation, exhaustion, and typhus. The dead Jews were buried in a nearby ancient Jewish cemetery dating back to 1183.[31]

The Giado concentration camp, 235 kilometers south of Tripoli, was set up in a former old military camp. The camp consisted of long barracks surrounded by barbed wire, with a machine gun looking down upon the camp from an opposite hill in order to prevent escape. One of the barracks served as a jail, but prisoners accused of several crimes were sent to prison in Tripoli. The camp commander, General Ettore Bastico, was known for his anti-Semitic outlook and humiliation of prisoners. His assistant, Major Commadant Guerriero Modestino, was more sympathetic. The camp guards were Italians and Arabs. Jews brought from Cyrenica traveled five days to reach the camp and slept outside en route. In the camp the family unit was kept together. Sanitary conditions were despicable. The camp officials fed the prisoners 100–150 grams of bread a day, and there was a small weekly provision of rice, macaroni, oil, sugar, tea, and coffee. After several weeks, when a delegation of prisoners requested from the commander an increase in food quantities, he answered, "We didn't come here to support you, we give you food since it's not worth wasting bullets on you."[32] Only the males worked, and they cleared garbage, cleaned bathrooms, and moved rocks from place to place. Once a week, their tough task was to weed with a hoe and transport dirt for twelve hours a day. They were overseen by a *kapo* who was to worry about arranging the work list. The Jews received from the assistant head of the camp permission to set up a makeshift synagogue in one of the barracks. The typhus fever that broke out in Giado due to unhealthy sanitary conditions and hunger killed dozens of people daily. The makeshift solitary quarantine room was almost a death sentence, since those that transferred there never left. Roumani noted, "Those who were interned in Giado faced many hardships and bad conditions which resulted in the breakout of typhus in the camp causing the death of young and old members of several families."[33]

Iris Mozzeri's story was recently published in the *Yad Vashem Quarterly Magazine*. Here is an excerpt:

Iris Mozzeri—born in 1932 in Benghazi, Libya, to the Habibs, a Jewish traditional family of Jewish dignitaries. Iris had four sisters and two brothers. In 1941, on Passover, an Italian pogrom in the town left much destruction. The Jews fled to shelter in the synagogue. Shortly afterwards, Iris's parents, along with other Jewish families, left Benghazi and via back roads reached the village of Qufiyya. In 1942, the Italian authorities entered the village and took the entire family on a five-day march to the Giado (Jadu) camp in the Libyan desert—a place of unbearable hunger and thirst, onerous heat, and rampant typhus and other diseases. Iris's mother, Viola, her oldest brother Haim, and two paternal uncles, Victor and Isaac, succumbed to the harsh conditions. . . . Iris and her brothers became seriously ill with typhus. They were not treated until the arrival of the British. They returned to Benghazi in the summer of 1943.[34]

One morning in January 1943 in Giado, several days before the Allies arrived, all the inmates were amassed in formation in front of the flagpole to face the machine guns. Rabbi Gian was dragged by force and was placed in front of everyone. The rumor had spread that the Italians were only waiting for a phone call to order them to start shooting, but nothing happened. Several days later, the Italian guards fled from the camp, and 200 Jews, who still retained a little strength, also exploited the opportunity, ripped through the fence, and fled. Several weeks later the British liberated the camp and found many very sick people who could not move. The more severe cases were taken to a hospital in Tripoli, and those less sick were taken to Gharian for medical supervision. Many died en route or in the hospital.

Some 300 Jews who were British subjects were sent to prison camps in Italy. British Jews from Libya had arrived in Italy as early as January 1942. After the German conquest of Italy on 8 September 1943, they were taken to build fortifications in Italy, and in the beginning of 1944, 100 were transferred to the Innsbruck camp, and 200 were taken to Bergen-Belsen.[35] A total of 370 Jews of British citizenship were deported from Libya to Bergen-Belsen in four transports. The first deportation was from Civitella del Tronto, two were from Fusili de Carpi, and one departed from Arezzo. The first transport arrived in Bergen-Belsen in January 1944, and the last arrived in August 1944. Most left Bergen-Belsen in November–December 1944. Most were compelled to perform difficult forced labor, suffered from beatings by the SS, and did not enjoy preferential status.

One group of Libyan Jews from a transport of eighty-three people were in Bergen-Belsen only three weeks.[36] Most of the Libyan Jews in Bergen-Belsen were released from the camp in November and transferred to the prisoner-of-war camp in Biberach-Riss in southern Germany, near the Swiss border. Another group of Libyan Jews left Bergen-Belsen only in January 1945, when the situation there was already severe, and they were taken to the German camp for British prisoners, Wurzach. The Libyan Jews were in both Biberach-Riss and Wurzach until the Free French Army liberated them in April 1945. Another group of Libyan Jews reached Lisbon, Portugal, and from there went to American DP (displaced person) camps in Morocco and Algeria until the beginning of 1945.

In the Innsbruck-Reichenau camp in western Austria, more than 100 Libyan Jews of British nationality were imprisoned. These Jews were brought in closed cattle cars straight from the Bazano prison camp in Italy in October 1943. The men were separated from the women and all were given neck tags, but they remained in civilian dress. The men worked from 5 A.M. to 7 P.M. paving roads, in construction, or in a cement factory in the area. Some cleaned the camp or removed snow. The Libyan women worked mostly in gardening and had it easier than the men. In this small satellite camp of Dachau, the German guards were very cruel to the Libyan and other Jews. For keeping Jewish laws and practices, like praying, the Libyan Jews were beaten, put in jail cells, and sprayed with cold water. The camp was surrounded by barbed wire, and the elderly of the Libyan Jews did not succeed in enduring the tough conditions, especially the beatings, the hunger, crowding, and the cold weather. Some of them died in the camp. The Libyan Jews tried to keep kosher, and were admired by the Ashkenazic Jewish inmates for this, but this also contributed to their deaths. The total number of deaths is not known, but most of the Libyans in the camp did survive. In April 1944 they were transferred to the Vittel Camp in France until the liberation.[37]

In early 1942, after negotiations between January and March 1942 between the Italian and French authorities, 1,600 Jewish French subjects from Tripolitania and Cyrenica were transferred to Tunisia.[38] The Italians transported them to the border and forbade them from taking gold or money with them. Some went to the Jewish communities in Tunis or Gabes, but most were put in a detention camp seven kilometers from Sfax. Several families were crowded together in individual cabins and slept on boards. Hygienic conditions were terrible, and there was no running water. In the absence of toilets, people performed their private necessities outside the camp in pits. Many were bitten by scorpions, and there was no medical treatment in the camp. The Jewish community of Sfax agreed to provide a doctor and food packages. The gendarme guarded the camp and often robbed the inmates of their meager possessions. The Jews convinced the French to allow the Jews themselves to guard the camp, and for a year they lived as a closed, autonomous body. They traded with the nearby Arab villages. Eventually, the Sfax Jewish community halted assistance, and the French authorities did not intervene for better or for worse. When the Germans conquered Tunisia in November 1942, the camp was overseen by a joint German–Italian command. This distant camp remained practically neglected, but once a week the German officials recruited Jews for forced labor, mostly for stonecutting. In order to avoid this difficult work, Jews tried to hide or not sleep in the camp. Even when the camp was liberated, the Libyan Jews still were left in a difficult situation because they could not return to their homes in Libya since there was a lack of transportation. A different group of more than 400 from Tripolitania had gone to La Mersa, the satellite city of the capital, Tunis, where they lived in rickety shacks on the seashore. In crowded conditions, with poor sanitation, broken toilets and sewers, and not enough food, they lived there throughout the German occupation and for six months afterward. For a year after the liberation from the Germans until the summer of 1944, there were still found throughout Tunisia and Algeria some 1,000 Jewish Libyan refugees.

Italy did not have a reputation for being harsh in operating its labor camps and its treatment of forced Jewish workers in Tunisia. It made sure that its Jewish nationals in Tunisia, as in Salonika or in northern France, did not have to wear the yellow star. Several Italian military men were distinguished in their efforts to assist Jews in Tunisia. Captain Corsi and Sergeant Gallese made noteworthy contributions in their assistance to Jews. Gallese was brought before a military tribunal for his acts and was punished by being demoted a rank.[39]

Italy was officially anti-Semitic in World War II but acted paradoxically and altruistically in saving Jews in the occupied territories of the Balkans. In Italy Jews could be arrested for any reason, and in German-occupied areas Italy did everything that it could to protect Jews. The Italian army, diplomatic corps, and Foreign Ministry did its utmost to protect all Jews in the occupied territories, with the exception of North Africa.[40] Italy opposed the quisling Vichy government in North Africa and feared that it would initiate measures to deport Jews in its territories as it did in France. However, paradoxically, there was no hesitancy on Italy's part to deport English subjects in Libya to camps in Italy, deport the foreign national Jews to Tunisia, and expose them to potential German danger. Italy created labor camps for its foreign nationals, as well as its own nationals, which turned out to be death machines through diseases, hard labor, and torture. It was rare that Italian troops acted violently and abusively against Jews in the occupied Balkans, but it was more frequent in Italy. Italian behavior toward the Jews was irrational, sometimes cruel to devoted citizens and altruistically warm to foreigners. Italian behavior toward Jews was based more on emphathy than rationally or ideologically motivated. Italian behavior toward the Greek Jews—those who paradoxically had fought so hard and valiantly in Albania against the invading Italians from 28 October 1940 to April 1941—reflected a stream of humanitarianism. Again, paradoxically, those same Greek Jews who resented Italy's attack on Greece in 1940 resented Italy's surrendering its command to the Germans. In 1940 Greek Jews were fighting for Greece against Italy for patriotic reasons. In 1943 Greek Jewry was saddened to see the Italian army leave Greece. Italian soldiers were left to be massacred by the German army, and Greek Jewry would now be vulnerable to death at the hands of the Germans and their annihilation factories in Poland.

While Italy deserves to be remembered and thanked for its altruistic actions on behalf of Jews in France, Yugoslavia, Albania, and Greece, its role in the death process of Jews in Libya in the Giado camp and elsewhere not only deserves to be condemned but also is an important and neglected part of World War II Holocaust historiography. In World War II, there were altruistic individuals, but no government or entire people were either entirely altruistic or genocidal. North Africa is a dark chapter in Italy's history as an occupier in World War II. Despite its altruism, at home and abroad in its occupied zones, Italy assisted in the death process of Jews and was manipulated into being a partner in the Nazi "Final Solution" against the Jews. In the end, Italy lost the war and lost its humanity, and it was responsible for Jewish deaths.

NOTES

1. Minna Rozen et al., eds., *Daniel Carpi Jubilee Volume, a Collection of Studies in the History of the Jewish People Presented to Daniel Carpi upon his 70th Birthday by His Colleagues and Students* (Tel Aviv: Tel Aviv University, Humanities Faculty and Hayim Rosenberg School for Jewish Studies, 1996), p. 188.

2. Ibid., p. 194.

3. Ibid., p. 197.

4. Ibid., pp. 198–199.

5. Menachem Shelach, ed., *History of the Holocaust: Yugoslavia* (Jerusalem: Yad Vashem, 1990) p. 229. (In Hebrew)

6. Rozen, *Daniel Carpi*, p. 201.

7. Ibid., p. 204.

8. Jonathan Steinberg, *All or Nothing, the Axis and the Holocaust 1941–1943* (London and New York: Routledge, 1990), pp. 126–127.

9. Harriet Pass Freidenreich, *The Jews of Yugoslavia, a Quest for Community* (Philadelphia: Jewish Publication Society of America, 1979), p. 192.

10. Rozen, *Daniel Carpi*, p. 202.

11. Daniel Carpi, ed., *Italian Diplomatic Documents on the History of the Holocaust in Greece (1941–1943)* (Tel Aviv: Chair for the History and Culture of the Jews of Salonika and Greece, The Diaspora Research Institute, Tel Aviv University, 1999), pp. 17–18.

12. Yitzchak Kerem, "Rescue Attempts of Jews in Greece in the Second World War," *Pe'amim* 27 (1986): 77–109. (In Hebrew)

13. Carpi, *Italian Diplomatic Documents*, p. 30.

14. Ibid., p. 19.

15. Ibid., p. 23.

16. Ibid., p. 29.

17. Kerem, "Rescue Attempts," pp. 91–92.

18. Carpi, *Italian Diplomatic Documents*, p. 36.

19. Ibid., p. 41.

20. Ibid., pp. 42–43.

21. Ibid., pp. 46–47.

22. Ibid., pp. 47–48.

23. Steven Bowman, "Jews in Wartime Greece," *Jewish Social Studies* 48, no. 1 (Winter 1986): 45–62.

24. Daniel Carpi, "Notes on the History of the Jews in Greece during the Holocaust Period. The Attitude of the Italians (1941–1943)," in *Festschrift in Honor of Dr. George S. Wise* (Tel Aviv: Tel Aviv University, 1981), pp. 25–62.

25. Yitzchak Kerem, "Corfiote Triestians: A Jewish Diasporic Community from Greece," *Proceedings of the Eleventh World Congress of Jewish Studies, Division B: The History of the Jewish People*, vol. 3: *Modern Times* (Jerusalem: World Union of Jewish Studies, 1994), pp. 187–194.

26. Irit Abramski-Bligh, ed., *Pinkas Hakehillot, Libya—Tunisia, Encyclopedia of Jewish Communities from Their Foundation till after the Holocaust* (Jerusalem: Yad Vashem, 1997), pp. 61, 120. (In Hebrew)

27. Renzo De Felice, *Jews in an Arab Land, Libya, 1835–1970* (Austin: University of Texas Press, 1985), p. 173.

28. Ibid., pp. 179–180.

29. Abramski-Bligh, *Pinkas Hakehillot*, p. 160. See also Maurice M. Roumani, "Aspects of the Holocaust in Libya," in Solomon Gaon and M. Mitchell Serels, eds., *Del Fuego*,

Sephardim and the Holocaust (New York: Sepher-Hermon Press, 1995), pp. 122–128.

30. Abramski-Bligh, *Pinkas Hakehillot*, p. 67.

31. Ibid., p. 167.

32. Ibid., pp. 120–121.

33. Roumani, "Aspects," p. 126.

34. Galia Limor, "Six Survivors Remember: Torch Lighters 1999," *Yad Vashem Quarterly Magazine* 13 (Spring 1999): 10–11.

35. Ibid., p. 120.

36. Ibid., pp. 64–65.

37. Ibid., p. 65.

38. Ibid., pp. 65–66.

39. Daniel Carpi, *The Italian Authorities and the Jews of France and Tunisia during the Second World War* (Jerusalem: Zalman Shazar Center for Jewish History, 1993), p. 291. (In Hebrew)

40. Susan Zuccotti, *The Italians and the Holocaust, Persecution, Rescue, Survival* (New York: Basic Books, 1987), pp. 74–75.

26

The Priebke Trial(s)

David Travis

INTRODUCTION

The Erich Priebke trial—actually, three trials in all—held in Italy between 1996 and 1998 tells the story of how guilt and responsibility for war crimes surfaced in Italy five decades after World War II. It is also the story of the complicated and sometimes contradictory path taken to address these issues. Finally, these trials are about the importance of historical memory today and about the power of indignation, outrage, and shame in offering partial justice to the victims of one of the great tragedies of this century.

Many people—primarily those in the Italian-Jewish communities, especially the community of Rome—held onto a historical memory with enough determination to put these issues before the public and keep them there despite a myriad of problems. They offered a lesson in the importance for democratic life today in pursuing justice for crimes committed long ago. We also learn in this story how much the history of Jews in Italy is identical to the history of Italy.

All of this takes place in Rome and covers a fifty-four-year period, starting with a war crime in 1944 and concluding with a conviction in 1998.

BACKGROUND: THE CRIME

It began on the via Tasso at number 145, only a few yards from one of the pope's holiest churches, St. John in Lateran. A building on via Tasso was the Gestapo headquarters in the capital city under German occupation. On 24 March 1944, SS captain Erich Priebke, thirty-one years old, received the orders that he had been trained for ten years to carry out. In retaliation for an Italian partisan attack on German soldiers that had taken place the previous day, 330 civilians were to be murdered.

The circumstances of the German occupation of Italy are very complicated;

simply put, Hitler's military had not been convinced that Italy remained a loyal ally after the Italian king had dismissed Mussolini in July 1943. When General Eisenhower announced the armistice with the Allied forces on 8 September 1943, the Germans invaded. From the Austrian border south to Naples, most Italians had no choice but to see their country overrun.

The Germans reinstated Mussolini in northern Italy, but the Republic of Salò was a puppet government, and while Mussolini pretended again to be the Duce, the Germans literally called the shots. The deportation of Italian Jews began almost immediately. The first 1,000 were seized from the ghetto in Rome in October 1943.

A domestic Resistance movement began to grow in central and northern Italy. Limited in numbers and in their ability to wage war, the partisans did what they could. As in the rest of occupied Europe, this most often meant harassment, sabotage, and occasionally assassination of enemy troops.

On 23 March 1944 a small group of partisans operating in Rome's city center carried out the most audacious attack yet. Every afternoon on their return to the barracks, a German patrol marched along the via Rasella, a narrow street that heads steeply uphill behind the Piazza Barberini. The *partigiani* (partisans) placed nearly 100 kilograms of explosives in the handcart of a street sweeper, and left the cart in front of the Palazzo Tittino. The bomb exploded just as the patrol passed by. Twenty-six soldiers were killed instantly; seven more died within a few hours.

The Germans reacted immediately, opening fire on anything and everything. The bullet holes are still visible on some of the buildings. Late that night, Herbert Kappler, the commander of the Gestapo in Rome, received his orders from Germany. Ten civilians were to be killed for every solider who had died. The next day, Kappler turned the matter over to his subordinate, Erich Priebke, who simply emptied the jail in via Tasso of all of its 135 prisoners; 200 more were taken from another prison. Jews awaiting deportation were among those included. The total should have been 330, but somewhere along the line Priebke made a mistake and included five men too many.

The building on the via Tasso today houses the Museum of the Liberation of Rome. Chronic underfunding has produced a simple and Spartan—but, for those very reasons, a powerful—museum, whose rooms remain exactly as the Gestapo left them, including the cells with the prisoners' names and messages scratched into the walls.

Fifty-five years ago, on that afternoon, the Germans loaded their prisoners into trucks and drove to an unused quarry a few kilometers along the via Ardeatine. Priebke stood at the entrance and checked off the name of each prisoner. The men had their hands tied behind their backs and were marched in pairs the fifty yards into the cave, forced to kneel down, and then shot. Priebke executed several men himself.

For decades, the Fosse Ardeatine massacre was remembered both within Italy and elsewhere as a crime against Jews. In reality, those murdered by the Germans represented a cross-section of the population of Rome. Of the victims, 257 were civilians, 66 were military men, and 12 were never identified. Most had been arrested on political charges, as antifascists; 28 were less than twenty years old, and the youngest was only fifteen. Seventy-five Jews from Rome were among the victims.

It took nearly three hours to kill all the prisoners. The Germans then closed the cave's entrance with an explosion, sealing the "tomb" (the *fosse*). Several days later, two young boys, playing in the quarry, found their way into the cave and came across the bodies. By the end of the month, the clandestine Resistance movement had told the city about the Fosse Ardeatine massacre. German authorities had notified the families of the victims only that their relatives had died in custody.

Today a memorial stands at the Fosse Ardeatine site. Several thousand people a year visit the former quarry and the monumental *sacrario* (sanctuary) (built in 1949) that shelters the tombs of the victims.

1944–1995

Erich Priebke left Rome in the German retreat of June 1944, surrendered near Bolzano, and was held by the English in a prison camp at the end of the war. His name appeared on a list of "war criminals" wanted by the Allies, and American officers interrogated him about the Fosse Ardeatine in 1946. Later that year, Priekbe escaped, and in his case, as in so many others, no serious effort was made to find him. Priebke's name figured on the list of witnesses (though not among the defendants) when the perpetrators of the Fosse Ardeatine massacre first went on trial in 1948, but Priebke could not be found to give evidence. His superior officer, Kappler, was tried, convicted, and then sentenced to life imprisonment, with the final verdict issued in 1953. Five lower-ranking officers, however, were found "not guilty" at the same trial because the court determined that they had acted only in obedience to Kappler's orders.

No one saw Erich Priebke until May 1994, when ABC correspondent Sam Donaldson, apparently acting on a tip from the Wiesenthal Center, "found" Priebke living an open life in a quiet suburb of Bariloche, a resort town in western Argentina. The interview was aired on Italian television the next day. A prosecutor for the Military Tribunal asked the Italian government to apply for Priebke's extradition from Argentina. In the meantime, Priebke was arrested.

The Italian request went forward at a very slow pace under two governments for the next eighteen months. Finally, early in November 1995 Argentina granted Italy's extradition request, and on 21 November Priebke arrived back in Rome and was imprisoned.

1996: THE FIRST TRIAL

A complicated legal issue had to be resolved before the trial could even begin: Who should try Erich Priebke? The case eventually went to a Military Tribunal; however, the highest civil court, the Court of Cassation, set an important precedent by allowing civil plaintiffs to constitute themselves as part of the prosecution. Two organizations were admitted: the Italian Jewish Communities, led by the community of Rome, and the Association of the Families of the Victims of the Fosse Ardeatine. Each had its own lawyer.

These two associations had followed the Priebke case from the moment that he had turned up in Argentina. The Italian Jewish Communities, in particular, worked hard to keep the extradition issue alive; some of its members had even traveled to Argentina to give evidence at the extradition hearing. Once Priebke was back in an Italian jail, the Jewish community and its leaders repeatedly spoke about the historical significance of this trial and the importance of situating the tragedy of the Fosse Ardeatine in the larger context of Germany's war in Europe, not only in the need to reach a verdict on Erich Priebke the individual. The trial began in May 1996.

From the outset, however, it was clear that the Military Tribunal was not up to the task of judging a war criminal. Today's military tribunals specialize in the contemporary questions of obligatory military service: chronic return to the barracks after hours, disobedience to orders, initiation rites subjected on new recruits, and so on. Nothing over the past decades had prepared the military for this case; the tribunal tackled this trial without the historical culture to gauge its importance and, as it turns out, without the professionalism even to judge the crime.

The composition of the tribunal only compounded the mistake of assigning jurisdiction to the military. The court's president, Judge Agostino Quistelli, quickly became the object of almost as much attention as Priebke. Giving the clear impression of wishing to hurry the case along, Quistelli limited the number of witnesses allowed to testify to only thirty, reducing from 100 the names submitted to the court. Many survivors, many of them Jews, were thereby denied the right finally to deliver a formal account of the torture and murder that were the daily stuff of the Gestapo in Rome. Citing the expenses involved, Judge Quistelli refused to transfer the proceedings to a larger courthouse with more room for the public. Claiming that the "facts" about the German occupation of Rome were already well known, Quistelli also allowed only one historian to present an account of the war and the Resistance.

Even worse, Quistelli and another judge had apparently made up their minds before the trial began. In 1995, before Priebke even arrived in Italy, Quistelli voiced the opinion that the whole undertaking was simply useless because too many years had passed for justice to be rendered. The judge also believed—and said so—that a jail sentence for an eighty-year-old man was inhumane. Motions to disqualify the judges were rejected by Quistelli and confirmed by a military appellate court.

The first trial ended on 31 July 1996. The judges were back in the courtroom with a verdict and a sentence at 6 P.M. the next day. Quistelli's court found Priebke "guilty," but, shockingly, "not punishable" and ordered his immediate release.

There was no question of Priebke's guilt; the man himself had admitted his role at the Fosse Ardeatine but claimed that he had merely followed orders. While the Military Court did convict Priebke on multiple counts of first-degree murder, it then took into consideration a number of mitigating and extenuating circumstances in its sentence: Priebke's advanced age, his good behavior since the end of the war, his conversion to Catholicism in 1948, and the fact that he had made no attempt to hide or change his identity in Argentina. Furthermore, the court accepted the defense argument that Priebke had no choice but to follow his orders. It also asserted that Priebke had expressed remorse for his actions in 1944, though the defendant had never offered this apology in (or out) of court.

When the verdict and the sentence reached those waiting outside the tribunal, disbelief quickly gave way to fury. The public, perhaps 150, mostly from the Jewish community and families of the victims, forced its way into the building and toward the courtroom, hurling insults equally at the tribunal, at Priebke, and at his defense attorney. By 11 P.M., nearly 1,000 protesters had surrounded the courthouse, which was under a virtual siege. Pushing and shoving came to blows, and the crowd nearly overwhelmed the tiny police guard. The angry protest— carried on television—had an enormous impact on public opinion, much more than the months of the trial itself. Apologies were offered the next day for the violent reaction to the sentence.

The newspapers captured the shock and shame in the headlines Friday morning: "La Vergogna Priebke" (The Shame of the Priebke Trial), "Nuremberg, all'Italiana" (Nuremberg, Italian-Style), or (even more critical) "Italia cialtrona" (Shoddy Italy). The military tribunal had clearly failed to deliver justice. Paola Severino, lawyer for the Union of the Jewish Communities, commented in *La Repubblica*, "This is the worst possible sentence both because it has no merit or basis, but also because the Tribunal has simply avoided giving an answer." Tullia Zevi, president of the Italian Jewish Communities, spoke for all: "[This was] [a] terrible sentence, and we have lost a great opportunity to issue a definitive condemnation of the system that ruined Europe fifty years ago and of the men who made it all possible."[1]

What about Priebke? The near-siege of the courthouse made it impossible to release him. Along with the judges and his defense attorney, Priebke remained in the back rooms under police guard for the rest of the evening. Hoping to diffuse the situation, the Minister of Justice himself, Giovanni Maria Flick, showed up at the courthouse and entered into frenetic consultations, trying to find a solution to the "stand off." He found an answer in extremis—Priebke was released just after midnight (as the court had ordered), but he was then immediately rearrested, in the expectation that a German request for extradition would soon arrive in Italy. The crisis had passed, the judges were free to go home, and Priebke went back to jail just after 2 A.M. The whole episode, however, showed unmistakable signs of having been hurriedly patched together.

Rome's mayor, Francesco Rutelli, set aside the Piazza Campidoglio in front of the city hall for a public protest three days later. Several thousand turned out and, joined by the leading members of government and the Parliament, demanded a just sentence on appeal. Mayor Rutelli also announced that the city of Rome would constitute itself as another "injured party," and he ordered the lights of the city's historic monuments turned off as a sign of protest.

A moving ceremony followed. Three speakers read the names of all 335 victims, and, as is common in Mediterranean Europe, the public—several thousand—applauded as each speaker finished a page of thirty names. The piazza burst into sustained applause at the conclusion of this memorial. It was a powerful and contained display of mourning, outrage, and shame.

1997–1998: TWO MORE TRIALS

Public protest set in motion something of a "virtuous cycle." Even before an appeal could be heard, the Court of Cassation accepted the prosecution's and the civil plaintiffs' earlier argument that the judges of the Military Tribunal should have disqualified themselves. The first trial—its evidence, verdict, and sentence—was thrown out, and the higher court ordered a second trial. Jurisdiction was again given to the military justice system, but the stage was set for a more impartial examination of the case.

In the meantime, Priebke was released from jail but placed under house arrest while waiting for the trial to begin. Conceding such a provision to a man on trial for war crimes raised a passionate public debate, but Priebke remained in a monastery outside Rome.

The second trial started in April 1997. The defense team kept Priebke out of court; an icy demeanor and a refusal to express remorse made Priebke his own worst enemy, even without offering a word of testimony. The prosecution again recommended a guilty verdict and a life imprisonment sentence. The Military Tribunal reached its conclusions in July 1997: guilty (again, as in the first trial) but this time punishable. The court had accepted an important principle for the first time in Italy: "war crimes" have no statute of limitations. This meant that the maximum sentence was now life imprisonment; however, the court again cited mitigating circumstances and reduced Priebke's jail sentence to only fifteen years, and ten of those were canceled due to various amnesties issued since 1945. Since Priebke had already served three years and four months following his arrest in Argentina, it looked as if a man just convicted of a war crime would be free in only twenty months.

Protest again rained down on the court. Rome's chief rabbi Elio Toaff claimed in the press that "nothing has really changed since [the first trial] last year." Toaff "would have wanted to see Priebke judged not only for the crimes he committed but for the evil ideology that he represented" and concluded that "Italy has lost the chance to condemn Nazism in court."[2] The positive element of the sentence—and it was an extremely important one—was the affirmation that war crimes remain punishable forever. Tullia Zevi again underlined this fact, noting that "though we would have preferred a different sentence, the trial took place at a time when Italy is considering eliminating the penalty of life imprisonment entirely. Life imprisonment would (certainly) have sent a stronger message . . . a declaration by the Italian Republic that you cannot cancel certain crimes; (but) the end result for Priebke would be the same."[3]

The prosecution and the civil plaintiffs appealed. A third Priebke trial—really an appeal of the sentence from the second—began in January 1998. It finished its work early in March, and after eight hours of deliberations, the judges offered their sentence. As in both of the earlier trials, the verdict was "guilty." As in the second trial, the conclusion was "punishable." But finally, in this third trial, the sentence was life imprisonment. The court decided that the brutality of this crime did not allow the application of any generic mitigating circumstances (age, conduct since the war, etc.). Therefore, the penalty for murder, life imprisonment, had to be applied in full. This, too, was a new decision in an Italian court. Nine months later, the highest court, the Court of Cassation, upheld this decision. The last issue was imprisonment, and early in 1999 Priebke's defense lawyers successfully argued for "house arrest" for the term of the life sentence.

The Priebke trials had come to a conclusion. The president of the Jewish Community of Rome, Sandro Di Castro, summarized: "This is a condemnation by history and by the Italian people of a horrendous crime, which for no reason must ever be forgotten. We can all now rest a bit more easily."[4] De Castro's opinion was shared by some, but not by all, even within the Jewish community.

CONSIDERATIONS: STEPS FORWARD

Between extradition and three trials, Erich Priebke, eighty-four years old, had been in the public eye for nearly five years. A "guilty" verdict on the charge of "war crimes" and a life imprisonment sentence had finally been reached, but praise alternated with deep concern over the limits of the trials. Let me review both positions.

Maybe of greatest importance, "war crimes" were placed alongside "crimes against humanity" as knowing no statute of limitations in Italy. The last trial also corrected two earlier, horrible mistakes; it threw out the notion that mitigating or extenuating circumstances could reduce the penalty for a war crime; second, it rejected the defense of "just following orders," accepted for five junior officers in the 1948 trial of the Fosse Ardeatine. Italy had returned to the principles established by the Nuremberg War Crimes Trial. Hannah Arendt's argument, from the Eichmann trial in Jerusalem in 1961, on the difference between "obedience" and "support" had found its way into the courts.

As well, the shameful sentences issued in the first and second trials probably destroyed the reputation of the Military Tribunals, and there is some reason to expect that—as the Italian Constitution states—they will no longer be part of the justice system in times of peace.

The trial also directly addressed a very delicate current in Italian public opinion: the notion, first put forward by Judge Quistelli but picked up on a wider basis, that the trial of an eighty-four-year-old man was outright persecution. Instead, reaffirmed was the principle that certain crimes know no statute of limitations—not only legally, but also "culturally." The sentiment expressed, for example, in the headline of the conservative newspaper *Il Giornale*—"They are going to retry Grandpa Priebke"[5]—remained an isolated one. Priebke's "house arrest" later demonstrated a reasonable concern for his age; the few attempts to consider an official "pardon" or an act of clemency have not been officially formulated.

The historical discussion during the months of these trials was of great value as well. The testimony of some survivors of the via Tasso—Jews and others—offered long-overdue reflection on events either forgotten or never known.

The Priebke trial also introduced a very important new element to the understanding of war crimes generally and to this war crime in particular. The combined efforts of both of the civil plaintiffs—the Jewish Communities and the Association of the Families of the Victims—made the public aware that Priebke's was a crime against all Italians, of all classes, religions, and cultures—in other words, a crime against the nation, not just against some members of the nation. Di Castro said: "The drama of the Fosse Ardeatine concerns us Jews only in a small part; on that day (in 1944), above all, many, many Romans died. And I believe that we Jews will have won our battle for historical memory the day in which all of civil society realizes that Nazism was a tragedy for all, and not just for the Jews."[6] The Priebke trial was an important step in this direction for the country and the Jewish community.

The trial also led many schoolteachers and, then, the Minister of Education to insist on giving greater attention to the key political and moral issues of the twentieth century. A major reform of the national school curriculum emphasizing contemporary history was announced within a few months after the first Priebke trial.

Questions about "who was really responsible" for the Fosse Ardeatine massacre were raised, too; attempts made to blame the partisans failed. The vice president of Rome's Jewish community, Riccardo Pacifici, commented on a 1997 court case filed against the partisans for the bombing in via Rasella :

We're uneasy because the re-opening of this case . . . matches the interests of those who wish to "re-write history," accusing those Italian citizens who courageously decided to fight for the freedom of Italy and all of Europe against a foreign army of occupation that spread brutal terror. We're concerned because this tendency sets in motion a process whose purpose is to place those who fought for tyranny and those who fought for freedom on the same level.[7]

Finally, the guilty verdict and life imprisonment sentence reaffirmed that antifascism—the foundation of the Italian Republic and its original moral claim to democratic governance—still really matters.

CONSIDERATIONS: THE LIMITS

Criticism of the case was very common, maintaining that, despite the last verdict and sentence, the Priebke trial was too close a call and much less than it should have been.

First, the three trials were marked by a lack of attention to detail that often verged on incompetence. The extradition request was poorly managed by two successive governments and the last-minute efforts of the Minister of Justice to block Priebke's release in 1996—all conveyed the image of a state that rose to the moral and legal challenge presented by the Priebke trial only when forced to, only at the last moment, and then not very well at that.

The assignment of this case to a military tribunal was a legal mistake made twice; Priebke was not a soldier but a member of the Gestapo, the police force of a political party. Numerous cases in Germany have established the distinction between the police force of the Nazi Party and the regular German military; none of the documents submitted to the court on this issue were apparently even translated. The Nuremberg War Crimes Trial established the Gestapo as a criminal organization; no citation of this fact was included in the Priebke trials. These arguments would have forced the trial into the civil court system, whose greater professionalism and higher standards of justice would have prevented a series of errors. A civil court would have also given a wider historical reading to a trial, which should have been as much about Nazism as against a murderer.

For many, the Priebke trial also represented a missed opportunity to explore a dark corner of recent Italian history. Jews were taken to the Fosse Ardeatine because they were in prison; and they were in prison because the Gestapo had seized them as a first step toward deportation and death, the fate that hundreds had already suffered since the German occupation of Italy in the fall of 1943.

This was where the Racial Laws of 1938 and continued collaboration with the Republic of Salò had led the nation by 1944. There is still little critical historical or popular reflection on the racial laws (or on Italy's record as a colonial power in the late 1930s). The first half of Roberto Benigni's film *Life Is Beautiful* has done something to soften up the ground for a wider consideration of what anti-Semitism as official fascist policy started. But this has only just begun. In 1994 Victor Emmanuel IV, the current "pretender" to the Italian throne living in exile in Switzerland, was asked if an official apology for his grandfather's signature to the racial laws in 1938 wouldn't help ease the reentry of the royal family into Italy. The grandson replied that, in actual practice, the racial laws weren't that bad in Italy. Tragically, this is a widely held opinion.

Collaboration with the Republic of Salò has largely disappeared from Italy's memory of itself between 1943 and 1945. Hundreds of the political prisoners arrested and the Jews subject to deportation had been turned in by other Italians working with Mussolini's fascists and the Germans, in some cases up until just days before Allied troops arrived. In France the Maurice Papon trial (which took place at the same time as the second Priebke trial) opened up the issue of collaboration for national reconsideration. These ugly, uncomfortable, but necessary truths have yet fully to surface in Italy.

Another element missing from the Priebke trials is the story of his life from 1946 to 1994. How had he escaped from Italy and avoided the charge of war crimes? Was his conversion to Catholicism in 1948 a sign of religious conviction or an element in his escape to South America? How did he make it to Argentina, and how did he provide for himself in Bariloche? Answers to these questions came out in France during the trial of Klaus Barbie in the 1980s. None, however, emerged during the Priebke trials.

Finally, the Priebke case has not yet served to accelerate the investigation of hundreds of other men also charged with war crimes. The military tribunals "temporarily" closed their files—illegally—between 1945 and 1949. Many individuals still have to account for their actions in Italy during the war. Two, for example, popped up during the Priebke trial. One, Karl Hass, was still in Italy; he had been Hitler's interpreter in Rome, he had been present at the Fosse Ardeatine, and, after the war, he had worked for the Italian military intelligence services. A second man—who had set and detonated the explosives at the quarry—had lived in southern Austria under his own name since 1948 but war crimes investigators had never searched for him.

CONCLUSION

These are all legitimate criticisms of the Priebke trials, but every trial of war crimes or crimes against humanity, from Nuremberg, to Jerusalem, to Lyons and now Rome, has been marked by furious debates over jurisdiction, procedure, evidence, and sentencing. In this, Italy's trial of Priebke may not be all that different, and by Italian standards of justice, Priebke's case was dealt with quickly: two and a half years from start to finish. Other criminal cases, from first trial through the appeals process, can easily stretch out for five to seven years.

What overall conclusion can be made regarding the Priebke trials? The determination in Italy in the late 1990s to prosecute war crimes—even through all the twists, turns, and contradictions of the Priebke trials—strengthens the argument that these crimes, wherever and whenever they are committed, will be pursued and judgment rendered, years—even fifty years—later. The Jewish communities of Italy and the families of the victims of the Fosse Ardeatine helped to deliver this message from Italy; and there are few more important messages about justice to be made in these weeks of war (April 1999) in the Balkans.

CHRONOLOGY

23 March 1944: *Partigiani* attack German troops in via Rasella. Thirty-three German soldiers die.

24 March 1944: Order received for retaliation. 200 prisoners taken from Regina Coeli prison; 135 prisoners taken from Gestapo prison in via Tasso. Seventy-five Jews are among the prisoners. Driven to the Fosse Ardeatine (an abandoned quarry outside Rome); all prisoners are killed. Captain Erich Priebke, Gestapo, in charge.

6 May 1994: ABC journalist Sam Donaldson interviews Erich Priebke in Bariloche, Argentina.

7 May 1994: Priebke interview aired on Italian television.

8 May 1994: Priebke is arrested by Argentine police.

9 May 1994: Italy announces its intention to apply for extradition.

August 1995: Italy submits documentation and its formal request for Priebke's extradition.

2 November 1995: Argentina grants Italy's extradition request after adding "crimes against humanity" to the Italian foreign minister's charge of "war crimes."

21 November 1995: Priebke arrives in Italy and is placed in the prison at Forte Boccea in Rome.

28 February 1996: Court of Cassation sets a precedent by allowing the *parte civile*—the Italian Jewish Communities and the Association of the Families of the Victims of the Fosse Ardeatine—to take part in a trial held in a Military Tribunal.

24 March 1996: Court of Cassation fully excludes the possibility of hearing the Priebke case in civil court.

3 April 1996: Preliminary hearings begin. Priebke proclaims his innocence, declaring that he risked his own life if he hadn't followed orders.

8 May 1996: First Priebke trial begins.

10 July 1996: Public prosecutor Intelisano asks Judges Quistielli and Rocchi to disqualify themselves on the grounds that they expressed an opinion favorable to Priebke's defense in 1995. Judge Quistelli rejects this request, and the Appeals Court confirms this decision a few days later.

15 July 1996: Prosecution case against Priebke closes with demand for a guilty sentence and life imprisonment.

30 July 1996: Appeals Court rejects a second request to disqualify Judges Quistelli and Rocchi, presented by the *parte civile* representing the Jewish Communities and the Association of the Families of the Victims of the Fosse Ardeatine.

1 August 1996: Military tribunal declares Priebke "guilty, but not punishable." Priebke is convicted on multiple, first-degree murder charges, but the statute of limitations (twenty years) for this crime, plus "generic" mitigating and special extenuating circumstances reduce his thirty-year jail sentence to zero. The court orders Priebke released. Public protest turns into a siege of the courthouse that lasts for several hours, until after midnight. Neither the judges nor Priebke is safe to leave. Justice Minister Flick arrives at the courthouse at 9 P.M.

2 August 1996: Priebke is released at 1 A.M. and then immediately rearrested, citing an expected request from Germany for his extradition. Rome's mayor, Franceso Rutelli, turns off the lights on city monuments in protest over the Military Tribunal's decision.

5 August 1996: Rome's mayor, Francesco Rutelli, calls for public demonstration in Piazza Campidoglio.

10 August 1996: Priebke's defense attorneys challenge Priebke's second arrest before the Cassation Court. The arrest is later upheld.

15 October 1996: Cassation Court accepts the prosecution and "civil party" motions to disqualify Judges Quistelli and Rocchi. Cancels verdict and sentence

and orders a second trial for Priebke.

10 February 1997: Cassation Court determines that a military tribunal will again hear the Priebke trial.

18 March 1997: Despite much protest, Priebke is released from jail and placed under house arrest in a monastery in Frascati (near Rome) while waiting for the trial to begin.

14 April 1997: The second Priebke trial begins.

27 June 1997: Prosecution's case ends with a request for a guilty verdict and life imprisonment.

22 July 1997: Military tribunal issues its sentence; guilty verdict and jail sentence establishes principle that there is no statute of limitations on war crimes. Priebke is still convicted on multiple first-degree murder charges but now sentenced to fifteen years in prison (ten years to be pardoned as part of the general amnesty of 1945, three years and four months already served since his arrest in Argentina).

October 1997: Appeal filed.

27 January 1998: Appeal trial begins.

7 March 1998: Appeal trial concludes with a guilty verdict and a sentence of life imprisonment to be served in a military prison.

17 November 1998: Court of Cassation confirms the life imprisonment sentence. A few months later, the prison sentence is converted into "house arrest."

NOTES

1. *La Repubblica*, 2 August 1996, p. 1.
2. *La Repubblica*, 23 July 1997, p. 1.
3. Ibid.
4. *La Repubblica*, 17 November 1998, p. 1.
5. *Il Giornale*, 16 October 1996, p. 1.
6. *La Repubblica*, 30 June 1997, p. 1.
7. Ibid.

Part V

PRIMO LEVI

27

Deporting Identity:
The Testimonies of Primo Levi
and Giuliana Tedeschi

H. Marie Orton

Over the past decade, the Shoah in Italy has received increasingly greater critical and social attention, due in part to the wide diffusion of Primo Levi's writing and the adjacent critical response and historical inquiries that have steadily expanded since his premature death in 1987. Though now international best-sellers, Levi's Holocaust writings elicited little critical attention before 1984. Levi, like the majority of Italian writers and scholars until recently, never used the terms "Holocaust" or "Shoah" but instead referred exclusively to "*la deportazione*." This tendency in Italy to identify the genocide as "deportation" has to do with the events specific to the Italian context. While Italy instituted its own series of racial laws in 1938, aligned with Germany the following year, and in 1940 began building its own camp system, actual deportations of Italian Jews (as well as Jews in Italian-controlled war zones) to Nazi death camps followed almost immediately the fascist "betrayal" of the Nazi alliance and the subsequent Nazi invasion of Italy in September 1943.[1] The contemporaneous deportation of tens of thousands of Italian resistance fighters (*partigiani*) to Nazi camps and the early presence of volunteer civilian workers from Italy to the Third Reich have contributed to the Italian formation of the concept of *la deportazione*.[2] In the testimonies of two Jewish Auschwitz survivors, Primo Levi and Giuliana Tedeschi, the deportation stands as the dominant metaphor of the annihilation of identity that they experienced in the Lager. Deportation in these two testimonies means displacement, dehumanization, violence to the body, and violence to identity. The displacement/estrangement metaphor stands central in each testimony for understanding the destruction of identity, for it reveals that though their bodies returned, their identities did not survive Auschwitz-Birkenau.

The testimonies of Levi and Tedeschi aim to reverse the process that Hannah Arendt termed "mastering the past"[3] or the making of meaning for history through narrative that involves imposing a totalizing interpretation of experience.

Conversely, Levi's and Tedeschi's narratives, in reconfiguring their own identities, also reconfigure the historical context that bounded those identities. Their narratives seek to exorcise their past by "un-explaining" the deportation. Both survivors show that no "final" meaning can be assigned to the tragedy; they write to witness and preserve but not explain or "master" the past, for Auschwitz defies logical explanation. Their testimonies bear witness to the ways in which the violence of Auschwitz systematically destroyed not only bodies but identities. Central to the project of "un-mastering" the past are Levi's and Tedeschi's delineations of the relationships between identity and space and between identity and language in the camps. This study uses Gilles Deleuze and Felix Guattari's idea of "deterritorialization," the displacement of the subject and the space from which it speaks, as the mechanism of destruction that typifies the Lager machine. The concept of "space" in Levi's and Tedeschi's works is multifaceted, including physical space, the relationship to community, the "space" of language, and the discursive "space" of their texts.

ESTRANGEMENT FROM THE BODY, ESTRANGEMENT FROM COMMUNITY: DISMEMBERMENT

Primo Levi was captured in Aosta, Italy, together with a group of partisans in December 1943, was imprisoned in Fossoli at the end of January, and was deported to Auschwitz the following month, where he remained until the liberation in January 1945. The first account of his witness, *Se questo è un uomo* (Survival in Auschwitz) was published in 1948.[4] Giuliana Tedeschi was arrested "for racial motives" together with her husband on 8 March 1944; they were sent first to the camp in Fossoli, Italy, then to Maastricht in Holland before arriving in Birkenau in October. She was transferred to Auschwitz during the final months of the war. Her husband never returned from the camps, but her two infant daughters avoided capture, for Tedeschi entrusted them to their Catholic nurse, who hid and cared for them until Tedeschi's return. Her account, *C'è un punto della terra . . .* (There is a Place on Earth . . .), was published in 1988.[5] While Levi and Tedeschi did not know each other in the camps, they formed a friendship after their return and traveled together to public schools in Italy to educate students regarding the Lager. They also returned to Auschwitz together for a memorial service in 1963, and Tedeschi, who is currently living in Turin, intends to publish a joint edition of their testimonies.[6]

In the two accounts considered here, an intimate relationship exists between physical space and the writers' narration of identity. Deleuze and Guattari's concept of deterritorialization makes explicit a relationship between the subject and space; the subject speaks from a certain space, and the deterritorialized subject, the subject in exile, cannot speak from a determined space but rather shows a "vector of influence." The identity constructed by the narrators is then bounded by that "vector of influence." In these two narrations, the motif of exile or "deportation" ("estrangement," to use Deleuze and Guattari's term) is this "vector of influence." Tedeschi's and Levi's narrations reveal multiple exiles or estrangements that impinge directly on identity and, indeed, are the motor that move the annihilation of their identities. First, their bodies are exiled to Auschwitz in Poland; then, within the camp itself, their bodies are exiled to certain small corners of the Lager and there not allowed sufficient space to accommodate them; further, camp power structures do not allow the prisoners to construct a space (neither a physical space nor "space" in the sense of community). Finally, even their bodies become a space from which their identities are estranged by the force of violence.

Auschwitz includes a spatial hierarchy; the lowest-status prisoners (Jews) have the least space allowed them and the least freedom of movement. Both Levi and Tedeschi report that they were prisoners for months before they realized that Auschwitz-Birkenau contained more barracks besides their own—they are exiled from Italy but they are exiled within the camp as well. From the suffocating deportation in cattle cars to the sleeping berths with three to eight prisoners, inadequate physical space is another torturous deprivation of the camp, like starvation rations and inadequate clothing. In the Lager, physical confinement is a life-and-death issue in two senses: first, those who do not remain in their assigned spaces are executed, and second, as revealed in Levi's chilling account of the selection of 1944, death is routinely meted out to thousands of prisoners arbitrarily with the justification of "making more room."

In the Lager, confinement *of* the body also spells confinement *from* the body, for the prisoners have the sense that their bodies are not their own. Both Levi and Tedeschi equate this invasion and estrangement with death. As Levi reports, the prisoners are not allowed control over the space of their own bodies, as is evident in his retelling of being tattooed upon entering the camp: "In an instant, with an almost prophetic intuition, the reality becomes apparent—we have reached the bottom. Further than this one cannot go . . . they will even take away our names. *Häftling* [prisoner]: I learned that I am a *Häftling*. My name is 174517; we have been baptized, we will carry the mark tatooed on our left arms until we die."[7] Here Levi transforms the image of the Christian rite of baptism, which symbolically removes the "mark" of sin and celebrates the beginning of a new life, into an opposing ritual—the imposition of a mark, but a mark that erases identity and itself suggests that the bearer of the tattoo will not live for long. Indeed, Levi's claim that "we will carry the mark until we die" foregrounds the prisoners' desperate condition and eminent death. Levi relates the act of being tattooed in his chapter entitled "Initiation." Indeed, with the act of the tattoo, the violence of the camp does mark an initiation, the beginning of the extinction of the prisoners' identities and their lives. Furthermore, Levi's use of the image of baptism implicitly charges the reader to determine where (in this scene) the actual sin lies.

The most extreme example of Tedeschi's estrangement from her identity is her confinement to the *Blocco delle esperienze*, the medical experiments of sterilization. The space of her body becomes the stage upon which the Lager acts out the most invasive and destructive aspect of her confinement. In her retelling, Tedeschi strives to distance herself from having to recount the horrific memory, thus replacing the invasion or loss of space of the experiments with a space created by narrative distance. First, she explains her story through the voice of other women (that of the Greek prisoners); second, she diffuses the invasion to her body by casting this as the experience of a group ("the Italians"), and third, she repeatedly interrupts her narration with ellipses:

The check-up went on all morning: listening to your breathing, measurements, photographs. . . . There was no time for the Italians that first day or the next. Gradually we realized we were being looked at differently by the other prisoners. When we went by, we heard, "I don't envy them, that's for sure; they're going to the Experimentation Block. They keep them there as guinea pigs."

The news was confirmed by some Greeks who had already been in the camps for quite a few months. They told of appalling surgical operations, the removal of genital organs, mysterious injections with unknown effects repeated on several occasions, maybe in an attempt to produce sterility, abdomens marked by monstrous scars . . .

Guinea pigs, human guinea pigs, material used by doctors for racial studies!

Strangely, the Greeks telling the stories, who had all been in the camp a long time, were not upset. "Better this way, girls," they said, "better than dying. They'll treat you a little bit better, and you don't have to go and work. You won't die!"

I was overcome by a wild desperation. My deepest, most intimate femininity, was anguished and rebelled. I thought of my body brutally mutilated. . . . "This body, this body, do you understand, it's not mine anymore. . . . I want a child, another child!" Memories of early motherhood, its infinite, overwhelming sweetness, flooded back like a torture, a physical need.[8]

Tedeschi truncates and re-begins this retelling four times, without ever stating what was done to her; rather, she records only fragments. The dramatic contrast between her horror at the medical experiments and her sweet memories of becoming a mother makes plain that mutilation of the body spells mutilation of the identity. This contrast, rendered more extreme by the placid attitude of the Greek women, reveals that any increased chance of survival offered by the new assignment is actually worse than death. Her self-silencing of this experience suggests that language is inadequate to the task and also re-creates on a textual level a "mutilation" of the self.

In Levi's account as well, the alienation of the narrator from the body is equivalent to the death of the body and death of the identity. As the external characteristics of the body change, the body no longer successfully functions as a means to mark identity. Levi says that "already my own body is no longer my own: my belly is swollen, my limbs emaciated, my face is thick in the morning, hollow in the evening; some of us have yellow skin, others grey. When we do not meet for a few days we hardly recognize each other."[9] The eminence of death marks the prisoners' bodies and is simultaneously a sign of the death of the identity.

The fact that prisoners become unrecognizable to each other from one day to the next extends the alienation of the individual from identity to incorporate the alienation of the individual from the community of prisoners, as well. Indeed, the second prong of the torture of spatial confinement is that it prevents the prisoners from constructing a "space" of their own or any sense of a community "space." Levi and Tedeschi describe how prisoners are continually reassigned to different quarters and work *Kommandos* arbitrarily, which prevents them from establishing connections or community. Tedeschi calls this "the constant nightmare of becoming isolated, uncomprehended by others, and hence their victims."[10] Being forced from a familiar space is tantamount to death. Absence lays bare one of the fundamental paradoxes of the Lager—prisoners are constantly together but always alienated.

As Levi explains, in the Lager, the violence of relationships in the camps makes community impossible; in the battle for survival, every person lived "at other people's expense" and was therefore "desperately and ferociously alone."[11] In his final text dedicated to his experiences in Auschwitz, *I sommersi e i salvati* (The Drowned and the Saved),[12] published shortly before his death, Levi dedicates several chapters to examining the role of violence in the camp structure. Levi articulates clearly that the camp power structure depended directly upon fostering hostility among the inmates:

The arrival in the Lager was indeed a shock because of the surprise it entailed. . . . One entered hoping at least for the solidarity of one's companions in misfortune, but the hoped-for allies except in special cases, were not there; there were instead a thousand sealed off monads, and between them a desperate covert and continuous struggle. This brusque revelation, which became manifest from the very first hours of imprisonment, often in the instant form of a concentric aggression on the part of those in whom one hoped to find future allies, was so harsh as to cause the immediate collapse of one's capacity to resist. For many it was lethal, indirectly or even directly.[13]

As Levi elucidates, the impossibility of community within the Lager was itself deadly to the prisoners, even upon entry in the camps. Here the nexus between the body and the identity becomes very clear, for the estrangement from the body (the communal body as well as the physical body) spells the death of both. For Levi, the fact that the Lager forced everyone within its walls to become the potential enemy of everyone else is synonymous with the total moral collapse of Auschwitz.

Levi makes equally clear that, inversely, the inclusion in a community structures identity. In *Survival in Auschwitz* Levi recounts how, during the final days before the arrival of the liberating Russian troops, he and two French prisoners work together to care and provide for their eleven fellow inmates in the Ka-Be (sick ward). The bedridden inmates, out of gratitude, volunteer a portion of their tiny store of bread for the three "workers." For Levi, this impulse of group solidarity signals his regaining a "human" identity. The spontaneous gratitude and sharing of bread spells the end of the Lager:

Only a day before a similar event would have been inconceivable. The law of the Lager said: "eat your own bread, and if you can, that of your neighbour," and left no room for gratitude. It really meant that the Lager was dead.

It was the first human gesture that occurred among us. I believe that that moment can be dated as the beginning of the change by which we who had not died slowly changed from *Häftlinge* to men again.[14]

The Ka-Be, previously held as a place of death, now becomes a place of healing in the moment when human exchange becomes one of gratitude instead of violence. In Levi's account, to reestablish a community means to be reborn—he even casts the rebirth as a collective experience: "We became men again." While violence alienates the self from community, inversely, the reterritorialization of self is facilitated by a sense of community.

Tedeschi's narration distinguishes itself from Levi's in its consistent references to acts of sharing and mutual concern among the female prisoners. Nonetheless, Tedeschi's narration never assumes that such acts are typical or frequent. She never suggests that such acts construct an actual community for the women; rather, she contrasts these acts of nurturing and sharing with the context of violence surrounding them. As in many other accounts by female survivors,[15] Tedeschi tells of constructing a small group that follows a kind of family structure: Zilly, an inmate from France, takes on the role of "mother," another acts as "aunt" or "grandmother," and Tedeschi's friend Olga is like a sister to her. Tedeschi actually equates her physical survival as well as the survival of her identity with the cohesion of her group. When the group shrinks due to executions, death from illness, and transfers, she "unravels": "I felt I was alone for the first time, perhaps to remain alone forever. Prison life is like a piece of knitting whose stitches are strong as long as they remain woven together; but if the woolen strand breaks, the invisible stitch that comes undone slips off among the others and is lost."[16] The women create a space for each other and maintain that space. When sixteen women from Tedeschi's barrack are selected for the "Experiment Block," only one returns. The women in the barrack, however, still preserve the physical space that those women occupied: "In the next bunk their places were empty—one, two, three . . . fourteen, fifteen. Those spaces screamed. Where one or two were missing, the remaining women would have preferred to be crushed together as they had been before, and that night they huddled close to each other and the spaces stayed empty."[17] Preserving a physical place for the women who disappear parallels the process of witnessing, for it echoes the remembrance kept by survivors of those companions who did not survive.

ESTRANGEMENT FROM LANGUAGE: ENCRYPTION

In the Lager, language is polluted by violence and can therefore communicate only the camp business of dehumanization. Levi explains that "normal" language is insufficient to express the severity of the Lager's condition: words such as "hunger," "pain," and "fear" are created and used by those who are free, and the words cannot re-create the entirety of the Lager brutality.[18] In the context of the Lager, these words signify much more extreme conditions, and Levi posits the possibility of the Lager's creating its own language: "If the Lagers had lasted longer a new, harsh language would have been born; and only this language could express what it means to toil the whole day in the wind, with the temperature below freezing, wearing only a shirt, underpants, cloth jacket and trousers, and in one's body nothing but weakness, hunger and knowledge of the end drawing nearer."[19]

However, both testimonies give evidence that a new language was indeed created in the Lager, one in which violence becomes fused to language and becomes a language. Like control over space, control over language is an affirmation of the Lager's domination of the prisoners. The language of the camp involves a sign system created by violence in which there is no longer a moral referent; violence has inverted the moral universe and creates a different ethics in which survival takes the place of morality. Rather than the idea of morality, the idea of survival is the greatest good, an inversion of the moral universe that could not come about without violence.

Tedeschi's and Levi's narrations describe how violence, because it is omnipresent in the Lager, becomes a language and actually develops different registers and meanings. The narrators describe how violence is used to communicate things as varied as warning, cruelty, encouragement, amusement but is, in every case, used to maintain the power structures of the camp. In this language of violence that they describe, silence and threat become crucial elements used to maintain the Lager's power structures, and threat particularly becomes an intrinsic element in the camp's language of violence. Tedeschi's and Levi's narrations also concur that, despite the linguistic variety in the camp, the language of violence is universally understood. In Levi's and Tedeschi's narratives, the narrators' identities are attacked by the camp's language of violence in two ways: the language of the camp dehumanizes them and also attempts to cancel out the linguistic difference between different nationalities. Because it is violence at work, it prevents, rather than creates, a community.

Levi's account couples images of linguistic estrangement or deterritorialization with images of confinement and dispersion by comparing the crematorium at Buna to the biblical Tower of Babel:

The Carbide Tower, which rises in the middle of Buna and whose top is rarely visible in the fog, was built by us. Its bricks were called *Ziegel, briques, tegula, cegli kamenny, bricks, téglak*, and they were cemented by hate; hate and discord, like the Tower Babel, and it is this that we call it:—*Babelturm Bobelturm*; and in it we hate the insane dream of grandeur of our masters, their contempt for God and men, for us men.

And today just as in the old fable, we all feel, and the Germans themselves feel, that a curse—not transcendent and divine, but inherent and historical—hangs over the insolent building based on the confusion of languages and erected in defiance of heaven like a stone oath.[20]

Levi's description recalls from the biblical story the hubris of the people of Babel, and he applies that hubris to the Nazi program. Michael Tager suggests that the biblical metaphors that Levi uses imply "the epic scale of the suffering and evil present" in Auschwitz and also links "the linguistic confusion of the camp to its horrible moral chaos. . . . Babel in the camp resulted not only from the multiplicity of languages spoken by the inmates but from the attempt to negate language through violence. The diverse linguistically-based identities of the inmates were destroyed, and replaced by one identity based on race (as the Nazis understood it) that signified a sub-human status."[21]

The Nazi program used the difference of certain people to consolidate its own identity through the vilification of "non-Aryans." The violence inherent in reducing an identity to *Häftling* finds its logical end in the violence of the crematorium, the ultimate domination and "solution." The narrator's conservation of the linguistic diversity of the Lager inmates is not only a unique stylistic choice; Levi's preservation of linguistic difference is one way in which he reinstates in his text the individuality of all the *Häftlinge*.

The "new" language created by the Lager is a kind of universal dialect understood by all nationalities within the camp, a language that has meaning only within the hermetic world of the Lager and that could communicate only about the life in the camp. Along with the development of actual terms such as *Häftling*, *sabotaggio* (any transgression of camp regulations), *organizzare* (to find, trade, or pilfer), Canada (the work detail that emptied the arriving train cars). amd *musalmanni* (inmates who were nearly dead), the camp gave birth to a communicative system based in violence. An illustrative example is Levi's recollection that the Kapo's clubs were called *der Dolmetscher* (the interpreter).[22] The violence of the camp neutralizes normal linguistic markers and becomes itself the universally understood dialect. Violence becomes the universal camp language because it is universally inscribed on every inmate's body; violence "writes" on the body—its signs are bruises, broken bones, blood, the tattoo, the code of the camp's hierarchy. The body carries the signs of violence and becomes the site where the discourse of violence becomes flesh.

In the language of the camp, the crematorium becomes the supreme symbol of violence, a fundamental reference point in the universal camp dialect. The crematorium is the maximum symbol of confinement and dispersion—inside the crematorium, bodies are confined and subsequently dispersed as smoke and ashes; the crematorium spells annihilation of body and identity, for no trace of either remains. Tedeschi equates the rhetoric of constant threat of death with the economy of power continually reinforced in the Lager by physical violence. The threat of the crematorium becomes a part of daily language in every common exchange; it becomes intrinsic to the camp dialect that is universally understood. For over a year, Tedeschi survived the Lager at Birkenau, where the presence of the two huge crematoria used for the prisoners from Auschwitz I, II, and III conditioned the language in the camp. The continual threat, whether verbalized or not, of being sent to the crematorium remains constantly before the prisoners, just as the flame of the crematorium is always visible against the gray sky:

"Is it burning? Can you see the flame? Is there smoke?" . . .

"Kreamatorium . . . crematorio . . . crématoire," the women began to mutter: everybody whispered the word, and everybody understood it in every language. They couldn't take their eyes off the chimney. The message passed from one to the next and the tension grew. Nightmares were becoming reality. "In rows of five—*pente kai pente—zu fünf nach Krematorium.*[23]

Threat and reality merge in Tedeschi's description, for she describes walking past the crematorium as equivalent to walking into it. Tedeschi truncates her own retelling with ellipses, thus re-creating in the text the sense of life's being truncated by entering the crematorium. The crematorium represents the final silence imposed by the Lager; the flame cuts off forever all communication and burns out all traces of identity. The flame and its smoke become a line of writing that all the inmates can read, a writing that represents the ultimate deterritorialization, for that smoke is the material dispersion of their bodies into space.

WITNESSING: TEXT AS SPACE

Jean-François Lyotard asserts that literature written by camp survivors "does not say the unsayable, but says that it cannot say it." For Lyotard, witnessing can only be speaking the "forgetting of the recollection," or "negative" witnessing; to record experience in language is impossible but "to bear witness to this impossibility remains possible."[24] The estrangement-confinement theme that runs through both Levi's and Tedeschi's witness is especially evident in their self-consciousness about the act of writing their witness. Their texts become a space—a body—in which they can reinscribe their identities and reconstruct a sense of community. Ironically, however, in constructing the identity of "survivor," the text synonymously functions as a memorial to the identity and community that did not survive Auschwitz. For in de-scribing (the act of attempting to reclaim identity through writing), the narrators are re-inscribing the violence that destroyed identity.

In her narrative, Tedeschi actually assumes the voices of other women to tell her own story and writes their words and thoughts, which she claims were never spoken. For example, "'Lucky so and so,'" Olga immediately thought. 'She's got shoes, she can walk.'"[25] "[Bianca] told nobody what she had seen, that in the pit, all lying next to each other, a host of human heads were roasting slowly like chestnuts on the grate."[26] By inscribing other women's voices into her narrative, or by speaking the unspoken thoughts of her companions, Tedeschi manifests the solidarity of the group in which she takes part. Her text becomes a communal voice of group testimony and allows those to speak who did not return. At the same time, in writing, Tedeschi constructs a new identity, that of survivor. Her technique of incorporating other women's voices creates a space for the other women within her text and, in a sense, allows them to survive through her narrative.[27]

In Levi's text, his writing becomes a space in which individual identity can be reinscribed. The text becomes a space (a body) over which he has a measure of control. In The Drowned and the Saved, Levi claims that there are two kinds of survivors—those who speak and those who are silent. He includes himself with the first group and claims that he and the other "talkers" "speak because, at varied levels of consciousness, they perceive in their (even by now distant) imprisonment the center of their life, the event that for good or evil has marked their entire existence."[28] In Survival in Auschwitz, Levi connects writing to the existence of identity and his awareness of his human identity. Writing can happen only when he remembers that he was once a "man"; in the text of Survival in Auschwitz, the narrator claims that he begins writing while working in the chemistry lab, when he feels "the old ferocious longing to feel myself a man, which attacks me like a dog the moment my conscience comes out of the gloom. Then I take my pencil and notebook and write what I would never dare tell anyone."[29] Levi's act of writing distances, rather than unites, him to an audience—his writing is the *mise-en-abime* (placing in the abyss) of the exile, one who writes what no one will read. Lawrence L. Langer takes issue with the notion of "sharing" the survivor's experience through testimony, asserting instead that testimony does not "serve" but can only "preserve."[30] In the space of his text, Levi does not attempt to reestablish a link with the imagined (and negated) "community" or reader; rather, the re-writing of his violated humanity lies with the power of language to exorcise the experience. However, as Levi and Tedeschi repeatedly emphasize, the act of writing only reveals the limits of language, and witnessing becomes "creating the paradox of the inaudible silence."[31] Levi's and Tedeschi's texts reinforce that the task of their narrations is not an attempted act of recovering the identity of their pre-Lager experience. Rather, the opposite is the case: these texts memorialize the identity that was annihilated at Auschwitz-Birkenau. These narrators' project of suggesting a universal human identity is profoundly connected to their project of witnessing. Both speak as a voice constituent of a universal humanity and, with their witness, implicitly impel the reader to judge the crimes against humanity to which they testify.

NOTES

1. For a detailed study of the condition of the Jews during the fascist years, see Renzo de Felice, *Storia degli ebrei italiani sotto il fascismo* (Turin: Einaudi, 1993); Meir Michaelis, *Mussolini and the Jews: German–Italian Relations and the Jewish Question in Italy 1922–1945* (London: Clarendon Press, 1978).

2. According to G. Lazzero Ricciotti, *Gli schiavi di Hitler* (Milan: Mondadori, 1996), the first voluntary civilian laborers from Italy arrived in Germany in the middle of March 1938 and numbered in the tens of thousands by the time of the Italian armistice with the Allied troops on 8 September 1943 (p. 5). In addition, over 800,000 Italian troops were located behind German lines at announcement of the armistice, thousands of whom were taken prisoner as "betrayers" and forced into slave labor (p. 32). Ricciotti's concluding statistics indicate that over 45,000 Italians perished in Nazi camps, including 33,000 "political" prisoners, 3,000 civilian workers and former fascist soldiers, and over 7,000 Jews (p. 277).

3. Hannah Arendt, *Men in Dark Times* (New York: Harcourt, Brace, and World, 1968), pp. 21–22.

4. Primo Levi, *Se questo è un uomo* (Turin: Einaudi, 1989). As Levi explains in the appendix to his text written in 1976 for the edition still used in the Italian schools, he wrote *Se questo è un uomo* immediately upon his return from the camps in 1946; the manuscript was accepted by the small Torinese publishing house of De Silva in 1947, and 2,500 copies were published. Ten years later, the text was accepted by the Einaudi publishing house, after which its circulation increased dramatically, it was translated into numerous languages, and it was adapted for the radio and theater (Appendix, pp. 328–329).

5. Giuliana Tedeschi Fiorentino, *C'è un punto della terra . . .* (Florence: Giuntina,

1988). Tedeschi published an earlier form of her testimony in 1946 under the title *Questo povero corpo* (This Poor Body), which had a very narrow circulation and was never translated from the Italian.

    6. Alberto Cavaglion, ed., *Primo Levi: Il presente del passato* (Milan: Franco Angeli, 1990), pp. 233–234.

    7. Primo Levi, *Se questo è un uomo*, p. 23; all translations are my own.

    8. Tedeschi, *C'è un punto*, pp. 44–45.

    9. Levi, *Se questo è un uomo*, p. 32.

    10. Tedeschi, *C'è un punto*, p. 56.

    11. Levi, *Se questo è un uomo*, p. 80.

    12. Primo Levi, *I sommersi e i salvati* (Turin: Einaudi, 1986). All citations are from Primo Levi, *The Drowned and the Saved*, translated by Raymond Rosenthal (New York: Summit Books, 1988).

    13. Ibid., p. 38.

    14. Levi, *Se questo è un uomo*, p. 145.

    15. Marlene E. Heinemann, *Gender and Destiny: Women Writers and the Holocaust* (New York: Greenwood Press, 1986); Joan Ringelheim, "The Unethical and the Unspeakable: Women and the Holocaust," *Simon Wiesenthal Center Annual*, vol. 1 (New York: Chappaqua, 1991); Carol Rittner and John K. Roth, eds., *Different Voices: Women and the Holocaust* (New York: Paragon House, 1993).

    Ringleheim, Heinemann, Ritter, and Roth consider the writings of female deportees from all of Europe and attribute women's greater ability to survive to their ability to maintain positive, helping relationships. Heinemann's research concurs that women in the Lager reconstructed "family" groups and also attributes their higher survival rate to women's ability to establish emotional relationships. Ringleheim's research sustains that more women were actually deported than men; more women were immediately gassed upon arrival, and thus fewer women than men were admitted to the camps. Yet of those prisoners who were admitted, a higher percentage of women than men survived to liberation, even though, in general, conditions were much more severe in the women's camps. Liliana Picciotto Fargion's statistics of admission and survival rates of Italian deportees (*Il libro della memoria: gli ebrei deportati dall'Italia* [Milan: Mursia, 1991]) are consonant with Ringleheim's and Heinemann's statistical findings of European deportees in general.

    16. Tedeschi, *C'è un punto*, p. 124.

    17. Ibid., p. 47.

    18. Levi, *Se questo è un uomo*, p. 112.

    19. Ibid., p. 113.

    20. Ibid., p. 66.

    21. Michael Tager, "Primo Levi and the Language of the Witness," *Criticism* 35, no. 2 (Spring 1993): 284.

    22. Cesare Segre, "Primo Levi nella Torre di Babele," *Primo Levi as Witness* (Proceedings of the Symposium at Princeton University, 30 April–2 May 1989), p. 87.

    23. Tedeschi, *C'è un punto*, pp. 93–94.

    24. Jean-François Lyotard, *Heidegger and the "Jews,"* translated by Andreas Michel and Mark Roberts (Minneapolis: University of Minnesota Press, 1990), p. 47.

    25. Tedeschi, *C'è un punto*, p. 20.

    26. Ibid., p. 92.

    27. According to Heinemann's study of concentration camp narratives, all narrators portray themselves as survivors, never as heroes, and rarely as victims and consistently minimize their own role in their survival, which they invariably attribute to chance (p. 24).

    28. Levi, *Se questo è un uomo*, p. 149. During his career, Levi referred to *Se questo è un*

uomo in several different ways. On different occasions, he termed this first work a book written to *sfogarsi* (to vent); however, Levi records in *I sommersi e i salvati* that in 1959 he was offered the possibility to publish *Se questo è un uomo* in German translation and claims that his relationship to the book then became clear: "When I heard of that contract, everything changed and became clear to me: yes, I had written the book in Italian, for Italians, for my children, for those who did not know, those who, willingly or not, had assented to the offense; but its true recipients, those against whom the book was aimed like a gun were they, the Germans. Now the gun was loaded" (p. 168).

29. Levi, *Se questo è un uomo*, p. 128.

30. Lawrence Langer, *Admitting the Holocaust* (Oxford: Oxford University Press, 1995), p. 18.

31. Ibid.

28

Narrating Auschwitz:
Linguistic Strategies in
Primo Levi's Holocaust Memoirs

Eva Gold

The theme of language in the Holocaust works of Primo Levi is a complex issue. In order to understand the author's methods for rendering his memoirs believable to the public, it is necessary to examine his position with regard to the functions and dysfunctions of language and communication within the Lager and in subsequent descriptions of it, as well as his own strategic use of language to serve his larger purpose: constructing a credible Holocaust narrative.

One of the most disturbing realities concerning language in the literature of the post–World War II era is that certain terms lost much of their value as a result of how their meanings were corrupted during the war. In addition, words took on meanings that they had never had, and this altered language as a system irreversibly. Irreparable harm was done to the existing language by the events of the war, and the events of the war subsequently could not be described by language. As Susan Tarrow writes, "Levi had no illusions about the shortcomings of language. . . . The Holocaust is beyond words but its tale must be told."[1]

There are numerous examples of these problems in Levi's works, as well as in other authors' and critics' writings on the Holocaust. It is by now well known that, in their propaganda, the Nazis relied heavily on the altering of language, that is, on certain semantic shifts, to be able to carry out their plan of annihilation. In *After Babel*, George Steiner discusses the Nazi Party's use of peace terminology to gain public support. He writes:

Nazism and Stalinism . . . pilfer and decompose the vulgate. In the idiom of fascism and communism, "peace," "freedom," "progress," "popular will" are as prominent as in the language of representative democracy. But they have their fiercely disparate meanings. . .
  When antithetical meanings are forced upon the same word, . . . when the conceptual reach and valuation of a word can be altered by political decree, language loses credibility.[2]

The most striking example of this was the very sign over the entrance to

Auschwitz, *Arbeit Macht Frei*. This concept that work would lead to freedom (quite fitting, perhaps, in civilization) is clearly ironic and perverse in the setting of a camp where, if one followed the rules as dictated by the SS, one would surely die in a matter of months. As camp labor was designed to exploit and ultimately kill the worker, this equation of work with freedom was one of many linguistic violences that we find in camp language. Levi describes the maxims accompanying the "curious didactic frescoes" on the bathroom walls in Auschwitz, for example, *Ein Laus, dein Tod* (a louse is your death) and *Nach dem Abort, vor dem Essen, Hände waschen, nicht vergessen* (after the latrine, before eating, wash your hands, do not forget),[3] which are clearly intended to mock the prisoners forced to live in filth and squalor by their oppressors. In addition, as Levi points out, while attempting to keep clean may have had a certain psychological/spiritual value, it was also an activity that required the use of a large amount of calories and energy, which the severely undernourished prisoners could not spare.

The Nazis distorted meanings both to disorient and confuse their victims as well as to ensure the collaboration of the German people. Nancy Harrowitz addresses the issue of the Nazis' use of euphemism to justify the killing of millions in her essay "Representations of the Holocaust." She writes: "The Jews were referred to as vermin, and a whole rhetoric of euphemisms adopted in an effort to rely on the force of figurative language to back up a political agenda of genocide."[4] By reducing their victims to "vermin," the Nazis rendered their task acceptable. In *Language and Silence*, George Steiner addresses the effectiveness of this strategy as well:

They spoke of having to "liquidate vermin." Gradually, words lost their original meaning and acquired nightmarish definitions. *Jude, Pole, Russe* came to mean two-legged lice, putrid vermin which good Aryans must squash, as a party manual said, "like roaches on a dirty wall." "Final solution," *endgültige Lösung*, came to signify the death of six million human beings in gas ovens.[5]

Levi provides examples of the effectiveness of linguistic maneuvers used by the Nazis throughout *Se questo è un uomo* (better known in English as *Survival in Auschwitz*). His first contact with the German troops, in fact, while still in a transit camp in Italy, constitutes Levi's first encounter with this linguistic device. The words *Wieviel Stück?* (how many pieces?), used to describe men, show that the Nazis were not unaware of the importance of names and thus of renaming their enemies. In *Testimony*, Shoshana Felman refers to an interviewee in the film *Shoah* and gives the following example of the Nazis' renaming of human beings (which consisted of attributing to the human a definition generally used for the inanimate). She writes: "The Germans even forbade us to use the words 'corpse' or 'victim.' The dead were blocks of wood, shit. The Germans made us refer to the bodies as *Figuren*, that is, as puppets, as dolls, or as *Schmattes*, which means 'rags.'"[6]

It was, Levi tells us, forbidden for the SS soldiers to use the word "men" when referring to the prisoners. He relays the following episode to illustrate this point:

aware of the power of language and names, the SS prevented their men from addressing the prisoners as human beings:

On the work yard, the rookie Kapo of a squad made up mostly of Italians, French and Greeks, had not realized that one of the most feared SS supervisors had approached him from behind. He turned around suddenly, stood at attention, completely flustered, and enunciated the prescribed *Meldung*: "Kommando 83, forty-two men." In his flustered state, he had actually said "zweiundvierzig Mann," "men." The SS officer corrected him in a gruff, paternal tone: that's not how you say it, you say "zweiundvierzig Häftlinge" (forty-two prisoners). He was a young Kapo and therefore forgivable, but he had to learn the trade, the social conventions and the hierarchical distances.[7]

Linguistic ability as well as the ability to accept the dangers that became associated with trying to understand presented themselves in the camp immediately as a criterion for survival. Upon arrival at the camp, the SS men call for an interpreter among the prisoners with the words *Wer kann Deutsch*?, which Levi leaves in the original German, and Flesch, a fellow Jewish prisoner, volunteers to be the group's interpreter. Levi empathizes with Flesch, who must translate the unspeakable (and hence untranslatable) because understanding is a burden that he must first face alone and then pass on to the others.

Paradoxically, understanding is not a source of empowerment but rather an experience that demoralizes, precisely because that which one is called upon to understand and communicate is irrational, and therefore to understand it is potentially damaging. There is no dialogue on the part of the SS officers, and therefore communication is rendered impossible. For the same reason, the attempt to establish communication through questions is futile and potentially dangerous, as breaking the wall of "silence" between the SS and the Jewish prisoners would constitute a challenge to the established order. The effect of this forced participation in this first assault on the language is traumatic for the interpreter. Recounting Flesch's translation of the SS officer's orders, Levi writes: "The officer says you must be quiet, because this is not a rabbinical school. One sees the words which are not his, the bad words, twist his mouth as they come out, as if he were spitting out a disgusting mouthful."[8]

Here, Levi finds himself in a predicament with which he would have to come to terms throughout his career as a Holocaust memorialist: the dilemma of being burdened with a duty to report what he saw, a task rendered perhaps impossible not only because of the nature of memory and testimony but also because the necessary linguistic tools did not exist. Describing his first encounter with the Nazi initiation process designed to strip the prisoners of their humanity, Levi tells us: "For the first time we realized that our language lacks words to express this offense, the demolition of a man."[9]

On another level, linguistic confusion and failure in the camps were an integral part of the Germans' plan. Aware that communicating is a vital human need, the SS rendered it as difficult as possible for the prisoners to gain access to information and, consequently, to communicate successfully. After the first day, in fact, nothing was translated for the non-German speakers. This not-understanding became a part of everyday life, which provoked a terror that translated into nightmares of confronting incomprehensible orders: "One awakes at every moment, frozen with terror, limbs shaking, under the impression of an order shouted in voice full of fury in a language not understood."[10] Orders had to be obeyed, yet they were never properly communicated. In fact, the SS counted on the not-understanding of the prisoners to add to their state of misery as well as to reduce their numbers more quickly. It was an intentional (and, to the SS, useful) element of camp life. Levi writes: "The confusion of languages is a fundamental component of the way of life here: one is surrounded by a perpetual babel, in which everyone screams orders and threats in languages never heard before, and woe betide anyone who fails to grasp the meaning quickly. No one has any time here, no one has patience, no one listens to you."[11]

Levi-prisoner learns that *nessuno qui parla volentieri* (no one here speaks willingly) and that *Hier ist kein Warum* (there is no why here).[12] What are the effects on humanity of a system where "why," the most natural and spontaneous of human responses to the incomprehensible, is abolished? Levi's answer to why certain acts that outside the camp are natural and spontaneous to a person, were forbidden inside the camp illustrates how camp language adapted itself to the camp's sinister reality: "The explanation is repugnant but simple: in this place everything is forbidden, not for hidden reasons, but because the camp has been created for that very purpose."[13] The Nazi Lager's purpose was to annihilate any and all human characteristics in its victims. This plan was carried out, in part, by removing from them what was for Levi the innately human system of language. As the rules of life and community had undergone a complete perversion, so, then, did the language that was called on to describe them. There could be no "why," as the very concept of "why" presupposed a social and linguistic system that had been eliminated.

The Nazis manipulated the signifier–signified relationship in their assigning of a number (and the consequent removal of a name) to each prisoner. Since their names were no longer human ones, they were rendered subhuman to their oppressors. Roll calls, which were excruciatingly long and at which many died of cold and fatigue, consisted not of a calling of names (names belonging to human beings) but rather of numbers. Clearly, among its purposes was demonstrating to the prisoners that they were no longer human. This "objectifying" of the human subject led to the prisoners' loss of desire to carry out the uniquely human act of speech. Even the civilians working in and around the camp treated the prisoners with disdain for their apparent lack of a language similar to their own:

We are in fact the untouchables to the civilians. . . . They hear us speak in many different languages, which they do not understand and which sound to them as grotesque as animal voices. . . .They know us as thieves and untrustworthy, muddy, ragged and starving, and mistaking the effect for the cause, they judge us worthy of our degradation. . . .Who could distinguish one of our faces from the others? For them we are "Kazett," singular neuter.[14]

The quick adaptation of the prisoners to the new linguistic system is illustrated also by their attaching meaning to the numbers (rather than to names) to identify a prisoner's place of origin, as well as his level of experience and degree of ingenuousness:

As for the high numbers, they have an essentially comic air about them, as is associated with the terms "freshman" or "conscript" in normal life. The typical high number is a corpulent, docile and stupid fellow, whom one can convince that leather shoes are distributed at the infirmary to individuals with delicate feet, as well as to run there and leave his bowl of soup "in your custody": you can sell him a spoon for three rations of bread; you can send him to one of the most ferocious of the Kapos to ask him (this happened to me!) whether it is true that his is the *Kartoffelschälkommando*, the "Potato Peeling Command," and if one can be enrolled in it.[15]

In this passage Levi illustrates that certain terms were different in Auschwitz and also shows that if one took terms too literally (and missed the irony of camp language), he would not survive. One example in the passage is "in custody," which evidently in the camp acquired a meaning quite different from that in our world. Here, one who surrendered his soup to another's custody would never see it again, as camp law dictated that hunger must be satisfied in any way possible. Levi also uses the term *comicità* with irony, illustrating that what was comic in the perverse world of Auschwitz were the very discomfort and confusion of the new prisoners, as yet unacquainted with the new and strikingly different laws of survival that they were encountering for the first time.

In the following episode, Levi is forced to come to terms with the implications of his own number, which pegs him as a member of a decidedly underprivileged group. Having badly injured his foot while working, Levi must present himself for medical attention. At roll call, the prisoners in need of care line up, at which point their belongings are taken from them. Levi's ignorance of this fact provokes laughter by the crowd of prisoners present, who see the explanation for his ingenuous behavior in his number: "[T]hey look at my number and shake their heads: from one with so high a number, any stupidity can be expected."[16] While waiting in line in the camp infirmary, Levi makes the mistake of asking information of a fellow prisoner who is Aryan and therefore privileged. Here, as well, Levi's number is a cause of humiliation:

Then one of them took my arm and looked at my number and they both laughed even harder. Everyone knows that the 17400s are the Italian Jews, the well-known Italian Jews who arrived two months ago, all lawyers, all with degrees, there were over a hundred of them and now there are only forty; the ones who do not know how to work, and whose bread gets stolen, and who are knocked around from morning to the evening. The Germans call them *zwei linke Hände* (two left hands), and even the Polish Jews despise them as they do not speak Yiddish.[17]

Levi's behavior, personal history, and identity are explained by his number, which has substituted for his name.

In Auschwitz the German language itself also underwent harsh changes, and "Lager jargon" became for Levi an acquired tongue. He notes that certain new terms were universally adopted to describe certain activities that were born of life in the camp. For example, *Essen* (to eat) is replaced by *Fressen* (the German verb to describe the eating of animals, rather than humans). The way to say "never" in the camps becomes *Morgen früh* (tomorrow morning).[18] Due to the distorted rules of life and survival in the Lager, Levi emerged with the knowledge of only a certain, very specific vocabulary in his acquired "language." At the end of his chemistry exam at Auschwitz, for example, he realizes he is without the vocabulary necessary to take leave of his interviewer and writes: "For a moment I struggle, trying to come up with a suitable formula of saying goodbye, but in vain. In German, I know how to say to eat, to work, to steal, to die . . . but I do not know how to address a person in a respectful manner."[19]

Levi describes the new language necessary to reproduce the new realities of life at Auschwitz:

Just as this hunger of ours is not the sensation of missing a meal, so our way of being cold has need of a particular word. We say "hunger," we say "tiredness," fear," "pain," we say "winter" and they are different things. They are free words, created and used by free men. . . . If the Lagers had lasted longer, a new, bitter language would have been born; the language necessary to explain what it means to toil the whole day in the wind, in sub-zero temperatures, wearing only a shirt, underpants, cloth jacket and trousers, and in one's body nothing but weakness, hunger and knowledge of the inevitable end.[20]

Given that the experiences that the camp produced could not be rendered by ordinary language, a new language would be necessary to describe its events.

The ultimate result of all this was the prisoners' loss of faith in language, which could no longer be trusted to convey truth, as it had been completely violated and destroyed by the Nazi system.

Many critics have sustained the absolute impossibility of writing literature and poetry after Auschwitz. Theodor Adorno's assertion that art is impossible (and hence that it is no longer possible to write poetry/literature) after Auschwitz is perhaps the best known of these theories. Adorno's position, however, was not shared by Levi, who felt that post-Auschwitz literature was not only possible but essential. In *The Drowned and the Saved*, Levi insists on the need to communicate and writes: "To deny that communication is possible is false; one always can."[21] Yet his writing in *Survival in Auschwitz* strongly suggests that communication in the Lager was a challenge for both Levi-prisoner and Levi-author. We immediately see that relaying the Auschwitz experience required certain linguistic strategies if the author were to convey the horrors brought on by the linguistic difficulties that were an inherent part of this ordeal.

The first lesson that the prisoners learn upon arrival is that not only are they unfamiliar with the language, but the act of speech and of understanding is forbidden to them. In order to survive one had to renounce the effort to understand: "And we have learned yet other things, more or less quickly, each according to his native intelligence: to reply *Jawohl*, never to ask questions, and to always pretend to understand."[22] Paradoxically, *not* understanding (or at least pretending not to try to understand) became a necessary condition for survival.

Levi also comments on the linguistic trauma undergone by native German speakers who were forced to suffer the violence done to their mother tongue. He uses Jean Améry as an example of a German speaker who deeply suffered the corruption of German:

Améry-Mayer also affirms that he suffered from the mutilation of language that I mentioned in chapter four: and yet German was his language. He suffered from it in a way different from we who, not knowing German, were reduced to the condition of deaf mutes: in a way, if I may, that was more spiritual than material. He suffered from it *because* German was his language, because he was a philologist who loved his language, the way a sculptor would suffer at seeing one of his statues defaced or amputated. The suffering of the intellectual was therefore different, in this case, from the suffering of the uncultured foreigner: for the foreigner, Lager German was a language he did not understand (and which fact put his life at risk); for the German intellectual, it was a barbaric jargon that he did understand but that scorched his mouth when he tried to speak it. One was a deportee, the other a stranger in his own country.[23]

For both German and non-German native speakers, language was damaged and therefore could no longer be seen as an ally or a tool with which one could seek to work toward survival. Levi insists that it was the cause of profound pain in the speaker. By reminding us that the intellectual tended to suffer more deeply in the camps and that the linguistic obstacles that he found in Auschwitz were painful and confusing, Levi invites the reader to make an even greater effort to comprehend his story and to accept that his survival was indeed the result of a struggle that was painful, both physically and spiritually.

What does the loss of meaning of certain terms or the inadequacy of meaning of others mean to the Holocaust memorialist? How did Levi deal with this problem? In *Testimony*, Shoshana Felman speaks of the loss of language, recognizing that in all Holocaust literature there are both a need to speak and a simultaneous awareness that language is not commensurate with the experience.

James Young devotes his essay "Figuring and Refiguring the Holocaust—Interpreting Holocaust Metaphor" to the Nazi Lager's semantic contribution to language. Not only did the Nazis use a certain rhetoric to gain public support among the German people, but they also used a historical terminology familiar to the Jews to ensure their compliance with, and acceptance of, the persecution. He analyzes David Roskies' assertion that "during the Holocaust the literal and the practical may even have been fatally interdependent":[24]

[T]he Nazis seemed to understand all too well the historically minded—which is to say analogically minded—nature of the Jews. By re-instituting the Renaissance ghetto, the medieval yellow star, and the seventeenth century Jewish councils, for example, the Germans "thereby created a world that was both utterly terrifying and strangely familiar."[25]

The Jews thus saw the Nazi persecution as merely one more in a series of historical persecutions. Young writes: "By thus lulling their victims into analogy, as it were, by recreating all previous persecutions, the Nazis were actually able to screen from view *the difference* of the present persecution until it was too late."[26] This was a first step in making the Jews accomplices to their own destruction, which made the telling of these events practically impossible. Levi writes of the difficulty of putting into words events in which, in some sense, the Jews felt that they had been participants: "[I]t had to be the Jews who put the Jews into the ovens; it had to be shown that the Jews, sub-race, sub-human, bow to any humiliation, even to destroying themselves."[27]

In light of all the damage and manipulation done to language, how does Levi, in turn, use it to, in a sense, beat the Nazis at their own linguistic game? That is, how does he tell the story that the Nazis had sought to make untellable by employing similar linguistic tactics? As the Nazis counted on linguistic confusion to disorient the prisoner/victim, so does Levi in order to disorient the reader and pull him or her into the Lager universe. Levi's constant use of foreign words, which he could have easily translated into Italian, helps him to achieve one of his communicative goals: forcing the reader to relive his situation (albeit to a very limited extent).

Survival in Auschwitz contains many examples of this. Beginning with *Wieviel Stück?* and *Arbeit Macht Frei*, Levi carries on this use of foreign words to contribute to the readers' discomfort, which he hopes will ultimately lead to his or her identification with the author's own plight. Upon arrival at Auschwitz, as soon as the doors of the train open, "the dark echoed with foreign orders and with that barbaric barking of Germans in command which seems to give vent to century-old anger."[28] Once in the camp, Levi, having studied some German in school, explains that he understood the meanings of the numerous written prohibitions found throughout the camp. One of the first, *Wassertrinken Verboten*, symbolizes what will be a theme of Auschwitz: restrictions that deny even the most basic of human needs. Levi, in fact, attributes his having survived, in part, to his basic knowledge of the German language. One of the first things that Levi learns about himself in the camps is his role within the structure. He writes: "*Häftling*: I have learned that I am a *Häftling*" (prisoner).[29] The consequence of this new role, which can be expressed only by a German word, is a new name: "My name is 174517; we have been baptized, we will bear the tattoo on our left arm for as long as we live."[30] In order to survive, Levi tells us, he had to adjust to the sound of his new "name" in German, as actual names were never used in the camp: "only by 'showing one's number' can one receive bread and soup . . . it took weeks and months for us to learn its sound in German."[31] As far as the Nazis were concerned, in fact, their real names no longer existed. Their prisoners were not human but rather "pieces," numbers, as their tattoos suggest.

Perhaps the most significant use of German in *Survival in Auschwitz* appears in the context of Levi's being told about the exterminations, indeed the most incommunicable concept, clearly out of the frame of reference of human thought. When told by another prisoner that certain illnesses should not be reported, as they prohibit the victim from working and would therefore mean certain selection for the gas chamber, Levi himself proves unwilling to believe and writes:

I still have a fairly confused idea about this kind of danger. Everyone talks about it indirectly, by allusions, and when I ask about it they look at me and are silent.

So is it true what one hears of selections, of gas, of crematoriums? . . .

So *"der Italeyner"* does not believe in selections? Schmulek would like to speak German but speaks Yiddish; I can barely understand him, and only because he wants to be understood. He silences Walter with a sign, he will persuade me:

"Show me your number: you are 174517. This numbering began eighteen months ago and applies to Auschwitz and the dependent camps. There are now ten thousand of us here at Buna-Monowitz; perhaps thirty thousand between Auschwitz and Birkenau. *Wo sind die Andere?* Where are the others?"

"Maybe transferred to other camps?" I suggest.

Schmulek shakes his head, and he turns to Walter:

"Er will nix verstayen, he does not want to understand."[32]

Levi's use of German and Yiddish here is not necessary to recount this dialogue. In fact, he has translated all of what was said except for *Wo sind die Andere* and *Er will nix verstayen*. These are the two central ideas in the discourse, and they are made more powerful by being said twice, first in the foreign language and then in Italian. Levi wants us to read it in German, the language of the offense; he is astutely using German to bear witness to its own crimes.

Throughout the telling of the infirmary episode, Levi reminds the reader of the linguistic difficulties that he encountered, as well as of the harshness and cruelty of the German language itself, by inserting German expressions into his text. After being examined, he is told: *Nummer hundertvierundsiebzigtausend funfhundertsiebzehn, kein Fieber* and declared, *Arztvormelder*, of which he says: "What it means I do not know, but this is certainly not the place to ask for explanations."[33] Subsequently proclaimed *Aufgenommen, Block dreiundzwanzig*, he writes: "I stand there with my mouth open, waiting for some other indication, but someone yanks me brutally backwards, throws a gown on my bare shoulders, hands me a pair of sandals, and pushes me into the open." He then discovers that Block 23 is the "Schonungsblock: who knows what it means?"[34] These terms are left in German to illustrate the impact of not understanding and the complete, intentional lack of communication within the camp structure. In this chapter Levi recounts a cruelty that is, for him, best left in the original German, where it finds its truest expression. The same non-Jewish prisoners (one of whom is an infirmary nurse) who derided him because of his number (indicating that he was an Italian Jew) poke at his skin, mocking him for his frailty and undernourishment. Of this humiliation, Levi writes:

I wish I had never spoken to the Pole: I feel as if I had never in all my life undergone an offence more atrocious than this. The nurse, meanwhile, seems to have finished his demonstration in this language which I do not understand and which sounds terrible to me.

He turns to me, and in quasi-German, charitably, sums it up for me: "*Du Jude kaputt. Du schnell Krematorium fertig*" (You Jew, done for. You soon in crematorium.)[35]

Levi uses the original German to ensure that the reader encounter the jolting strangeness of camp jargon.

As German is the language of the oppressor, Levi dreams of telling his story in Italian (in his case the language of the oppressed). He tells of his yearning to turn his experiences into narration, specifically insisting that he be able to do so in his language with an interlocutor who understands. In his dream: "And a woman would pass, and she would ask me 'Who are you?' in Italian, and I would tell her in Italian, and she would understand, and she would give me food and shelter. And she would not believe the things I tell her, and I would show her the number on my arm, and then she would believe me."[36] To communicate successfully becomes a dream of the prisoners, just as to be able to find someone willing to listen was perhaps Levi's purpose in writing.

In addition to adopting very specific linguistic strategies, Levi also takes, in a sense, the very act of recording his Auschwitz experiences directly from the Nazis, as this mirrors the Nazi custom of meticulously recording every event and detail of the inhumanities that they committed (which is curious, considering they were seeking to create "an event without a witness"). George Steiner describes what happened under the Third Reich:

Not silence or evasion, but an immense outpouring of precise, serviceable words. It was one of the peculiar horrors of the Nazi era that all that happened was recorded, catalogued, chronicled, set down; that words were committed to saying things no human mouth should ever have said and no paper made by man should ever have been inscribed with. It is nauseating and nearly unbearable to recall what was done and spoken, but one must. In the Gestapo cellars, stenographers (usually women) took down carefully the noises of fear and agony wrenched, burned or beaten out of the human voice. The tortures and experiments carried out in live beings at Belsen and Matthausen were exactly recorded. The regulations governing the number of blows to be meted out on the flogging blocks at Dachau were set down in writing. When Polish rabbis were compelled to shovel out open latrines with their hands and mouths, there were German officers there to record the fact, to photograph it, and to label the photographs.[37]

While analyses of language and the problems associated with its use and reliability are present to varying degrees in all of Levi's Holocaust works, nowhere are they more evident than in his final book, *The Drowned and the Saved*. Here, Levi addresses this issue explicitly. Aware that the tools for making others understand are "language and conceptual thought,"[38] Levi proceeds to explain the perversion of language in the Lager at a distance of over forty years. The chapter "Communicating" begins with a refutation of the statement that the general human condition is one of incommunicability: "In today's normal world . . . it almost never happens that one runs into a true linguistic barrier, i.e., finds oneself face to face with a human being with whom one must absolutely establish communication or die, and is unable to do so."[39] Having found himself in a situation in which the language that he knew was incommensurate with the events that he was experiencing and in which he was unable to comprehend much of what was happening because of an unwillingness on the part of others (the SS, the other prisoners, etc.) to communicate, Levi refuses to accept that under normal circumstances one could find himself in a situation that would justify the choice not to communicate. In order to further strengthen his credibility as the ideal narrator of the camp history, he tells his readers that he is among the few who are truly acquainted with the inability to communicate and that despite that (or perhaps because of it), he chooses to use language to give testimony to his experiences. His refuting of these theories of incommunicability (Levi uses the term a bit differently than was intended in these theories; he defines it as a situation in which there is no communication or a state of linguistic confusion, which renders the natural flow of information and dialogue impossible or at least extremely problematic) is a way to legitimize his own writing, declaring it a duty rather than a choice. In response to the complaint that incommunicability was a "life sentence inherent to the human condition" Levi writes: "Except for cases of pathological incapacity, one can and must communicate. . . . To refuse to communicate is a fault; we are biologically and socially predisposed [to communication]."[40]

Levi describes what he considers normal and acceptable degrees of incommunicability, in comparison to the condition of the non-German prisoner in Auschwitz. While a tourist on vacation can usually overcome the minor discomfort of not understanding the foreign language, and the immigrant can generally remedy his situation of unfamiliarity with the language and customs of the host country (through school and work, he can acclimate himself; in addition, neighbors, family, and the belongings that he brings with him from home provide a certain degree of comfort), the camp prisoner had to deal with linguistic barriers that were often insurmountable and sometimes fatal: "We saw incommunicability in a more radical manner. . . . We immediately realized, from our very first contacts with the scornful men with the black badges, knowing German was a watershed."[41]

German became a means of dividing the human being from the nonhuman. The SS conveyed the message that German was the only true language; one who spoke no German essentially spoke no language worth speaking (which proved ultimately to be true, as German was often the difference between life and death). The SS were unable to perceive as human anyone who did not belong to their own cultural and linguistic background:

With those who understood them and answered in an articulate manner, they established a semblance of human relationship. With those who did not understand them the SS men reacted in a manner that stupefied and frightened us: the order that had been pronounced in the calm voice of one who knows he will be obeyed, was repeated word for word in a loud, angry voice, then screamed at the top of his lungs as if he were addressing a deaf person or, better yet, a household pet, who responds more to the tone than the content of the message.[42]

As speaking German became synonymous with being human, those prisoners incapable of understanding it were faced with doubts about their own humanity, which certainly explains, in part, the difficulty of narrating one's experiences. The crisis of the written word addressed by critics such as Steiner and Blanchot as well as Adorno and Celan stems from the violence done to language, of which Levi writes. In the camps, the transition from words to blows was natural, as the language of the oppressor already represented a perversion of human language:

If anyone hesitated (and everyone hesitated because they did not understand and were terrified) the blows fell, and it was evident that they were a variant of the same language: the use of the word to communicate thought, this necessary and sufficient mechanism for humans to be human, had fallen into disuse. This was a signal: for those people we were no longer men.[43]

Thus, in the camps, "language" came to mean "German." In other words, believing in only one real civilization, the SS convinced themselves (and imposed on the prisoners as a camp rule) that he who did not speak German was not part of the civilized world:

[A]n uncultured man . . . does not know how to distinguish clearly between those who do not understand his language and those who do not understand *tout court*. It had been driven into the heads of the young Nazis that there existed only one civilization in the world, the German civilization; all others, present or past, were acceptable only inasmuch as they contained some German elements. Thus, whoever did not understand or speak German was by definition a barbarian; if he insisted on trying to express himself in his own language—or rather in his own *non*-language—he had to be beaten into silence and put back in his place, pulling, carrying, and pushing, because he was not a *Mensch*, not a human being.[44]

As he tells in *Survival in Auschwitz*, Levi reminds us here that, as a result, adapting to Lager German was an absolute necessity to survival. Levi found his German-language training inadequate: "I realized that the German of the Lager— skeletal, screamed, studded with obscenities and imprecations—was only vaguely related to the precise, austere language of my chemistry textbooks."[45] In fact, he writes, "I did not realize then—and I realized this only much later—that the Lager's German was a language apart: to say it precisely in German, it was *orts- und zeitgebunden,* tied to place and time."[46] It was, indeed, so foreign, that even years later in his last book he needed German terminology to describe it. In his interview with Ferdinando Camon many years later, he reiterates the importance of communicating successfully. When asked whether not being able to communicate linguistically was fatal, Levi responds that the linguistic isolation forced on the prisoners was as significant a factor as cold or hunger in the death of many.

Finally, after his experiences have forced the Lager language upon him, Levi uses this Lager German to substantiate much of what he writes. Levi recounts an episode in which he uses, many years later, an expression from Lager German at a business meeting at Bayer, *Jetzt hauen wir ab*:

It was if I had said, "Now let's get the hell out of here." They looked at me in astonishment:

the term belonged to a different linguistic register from the one in which our preceding conversation had been conducted and is certainly taught in "foreign language" courses in school. I explained to them that I had not learned German in school but rather in a Lager called Auschwitz; this gave rise to some embarrassment, but since I was there as buyer they continued to treat me with courtesy. I realized later that my pronunciation is coarse, but I deliberately have not tried to make it more genteel; for the same reason, I have never had the tattoo removed from my left arm.[47]

What is Levi telling us about language, more specifically, about the language that he chooses to use? German is clearly the language of the oppressor, which in Levi's text becomes a sort of antilanguage, as it has been transformed into blows and other inhuman forms of expression.

In an essay, Fabio Girelli-Carasi examines the way in which Levi proposes Italian as the language of humanity, left unscathed by the atrocities of the war. He writes:

The inability to relate to the content of the words, to belong to the discourse of the Lager, may in fact have contributed to his enhanced ability to function as an observer of the linguistic reality in its unfolding. Furthermore, because he was reduced to silence, I would venture to say that his language, Italian, was preserved uncorrupted throughout the ordeal of the Lager, and that he found it still uncontaminated inside himself, his family and nation, when he began to write. The language outside the Lager, before and after the event, had not been changed by it. Italian is ignorant of the Holocaust.[48]

As Steiner maintained that the German language itself had some guilt to bear with regard to the Holocaust, here Girelli-Carasi suggests that Italian is guiltless (at least linguistically). I agree that Levi perceived Italian as not only innocent of any crime but also a kind of spiritual savior for him. By illustrating that his language (Italian) is untouched by Auschwitz and ignoring the damage done to Italian under Mussolini, he reiterates his standing as an ideal Holocaust narrator. Unlike Paul Celan, Levi argues that he can continue to trust his mother tongue, as it remained outside the world of Auschwitz, a fact that would render an Italian account of the events the most reliable.

As a chemist, Levi was able to use his position as a scientist to render his discourse more objective in nature. Similarly, he was obliged to adopt certain linguistic strategies in order to render the experiences of camp life as authentic as possible. The problematic nature of the referentiality of language was an issue that Levi was forced to confront in Auschwitz. As we have seen, this experience taught him to most effectively employ the strategies that he learned there to his own writing. In this way, Levi takes an "event without a witness" and forces language, a system damaged in many ways by the Holocaust, to bear witness to the crimes committed against it.

NOTES

1. Susan Tarrow, ed., *Reason and Light* (Ithaca, NY: Cornell University Press, 1990),

p. 5.

2. George Steiner, *After Babel: Aspects of Language and Translation* (New York and London: Oxford University Press, 1975), p. 34.

3. Primo Levi, *Se questo è un uomo* (Turin: Einaudi, 1958, 1976), p. 46. (All translations from the Italian are by Eva Gold.)

4. Nancy A. Harrowitz, "Representations of the Holocaust: Levi, Bassani, and the Commemorative Mode," in Tarrow, *Reason and Light*, p. 38.

5. George Steiner, *Language and Silence: Essays on Language, Literature and the Inhuman* (New York: Atheneum, 1967), p. 100.

6. Shoshana Felman and Dori Laub, *Testimony: Crises of Witnessing in Literature, Psychoanalysis and History* (New York: Routledge, 1992), p. 210.

7. Primo Levi, *I sommersi e i salvati* (Turin: Einaudi, 1986, 1991), pp. 71–72.

8. Levi, *Se questo*, p. 26.

9. Ibid., p. 29.

10. Ibid., p. 77.

11. Ibid., p. 44.

12. Ibid., p. 32.

13. Ibid., p. 25.

14. Ibid., p. 153.

15. Ibid., p. 31.

16. Ibid., p. 57.

17. Ibid., p. 59.

18. Ibid., p. 168.

19. Ibid., p. 136.

20. Ibid., pp. 155–156.

21. Levi, *I sommersi*, p. 69.

22. Levi, *Se questo*, p. 37.

23. Levi, *I sommersi*, p. 109.

24. David Roskies, *Against the Apocalypse: Responses to Catastrophe in Modern Jewish Culture* (Cambridge and London: Harvard University Press, 1984), p. 94.

25. James Young, *Writing and Rewriting the Holocaust: Narrative and the Consequence of Interpretation* (Bloomington: Indiana University Press, 1988), p. 191.

26. Ibid., p. 94.

27. Levi, *I sommersi*, pp. 37–38.

28. Levi, *Se questo*, p. 19.

29. Ibid., p. 30.

30. Ibid.

31. Ibid.

32. Ibid., pp. 63–64.

33. Ibid., p. 56.

34. Ibid., p. 58.

35. Ibid., p. 59.

36. Ibid., p. 52.

37. George Steiner, *Language and Silence* (New York: Atheneum, 1967), pp. 99–100.

38. Levi, *I sommersi*, p. 24.

39. Ibid., p. 68.

40. Ibid., pp. 68–69.

41. Ibid., p. 70.

42. Ibid.

43. Ibid.

44. Ibid., p. 71.

45. Ibid., p. 75.

46. Ibid., p. 76.

47. Ibid., pp. 77–78.

48. Fabio Girelli-Carasi, "The Anti-Linguistic Nature of the Lager in the Language of Primo Levi's *Se questo è un uomo*," in Tarrow, *Reason and Light*, p. 49.

The Tower of Babel:
Language and Power in
Primo Levi's *Survival in Auschwitz*

Anna Petrov Bumble

In his book *Language and Symbolic Power* French philosopher and sociolinguist Pierre Bourdieu analyzes the relationships between language and power in great detail.[1] Bourdieu argues that language as "the relations of communication *par excellence*—linguistic exchanges—are also relations of symbolic power in which the power relations between speakers or their respective groups are actualized."[2] One of the best literary examples supporting Bourdieu's theory is Levi's *Survival in Auschwitz*, as it is through his unique understanding of the importance of language that Primo Levi is capable of illuminating the Nazi philosophy behind the "Final Solution." Symbolic power of language is a key concept in *Survival in Auschwitz* since, through this technique, Levi actualizes his relationships with the world of the camp. In this context, Levi's emphasis on the functions of language in the camp and consequently on the balance of power is of the utmost importance for our understanding of the Holocaust experience.

The first step in Levi's attempt to adjust to the new reality of the camp is to realize the significance of linguistic chaos. After arriving at Auschwitz, the protagonist, the young Italian chemist Primo Levi, is exposed to a stunning multiplicity of European languages heard and spoken in the camp. Throughout the narrative, Levi describes the nationalities present at the camp and illustrates their interactions among themselves and with the Germans.

The confusion of languages is a fundamental component of the manner of living here: one is surrounded by a perpetual Babel, in which everyone shouts orders and threats in languages never heard before, and woe betide whoever fails to grasp the meaning. No one has time here, no one has patience, no one listens to you; we latest arrivals instinctively collect in the corners, against the walls, afraid of being beaten.[3]

European peoples, Jews, Poles, Greeks—all can be found in the camp. Each group's status corresponds to, and sometimes is even directly dependent on, its language and national background. Levi describes multiple individuals, himself included, whose chances of survival increase just by virtue of knowing foreign languages. In a conversation with Philip Roth, Levi outlined three main components that enhance a prisoner's odds: "I insist there was no general rule, except entering the camp in good health and knowing German. Barring this, luck dominated."[4]

It is important to emphasize that Auschwitz was not only the place where the German language attempted to structure the life of the camp and to expunge the memories of the prisoners but also the epitome of linguistic chaos. Multilingual confusion influenced the psychological stability of the prisoners and negatively affected their ability to understand their new reality. In Fedinando Camon's *Conversations with Primo Levi*, it is evident that Primo Levi was acutely aware of this linguistic chaos and its devastating affect on Italian prisoners in Auschwitz. In the chapter "The Sin of Being Born," Levi explains the lack of all prisoners' awareness that they are suffering a common injustice in the following way:

The fundamental reason [for the lack of unity among the prisoners, even Jews] was the lack of communication. . . Few of us Italian Jews understood German or Polish—very few. Under those conditions the language barrier was fatal. Almost all Italians died from it. Because from the very first days they didn't understand the orders, and this wasn't allowed, wasn't tolerated.

I—I've always said I was lucky—I found I had a little bit of the German language at my command, as a chemist I'd studied it, and so I was able to establish some sort of communication with the non-Italians, and this was essential for understanding where I was living, the rules of the place.[5]

Remembering Dante thus becomes in itself an attempt on Levi's part to bring order to the "indecipherable inferno" of the concentration camp,[6] characterized by linguistic chaos and the severance of all cultural ties. Risa Sodi quotes Levi by writing that "one clings to the atavistic notion that the world may be terrible but always decipherable."[7] The world of the Lager is, however, not only violent and dehumanizing but also indecipherable (*ne pas chercher de comprendre*). The reader thus is compelled to follow Levi's experience, going through the same stages: overwhelming linguistic chaos, alteration of individuality and identity, and finally abandonment of familiar thinking patterns. In the words of Fabio Girelli-Carasi, "[I]mplicit in the term Holocaust is a phenomenon whose enormity has defied all attempts at comprehension and definition, causing the surrender of our power of categorization and rational understanding."[8] The camp forces Levi to "unlearn" familiar notions and learn new, dehumanizing categories.

Notwithstanding the position of the "master language" as an object of hatred, learning German was compulsory for survival. Levi provides the reader with several situations that reflect the importance of understanding the basics of the German language to both maintain physical survival and on occasion to promote one's status. In the chapter "The Drowned and the Saved," Levi explores the permeable boundary between good and evil in the human soul, which is invaluable for understanding the history of the Holocaust. He emphasizes survival benefits gained by learning the German language. Since language is the key to the written and unwritten laws of the camp, it is also the key to the preservation of the prisoners' mental stability and avoidance of becoming a "musselman." Levi describes "the drowned," those who lose the will to struggle and have neglected not only their bodies but also their identity and the sense of their own humanity. He writes: "[T]hey are beaten by time, they do not begin to learn German, to disentangle the infernal knot of laws and prohibitions until their body is already in decay, and nothing can save them from selections or from death by exhaustion."[9]

Upon the arrival of an Italian train to Auschwitz containing 650 "Stück" of Italian Jews, the atmosphere encompassed by confusion and the fear of the unknown, one prisoner volunteers to be a translator from German to Italian. The job, however, immediately evokes in him feelings of hatred and revulsion as he is confronted with the power of the German language over people's lives:

The door opens, and a German enters; it is the officer of before. He speaks briefly, the interpreter translates. "The officer says you must be quiet, because this is not a rabbinical school." One sees the words which are not his, the bad words, twist his mouth as they come out, as if he was spitting out a foul taste. We beg him to ask what we are waiting for, how long we will stay here, about our women, everything; but he says no, that he does not want to ask. This Flesch, who is most unwilling to translate into Italian the hard cold German phrases and refuses to turn into German our questions because he knows that it is useless.[10]

One rarely thinks of language as an intrinsic part of the Nazi war machine. For the Auschwitz prisoners assembled from all over Europe, coping with the symbolic power of language over human lives is not an easy task. It is not only the power to pronounce the sentence of life or death; it is also the power of naming.

The process of dehumanizing by replacing the real name of a person with a six-digit number is the result of the controlling power that naming holds over people. In a chapter called "Rites of Institution," Bourdieu points out that naming is a systematic ritual adopted by an institution of political power. The ritual of naming is constructed by recognizing the criteria of distinction among people; thus, linguistic power imposes a specific vision of social structure on the constituency of any nation. Furthermore, Bourdieu points out that "social science must take account of the symbolic efficacy of rites of institution, that is, the power they possess to act on reality by acting on its representation."[11] A person's hair is shaved, his personal belongings are taken away (all these are symbolic signs of power), and his own name is replaced by an anonymous reference, "*Häftling*." Levi does not fail to illuminate the devastating results of these actions on the psychological stability of the inmates and their sense of individuality: "Imagine now a man who is deprived of everyone he loves, and at the same time of his house, his habits, his clothes, in short, of everything he possesses: he will be a hollow man, reduced to suffering and needs, forgetful of dignity and restraint, for he who loses all often easily loses himself."[12]

These actions transform the representation the person has of himself and impose on the person a new vision of the universe—he or she is not a human being anymore but a nameless slave. A clear understanding of the nature of this transformation provides the reader with yet another perspective of Levi's phrase, "I have learnt that I am Häftling. My number is 174517; we have been baptized, we will carry the tattoo on our left arm until we die."[13] As Wade Kelson observes in his article "Primo Levi and the Humanness of Cultural Understanding," by the transition from "cultural margins of Italy"—the detention camp near Modena—to the very bottom of humanity in Auschwitz, "Levi entered a deeply marginalized world characterized by the vacuity of cultural centering."[14] From a member of the Jewish minority in Italy, Primo Levi was declassed into a nonentity and brutalized into a nonhuman, and all conceivable effort was made to deprive him of his intellectual and spiritual individuality, cultural connection to his home country, and awareness of his own humanity.

By replacing a prisoner's name with a number, the Nazi ideology restructured that prisoner's life and deprived him or her of a familiar identity. In Bourdieu's words,

The act of Institution is thus an act of communication, but of a particular kind: it *signifies* to someone what his identity is, but in a way that both expresses it to him and imposes it on him by expressing it in front of everyone (*kategorein*, meaning originally, to accuse publicly) and thus informing him in an authoritative manner of what he is and what he must be.[15]

In this context, our next point of interest is to find out what Levi's identity was before the war. In his essay "Beyond Survival," Levi wrote: "I accepted the condition of being a Jew only as a result of the racial laws enacted in Italy in 1938, when I was 19 years old, and of my deportation to Auschwitz, in 1944."[16] This statement is fully understood in the context of the history of Jewish emancipation in Italy, assimilation of Italian Jewry, and its profound integration into the social and cultural life of the country. According to Cecil Roth's *The History of the Jews of Italy*, "some 8 percent of the university professors in 1930 were Jews; while in the standard Italian handbook of contemporary biography, 169 out of the 2,515 notables listed, or 6.72 percent, belonged to Jewish families, though the proportion of the Jews in the country was only about one-tenth of one percent"[17] after the emancipation had reached its culmination in 1909, when Luigi Luzzatti became the first Italian Jewish prime minister. Only in the atmosphere of the totalitarian regime of the late 1930s to early 1940s did the legacy of Jewish emancipation in Italy start to crumble. "Like most Jews of ancient Italian descent," Levi writes in "Beyond Survival," "my parents and grandparents belonged to the middle class, and they had thoroughly assimilated the language, customs, and ethical attitudes of the country. Religion did not count much in my family."[18] Ironically, in Auschwitz Levi learns about Judaism and East European Jewish culture through his encounters with a Yiddish linguistic environment.

Levi's connection to his Italian background is personified in the non-Jewish Italian civilian worker Lorenzo. Lorenzo feeds Primo with his bread and soup ration every day for six months, gives Primo his vest, and sends a postcard to Italy on Levi's behalf. Not only does Lorenzo not consider himself superior due to his race, but, more importantly, he never expects any reward "because he [is] good and simple and [does] not think that one [does] good for a reward."[19] Furthermore, Lorenzo's actions remind Primo of the world outside the camp, of his home country, and of the connection between *all* Italians.

I believe that it was really due to Lorenzo that I am alive today; and not so much for his material aid, as for his having constantly reminded me by his presence, by his natural and plain manner of being good, that there still existed a just world outside our own, something and someone still pure and whole, not corrupt, not savage, extraneous to hatred and terror; something difficult to define, a remote possibility of good, but for which it is worth surviving. . . . Lorenzo was a man; his humanity was pure and uncontaminated, he was outside this world of negation. Thanks to Lorenzo, I managed not to forget that I myself was a man.[20]

Levi's transformation in the death camp during which he, although lacking a traditional Jewish upbringing, becomes an individual aware of his Jewish identity dominates *Survival in Auschwitz*. Levi's education both in lyceum and in the University of Turin endowed him with a love and fine appreciation of rich Italian culture, literature, and language. As a result of his education, Levi became saturated with European humanist ideals. During the most difficult times in the camp Lorenzo reminds Levi of his identity in a time of despair and spiritual vacuum. "The Nazis contaminated everything, including language, that repository of culture, thought and feeling," observes Anthony Rudolf in his essay "The Shoreline of the Heart." "Primo Levi, trusting language, especially Italian, salvaged and reasserted truth through language, went with its grain."[21] Through Levi's humanist ideals, which manifest themselves in his literary work, we get a glimpse of the horrifying experience of the camps.

In his comprehensive article on the literary strategies that Levi employs in order to convey the historical reality of the Holocaust, Gian Paolo Biasin suggests that two qualities of Levi's language—physicality and spirituality—help him to survive the dehumanizing ordeal of the concentration camp. These two qualities are reflected in the text of *Survival in Auschwitz*. With their help, Levi not only mirrors his experiences but rearranges historical truth so as to produce the deepest impact on his readers. According to Biasin, physicality

guides the exactness with which he describes the organization of the Lager, its economy, its hierarchical system, its maddeningly complicated rules that made of it "a negative utopia"; it also presides over the description of the Buna factory, the laboratory, the chemicals used for hygienic purposes when the Nazis abandoned the sick for their fate before the arrival of the Russians.[22]

Spirituality, on the other hand, is present throughout the text of *Survival in Auschwitz* in the extraordinary multiplicity of intertextual references and allusions, the most important of which are the references to the Bible,[23] classical mythology,

Dante, and Machiavelli. Levi's exploration of relationships between language and power, especially the reference to Machiavelli, should not escape our notice. As Biasin points out, "the memory of Machiavelli's *The Prince* is subtly interwoven in the analysis of the character of Alfred L. and the considerations on the relationship between being strong and being feared and on the importance of the appearance of power."[24] Indeed, one may think of Machiavelli when confronted with the measured and calculated steps that Alfred L. undertakes in order to obtain a prominent position in the hierarchy of the Lager. "L. knew that the step was short from being judged powerful to effectively becoming so, and that everywhere, and especially in the midst of the general leveling of the Lager, a respectable appearance is the best guarantee of being respected."[25] This illumination of Alfred L.'s character brings us back to Bourdieu's idea that certain symbolic acts possess a special power "to act on reality by acting on its representation." In *Survival in Auschwitz*, some people change their representation voluntarily in order to conform to their environment; others, like Levi, struggle to preserve the representation of themselves in spite of the abuse that they suffer from powerful institutions.

Deprived of his name, Levi focuses on preserving his identity through language. As Sander L. Gilman points out, "language becomes for Levi the key to his survival in Auschwitz—language, not chance, is what prevents him from becoming a 'musselman.'"[26] The preservation of beautiful Italian speech, primarily through the recollections from Dante's *Commedia Divina*, is Levi's way of escaping the demoralizing influence of the "Lager jargon." Thus, writing his Italian name on the bottom of the soup bowl, teaching Italian to Jean, the *Pikolo* (messenger-clerk), and trying to recall Dante's poetry are the steps that he takes to recover the symbolic power of language, of which the prisoners were deprived by the dehumanizing conditions of the concentration camp. As Zvi Jagendorf suggests in his article "Primo Levi Goes for Soup and Remembers Dante," the lines of Dante's poetry, namely, the Canto of Ulysses, "remembered, spoken (and heard) by Primo in the camp, will, he hopes, communicate a different kind of message: that slaves can make themselves free by daring to contemplate words whose burden is the incitement to adventure and the exercise of the will."[27] Primo Levi's literary journey with Jean ends in the soup queue, where they must confront reality: hunger, deprivation, and the invasion of cacophony into their private linguistic space. "Kraut und Rüben," "Kaposzta és Répak"—sounds of German and Polish languages clash with Italian poetry. The hell envisioned by Dante becomes a man-made hell of the camp. Jagendorf writes:

> The closing sentences of the chapter mimic the chaotic dance of memory and oblivion in a kind of counterpoint to the shadowy theme of providence. There is a pattern in the text, but it is an imperfect memory or an intuition which perhaps cannot be conveyed to a listener or a reader. "Kraut und Rüben," on the other hand, is certain. It is the sound of the slaves ("Those just arrived press against our backs") huddled up together and squawking for food. This is cacophony, the authentic sound of hell.[28]

The image of the Tower of Babel thus corresponds to the image of the concentration camp as hell, where the variety of languages becomes "the sound of the slaves." Preservation of one's mother tongue becomes one of the most potent attempts to remind the prisoners of their humanity, which is being gradually reduced to an animal state. Levi emphasizes the power of Dante's poetry over him when the chapter "The Canto of Ulysses" culminates with the following lines:

> "Think of your breed; for brutish ignorance
> Your mettle was not made; you were made men,
> To follow after knowledge and excellence."

As if I also was hearing it for the first time: like the blast of a trumpet, like the voice of God. For a moment I forget who I am and where I am.[29]

Many critics who analyze Levi's works note the power that language has in his work. Regarding Levi's fascination with Dante's Ulysses, Nicholas Patruno suggests, "Levi's use of Dante is an example of his belief that literature can help bolster human endurance in suffering and provide uplifting moments that strengthen one's resistance."[30]

Dante's "The Canto of Ulysses" is a paramount example of the symbolic power of language; it brings order to Levi's understanding of the world and, even more important, to his understanding of himself and his place in the world. *Survival in Auschwitz* rejects the sentimental optimism characteristic of some contemporary literary and cinematographic works. "There is no final solace, no redeeming truth, no hope that so many millions may not have died in vain. They have," says Lawrence Langer in his essay "The Americanization of the Holocaust on Stage and Screen." "But the American vision of the Holocaust . . . continues to insist that they have not, trying to parlay hope, sacrifice, justice, and the future into a victory that will mitigate despair."[31] The language of Levi's work is dark; it portrays human drama of unthinkable dimensions and leaves no place for hope.

Often compelled to tell their story and relate the message to the general public, Holocaust survivors seek new ways to express their experience in terms understandable by an "average" individual. For Primo Levi, an attempt to understand the world of the concentration camps and to dissect its inner workings gives the power of knowledge, which is valuable after the fact but crucial for survival during the ordeal. The symbolic power of language becomes real power in the "concentration camp universe," which allows the prisoners—provided they are willing to learn and barring random acts of violence—to start a process of adjusting to the new conditions. In addition to realizing the significance of linguistic chaos, changes of representation through naming rituals, and the profound necessity to hold on to one's cultural background, Primo Levi illustrates two other parallel processes: "unlearning" the humanist ideals and old meanings of the familiar words and learning new meanings of the same words and the reality that they describe.

One of the scenes from the chapter "On the Bottom" is exemplary in this respect. Along with other new arrivals, Levi asks a veteran inmate questions that show his naïveté and thinking in terms of life outside the camp. Inside, however, everything is different, and he must learn various new concepts. To Levi's question whether the toothbrushes will be given back, his French interlocutor answers, "Vous n'êtes pas à la maison." One is not at home anymore, and he better forget his home because "the only exit is by way of the Chimney."[32] Levi admits that he does not understand what the phrase means until he learns a new meaning of the word "Chimney" and its role in the prisoners' lives.

Another way of learning new meanings of familiar words along with new concepts acts as Levi's method of scientific observation that would yield data necessary for coping with the oppression of the Lager. Levi avoids impressionistic writing; through systematic thinking, he attempts to analyze the workings of the camp. Out of his struggle to preserve the ability of rational understanding, Levi emerges as a writer exceptionally qualified to bear witness to the true nature of a concentration camp universe. One of the most fascinating examples of Levi's scientific thinking is his explanation of how bad shoes can cause a person's death. In our thinking patterns, there is no particular logical connection between shoes and death. In the language of a science textbook, Levi fills the gap in our knowledge as he takes the reader through the logical steps of his analysis:

And do not think that shoes form a factor of secondary importance in the life of the Lager. Death begins with the shoes; for most of us, they show themselves to be instruments of torture, which after a few hours of marching cause painful sores which become fatally infected. Whoever has them is forced to walk as if he was dragging a convict's chain; he arrives last everywhere, and everywhere he receives blows. He cannot escape if they run after him; his feet swell and the more they swell, the more the friction with the wood and the cloth of the shoes becomes insupportable. Then only the hospital is left: but to enter the hospital with a diagnosis of 'dicke Füsse' (swollen feet) is extremely dangerous, because it is well known to all, and especially to the SS, that here there is no cure for that complaint.[33]

Lager economy and intricacies of the black market are another example of Levi's profound desire to play the role of an observer in a scientific experiment undertaken by the Germans on living human beings. Logical analysis of the events and personalities helps him to preserve his own humanity while observing a kind of Darwinian struggle for the survival of the fittest and the meanest. Language becomes Levi's tool for learning the rules of the Lager.

Aiming at an exploration of Primo Levi's description of the symbolic power of language during the Holocaust, it is helpful to turn to yet another literary theorist, Russian philosopher Mikhail Bakhtin. Linguistic relations, as suggested by Bourdieu, are the foremost relations of power. In the context of *Survival in Auschwitz*, however, it is primarily the power struggle through the dialogue of two voices—that of the perpetrators and the other of the victims—that makes it a fascinating, multilayered literary work. The principle of dialogism as a fundamental and underlying principle of existence, thinking, and literature was developed by Bakhtin in the 1930s. Since his rediscovery in the 1980s, scholars have applied Bakhtin's theory to literary texts whose complicated narrative structure requires a detailed analysis, succeeding in reaching a new level of understanding of many works.

Dialogism is defined by one of Bakhtin's principal scholars, Michael Holquist, as "an epistemology based on the assumption that knowing an entity (a person or a thing) is to put this entity in a relation of simultaneity with something else, where simultaneity is understood as not being a relation of equality or identity."[34] Understanding the potential hidden in this definition leads many literary critics and historians to a positive response to Bakhtin's theory. If a person has a tendency to understand himself or herself only in terms of the other, whoever it may be, and acknowledge himself or herself in relation to the world, the other becomes a partner in the dialogue; even more—he or she becomes an absolutely necessary requirement for a person's definition of the self. Holquist emphasizes that the word dialogue suggests that "two people who are different are talking to each other (but not saying the same thing)."[35] Victims and perpetrators in the conditions of the concentration camp are different by definition. By pointing out the fact that all the participants of a dialogue are supposed to get an equal chance to participate, Bakhtin rejects the idea of one dominant voice, which is exactly the Nazi ideal for all occupied and oppressed nations and people. It is precisely the multiplicity of voices that makes the novel a different type of genre and the events narrated in the novel sound more vivid and realistic.

Another issue of interest may be Bakhtin's notion of heteroglossia. As he writes in "Discourse in the Novel,"

at any given moment of its historical existence, language is heteroglot from top to bottom: it represents the co-existence of socio-ideological contradictions between the present and the past, between different epochs of the past, between different socio-ideological groups in the present, between the tendencies, schools, circles and so forth, all given bodily form. These "languages" of heteroglossia intersect each other in a variety of ways, forming new socially typifying "languages."[36]

Once again all human beings are given a voice; however weak or subordinate this voice may be, it is always there. The Nazi war machine, on the other hand, was based on the notion of uniformity and suppression of any independent speech. Such notions as heteroglossia presuppose the existence of diversity and imply a certain equality of rights that various voices may have in the novel (as well as in real life). Those can be methodologically juxtaposed to the concentration camp universe, which is dehumanizing in its uniformity. In Bakhtin's philosophy, there is no one hegemonic dominant voice that subdues all the rest of the possible voices. Even more—it is implied that the socioideological situation is constantly changing, creating new voices that are "hybrids" of the voices of different social status, education, and experience. Levi's *Survival in Auschwitz* represents an extraordinarily rich plethora of different voices, all possible languages, religions, and nationalities, which are unified by one historical fact—all of them are subject to annihilation on the basis of presumed racial inferiority.

In *Survival in Auschwitz*, the symbolic power of language is tightly intertwined with memories and dreams. Levi's memories from times predating his internment in the camp, as they are described in the chapter "Chemical Examination," serve to boost Levi's confidence in his intellectual abilities. He recognizes the "sense of lucid elation," the excitement that comes with the "spontaneous mobilization of all my [Levi's] logical faculties and all my knowledge."[37] Memories of home, homemade food like spaghetti, and even the memories of previous intellectual achievements—all serve the purpose of preservation of the humanity of "Häftlinge."

In the conditions of a concentration camp, the power of naming generates a situation where a certain word becomes 'overweight' with symbolic meaning. Patruno observes:

In the third chapter, "Initiation," bread becomes a constant obsession, and the word for it is one quickly learned in several languages: *Brot-Broit-chleb-pain-lechem-kenyer*. . . . Food becomes the fixation that will intrude in dreams and play tricks on vision. Many prisoners will smack their lips and move their jaws in their sleep in a collective dream reminiscent of the myth of Tantalus, who was condemned not to be able to grasp the food and water within his reach.[38]

Dreams are the field where the symbolic power of the language is especially visible, since subconsciousness transforms the trauma of the daytime into the nightmare. The collective dream about food and the nightmares described later in the book correspond to the Freudian notion of trauma. Cathy Caruth, in her book *Unclaimed Experience*, points out that in Freudian text, "the term *trauma* is understood as a wound inflicted not upon the body but upon the mind."[39] In the chapter "Our Nights," Levi describes the recurrent dream that he and other prisoners have every night. It is a dream about a train coming to Buna, the sound of the train engine, the whistle that regulates the time, and the scene of storytelling. In this particular scene, Levi shows language's failure to describe the horrors of the camp experiences. He notices that his listeners do not follow his story; "in fact, they are completely indifferent."[40]

Caruth answers Levi's question, "Why is the pain of every day translated so constantly into our dreams, in the ever-repeated scene of the unlistened-to story?" in the following way:

[T]he wound of the mind—the breach in the mind's experience of time, self, and the world—is not, like the wound of the body, a simple and healable event, but rather an event that . . . is experienced too soon, too unexpectedly, to be fully known and therefore not available to consciousness until it imposes itself again, repeatedly, in the nightmares and repetitive actions of the survivor.[41]

The symbolic power of language permeates the dreams as does anything else in the camp. The language, therefore, serves a double function: it contributes to the survival chances through the ability of some prisoners to communicate better than others and through reawakening the prisoners' desire to preserve their identity, but it also translates evil into their dreams and frustrates their attempts to make sense of the surrounding world.

Going back to our initial premise that Levi's *Survival in Auschwitz* is an example of the intricate relations between language and power, we can conclude that these relations are threaded throughout the texture of the novel as the genius of Levi's literary imagination reconstructs the historical reality of the Holocaust. However, not only do the relations of power between "the slaves" and "the masters" enrich the depth of the novel, but they also elucidate the symbolic relations between good and evil within the human soul, between horrible reality and nightmares, between desire to make an order of things and failure to understand the "indecipherable inferno."

NOTES

1. Pierre Bourdieu, *Language and Symbolic Power* (Cambridge: Harvard University Press, 1991).

2. Ibid., p. 2.

3. Primo Levi, *Survival in Auschwitz*, translated by Stuart Woolf (New York: Simon and Schuster, 1996), p. 38.

4. Philip Roth, "Interview with Primo Levi by Philip Roth," in Levi, *Survival in Auschwitz*, p. 180.

5. Ferdinando Camon, *Conversations with Primo Levi*, translated by John Shepley (Marlboro, VT: Marlboro Press, 1989), pp. 23–24.

6. Risa Sodi, *A Dante of Our Time. Primo Levi and Auschwitz* (New York: Peter Lang, 1990), p. 35.

7. Ibid., p. 34.

8. Fabio Girelli-Carasi, "The Anti-Linguistic Nature of the Lager in the Language of Primo Levi's *Se questo è un uomo*," in *Reason and Light. Essays on Primo Levi*, edited by Susan Tarrow, Western Societies Program Occasional Paper # 25 (Ithaca: Cornell University Center for International Studies, 1990), p. 40.

9. Levi, *Survival in Auschwitz*, p. 90.

10. Ibid., p. 24.

11. Bourdieu, *Language and Symbolic Power*, p. 119.

12. Levi, *Survival in Auschwitz*, p. 27.

13. Ibid., p. 27.

14. Wade Kelson, "Primo Levi and the Humanness of Cultural Understanding," in *Cultural Dialogue and Misreading*, edited by Mabel Lee and Meng Hua (Sydney, Australia: University of Sydney and Wild Peony, 1997), p. 397.

15. Bourdieu, *Language and Symbolic Power*, p. 121.

16. Primo Levi, "Beyond Survival," *Prooftexts: A Journal of Jewish Literary History* 4, no. 1 (1984): 9–21, quote on p. 9.

17. Cecil Roth, *The History of the Jews of Italy* (Philadelphia: Jewish Publication Society of America, 1946), p. 480.

18. Levi, "Beyond Survival," p. 9.

19. Levi, *Survival in Auschwitz*, p. 119.

20. Ibid., pp. 121–122.

21. Anthony Rudolf, "The Shoreline of the Heart," in *At an Uncertain Hour: Primo Levi's War against Oblivion* (London: The Menard Press, 1990), pp. 46–47.

22. Gian Paolo Biasin, "Our Daily Bread-Pane-Brot-Broid-Chleb-Pain-Lechem-Kenyer,"

in *Primo Levi as Witness*, edited by Pietro Frassica (Fiesole: Casalini Libri, 1990), p. 11.

23. Levi writes about one of the characters in "The Drowned and the Saved," *Survival in Auschwitz*: "Henry was inhumanly cunning and incomprehensible like the Serpent in Genesis" (p. 100).

24. Ibid., p. 11.

25. Levi, *Survival in Auschwitz*, p. 94.

26. Sander L. Gilman, "To Quote Primo Levi: 'Redest keyn jiddisch, bist nit kein jid' ['If you don't speak Yiddish, you're not a Jew']," *Prooftexts* 9 (1989): 139–160, quote on p. 142.

27. Zvi Jagendorf, "Primo Levi Goes for Soup and Remembers Dante," *Raritan* 2, no. 4 (1993): 31–51, quote on p. 39.

28. Ibid., p. 46.

29. Levi, *Survival in Auschwitz*, p. 113.

30. Nicholas Patruno, *Understanding Primo Levi* (Columbia: University of South Carolina Press, 1995), p. 22.

31. Lawrence L. Langer, "The Americanization of the Holocaust on Stage and Screen," in *Admitting the Holocaust. Collected Essays.* (New York: Oxford University Press, 1995), p. 158.

32. Levi, *Survival in Auschwitz*, p. 29.

33. Ibid., p. 35.

34. Michael Holquist, *Dialogism. Bakhtin and His World* (London and New York: Routledge, 1990), p. 157.

35. Ibid., p. 40.

36. Mikhail Mikhailovich Bakhtin, "Discourse in the Novel." in *The Dialogic Imagination. Four Essays*, edited by Michael Holquist and translated by Carol Emerson and Michael Holquist (Austin: University of Texas Press, 1981), p. 291.

37. Levi, *Survival in Auschwitz*, p. 106.

38. Patruno, *Understanding Primo Levi*, p. 15.

39. Cathy Caruth, *Unclaimed Experience. Trauma, Narrative, and History* (Baltimore and London: Johns Hopkins University Press, 1996), p. 3.

40. Levi, *Survival in Auschwitz*, p. 60.

41. Caruth, *Unclaimed Experience*, p. 4.

Part VI

"THE LANGUAGE OF
THE WITNESS":
HOLOCAUST SURVIVORS SPEAK

I believe in reason and in discussion as supreme instruments of progress, and therefore I repress hatred even within myself: I prefer justice. Precisely for this reason, when describing the tragic world of Auschwitz, I have deliberately assumed the calm, sober language of the witness . . .

Primo Levi, "Afterword: The Author's Answers
to His Readers' Questions," translated by
Ruth Feldman in *The Reawakening*
(New York: Macmillan, 1987), p. 196.

30

Dante Almansi, President of the Union of Italian Jewish Communities

Renato J. Almansi

No history of the tragedy that befell the Italian Jews under fascism could be complete without a biography illustrating the character and deeds of the man who, very shortly after the enactment of Mussolini's anti-Jewish legislation, became the president of the Union of the Italian Jewish Communities and who wholly dedicated himself to the heartbreaking and dangerous task of helping the Jews of Italy as well as a large number of foreign Jews who had fled into Italy to escape the Nazi persecution.

My father, Dante Almansi, was the man who accepted that awesome responsibility in the most difficult period in the many centuries in which Jews had lived on the Italian peninsula; it was a position that offered no personal advantages of any kind and promised only difficulties and dangers, but he accepted it because he thought that, despite the difficulties, he might be able to be of help. He was a very idealistic and, at the same time, a determined and very practical kind of man. The results of his work are written in the books of history. The most detailed and authoritative of them is *Storia degli ebrei italiani sotto il fascismo*,[1] in which Renzo De Felice describes, in various aspects, the amount of dedication, courage, and wisdom that my father displayed in the performance of his duties. A great source of information on this subject also is the official papers of the Union, which are preserved at the Union of the Italian Jewish Communities in Rome.

In this chapter I present a general outline of my father's life, with special attention to his work as president of the Union. Also, since after the liberation of Rome he was considered by the Allies "a fascist" and therefore a person to be removed from office, I give a number of details about my father's relationship to the fascist regime and discuss the origins of the difficulties that he met when the Allies took over Rome.

My father was born in Parma, Italy, on 15 September 1877. He received his law degree in 1900. He had originally intended to enter private practice and to specialize in corporate law, but sudden severe financial reverses in the family obliged him to seek government employment immediately after his graduation. At first my father was attached to the governmental prefectures of Modena and Parma, where he worked as *segretario di prefettura*. Very early he developed a special interest and expertise in matters of local administration, which persisted throughout his lifetime. He became very competent in problems of local administration, taxation, and public works, as in the construction of hospitals, electrification works, aqueducts, and public housing. He considered politics generally unproductive and a boring waste of time and often regretted the time, money, and effort that went into sterile politics while so many worthwhile projects that could improve the people's quality of life correspondingly suffered.

In keeping with these interests, he was sent as *regio commissario* (government-appointed mayor) to reorganize several small municipalities. In 1915 my father took the competitive examination to enter a career leading to becoming a prefect, an official who is the governmental representative in a province. From 1915 to 1918 he was *sottoprefetto* in Ariano di Puglia and between 1918 and 1919 in Terni. This was the postwar period, characterized by great political turmoil; there were labor strikes, looting, communist agitation, and occupation of factories. Terni was a particularly difficult place because of the presence of a large armaments factory that held over 1 million rifles and a very large amount of ammunition. Its fall to the communists would have been a national disaster. My father handled the situation very successfully, with the result that, despite the turmoil that prevailed in most of Italy at that time, nothing serious happened, and only a few stores were looted. This brought him to the attention of the Ministry of the Interior, and in 1919 he was called to Rome as a section chief of the General Directorship of Police. While there, he was promoted to division chief (equivalent to vice prefect) and became the vice director of the Italian Police.

During that time he observed, with great misgivings, the rise of fascism. Although not formally attached to any political party, his own personal preference was for the socialist parties, which had gained support in Italy prior to World War I. He greatly admired their social concern and the great strides that the socialists had made, particularly in the field of education. He loathed the illegality of the fascist squads and their use of violence.

Characteristic of his orientation is the following episode. On the day that Mussolini was called to the premiership (28 October 1922), I was walking with my father when a special edition of a newspaper came out with the news that Mussolini had been appointed prime minister. Since a "state of siege" had been declared, I asked my father whether it was legal for newspapers to be published freely while a "state of siege" existed. He answered, "No, but how lawful will fascist law be?" At the time of the march in Rome, my father was forty-five years old.

The day that General De Bono took office as director of the Italian police, my father introduced him to the staff and presented his own resignation, which De Bono refused to accept. Two and a half months later, in December 1922, my father's promotion to prefect took place. De Bono asked him to remain, but my father politely declined, alleging his wish to reach the culmination of his chosen career. In reality, he was not happy about being with the police under fascism.

He was sent to Caltanissetta, Sicily, in January 1923 and remained there until February 1924. A fascist deputy, Damiano Lipani, hinted several times to him that he should join the Fascist Party. My father had not done so previously, and he had no such intention. He had not even taken party membership in Rome before his promotion. When Lipani realized that his hints had gone unheeded, one day he appeared at my father's office, accompanied by a small delegation, and presented him with a small Fascist Party card ad honorem, virtually drafting him into the party. Had my father refused membership, he might have been discharged from government service, a prospect that a responsible family man of his age and with no personal financial means could certainly not contemplate. My father, in a brief speech, said that if being a fascist meant respect for the law, honesty, and love for one's country, he considered himself to have always been one. Lipani did not understand the fundamental reservation attached to this statement.

At the beginning of February 1924, my father was unexpectedly recalled by De Bono to the general direction of the police. This order came as an unpleasant surprise but left him with no choice.

In June 1924 the socialist deputy Matteotti was murdered. This assassination was extensively discussed in our home. My father had no evidence and no reason whatsoever to believe that De Bono had been guilty of any wrongdoing in connection with the crime. No one has ever proven otherwise. When my father was called as a witness at the De Bono trial, he testified truthfully to all he knew in this matter. Because of the very strict separation that existed at the General Directorate between the party people (De Bono and his secretary, Captain Butturini) and the career people, De Bono, if guilty of any wrongdoing, would have no reason to confide to my father dangerous party secrets. My father was totally cleared of any suspicion of wrongdoing by the attorney for the Matteotti family.

After De Bono left office, my father remained with his successor, Crispo-Moncada, but in October 1924 he was sent back to the provinces and was prefect of Avellino for one and a half years. The local fascist deputy was De Marsico, whom my father deeply disliked and mistrusted because he considered him to be an opportunist. They had a very cold and distant relationship. In 1925–1926 my father was prefect of Reggio Emilia. He got along very well with the local fascist deputy (whose name I do not remember), whom he considered to be a person of great integrity and highly dedicated to public service. In 1927 my father was prefect of Macerata for less than a year. There he engaged in a fierce struggle with the local fascist deputy, Count Serafino Mazzolini, whom he considered a pernicious individual. He fully knew that he was risking his entire career by contesting Mazzolini, since Mazzolini, a member of the extremist wing of the Fascist Party, was strongly backed by the party. My father made it impossible for Mazzolini to continue his activities in Macerata, so he was sent away and given an important-sounding, but insignificant, job in Brazil. But the party had its revenge on my father. He was relieved of his duties and left temporarily without an assignment.

During that time, he decided to seek a place as sheltered as possible from politics, and he let it be known that he would be pleased to receive an administrative assignment. This materialized in the summer of 1927, when he was appointed *regio commissario* of Naples, a position that he held for two and a half years. The city of Naples was in deep financial difficulties, and its administrative functioning needed a complete overhaul. This was my father's happiest time. He consolidated all the city's debts, arranged for their gradual repayment, improved the taxation system immeasurably, executed many improvements in public services, instituted the pasteurization of the city's milk (a pioneering undertaking at the time), and started a large-scale public housing venture. All these projects ended when he was relieved of his post to allow an incompetent member of the Neapolitan nobility to represent the city at the impending wedding of the prince of Piedmont.

Even so, the success of the Naples mission was so considerable that he was allowed to choose his next assignment. He could have asked for an important prefecture, such as Rome or Milan, but he preferred a quiet administrative position, which would remove him from politics. He therefore asked for the position of councilor at the *Corte dei Conti*, an administrative post of a semijudicial type in which his function was to make rulings on the legality of government expenditures. Actually, in the main, his work consisted of passing legal opinions in pension cases. By law he could not be removed before the age of seventy. He held this position from 1927 until his discharge from government service in 1938 in accordance with the new racial laws modeled after the Nazi Nuremberg laws of 1935.

From 1935 to 1937 he was chief of cabinet for the Minister of Finance, Guido Jung, and he was very happy in this post, both because he enjoyed the work and because of his close personal friendship with Jung, a man of high personal integrity. Together they engineered, in the greatest secrecy, the "conversion" of Italy's public debt, a huge financial operation, the knowledge of which would have permitted a less honest man to reap large financial gains. My father left government service a poor man, as he had always been.

It seems fitting here to say something about my father's personal finances. He started with nothing, and throughout his working life he lived only on his salary (it is well known that government employees are not well paid in Italy). When he left government service, he had almost no savings; all he had was his government pension. During the Nazi occupation of Rome, although in hiding, he was obliged to go to the Pension Office to collect his monthly pension under his real name, a highly dangerous undertaking at the time.

When the Allied troops entered Rome, my father was penniless. During the German occupation of Rome, my family underwent unimaginable deprivations. Upon his death, he left no money; his only legacy was the equity in a modest condominium of government employees that he had purchased, with a fifty-year mortgage, about twenty-five years previously.

After his discharge from his government post because of the anti-Semitic legislation, my father was forcibly idle until November 1939, when he was appointed president of the Union of the Italian Jewish Communities. His deeply ingrained ethical beliefs and religious feelings unquestionably motivated him to accept this dangerous appointment. Although he was only minimally observant of religious forms (he fasted and went to the synagogue only on Yom Kippur), he felt a deep obligation to do what was right. He considered human life a mission and conducted his own life accordingly.

From this point on I can offer very little from my personal knowledge, as I came to the United States in September 1939. After describing the difficulties that had developed in the Union that necessitated a new leadership, Renzo De Felice writes in his book *Storia degli ebrei italiani sotto il fascismo*:

[A]fter a series of frenzied searches and negotiations, a man was finally found in the person of the ex-prefect and ex-councilor of the Court of Accounts, Dante Almansi. He was an old gentleman, small in stature and almost insignificant, who, up to that time had never had anything to do with the administrative and moral life of Italian Judaism. It was because of his firmness and sagacity that the Union became once again the catalyst for the Jews from the end of 1939 to the liberation of Rome. All the Italian Jews had a proud, dignified and active representation and the thousands of foreign Jews could be helped in a concrete way to live in Italy and to emigrate abroad.[2]

In a firm and dignified way he succeeded in establishing a sort of useful collaboration with the police chief, whom he had known for years, on concrete, practical problems such as concession of passports and exit visas and avoidance of expulsion of German Jews who had been able to enter Italy. The most important of his successes was the creation of the Delasem (an acronym for Delegation for Assistance in Emigration), which helped the emigration in all possible ways and also offered material assistance. Altogether, from 1939 to 1943 the Delasem was able to organize the emigration of about 5,000 Jews. The charitable work not only was directed toward free individuals but also included internees both free and in concentration camps: about 500 in Rhodes, 200 in Albania, and 2,000 in Slovenia and Dalmatia. In 1942 the Delasem was assisting 9,000 Jews and had extended its field of action, besides Italy, to the occupied areas of Yugoslavia. The assistance included not only the care of material needs (subventions, blankets, clothing, medicines) but also religious assistance (prayer books, matzos, etc.) and moral assistance (search for relatives, establishing contact with them). The assistance also took into consideration the age and even the particular religious rite practiced by the individual.

The Union was extremely active in the field of education since Jews had been barred from all schools. Elementary schools, higher education courses, and schools of chemistry, commerce, and engineering were created in many localities, some of them staffed by professors of international reputation.

The work of the Union was very complex. It covered not only Italy, where the beneficiaries were widespread, often in very small and remote localities, but also areas where Italian troops were operating, as in Croatia. Also, external circumstances often were changing unpredictably, and the assisted people had, at times, very particular problems and needs.

Many extremely devoted persons participated in this work; in Rome Lelio Valobra, the vice president of the Union, flew (in Italian military planes) to

Dalmatia and Slovakia to contact the Italian military authorities to avoid the shipment to Croatia of Jewish refugees. Also, in Rome Settimo Sorani was extremely active. Once he was captured by the Germans but succeeded in deceiving them and was released. He has written a very interesting book on his work. The Capuchin monk Benoît-Marie (Father Benedetto) was extremely active, first in France and subsequently in Rome, where in 1943 he participated very actively in the work of the Delasem, providing refuge in religious institutions to many people in danger of shipment to the death camps. After the war he was awarded a gold medal by the Union of the Italian Jewish Communities for the enormous amount of work he had done in Rome as well as in France. In Milan, an engineer, I. Kalk, operated a very successful organization of assistance.

De Felice writes further:

The years 1940, 1941, 1942, 1943 up to the fall of Fascism were for the Union years of serious and concrete work which, in a short time and in keeping with the general situation in Italy and that of the Jews in particular, gave back to the Union its character as a catalyst of Italian Judaism and as its moral guide. Not without a reason, the memory of Almansi has remained—despite the unfair attacks from some exiles who had just come back to Italy who had not, for that reason, lived the harsh realities of those years in Italy—one of the most pure and beautiful features of that terrible period. The contacts with the government, always marked by dignity and firmness, were limited to the strictly necessary.[3]

The occupation of Rome by the Germans after Mussolini's fall was the final tragedy for the Italian Jews. On 28 September 1943 the Germans ordered my father and the president of the Roman Jewish community, Ugo Foa, to come to the German Embassy, where SS Major Kappler, commander of the German occupation, notified them that within thirty-six hours they expected to receive fifty kilos of gold from the Jewish community of Rome. If this order was not complied with, 200 Jews would be deported to Germany to go to the Russian front or would be "made harmless in some other way." This extortion could not be resisted. After the gold had been collected, my father and Foa went back to pay the ransom. At first the Germans contended that the amount was five kilos short of what had been requested, and only after a difficult debate did they consent to reweigh it and found that the amount was indeed correct. In spite of that, on 16 October, a German detachment surrounded the old Roman ghetto and began the deportation of all Jews whom they were able to round up.

On that day, at about 7 A.M., my family was called by a former maid who had heard about the German action and told them to leave their home immediately. They went to the home of a neighbor and contacted a friend of ours, Dr. G. Lapponi, who took them in right away. As soon as he reached Dr. Lapponi's home, my father contacted the other Jewish leaders, and on the same day he met with them in a dairy shop to try to organize, if possible, the rescue of those who had been captured by the Nazis. An urgent appeal was sent to Pope Pius XII, but the Germans captured the messenger so that nothing useful was achieved.

The frightful danger of those days never prevented my father from doing his duty. Every day, throughout the German occupation, he met with the other leaders, and together they organized whatever essential activities were needed and were possible. These meetings occurred daily, at different street corners or in milk shops designated from day to day throughout the month when my father was the guest of Dr. Lapponi, as he did not want to put his host in danger. Later, when he was able to rent a little apartment with the help of forged identity papers, these meetings were regularly held there. In that apartment they lived, always in fear of discovery, until the Allies liberated Rome on 4 June 1944. In the words of R. Cantoni, "when the deportations started and concealment was our only refuge, Almansi, from his hiding place directed and was in constant contact with those activists who were engaged in helping with money, food, ration cards, and advice. . . . Almansi's conduct in that period was so admirable that we all felt it an offense and an injustice that the liberating Allies did not leave him in his post after the occupation of Rome."[4]

Very soon after the Allied armies entered Rome, the military government found itself confronted with a puzzling problem: the survivors of the Jewish community, particularly those living in the old ghetto, who were very religious and who had suffered so much from the deportations, at that time seemed to be interested in one thing only: to get rid of Rabbi Zolli at all costs. In fact, they had even gone so far that they had demonstrated against him in the course of a religious service. This appeared very strange to Colonel Poletti, the Allied military governor of Rome, who decided to place the handling of Jewish affairs in the hands of Captain Maurice Neufield, who, being a Jew, perhaps might have been able to understand them better. This, unfortunately, did not happen at all. Captain Neufield unfortunately did not know—or, if he later learned it, he minimized—the fact that the antagonism to Zolli was motivated by the fact that Zolli, throughout the German occupation of Rome, had disappeared completely, had not participated in any way in the work of the Jewish leaders, had remained for nine months totally unavailable, and had reappeared as soon as the Allies entered Rome. All the Jews felt that, at least, he should have brought to them a word of consolation and hope; his behavior was not their idea of what a good rabbi should have done. Rejected by his flock and asked to resign in June 1944, Zolli turned toward the Americans. Captain Neufield, who certainly had the best of intentions but little understanding of the people with whom he was dealing, eagerly supported him. He thought that the leadership of the Union was composed of fascists to be eliminated and decided that the only person through whom the Allies could best reach the Jews of Rome was the rabbi.[5] So he protected Zolli by postponing an election, which would have been unfavorable to him, and made possible his reintegration as Chief Rabbi of Rome on 21 September 1944.

In 1971 I visited Neufield at his home in Ithaca, New York, and I had a long conversation with him about that period. He emphasized to me the fact that he had done all he could to support Rabbi Zolli and spoke of the shock that Zolli's most unexpected conversion to Catholicism had caused him. At that point he had broken off any relationship with him. He certainly had felt very much betrayed by Zolli. Neufield accepted the idea that a manuscript that I was preparing about my father be included in the collection of his papers, which are preserved at the Library of Congress in Washington, D.C.[6] Well before my visit, in 1946, he must have already thought back a great deal over that period and had written an article in which he spoke of the "chaos" and of "the administrative confusion" created by the Allies and said that the Allies "had ruled, even at the highest levels, with limited political and administrative vision of things" and that "the personnel of the AMG [Allied Military Government] was low in numbers, training, and political understanding."[7]

My father resigned from the presidency of the Union on 1 October 1944. As the idealistic and active man that he was, he would have liked to participate in the reconstruction of Italian Jewry, for which he had fought so hard in its darkest times. He had the right to feel that, after all he had done and after all the personal risks that he had taken, he should not have been obliged to resign under fire, yet from the time of the liberation of Rome, he had known that his job was actually finished. He had seen the Italian Jews through their greatest torment and had fully done his duty as best as he could. He was then sixty-eight years old and seriously ill (his illness had begun much earlier but had become more severe around 1940). He knew he had little time left, and his greatest desire was to see me again and meet my family. This ardent wish is expressed over and over again in letters that I still preserve. As soon as circumstances permitted, in October 1946 he and my mother came to the United States to my home. He was a tired old man, but his eyes still glittered, and his face smiled when he was talking of his most important creation, the Delasem. His health further deteriorated, and after about twenty months he decided to return to Italy to see my sister and her family before his death. He died in Rome, five months after his return, on 4 January 1949.

NOTES

1. Renzo De Felice, *Storia degli ebrei italiani sotto il fascismo* (Turin: Einaudi, 1993), recently published in English as *The Jews in Fascist Italy: A History*, translated by Robert L. Miller (New York: Enigma Books, 2001).

2. Ibid., p. 426.

3. Ibid., p. 428.

4. R. Cantoni, "Dante Almansi," *Jerusalem* (13 January 1949).

5. C. L. Newmann, *A "Chief Rabbi" of Rome Becomes a Catholic* (New York: Renaissance Press, 1945).

6. Copies of this manuscript, "Dante Almansi," are also to be found at the Jewish Theological Seminary in New York City; at the Yivo Institute for Jewish Research; New York Public Library, 42nd Street Branch; the University of Tel Aviv Institute for Zionist Research; and Yad Vashem, Jerusalem; Union of the Italian Jewish Communities, Rome.

7. M. Neufield, "The Failure of the Allied Military Government in Italy," *Public Administration Review* (April 1946).

31

Reflections on an Italian-Jewish Life

Lucia Servadio Bedarida

I am an Italian Jew. My forefathers settled in Sicily, Italy, around the fourteenth century. The genealogical family tree shows that a Simone Servadio settled in Palermo in 1350. Then in the fifteenth century there is Elia de Servadio, followed by Servadio Obadia. The Italian translation of the Hebrew name Obadia is Servadio (Servant of God). At that time Sicily had fallen under Spanish rule, and an edict was issued to expel all the Jews from the island, where they had lived peacefully and splendidly for centuries. Part of the Obadias settled in Tuscany, part in the Marche, especially in Ancona, where I was born in 1900.

By then the Jewish population was already emancipated, with the same rights and duties of any Italian citizen. There were no ghettos, no restrictions, no quotas. We lived where we liked, we traveled as we wished, we chose the professions that we wanted. My brothers and I attended public school and later the university. I graduated from the Faculty of Medicine in Rome in 1922. Our family frequented non-Jewish friends, and we were accepted as their peers. Our daily life went on normally until I was an adult. Therefore, it was a great shock when the anti-Semitic campaign was launched by the fascist government to brainwash the country; newspapers, radio, conferences, books were preparing the promulgation of the "racial laws" announced to the Italians in September 1938. Newspapers were leading a campaign of smear and accusations in order to convince the people that the racial laws were well founded and justified. It was around 1941 or 1942 when a particularly poisonous and insulting article appeared in an important newspaper. One of my brothers, Lucio, who had always been a fighter for justice and human rights (he later joined the partisans) was so infuriated by this despicable attack against the Jews that he went to the newspaper's headquarters, waited for the author of the article to come out, and punched him a few times. My brother was arrested and sent to *confino* (domestic confinement or internment) in a small house in the mountains, far away from home, family, and friends. He was there for many months.

I do not know all the exact details of this event, as at that time I was already in Morocco. I am mentioning this episode to point out that even before the big roundup and the "Final Solution," in Italy, too, the Jews were harassed and persecuted. First came the law expelling foreign Jews. These were, for the most part, young people not accepted in the universities of their own countries. Mussolini had invited them to attend Italian universities, helped them financially to obtain a degree, and prompted them to stay to exercise their profession. Then came the law against Italian Jews. Children could not attend public school; all civil servants were dismissed from their job, including my husband, who was chief surgeon in a public hospital. We had to return our membership cards to clubs, associations, and societies; the Aryans were admonished not to protect or help the Jews.

We were the only Jewish family in a small town in Abruzzo, where we were respected and admired. We were obliged to belong to the Fascist Party, where they gave us high-ranking positions. We felt rejected, lonely, and sad. For the preceding reasons we decided that the time had come to leave Italy and to immigrate wherever possible.

My husband and I spent weeks in Rome going from one consulate to another. No country was willing to open its borders to us. Somebody who had told us that he was a big shot in Ecuador's embassy and to whom my husband had paid a high sum, had informed us that there was the possibility of a visa and a job in Quito, Ecuador's capital. We bought passage on a ship, and we bought trunks that we filled for the big move. At the last minute the visa was refused, and the money was kept. We finally heard about Tangier. We received a letter from Dr. Shakin, a Hungarian ex-student of my husband, one of the first group of expelled Jews. He was asking if my husband was willing to direct a surgical clinic not yet built.

Tangier was, at that time, an international city in the north of Morocco, and Italy was a member of the International Government. For this reason we did not need a visa, and our medical degrees were recognized. Moreover, there was an excellent Italian school to which our children could be admitted and receive a high school education.

Leaving our three girls temporarily with my mother, my husband and I went to Tangier. We liked the city, the position, the ambience, the climate, and we began to prepare for our new life. During our absence my brother Luxardo, who lived in Padova, invited my youngest daughter, Adria, to spend some time with his family, thus reducing my mother's burden of caring for our three girls. Adria was then six years old. They arranged that she would travel by train from Pescara to Bologna with a friend of ours, who then would continue her trip. In Bologna my sister-in-law, a Catholic, was to meet her and bring her to Padova. To give Adria's schedule, my mother sent a very concise telegram: "Adria Bologna 8 A.M., red ribbon on lapel." The encounter occurred with no problems, until the police arrived at our house in Pescara and turned our apartment upside down. They went to my mother's desk, took letters and her address book, and asked her to follow them to the police station. Simultaneously, the same happened at my brother's house in Padova. My little Adria was so frightened that, she later recounts, she wet her aunt's pink couch, and for a long time she had nightmares.

My mother was interrogated at the police station, where she explained that she was temporarily in Pescara to care for her three granddaughters: Paola, Mirella, and Adria. At the name Adria, the policeman apologized for the misunderstanding. The telegram had been censored, and the censor had mistaken Adria for the town of Adria, near Bologna, and had imagined a big plot of espionage and smuggling. Nevertheless, my mother was followed in the streets for one week. This episode demonstrates how, by that time, we were watched and considered enemies. I returned to Italy to fetch our girls and bring them to Morocco. But we still believed that nothing terrible would happen in Italy; we were still Italian citizens, very much attached to our country, and when we left for Tangier, we left our apartment as it was, with all its furniture and household goods.

In Tangier we began our new life, and it was a relatively good one. We escaped the horrors of the war, we never went hungry, we never saw Nazi troops, and we were not aware of the extermination camps and the "Final Solution"; for all these reasons we were very thankful to Morocco, a generous and beautiful country. But it was not so for my mother and grandmother, living in Torino. In 1944 they were rounded up by the Nazis and the fascists of the Salò Republic and deported to Fossoli, the concentration camp for Italian Jews near Modena. They lived there for one month in terrible conditions and in June were transferred to Auschwitz on a cattle train, with no food and no latrine. They were immediately gassed.

My grandmother, Nina Levi Vitale, was eighty-nine, and her daughter, my mother, Gemma Vitale Servadio, was sixty-five. Notes and postcards written by my mother from the concentration camp at Fossoli to non-Jewish friends and relatives were a desperate call for help; she'd ask for food, clothing, money, and toilet articles. These notes, by my and my brothers' decision, are now in the archives of the Holocaust National Museum in Washington, where they will be part of the historical testimony of the Nazi's ferocity. Only this way will we have avoided their dispersion or destruction by forgetful future generations.

One of the people who researched their unfortunate conditions was my uncle Adolfo Vitale. His name appears on the first page and many times again in the book of Liliana Picciotto Fargion, *Il libro della memoria*, the most complete work on the Italian Holocaust.[1] After a life full of activities as a salesman, a military man, an aviator, colonialist, and politician, he was dismissed from his high rank in Cirenaica and went to Paris. When the city was occupied by the Nazis, he went to the south of France and later joined us in Tangier. There he worked so well for the U.S. delegation that after the war he was sent to Rome with one of the first allied convoys. He created the Comitato di Ricerche Deportati Ebrei (CRDE) (Committee for Research on Deported Jews). In 1946 Adolfo went to Poland to represent the Italian government at the trial of the war criminal Rudolf Ferdinand Hess, Auschwitz commander. He also represented the Union of Italian Jewish Congregations, his committee, and the survivors of the extermination camps. In presentations he gave in Rome and Milan he related all the horrors, atrocities, and cruelties perpetrated in the camps against the people living there, prior to and after their death. He brought back a picture of Hess, with whom he had a private conversation, some crystals of the poison used to gas the victims, ciclon and potassium cianure, and some ashes from the crematorium, which he religiously kept for the rest of his life.

His impression of Hess was one of calm and firm belief that he had been a military man who had done his duty and obeyed orders. He accepted his punishment, death, stating that he would behave in the same way if ordered to do so again.

I would like to mention an anecdote about a child's reaction to the Nazi's persecutions. Gaia Servadio was born in 1938 in Padova to my brother Luxardo and Bianca Prinzi, a Catholic. Today she is a well-known journalist, novelist, and television personality in Italy and England. In her book *Un'infanzia diversa*[2] (A Different Childhood), she describes her life with the mentality of a little girl. She speaks of how she moved from place to place without understanding the reason and how she gave her real name when she had been taught by her parents to give a false one, and, above all, she describes the cold and hunger that she suffered and the bombardments.

In Morocco we had no news of the Italian relatives and had no idea that genocide was taking place. We were busy in our professional activity, integrating ourselves more to the local life and culture. We were studying languages because we had to deal with various nationalities: French, Spanish, English.

At the end of the war we had to think of our girls' future, and locally there was no opportunity to pursue a higher education. From Rome, my uncle would write about the confusion and moral laxity existing in Italy and suggested not to send our girls there. So we thought of the United States, considered, at that time, the "caput mundi." With the support of the consulate, where they found a job and an affidavit from a cousin who was a resident, we were able to obtain visas for two of our daughters. In September 1946 we accompanied them to Cadiz, where they embarked on a Spanish ship.

The separation from our two daughters, then nineteen and twenty-two, was a very traumatic one. We were sending them to an unknown country, hoping for a better future, yet we were torn by guilt. Once in the States, they were able to make a new life by studying, working, marrying, and having a family. Later, even the third daughter, after studying fashion design in Italy, joined the sisters in the New World.

My husband and I stayed in Tangier. He could not face a new change of life; his health was failing, having had in 1951 and 1958 a heart attack, and consequently closed the clinic. He died in September 1965. A correct and honest man in all the manifestations of life, he loved his family and was loved by all. My oldest daughter was with me during that painful and difficult time. It took four months to have him buried in the Bedarida Mausoleum in Turin.

Alone in Tangier, my professional activity had increased. I refused my brother's proposal to move to Rome and work there. I was already in my late sixties and felt too old to start a new life. In Tangier I had many good friends.

Members of my family, scattered all over, visited me frequently. Apart from my work I had many interesting social activities. I wrote and published many articles, including a proposal for the establishment of an international university in Tangier, an essay on Dante and medicine, and a study of ancient Arab medicine and its influence on the modern medical mind, which was even read by King Hassan II in 1967.

Should you ask me which was the most memorable experience of my professional life, I would have to say that it was the delivery of the third child of my youngest daughter. In the delivery room I found myself, above all, as a doctor but also as a mother having the responsibility of two lives of my own flesh and blood.

My job was satisfactory, but all the big and small difficulties of daily life had to be dealt with: discussions with the landlords, failure of telephone service, theft of a car, unreliable help, nurses, cleaning ladies, and so on. I fractured my leg twice; a cataract operation to my right eye rendered my work more difficult. At the end of 1979 I was hit by a taxi, fracturing two ribs and sustaining such a head wound that I was in a coma for three days. Friends and colleagues surrounded me with loving attention and care. One of my daughters also came to care for me, but it was obvious that I could no longer be alone. I gave my resignation to the Public Health Office. The demonstration of affection of the people working with me was really very moving. It was a painful decision to leave Morocco and join my daughters in the United States. I arrived here in May 1981, and I cannot say I have ever fully integrated. "Trees, if transplanted old, cannot take roots easily," says an old proverb. I have lost my independence, my profession, my own home that was always open to friends and family; the climate is harsh, the language difficult to comprehend as my hearing fails. We live far from New York City, which makes it difficult to enjoy its cultural life. Some local bridge parties amuse and distract me and keep my memory and mind alive. Two intraocular implants of the crystalline lens have improved my vision, and I am happy to say I can read, write, and sew.

I travel often—sometimes with a little difficulty but nevertheless always with an increasing desire. I go to Italy, where I feel at home and where I want to be buried, to Morocco, where some of my good friends still live, and to Brazil, where my only surviving brother lives. As time goes on, I receive news of beloved friends and relatives dying or seriously ill, and this is the worst part of aging. For this reason, perhaps, I look for the support of my grandchildren, following them in the good and bad moments of their lives. In a week I will celebrate the bas mitzvah of my first great-granddaughter, and I have just received the news that my last great-granddaughter, seven months old, is out of danger after very serious and difficult surgery.

I conclude now, as I do not want to take advantage of your patience. Thank you.

NOTES

1. Liliana Picciotto Fargion, *Il libro della memoria: Gli ebrei deportati dall'Italia*

(1943–1945) (Milan: Mursia, 1991).
    2. Gaia Servadio, *Un'infanzia diversa* (Milan: Rizzoli, 1988).

Part VII

EPILOGUE

32

The Survival of
"the Most Ancient of Minorities"

Stephen Siporin

My purpose in this chapter is to describe new cultural expressions and initiatives undertaken by Italian Jews over the last twenty-five years and to analyze them in a context usually described as the decline of Italian Jewry. The first surprise: there have been many cultural innovations since the 1970s. Still, there are questions: Are these changes signs of vitality or of devolution? Are they the last gasps of a dying society or evidence of dynamism? Are we witnessing sunset or sunrise?

Scholarly consensus suggests that Italian Jewry is experiencing its twilight years. H. Stuart Hughes' *Prisoners of Hope: The Silver Age of the Italian Jews 1924–1974*, assumed the long decline of Italian-Jewish culture with its reference to "the silver age," which, as we know, always follows a golden age.[1] Writing in 1983, Hughes says that "a residual ethnic consciousness maintained itself throughout what I have called their Silver Age and into the last quarter of the twentieth century,"[2] intimating continuing cultural devolution. Cecil Roth, the great historian of Italian Jewry, described the decline of religiosity and communal life throughout the nineteenth and early twentieth centuries: in 1830 Italy's 108 synagogues opened twice daily, but by 1930, only 38 opened, half of them irregularly.[3] In 1976 Sergio Della Pergola, a leading demographer of world Jewry, himself an Italian Jew who had immigrated to Israel, painted a bleak statistical portrait of Italian Jewry in his *Anatomia dell'ebraismo italiano*. Projecting rapid decline in Italy's small and medium-sized Jewish communities outside Rome and Milan, he stated that "in the future, Italian Judaism will be increasingly polarized between the communities of Rome and Milan, and it will appear more and more to be either Roman or foreign in origin, while the remaining sectors of the Jewish community *proceed rapidly down the road of their demographic sunset*"(emphasis added).[4] The population loss in Venice, the Jewish community where I did fieldwork in 1978, confirms Della Pergola's projection for the small communities. From 1956 to 1965 the population declined from 1,091 to 844 and to 788 in 1975.[5]

The diminishing population had fallen to 500 twenty years later, in 1995.[6]

There is much to regret and much to mourn—and there is no denying the losses. Italian Jewry today is not experiencing a population explosion, a religious revival, or a full-fledged renewal movement. Nevertheless, culture critics are often too quick to pronounce the death sentence. An apt analogy may exist in the American West; during the nineteenth century, many Americans assumed that Native Americans were doomed and were vanishing. It was thought that they would assimilate, and reservations were expected to "terminate" as Native Americans melted into the general American population. Native Americans obviously haven't vanished—in fact, some tribes are much more numerous than they ever were before. But more to the point is the fact that they have changed in unpredicted ways and still remained Native Americans.

Native Americans invented new social events, like the powwow; new art forms, like beadwork; new foods, like fry bread; and uncounted new stories, told in English. These new expressions became rallying points for besieged Native societies. Cultural change that is based in tradition is key to a group's survival—but change is too often mistaken by outsiders for cultural degradation. I would like to suggest that just as Native Americans met impending doom with cultural creativity, there *are* dynamic expressions of Italian-Jewish life today (unforeseen just a short time ago) and that their identification, description, and analysis may eventually give us new perspectives on a culture that is not as ready to die as many may have thought.

What are these dynamic expressions? Here I identify and examine several categories and instances of cultural innovation that have arisen, beginning in the 1970s.

The first category is public festivals that celebrate Jewish Italian life. "On Sunday, June 5, 1977, from 9:30 A.M. to well past midnight, a 'happening' took place in Rome's via Portico d'Ottavia. . . . The ghetto of Rome . . .celebrated its first official *festa*, timidly launched under the title 'Rendezvous at Portico d'Ottavia.'"[7]

Thus wrote Lisa Palmieri-Billig, an American journalist and participant in the event. Technically, what she wrote was false. Jewish festivals, like Passover and Rosh Hashanah, have been going on in Rome for over 2,000 years. But these are traditional, private festivals for insiders, members of the Jewish community—not public events, like the Rendezvous, which was aimed as much at outsiders as insiders. Something new was initiated when Roman Jews embraced the local custom of summer neighborhood festivals, making their own *festa* into a showcase and celebration of Jewish culture—including Jewish foods, music, speeches, a model of the ghetto, and even a recital of poems in *giudeo-romanesco*, the Roman-Jewish dialect.[8]

A somewhat different, but parallel, "Jewish Culture Festival" was held in Venice on 19–26 November 1995. Like the festival in the old Roman ghetto, this event was designed to appeal to outsiders as well as insiders. It was more "highbrow," featuring films, performances, and lectures. The "Jewish Culture Festival" is a biennial event, and it was held for the second time in 1997.

Organizers (and others) hope to build support for the establishment of an international Jewish study center in the old ghetto.

A similar festival—a series of public exhibitions, lectures, and plays—under the title "Shalom Trieste" was initiated recently, and a Jewish film festival was begun in 1998 in Pitigliano. Pitigliano is a small town in southern Tuscany that was once known as "the Little Jerusalem" but is now home to fewer than five Jews.

The case of Pitigliano raises questions about cultural innovations that will be pursued in the next section and later in this chapter. If only a few or even no Italian Jews are involved in an initiative that has Jewish content, can we really speak of such public events as instances of Jewish cultural innovation? (Can Boy Scout versions of Native American rituals be considered Native American?) Perhaps cases like Pitigliano indicate the irony of how, in the course of a mere half century, an ethnic culture can pass from being a target for destruction to being a commodity for promotion.

My second category in this catalog of innovation is the restoration of synagogues and other Jewish sites in places like Pitigliano, Venice, and elsewhere. The synagogue of Pitigliano offers a striking example: a synagogue restored, in 1995,[9] not for Jewish worship—since the Jews are gone—but as a historical monument and tourist attraction. As is the case with the festivals mentioned earlier, the restoration of the synagogue of Pitigliano and many of the cultural initiatives described here were funded by Jewish organizations from both inside and outside Italy, private donors, and Italian government agencies (especially at the regional and local levels). What does this cultural conservation effort mean? Increasing local and regional income from tourism obviously provides one kind of motivation, but it seems that restoration serves more than one group.

To understand the meaning of restoring synagogues requires a larger context. In 1978 in Padova I interviewed an elderly Jewish businessman. When I asked him about the future of the main synagogue of Padova, then in disrepair, he became upset and told me that the state should pay to fix it since in less than 100 years all such properties would belong to the state. He said that he was not interested in contributing to future tourist attractions, where people will come, as they do now to see Etruscan ruins, saying, "This is where the Jews *used* to live." He preferred to donate to Israel or to some American Jewish cause in which he could support living Jewish culture that has a future.[10] Thus spoke a man whose ancient Italian-Jewish name, since he had three daughters and no sons, would come to an end with him.

What has Italian Jewry done about its precious physical heritage—the synagogues and all their appurtenences, representing hundreds of years of Jewish life in scores of communities throughout northern Italy? In the 1940s, 1950s, and 1960s, the furnishings of many Italian synagogues were removed and sent to Israel, where they were incorporated into synagogues there. Such was the case with objects from the ancient synagogues of Busseto, Moncalvo, Reggio Emilia, San Daniele del Friuli, and Trino, among others. Even whole synagogues, in places like Conegliano and Vittorio Veneto, were disassembled and then reassembled in Israel. Others fell into disrepair and even had to be abandoned. This general approach implied that there was no point in maintaining historic synagogues in cities depopulated of their Jews[11]—an attitude not so very different from that of my informant in Padova.

The restoration and preservation of a synagogue like the one in Pitigliano thus represents a dramatic break with the earlier approach. As Annie Sacerdoti put it, "A fervor of restorations, repairs, and documentation was started in the 1970s. This was assisted with contributions from the Assessors of Cultural Possessions. There has now been a reversal of tendencies . . . destruction and abandonment has been transformed into restoration."[12] Economics may motivate the regional tourism office, but why are Italian Jews now contributing to such restoration, too? Clearly, something fundamental has changed since the 1960s.

The appearance of guidebooks to Jewish Italy forms a third category of cultural innovation. Most notable is the Jewish Itineraries Series,[13] a number of guidebooks that consider Italian-Jewish history and its physical monuments regionally. Titles thus far include *Emilia Romagna* (1992), *Lombardia* (1993), *Piemonte* (1994), *Toscana* (1995), and *Veneto* (1997). They are published in Italian and English and contain attractive color photos and erudite historical narratives. Each guide includes an impressive bibliography and an extensive glossary useful to anyone unfamiliar with Jewish religious terminology. The guidebooks even include phone numbers of local contacts who will admit visitors to Jewish sites that are not regularly accessible to the public. This series appears to be an extension and elaboration of an original one-volume book, *Guide to Jewish Italy*, by Annie Sacerdoti, translated into English in 1989.

These guidebooks are for the serious tourist—Jew or non-Jew. What does the appearance of guidebooks to Jewish Italy at this moment in history tell us? Is there some sort of confluence of events occurring now that was not imaginable in the 1950s? Are Italian Jews educating themselves at the same moment that they educate tourists? Does the process rally culture or commodify it? Does the conservation of cultural heritage inevitably do both?

The appearance of cookbooks publicizing Italian-Jewish cuisine for a broad public provides a fourth category. Until the 1980s there were only two Italian-Jewish cookbooks available, and one was an expanded edition of the other. Today there are several, and their number continues to increase. They include, in chronological order:

1930s (1)	*Poesia Nascosta* (1931)[14]
1970s (1)	*La cucina nella tradizione ebraica* (1970)[15]
1980s (2)	*The Classic Cuisine of the Italian Jews: Traditional Recipes and Menus and a Memoir of a Vanished Way of Life* (1981)[16]
	Dal 1880 ad óggi: La cucina ebraica della mia famiglia (1982)[17]
1990s (4)	*The Classic Cuisine of the Italian Jews II: More Menus, Recipes, and Recollections* (1992)[18]
	Italian Jewish Cooking (1993)[19]
	Le ricette di casa mia: La cucina casher in una famiglia ebraica italiana (1993)[20]
	Cucina Ebraica: Flavors of the Italian Jewish Kitchen (1998)[21]

Some of these cookbooks, published only in English, mainly for an American audience, are riding the wave of the insatiable contemporary appetite for new cuisines. The relevance of this phenomenon for my study is that it lends Italian-Jewish cooking an international aura of exoticism and prestige. Outside interest and excitement may kindle internal interest and pride, too.

I suggested in my article "From *Kashrut* to *Cucina Ebraica*: The Recasting of Italian Jewish Foodways"[22] that Jewish food in Italy had made a transition from a religious to an ethnic tradition—that new cookbooks had gradually left behind their role of delineating the rules of *kashrut* (regulations for ritual purity, such as not eating pork and not serving meat dishes and milk dishes at the same meal) and had come to promote the nostalgic values of *cucina ebraica* (Jewish-style cooking). Thus, Jewish cooking in Italy is now conceived of as parallel to regional cooking (the cuisine paradigm in "a nation of regions") and was made desirable for non-Jews as well as Jews because of its attributed distinctiveness and homey, sentimental value.

On the other hand, the most recent Jewish cookbook published in Italy for Italians, *Le ricette di casa mia: La cucina casher in una famiglia ebraica italiana*, stresses *kashrut* even in its title, perhaps indicating an even newer "innovation"— an innovation that is the most conservatively Jewish of all.

Nevertheless, like the other cultural categories that I have mentioned, food has been gaining Italian Jews a certain validation in the larger, national context during the period of the past twenty-five years; that is, Jewish culture has gone public. Have the ensuing positive feedback and recognition been a kind of encouragement, leading to more innovation, too?

Yet another recent means of celebrating Italian-Jewish culture has been found in the curating of major art exhibitions on Italian Jewry within Italy and in the United States. This high-art model presents Italian-Jewish culture aesthetically and appeals to Italians, Italian Jews, and to the larger world, thus bringing prestige to the heritage of Italian Jewry. It rallies and educates, even though it looks mainly to the past.

The most outstanding example was the exhibition and catalog *Gardens and Ghettos: The Art of Life in Jewish Italy*, a major exhibition shown in New York (1989) and Italy (Ferrara).[23]

Other exhibitions include Ebrei a Torino (Turin, 1984), Jewish Art and Culture in Emilia-Romagna/Arte e cultura ebraiche in Emilia-Romagna (San Francisco, 1989, and Italian sites in Emilia-Romagna),[24] and Ebrei Piemontese: Jews of Piedmont (New York, 1998).[25] Since these exhibitions appeared during the same time frame as the other four categories of cultural innovation, we may see all of them as part of the same fabric, the same cultural phenomenon—which is one of dynamism rather than stagnation.

My sixth and final category is different from the others. It involves an innovation that was imposed on the Italian-Jewish community, rather than emerging from it. I am referring to the appearance and residence of ultra-Orthodox Jews (from the Habad Lubavitcher Hasidic sect) in Venice and Milan. I will briefly describe the situation in Venice.

Seeing Hasidic Jews in the ghetto of Venice during a short visit there in 1996 was a shock to me. They hadn't been there in 1978, when I lived in the ghetto area doing fieldwork for nine months, or in 1985, when I made another short visit to Venice. In 1996 they were not only visible but also ran their own shops (promoting Lubavitcher Hasidism) and a glatt-kosher restaurant. They were prominent participants (even leaders) in the synagogue services. I was shocked because the Hasids were simultaneously appropriate (being Jews) and inappropriate (not being Italian) in the ghetto area. Their brand of Judaism was of such a different style from that of Venetian and Italian Jews that they seemed to represent a kind of colonialism—particularly since their presence indicated an effort to convert Venetian Jews to their form of orthodoxy. I wondered if they had imposed themselves on the community and how Venetian Jews felt about them. I spoke to Venetian Jews briefly while I was there and later corresponded with Jewish friends from Venice. I found out that I was not entirely wrong or alone in my reaction.

One friend wrote:

They came probably 15 years ago. The start was a shock, because they tend to impose on you and on your ways. We had various chances of struggle and fought harshly. Now, thanks to the rabbi who is quite positive about his and their roles, we have come to a sort of gentlemen's agreement: they behave as they like but respect us and our traditions. In synagogue they behave as we expect them to do. But we keep very fast and close to our traditions.[26]

My concern had been that a foreign force that was Jewish itself could be the undoing of this community's local traditions—what neither the Nazis or assimilation could accomplish, another Jewish group, ironically, might. What a loss it would be, for example, if the singing of the unique Venetian Passover song "Capretto" were to be replaced by the widespread Ashkenazic version, "Had Gadya." Perhaps that will be the case, but I am somewhat reassured that a community that has absorbed other Jewish traditions repeatedly in the past will do so once again. After all, the original official Jewish community of Venice was Ashkenazic, and its first synagogue was called the *scola todesca*. Then came Spanish and Portuguese Jews, who brought their traditions and built the *scola levantina* and the *scola spagnola*. The Italian Jews were seemingly always there in the background, the poorest sector of the population, absorbing and assimilating the many layers of Jewish immigrants. Maybe the Lubavitchers are just the latest phase. Although they import foreign Jewish institutions and attitudes that Italian Jews must face and interact with, perhaps they will add to the Jewish mix, and, ultimately, they may help the community survive.

My six categories as well as other cultural expressions—like the explosion of Italian-Jewish literature in the 1980s and 1990s, described by Professor Raniero Speelman elsewhere in this volume—bespeak ferment rather than stagnation. I do not claim that all of these developments are entirely positive or that they can be reduced to one meaning; I want only to say that they do warrant a look at Italian Jews today as they come to terms with a world that is far different from that of their fathers and mothers. Perhaps it will be a world in which their ancient identity persists.

There is nothing conclusive in what I have presented here. Simply, it is clear that something that we might call "Italian-Jewish culture" is active, even "hot." What this means is another story. Does this activity point to a dynamic Italian-Jewish people or to capitalistic commodification? Or both? If both, what are the proportions?

If nothing else, this investigation may lead us to ask what survival means. "Survival," when we get beyond the biological and the individual, has to do with the corporate nature of society and culture—the continuity of a group's sense of itself over time. The content—what that group fixes on as its means of self-identification—may be constantly changing while the corporate sense endures. There is a paradox here. Italian Jews have survived twenty centuries, culturally and socially, but we wonder about their future. How much can they change and still be Italian Jews? We don't question the "Jewish credentials" of seventeenth century Roman ghetto dwellers, yet surely they were far different from their ancestors who settled in Rome more than seventeen centuries earlier. If we could put members of these two historic groups of Jews together, face to face, one wonders to what extent they would recognize each other as belonging to the same group, but both, surely, are Jews, and both their cultures, with points in common and points of divergence, are surely Jewish.

This phenomenon is easier to imagine when placed in the past than in the present, but might not someone, two centuries from now, look at the cultural dynamics of Italian Jews in the year 2000 and remark on their continuity with, not just their divergence from, their two millennia of history?

NOTES

1. Hughes actually claims that Italian Jewry experienced two golden ages. He identifies the first with the preghetto Renaissance and the second with the first two decades of the twentieth century, when Jews participated fully and prominently in Italian national life. H. Stuart Hughes, *Prisoners of Hope: The Silver Age of the Italian Jews 1924–1974* (Cambridge: Harvard University Press, 1983), pp. 16–20.

2. Ibid., pp. 150–151.

3. Cecil Roth, *History of the Jews of Italy* (Philadelphia: Jewish Publication Society, 1946), p. 506.

4. Sergio Della Pergola, *Anatomia dell'ebraismo italiano: Caratteristiche demografiche, economiche, sociali, religiose, e politiche di una minoranza* (Roma: Carucci, 1976), p. 154. The original reads, "in futuro l'ebrasimo italiano sarà polarizzato in misura crescente fra le comunità di Roma e di Milano, e apparirà sempre più di origine romana o di recente origine straniera, mentre i rimanenti settori della comunità ebraica proseguiranno rapidamente sulla strada del loro tramonto demografico."

5. Ibid., p. 60.

6. Ruth Gruber, "Life in Venice: Jewish Festival a Hit," *Forward*, 8 December 1995, p. 2.

7. Lisa Palmieri-Billig, "Jews of Rome," *Hadassah Magazine* (October 1977): 14.

8. Ibid., pp. 14–15.

9. Dora Liscia Bemporad and Annamarcella Tedeschi Falco, eds., *Tuscany Jewish Itineraries: Places, History and Art* (Venice: Marsilio, 1995), p. 137.

10. Personal field notes, 6 October 1978.

11. Sometimes furnishings went to functioning synagogues in larger Jewish communities in Italy, like Turin or Florence.

12. Annie Sacerdoti, *Guide to Jewish Italy* (Brooklyn: Israelowitz Publishing, 1989), p. 17.

13. Edited by Annie Sacerdoti and published by Marsilio Editore, in Venice.

14. Ines De Benedetti, *Poesia Nascosta* (Milano: Adei, 1949 [1931]).

15. Giuliana Ascola Vitali-Norsa, *La cucina nella tradizione ebraica* (Milano: Adei, 1970).

16. Edda Servi Machlin, *The Classic Cuisine of the Italian Jews: Traditional Recipes and Menus and a Memoir of a Vanished Way of Life* (New York: Dodd, Mead, 1981).

17. Donatella Limentani Pavoncello, *Dal 1880 ad óggi: La cucina ebraica della mia famiglia* (Rome: Carucci, 1982).

18. Edda Servi Machlin, *The Classic Cuisine of the Italian Jews II: More Menus, Recipes, and Recollections* (Croton-on-Hudson, NY: Giro, 1992).

19. Mira Sacerdoti, *Italian Jewish Cooking* (London: Robert Hale, 1993).

20. Milka Belgrado Passigli, *Le ricette di casa mia: La cucina casher in una famiglia ebraica italiana* (Firenze: La Giuntina, 1993).

21. Joyce Goldstein, *Cucina Ebraica: Flavors of the Italian Jewish Kitchen* (San Francisco: Chronicle Books, 1998).

22. *Journal of American Folklore* 107 (1994): 268–281.

23. The catalog is Vivian B. Mann, ed., *Gardens and Ghettos: The Art of Life in Jewish Italy* (Berkeley: University of California Press, 1989).

24. The exhibition catalog is *Arte e cultura ebraiche in Emilia-Romagna/Jewish Art and Culture in Emilia-Romagna* (Milano: Arnoldo Mondadori, 1989).

25. Catalog forthcoming.

26. Personal E-mail communication, 19 September 1998.

A Selected Bibliography, 1996–1999

James Tasato Mellone

Research on the Jews of Italy can begin with the following authoritative bibliographies:

Consonni, Manuela, M. *Biblioteca italo-ebraica: bibliografia per la storia degli ebrei in Italia, 1986–1995*. Edited by Shlomo Simonsohn. Rome: Menorah, 1997.

Luzzatto, Aldo. *Biblioteca italo-ebraica: bibliografia per la storia degli ebrei in Italia, 1974–1985*. Milan: Franco Angeli, 1989.

Luzzatto, Aldo and Moshe Moldavi. *Bibliotheca italo-ebraica: bibliografia per la storia degli ebrei in Italia, 1964–1973*. Edited by Daniel Carpi. Rome: Carucci, 1982.

Milano, Attilio. *Bibliotheca historica italo-judaica*. Florence: Sansoni, 1954.

———. *Bibliotheca historica italo-judaica*. Florence: Sansoni, 1964.

The preceding books are comprehensive, yet not exhaustive, in their coverage. The following is a continuation, covering selected studies in English, Italian, French, German, and Spanish.

ANCIENT ROME AND MEDIEVAL ITALY

Bonfil, Roberto. "Giustizia, giudici e tribunali nelle comunità ebraiche dell'occidente cristiano." In *La Giustizia nell'Alto Medioevo (secoli IX–XI): 11–17 aprile 1996*, 931–973. Spoleto: Centro italiano di studi sull'alto Medioevo, 1997.

———. *Tra due mondi: cultura ebraica e cultura cristiana nel Medioevo*. Naples: Liguori, 1996.

Bucaria, Nicolo, ed. *Gli ebrei in Sicilia, dal tardoantico al Medioevo: studi in onore di mons. Benedetto Rocco*. Palermo: Flaccovio, 1998.

———. "L'archeologia giudaica in Sicilia." *Materia Giudaica* 3 (1997): 44–49.

———. *Sicilia judaica: guida alle antichità giudaiche della Sicilia*. Palermo: Flaccovio, 1996.

Congresso internazionale dell'AISG (9th Congress, 1992: Potenza and Venosa). *L'ebraismo dell'Italia meridionale peninsulare dale origini al 1541: società, economia, cultura*. Galatina: Congedo, 1996.

Donfried, Karl P. and Peter Richardson, eds. *Judaism and Christianity in First-Century Rome*. Grand Rapids, MI: William B. Erdmanns, 1998.

Gebbia, Clara. *Presenze giudaiche nella Sicilia antica e tardoantica.* Rome: G. Bretschneider, 1996.

Levi, Joseph Abraham. "'La ienti de Sion': Linguistic and Cultural Legacy of an Early Thirteenth-Century Judeo-Italian Kinah." *Italica* 75, no. 1 (Spring 1998): 1–21.

Liberanome, Daniele. "Gli ebrei al tempo di Teodorico e il ruolo della Chiesa di Roma." *Rassegna Mensile di Israel* 64, no. 3 (September/December 1998): 21–40.

Limor, Ora. "Die Disputationen zu Ceuta (1179) und Mallorca (1286): Zwei antijudische Shriften aus dem mittelalterlichen Genua." *Jewish History* 10, no. 2 (1996): 138–139.

Noy, David. "Writing in Tongues: The Use of Greek, Latin and Hebrew in Jewish Inscriptions from Roman Italy." *Journal of Jewish Studies* 48, no. 2 (1997): 300–311.

Pavoncello, Nello. "Antiche famiglie ebraiche italiane: 1. Gli Ascarelli." *Rassegna Mensile di Israel* 63, no. 1 (January/April 1997): 135–140.

Perani, Mauro. "La 'Genizah italiana': caratteri generali e rapporto su quindici anni di scoperte." *Rivista Biblica* 45, no. 1 (1997): 31–70.

Rossana, Urbani and Guido Nathan Zazzu. *The Jews in Genoa*. Vol. 1: *507–1681*. Boston: Brill, 1999.

Simonsohn, Shlomo. *The Jews in Sicily*. Vol. 1: *383–1300*. Boston: Brill, 1997.

Slingerland, H. Dixon. *Claudian Policymaking and the Early Imperial Repression of Judaism at Rome*. Atlanta: Scholars Press, 1997.

Toaff, Ariel. *Love, Work and Death: Jewish Life in Medieval Umbria*. Translated by Judith Landry. London: Littman Library of Jewish Civilization, 1996.

Williams, Margaret H. "The Jews of Early Byzantine Venusia: The Family of Faustinus I, the Father." *Journal of Jewish Studies* 50, no. 1 (Spring 1999): 38–52.

RENAISSANCE AND EARLY MODERN ITALY

Alfie, Fabian. "Immanuel of Rome, Alias Manoello Giudeo: The Poetics of Jewish Identity in Fourteenth-Century Italy." *Italica* 75, no. 3 (Autumn 1998): 307–329.

Allegra, Luciano. "Conversioni dal Ghetto di Torino." *Dimensioni e Problemi della Ricerca Storica* no. 2 (1996): 187–202.

———. *Identità in bilico: il ghetto ebraico di Torino nel Settecento*. Turin: Zamorani, 1996.

Artocchini, Carmen. "Presenze ebraiche a Piacenza dalla metà del XVI sec. all'unità d'Italia." *Archivio Storico per le Province Parmensi* 47 (1996): 143–160.

Attias, Jean-Christophe. "Isaac Abravanel: Between Ethnic Memory and National Memory." *Jewish Social Studies* 2, no. 3 (1996): 137–155.

Bardelle, Thomas. *Juden in einem Transit- und Bröckenland: Studien zur Geschichte der Juden in Savoyen-Piemont bis zum Ende der Herrschaft Amadeus VIII*. Hannover: Hahnsche Buchhandlung, 1998.

Belkin, Ahuva, ed. *Leone de 'Sommi and the Performing Arts*. Tel Aviv: Yolanda and David Katz Faculty of the Arts, Tel Aviv University, 1997.

Bonfil, Roberto. "Dubious Crimes in Sixteenth-Century Italy: Rethinking the Relations between Jews, Christians, and 'Conversos' in Pre-Modern Europe." In *The Jews of Spain and the Expulsion of 1492*. Edited by Moshe Lazar and Stephen Halczer. Lancaster, CA: Labyrinthos, 1997, pp. 299–310.

Botticini, Maristella. "New Evidence on Jews in Tuscany, c. 1310–1435: The Friends and Family Connection Again." *Zakhor* 1 (1997): 77–93.

Calabi, Donatella. "Les quartiers juifs entre 15ᵉ et 17ᵉ siecle: quelques hypotheses de travail." *Annales: Histoire, Science Sociales* 52, no. 4 (1997): 777–797.

Campanini, Saveria. "'Peculium Abrae,' la grammatica ebraico-latina di Avraham de Balmes." *Annali di Ca'Foscari* 36, no. 3 (1997): 5–49.

Cassandro, Michele. *Intolleranza e accettazione, gli ebrei in Italia nei secoli XIV–XVIII: lineamenti di una storia economica e sociale.* Turin: G. Giappichelli, 1996.

Colafemmina, Cesare. *Per la storia degli ebrei in Calabria: saggi e documenti.* Soveria Mannelli: Rubbettino, 1996.

Colbi, Paolo S. "Note su di un'antica famiglia Levi, residente a Trieste fin dall'inizio del Seicento." *Rassegna Mensile di Israel* 63, no. 1 (January/April 1997): 121–134.

Cooperman, Bernard Dov. "Portuguese 'Conversos' in Ancona: Jewish Political Activity in Early Modern Italy." In *In Iberia and Beyond: Hispanic Jews between Cultures.* Newark: University of Delaware Press, 1998, pp. 297–352.

Cortese, Ennio. "Mutui ebraici usurari e svalutazione della moneta: Pinamonte da Vimercate e le fortune canonistiche di un suo lodo arbitrale." *Studia Gratiana* 28 (1998): 199–212.

Cozzi, Gaetano. *Giustizia 'contaminata': vicende giudiziarie di nobili ed ebrei nella Venezia dei Seicento.* Venice: Marsilio, 1996.

De León-Jones, Karen Silva. *Giordano Bruno and the Kabbalah: Prophets, Magicians, and Rabbis.* New Haven, CT: Yale University Press, 1997.

Di Leone Leoni, Aron. "I marrani di Coimbra denunciati al papa all'Inquisizione portoghese nel 1578: il loro status giuridico in diversi stati italiani." *Zakhor* 2 (1998): 73–109.

———. "Nuove notizie sugli Abravanel." *Zakhor* 1 (1997): 153–206.

———. "Per una storia della nazione tedesca di Ferrara nel Cinquecento." *Rassegna Mensile di Israel* 62, no. 1/2 (January/August 1996): 137–168.

Dubin, Lois C. *The Port Jews of Habsburg Trieste: Absolutist Politics and Enlightenment Culture.* Stanford, CA: Stanford University Press, 1999.

Durissini, Daniela. "Credito e presenza ebraica a Trieste (XIV–XV secolo)." *Zakhor* 1 (1997): 25–76.

Filippini, Jean Pierre. *Il porto di Livorno e la Toscana, 1676–1814.* Naples: Edizioni Scientifiche Italiane, 1998.

Foa, Anna. "The Jews of Rome." In *Rome, Amsterdam: Two Growing Cities in Seventeenth-Century Rome.* Edited by Peter van Kessel and Elisja Schulte van Kessel. Amsterdam: Amsterdam University Press, 1997.

Goetschel, Roland, ed. *1492: l'expulsion des juifs d'Espagne.* Paris: Maisonneuve et Larose, 1996.

Harrán, Don. "'Dum recordaremur Sion': Music in the Life and Thought of the Venetian Rabbi Leon Modena (1571–1648)." *Association for Jewish Studies Review* 23, no. 1 (1998): 17–61.

Ioly Zorattini, Pier Cesare. "Domenico Gerosolimitano a Venezia." *Sefarad* 58, no. 1 (1998): 107–116.

Jacopetti, Ircas Nicola. *Ebrei a Massa e Carrara: banche, commerci, industrie dal XVI al XIX secolo.* Florence: Edifir, 1996.

Kirn, Hans-Martin. "Antijudaismus und spätmittelalterliche Bussfrömmigkeit: die Predigten des Franziskaner Bernhardin von Busti (um 1450–1513)." *Zeitschrift für Kirchengeschichte* 108, no. 2 (1997): 147–175.

Knoch-Mund, Gaby. "Disputationsliteratur als Instrument antijüdischer Polemik: Leben und Werk des Marcus Lombardus, eines Grenzgangers swischen Judentum und Christentum im Zeitalter des deutschen Humanismus." *Shofar* 17, no. 3 (1999): 179.

Kuyt, Annelies. "With One Foot in the Renaissance: Shlomoh Almoli and His Dream Interpretation." *Jewish Studies Quarterly* 6, no. 3 (1999): 205–217.

Lattes, Yaakov Andrea. "Aspetti politici ed istituzionali delle comunità ebraiche in Italia nel Cinque-Seicento." *Zakhor* 2 (1998): 21–37.

Lelli, Fabrizio. "L'educazione ebraica nella seconda metà del '400: poetica e scienze naturali nel *Hay ha-'Olamim* di Yohanan Alemanno." *Rinascimento* 36 (1996): 75–136.

Liscia Bemporad, Dora and Ida Zatelli, eds. *La cultura ebraica all'epoca di Lorenzo il Magnifico: celebrazioni del V centenario della morte di Lorenzo il Magnifico*. Studi, Accademia Toscana di Scienze e Lettere La Colombaria. Florence: Olschki, 1998, p. 170.

Luzzati, Michele, ed. *La sinagoga di Pisa: dale origini al restauro ottocentesco di Marco Treves*. Florence: Edifir, 1997.

Malkiel, David. "The Inheritance Tale in Immanuel of Rome's Mahbarot." *Prooftexts* 16, no. 2 (May 1996): 169–173.

Melzi, Robert C. "The Flight of Jews into Italy and the Testimony of Some Italian Renaissance Plays." *Annali d'Italianistica* 14 (1996): 542–552.

Meron, Orly. "The Dowries of Jewish Women in the Duchy of Milan (1535–1597): Economic and Social Aspects." *Zakhor* 2 (1998): 127–137.

Muzzarelli, Maria Giuseppini, ed. *Verso l'epilogo di una convivenza: gli ebrei a Bologna nel 16° secolo*. Florence: Giuntina, 1996.

Orfali, Moise. "Il 'Danielillo' da Livorno: testo e contesto." *Zakhor* 1 (1997): 207–220.

Panato, Giuseppina. "I patti fra gli ebrei di Castel Goffredo e in Gonzaga nel Cinquecento." *Zakhor* 2 (1998): 39–71.

Parisi, Susan. "The Jewish Community and Carnival Entertainment at the Mantuan Court in the Early Baroque." In *Music in Renaissance Cities and Courts: Studies in Honor of Lewis Lockwood*. Edited by Jessie Ann Owens and Anthony M. Cummings. Warren, MI: Harmonie Park Press, 1997, pp. 293–305.

Patroni Griffi, Filena. "Documenti inediti sulle attività economiche degli Abravanel in Italia meridionale (1492–1543). *Rassegna Mensile di Israel* 63, no. 2 (May/August 1997): 27–38.

Pellegrini, Paolo. "Medici ebrei a Terni fra Tre e Quattrocento." *Zakhor* 2 (1998): 113–125.

Petruccioli, Attilio, ed. *Sefarad: architettura e urbanistica ebraiche dopo il 1492*. Como: Dell'Oca, 1996.

Pironio, Lara. "L'insediamento ebraico di San Daniele del Friuli nel Settecento." *Rassegna Mensile di Israel* 65, no. 2 (May/August 1999): 31–80.

Pisa, Franco. "Sulle attività bancarie locali nell'Italia dei secoli XIV–XVI." *Zakhor* 1 (1997): 113–149.

Ravid, Benjamin C. I. "Christian Travelers in the Ghetto of Venice: Some Preliminary Observations." In *Between History and Literature: Studies in Honor of Isaac Barzilay*. Edited by Stanley Nash. Tel Aviv: Hakibbutz Hameuchad, 1997, pp. 111–150.

Ritter-Santini, Lea. "Die Erfahrung der Toleranz: Melchisedech in Livorno." *Germanisch-Romanische Monatsschrift* 47, no. 3 (1997): 317–362.

Salvadori, Roberto G. "Famiglie ebraiche di Monte San Savino (1627–1799): attività economiche e rapporti sociali." *Zakhor* 2 (1998): 139–154.

———. *1799: gli ebrei italiani nella bufera antigiacobina*. Florence: Giuntina, 1999.

Schoeps, Julius Hans. "Justizfolter und Geständnis: der Trienter Ritualmordprozess von 1475." *Zeitschrift für Religions- und Geistesgeschichte* 49, no. 4 (1997): 377–381.

Segre, Renata. "Sephardic Refugees in Ferrara: Two Notable Families." In *Crisis and Creativity in the Sephardic World, 1391–1648*. Edited by Benjamin Gampel. New York: Columbia University Press, 1997, pp. 164–185.

Shapiro, James. *Shakespeare and the Jews*. New York: Columbia University Press, 1996.

Sloan, Dolores J. "Ferrara: Spiritual Haven for Conversos in the Early Renaissance." *Halapid* 7, no. 2 (Spring 1999): 1–2.

Steinbach, Marion. "Judische Bankiers im Venedig der Renaissance: eine Symbiose gemass den Maximen der Staatrason." In *Shylock? Zinsberbot und Geldverleih in judischer und christlicher Tradition*. Edited by Johannes Heil and Bernd Wacker. Munich: Fink, 1997, pp. 81–100.

Stow, Kenneth R. "Church, Conversion, and Tradition: The Problem of Jewish Conversion in Sixteenth Century Italy." *Dimensioni e Problemi della Ricerca Storica* no. 2 (1996): 25–34.

———. "Corporate Double Talk: Kehillat Kodesh and Universities in the Roman Jewish Sixteenth Century Environment." *Journal of Jewish Thought and Philosophy* 8, no. 2 (1999): 283–301.

———. *The Jews in Rome*. Vol. 2: *1551–1557*. Boston: Brill, 1997.

Tamani, Giuliano, ed. *L'attività editoriale di Gershom Soncino, 1502–1527: atti di convegno, Soncino, 17 settembre 1995*. Soncino: Edizioni dei Soncino, 1997.

Tamburini, Filippo. *Ebrei saraceni cristiani: vita sociale e vita religiosa dai registri della Penitenzieria apostolica, secoli 14.-16.* Milan: Istituto di Propaganda Libraria, 1996.

Testuzza, Giorgio. "Fuga di un 'Marrano'? dalla Spagna a Roma: Juan Arias Davila, vescovo di Segovia (1461–1497)." *Rassegna Mensile di Israel* 64, no. 3 (September/December 1998): 41–52.

Tirosh-Samuelson, Hava. "Theology of Nature in Sixteenth-Century Italian Jewish Philosophy." *Science in Context* 10, no. 4 (1997): 529–570.

Toaff, Ariel. "Maestro Laudadio de Blanis e la banca ebraica in Umbria e nel Patrimonio di San Pietro nella prima metà del Cinquecento." *Zakhor* 1 (1997): 95–112.

Toniolo, Alberta. "Los sefarditas españoles y la sedería italiana en la primera edad moderna." *Revista de Historia Industrial* no. 12 (1997): 43–73.

Treue, Wolfgang. "Kirche im Konflikt: die Auseinandersetzungen um den Trienter Judenprozess." *Das Jüdische Echo* 46 (1997): 167–174.

———. *Der Trienter Judenprozess: Voraussetzungen, Abläufe, auswirkungen (1475–1588)*. Hannover: Hahn, 1996.

Turniansky, Chava. "La letteratura yiddish nell'Italia del Cinquecento." *Rassegna Mensile di Israel* 62, no. 1/2 (January/August 1996): 63–92.

Van Boxel, Piet. "Dowry and Conversion of the Jews in Sixteenth-Century Rome: Competition between the Church and the Jewish Community." In *Marriage in Italy, 1300–1650*. Edited by Trevor Dean and K.J.P. Lowe. New York: Cambridge University Press, 1998.

Vargon, Shmuel. "Isaiah 56:9–57:13: Time of the Prophecy and Identity of the Author according to Samuel David Luzzatto." *Jewish Studies Quarterly* 6, no. 3 (1999): 218–233.

Veronese, Alessandra. *Una famiglia di banchieri ebrei tra XIV e XVI secolo: i da Volterra Reti di credito nell'Italia del Rinascimento*. Pisa: ETS, 1998.

———. "La presenza ebraica nei territori del Ducato di Urbino: prime testimonianze e alcune notizie sul materiale archivistico di Gubbio, Cagli e Casteldurante." *Materia Giudaica* 3 (1997): 32–38.

Weinstein, Roni. "Rituel du marriage et culture des jeunes dans la societé judéo-italienne, 16ᵉ-17ᵉ siècles." *Annales: Histoire, Science Sociales* 53, no. 3 (1998): 455–479.

Wolfson, Elliot R. "Tiqqun ha-Shekhinah: Redemption and the Overcoming of Gender Dimorphism in the Messianic Kabbalah of Moses Hayyim Luzzato." *History of Religions* 36, no. 4 (1997): 289–332.

Yaffe, Martin D. *Shylock and the Jewish Question*. Baltimore, MD: Johns Hopkins University Press, 1997.

Zanardo, Andrea. "'Lor corpa fu d'essere sedotti': un processo dell'inquisizione modenese ad ebrei neofiti." *Nuova Rivista Storica* 80, no. 3 (1996): 525–592.

Zöller, Sonja. "Abraham und Melchisedech in Deutschland Oder: von Religionsgesprächen, Unbelehrbarkeit und Toleranz zur Rezeption der beiden Juden aus

Giovanni Boccaccio's 'Decamerone' in der deutschen Schwankliteratur des 16. Jahrhunderts." *Aschkenas* 7, no. 2 (1997): 303–339.

RISORGIMENTO AND LIBERAL ITALY

Arian Levi, Giorgina and Giulio Disegni. *Fuori dal ghetto: il 1848 degli ebrei*. Rome: Editori Riuniti, 1998.

Aslanov, Cyril. "Elia Benamozegh scrittore trilingue: il fattore della lingua nelle sue opere." *Rassegna Mensile di Israel* 63, no. 3 (September/December 1997): 29–42.

Bernardini, Paolo. *La sfida dell'uguaglianza: gli ebrei a Mantova nell'età della rivoluzione francese*. Rome: Bulzoni, 1996.

Capuzzo, Ester. *Gli ebrei nella società italiana: comunità e istituzioni tra Ottocento e Novecento*. Rome: Carocci, 1999.

Cavaglion, Alberto. "Una famiglia ebraica fra Risorgimento e Resistenza." *Rassegna Mensile di Israel* 64, no. 1 (January/April 1998): 23–30.

Del Regno, Filomena. "Un archivio ottecentesco: le carte di Isacco Artom presso il Centro Bibliografico." *Rassegna Mensile di Israel* 64, no. 1 (January/April 1998): 13–22.

Di Porto, Bruno. "Valdesi ed ebrei, le due storiche minoranze religiose dal Risorgimento alla Repubblica." *Rassegna Mensile di Israel* 64, no. 1 (January/April 1998): 7–12.

Dubin, Lois C. "The Rise and Fall of the Italian Jewish Model in Germany: From Haskalah to Reform, 1780–1820." In *Jewish History and Jewish Memory: Essays in Honor of Yosef Hayim Yerushalmi*. Edited by Elisheva Carlebach, John M. Efron, and David N. Myers. Hanover, NH: University Press of New England, 1998, pp. 271–295.

Faar, José. "The Hebrew Species Concept and the Origin of Evolution: R. Benamozegh's Response to Darwin." *Rassegna Mensile di Israel* 63, no. 3 (September/December 1997): 43–66.

Gentile, Emilio. "The Struggle for Modernity: Echoes of the Dreyfus Affair in Italian Political Culture, 1898–1912." *Journal of Contemporary History* 33, no. 4 (October 1998): 497–511.

Gopin, Marc. "An Orthodox Embrace of Gentiles?: Interfaith Tolerance in the Thought of S. D. Luzzatto and E. Benamozegh." *Modern Judaism* 18, no. 2 (1998): 173–195.

Grantaliano, Elvira. "Le minoranze religiose a Roma sotto il governo pontificio: gli ebrei nei fondi documentari dell'Archivio di Stato." *Rassegna Mensile di Israel* 64, no. 1 (January/April 1998): 71–82.

Guetta, Alessandro. "Le statut de l'hebreu selon les intellectuelles juifs italiens du XIXe siecle." *Revue de l'Histoire des Religions* 213, no. 4 (1996): 485–500.

———. "Qabbalà e Cristianesimo nella filosofia di Benamozegh." *Rassegna Mensile di Israel* 63, no. 3 (September/December 1997): 21–28.

Kertzer, David I. *The Kidnapping of Edgardo Mortara*. New York: Knopf, 1997.

Luzzatto Voghera, Gadi. *Il prezzo dell'eguaglianza: il dibattito sull'emancipazione degli ebrei in Italia, 1781–1848*. Milan: Franco Angeli, 1998.

———. "'Primavera dei popoli' ed emancipazione ebraica: due lettere dell'aprile 1848." *Rassegna Mensile di Israel* 64, no. 1 (January/April 1998): 83–86.

Milano, Roberto, ed. "Dal diario di Ella Tagliacozzo, volontario garibaldino." *Rassegna Mensile di Israel* 64, no. 1 (January/April 1998): 87–94.

Millo, Anna. *Storia di un borghesia: la famiglia Vivante a Trieste dall'emporio alla Guerra mondiale*. Gorizia: Libreria editrice goriziana, 1998.

Morselli, Marco. "Un progretto editoriale per le opere di Elia Benamozegh." *Rassegna Mensile di Israel* 63, no. 3 (September/December 1997): 79–88.

Pisa, Beatrice. "Ernesto Nathan e la 'politica nazionale.'" *Rassegna Storica del Risorgimento* 84, no. 1 (1997): 17–66.

Sofia, Francesca. "Stato moderno e minoranze religiose in Italia." *Rassegna Mensile di Israel* 64, no. 1 (January/April 1998): 31–48.

Toscano, Mario. "Risorgimento ed ebrei: alcune riflessioni sulla 'nazionalizzazione parallela.'" *Rassegna Mensile di Israel* 64, no. 1 (January/April 1998): 59–70.

Toscano, Mario and Claudio Magris, eds. *Integrazione e identità: l'esperienza ebraica in Germania e Italia dall'illuminismo al fascismo*. Milan: Franco Angeli, 1998.

Vitale, Micaela, ed. *Il matrimonio ebraico: le ketubbot dell'Archivio Terracini*. Pubblicazioni dell'Archivio per le tradizioni e il costume ebraici Benvenuto e Alessandro Terracini, no. 1. Turin: S. Zamorani Editore, 1997.

Zini, Rav Eliahu. "Due maestri del nostro tempo: i rabbini Elia Benamozegh e Avraham Itzhak Hacohen Kuk." *Rassegna Mensile di Israel* 63, no. 3 (September/December 1997): 67–78.

FASCIST ITALY

Afonso, Rui C. "Count Giuseppe Agenore Magno." *Portuguese Studies Review* 5, no. 1 (1996): 12–21.

Amodio, Paolo, Romeo de Maio, and Giuseppe Lissa, eds. *La sho'ah: tra interpretazione e memoria*. Naples: Vivarium, 1999.

Anissimov, Myriam. *Primo Levi, ou la tragédie d'un optimiste: biographie*. Paris: Lattés, 1996. *Primo Levi: The Tragedy of an Optimist*. Translated by Steve Cox. New York: Overlook, 1998.

Barozzi, Federica. "I percosi della sopravvivenza: salvatori e salvati durante l'occupazione nazista di Roma (8 settembre 1943–4 giugno 1944)." *Rassegna Mensile di Israel* 64, no. 1 (January/april 1998): 95–144.

Belpoliti, Marco, ed. *Primo Levi: conversazioni e interviste, 1963–1987*. Turin: Einaudi, 1997. *Primo Levi: The Voice of Memory*. Translated by Robert Gordon. New York: Free Press, 2001.

Biagini, Furio. *Mussolini e il sionismo*. Milan: M & B, 1998.

Bosworth, Richard J. B. "Explaining 'Auschwitz' after the End of History: The Case of Italy." *History and Theory* 38, no. 1 (1999): 84–99.

Bravo, Anna and Daniele Jalla. "Una misura onesta: gli scritti di memoria della deportazione dall'Italia, 1944–1993." *Holocaust and Genocide Studies* 13, no. 2 (Fall 1999): 278–279.

Broggini, Renata. *La frontiera della speranza: gli ebrei dall'Italia verso la Svizzera, 1943–1945*. Milan: Mondadori, 1998.

Burger, Harry. *Biancastella: A Jewish Partisan in World War II*. Niwot: University Press of Colorado, 1997.

Burrin, Pihlippe. "Political Religion: The Relevance of a Concept." *History and Memory* 1/2, no. 9 (Fall 1997): 321–349.

Calabrese, Rita. "Oltre la scrittura della Shoà: alcune voci 'femminili.'" *Rassegna Mensile di Israel* 64, no. 3 (September/December 1998): 87–116.

Cattaruzza, Marina. "Il ruolo degli 'uomini communi' nello sterminio degli ebrei europei." *Storia della Storiografia* no. 30 (1996): 141+.

Cavaglion, Alberto. *Per via invisible*. Bologna: Il Mulino, 1998.

Caviglia, Stefano. *L'identità salvata: gli ebrei di Roma tra fede e nazione, 1870–1938*. Rome: Laterza, 1996.

Cohen, Kate. *The Neppi Modona Diaries: Reading Jewish Survival Through My Italian Family*. Hanover, NH: University Press of New England, 1997.

Collotti, Enzo, ed. *Razza e fascismo: la persecuzione contro gli ebrei in Toscana, 1938– 1943*. Rome: Carocci, 1999.

Coppa, Frank J., ed. *Controversial Concordats: The Vatican's Relations with Napoleon, Mussolini, and Hitler*. Washington, DC: Catholic University of America Press, 1999.

Cornelius, Sarah T. "In Defence of Superior Orders and Erich Priebke." *Patterns of Prejudice* 31, no. 1 (1997): 3–19.

Cornwell, John. *Hitler's Pope: The Secret History of Pius XII*. New York: Viking, 1999.

Coslovich, Marco. "I percorsi della sopravvivenza: storia e memoria della deportazione dall'Adriatisches Kustenland." *Holocaust and Genocide Studies* 13, no. 2 (Fall 1999): 276–278.

Debenedetti, Giacomo. *The Sixteenth of October 1943 and Other Wartime Essays*. Translated by Judith Woolf. Leicester, UK: University Texts, 1996.

De Felice, Renzo. *The Jews in Fascist Italy: A History*. Translated by Robert L. Miller; edited by Stanislao G. Pugliese. New York, Enigma Books, 2001.

Della Coletta, Cristina. "La cultura del giardino: miti e appropriazioni letterarie nel *Giardino dei Finzi-Contini*." *MLN* 113, no. 1 (January 1998): 138–163.

DeMichaelis, Cesare G. "Il Principe N. D. Ževaxov e i *Protocolli dei Savi di Sion* in Italia." *Studi Storici* 37, no. 3 (1996): 747–770.

Dickie, John. "'Largo Bottai': An Attempt to Construct a Common Italian History." *Patterns of Prejudice* 31, no. 2 (1997): 7–14.

Di Porto, Stefano. "La temuta protesta dei senatori ebrei per le leggi antiebraiche." *Rassegna Mensile di Israel* 64, no. 2 (January/April 1998): 69–80.

Fabre, Giorgio. *L'elenco: censura fascista, editoria e autori ebrei*. Turin: Zamorani, 1998.

Fargion, Liliana Picciotto. "Il libro della memoria: gli ebrei deportati dall'Italia, 1943– 1945." *Holocaust and Genocide Studies* 13, no. 2 (Fall 1999): 272–276.

Finzi, Roberto. *L'università italiana e le leggi antiebraiche*. Rome: Edizione Riuniti, 1997.

Fubini, Guido. *Lungo viaggio attraverso il pregiudizio*. Turin: Rosenberg Sellier, 1996.

Garti, Itzhak. "The Living Conditions of Jewish Refugees from Yugoslavia Held as Civilian Prisoners of War in Fascist Italy up to the Fall of the Regime in July 1943." *Yad Vashem Studies* 25 (1996): 343–360.

Goldman, Louis. *In the Sight of God and Man*. Harrison, NY: Delphinium, 1996.

Gordon, Robert S. "'Per mia fortuna . . .': Irony and Ethics in Primo Levi's Writing." *Modern Language Review* 92, no. 2 (1997): 337–347.

———. "Primo Levi's *If This Is a Man* and Responses to the Lager in Italy, 1945–47." *Judaism* 48, no. 1 (Winter 1999): 49–57.

Impagliazzo, Marco, ed. *La resistenza silenziosa: leggi razziali e occupazione nazista nella memoria degli ebrei di Roma*. Milan: Guerini e Associati, 1997.

Kappler, Herbert. *Lettere dal carcere, 1948–1950*. Rome: Maurizio Edizioni, 1997.

Kurlansky, Mark. "The Italian Connection." *Partisan Review* 63, no. 1 (1996): 131–139.

Levi, Fabio. *L'identità imposta: un padre ebreo di fronte alle leggi razziali di Mussolini*. Turin: S. Zamorani, 1996.

———. *Le case e le cose: la persecuzione degli ebrei torinesi nelle carte dell'EGELI, 1938–1945*. Turin: Compagnia di San Paolo, 1998.

———, ed. *I ventenni e lo sterminio degli ebrei: le risposte a un questionario proposto presso la Facoltà di lettere di Torino*. Turin: Zamorani, 1999.

Marchione, Margherita. *Yours Is a Precious Witness: Memoirs of Jews and Catholics in Wartime Italy*. New York: Paulist Press, 1997.

Markovizky, Jacob. "The Italian Government's Response to the Problem of Jewish Refugees, 1945–1948." *Journal of Israeli History* 19, no. 1 (Spring 1998): 23–39.

Mendel, David. "Italy, Great Britain and Jewish Identity: A Personal Comment on Primo

Levi." *European Judaism* 31, no. 2 (Autumn 1998): 81–90.

Michaelis, Meir. "Italy." In *The World Reacts to the Holocaust*. Edited by David S. Wyman. Baltimore, MD: Johns Hopkins University Press, 1996, pp. 514–553.

———. "Mussolini's Unofficial Mouthpiece: Telesio Interlandi, *Il Tevere* and the Evolution of Mussolini's Anti-Semitism." *Journal of Modern Italian Studies* 3, no. 3 (Fall 1998): 217–240.

Momigliano Levi, Paolo and Piero Lucat, eds. *Storia e memoria della deportazione: modelli di ricerca di communicazione in Italia e in Francia*. Florence: Giuntina, 1996.

Neppi, Enzo. "Sopravvivenza e vergogna in Primo Levi." *Strumenti Critici* 11, no. 3 (1996): 479–500.

Passalecq, Georges and Bernard Suchecky. *The Hidden Encyclical of Pius XI*. New York: Harcourt Brace, 1997.

Patruno, Nicholas. "Understanding Primo Levi." *Shofar* 15, no. 2 (Winter 1997): 116–123.

La persecuzione degli ebrei durante il fascismo: le leggi del 1938. Rome: Camera dei deputati, 1998.

Phayer, Michael. *The Catholic Church and the Holocaust, 1930–1965*. Bloomington: Indiana University Press, 2000.

Piazza, Bruno. "Perche gli altri dimenticano: un italiano ad Auschwitz." *Holocaust and Genocide Studies* 13, no. 2 (Fall 1999): 280–281.

Pugliese, Stanislao G. *Carlo Rosselli: Socialist Heretic and Antifascist Exile*. Cambridge, MA: Harvard University Press, 1999.

———. "Bloodless Torture: The Books of the Roman Ghetto under the Nazi Occupation." *Libraries & Culture* 34, no. 3 (Summer 1999): 241–253.

Raiber, Richard. "Generalfeldmarschall Albert Kesselring, Via Rasella, and the 'Ginny Mission.'" *Militärgeschichtliche Mitteilungen* 56, no. 1 (1997): 96–106.

Rimini, Cesare. *Una carta in più*. Milan: Mondadori, 1997.

Ryan, Donna F. *The Holocaust and the Jews of Marseille: The Enforcement of Anti-Semitic Policies in Vichy France*. Urbana: University of Illinois Press, 1996.

Sarfatti, Michele. "Fascist Italy and German Jews in Southeastern France in July 1943." *Journal of Modern Italian Studies* 3, no. 3 (Fall 1998): 318–328.

———. "Der Novemberpogrom 1938 in Deutschland und die antijòdische Politik des italienischen Achsenpartners." *Zeitschrift fòr Geschichtswissenschaft* 46, no. 11 (1998): 1007–1013.

———. "La persecuzione antiebraica nel periodo 1938–1943 e il suo difficile ricordo." In *Italia 1939–1945: storia e memoria*. Edited by Anna Lisa Carlotti. Milan: Vita e Pensiero, 1996, pp. 73–85.

Smolensky, Eleonora M. *Tante voci, una storia: italiani ebrei in Argentina, 1938–1948*. Bologna: Il Mulino, 1998.

Sohn, Sigrid. "Sulla vita culturale e la nascita della resistenza nei ghetti durante la seconda guerra mondiale: alcuni canti Yiddish." *Rassegna Mensile di Israel* 62, no. 1/2 (January/August 1996): 349–362.

Tagliacozzo, Franca. "Memoria e catarsi: didattica della storia dopo Auschwitz." *Rassegna Mensile di Israel* 63, no. 1 (January/April 1997): 107–120.

Toscano, Mario. "Marcello Ricci: una testimonianza sulle origini del razzismo fascista." *Storia Contemporanea* 27, no. 5 (1996): 879–897.

Villani, Cinzia. *Ebrei fra leggi razziste e deportazioni nelle province di Bolzano, Trento e Belluno*. Trento: Società di Studi Trentini di Scienze Storiche, 1996.

Walston, James. "History and Memory of the Italian Concentration Camps." *Historical Journal* 40, no. 1 (1997): 169–183.

Walter, Katharina. "Die Judenpolitik unter Mussolini: Standpunkte und Entwicklungen der Forschung." *Zeitgeschichte* 24, no. 1/2 (1997): 3–29.

Weiss, Beno. "The Inferno of Auschwitz." *Shofar* 15, no. 2 (Winter 1997): 116–123.

Woolf, Judith. "Silent Witness: Memory and Omission in Natalia Ginzburg's *Family Sayings*." *Cambridge Quarterly* 25, no. 3 (1996): 243–262.

Wygoda, Hermann. *In the Shadow of the Swastika*. Urbana: University of Illinois Press, 1998.

Zapponi, Niccolà. "L'oracolo azzittito: Margherita G. Sarfatti." *Storia Contemporanea* 27, no. 5 (1996): 759–777.

Zittoun, Tania. " 'Non sono tutti fascisti': immagini di sé e degli altri nei ragazzi della scuola ebraica." *Rassegna Mensile di Israel* 62, no. 3 (September/December 1996): 155+.

Zuccotti, Susan. "The Italian Racial Laws, 1938–1943: A Reevaluation." In *Fate of the European Jews, 1939–1945: Continuity or Contingency?* Edited by Jonathan Frankel. New York: Oxford University Press, 1997, pp. 133–152.

———. *Under His Very Windows: The Vatican and the Holocaust*. New Haven: Yale University Press, 2000.

CONTEMPORARY ITALY

Funzioni dei Centri di storia e cultura ebraica nella società contemporanea: atti del convegna, Milano, 3 febbraio 1997. Milan: Librificio-Proedi, 1998.

Nirenstajn, Alberto, ed. *Come le cinque dita di una mano: storie di una famiglia di ebrei da Firenze a Gerusalemme*. Milan: Rizzoli, 1998.

Pezzana, Angelo and Dan Vittorio Segre. *Quest'anno a Gerusalemme: gli ebrei italiani in Israele*. Milan: Corbaccio, 1997.

Piussi, Anna Maria, ed. *E li insegnerai ai tuoi figli: educazione ebraica in Italia dalle leggi razziali ad oggi*. Florence: Giuntina, 1997.

———. *Presto apprendere, tardi dimenticare: l'educazione ebraica nell'Italia contemporanea*. Milan: Franco Angeli, 1998.

Sarfatti, Michele, ed. *Il ritorno alla vita: vicende e diritti degli ebrei in Italia dopo la seconda guerra mondiale*. Florence: Giuntina, 1998.

MISCELLANEOUS

Alhadeff, Gini. *The Sun at Midday: Tales of a Mediterranean Family*. New York: Pantheon, 1997.

Benuzzi, Angelo, ed. *Il ghetto riscoperto, Bologna: recupero e rinascita di un luogo*. Bologna: Grafis, 1996.

Castelnuovo, Antonella, Giovanna Pons, and Gabriella Rustici, eds. *Ebrei e protestanti nella storia d'Italia: modelli per un'educazione interculturale*. Milan: Franco Angeli, 1996.

De Benedetti, Claudia, ed. *Hatikwà, il cammino della speranza*. Vol. 1: *gli ebrei e Padova*. Padua: Papergraf, 1998.

Hassine, Juliette, Jacques Misan-Montefiore, and Sandra Debenedetti Stow, eds. *Appartenenza e differenza: ebrei d'Italia e letteratura*. Florence: Giuntina, 1998.

Lattes, Yaakov A. "The Constitutional Documents of the Italian Jewish Community." *Jewish Political Studies Review* 8, no. 3/4 (Fall 1996): 11–65.

Lévy, Lionel. *La communauté juive de Livourne, le dernier des livournais: essai*. Paris: Harmattan, 1996.

———. *La nation juive portugaise: Livourne, Amsterdam, Tunis, 1591–1951*. Paris: Harmattan, 1999.

Luzzati, Michele, ed. *Gli ebrei di Pisa, secoli 9°–20°: atti del convegno internazionale, Pisa, 3–4 ottobre 1994*. Pisa: Pacini, 1998.

Mazzamuto, Salvatore. "Ebraismo e scienza giuridica nell'Italia moderna." *Diritto Ecclesiastico* 108, no. 2 (1997): 355–362.

Miething, Christoph, ed. *Judentum und Moderne in Frankreich und Italien*. Tòbingen: M. Niemeyer, 1998.

Ruderman, David B. "Cecil Roth, Historian of Italian Jewry: A Reassessment." In *The Jewish Past Revisited: Reflections on Modern Jewish Historians*. Edited by David N. Myers and David B. Ruderman. New Haven, CT: Yale University Press, 1998, pp. 128–142.

Toaff, Ariel. *Mostri giudei: l'immaginario ebraico dal medioevo alla prima età moderna*. Bologna: Il Mulino, 1996.

Vivanti, Corrado, ed. *Gli ebrei in Italia. I. Dall'alto medioevo all'età dei ghetti. II. Dall'emancipazione a oggi*. Storia d'Italia, Annali, 11 vols. Turin: Einaudi, 1996.

Index

Aaron, 70
Abraham, 69, 70, 160
Absalom, 69
Accademia dei Faticanti, 19
Acquaviva, Sabino, 183
Action Française, 233
Adorno, Theodor, 326
Aeneas, 270
After Babel, 315
Alba, 17
Alessandria, 170
Alexander VIII, Pope, 20, 25
Alfieri, Vittorio, 133
Alfonso, King, 111
Allason, Barbara, 252
Allied Military Government, 353
Almansi, Dante, 345–352
Alvarez, Ferdinando, 101–103
Alvarez, Leocadia, 101–103
Ambrosio, Giovanni. *See* Ebreo, Guglielmo
Améry-Mayer, Jean, 321
Anatomia dell'ebraismo italiano, 361
Anau, Salvatore, 139
Ancona, 91, 93, 94, 97, 353
Annibaldi family, 51
anti-fascism, 5, 6, 7, 147, 148, 149, 150, 177, 265–266
anti-Risorgimento, 269
anti-Semitism, 1, 2, 3, 4, 13–31, 35–47, 59–66, 91–98, 105–114, 124–129, 139, 142–145, 182, 192, 198, 203– 214, 217, 218, 219–220, 222, 226– 227, 231–240, 247–256, 259–271, 275–286, 297
Antonelli, Alessandro, 173
Antonius Pius, 15
Anzelotti, Fulvio, 184
Appartenenza e differenza: Ebrei d'Italia e letteratura, 193, 195
Aquileia, 220
Aragon court (Naples), 77
Arba' a Turim, 79
Arbanquanfot, 113
Archival Law of 1968, 54
archives, 51–55
Archivio Centrale dello Stato (ACS), 54, 252
Archivio storico capitolino, 53
Arendt, Hannah, 295, 303
Argoli, Alessandro, 103
Artom, Eugenio, 132, 211, 263
Artom, Guido, 183, 185, 186
Artom, Isacco, 53, 262
Ascoli, Max, 6
Ashkenazim, 59, 79, 83, 169, 180, 219, 260
Assicurazioni Generali, 222
assimilation/secularization, 5, 14, 131– 136, 139–145, 177, 218
Assisi, 20, 21, 23
Association of the Families of the Victims of the Fosse Ardeatine, 292, 296, 299

Asti, 170
Astrologo, Sergio, 183
Augustus, 3, 15, 38, 40, 254
Auschwitz, 194, 203, 204, 208, 209,
    210, 268, 278, 281, 304, 305–313,
    315–327, 331–341, 343
Austria, 234–235

Baal-Shem Toe, 157–158
Badoglio, Pietro, 208, 277
Bakhtin, Mikhail, 338–339
Balabanoff, Angelica, 248
Balbo, Italo, 282
Ballerini, R., 264
Balsdon, J. P. V. D., 36, 44–45
Bandiera, Irma, 211
bar Isaac, Semeon, 79
Barbie, Klaus, 297
Basilica of Maxentius, 174
Bassani, Giorgio, 8, 157, 162, 165,
    178, 186, 188
Bastianini, Giuseppe, 277, 280
Bastico, Ettore, 283
Bazano prison camp, 285
Bazlem, Bobi, 177
Bedarida, Adria, 354
Belardini, Gaspare, 81
Bemporad, Remo, 184
Bemporad (publishing house), 192
ben Asher, Jacob, 79
ben Daniel, R. Abraham, 97
Benardini, Gene, 232
Benedetto, Abraham, 171
Benedetto, Nathan, 171
Benedetto, P. Marie (Benoît-Marie),
    350
Benedict XIV, Pope, 19, 23
*Benevolence and Betrayal: Five Italian
    Jewish Families under Fascism*,
    196, 204
Benigni, Roberto, 191, 247, 297
Bergen-Belson, 209, 279, 284
Berliner, Abraham, 101
Berneri, Camillo, 255–256
Bernini, Gian Lorenzo, 169, 170
Bertolotti, Antonino, 101, 102
Bianchi, Lidia, 211
Bianchini, Angela, 184
Bianchini, Marcella, 184
Biasin, Gian Paolo, 335

Biblioteca Apostolica Vaticana, 102
Biella, 170
Bitone, 112
Blanchot, Maurice, 326
Bologna, 25
Bon, Gherardi, 226
Bonano, Monsignor (bishop of Patti),
    107
Bonfil, Robert, 83
Boniface VIII, Pope, 16, 27
Borgongini Duca, Monsignor, 237
Bourdieu, Pierre, 331, 333, 334
Bova Marina, 169
Brandes, George, 124, 128
Bravo, Anna, 194, 198
Bricarelli, Chiara, 184, 196
British Eighth Army, 207, 227
British Intelligence Service, 5
Bruck, Edith, 179
Buber, Martin, 8
Buchenwald, 209
Bulgaria, 259

Caetani family, 51
Cain, 72
Caligula, 36, 38
Calixtus III, Pope, 18
Calvino, Italo, 180
Camilla of Aragon, 80
Camon, Ferdinando, 326, 332
Canepa, Andrew, 4
Cantoni, R., 351
capitoli, 21, 23, 52, 61
Caracciolo, Nicola, 204
Carbonari, 261
Cardinal Borromeo, 81
Carmagnola, 170, 171
Carpi, Aldo, 196
Carpi, Daniel, 276, 280
Carpi, Fabio, 182
Caruth, Cathy, 340
Cary, Earnest, 45
Casale Monferato, 25, 170, 171–172,
    187
Casnedi, Maria Sofia, 184, 196
Cassuto, Umberto, 61, 62–63, 64
Castel Gandolfo, 235
Castelnuovo, Enrico, 141–144
Castiglione, 112
Castruccio, Giuseppe, 278, 279, 280

catacombs, 169
Catania, 110
Catholic Popular Party, 231, 271
Catholicism/Catholic Church, 1, 2, 15,
    16, 17, 24, 51, 60, 101–103, 105–
    114, 194, 231, 231–240, 267, 271
Cavaglion, Alberto, 184
Cavour, Camillo Benso Count, 53, 262,
    263, 269
C'è un punto della terra, 304–312
Celan, Paul, 326, 327
Centro Bibliografico dell'Unione delle
    Comunità Ebraiche Italiane, 53,
    102
Centro di documentazione ebraica
    contemporanea, 53
Chabauty, E. A., 263
Cherasco, 21, 170, 171
Chieri, 170
Chiesa, Eugenio, 6
Choral Temple (Bucharest), 174
"Christian," 105
Ciano, Galeazzo, 237, 238, 256
Cicero, 41
circumcision, 15
La Civiltà Cattolica, 4, 234, 237, 264,
    268, 271
Claudius, 37, 38, 39, 45–46, 47
Clement VIII, Pope, 81
Clement XIII, Pope, 19, 23
Clinton, William Jefferson, 214
Coen, Fausto, 182
Coen, Maurizio, 182
Cogni, Giulio, 234
Coifmann, Lattes, 182
Cole, G. D. H., 266
Comitato di Richerche Deportati Ebrei
    (CRDE), 355
communism, 5, 160, 161
Comprehensive Laws on Jewish
    Communities (1931), 221
condotta, 17, 21, 27, 52
confino, 353
Consiglio del Popolo, 61, 62, 64
Constantine the Great, 13,15
Constantinople, 125
Constantius II, 15, 22, 28
Contra Christianos, 16
conversos, 67, 101
cookbooks, 364–365

Coreggio, 260
Corpus Juris Canonici, 125
Cortona, 61
Coryat, Thomas, 128
Cosimo de Medici, 68
Coston, Henry, 251
Coughlin, Charles E. Father, 234
Council of Basle, 24
Council of Orleans, 15, 21
Council of Rheims, 125
Council of Rome, 125
Council of Trent, 2, 81
Counter-Reformation, 81, 82, 83, 260,
    261, 264
Court of Cassation, 291, 294, 295, 299,
    300
Cremona, 81, 97
Crisi, Andrea, 112
Crisi, Bartolomeo, 112
Croce, Benedetto, 159, 210, 211
Crusades, 198
Cum Nimis Absurdum, 2, 16–17, 18,
    20, 25, 29
Cuneo, 170

D'Annunzio, Gabriele, 218, 255, 265
d'Azeglio, Massimo, 261
d'Este, Borso, 52
d'Este, Isabella, 77
da Messina, Bonavoglia, 108
Dachau, 5, 268
Dalla Torre, Giuseppe, 232
Dalmatia, 223
dance, 77–84
Dannecker, Theodor (SS
    Hauptsturmführer), 208
Dante, 21, 82, 133, 332, 336, 337
Datill, Abraham, 17, 23, 27, 28–29
Davar, 252
David, 69
de Medici family, 67
de Medici, Lorenzo, 77
de Servadio, Elia, 353
de Troyes, Rashi, 124
de Tuleda, Benjamin, 131
De Bono, Emilio, 346, 347
De Carlo, Andrea, 185
De Felice, Renzo, 6, 266, 345, 349,
    350
De Sica, Vittorio, 247

De pratica seu arte tripudii, 77–78
de' Sommi, Leone, 82
Debenedetti, Antonio, 178, 181–182,
    184, 185, 186, 188
Debenedetti, Giacomo, 186
Debenedetti, Paolo, 186
Del Monte, Crescenzo, 120
Delasem, 206, 220, 350, 352
Deleuze, Gilles, 304–305
Della Pergola, Sergio, 361
della Rovere, Vittoria, 68
della Rovere II, Guidobaldo (Duke of
    Urbino), 95, 96
Della Seta, Fabio, 8, 184, 196
Demme, Jonathan, 186
Demografia e Razza, 4, 53–54, 205,
    221
Denmark, 259
Desbuquois, Gustave, 236
Di Cori, Bruno, 184
Di Giovanni, Giovanni, 105–114
Di Castro, Sandro, 295, 296
dialogism, 338–339
Diaspora, 8, 67, 110, 132, 133, 169,
    195
Diaz, Raphael, 68
La differenza invisibile, 196
Dio, 42, 45, 46, 47
Diplomatic Code of Sicily, 106
Disraeli, Benjamin, 127
Divini Illius Magistri (1929), 233
Dodici Boniviri, 61
Dollfuss, Engelbert, 254
Domenico di Piacenza, 77, 78, 83
Dominicans, 109
Donaldson, Sam, 291, 298
Donati, Angelo, 213
Draper, John W., 129
The Drowned and the Saved, 178, 307,
    311, 324
Drummont, Edouard, 263
Dubrovnik, 95
Duchy of Savoy, 17, 21, 23, 26, 27, 30

L'Ebraismo della Sicilia, 105–114
*Ebrei in Italia: un problema di
    identità*, 196
Ebreo, Deodato, 80, 83
Ebreo, Guglielmo (aka Giovanni
    Ambrosio), 77–84

Ebreo, Leone, 81
Ebreo, Moise, 81
Eco, Umberto, 178, 183
Edict of Caracalla, 13
Editto Supra Gli Ebrei, 17, 19, 23, 28,
    29
L'educatore israelita, 173
Eichmann, Adolf, 208
Eiffel Tower, 173
Einstein, Albert, 251
Eli, 69–70
Elkann, Alain, 182, 184, 185, 187, 196
emancipation, 260, 261, 271
Emeq ha-Bakha, 92–93
Encyclopedia Judaica, 102
Enlightenment, 260
Ercole II, 52
Esecutori contro la Bestemmia, 18
Ethiopia, 231, 250, 269
Eugenius IV, Pope, 16, 18, 19, 23, 27,
    65
Eve, 69, 71–72
exhibitions, 365

Fargion, Liliana Picciotto, 195, 196,
    198, 205, 208, 209, 355
Farinacci, Roberto, 3, 4, 232–233, 237,
    238
fascism, 3, 147–153, 157, 183, 184,
    191–199, 203–214, 217–227, 231–
    240, 247–256, 259, 346–352
Fascist Grand Council, 218, 224
Feast of the Tabernacles, 113
Federal Hate Crimes law, 214
Federico di Montefeltro, 77
Felman, Shoshana, 316, 321
Ferdinand, King, 111, 112
Ferme, 19
Ferramonti (concentration camp), 203,
    204, 207
Ferrara, 80, 82, 91, 93, 97, 120, 209
festivals, Jewish, 362–363
Final Solution, (see Holocaust)
Finale, 25
Finzi, Aldo, 3
Flaubert, Gustav, 159
Flick, Giovanni Maria, 293, 296, 299
Florence, 13, 20, 23, 27, 28, 59–66,
    209
Foa, Anna, 184

Foà, Arnoldo, 182
Foa, Ugo, 209, 350
Foa, Vittorio, 6, 177, 184
Fölkel, Ferruccio,177
Fool, 79
formula di giuramento, 51
Fortini, Franco (Lattes), 178–179
Fosse Ardeatine, 204, 290–291, 298,
    299
Fossoli (prison), 209, 355
Fourth Lateran Council (1215), 16, 21
Fra Matteo da Ponsecco, 24
Franciscan Friars Minor, 125, 126
Frank, Tenney, 37
Frederick II (Holy Roman Emperor),
    22, 110, 111
Frederick III, 77
Freemasonry, 262
Freidenreich, Harriet Pass, 277–278
French Revolution, 260, 261
Frend, W. H. C., 36, 39
Freud, Sigmund, 177
Friends of Israel, 233
Frigessi, Arnoldo, 222
Friuli, 18, 19, 23
Fubini, Guido, 184

Gaius, 38, 43, 44, 45, 46
The Garden of the Finzi-Contini (film),
    247
The Garden of the Finzi-Contini
    (novel), 165
Garibaldi, Giuseppe, 262
Garosci, Aldo, 253
Geloso, Carlo, 280–281
General Archive Administration, 54
Genoa, 17, 25, 29
Gentile, Giovanni, 267
Gentili Tedeschi, Eugenio, 184
German Romanticism, 134
Gestapo, 289, 292, 297
ghetto, 2, 170, 196
Giado (concentration camp), 283–284,
    286
Gini, Corrado, 220
Ginzburg, Carlo, 186
Ginzburg, Leone, 6, 7, 150, 151, 177,
    186, 211, 253, 254
Ginzburg, Natalia, 7, 141, 147–153,
    157, 162, 165, 177, 178, 185, 186,

187, 254
Il gioco dei regni, 157–166
Gioco della Cieca, 82
Giorgini, G. B., 261
Girelli-Carasi, Fabio, 327, 332
Giuseppe of Sicily, 77, 83
Giustizia e Libertà, 148, 210–211, 252,
    255
Givat Brenner Kibbutz, 5
Gli ebrei in Italia, 4
Goldmann, Nahum, 267
Gonfalonieri delle Società del Popolo,
    61
Gonzaga, Annibale, 82
Gonzaga, Vincenzo Duke, 82
Gordon, M. M., assimilation model,
    14–15, 18–31
Gorizia, 25
Gramsci, Antonio, 3, 132, 139, 270
Grand Duchy of Tuscany, 19
Graziani, Rodolfo, 282
Gregory XIII, Pope, 81
Gregory, Saint, 16, 18, 30, 112, 114
Guarini, Battista, 82
Guattari, Feliz, 304–305
guidebooks, 364
Gundlach, Gustav, 236
Gunzberg, Lynn, 2, 3, 4, 191–192, 204

Ha-Kohen, Abraham Menahen Porto,
    97
Ha-Kohen, Joseph, 92–93, 94, 95
Habad Lubavitcher, 365–366
Hadrian, 15
Halevi, Jacob, 81, 83
Hanna, 71, 72
Harrowitz, Nancy, 316
Hasidic Jews, 365–366
Haskalah, 260
Hass, Karl, 298
Hasson, Vital, 280
Hebel, 72
Hebra Ba'ale Teshuba, 67
Hebra de Cazar Orfas e Donzelas, 68
Hebra Ghemilut Hasadim, 67
Hebra Malbish Arumim, 68
Hebra Mohar ha-Betulot, 67–68
Hebraeorum gens, 91
Hebrew, 1, 5, 6, 53, 68, 119, 120, 121–
    122, 131, 159, 172, 260

Hebrew prophets, 7
Hebrew University, 267
Hegel, G. W. F., 159
Heine, Heinrich, 134–136
Herod Agrippa, 37
Hess, Rudolf, 355
heteroglossia, 339
Himmler, Heinrich, 209
History of the Jews of Venice, 132
History of the Yiddish Language, 119
Hitler, Adolf, 4, 204, 205, 211, 212,
    232, 235, 237, 247, 249, 250, 254,
    264, 267, 269–270, 276
Hochhuth, Rolf, 239
Holocaust, 53, 165, 177–178, 179, 180,
    182, 183, 184, 191, 192, 193, 194,
    195, 196, 198, 203–214, 231, 236,
    259, 275, 303–341, 345–352
Holquist, Michael, 339
Holy Roman Inquisition, 83, 102, 106,
    112
Homer, 82
Honorarius, 15, 17, 19
Howells, William Dean, 125
Hughes, H. Stuart, 1, 361
Humani Generis Unitas, 233, 236, 237
humanism, 1, 270–271

ibn Yahya, Gedaliah, 92
L'idea sionistica, 144
identity, 1–8, 139–146, 191–199, 217–
    227, 264, 303–312, 361–367
igronim, 93–94
Index Librorum Prohibitorum, 17, 234
Un'infanzia diversa, 356
Innocent III, Pope, 18, 24, 26, 29, 30
Interlandi, Telesio, 3,4
Isaac, 1, 69, 70, 72
Isaac, Jules, 231–232
Israel, 6, 8, 92, 94, 127
Israel (newspaper), 143, 249, 251
Istria, 223
Italian Army, 275–286
Italian Communist Party, 160, 165
Italian Foreign Office, 237
Italian Military Intelligence Service,
    278
Italian Zionist Federation, 251
Ivrea, 170

Jabotinsky, Vladimir, 239, 267
Jacob, 1, 69
Jagendorf, Zvi, 336
Janaczek, Helena, 179
Jarre, Marina, 165
Jesurum, Stefano, 184, 185, 188, 196
Jesus, 35, 36, 110
Jewett, Robert, 46
Jewish Agency, 239
Jewish anti-fascism, 6
Jewish Cemetery (Venice), 169
Jewish resistance, 210
*The Jews in Florence in the Age of the
    Renaissance*, 61
John XXIII, Pope, 239
John Paul II, Pope, 194
Joint Distribution Committee, 206
Jona, Davide, 184
Joseph, 69
Joseph, Bernard, 239
Josephus, 40, 110
Judeo-Italian, 119–122
Julius III, Pope, 16
Julius Caesar, 3, 15, 254, 259
Jung, Guido, 3, 267, 348
Juster, Jean, 36
Justinian, 27

Kafka, Franz, 182, 185
Kalk, I., 350
Kappler, Herbert (SS Major/Captain),
    208, 209–210, 290, 291, 350
kashrut, 3, 365
Kaufmann, David, 94
Kedem, Bene, 119, 120
Kelson, Wade, 334
Kingdom of Naples, 55
Kraeling, Carl, 45
Krenzki, Kurt von, 279
Krinsky, Carol Herselle, 173
Kulturkampf, 237

La Farge, John, 233, 235–236, 239
La Piana, Giorgio, 37, 38
Ladino, 119, 120, 260
Lago, Marcello, 180
Langer, Lawrence L., 312, 337
Lapponi, G., 350, 351
Laski, Neville, 234
Lateran Accords (1929), 233, 238, 239,

259, 267
Lateran Council (1139), 125
Lecco, Alberto, 188
Ledochowski, Wlodimir, 236
Leo I, Pope, 125
Leo III, Pope, 16
Leo X, Pope, 263–264
Leon, Harry J., 38, 39, 40
Lessico famigliare, 147–153, 165
Levi, Augusto, 251
Levi, Carlo, 6, 7, 165, 177, 185, 188, 252, 255
Levi, David, 132
Levi, Donatella, 184
Levi, Franco, 184
Levi, Giuseppe, 252
Levi, Lia, 182, 183, 184, 185, 188, 196
Levi, Mario, 252, 253
Levi, Paolo, 182
Levi, Primo, 6, 7, 162, 165, 177, 178, 182, 183, 185, 186, 187, 188, 191, 194, 260, 303–312, 315–327, 331–341, 343
Levi Vitale, Nina, 355
Levi-Bianchini, Marcella, 184
Levi-Montalcini, Rita, 184
Library of Congress, 353
Il libro della memoria. Gli ebrei deportati dall'Italia, 196, 198
Libya, 275, 276, 281
The Life of Judah, 81
Limentani, Giacometta, 164, 182, 188
Lipani, Damiano, 347
La Livornina, 67
Livorno, 25, 30, 67–73, 102, 120
Loewenthal, Elena, 178
London, 124
Lorenzo, 334–335
Los Sitibundos, 68
Lospinoso, Guido, 213
Lot, 70
Louis II, 24
Loy, Rosetta, 165
Lucius Flaccus, 37
Ludwig, Emil, 249
Lueger, Karl, 263
Luzzati, Emanuele, 182
Luzzatti, Luigi, 2, 334
Lyotard, Jean-Françoise, 310
Lyttleton, Adrian, 250

Machiavelli, Niccolo, 336
Mackensen, August von, 277
Maestro, Roberto, 184
Magnarelli, Paolo, 184
Mahler, Raphael, 261
Maimonedes, 79
malaria, 207
Malatesta family, 77
Manchester Guardian, 250
"Manifesto of the Racial Scientists," 4, 235
Manin, Daniele, 261
Mantua, 79, 81, 91, 93, 94, 96, 97, 124
Marchiani, Irma, 211
Margulies, Samuel, 143
Mariotto da Perugia, 78, 80, 83
marranos, 67, 260
Martin V, Pope, 16, 17, 23, 26, 27
Massarani, Tullo, 131–136
Massarano, Isachino, 82, 83
massari, 25
Matteotti, Giacomo, 231, 265, 347
Maurensig, Paolo, 177, 181
Maurras, Charles, 233
May, Gaston, 37, 41
Mazzini, Giuseppe, 2, 133–134, 261, 262
Mazzolini, Count Serafino, 347
"Measures for the Defense of the Italian Race," 238
Mein Kampf, 249
Memoirs of a Fortunate Jew, 7–8
Memorie Venete, 125
Merci, Lucillo, 278, 279
meschita, 109
Michaelis, Meir, 247, 249, 276, 278
Michal, 71, 72
Michelstaedter, Carlo, 177, 188
Military Tribunal, 291–300
Millu, Liana, 178, 196, 197
Ministry of the Interior, 53, 54
Mishne Torah, 79
mitzwe-tanz, 83
Mocenigo I, Alvise, 95
Modena, 21, 25, 27, 206
Modena, Leone, 81, 83, 260
Modestino, Guerriero, 283
Modigliani, Giuseppe Emanuele, 6, 253
Moisis, Saul M., 279–280

Mole Antonelliana, 173, 174
Molinari, Maurizio, 195
Momigliano, Arnaldo, 3, 8, 46, 47,
   132, 139, 184
I Moncalvo, 141–144
Mondadori (publishing house), 192
Mondovi, 170
money-lending, 20–21, 59–66, 91, 110,
   125–126
Monferato, 25
Monte di pietà, 21, 125, 126
Montepulciano, 61
Morante, Elsa, 162, 165, 177, 178,
   182, 185, 186, 188
Morante, Marcello, 186
Moravia, Alberto, 5, 7, 165, 177, 187,
   188, 193
Morazzini, Marta, 165
moresca/moresche, 78, 80, 81
Morgari, Oddino, 253
Morley, John F., 209
Morpurgo, Edgardo, 222
Morpurgo, Elena, 184
Morpurgo, Lisa, 182
Moses, 70
Moses of Sicily, 77
Mosse, George, 247
Mosseri, Mark, 278
Mozzeri, Iris, 283–284
Murat, Joachim, 8
Museum of the Liberation of Rome,
   290
Mussolini, Benito, 2, 3, 4, 152, 193,
   203, 204, 208, 212–213, 219, 231,
   232, 233, 237, 238, 247–248, 249,
   250, 251, 254, 255, 256, 259, 265,
   266–269, 270, 276, 277, 282, 283,
   290, 327, 346, 354

The Name of the Rose, 178
Naples, 25
Napoleon, 2, 25, 263
Nathan, Ernesto, 5, 263
Nathan, Virginia, 184
National Endowment for the
   Humanities, 102
National Socialism, 3, 4, 5, 203–214,
   231–240, 250, 269, 286, 289–300,
   303–312, 315–327, 331–341
Native Americans, 362

Nazis/Nazism (see National Socialism)
Negri, Paride (General), 212
Neri, Emilio, 278
Nero, 36
Neufeld, Maurice, 351–352
Nicholas V, Pope, 19
Noah, 70
Nogara, Bernardino, 233
Non abbiamo bisogno (1931), 232, 234
North Africa, 259, 275
La nostra bandiera, 255
La Nuova Italia (publishing house),
   192
Nuove prison (Turin), 211
Nuremberg Laws, 218
Nuremberg War Crimes Trial, 295, 297

Obadia, Servadio, 353
Olivetti, Adriano, 148
Ombres, Rossana, 187
On the Civil Emancipation of the Jews,
   261
On the Unity of the Human Race (see
   Humani Generis Unitas)
Oneg Sciabbath, 252
Orano, Paolo, 4
Orlando, Vittorio, 265
Orthodox Judaism, 260
L'Osservatore Romano, 234, 235, 236,
   237, 238
Ostia Antica, 169
Ostjuden, 269
Otherness, 195, 199
Ottolenghi, Massimo, 182
Ovadia, Moni, 180
Ovazza, Ettore, 7
OVRA (fascist secret police), 254

Pacifici, Alfonso, 133
Pacifici, Emanuele, 184, 196
Pacifici, Riccardo, 296
Padua, 26, 81, 124
paganism, 1
Palazzo Titino, 290
Palermo, 106
Palmieri-Billig, Lisa, 362
Papal States, 2, 24, 91–98, 140, 170
Papon, Maurice, 297
parallel nationalization, 270
Parker, R. B., 123

Parma, 19, 30
Partito d'Azione, 211
Pasqualigo case, 133
Passover, 15, 113, 253
Pastor, Ludwig Freihen von, 101
La Patria, 139
Patruno, Nicholas, 337
Paul IV, Pope, 18, 21, 23, 25, 29, 91,
    92, 94
Pavese, Cesare, 150
Pecci family, 81
Pekelis, Carla, 196–197
Penso de la Vega, José, 68–73
Perugia, 21, 24
Pesaro, 91, 92, 93, 94, 95, 96, 97
Petrarch, 82
Pezzena, Angelo, 184, 196
Philo, 43, 45, 110
philo-Semitism, 192, 259–264
Piacenza, 30
Piazza, Brunetto, 186
Piazza, Bruno, 177, 186
Piazza, Giulio, 186
Piazza, Maria Luisa, 186
Piazza Barberini, 290
Piazza Campidoglio, 293
Picard, Louis, 232
Il Piccolo, 222
Pieche, Giuseppe, 277
Piemonte, 170–175
Pietromarchi, Luca, 276
Pilate, 35
Pinhas, 69
Pisa, 102
Pitigliano ("Little Jerusalem"), 363
Pitigrilli, (pseudonym of Dino Segre),
    252
Pius IV, Pope, 91
Pius V, Pope, 91, 92, 96
Pius VI, Pope, 17, 26, 28
Pius IX, Pope, 25, 140, 233, 261, 262–
    263
Pius XI, Pope (Achille Ratti), 231–240,
    259, 267, 268
Pius XII, Pope (Eugenio Pacelli), 204,
    208, 209–210, 234, 350
pizmon, 79
Pizzoli, 153
Plateia Eleftherias, 279
PNF (Partito Nazionale Fascista), 3,

218, 222, 265, 268
Poliakov, Leon, 270
Pompey, 110, 259
Il Popolo d'Italia, 224, 232, 250, 253
Prato, 62
Pressburger, Giorgio, 179–180, 186
Pressburger, Nicola, 179, 186
Preziosi, Giovanni, 256, 269
Priebke, Erich, 204, 289–300
Priori of Assisi, 20
Prisoners of Hope: The Silver Age of
    the Italian Jews 1924–1974, 361
Pro Cultura, 143, 265
Propaganda Fide, 237
protocolli, 53
"Protocols of the Elders of Zion," 4,
    38, 266
Provenzalo, Moses, 97
Pubblica Sicurezza, 54
Pugliese, Emanuele, 2, 268
Purim, 17, 79, 81, 113

queen of Sheba, 80
Quistelli, Agostino, 292, 295, 299

Rab, 212, 278
Rabbi Gian, 284
Racial Laws (1938), 3, 4–5, 7, 8, 53,
    147–153, 184, 193, 203, 204, 205,
    217, 221, 223, 232, 256, 280, 281,
    297, 348, 353
"Racial Manifesto," 219, 235, 236,
    237, 268–269, 280, 281
Radigales, Sebastian Romero, 279
Radin, Max, 39, 40
Rainer, Friedrich Gauleiter, 227
Ratti, Achille (see Pope Pius XI)
Ravensbruch, 209
Rebecca, 72
Reberschak, Sandra, 185, 187
Red Biennium, 265
Reform Judaism, 260
Regge, Tullio, 177
Reggio, 25
Il Regime fascista, 4, 238
Regina Coeli (prison), 54, 211, 298
Reich Citizen's Law, 218
Reich Interior Ministry (Citizenship
    and Race Section), 227
Renaissance, 260, 261, 271

"Report to the Duce on Demography and Race," (1940), 221
Repubblica Sociale Italiana (RSI; Salò Republic), 4, 53, 208, 290, 297
Republic of Rome, 261
Resistance, 7, 194, 210–211, 290
Il Resto del Carlino, 218
Revere, Giuseppe, 135–136, 261
Reverenda Camera Apostolica, 52
Rhodes, 209, 280
Rimini, Cesare, 184
Risorgimento, 2, 52, 136, 139, 141, 170, 262, 263, 265, 269
Riunione Adriatica di Securità, 222
Rivista israelitica, 143
Roatta, Mario, 276
Rocco, Alfredo, 3, 219
Rochlitz, Joseph, 204
Roman Republic/Empire, 13, 15, 28, 35–47, 51, 59, 219
Romanticism, 134
Romanus Pontifex, 91
Rome, 1, 2, 3, 4, 13, 15, 16, 17, 20, 21, 22, 24, 25, 28, 30, 59, 91, 93, 94, 97, 101–103, 131, 139, 140, 141, 169, 185, 196, 204, 208, 209–210, 289–300
Romulus, 270
Rondina, F. S., 264
Rosani, Rita, 211
Rosenberg, Riccardo, 278
Roskies, David, 321
Rosselli, Aldo, 184, 186
Rosselli, Amelia, 6–7, 186
Rosselli, Carlo, 5, 6, 7, 151, 186, 187, 210–211, 253, 265
Rosselli, Nello, 5–6, 7, 151, 186, 187, 210–211, 265–266
Rossi, Gianfranco, 186, 188
Rotella rossa, 114
Roth, Cecil, 3, 80, 101, 127, 132, 248, 260, 271, 334, 361
Roth, Philip, 332
Rothchild, Jon, 181
Rothschild Miscellany, 79
Rudolf, Anthony, 335
Rumbach Street Synagogue (Budapest), 174
Ruppin, Arthur, 217–218
Rutelli, Francesco, 293, 299

Ruth, 72

Saba, Umberto, 177, 188, 193
Sacerdoti, Annie, 364
Sacerdoti, Giancarlo, 184
Sacred College of Seminaries, 234
Saint Gregory, 110
Saint Paul, 36
Saint Peter's Basilica, 169, 170
Salingar, Leo, 127–128
Salomone da Riva, 52
Salomone di Buonaventura, 20
Salomone Rossi, 82–83
Saloniccio, Avraham, 281
Salonika, 197, 213, 267, 275, 278, 279, 280, 281
Saluzzo, 170, 172–173
Salvatore, Paolo, 207
Salvatorelli, Luigi, 266, 269
San Sabba (La Risiera concentration camp), 207–208
San Gimignano, 61
San Vittore (prison), 54
Sanudo, Marin, 124
Sarah, 71, 72
Sardinia, 59
Sarfatti, Gianfranco, 7
Sarfatti, Margherita, 3, 248
Sarfatti. Michele, 2
Saul, 72
scholae (synangogues), 53
Scholae siciliane, 55
Sciarch, Giacomo, 111
Scott, Charles Alexander, 262
Scramuzza, Vincent, 36, 38
Se non ora, quando?, 178
Se questo è un uomo (see *Survival in Auschwitz*)
Second Vatican Council, 259
Segre, Augusto, 182, 184
Segre, Cesare, 184
Segre, Dan Vittorio, 7–8, 184, 185, 219
Segre, Mordechai, 172
Segre, Renzo, 184
Segre Amar, Sion, 177, 183, 185, 252, 253, 254
Sejanus, 39
Senigallia, 95
Sephardim, 59, 67–73, 169, 219
Septimus Severus, 15, 30

Sereni, Ada, 184, 185, 196
Sereni, Clara, 157–166, 185, 186
Sereni, Emilio, 6, 161, 165
Sereni, Enzo, 5, 6, 161, 266
Sermoneta, 51
Servadio, Gaia, 356
Servadio, Lucio, 353–354
Servadio, Simone, 353
Servi, Flaminio, 132, 139
Severino, Paola, 293
Sforza, Costanzo, 80
Sforza, Francesco, 77
Shakespeare, William, 123–129
Shalshelet ha-Kabbalah, 92
Shire, William L., 235
Shmulevics, Lev, 158, 163
Shmulevics, Xenia, 158, 163
Shoah (see Holocaust)
Shylock, 123–129
Sicily, 24, 55, 59, 105–114, 353
Sicut Judeis, 16, 26
Siena, 78, 209
Silvera, Miro, 180–181
Sirovich, Livio Isaak, 185
Smallwood, E. Mary, 36, 47
Sodi, Risa, 332
Solin, Heikki, 37
Solomon, 72
Solomon's temple, 170
I sommersi e i salvati (see *The Drowned and the Saved*) 178
Sonne, Isaiah, 92
Sonnino, Sidney, 2
Soprintendenza ai Monumenti della regione Piemonte, 171
Sorani, Settimo, 350
Spada, Giovanni Battista, 103
Spanish Civil War, 269
Speelman, Raniero, 366
Spiliakos, Dimitri, 279
Spinoza, 132
Springer, Elisa, 179, 196, 198
squadristi, 265
SS, 316–318, 325
Stalinism, 315
Starhemberg, Prince, 254
Statuti, 51
Stavisky affair, 251
Steiner, George, 315, 316, 324, 327
Stendhal, 159

Stern, Menahem, 38
Stille, Alexander, 195–196, 204, 208
Stock, Lionel, 219
La Storia, 178
Strangers at Home: Jews in the Italian Literary Imagination, 191–192, 204
Strauss, Leo, 105
Streicher, Julius, 264
Studi di letteratura e d'arte, 131
Stuparich, Giani, 177, 185
Sturzo, Luigi, 271
Suetonius, 38, 39, 46
Sukkoth, 79
Super Gregem Dominicum, 23
Survival in Auschwitz, 178, 304–312, 316–327, 331–341
Suvich, Fulvio, 222
Svevo, Italo, 7, 165, 177, 186, 188, 193
Syllabus of Errors, 262, 264
synagogues, 169–175, 363–364
Synod of Gerona, 29
Syracuse (Sicily), 110

tabarro rosso, 23
Tager, Michael, 309
Tagliacozzo, Mario, 184
Taled, 113
Talmud, 17
Tamaro, Susanna, 177, 182, 185–186
Tangier, 354, 355, 356–367
Tardini, Domenico, 239
Tarrow, Susan, 315
Tarsia, 204
Tedeschi, Giuliana, 197, 303–312
Tedeschi, Nedelia, 196
Templegasse Synagogue (Vienna), 174
Terracini, Umberto, 6
tevah, 170, 171, 172, 173
Il Tevere, 4, 249, 250, 251, 252, 253, 254
Theodosius the Great, 15, 30
Third Lateran Council, 21
The Tiber Afire, 8
Tiberius, 24, 36, 39, 40, 41, 42, 43, 46
Tito, 212, 278
Titus, 110, 259
Toaff, Elio, 185, 187, 196, 294
tolleranza, 21

Tomizza, Fulvio, 183
Torah, 15
Torquemada, 108, 113
Torres, Valeri, 278
Tower of Babel, 173, 309, 336–337
Treblinka, 268
La Tregua, 178
Treves, Claudio, 6, 253
Treves, Marco, 173–174
Treves (publishing house), 192
Treves Alacalay, Liliana, 185, 196
Trevi, Emanuele, 178
Tribunale criminale del Governatore, 52
Trieste, 20, 23, 25, 177, 185, 217–227
Tunisia, 275–276, 286
Turati, Filippo, 148
Turin, 25, 173, 177

Ufficiali al Cattaver, 18
Union of Jewish Communities, 53, 54, 268, 291–292, 293, 296, 345–352, 355
Urban II, Pope, 16
Urban VIII, Pope, 101
Urbino, 77, 78, 91, 93, 94–95
Ustasha, 211–212
usury, (see money-lending)
Uziel, Shlomo, 279, 280

Valerian III, 19, 28
Valobra, Lelio Vittorio, 206, 349–350
Varadi, Max, 184
Vassale, Vera, 211
Vastavillani, Cardinal, 21
Vatican, 3, 4, 52, 204, 205, 209–210, 231–240
Vatican Radio, 234, 238
Venice, 2, 18, 19, 20, 23, 24, 25, 26, 28, 30, 120, 123, 127, 128, 170, 171, 209, 366
Vercelli, 25, 170, 173–174
Verona, 124
Il Vessillo Israelitico, 132, 139, 144
via Rasella, 290, 296, 298
via Tasso, 289, 298
Vichy, 212–213, 275, 276
Vico, Giambattista, 133
Victor Emmanuel III, 4, 263

Victor Emmanuel IV, 297
Vigevani, Alberto, 178
Vigevano, Roberto (Ruve Masada), 181
Villa Emma, 206
Virgil, 3, 254
Vita di Carlo Rosselli, 253
Vita-Finzi, Paolo, 185
Vitale, Adolfo, 355
Vitale Servadio, Gemma, 355
Vitelleschi, Pietro Nobili, 278
Voghera, Giorgio, 177, 184
Voghera, Guido, 177
Volpi di Misurata, Conte, 222
Von Bismarck, Prince Otto, 276
von Ribbentrop, Joachim, 212–213, 276

Wagner, Otto, 174
Weinreich, Max, 119
Weiss, John, 266
Weizmann, Chaim, 260–261, 267
Williams, Margaret H., 36, 38, 40–42
Willrich, Hugo, 43, 44
women, 53, 69–73, 164, 165–166, 172, 197, 211, 231, 306

Xemona, 131

Yawn, Lila, 102
Yiddish, 5, 119, 120, 121, 260
Young, James, 321–322
Yugoslavia, 206, 275, 276

Zaban, Luisa, 184, 185
Zaban, Silvia, 184, 185
Zamboni, Guelfo, 278, 278–279, 280
Zango, Camus, 283
Zargani, Aldo, 184, 185
Zevi, Tullia, 293, 294
Zielinski, Thaddée, 38
Zionism, 3, 4, 5–6, 8, 37, 143, 144, 145, 157, 160, 161, 220, 239, 248, 250, 251–252, 254–255, 264, 265, 267
Zolli, Rabbi Eugenio, 351–352
Zuccotti, Susan, 206, 210, 213–214, 247
Zunz, Leopold, 131

About the Contributors

RENATO J. ALMANSI was the son of Dante Almansi, president of the Union of the Italian Jewish Communities from November 1939 until October 1944. A physician in New York City, he died in January 2000, nine months after the conference at Hofstra University.

LUCIA SERVADIO BEDARIDA's ancestors settled in Italy sometime in the fourteenth century. In 1938 she was working as a radiologist and, with her husband, went to Tangier, where they established a private medical clinic. Both her mother and grandmother perished in the Holocaust. Between 1960 and 1980 she worked for the Moroccan Ministry of Health. In 1980 she emigrated to the United States and now lives in Cornwall-on-Hudson, New York.

ANNA PETROV BUMBLE is a Ph.D. candidate in Near Eastern and Judaic studies at Brandeis with major interest in Jewish literatures all over the world, especially Yiddish literature of the nineteenth century and American Jewish literature of the twentieth century. She received her B.A. from Tel Aviv University and an M.A. in comparative literature from Pennsylvania State University.

MARYANN CALENDRILLE has been conducting independent research on the history of Jews in Italy during World War II for several years. She has taught college English for many years and currently co-owns an independent bookstore, Canio's Books, in Sag Harbor, New York. She is a published poet and journalist.

FRANK J. COPPA is currently Professor of History at St. John's University, Director of its doctoral program in modern world history, and Chair of St. John's Symposium on Vatican Studies. An associate in the Columbia University Seminar on Modern Italy, he is general editor of the Peter Lang series, Studies in Modern

European History. He is the author of monographs on Giovanni Giolitti, Camillo di Cavour, Pope Pius IX, and Giacomo Antonelli and has written articles on Mazzini, Garibaldi, and Victor Emmanuel among others, and various aspects of liberal, fascist, and post–World War II Italy. He is the author of *The Origins of the Italian Wars of Independence* (1992) and *The Modern Papacy since 1789* (1998). He has edited more than half a dozen volumes, including the *Dictionary of Modern Italian History*, *Modern Italian History: An Annotated Bibliography*, and, most recently, *Encyclopedia of the Vatican and Papacy* (1999) and *Controversial Concordats: The Vatican's Relations with Napoleon, Mussolini, and Hitler* (1999). He has published articles on the Vatican in the interwar period and during World War II. Currently, he is editing a volume on notable popes.

ROBERTO MARIA DAINOTTO, Assistant Professor of Italian at Duke University, is the author of *Place in Literature: Regions, Cultures, Communities* (2000). He has taught courses on various aspects of nineteenth- and twentieth-century Italian literature and culture at the New School for Social Research, Sarah Lawrence College, and New York University. His current interests include Risorgimento memoirs, fascist propaganda, and post-war narrative and cinema. His contributions have appeared in the journals *Critical Inquiry*, *Rivista di Studi Nord-Americani*, *Postmodern Culture*, *Studio*, and *Italian-Americana*, and in various essay collections. At present, he is completing a book on the rhetorical construction of the regionalist novel and the idea of Europe.

ABRAHAM DAVID is a specialist in Jewish history and historiography of the Middle Ages. Between 1964 and 1968 he was involved with the Hebrew Bibliography Project at the National and University Library at the Hebrew University; from 1968 to 1971 he was a member of the editorial staff of the *Encyclopaedia Judaica*. Since 1971 he has been Senior Researcher at the Institute of Microfilmed Hebrew Manuscripts, Jewish National and University Library, Hebrew University and is the supervisor of the S. D. Goitein Laboratory for Genizah Research. In 1980–1981, 1986–1987 and 1989, he was a Visiting Scholar at the Center for Jewish Studies at Harvard University and in the summer of 1985 a Visiting Scholar at the Oxford Center for Postgraduate Studies, Oxford University. He has published more than 130 articles and papers on Jewish history in Hebrew, English, German, Spanish, French and Swedish. He is the author of several full-length monographs including *A Hebrew Chronicle from Prague, c.1615* (1993), *Me-Italyah li-Yerushalayim* (with M. E. Artom, 1997), *To Come to the Land, Immigration and Settlement in 16th-Century Eretz-Israel* (1999) and *In Zion and Jerusalem, The Itinerary of Rabbi Moses Basola (1521–1523)* (1999).

FABIO GIRELLI-CARASI is Associate Professor of Modern Languages at CUNY-Brooklyn College. He has published several articles on literary criticism and cultural studies and has written extensively on the works of Primo Levi. He is the recipient of several grants. In addition to academic research, he is a contributor to Italian magazines and newspapers on political, social and cultural issues. Currently, he is working on a book on Italian-Jewish memoirists.

EVA GOLD is Lecturer of Italian language and literature at SUNY Stony Brook. She received a Ph.D. in 1996 in Italian literature from New York University, an M.A. in 1990 from Middlebury and her Bachelor's degree in 1988 from Northwestern University (in film studies). She was a Fulbright Fellow from 1995 to 1997 in Milan and Rome.

SAMUEL GRUBER is Director of the Jewish Heritage Research Center (Syracuse, New York); Research Director of the U.S. Commission for the Preservation of America's Heritage Abroad, Jewish Heritage Program Consultant for the World Monuments Fund and President of the International Survey of Jewish Monuments, for which he edits "Jewish Heritage Report." He is co-author of *Survey of Historic Jewish Sites in the Czech Republic* (1995) and *Survey of Historic Jewish Sites in Poland* (1994, second revised edition, 1995) and author of *Synagogues* (1999), as well as numerous reports, articles and exhibition essays about medieval architecture, Jewish art and architecture and historic preservation. He is a Fellow of the American Academy in Rome and serves on many international boards and commissions.

LYNN M. GUNZBERG taught at the University of California at Santa Cruz before joining the faculty of Brown University. She is the author of *Strangers at Home: Jews in the Italian Literary Imagination*. She is currently Associate Dean of the College and Adjunct Associate Professor of Italian Studies at Brown.

MAURA E. HAMETZ is an Assistant Professor of history at Old Dominion University, Norfolk, Viriginia. Her research focuses on the city of Trieste in the twentieth century. She is currently a German Marshall Fund Fellow 1999–2000, completing a manuscript exploring Trieste's affiliations with Central Europe after 1918.

H. WENDELL HOWARD is a writer, musician (Choral Conductor) and Professor of English at St. John Fisher College in Rochester, New York. His poems, articles, scholarly essays, satires and other writings—numbering well over 100—have appeared in journals, periodicals, and volumes throughout the United States and Canada. His book of poems, *In Praise of Women*, was published in 1999.

GEORGE JOCHNOWITZ is Professor Emeritus of linguistics at the College of Staten Island, CUNY. He is especially interested in the dialects of the Jews of Italy and southern France. He also taught linguistics in Baoding, China, in 1984 and again in 1989 and has written about the events of Beijing Spring in 1989.

YITZCHAK KEREM is a historian on the Jews of Greece and the Sephardim at Aristotle University in Thessaloniki, Greece, and the Hebrew University of

Jerusalem, as well as Yad Vashem in Jerusalem. He recently founded the Institute of Hellenic-Judaic Studies at the University of Denver and serves as its Director. He makes films on Greek and Sephardic Jewry, as well as contributing to historical museums and exhibitions.

NANCY GOLDSMITH LEIPHART teaches Italian language, literature, vocal diction and the humanities, and is the Assistant Dean of the Division of General Studies at the North Carolina School of the Arts in Winston-Salem. She has participated in two National Endowment for the Humanities Summer Seminars, "Chaucer and Boccaccio" at Stanford University and "Palace Culture in Renaissance and Baroque Rome" at the American Academy of Rome. She was also a recipient of a Fulbright Summer Seminar to central and northern Italy, an American Association of Teachers of Italian grant to Siena, and a Renaissance Society of America/Mellon grant for paleography and dissertation research. Her current interests include the Jews of Italy, particularly the sixteenth- and seventeenth-century communities of Rome, Venice, Ferrara and Mantova; early modern art patronage in Italy of artists and musicians; seventeenth-century opera; and early performance practice and staging in temporary and permanent palace theaters.

JULIA R. LIEBERMAN teaches Spanish language and literature at Saint Louis University, St. Louis, Missouri. She is the author of *El teatro alegórico de Miguel (Daniel Leví) de Barrios*, published in 1996.

MICHELE LUZZATI is Full Professor of medieval history at the University of Pisa (Italy). He was assistant professor of history at the Scuola Normale Superiore of Pisa (1970–1983). After becoming "Libero docente" of medieval history (1971), he was also charged with the courses in medieval history at the University of Pisa from 1971 to 1983. He was later nominated Associate Professor of Medieval History at the Scuola Normale Superiore di Pisa (from 1983 to 1986) and Full Professor of the same discipline at the University of Sassari (from 1986 to 1989). He is President of the Associazione Italiana per lo Studio del Giudaismo, member of the committee of the journal *Quaderni Storici*, and member of the Centro di Cultura Medievale of the Scuola Normale Superiore of Pisa. His main areas of research are the economic and social history of the last centuries of the Middle Ages and of the Renaissance and the history of the Jews in Italy from the Middle Ages until today. His publications include many essays and the following works of Jewish interest: *La casa dell'ebreo. Saggi sugli ebrei a Pisa e in Toscana nel Medioevo e nel Rinascimento* (1985); *Banche e banchieri a Volterra nel Medioevo e nel Rinascimento* (with Alessandra Veronese, 1993); *Ebrei di Livorno tra due censimenti (1841–1938). Memoria familiare e identità* (1990); *L'Inquisizione e gli Ebrei in Italia* (1994); *Le tre sinagoghe. Luoghi di culto e vita ebraica a Livorno fra Seicento e Novecento* (1995); *La sinagoga di Pisa. Dalle origini al restauro ottocentesco di Marco Treves* (1997); and *Gli ebrei di Pisa (secoli IX-XX)* (1998).

JAMES TASATO MELLONE is Social Sciences Librarian and Assistant Professor at Queens College, City University of New York. He is a book reviewer for *Kirkus Reviews*, *Library Journal*, and *History: Reviews of New Books*, an abstracter for Historical Abstracts, and the author of the forthcoming *Fascist Italy: A Bibliography of Works in English, 1919–2000* (Greenwood).

ELISABETTA PROPERZI NELSEN is an Assistant Professor of Italian at San Francisco State University and coordinator of the Italian Program in the same university. She has published scholarly articles on Elsa Morante, Dacia Maraini and Italo Calvino. At present she is working on a book on Baroque poetry, which has been her first literary passion since her years at the University of Florence.

LUC NEMETH is a specialist of the fascist period and has recently published articles in *L'Homme et la Societe*, *Italia contemporanea*, and *Les Temps Modernes*. He is currently writing the biography of the anarchist Michele Schirru, condemned to death in 1931 for his attempted assassination of Benito Mussolini.

CLAUDIA NOCENTINI, having taught in various universities in the U.K., now lectures in Edinburgh. Her area of research is contemporary Italian literature, and she has just published a volume titled *Italo Calvino and the Landscape of Childhood*.

H. MARIE ORTON is an Assistant Professor of Italian at Truman State University in Missouri. Her current research projects include the narratives of female Auschwitz survivors from Italy and portrayals of the Shoah in film.

MICAELA PROCACCIA is an Archivist for the Ministry of Cultural Heritage and Activities of the General Archive Administration in Rome, Italy. She is responsible for the religious archives in the Ministry of Culure and is a member of the Council of the Jewish Cultural Heritage Foundation. She has collaborated with the Survivors of the Shoah Visual History Foundation by organizing training sessions for interviewers in Italy. She is the author of several essays on the history of Italian Jews and, with Bice Migliau, of *Lazio: itinerari ebraici. I luoghi, la storia, l'arte* (1997).

STANISLAO G. PUGLIESE is Associate Professor of modern European history at Hofstra University, where he directed "The Most Ancient of Minorities." He is a former Visiting Research Fellow at the Italian Academy for Advanced Studies at Columbia University. He is a specialist on twentieth-century Italian history, fascism and anti-fascism, and his articles have appeared in scholarly journals in Italy and the United States. He is the author of *Carlo Rosselli: Socialist Heretic and Antifascist Exile* (1999) which won the 2000 Premio Internazionale "Ignazio Silone," and *Italian Fascism and Anti-Fascism: A Critical Anthology* (2000). He is currently working on a biography of Ignazio Silone (to be published by Farrar, Straus & Giroux), a general history of Italy and a study of the Italian antifascist

Resistance tentatively titled "Poems before Death: Graffiti from a Nazi Prison in Rome, 1943–1944."

SALVATORE G. ROTELLA is President of Riverside Community College, a three-campus system, in Southern California. He is Chancellor Emeritus of the City Colleges of Chicago. He has held teaching assignments in political science and public administration at the Illinois Institute of Technology, Chicago; St. John's University, New York; and the City Colleges of Chicago. Additionally, he has been Visiting Professor in the Graduate School of Loyola University, Chicago, and SUNY Stony Brook. His research and publications are in comparative government and topics related to educational administration. For the past twenty years, he has done extensive research and made presentations on the Jews of Sicily.

FREDERICK M. SCHWEITZER has been a member of the History Department of Manhattan College since 1960. His life's work was inspired by the great ecumenist A. Roy Eckhardt. He specializes in modern British and European history, Jewish history and Catholic-Jewish relations. He is the author of *A History of the Jews since the First Century A.D.* (1971); co-edited *Jewish-Christian Encounters over the Centuries* (1994); and has written many essays and reviews on the Holocaust, World War II, and related subjects; he is a frequent speaker at scholarly conferences on these themes. With Marvin Perry he is completing a book on *Myths about Jews.*

STEPHEN SIPORIN is presently Associate Professor in the Departments of English and History at Utah State University, where he is also an Associate of the Folklore Program. He is a specialist on the folklore of Italian Jews and has published extensively on the subject. Most recently, he conducted research on the Jewish community in Pitigliano, Italy.

DIXON SLINGERLAND, between 1973 and 1979, was Pastor at St. Jacobi Lutheran Church in Brooklyn, New York. Since 1979 he has been Professor and Department Chair of religious studies at Hiram College. Professor Slingerland is the author of *Claudian Policymaking and the Early Imperial Repression of Judaism at Rome* (1997) and *The Testaments of the Twelve Patriarchs: A Critical History of Research* (1977; reprint, 1999), as well as several articles on religious history.

BARBARA SPARTI is a dance historian specializing in fifteenth- to seventeenth-century Italian dance. She was "Distinguished Visiting Professor" at the University of California, Los Angeles, in 1990 and has also taught and lectured at UC Santa Cruz, as well as at Tel Aviv University and the Hebrew University in Jerusalem. Her edition and English translation of Guglielmo Ebreo's 1463 dance treatise was published by Oxford University Press in 1993. She has also published various articles on Italian Renaissance and Baroque dance in specialized journals focusing on such problems as dance music, iconography and the socioeconomic, political, and aesthetic contexts of dance. She founded and directed the company Gruppo di

Danza Rinascimentale (1975–1988), which performed throughout Italy and Europe. She has choreographed period operas and plays for stage and television. Since 1973 she has been teaching practical courses in Italian fifteenth- to seventeenth-century dance in Italy, Europe, North America and Japan, as well as at the Rubin Academy of Music and Dance in Jerusalem.

RANIERO M. SPEELMAN prepared the critical edition of the Tuscan version of the *Bestiaire d'Amours* by Richart de Fornival. He works as Associate Professor of Italian literature at Utrecht University, the Netherlands, teaching primarily Italian Renaissance literature, and is a specialist on contemporary Italian-Jewish literature, as well as on the relationships between Italy and the Ottoman Empire. He has translated the collected essays, most short stories and poems of Primo Levi. He is now preparing the critical edition of the complete documents regarding the Peace Treaties between Venice and the Ottomans in 1502–1503 and studying the *Lettere informative delle cose de' Turchi* by Pietro Businello (1744).

SANDRA TOZZINI is Assistant Professor of Law at the University of La Verne College of Law. She served as a law clerk at the California Supreme Court and a Teaching Fellow at Santa Clara University School of Law.

DAVID TRAVIS is the Director of New York University's Italian Program in Florence, Italy. He is a specialist on contemporary Italian politics and society. He was a Junior Research Fellow at St. Anne's College, Oxford University, and has received a Fulbright Scholarship and a research grant from the Fondazione Luigi Einaudi. He is the author of *Italy: The Land and People* and many articles on contemporary Italy.

Recent Titles in
Contributions in Ethnic Studies

Latino Empowerment: Progress, Problems, and Prospects
Roberto E. Villarreal, Norma G. Hernandez, and Howard D. Neighbor, editors

Contemporary Federal Policy Toward American Indians
Emma R. Gross

The Governance of Ethnic Communities: Political Structures and Processes in Canada
Raymond Breton

Latinos and Political Coalitions: Political Empowerment for the 1990's
Roberto E. Villarreal and Norma G. Hernandez, editors

Conflict Resolution: Cross-Cultural Perspectives
Kevin Avruch, Peter W. Black, and Joseph A. Scimecca, editors

Ethnic and Racial Minorities in Advanced Industrial Democracies
Anthony M. Messina, Luis R. Fraga, Laurie A. Rhodebeck, and Frederick D. Wright, editors

Asian and Pacific Islander Migration to the United States: A Model of New Global Patterns
Elliott Robert Barkan

Semites and Stereotypes: Characteristics of Jewish Humor
Avner Ziv and Anat Zajdman, editors

Irish Illegals: Transients Between Two Societies
Mary P. Corcoran

The Germanic Mosaic: Cultural and Linguistic Diversity in Society
Carol Aisha Blackshire-Belay, editor

A Legal History of Asian Americans, 1790-1990
Hyung-chan Kim

An Ethnic History of Russia: Pre-Revolutionary Times to the Present
Tatiana Mastyugina, Lev Perepelkin, Vitaly Naumkin, and Irina Zviagelskaia, editors